TRUTH AND METHOD

TRUTH AND METHOD

Hans-Georg Gadamer

Second, Revised Edition
Translation revised by Joel Weinsheimer and Donald G. Marshall

continuum
LONDON • NEW YORK

Continuum

The Tower Building
11 York Road
London SE1 7NX

80 Maiden Lane
New York, NY 10038

www.continuumbooks.com

Copyright © 1975 and 1989 by Sheed & Ward Ltd and the
Continuum Publishing Group.
First published 1975; second edition 1989; this edition 2004.
Reprinted 2006. All rights reserved.

ISBN 08264 7697X

Typeset by Interactive Sciences Ltd, Gloucester
Printed in the United States

Catch only what you've thrown yourself, all is
mere skill and little gain;
but when you're suddenly the catcher of a ball
thrown by an eternal partner
with accurate and measured swing
towards you, to your center, in an arch
from the great bridgebuilding of God:
why catching then becomes a power—
not yours, a world's.

—Rainer Maria Rilke

XX – XXIV
XXV – XXXIV
267 – 306 / 307 – 371
383 – 436
436 – 484

Contents

CONTENTS

Translators' Preface

Truth and Method is one of the two or three most important works of this century on the philosophy of humanistic studies. The book is powerful, exciting, but undeniably difficult. Published when Gadamer was sixty, it gathers the ripe fruit of a lifetime's reading, teaching, and thinking. Because it is immersed in German philosophy and scholarship, the book is even more challenging for an American reader. An emerging body of commentary in English as well as the many shorter essays Gadamer has, happily, lived to write and which are increasingly available in translation provide additional means of access to his thought. *Truth and Method*, however, remains his *magnum opus*, the comprehensive and integrated statement of his rich and penetrating reflections.

The first edition of 1960 was revised and the footnotes updated for the second and again for the third edition, and then for the last time for inclusion in Gadamer's ten-volume *Gesammelte Werke*. An English translation based on the second edition appeared in 1975. Gadamer teaches us that the idea of a perfect translation that could stand for all time is entirely illusory. Even apart from the inevitable mistakes that reflect limits of erudition or understanding, a translation must transpose a work from one time and cultural situation to another. Over the past decade, both philosophical and literary study have become increasingly interested in the thinkers and issues that figure prominently in Gadamer's work. This altered situation presents difficulties, but also opportunities for bringing Gadamer's thought more fully into the contemporary cultural dialogue. We have undertaken a thorough revision of the earlier translation of *Truth and Method*, based on the German text for the *Gesammelte Werke*, but using the fourth edition to correct some obvious errors. We have aimed at accuracy, not according to an abstract standard, but specifically to help his contemporary American readers understand Gadamer more fully; and we have tried to make our translation as readable and often powerfully eloquent as Gadamer's German. We have no illusion that our revised translation will speak clearly into every future situation, but we have been conscious that our version will have to stand for an indefinite length of time and have therefore aimed always to serve as a bridge, not an obstacle, between Gadamer and his readers.

Some notes on important German terms and our translation of them will be helpful. The impossibility of translating even key terms the same way every time they occur is not due simply to the obvious fact that the range of meanings of the German word does not match precisely the range of any single English word. More telling is the fact that Gadamer's language resists hardening into a terminology, a technical language with stipulated, univocal meanings. He remains always responsive to the flexible usage of actual words, not simply in their "ordinary" meanings, but as they respond to the movement of thinking about particular subject matters.

Bildung is translated by "culture" and related forms such as "cultivation," "cultivated." In Part One, I.1.B.i., Gadamer defines *Bildung* as "the properly human way of developing one's natural talents and capacities." The term has the flavor of the late-eighteenth and nineteenth centuries and played a key role throughout German-speaking Europe. Gadamer uses the term throughout the book, but he is not uncritically taking up the whole mode of thought the term conveys. Specifically, he questions it in its association with the aesthetic taken as an ideal of life. And in other writings, he has made clear that we cannot simply ignore the fact of later critiques of the concept, particularly the suspicion that "culture" and "cultivation" are simply instruments of bourgeois domination. What remains important is the concept that a self can be formed without breaking with or repudiating one's past and that this formation cannot be achieved by any merely technical or methodical means.

Gadamer notes that within *Bildung* is the root word *Bild*, "form," "image," and more particularly, "picture." "Cultivation" is a process of "forming" the self in accordance with an ideal "image" of the human. Art, as a general capacity to form "images" or representations of experience, played a special role in the conception of *Bildung*. Gadamer appropriately turns to a consideration of the aesthetic and especially, at the end of Part One, the "picture." The interrelations of *Urbild*, "original"; *Vorbild*, "model";

Abbild, "copy"; *Bild*, "picture"; and *Einbildungskraft*, "imagination," cannot be reproduced in English. The conceptual argument is clear enough, but what is missed is not simply some verbal pyrotechnics, but an example of what Gadamer in Part Three describes as the preparatory conceptual work ordinary language accomplishes through the formation of word families and other devices.

What Gadamer wants to draw out is the temporality of art. While it is doubtless a product of a particular historical era and a particular artist's life history, we nevertheless encounter even an artwork from long ago as immediately present. We may therefore think art must transcend mere history and derive from a "timeless" realm of the beautiful. But Gadamer tries carefully to dismantle such a line of thought. Its most penetrating representative is Kant and the line of aesthetics that derives from him. According to this view, *Erlebnisse*, "experiences," seen as the enduring residue of moments lived in their full immediacy, are the material artistic genius transforms into works of art. The artwork begins in "experiences," but rises above them to a universal significance which goes beyond history.

German has two separate words for "experience": *Erlebnis* and *Erfahrung*. In his discussion of aesthetics (Part One, I.2.B.), Gadamer is almost always speaking of *Erlebnis* and distinguishing what remains valid from what must be rejected in the line of thought it implies. At a much later stage (Part Two, II.3.B.), Gadamer brings his discussion of the concepts of "history" and "tradition" to a climax with an analysis of *Erfahrung*, which provides the basis in our actual lives for the specifically hermeneutic way we are related to other persons and to our cultural past, namely, dialogue and especially the dialogue of question and answer. This kind of "experience" is not the residue of isolated moments, but an ongoing integrative process in which what we encounter widens our horizon, but only by overturning an existing perspective, which we can then perceive was erroneous or at least narrow. Its effect, therefore, is not simply to make us "knowing," to add to our stock of information, but to give us that implicit sense of broad perspectives, of the range of human life and culture, and of our own limits that constitutes a non-dogmatic wisdom. *Erlebnis* is something you have, and thus is connected with a subject and with the subjectivization of aesthetics. *Erfahrung* is something you undergo, so that subjectivity is overcome and drawn into an "event" (*Geschehen*) of meaning. Gadamer typically uses the term *Erlebnis* with a critical overtone, and the term *Erfahrung* with a positive one. Because the more concentrated discussion of *Erlebnis* is widely separated from that of *Erfahrung*, the local context is fairly clear. But throughout the book, Gadamer returns to his critique of *Erlebnis* and of the aesthetics based on it. We have tried to mark these returns by some special phrases: *Erlebnis* permits a plural, "experiences," whereas *Erfahrung* is normally integrative and hence singular; "art of experience," "art based on experience," or "aesthetics of experience" are intended to hint a neologism, a special way of conceiving "experience," whereas the "experience of art" translates *Erfahrung* in its range from neutral to decidedly positive. We have sometimes inserted the German in parentheses, particularly where Gadamer shifts from one term to another, so that the reader can be alert to the distinction.

Against the idea that the genius transforms "experiences" into artworks, Gadamer sets "transformation into structure" (*Verwandlung ins Gebilde*, Part One, II.1.B.). In a preparatory analysis of "play," Gadamer shows that play is not a subjective attitude of the players, but rather the players are caught up in the shaped activity of the game itself. Where this activity takes on enduring form, it becomes "structure," *Gebilde*. The root word maintains the line from *Bildung* to *Bild*, and thus anticipates the way even a picture transforms our world into a lasting shape, but does not thereby exit from that world into a timeless realm. In play, we do not express ourselves, but rather the game itself "presents itself." The term here is *Darstellung* and *sich darstellen*, which implies that something is immediately present, but as something with a shape or structure which is particularly brought out in presentation. The same term can be used for theatrical presentation, performance or recital of musical or other temporal works, or any exhibition. In the interrelations of "original" (*Urbild*) and "picture" (*Bild*), Gadamer wants to stress that we find not mimetic repetition or aestheticist displacement of the real, but a process best described in Neoplatonic language, where the original reality comes to its fullest self-presentation in the picture and where the tie between original and picture is never broken. But as art, this interrelation is fully real only each time it is represented, exhibited, brought into the actuality of our participation in it. Pictorial art is thus in its temporality not fundamentally different from the "reproductive" arts, what English calls "the performing arts." In re-presenting, the work of art performs a "total mediation" (*Vermittlung*). That is, what has been "transformed into structure" is made fully available to us once again. We have generally translated *Vermittlung* and related forms as "mediation," since this is the standard equivalent in philosophy. Occasionally, the context has led us to use "communication," but Gadamer does not conceive communication as the passing of information from one person to another. Rather, in communication some subject matter becomes mutually accessible for two or more people, while the medium which gives us this access withdraws from prominence.

In Part Two, Gadamer reviews the development of the "historical sciences" and their theory, particularly in nineteenth-century Germany, as well as what they contribute to our insight into "understanding." The humanistic discipline which particularly brought the resources of systematic historical study to bear on the literary and other texts that come down from the past was called "philology." The term has little currency in contemporary America, even in academic circles, but it remains common in Germany. We have occasionally used "criticism" or "literary criticism," particularly where the context implies an approach to texts which attends to their classic status, either as models of writing or as statements of a particular view, or where a contrast is drawn between the historian's approach and the approach a "philologist" finds it necessary to take, even as he claims to follow the historian. But we have freely used the term "philology" to remind the reader of the particular discipline Gadamer is describing.

Special attention needs to be drawn to Part Two, II.1.B.iv., and the key concept *wirkungsgeschichtliches Bewusstsein*, which we have translated as "historically effected consciousness," concurring with P. Christopher Smith's suggestion. We have tried to capture Gadamer's delineation of a consciousness that is doubly related to tradition, at once "affected" by history (Paul Ricoeur translated this term as "consciousness open to the effects of history") and also itself brought into being—"effected"—by history, and conscious that it is so. The term was originally translated as "effective-historical consciousness," and readers will encounter that expression in many English-language discussions of Gadamer. *Wirkung* is translated as "effect," while its adjectival and adverbial forms are usually translated as "actual," "real," sometimes "truly." Where something more emphatic seemed meant, we have rephrased or inserted the German. The reader should note the relation to *wirken*, "to work, to weave," and to *Wirklichkeit*, the real as something actual before us.

The double relation of historically effected consciousness to the past, Gadamer names "belonging." The German term is *gehören*, which contains the root *hören*, "listen to." In many languages, "to hear" and "to obey" are the same word. When we genuinely listen to another's insight into whatever we are seriously discussing, Gadamer suggests, we discover some validity in it, something about the thing itself that would not have shown itself simply within our own limited horizon. But this gain in insight is only possible where both participants in a conversation grant what "is due" to the subject matter (another sense of *gehören*). In that sense, participants in a conversation "belong" to and with each other, "belong" to and with the subject of their discussion, and mutually participate in the process which brings out the nature of that subject (Gadamer's standing example is the Platonic dialogues).

This ongoing conversation is *Überlieferung*, "tradition." English has no corresponding verb, nor any adjective that maintains the active verbal implication, nor any noun for what is carried down in "tradition." We have therefore admitted the neologism "traditionary text," and have sometimes used the phrase "what comes down to us from the past" or "handed down from the past" to convey the active sense of the German. We are likely to think of "tradition" as what lies merely behind us or as what we take over more or less automatically. On the contrary, for Gadamer "tradition" or "what is handed down from the past" confronts us as a *task*, as an effort of understanding we feel ourselves required to make because we recognize our limitations, even though no one compels us to do so. It precludes complacency, passivity, and self-satisfaction with what we securely possess; instead it requires active questioning and self-questioning.

The central question of Gadamer's investigation is the nature of "understanding," particularly as this is revealed in humanistic study. The German term is *Verstehen*, and Gadamer stresses its close connection with *Verständigung*, "coming to an understanding with someone," "coming to an agreement with someone," and *Einverständnis*, "understanding, agreement, consent." Instead of the binary implication of "understanding" (a person understands something), Gadamer pushes toward a three-way relation: one person comes to an understanding with another about something they thus both understand. When two people "understand each other" (*sich verstehen*), they always do so with respect to something. That something is never just an opinion (*Meinung, Gemeinte*), as when two people merely "exchange views." When we understand what someone says to us, we understand not just that person (his "psychology," for instance), nor just his or her "view," but we seriously consider whether that way of looking at a subject has some validity for us too. In this sense, even "self-understanding" (*Sichverstehen*) does not for Gadamer mean turning oneself into an object, but in German idiom, "knowing one's way around" in a certain matter.

What makes "coming to an understanding" possible is language, which provides the *Mitte*, the "medium" or "middle ground," the "place" where understanding, as we say, "takes place" (see especially Part Three, 3.B.). Language is the *Vermittlung*, the communicative mediation which establishes common ground. But Gadamer stresses that that ground is not established by any explicit agreement or "social contract" that could be negotiated in advance, nor by any purely psychological processes of "empathy" or "sympathy." As in play, it rests on a common willingness of the participants in conversation to lend themselves to the emergence of something else, the *Sache* or subject matter which comes to presence and presentation in conversation. We have generally reserved "objective" and related forms for *Gegenstand*, the German term which carries with it the whole set of philosophical problems that arose in the wake of Descartes' separation of "subject" from "object"; and we have translated *Sache* and related forms as "subject matter," or just as "thing."

Sprache and related forms present a special problem. In German, they are close to the common verb *sprechen*. But English forms such as "language," "linguistic," and even "speech" are Latinate or remote from our equivalent common verbs. English phrasing therefore looks stiffer and more formal than the German. We have generally used "verbal" and related forms or rephrased. Where Gadamer speaks of the *Sprachlichkeit* of our thinking, English idiom wants to put it completely differently: for instance, "what we think is always something we say or can say." Gadamer is thinking of language not as an entity or the object of scientific study, but as it inheres in the act of utterance and thus becomes an event, something historical.

Gadamer ends with a return to the central topic of aesthetics, namely, beauty. When something is "beautiful," its appearance strikes us with immediate self-evidence as valid. It "appears" or "shines" (*scheinen*), as a "phenomenon" (*Erscheinung*), and even though it may be a "mere" appearance, it may also have that special validity of what is visible that we call the "beautiful" (*Schöne*). Gadamer relates this experience to the self-evidentness of what strikes us as valid in material conveyed to us from the past and preserved in language. What is thus "evident" (*einleuchtend*) seems "self-evident" or "manifest" (*offenbar*, with the root meaning of standing "in the open") because it stands in the "light" (*Licht*) or is itself a "shining light" (*Leuchte*) that brings "enlightenment" (*Aufklärung*). These physical analogies are taken over in the mental "seeing" we call "insight" (*Einsicht*) and in phrases like, "you see what I'm saying." Because this insight is something that is not under our control, we say it "happens" (*geschehen*):

an idea "occurs" to us. Much of Gadamer's argument is directed to showing that understanding and the kind of "truth" that belongs to it has the character of an event, that is, something that belongs to the specific temporal nature of our human life.

A few frequently used special terms also invite comment. The Hegelian term *aufheben* we have almost always translated as "supersede." The German suggests what goes beyond, and thus cancels or makes obsolete, but at the same time preserves as something precedent, to which a relation is maintained. We have not hesitated to leave untranslated the Heideggerian term *Dasein*, "existence," "human being."

The German *Wissenschaft* suggests thorough, comprehensive, and systematic knowledge of something on a self-consciously rational basis. Gadamer certainly contrasts what we would call "the sciences" with the "humanities," but German keeps these close to each other by calling them "the natural sciences" and the "human sciences" (*Geisteswissenschaften*). By the latter, Gadamer does not mean what has been called in English the "human sciences," following the movement of structuralism and post-structuralism in recent French thought (and closer to what we call "the social sciences"). Gadamer notes the irony that the "untranslatable" German term *Geisteswissenschaften* itself originated as a translation of John Stuart Mill's English term "moral sciences." The lesson for translation is that the evolution of the term within German philosophy has given it an inflection that now diverges from any brief English equivalent. The word "scientific" still appears here in contexts that will momentarily puzzle the English-speaking reader, as when Gadamer speaks of "scientific" theology, where we would say rational or systematic theology. We have sometimes translated *wissenschaftlich* as "scholarly," where in the context "scientific" would have been positively misleading.

We have kept the brackets Gadamer uses to mark added material, which is especially frequent in the notes. We have not had time to check all of Gadamer's notes, but we have followed as consistently as possible American conventions of citation. We have provided English titles and citations, particularly for Gadamer's works, where the reference was to a whole work available in translation or to a separately marked part of it, rather than to a page number in a specific German edition. In the notes, the abbreviation *GW* is used for Gadamer's *Gesammelte Werke*, now in process of publication in ten volumes by J. C. B. Mohr.

We have divided our task as follows: Joel Weinsheimer translated the "Afterword to the Third Edition," and initially revised the translation of

Parts Two and Three, the Appendices, and Supplement I. Donald Marshall initially revised the translation of the "Preface to the Second Edition," Part One, Supplement II, and the notes for the whole work (translating all additions to the notes). Each of us carefully went over the other's work, and Joel Weinsheimer revised the whole text to make it more readable and stylistically consistent. It has been a collaborative project throughout, a case of mutual understanding in relation to a subject matter about which we both care deeply.

We wish to acknowledge the helpful suggestions of Robert Scharlemann of the University of Virginia, Jan Garrett of Western Kentucky University, and Ulrich Broich of the University of Munich. Richard Palmer of MacMurray College gave us particularly full and helpful remarks on the original translation of Part One and Part Two, I. Gadamer himself has kindly answered our questions about a number of particularly difficult passages. Our initial lists for changes in the translation emerged especially out of teaching *Truth and Method*, and thanks are due the students who provided the situation that gave thinking about what Gadamer said full and present actuality. The University of Minnesota funded the use of a Kurzweil optical scanner to transpose the first English edition into a computerized data base for word processing. This is undoubtedly a project made possible by modern technology.

To spouses and children who have accepted absence and absence of mind while we labored on this project, we express our thanks (in proper hermeneutic fashion, our experience has enabled us to recover the living truth behind these conventional and traditional phrases).

Though we have frequently altered the first translation, we and all English-speaking readers of Gadamer owe an enduring debt to its translator, W. Glen-Doepel, and to its editors, John Cumming and Garrett Barden.

Minneapolis
Iowa City
February, 1988

Introduction

These studies are concerned with the problem of hermeneutics. The phenomenon of understanding and of the correct interpretation of what has been understood is not a problem specific to the methodology of the human sciences alone. There has long been a theological and a legal hermeneutics, which were not so much theoretical as corrolary and ancillary to the practical activity of the judge or clergyman who had completed his theoretical training. Even from its historical beginnings, the problem of hermeneutics goes beyond the limits of the concept of method as set by modern science. The understanding and the interpretation of texts is not merely a concern of science, but obviously belongs to human experience of the world in general. The hermeneutic phenomenon is basically not a problem of method at all. It is not concerned with a method of understanding by means of which texts are subjected to scientific investigation like all other objects of experience. It is not concerned primarily with amassing verified knowledge, such as would satisfy the methodological ideal of science—yet it too is concerned with knowledge and with truth. In understanding tradition not only are texts understood, but insights are acquired and truths known. But what kind of knowledge and what kind of truth?

Given the dominance of modern science in the philosophical elucidation and justification of the concept of knowledge and the concept of truth, this question does not appear legitimate. Yet it is unavoidable, even within the sciences. The phenomenon of understanding not only pervades all human relations to the world. It also has an independent validity within science, and it resists any attempt to reinterpret it in terms of scientific method. The following investigations start with the resistance in modern science itself to the universal claim of scientific method. They are concerned to seek the experience of truth that transcends the domain of scientific method wherever that experience is to be found, and to inquire into its legitimacy. Hence the human sciences are connected to modes of experience that lie outside science: with the experiences of philosophy, of art, and of history itself. These are all modes of experience in which a truth is communicated that cannot be verified by the methodological means proper to science.

Contemporary philosophy is well aware of this. But it is quite a different question how far the truth claim of such modes of experience outside science can be philosophically legitimated. The current interest in the hermeneutic phenomenon rests, I think, on the fact that only a deeper investigation of the phenomenon of understanding can provide this legitimation. This conviction is strongly supported by the importance that contemporary philosophy attaches to the history of philosophy. In regard to the historical tradition of philosophy, understanding occurs to us as a superior experience enabling us easily to see through the illusion of historical method characteristic of research in the history of philosophy. It is part of the elementary experience of philosophy that when we try to understand the classics of philosophical thought, they of themselves make a claim to truth that the consciousness of later times can neither reject nor transcend. The naive self-esteem of the present moment may rebel against the idea that philosophical consciousness admits the possibility that one's own philosophical insight may be inferior to that of Plato or Aristotle, Leibniz, Kant, or Hegel. One might think it a weakness that contemporary philosophy tries to interpret and assimilate its classical heritage with this acknowledgment of its own weakness. But it is undoubtedly a far greater weakness for philosophical thinking not to face such self-examination but to play at being Faust. It is clear that in understanding the texts of these great thinkers, a truth is known that could not be attained in any other way, even if this contradicts the yardstick of research and progress by which science measures itself.

The same thing is true of the experience of art. Here the scholarly research pursued by the "science of art" is aware from the start that it can neither replace nor surpass the experience of art. The fact that through a work of art a truth is experienced that we cannot attain in any other way constitutes the philosophic importance of art, which asserts itself against all attempts to rationalize it away. Hence, together with the experience of philosophy, the experience of art is the most insistent admonition to scientific consciousness to acknowledge its own limits.

Hence the following investigation starts with a critique of aesthetic consciousness in order to defend the experience of truth that comes to us through the work of art against the aesthetic theory that lets itself be restricted to a scientific conception of truth. But the book does not rest content with justifying the truth of art; instead, it tries to develop from this starting point a conception of knowledge and of truth that corresponds to the whole of our hermeneutic experience. Just as in the experience of art we are concerned with truths that go essentially beyond the range of methodical knowledge, so the same thing is true of the whole of the human sciences: in them our historical tradition in all its forms is certainly made the *object* of investigation, but at the same time *truth comes to speech in it*. Fundamentally, the experience of historical tradition reaches far beyond those aspects of it that can be objectively investigated. It is true or untrue not only in the sense concerning which historical criticism decides, but always mediates truth in which one must *try to share*.

Hence these studies on hermeneutics, which start from the experience of art and of historical tradition, try to present the hermeneutic phenomenon in its full extent. It is a question of recognizing in it an experience of truth that not only needs to be justified philosophically, but which is itself a way of doing philosophy. The hermeneutics developed here is not, therefore, a methodology of the human sciences, but an attempt to understand what the human sciences truly are, beyond their methodological self-consciousness, and what connects them with the totality of our experience of world. If we make understanding the object of our reflection, the aim is not an art or technique of understanding, such as traditional literary and theological hermeneutics sought to be. Such an art or technique would fail to recognize that, in view of the truth that speaks to us from tradition, a formal technique would arrogate to itself a false superiority. Even though in the following I shall demonstrate how much there is of *event* effective in all *understanding*, and how little the traditions in which we stand are weakened by modern historical consciousness, it is not my intention to make prescriptions for the sciences or the conduct of life, but to try to correct false thinking about what they are.

I hope in this way to reinforce an insight that is threatened with oblivion in our swiftly changing age. Things that change force themselves on our attention far more than those that remain the same. That is a general law of our intellectual life. Hence the perspectives that result from the experience of historical change are always in danger of being exaggerated because they forget what persists unseen. In modern life, our historical consciousness is constantly overstimulated. As a consequence—though, as I hope to show, it is a pernicious short circuit—some react to this overestimation of historical change by invoking the eternal orders of nature and appealing to human nature to legitimize the idea of natural law. It is not only that historical tradition and the natural order of life constitute the unity of the world in which we live as men; the way we experience one another, the way we experience historical traditions, the way we experience the natural givenness of our existence and of our world, constitute a truly hermeneutic universe, in which we are not imprisoned, as if behind insurmountable barriers, but to which we are opened.

A reflection on what truth is in the human sciences must not try to reflect itself out of the tradition whose binding force it has recognized. Hence in its own work it must endeavor to acquire as much historical self-transparency as possible. In its concern to understand the universe of understanding better than seems possible under the modern scientific notion of cognition, it has to try to establish a new relation to the concepts which it uses. It must be aware of the fact that its own understanding and interpretation are not constructions based on principles, but the furthering of an event that goes far back. Hence it will not be able to use its concepts unquestioningly, but will have to take over whatever features of the original meaning of its concepts have come down to it.

The philosophical endeavor of our day differs from the classical tradition of philosophy in that it is not a direct and unbroken continuation of it. Despite its connection with its historical origin, philosophy today is well aware of the historical distance between it and its classical models. This is especially to be found in its changed attitude to the concept. However important and fundamental were the transformations that took place with the Latinization of Greek concepts and the translation of Latin conceptual language into the modern languages, the emergence of historical consciousness over the last few centuries is a much more radical rupture. Since then, the continuity of the Western philosophical tradition has been effective only in a fragmentary way. We have lost that naive innocence with which traditional concepts were made to serve one's own thinking. Since that time, the attitude of science towards these concepts has become strangely detached, whether it takes them up in a scholarly, not to say self-consciously archaizing way, or treats them as tools. Neither of these truly satisfies the hermeneutic experience. The conceptual world in which philosophizing develops has already captivated us in the same way that the language in which we live conditions us. If thought is to be conscientious, it must become aware of these anterior influences. A new critical consciousness must now accompany all responsible philosophizing which takes the habits of thought and language built up in the individual in his communication with his environment and places them before the forum of the historical tradition to which we all belong.

The following investigation tries to meet this demand by linking as closely as possible an inquiry into the history of concepts with the substantive exposition of its theme. That conscientiousness of phenomenological description which Husserl has made a duty for us all; the breadth of the historical horizon in which Dilthey has placed all philosophizing; and, not least, the penetration of both these influences by the impulse received from Heidegger, indicate the standard by which the writer desires to be measured, and which, despite all imperfection in the execution, he would like to see applied without reservation.

Foreword to the Second Edition

The second edition* of *Truth and Method* is virtually unaltered. It has found admirers and critics, and the attention it has received undoubtedly obliges the author to improve the whole by drawing on all the really valuable suggestions they have offered. And yet a line of thought that has matured over many years has its own stability. However much one tries to see through the critics' eyes, one's own generally pervasive viewpoint prevails.

The three years that have passed since the publication of the first edition have proved too short a time for the author to put the whole again in question, and to use effectively all that he has learned from criticism[1] and from his own more recent work.[2]

Perhaps I may once again briefly outline the overall intention and claim. My revival of the expression *hermeneutics,* with its long tradition, has apparently led to some misunderstandings.[3] I did not intend to produce a manual for guiding understanding in the manner of the earlier hermeneutics. I did not wish to elaborate a system of rules to describe, let alone direct, the methodical procedure of the human sciences. Nor was it my aim to investigate the theoretical foundation of work in these fields in order to put my findings to practical ends. If there is any practical consequence of the present investigation, it certainly has nothing to do with an unscientific "commitment"; instead, it is concerned with the "scientific" integrity of acknowledging the commitment involved in all understanding. My real

---

*This refers to the second German edition, not this second, revised English-language edition, which is based on the fifth German edition.—Eds.

concern was and is philosophic: not what we do or what we ought to do, but what happens to us over and above our wanting and doing.

Hence the methods of the human sciences are not at issue here. My starting point is that the historical human sciences, as they emerged from German romanticism and were imbued with the spirit of modern science, maintained a humanistic heritage that distinguishes them from all other kinds of modern research and brings them close to other, quite different, extrascientific experiences, especially those peculiar to art. Of course, this could also be explained in terms of the sociology of knowledge. In Germany (which has always been pre-revolutionary) the tradition of aesthetic humanism remained vitally influential in the development of the modern conception of science. In other countries more political consciousness may have entered into what is called "the humanities," "lettres": in short, everything formerly known as the humaniora.

This does not in the slightest prevent the methods of modern natural science from being applicable to the social world. Possibly the growing rationalization of society and the scientific techniques of administering it are more characteristic of our age than the vast progress of modern science. The methodical spirit of science permeates everywhere. Therefore I did not remotely intend to deny the necessity of methodical work within the human sciences (Geisteswissenschaften). Nor did I propose to revive the ancient dispute on method between the natural and the human sciences. It is hardly a question of different methods. To this extent, Windelband and Rickert's question concerning the "limits of concept formation in the natural sciences" seems to me misconceived. The difference that confronts us is not in the method but in the objectives of knowledge. The question I have asked seeks to discover and bring into consciousness something which that methodological dispute serves only to conceal and neglect, something that does not so much confine or limit modern science as precede it and make it possible. This does not make its own immanent law of advance any less decisive. It would be vain to appeal to the human desire for knowledge and the human capacity for achievement to be more considerate in their treatment of the natural and social orders of our world. Moral preaching under the guise of science seems rather absurd, as does the presumption of a philosopher who deduces from principles the way in which "science" must change in order to become philosophically legitimate.

Therefore in this connection it seems to me a mere misunderstanding to invoke the famous Kantian distinction between quaestio juris and quaestio facti. Kant certainly did not intend to prescribe what modern science must do in order to stand honorably before the judgment seat of reason. He asked a philosophical question: what are the conditions of our knowledge, by virtue of which modern science is possible, and how far does it extend? The following investigation also asks a philosophic question in the same sense. But it does not ask it only of the so-called human sciences (which would give precedence to certain traditional disciplines). Neither does it ask it only of science and its modes of experience, but of all human experience of the world and human living. It asks (to put it in Kantian terms): how is understanding possible? This is a question which precedes any action of understanding on the part of subjectivity, including the methodical activity of the "interpretive sciences" and their norms and rules. Heidegger's temporal analytics of Dasein has, I think, shown convincingly that understanding is not just one of the various possible behaviors of the subject but the mode of being of Dasein itself. It is in this sense that the term "hermeneutics" has been used here. It denotes the basic being-in-motion of Dasein that constitutes its finitude and historicity, and hence embraces the whole of its experience of the world. Not caprice, or even an elaboration of a single aspect, but the nature of the thing itself makes the movement of understanding comprehensive and universal.

I cannot agree with those who maintain that the limits of the province of hermeneutics are revealed in confrontation with extrahistorical modes of being, such as the mathematical or aesthetic.[4] Admittedly it is true that, say, the aesthetic quality of a work of art is based on structural laws and on a level of embodied form and shape that ultimately transcend all the limitations of its historical origin or cultural context. I shall not discuss how far, in relation to a work of art, the "sense of quality" represents an independent possibility of knowledge,[5] or whether, like all taste, it is not only developed formally but is also a matter of education and inculcation. At any rate, taste is necessarily formed by something that indicates for what that taste is formed. To that extent, it perhaps always includes particular, preferred types of content and excludes others. But in any case it is true that everyone who experiences a work of art incorporates this experience wholly within himself: that is, into the totality of his self-understanding, within which it means something to him. I go so far as to assert that the act of understanding, including the experience of the work of art, surpasses all historicism in the sphere of aesthetic experience. Admittedly, there appears to be an obvious distinction between the original world structure established by a work of art and its survival in the changed circumstances of the world thereafter.[6] But where exactly is the dividing line between the present world and the world that comes to be? How is the original life significance transformed into the reflected experience that is cultural significance? It seems to me that the concept of aesthetic non-differentiation that I have coined in this connection is wholly valid; here there are no clear divisions, and the movement of understanding cannot be restricted to the reflective pleasure prescribed by aesthetic differentiation.[7] It should be admitted that, say, an ancient image of the gods that was not displayed in a temple as a work of art in order to give aesthetic, reflective pleasure, and is now on show in a museum, retains, even as it stands before us today, the world of religious experience from which it came; the important consequence is that its world still belongs to ours. What embraces both is the hermeneutic universe.[8]

In other respects too, the universality of hermeneutics cannot be arbitrarily restricted or curtailed. No mere artifice of organization persuaded me to begin with the experience (Erfahrung) of art in order to assure the phenomenon of understanding the breadth proper to it. Here the aesthetics of genius has done important preparatory work in showing that the experience of the work of art always fundamentally surpasses any subjective horizon of interpretation, whether that of the artist or of the recipient. The mens auctoris is not admissible as a yardstick for the meaning of a work of art. Even the idea of a work-in-itself, divorced from its constantly renewed reality in being experienced, always has something abstract about it. I think I have shown why this idea only describes an intention, but does not permit a dogmatic solution. At any rate, the purpose of my investigation is not to offer a general theory of interpretation and a differential account of its methods (which Emilio Betti has done so well) but to discover what is common to all modes of understanding and to show that understanding is never a subjective relation to a given "object" but to the history of its effect; in other words, understanding belongs to the being of that which is understood.

Therefore I am not convinced by the objection that the performance of a musical work of art is interpretation in a different sense from, say, reaching understanding in reading a poem or looking at a painting. All performance is primarily interpretation and seeks, as such, to be correct. In this sense it, too, is "understanding."[9]

I believe that the universality of the hermeneutic viewpoint cannot be restricted even with respect to the multitude of historical concerns and interests subsumed under the science of history. Certainly there are many modes of historical writing and research. There is no need to assert that every historical observation is based on a conscious reflection on the history of effect. The history of the North American Eskimo tribes is certainly quite independent of whether and when these tribes had an effect on the "universal history of Europe." Yet one cannot seriously deny that reflection on effective history will prove to be important even in relation to this historical task. In fifty or a hundred years, anyone who reads the history of these tribes as it is written today will not only find it outdated (for in the meantime he will know more or interpret the sources more correctly); he will also be able to see that in the 1960s people read the sources differently because they were moved by different questions, prejudices, and interests. Ultimately historical writing and research would dissolve in indifference if it were withdrawn from the province of reflection on effective history. The hermeneutic problem is universal and prior to every kind of interest in history because it is concerned with what is always fundamental to "historical questions."[10] And what is historical research without historical questions? In the language that I use, justified by investigation into semantic history, this means: application is an element of understanding itself. If, in this connection, I put the legal historian and the practicing lawyer on the same level, I do not deny that the former has exclusively a "contemplative," and the other an exclusively practical, task. Yet application is involved in the activities of both. How could the *legal* meaning of a law be different for either? It is true that the judge, for example, has the practical task of passing judgment, and this may involve many considerations of legal politics that the legal historian (looking at the same law) does not consider. But does that make their legal *understanding* of the law any different? The judge's decision, which has a practical effect on life, aims at being a correct and never an arbitrary application of the law; hence it must rely on a "correct" interpretation, which necessarily includes the mediation between history and the present in the act of understanding itself.

Of course, the legal historian will also have to evaluate a correctly understood law "historically" as well, and this always means he must assess its historical importance; since he will always be guided by his own historical pre-opinions and pre-judgments, he may assess it "wrongly." This means that again there is mediation between the past and the present: that is, application. The course of history generally, including the history of research, teaches us this. But it obviously does not follow that the historian has done something which he should not have done, and which he should or could have been prevented from doing by some hermeneutic canon. I am not speaking of the errors of legal history, but of accurate findings. The legal historian—like the judge—has his "methods" of avoiding mistakes, and in such matters I agree entirely with the legal historian.[11] But the hermeneutic interest of the philosopher begins precisely when error has been successfully avoided. Then both legal historians and legal dogmaticians testify to a truth that extends beyond what they know, insofar as their own transient present is discernible in their acts and deeds.

From the viewpoint of philosophical hermeneutics, the contrast between historical and dogmatic method has no absolute validity. This raises a question about the extent to which the hermeneutic viewpoint itself enjoys historical or dogmatic validity.[12] If the principle of effective history is made into a universal element in the structure of understanding, then this thesis undoubtedly implies no historical relativity, but seeks absolute validity—and yet a hermeneutic consciousness exists only under specific historical conditions. Tradition, which consists in part in handing down self-evident traditional material, must have become questionable before it can become explicitly conscious that appropriating tradition is a hermeneutic task. Augustine has just such a consciousness in regard to the Old Testament; and, during the Reformation, Protestant hermeneutics developed from an insistence on understanding Scripture solely on its own basis (sola scriptura) as against the principle of tradition upheld by the Roman church. But certainly since the birth of historical consciousness, which involves a fundamental distance between the present and all historical tradition, understanding has been a task requiring methodical direction. My thesis is that the element of effective history affects all understanding of tradition, even despite the adoption of the methodology of the modern historical sciences, which makes what has grown historically and has been transmitted historically an object to be established like an experimental finding—as if tradition were as alien, and from the human point of view as unintelligible, as an object of physics.

Hence there is a certain legitimate ambiguity in the concept of historically effected consciousness (wirkungsgeschichtliches Bewußtsein), as I have employed it. This ambiguity is that it is used to mean at once the consciousness effected in the course of history and determined by history, and the very consciousness of being thus effected and determined. Obviously the burden of my argument is that effective history still determines modern historical and scientific consciousness; and it does so beyond any possible knowledge of this domination. Historically effected consciousness is so radically finite that our whole being, effected in the totality of our destiny, inevitably transcends its knowledge of itself. But that is a fundamental insight which is not to be limited to any specific historical situation; an insight which, however, in the face of modern historical research and of science's methodological ideal of objectivity, meets with particular resistance in the self-understanding of science.

We are certainly entitled to ask the reflective historical question: why, just now, at this precise moment in history, has this fundamental insight into the role of effective history in all understanding become possible? My investigations offer an indirect answer to this question. Only after the failure of the naive historicism of the very century of historicism does it become clear that the contrast between unhistorical-dogmatic and historical, between tradition and historical science, between ancient and modern, is not absolute. The famous querelle des anciens et des modernes ceases to pose real alternatives.

Hence what is here affirmed—that the province of hermeneutics is universal and especially that language is the form in which understanding is achieved—embraces "pre-hermeneutic" consciousness as well as all modes of hermeneutic consciousness. Even the naive appropriation of tradition is a "retelling" although it ought not to be described as a "fusion of horizons" (see p.537 below).

And now to the basic question: how far does the province of understanding itself and its linguisticity reach? Can it justify the philosophical universality implied in the proposition, "Being that can be understood is language"? Surely the universality of language requires the untenable metaphysical conclusion that "everything" is only language and language event? True, the patent objection implied by the ineffable does not necessarily affect the universality of language. The infinity of the dialogue in which understanding is achieved makes any reference to the ineffable itself relative. But is understanding the sole and sufficient access to the reality of history? Obviously there is a danger that the actual reality of the event, especially its absurdity and contingency, will be weakened and misperceived by being seen in terms of the experience of meaning.

Hence it was my purpose to show that the historicism of Droysen and Dilthey, despite the historical school's opposition to Hegel's spiritualism, was seduced by its hermeneutic starting point into reading history as a book: as one, moreover, intelligible down to the smallest letter. Despite all its protest against a philosophy of history in which the necessity of the idea is the nucleus of all events, the historical hermeneutics of Dilthey could not avoid letting history culminate in history of ideas. That was my criticism. Yet surely this danger recurs in regard to the present work? However, the fact that ideas are formed through tradition, especially through the hermeneutic circle of whole and part, which is the starting point of my attempt to lay the foundations of hermeneutics, does not necessarily imply this conclusion. The concept of the whole is itself to be understood only relatively. The whole of meaning that has to be understood in history or tradition is never the meaning of the whole of history. The danger of Docetism seems banished when historical tradition is conceived not as an object of historical knowledge or of philosophical conception, but as an effective moment of one's own being. The finite nature of one's own understanding is the manner in which reality, resistance, the absurd, and the unintelligible assert themselves. If one takes this finitude seriously, one must take the reality of history seriously as well.

The same problem makes the experience of the Thou so decisive for all self-understanding. The section on experience (Part Two, II.3.B) takes on a systematic and key position in my investigations. There the experience of the Thou throws light on the concept of historically effected experience. The experience of the Thou also manifests the paradox that something standing over against me asserts its own rights and requires absolute recognition; and in that very process is "understood." But I believe that I have shown correctly that what is so understood is not the Thou but the truth of what the Thou says to us. I mean specifically the truth that becomes visible to me only through the Thou, and only by my letting myself be told something by it. It is the same with historical tradition. It would not deserve the interest we take in it if it did not have something to teach us that we could not know by ourselves. It is in this sense that the statement "being that can be understood is language" is to be read. It does not mean that the one who understands has an absolute mastery over being but, on the contrary, that being is not experienced where something can be constructed by us and is to that extent conceived; it is experienced where what is happening can merely be understood.

This involves a question of philosophical methodology which was raised in a number of critical comments on my book. I should like to call it the "problem of phenomenological immanence." It is true that my book is phenomenological in its method. This may seem paradoxical inasmuch as Heidegger's criticism of transcendental inquiry and his thinking of "the turn" form the basis of my treatment of the universal hermeneutic problem. But I think that the principle of phenomenological demonstration can be applied to this term of Heidegger's, which at last reveals the hermeneutic problem. I have therefore retained the term "hermeneutics" (which the early Heidegger used) not in the sense of a methodology but as a theory of the real experience that thinking is. Hence I must emphasize that my analyses of play and of language are intended in a purely phenomenological sense.[13] Play is more than the consciousness of the player, and so it is more than a subjective act. Language is more than the consciousness of the speaker; so also it is more than a subjective act. This is what may be described as an experience of the subject and has nothing to do with "mythology" or "mystification."[14]

This fundamental methodical approach avoids implying any metaphysical conclusions. In subsequent publications, especially in my research reports "Hermeneutics and Historicism"[15] (cf. pp. 505–541 below) and "The Phenomenological Movement" (in *Philosophical Hermeneutics*, tr. David Linge [Berkeley: Univ. of California Press, 1976]), I have recorded my acceptance of Kant's conclusions in the *Critique of Pure Reason*: I regard statements that proceed by wholly dialectical means from the finite to the infinite, from human experience to what exists in itself, from the temporal to the eternal, as doing no more than setting limits, and am convinced that philosophy can derive no actual knowledge from them. Nevertheless, the tradition of metaphysics and especially of its last great creation, Hegel's speculative dialectic, remains close to us. The task, the "infinite relation," remains. But my way of demonstrating it seeks to free itself from the embrace of the synthetic power of the Hegelian dialectic, even from the "logic" which developed from the dialectic of Plato, and to take its stand in the movement of dialogue, in which word and idea first become what they are.[16]

Hence the present investigations do not fulfill the demand for a reflexive self-grounding made from the viewpoint of the speculative transcendental philosophy of Fichte, Hegel, and Husserl. But is the dialogue with the whole of our philosophical tradition—a dialogue in which we stand and which as philosophers, we are—groundless? Does what has always supported us need to be grounded?

This raises a final question, which concerns less the method than the contents of the hermeneutic universalism I have outlined. Does not the universality of understanding involve a one-sidedness in its contents, since it lacks a critical principle in relation to tradition and, as it were, espouses a universal optimism? However much it is the nature of tradition to exist only through being appropriated, it still is part of the nature of man to be able to break with tradition, to criticize and dissolve it, and is not what takes place in remaking the real into an instrument of human purpose something far more basic in our relationship to being? To this extent, does not the ontological universality of understanding result in a certain one-sidedness? Understanding certainly does not mean merely appropriating customary opinions or acknowledging what tradition has sanctified. Heidegger, who first described the concept of understanding as the universal determinateness of Dasein, means by this the very projectiveness of understanding—i.e., the futurality of Dasein. I shall not deny, however, that—among all the elements of understanding—I have emphasized the assimilation of what is past and of tradition. Like many of my critics, Heidegger too would probably feel a lack of ultimate radicality in the conclusions I draw. What does the end of metaphysics as a science mean? What does its ending in science mean? When science expands into a total technocracy and thus brings on the "cosmic night" of the "forgetfulness of being," the nihilism that Nietzsche prophesied, then may one not gaze at the last fading light of the sun setting in the evening sky, instead of turning around to look for the first shimmer of its return?

It seems to me, however, that the one-sidedness of hermeneutic universalism has the truth of a corrective. It enlightens the modern viewpoint based on making, producing, and constructing concerning the necessary conditions to which that viewpoint is subject. In particular, it limits the position of the philosopher in the modern world. However much he may be called to draw radical inferences from everything, the role of prophet, of Cassandra, of preacher, or of know-it-all does not suit him.

What man needs is not just the persistent posing of ultimate questions, but the sense of what is feasible, what is possible, what is correct, here and now. The philosopher, of all people, must, I think, be aware of the tension between what he claims to achieve and the reality in which he finds himself.

The hermeneutic consciousness, which must be awakened and kept awake, recognizes that in the age of science philosophy's claim of superiority has something chimerical and unreal about it. But though the will of man is more than ever intensifying its criticism of what has gone before to the point of becoming a utopian or eschatological consciousness, the hermeneutic consciousness seeks to confront that will with something of the truth of remembrance: with what is still and ever again real.

Notes

1 In addition to personal communications, I think especially of the following:

K. O. Apel, *Hegelstudien*, 2 (1963), 314–22.

O. Becker, "Die Fragwürdigkeit der Transzendierung der ästhetischen Dimension der Kunst (im Hinblick auf den I. Teil von *Wahrheit und Methode*)," *Philosophische Rundschau*, 10 (1962), 225–38.

E. Betti, *Die Hermeneutik als allgemeine Methodik der Geisteswissenschaften* (Tübingen, 1962).

W. Hellebrand, "Der Zeitbogen," *Archiv für Rechts– und Sozialphilosophie*, 49 (1963), 57–76.

H. Kuhn, "Wahrheit und geschichtliches Verstehen," *Historische Zeitschrift*, 193, no. 2 (1961), 376–89.

J. Möller, *Tübinger Theologische Quartalschrift*, 5 (1961), 467–71.

W. Pannenberg, "Hermeneutik und Universalgeschichte," *Zeitschrift für Theologie und Kirche*, 60 (1963), 90–121, esp. 94ff.

O. Pöggeler, *Philosophischer Literaturanzeiger*, 16, 6–16.

A. de Waelhens, "Sur une herméneutique de l'herméneutique," *Revue philosophique de Louvain*, 60 (1962), 573–91.

F. Wieacker, "Notizen zur rechtshistorischen Hermeneutik," *Nachrichten der Akademie der Wissenschaften (Göttingen), philos.–hist. Klasse* (1963), pp. 1–22.

2 See the following: "Einführung" to Martin Heidegger, *The Origin of the Work of Art*, English title, "Heidegger's Later Philosophy," in *Philosophical Hermeneutics*, tr. David E. Linge (Berkeley: University of California Press, 1976), pp. 213–28 (further references to this volume abbreviated *PH*).

"Hegel and the Dialectic of the Ancient Philosophers," in *Hegel's Dialectic: Five Hermeneutical Studies*, tr. P. Christopher Smith (New Haven: Yale University Press, 1976), pp. 5–34.

"On the Problem of Self-Understanding," in *PH*, pp. 44–58.

"Composition and Interpretation," in *The Relevance of the Beautiful and Other Essays*, tr. Nicholas Walker (Cambridge: Cambridge University Press, 1986), pp. 66–73.

"Hermeneutics and Historicism," Supplement I below.

"The Phenomenological Movement," in *PH*, pp. 130–81.

"The Nature of Things and the Language of Things," in *PH*, pp. 69–81.

"Über die Möglichkeit einer philosophischen Ethik," in *Sein und Ethos, Walberger Studien*, 1 (1963), 11–24 [*GW*, IV].

"Man and Language," in *PH*, pp. 59–68.

"Martin Heidegger and Marburg Theology," in *PH*, 198–212.

"Aesthetics and Hermeneutics," in *PH*, pp. 95–104.

3 E. Betti, op. cit.; F. Wieacker, op. cit.

4 Becker, op. cit.

5 In his *Traktat vom Schönen* (Frankfurt, 1935), Kurt Riezler attempted a transcendental deduction of the "sense of quality."

6 See H. Kuhn's recent work, *Vom Wesen des Kunstwerkes* (1961).

7 [The insistence on aesthetic experience, which Hans Robert Jauss urges, remains a narrowing. See his *Ästhetische Erfahrung und literarische Hermeneutik* (Frankfurt, 1979).]

8 The vindication of allegory, which is pertinent here, began some years ago with Walter Benjamin's major work, *The Origin of German Tragic Drama*, tr. John Osborne (1927; London: Verso NLF, 1977).

9 On this point I can invoke Hans Sedlmayr's papers despite their admittedly different emphasis, now collected as *Kunst und Wahrheit* (Rowohlts Deutsche Enzyclopädie, 71) especially pp. 87ff.

10 H. Kuhn, op. cit.

11 Betti, Wieacker, Hellebrand, op. cit.

12 K. O. Apel, op. cit.

13 Wittgenstein's concept of "language games" seemed quite natural to me when I came across it. See my "The Phenomenological Movement," cited in n. 2 above, pp. 173ff.

14 See my "Heidegger's Later Philosophy," cited n. 2 above, and the essay in the *Frankfurter Allgemeine Zeitung* of September 26, 1964, repr. *Kleine Schriften*, III, 202–11, *Heideggers Wege* (Tübingen, 1983), pp. 18–28 (*GW*, III).

15 See Supplement I below.

16 O. Pöggeler, op. cit., pp. 12f., has made an interesting suggestion about what Hegel would have said about this, through the mouth of Rosenkranz.

PART ONE

The Question of Truth as it Emerges in the
Experience of Art

1
Transcending the Aesthetic Dimension

I THE SIGNIFICANCE OF THE HUMANIST TRADITION FOR THE HUMAN SCIENCES

(A) THE PROBLEM OF METHOD

The logical self-reflection that accompanied the development of the human sciences in the nineteenth century is wholly governed by the model of the natural sciences. A glance at the history of the word Geisteswissenschaft shows this, although only in its plural form does this word acquire the meaning familiar to us. The human sciences (Geisteswissenschaften) so obviously understand themselves by analogy to the natural sciences that the idealistic echo implied in the idea of Geist ("spirit") and of a science of Geist fades into the background. The word Geisteswissenschaften was made popular chiefly by the translator of John Stuart Mill's *Logic*. In the supplement to his work Mill seeks to outline the possibilities of applying inductive logic to the "moral sciences." The translator calls these Geisteswissenschaften.[1] Even in the context of Mill's *Logic* it is apparent that there is no question of acknowledging that the human sciences have their own logic but, on the contrary, of showing that the inductive method, basic to all experimental science, is the only method valid in this field too. In this respect Mill stands in an English tradition of which Hume has given the most effective formulation in the introduction to his *Treatise*.[2] Human science too is concerned with establishing similarities, regularities, and conformities to law which would make it possible to predict individual phenomena and processes. In the field of natural phenomena this goal cannot always be reached everywhere to the same extent, but the reason for this variation is only that sufficient data on which the similarities are to be established cannot always be obtained. Thus the method of meteorology is just the same as that of physics, but its data is incomplete and therefore its predictions are more uncertain. The same is true in the field of moral and social phenomena. The use of the inductive method is also free from all metaphysical assumptions and remains perfectly independent of how one conceives of the phenomena that one is observing. One does not ascertain causes for particular effects, but simply establishes regularities. Thus it is quite unimportant whether one believes, say, in the freedom of the will or not—one can still make predictions in the sphere of social life. To make deductions from regularities concerning the phenomena to be expected implies no assumption about the kind of connection whose regularity makes prediction possible. The involvement of free decisions—if they exist—does not interfere with the regular process, but itself belongs to the universality and regularity which are attained through induction. What is programmatically developed here is a science of society, and research has followed this program with success in many fields. One only has to think of social psychology.

But the specific problem that the human sciences present to thought is that one has not rightly grasped their nature if one measures them by the yardstick of a progressive knowledge of regularity. The experience of the sociohistorical world cannot be raised to a science by the inductive procedure of the natural sciences. Whatever "science" may mean here, and even if all historical knowledge includes the application of experiential universals to the particular object of investigation, historical research does not endeavor to grasp the concrete phenomenon as an instance of a universal rule. The individual case does not serve only to confirm a law from which practical predictions can be made. Its ideal is rather to understand the phenomenon itself in its unique and historical concreteness. However much experiential universals are involved, the aim is not to confirm and extend these universalized experiences in order to attain knowledge of a law—e.g., how men, peoples, and states evolve—but to understand how this man, this people, or this state is what it has become or, more generally, how it happened that it is so.

What kind of knowledge is it that understands that something is so because it understands that it has come about so? What does "science" mean here? Even if one acknowledges that the ideal of this knowledge is fundamentally different in kind and intention from the natural sciences, one will still be tempted to describe the human sciences in a merely negative way as the "inexact sciences." Although Hermann Helmholtz's important and just comparison in his famous speech of 1862 between the natural and the human sciences laid great emphasis on the superior and humane significance of the human sciences, he still gave them a negative logical description based on the methodological ideal of the natural sciences.[3] Helmholtz distinguished between two kinds of induction: logical and artistic-instinctive induction. That means, however, that his distinction was basically not logical but psychological. Both kinds of science make use of the inductive conclusion, but the human sciences arrive at their conclusions by an unconscious process. Hence the practice of induction in the human sciences is tied to particular psychological conditions. It requires a kind of tact and other intellectual capacities as well—e.g., a well-stocked memory and the acceptance of authorities—whereas the self-conscious inferences of the natural scientist depend entirely on the use of his own reason. Even if one acknowledges that this great natural scientist has resisted the temptation of making his own scientific practice a universally binding norm, he obviously had no other logical terms in which to characterize the procedure of the human sciences than the concept of induction, familiar to him from Mill's *Logic*. The fact that the new mechanics and their triumph in the astronomy of Newton were a model for the sciences of the eighteenth century was still so self-evident for Helmholtz that the question of what philosophical conditions made the birth of this new science possible in the seventeenth century was utterly remote from him. Today we know what an influence the Paris Occamist school had.[4] For Helmholtz, the methodological ideal of the natural sciences needed neither to be historically derived nor epistemologically restricted, and that is why he could not understand the way the human sciences work as logically different.

At the same time there was the pressing task of raising one branch of knowledge—namely that of the "historical school," which was in fact in full flower—to logical self-consciousness. As early as 1843 J. G. Droysen, the author and founder of the history of Hellenism, wrote, "there is, I suppose, no field of knowledge that is so far from being theoretically justified, defined, and articulated as history." Droysen called for a Kant who, in a categorical imperative of history, "would show the living source from which the historical life of mankind flowed." He expressed the hope "that the more profoundly grasped idea of history will be the center of gravity in which the chaotic movement of the human sciences will gain stability and the possibility of further progress."[5]

The model of the natural sciences invoked here by Droysen is not intended in terms of a specific content—that is, a theoretical model of science to which the human sciences must be assimilated; on the contrary, he means that the human sciences must be firmly established as an equally autonomous and self-reliant group of sciences. Droysen's *Historik* attempts to carry out this task.

Even Dilthey, on whom the scientific method and the empiricism of Mill's *Logic* had a much stronger influence, retained the romantic, idealistic heritage in the concept of spirit (Geist). He always thought himself superior to English empiricism, because he vividly perceived what distinguished the historical school from all thinking in terms of the natural sciences and natural law. "The real empirical procedure that can replace prejudiced dogmatic empiricism can come only from Germany. Mill is dogmatic because he lacks historical training"—this was a note Dilthey made in his copy of Mill's *Logic*.[6] In fact all the arduous work of decades that Dilthey devoted to laying the foundations of the human sciences was a constant debate with the logical demand that Mill's famous last chapter made on the human sciences.

Nevertheless, Dilthey let himself be profoundly influenced by the model of the natural sciences, even when he was endeavoring to justify precisely the methodological independence of the human sciences. Two pieces of evidence will make this clear and will, as it were, point the way for our own investigation. In his obituary for Wilhelm Scherer, Dilthey emphasizes that the spirit of the natural sciences guided Scherer's procedure, and he attempts to give the reason why Scherer let himself be so influenced by English empiricism: "He was a modern man, and the world of our forebears was no longer the home of his spirit and his heart, but his historical object."[7] The antithesis shows that for Dilthey scientific knowledge obliges one to sever one's bond with life, to attain distance from one's own history, which alone makes it possible for that history to become an object. We may indeed acknowledge that Scherer and Dilthey's handling of the inductive and comparative methods was governed by genuine individual tact and that such tact presupposes a spiritual cultivation which indicates that the world of classical culture and the romantic belief in individuality survive in them. Nevertheless, it is the model of the natural sciences that guides their conception of themselves as sciences.

A second reference makes this particularly clear: Dilthey refers to the independence of the methods of the human sciences and substantiates it by appeal to their object.[8] At first blush, this sounds like good Aristotelianism and could indicate a genuine detachment from the scientific model. But in accounting for the independence of the methods of the human sciences Dilthey refers to the old Baconian aphorism, "to be conquered, nature must be obeyed,"[9] a principle which practically flies in the face of the classical and romantic heritage that Dilthey seeks to retain. Though his historical training accounts for his superiority over contemporary neo-Kantianism, it must be said that in his logical endeavors Dilthey did not really progress very far beyond the simple statements made by Helmholtz. However strongly Dilthey defended the epistemological independence of the human sciences, what is called "method" in modern science remains the same everywhere and is only displayed in an especially exemplary form in the natural sciences. The human sciences have no method of their own. Yet one might well ask, with Helmholtz, to what extent method is significant in this case and whether the other logical presuppositions of the human sciences are not perhaps far more important than inductive logic. Helmholtz had indicated this correctly when, in order to do justice to the human sciences, he emphasized memory and authority, and spoke of the psychological tact that here replaced the conscious drawing of inferences. What is the basis of this tact? How is it acquired? Does not what is scientific about the human sciences lie rather here than in their methodology?

Because the human sciences prompt this question and thus cannot be fitted into the modern concept of science, they remain a problem for philosophy itself. The answer that Helmholtz and his century gave to this question cannot suffice. They follow Kant in modeling the idea of science and knowledge on the natural sciences and seeking the distinctive feature of the human sciences in the artistic element (artistic feeling, artistic induction). But the picture that Helmholtz gives of work in the natural sciences is rather one-sided, seeing that he does not believe in "sudden flashes of intuition" (or in so-called "inspirations") and regards scientific work only as the "the self-conscious work of drawing iron-clad conclusions." He refers to John Stuart Mill's view that "in modern times the inductive sciences have done more to advance the methods of logic than all the professional philosophers."[10] They are, for him, the model of scientific method as such.

Now, Helmholtz knows that historical knowledge is based on a kind of experience quite different from the one that serves in investigating natural laws. Thus he seeks to determine why the inductive method in historical research proceeds under conditions different from those obtaining in the study of nature. To this end he uses the distinction between nature and freedom, which is the basis of Kantian philosophy. Historical study is different because in its domain there are no natural laws but, rather, voluntarily accepted practical laws—i.e., commandments. The world of human freedom does not manifest the same absence of exceptions as natural laws.

This line of thought, however, is not very convincing. Basing the inductive investigation of the human world of freedom on Kant's distinction between nature and freedom is not true to Kant's intentions; nor is it true to the logic of induction itself. Here Mill was more consistent, for he methodically excluded the problem of freedom. Moreover, Helmholtz's appealing to Kant without following out the consequences of doing so bears no real fruit, for even according to Helmholtz the empiricism of the human sciences is to be regarded in the same way as that of meteorology, namely with renunciation and resignation.

But in fact the human sciences are a long way from regarding themselves as simply inferior to the natural sciences. Instead, possessed of the intellectual heritage of German classicism, they carried forward the proud awareness that they were the true representatives of humanism. The period of German classicism had not only brought about a renewal of literature and aesthetic criticism, which overcame the outmoded baroque ideal of taste and of Enlightenment rationalism; it had also given the idea of humanity, and the ideal of enlightened reason, a fundamentally new content. More than anyone, Herder transcended the perfectionism of the Enlightenment with his new ideal of "cultivating the human" (Bildung zum Menschen) and thus prepared the ground for the growth of the historical sciences in the nineteenth century.[11] The *concept of self-formation, education, or cultivation* (Bildung), which became supremely important at the time, was perhaps the greatest idea of the eighteenth century, and it is this concept which is the atmosphere breathed by the human sciences of the nineteenth century, even if they are unable to offer any epistemological justification for it.

(B) THE GUIDING CONCEPTS OF HUMANISM

(i) Bildung (Culture)

The concept of *Bildung* most clearly indicates the profound intellectual change that still causes us to experience the century of Goethe as contemporary, whereas the baroque era appears historically remote. Key concepts and words which we still use acquired their special stamp then, and if we are not to be swept along by language, but to strive for a reasoned historical self-understanding, we must face a whole host of questions about verbal and conceptual history. In what follows it is possible to do no more than begin the great task that faces investigators, as an aid to our philosophical inquiry. Concepts such as "art," "history," "the creative," "worldview," "experience," "genius," "external world," "interiority," "expression," "style," "symbol," which we take to be self-evident, contain a wealth of history.[12]

If we consider the concept of Bildung, whose importance for the human sciences we have emphasized, we are in a fortunate situation. Here a previous investigation[13] gives us a fine overview of the history of the word: its origin in medieval mysticism, its continuance in the mysticism of the baroque, its religious spiritualization in Klopstock's *Messiah*, which dominates the whole period, and finally the basic definition Herder gives it: "rising up to humanity through culture." The cult of Bildung in the nineteenth century preserved the profounder dimension of the word, and our notion of Bildung is determined by it.

The first important thing to note about the usual content of the word Bildung is that the earlier idea of a "natural form"—which refers to external appearance (the shape of the limbs, the well-formed figure) and in general to the shapes created by nature (e.g., a mountain formation—Gebirgsbildung)—was at that time detached almost entirely from the new idea. Now, Bildung is intimately associated with the idea of culture and designates primarily the properly human way of developing one's natural talents and capacities. Between Kant and Hegel the form Herder had given to the concept was filled out. Kant still does not use the word Bildung in this connection. He speaks of "cultivating" a capacity (or "natural talent"), which as such is an act of freedom by the acting subject. Thus among duties to oneself he mentions not letting one's talents rust, but without using the word Bildung.[14] However when Hegel takes up the same Kantian idea of duties to oneself, he already speaks of Sichbilden (educating or cultivating oneself) and Bildung.[15] And Wilhelm von Humboldt, with his sensitive ear, already detects a difference in meaning between Kultur and Bildung: "but when in our language we say Bildung, we mean something both higher and more inward, namely the disposition of mind which, from the knowledge and the feeling of the total intellectual and moral endeavor, flows harmoniously into sensibility and character."[16]

9

Bildung here no longer means "culture"—i.e., developing one's capacities or talents. Rather, the rise of the word Bildung evokes the ancient mystical tradition according to which man carries in his soul the image of God, after whom he is fashioned, and which man must cultivate in himself. The Latin equivalent for Bildung is formatio, with related words in other languages—e.g., in English (in Shaftesbury), "form" and "formation." In German, too, the corresponding derivations of the idea of forma—e.g., "*Formierung*" and "*Formation*"—have long vied with the word Bildung. Since the Aristotelianism of the Renaissance the word forma has been completely separated from its technical meaning and interpreted in a purely dynamic and natural way. Yet the victory of the word Bildung over "form" does not seem to be fortuitous. For in Bildung there is Bild. The idea of "form" lacks the mysterious ambiguity of Bild, which comprehends both Nachbild (image, copy) and Vorbild (model).

In accordance with the frequent transition from becoming to being, Bildung (like the contemporary use of the German word "*Formation*") describes more the result of the process of becoming than the process itself. The transition is especially clear here because the result of Bildung is not achieved in the manner of a technical construction, but grows out of an inner process of formation and cultivation, and therefore constantly remains in a state of continual Bildung. It is not accidental that in this respect the word Bildung resembles the Greek physis. Like nature, Bildung has no goals outside itself. (The word and thing Bildungsziel—the goal of cultivation—is to be regarded with the suspicion appropriate to such a secondary kind of Bildung. Bildung as such cannot be a goal; it cannot as such be sought, except in the reflective thematic of the educator.) In having no goals outside itself, the concept of Bildung transcends that of the mere cultivation of given talents, from which concept it is derived. The cultivation of a talent is the development of something that is given, so that practicing and cultivating it is a mere means to an end. Thus the educational content of a grammar book is simply a means and not itself an end. Assimilating it simply improves one's linguistic ability. In Bildung, by contrast, that by which and through which one is formed becomes completely one's own. To some extent everything that is received is absorbed, but in Bildung what is absorbed is not like a means that has lost its function. Rather, in acquired Bildung nothing disappears, but everything is preserved. Bildung is a genuine historical idea, and because of this historical character of "preservation" it is important for understanding in the human sciences.

Thus even a preliminary glance at the linguistic history of Bildung introduces us to the circle of historical ideas that Hegel first introduced into the realm of "first philosophy." In fact Hegel has worked out very astutely what Bildung is. We follow him initially.[17] He saw also that philosophy (and, we may add, the human sciences, Geisteswissenschaften) "has, in Bildung, the condition of its existence." For the being of Geist (spirit) has an essential connection with the idea of Bildung.

Man is characterized by the break with the immediate and the natural that the intellectual, rational side of his nature demands of him. "In this sphere he is not, by nature, what he should be"—and hence he needs Bildung. What Hegel calls the formal nature of Bildung depends on its universality. In the concept of rising to the universal, Hegel offers a unified conception of what his age understood by Bildung. Rising to the universal is not limited to theoretical Bildung and does not mean only a theoretical orientation in contrast to a practical one, but covers the essential character of human rationality as a whole. It is the universal nature of human Bildung to constitute itself as a universal intellectual being. Whoever abandons himself to his particularity is ungebildet ("unformed")—e.g., if someone gives way to blind anger without measure or sense of proportion. Hegel shows that basically such a man is lacking in the power of abstraction. He cannot turn his gaze from himself towards something universal, from which his own particular being is determined in measure and proportion.

Hence Bildung, as rising to the universal, is a task for man. It requires sacrificing particularity for the sake of the universal. But, negatively put, sacrificing particularity means the restraint of desire and hence freedom from the object of desire and freedom for its objectivity. Here the deductions of the phenomenological dialectic complement what is stated in the *Propaedeutik*. In his *Phenomenology of Spirit* Hegel works out the genesis of a truly free self-consciousness "in-and-for-itself," and he shows that the essence of work is to form the thing rather than consume it.[18] In the independent existence that work gives the thing, working consciousness finds itself again as an independent consciousness. Work is restrained desire. In forming the object—that is, in being selflessly active and concerned with a universal—working consciousness raises itself above the immediacy of its existence to universality; or, as Hegel puts it, by forming the thing it forms itself. What he means is that in acquiring a "capacity," a skill, man gains the sense of himself. What seemed denied him in the selflessness of serving, inasmuch as he subjected himself to a frame of mind that was alien to him, becomes part of him inasmuch as he is working consciousness. As such he finds in himself his own frame of mind, and it is quite right to say of work that it forms. The self-awareness of working consciousness contains all the elements that make up practical Bildung: the distancing from the immediacy of desire, of personal need and private interest, and the exacting demand of a universal.

In his *Propaedeutic* Hegel demonstrates the nature of practical Bildung, of taking the universal upon oneself, by means of a number of examples. It is found in the moderation which limits the excessive satisfaction of one's needs and use of one's powers by a general consideration—that of health. It is found in the circumspection that, while concerned with the individual situation or business, remains open to observing what else might be necessary. But every choice of profession has something of this. For every profession has something about it of fate, of external necessity; it demands that one give oneself to tasks that one would not seek out as a private aim. Practical Bildung is seen in one's fulfilling one's profession wholly, in all its aspects. But this includes overcoming the element in it that is alien to the particularity which is oneself, and making it wholly one's own. Thus to give oneself to the universality of a profession is at the same time "to know how to limit oneself—i.e., to make one's profession wholly one's concern. Then it is no longer a limitation."

Even in this description of practical Bildung by Hegel, one can recognize the basic character of the historical spirit: to reconcile itself with itself, to recognize oneself in other being. It becomes completely clear in the idea of theoretical Bildung, for to have a theoretical stance is, as such, already alienation, namely the demand that one "deal with something that is not immediate, something that is alien, with something that belongs to memory and to thought." Theoretical Bildung leads beyond what man knows and experiences immediately. It consists in learning to affirm what is different from oneself and to find universal viewpoints from which one can grasp the thing, "the objective thing in its freedom," without selfish interest.[19] That is why acquiring Bildung always involves the development of theoretical interests, and Hegel declares the world and language of antiquity to be especially suitable for this, since this world is remote and alien enough to effect the necessary separation of ourselves from ourselves, "but it contains at the same time all the exit points and threads of the return to oneself, for becoming acquainted with it and for finding oneself again, but oneself according to the truly universal essence of spirit."[20]

In these words of Hegel the Gymnasium director, we recognize the classicist's prejudice that it is particularly in the world of classical antiquity that the universal nature of the spirit can most easily be found. But the basic idea is correct. To recognize one's own in the alien, to become at home in it, is the basic movement of spirit, whose being consists only in returning to itself from what is other. Hence all theoretical Bildung, even acquiring foreign languages and conceptual worlds, is merely the continuation of a process of Bildung that begins much earlier. Every single individual who raises himself out of his natural being to the spiritual finds in the language, customs, and institutions of his people a pre-given body of material which, as in learning to speak, he has to make his own. Thus every individual is always engaged in the process of Bildung and in getting beyond his naturalness, inasmuch as the world into which he is growing is one that is humanly constituted through language and custom. Hegel emphasizes that a people gives itself its existence in its world. It works out from itself and thus exteriorizes what it is in itself.

Thus what constitutes the essence of Bildung is clearly not alienation as such, but the return to oneself—which presupposes alienation, to be sure. However, Bildung is not to be understood only as the process of historically raising the mind to the universal; it is at the same time the element within which the educated man (Gebildete) moves. What kind of element is this? The questions we asked of Helmholtz arise here. Hegel's answer cannot satisfy us, for Hegel sees Bildung as brought to completion through the movement of alienation and appropriation in a complete mastery of substance, in the dissolution of all concrete being, reached only in the absolute knowledge of philosophy.

But we can acknowledge that Bildung is an element of spirit without being tied to Hegel's philosophy of absolute spirit, just as the insight into the historicity of consciousness is not tied to his philosophy of world history. We must realize that the idea of perfect Bildung remains a necessary ideal even for the historical sciences that depart from Hegel. For Bildung is the element in which they move. Even what earlier usage, with reference to physical appearance, called "perfection of form" is not so much the last state of a development as the mature state that has left all development behind and makes possible the harmonious movement of all the limbs. It is precisely in this sense that the human sciences presuppose that the scholarly consciousness is already formed and for that very reason possesses the right, unlearnable, and inimitable tact that envelops the human sciences' form of judgment and mode of knowledge as if it were the element in which they move.

The way that Helmholtz describes how the human sciences work, especially what he calls artistic feeling and *tact*, in fact presupposes this element of Bildung, within which the mind has a special free mobility. Thus Helmholtz speaks of the "readiness with which the most varied experiences must flow into the memory of the historian or philologist."[21] That may seem to be a description from an external viewpoint: namely, the ideal of the "self-conscious work of drawing iron clad conclusions," according to which the natural scientist conceives himself. The concept of *memory*, as he uses it, is not sufficient to explain what is involved here. In fact, this tact or feeling is not rightly understood if one thinks of it as a supervening mental competence which uses a powerful memory and so arrives at cognitive results that cannot be rigorously examined. What makes tact possible, what leads to its acquisition and possession, is not merely a piece of psychological equipment that is propitious to knowledge in the human sciences.

Moreover, the nature of memory is not rightly understood if it is regarded as merely a general talent or capacity. Keeping in mind, forgetting, and recalling belong to the historical constitution of man and are themselves part of his history and his Bildung. Whoever uses his memory as a mere faculty—and any "technique" of memory is such a use—does not yet possess it as something that is absolutely his own. Memory must be formed; for memory is not memory for anything and everything. One has a memory for some things, and not for others; one wants to preserve one thing in memory and banish another. It is time to rescue the phenomenon of memory from being regarded merely as a psychological faculty and to see it as an essential element of the finite historical being of man. In a way that has long been insufficiently noticed, forgetting is closely related to keeping in mind and remembering; forgetting is not merely an absence and a lack but, as Nietzsche in particular pointed out, a condition of the life of mind.[22] Only by forgetting does the mind have the possibility of total renewal, the capacity to see everything with fresh eyes, so that what is long familiar fuses with the new into a many leveled unity. "Keeping in mind" is ambiguous. As memory (mneme), it is connected to remembering (anamnesis).[23] But the same thing is also true of the concept of "tact" that Helmholtz uses. By "tact" we understand a special sensitivity and sensitiveness to situations and how to behave in them, for which knowledge from general principles does not suffice. Hence an essential part of tact is that it is tacit and unformulable. One can say something tactfully; but that will always mean that one passes over something tactfully and leaves it unsaid, and it is tactless to express what one can only pass over. But to pass over something does not mean to avert one's gaze from it, but to keep an eye on it in such a way that rather than knock into it, one slips by it. Thus tact helps one to preserve distance. It avoids the offensive, the intrusive, the violation of the intimate sphere of the person.

The tact of which Helmholtz speaks is not simply identical with this phenomenon of manners and customs, but they do share something essential. For the tact which functions in the human sciences is not simply a feeling and unconscious, but is at the same time a mode of knowing and a mode of being. This can be seen more clearly from the above analysis of the concept of Bildung. What Helmholtz calls tact includes Bildung and is a function of both aesthetic and historical Bildung. One must have a sense for the aesthetic and the historical or acquire it, if one is to be able to rely on one's tact in work in the human sciences. Because this sense is not simply part of one's natural equipment, we rightly speak of aesthetic or historical consciousness, and not properly of sense. Still, this consciousness accords well with the immediacy of the senses—i.e., it knows how to make sure distinctions and evaluations in the individual case without being able to give its reasons. Thus someone who has an aesthetic sense knows how to distinguish between the beautiful and the ugly, high and low quality, and whoever has a historical sense knows what is possible for an age and what is not, and has a sense of the otherness of the past in relation to the present.

If all that presupposes Bildung, then what is in question is not a procedure or behavior but what has come into being. It is not enough to observe more closely, to study a tradition more thoroughly, if there is not already a receptivity to the "otherness" of the work of art or of the past. That is what, following Hegel, we emphasized as the general characteristic of Bildung: keeping oneself open to what is other—to other, more universal points of view. It embraces a sense of proportion and distance in relation to itself, and hence consists in rising above itself to universality. To distance oneself from oneself and from one's private purposes means to look at these in the way that others see them. This universality is by no means a universality of the concept or understanding. This is not a case of a particular being determined by a universal; nothing is proved conclusively. The universal viewpoints to which the cultivated man (gebildet) keeps himself open are not a fixed applicable yardstick, but are present to him only as the viewpoints of possible others. Thus the cultivated consciousness has in fact more the character of a sense. For every sense—e.g., the sense of sight—is already universal in that it embraces its sphere, remains open to a particular field, and grasps the distinctions within what is opened to it in this way. In that such distinctions are confined to one particular sphere at a time, whereas cultivated consciousness is active in all directions, such consciousness surpasses all of the natural sciences. It is a *universal sense*.

A universal and common sense—this formulation of the nature of Bildung suggests an extensive historical context. A reflection on the idea of Bildung like that which lies at the basis of Helmholtz's thinking leads us far back into the history of this concept. We must pursue this context a little if we want to liberate the problem the human sciences present for philosophy from the artificial narrowness in which nineteenth-century methodology was caught. The modern concept of science and the associated concept of method are insufficient. What makes the human sciences into sciences can be understood more easily from the tradition of the concept of Bildung than from the modern idea of scientific method. It is to the *humanistic tradition* that we must turn. In its resistance to the claims of modern science it gains a new significance.

It would be worth making a separate investigation into the way in which, since the days of humanism, criticism of "scholastic" science has made itself heard and how this criticism has changed with the changes of its opponent. Originally it was classical motifs that were revived in it. The enthusiasm with which the humanists proclaimed the Greek language and the path of eruditio signified more than an antiquarian passion. The revival of the classical languages brought with it a new valuation of rhetoric. It waged battle against the "school," i.e., scholastic science, and supported an ideal of human wisdom that was not achieved in the "school"—an antithesis which in fact is found at the very beginning of philosophy. Plato's critique of sophism and, still more, his peculiarly ambivalent attitude towards Isocrates, indicate the philosophical problem that emerges here. Beginning with the new methodological awareness of seventeenth-century science, this old problem inevitably became more critical. In view of this new science's claim to be exclusive, the question of whether the humanistic concept of Bildung was not a special source of truth was raised with increased urgency. In fact we shall see that it is from the survival of the humanistic idea of Bildung that the human sciences of the nineteenth century draw, without admitting it, their own life.

At the same time it is self-evident that it is not mathematics but humanistic studies that are important here. For what could the new methodology of the seventeenth century mean for the human sciences? One has only to read the appropriate chapters of the *Logique de Port-Royal* concerning the rules of reason applied to historical truths to see how little can be achieved in the human sciences by that idea of method.[24] Its results are really trivial—for example, the idea that in order to judge an event in its truth one must take account of the accompanying circumstances (circonstances). With this kind of argument the Jansenists sought to provide a methodical way of showing to what extent miracles deserved belief. They countered an untested belief in miracles with the spirit of the new method and sought in this way to legitimate the true miracles of biblical and ecclesiastical tradition. The new science in the service of the old church—that this relationship could not last is only too clear, and one can foresee what had to happen when the Christian presuppositions themselves were questioned. When the methodological ideal of the natural sciences was applied to the credibility of the historical testimonies of scriptural tradition, it inevitably led to completely different results that were catastrophic for Christianity. There is no great distance between the criticism of miracles in the style of the Jansenists and historical criticism of the Bible. Spinoza is a good example of this. I shall show later that a logically consistent application of this method as the only norm for the truth of the human sciences would amount to their self-annihilation.

(ii) Sensus Communis

In this regard it is important to remember the humanistic tradition, and to ask what is to be learned from it with respect to the human sciences' mode of knowledge. Vico's *De nostri temporis studiorum ratione* makes a good starting point.[25] As its very title shows, Vico's defense of humanism derives from the Jesuit pedagogical system and is directed as much against Jansenism as against Descartes. Like his outline of a "new science," Vico's pedagogical manifesto is based on old truths. He appeals to the sensus communis, common sense, and to the humanistic ideal of eloquentia—elements already present in the classical concept of wisdom. "Talking well" (eu legein) has always had two meanings; it is not merely a rhetorical ideal. It also means saying the right thing—i.e., the truth—and is not just the art of speaking—of saying something well.

This ideal was proclaimed in the ancient world just as much by teachers of philosophy as by those of rhetoric. Rhetoric was always in conflict with philosophy and, in contrast to the idle speculations of the Sophists, claimed to teach true wisdom. Here Vico, himself a teacher of rhetoric, is in a humanistic tradition that stems from antiquity. This tradition is obviously important for the self-understanding of the human sciences; especially so is the positive ambiguity of the rhetorical ideal, which is condemned not only by Plato, but by the anti-rhetorical methodology of modern times. In Vico, we already find much of what will concern us. But apart from the rhetorical element, his appeal to the sensus communis contains another element from classical tradition. This is the contrast between the scholar and the wise man on whom the scholar depends—a contrast that is drawn for the first time in the Cynics' conception of Socrates—and its content is based on the distinction between the ideas of sophia and phronesis. It was first elaborated by Aristotle, developed by the Peripatetics as a critique of the theoretical ideal of life,[26] and in the Hellenistic period helped define the image of the wise man, especially after the Greek ideal of Bildung had been fused with the self-consciousness of the leading political class of Rome. Late Roman legal science also developed against the background of an art and practice of law that is closer to the practical ideal of phronesis than to the theoretical ideal of sophia.[27]

With the renaissance of classical philosophy and rhetoric, the image of Socrates became the countercry against science, as is shown, in particular, in the figure of the idiota, the layman, who assumes a totally new role between the scholar and the wise man.[28] Likewise the rhetorical tradition of humanism invoked Socrates and the skeptical critique of the Dogmatists. We find that Vico criticizes the Stoics because they believe in reason as the regula veri and, contrariwise, praises the old Academicians, who assert only the knowledge of not knowing anything; and the new ones, because they excel in the art of arguing (which is part of rhetoric).

Vico's appeal to the sensus communis undoubtedly exhibits a special coloring within this humanistic tradition. In this sphere of knowledge too there is a querelle des anciens et des modernes. It is no longer the contrast with the "school," but the particular contrast with modern science that Vico has in mind. He does not deny the merits of modern critical science but shows its limits. Even with this new science and its mathematical methodology, we still cannot do without the wisdom of the ancients and their cultivation of prudentia and eloquentia. But the most important thing in education is still something else—the training in the sensus communis, which is not nourished on the true but on the probable, the verisimilar. The main thing for our purposes is that here sensus communis obviously does not mean only that general faculty in all men but the sense that founds community. According to Vico, what gives the human will its direction is not the abstract universality of reason but the concrete universality represented by the community of a group, a people, a nation, or the whole human race. Hence developing this communal sense is of decisive importance for living.

On this communal sense for what is true and right, which is not a knowledge based on argumentation, but enables one to discover what is evident (verisimile), Vico bases the significance and the independent rights of rhetoric. Education cannot, he says, tread the path of critical research. Youth demands images for its imagination and for forming its memory. But studying the sciences in the spirit of modern criticism does not achieve this. Thus Vico supplements the critica of Cartesianism with the old topica. This is the art of finding arguments and serves to develop the sense of what is convincing, which works instinctively and ex tempore, and for that very reason cannot be replaced by science.

Vico's prescriptions have an apological air. They indirectly take cognizance of science's new concept of truth by the very fact that they defend the rights of the probable. As we have seen, he here follows an ancient rhetorical tradition that goes back to Plato. But what Vico means goes far beyond the defense of rhetorical persuasion. The old Aristotelian distinction between practical and theoretical knowledge is operative here—a distinction which cannot be reduced to that between the true and the probable. Practical knowledge, phronesis, is another kind of knowledge.[29] Primarily, this means that it is directed towards the concrete situation. Thus it must grasp the "circumstances" in their infinite variety. This is what Vico expressly emphasizes about it. It is true that his main concern is to show that this kind of knowledge lies outside the rational concept of knowledge, but this is not in fact mere resignation. The Aristotelian distinction refers to something other than the distinction between knowing on the basis of universal principles and on the basis of the concrete. Nor does he mean only the capacity to subsume the individual case under a universal category—what we call "judgment." Rather, there is a positive ethical motif involved that merges into the Roman Stoic doctrine of the sensus communis. The grasp and moral control of the concrete situation require subsuming what is given under the universal—that is, the goal that one is pursuing so that the right thing may result. Hence it presupposes a direction of the will—i.e., moral being (hexis). That is why Aristotle considers phronesis an "intellectual virtue." He sees it not only as a capacity (dunamis), but as a determination of moral being which cannot exist without the totality of the "ethical virtues," which in turn cannot exist without it. Although practicing this virtue means that one distinguishes what should be done from what should not, it is not simply practical shrewdness and general cleverness. The distinction between what should and should not be done includes the distinction between the proper and the improper and thus presupposes a moral attitude, which it continues to develop.

This idea propounded by Aristotle against Plato's "idea of the good" is in fact what Vico's point about the sensus communis goes back to. In scholasticism, say for St. Thomas, in elaborating on the *De Anima*,[30] the sensus communis is the common root of the outer senses—i.e., the faculty that combines them, that makes judgments about what is given, a capacity that is given to all men.[31] For Vico, however, the sensus communis is the sense of what is right and of the common good that is to be found in all men; moreover, it is a sense that is acquired through living in the community and is determined by its structures and aims. This concept sounds like natural law, like the koinai ennoiai of the Stoics. But the sensus communis is not, in this sense, a Greek concept and definitely does not mean the koine dunamis of which Aristotle speaks in the *De Anima* when he tries to reconcile the doctrine of the specific senses (aisthesis idia) with the phenomenological finding that all perception is a differentiation and an intention of the universal. Rather, Vico goes back to the old Roman concept of the sensus communis, as found especially in the Roman classics which, when faced with Greek cultivation, held firmly to the value and significance of their own traditions of civil and social life. A critical note directed against the theoretical speculations of the philosophers can be heard in the Roman concept of the sensus communis; and that note Vico sounds again from his different position of opposition to modern science (the critica).

There is something immediately evident about grounding philological and historical studies and the ways the human sciences work on this concept of the sensus communis. For their object, the moral and historical existence of humanity, as it takes shape in our words and deeds, is itself decisively determined by the sensus communis. Thus a conclusion based on universals, a reasoned proof, is not sufficient, because what is decisive is the circumstances. But this is only a negative formulation. The sense of the community mediates its own positive knowledge. One does not at all exhaust the mode of historical knowledge by saying that here one has to allow "belief in other people's testimony" (Tetens[32]) instead of "self-conscious deduction" (Helmholtz). Nor is it at all true that such knowledge has less truth value. D'Alembert is correct when he writes, "Probability operates principally in the case of historical facts, and in general for all past, present and future events, which we attribute to a kind of chance because we do not unravel the causes. The part of this knowledge whose object is the present and the past, although it may be founded on testimony alone, often produces in us a conviction as strong as that born from axioms."[33]

Historia is a source of truth totally different from theoretical reason. This is what Cicero meant when he called it the vita memoriae.[34] It exists in its own right because human passions cannot be governed by the universal prescriptions of reason. In this sphere one needs, rather, convincing examples as only history can offer them. That is why Bacon describes historia, which supplies these examples, as virtually another way of philosophizing (alia ratio philosophandi).[35]

This, too, is negative enough in its formulation. But we will see that in all these versions the mode of being of moral knowledge, as recognized by Aristotle, is operative. It will be important to recall this so that the human sciences can understand themselves more adequately.

Vico's return to the Roman concept of the sensus communis, and his defense of humanist rhetoric against modern science, is of special interest to us, for here we are introduced to an element of truth in the human sciences that was no longer recognizable when they conceptualized themselves in the nineteenth century. Vico lived in an unbroken tradition of rhetorical and humanist culture, and had only to reassert anew its ageless claim. Ultimately, it has always been known that the possibilities of rational proof and instruction do not fully exhaust the sphere of knowledge. Hence Vico's appeal to the sensus communis belongs, as we have seen, in a wider context that goes right back to antiquity and whose continued effect into the present day is our theme.[36]

We, on the contrary, must laboriously make our way back into this tradition by first showing the difficulties that result from the application of the modern concept of method to the human sciences. Let us therefore consider how this tradition became so impoverished and how the human sciences' claim to know something true came to be measured by a standard foreign to it—namely the methodical thinking of modern science.

In general, Vico and the unbroken rhetorical tradition of Italy do not directly influence this development, which was determined chiefly by the German "historical school." One can discern hardly any influence of Vico on the eighteenth century. But he was not alone in his appeal to the sensus communis. He has an important parallel in *Shaftesbury*, who had a powerful influence on the eighteenth century. Shaftesbury places the evaluation of the social significance of *wit* and *humor* under sensus communis and explicitly cites the Roman classics and their humanist interpreters.[37] As we have noted, the concept of the sensus communis undoubtedly reminds us of the Stoics and of the natural law. Nevertheless, it is impossible to deny the validity of the humanistic interpretation based on the Roman classics, which Shaftesbury follows. By sensus communis, according to Shaftesbury, the humanists understood a sense of the common weal, but also "love of the community or society, natural affection, humanity, obligingness." They adopt a term from Marcus Aurelius, koinonoemosune—a most unusual and artificial word, confirming that the concept of sensus communis does not originate with the Greek philosophers, but has the Stoical conception sounding in it like a harmonic.[38] The humanist Salmasius describes the content of this word as "a restrained, customary, and regular way of thinking in a man, which as it were looks to the community and does not refer everything to its own advantage but directs its attention to those things with which it is concerned, and thinks of itself with restraint and proper measure." What Shaftesbury is thinking of is not so much a capacity given to all men, part of the natural law, as a social virtue, a virtue of the heart more than of the head. And if he understands wit and humor in terms of it, then in this respect too he is following ancient Roman concepts that include in humanitas a refined savoir vivre, the attitude of the man who understands a joke and tells one because he is aware of a deeper union with his interlocutor. (Shaftesbury explicitly limits wit and humour to social intercourse among friends.) Though the sensus communis appears here mostly as a virtue of social intercourse, there is nevertheless a moral, even a metaphysical basis implied.

Shaftesbury is thinking of the intellectual and social virtue of sympathy; and on it, we recall, he based not only morality, but an entire aesthetic metaphysics. His successors, above all Hutcheson[39] and Hume, elaborated his suggestions into the doctrine of the moral sense, which was later to serve as a foil to Kantian ethics.

The concept of "common sense" acquired a quite central systematic function in *Scottish* philosophy, which was directed polemically against metaphysics and against its dissolution in skepticism, and built up its new system on the basis of original and natural judgments of common sense (Thomas Reid).[40] Doubtless this was influenced by the Aristotelian and scholastic tradition of the concept of sensus communis. Inquiry into the senses and their cognitive capacity comes from this tradition and is ultimately intended to correct the exaggerations of philosophical speculation. At the same time, however, the connection between common sense and society is preserved: "They serve to direct us in the common affairs of life, where our reasoning faculty would leave us in the dark." In their eyes, the philosophy of sound understanding, of good sense, is not only a cure for the "moon-sickness" of metaphysics, but also contains the basis of a moral philosophy that really does justice to the life of society.

The moral element in the concept of common sense or le bon sens has remained to the present day and distinguishes these from the German concept of "der gesunde Menschenverstand" ("sound understanding"). Take as an example *Henri Bergson's* fine speech on le bon sens given at the award ceremony in 1895 at the Sorbonne.[41] His criticism of the abstractions of natural science, of language and of legal thinking, his passionate appeal to the "inner energy of an intelligence which at each moment wins itself back to itself, eliminating ideas already formed to give place to those in the process of being formed" (p. 88), was called le bon sens in France. Naturally, the definition of this concept certainly contained a reference to the senses, but for Bergson it obviously goes without saying that, unlike the senses, le bon sens refers to the "milieu social": "while the other senses relate us to things, 'good sense' governs our relations with persons" (p. 85). It is a kind of genius for practical life, but less a gift than the constant task of "renewed adaptation to new situations," a work of adapting general principles to reality, through which justice is realized, a "tactfulness in practical truth," a "rightness of judgment, that stems from correctness of soul" (p. 88). Le bon sens, for Bergson, is, as the common source of thought and will, a "sens social," which avoids both the mistakes of the scientific dogmatists who are looking for social laws and those of the metaphysical utopians. "Perhaps there is, properly speaking, no method, but rather a certain way of acting." It is true that he speaks of the importance of classical studies for the development of this bon sens—he sees them as an attempt to break through the "ice of words" and discover the free flow of thought below (p. 91)—but he does not ask the contrary question, namely how necessary le bon sens is for classical studies—i.e., he does not speak of its hermeneutic function. His question has nothing to do with the sciences, but with the independent significance of le bon sens for life. We are emphasizing only the self-evidence with which the moral and political meaning of this concept dominated his mind and that of his hearers.

It is very characteristic of the human sciences' self-reflection in the nineteenth century that they proceeded not under the influence of the tradition of moral philosophy to which both Vico and Shaftesbury belong and which is represented primarily by France, the classical land of le bon sens, but under the influence of the German philosophy of the age of Kant and Goethe. Whereas even today in England and the Romance countries the concept of the sensus communis is not just a critical slogan but a general civic quality, in Germany the followers of Shaftesbury and Hutcheson did not, even in the eighteenth century, take over the political and social element contained in sensus communis. The metaphysics of the schools and the popular philosophy of the eighteenth century—however much they studied and imitated the leading countries of the Enlightenment, England and France—could not assimilate an idea for which the social and political conditions were utterly lacking. The concept of sensus communis was taken over, but in being emptied of all political content it lost its genuine critical significance. Sensus communis was understood as a purely theoretical faculty: theoretical judgment, parallel to moral consciousness (conscience) and taste. Thus it was integrated into a scholasticism of the basic faculties, of which Herder provided the critique (in the fourth "kritischen Wäldchen," directed against Riedel), and which made him the forerunner of historicism in the field of aesthetics also.

And yet there is one important exception: *Pietism*. It was important not only for a man of the world like Shaftesbury to delimit the claims of science—i.e., of demonstratio—against the "school" and to appeal to the sensus communis, but also for the preacher, who seeks to reach the hearts of his congregation. Thus the Swabian Pietist *Oetinger* explicitly relied on Shaftesbury's defense of the sensus communis. We find sensus communis translated simply as "heart" and the following description: "The sensus communis is concerned only with things that all men see daily before them, things that hold an entire society together, things that are concerned as much with truths and statements as with the arrangements and patterns comprised in statements. . . . "[42] Oetinger is concerned to show that it is not just a question of the clarity of the concepts—clarity is "not enough for living knowledge." Rather, there must be "certain anticipations and predilections present." "Fathers are moved without proof to care for their children; love does not demonstrate, but often against reason rends the heart at the beloved's reproach." Oetinger's appeal to the sensus communis against the rationalism of the "school" is especially interesting for us because he gives it an expressly hermeneutical application. For Oetinger, as a churchman, the important thing is the understanding of Scripture. Because the mathematical, demonstrative method fails here, he demands another, the "generative method"—i.e., the "organic presentation of Scripture—so that justice may be planted like a shoot."

Oetinger also made the concept of sensus communis the object of an extended and learned investigation, which is likewise directed against rationalism.[43] He sees in it the source of all truths, the very ars inveniendi, in contrast to Leibniz, who bases everything on a mere calculus metaphysicus (excluso omni gusto interno). According to Oetinger the true basis of the sensus communis is the concept of vita, life (sensus communis vitae gaudens). In contrast to the violent anatomization of nature through experiment and calculation, he sees the natural development of the simple into the complex as the universal law of growth of the divine creation and, likewise, of the human spirit. For the idea that all knowledge originates in the sensus communis he quotes Wolff, Bernoulli, and Pascal, Maupertuis' investigation into the origin of language, Bacon, Fenelon, etc. and defines the sensus communis as "the vivid and penetrating perception of objects evident to all human beings, from their immediate contact and intuition, which are absolutely simple."

From this second sentence it is apparent that Oetinger throughout combines the humanistic, political meaning of the word with the peripatetic concept of sensus communis. The above definition reminds one here and there ("immediate contact and intuition") of Aristotle's doctrine of nous. He takes up the Aristotelian question of the common dunamis, which combines seeing, hearing, etc., and for him it confirms the genuinely divine mystery of life. The divine mystery of life is its simplicity— even if man has lost it through the fall, he can still find his way back, through the grace of God, to unity and simplicity: "the activity of the logos, that is, the presence of God integrates diversity into unity" (p. 162). The presence of God consists precisely in life itself, in this "communal sense" that distinguishes all living things from dead—it is no accident that he mentions the polyp and the starfish which, though cut into small pieces, regenerate themselves and form new individuals. In man the same divine power operates in the form of the instinct and inner stimulation to discover the traces of God and to recognize what has the greatest connection with human happiness and life. Oetinger expressly distinguishes rational truths from receptivity to common truths—"sensible truths," useful to all men at all times and places. The communal sense is a complex of instincts—i.e., a natural drive towards that on which the true happiness of life depends, and to that extent an effect of the presence of God. Instincts are not to be understood, with Leibniz, as affects—i.e., as confusae repraesentationes—for they are not ephemeral but deeply rooted tendencies and have a dictatorial, divine, irresistible force.[44] Based on these instincts, sensus communis is of special importance for our knowledge, precisely because they are a gift of God.[45] Oetinger writes, "the ratio governs itself by rules, often even without God; but sense, always with God. Just as nature is different from art, so sense and ratio are different. God works through nature in a simultaneous increase in growth that spreads regularly throughout the whole. Art, however, begins with some particular part. . . . Sense imitates nature; the ratio, art" (p. 247).

Interestingly enough, this statement comes from a hermeneutical context, as indeed in this learned work the "*Sapientia Salomonis*" represents the ultimate object and highest example of knowledge. It comes from the chapter on the use (usus) of the sensus communis. Here Oetinger attacks the hermeneutical theory of the Wolffian school. More important than all hermeneutical rules is to be "sensu plenus." Naturally, this thesis is a spiritualistic extreme, but it still has its logical foundation in the concept of vita or sensus communis. Its hermeneutical meaning can be illustrated by this sentence: "the ideas found in Scripture and in the works of God are the more fruitful and purified the more that each can be seen in the whole and all can be seen in each."[46] Here what people in the nineteenth and twentieth centuries like to call "intuition" is brought back to its metaphysical foundation: that is, to the structure of living, organic being in which the whole is in each individual: "the whole of life has its center in the heart, which by means of common sense grasps countless things all at the same time" (Praef.).

More profound than all knowledge of hermeneutical rules is the application to oneself: "above all apply the rules to yourself and then you will have the key to understanding Solomon's proverbs" (p. 207).[47] On this basis Oetinger is able to bring his ideas into harmony with those of Shaftesbury who, as he says, is the only one to have written about sensus communis under this title. But he also cites others who have noted the one-sidedness of the rational method—e.g., Pascal's distinction between esprit géométrique and esprit de finesse. Nevertheless, for the Swabian Pietist what crystallizes around the concept of sensus communis is rather a theological than a political or social interest.

Of course other Pietist theologians have emphasized application against the dominant rationalism in the same way as Oetinger, as we can see from the example of Rambach, whose very influential hermeneutics also dealt with application. But when pietistic tendencies were supplanted in the later eighteenth century, the hermeneutic function of sensus communis declined to a mere corrective: that which contradicts the "consensus" of feelings, judgments, and conclusions—i.e., the sensus communis—cannot be correct.[48] In contrast to the importance that Shaftesbury assigned to the sensus communis for society and state, this negative function shows that the concept was emptied and intellectualized by the German enlightenment.

(iii) Judgment

This development of the concept of sensus communis in eighteenth-century Germany may explain why it is so closely connected with the *concept of judgment*. "Gesunder Menschenverstand" (good sense), sometimes called "gemeiner Verstand" (common understanding), is in fact decisively characterized by judgment. The difference between a fool and a sensible man is that the former lacks judgment—i.e., he is not able to subsume correctly and hence cannot apply correctly what he has learned and knows. The word "judgment" was introduced in the eighteenth century in order to convey the concept of judicium, which was considered to be a basic intellectual virtue. In the same way the English moral philosophers emphasize that moral and aesthetic judgments do not obey reason, but have the character of sentiment (or taste), and similarly Tetens, one of the representatives of the German Enlightenment, sees the sensus communis as a judicium without reflection.[49] In fact the logical basis of judgment—subsuming a particular under a universal, recognizing something as an example of a rule—cannot be demonstrated. Thus judgment requires a principle to guide its application. In order to follow this principle another faculty of judgment would be needed, as Kant shrewdly noted.[50] So it cannot be taught in the abstract but only practiced from case to case, and is therefore more an ability like the senses. It is something that cannot be learned, because no demonstration from concepts can guide the application of rules.

Consequently, German Enlightenment philosophy considered judgment not among the higher but among the lower powers of the mind. In this respect, it diverged considerably from the original Roman sense of sensus communis, while advancing the scholastic tradition. This was to be especially important for aesthetics. Baumgarten, for example, is quite certain that what judgment recognizes is the sensible individual, the unique thing, and what it judges in the individual thing is its perfection or imperfection.[51] It must be noted that by this definition judgment does not simply mean applying a pregiven concept of the thing, but that the sensible individual is grasped in itself insofar as it exhibits the agreement of the many with the one. Not the application of the universal but internal coherence is what matters. As we can see, this is already what Kant later calls "reflective judgment," and he understands it as judgment according to real and formal appropriateness. No concept is given; rather, the individual object is judged "immanently." Kant calls this an aesthetic judgment; and just as Baumgarten described the "iudicium sensitivum" as "gustus," so also Kant repeats: "A sensible judgment of perfection is called taste."[52]

We will see below that this aesthetic development of the concept of iudicium, for which Gottsched was primarily responsible in the eighteenth century, acquired a systematic significance for Kant, although it will also emerge that Kant's distinction between determinant and reflective judgment is not without its problems.[53] Moreover, it is difficult to reduce the meaning of sensus communis to aesthetic judgment. From the use that Vico and Shaftesbury make of this concept, it appears that sensus communis is not primarily a formal capacity, an intellectual faculty to be used, but already embraces a sum of judgments and criteria for judgment that determine its contents.

Common sense is exhibited primarily in making judgments about right and wrong, proper and improper. Whoever has a sound judgment is not thereby enabled to judge particulars under universal viewpoints, but he knows what is really important—i.e., he sees things from right and sound points of view. A swindler who correctly calculates human weakness and always makes the right move in his deceptions nevertheless does not possess "sound judgment" in the highest sense of the term. Thus the universality (Allgemeinheit) that is ascribed to the faculty of judgment is by no means as common (gemein) as Kant thinks. Judgment is not so much a faculty as a demand that has to be made of all. Everyone has enough "sense of the common" (gemeinen Sinn)—i.e., judgment—that he can be expected to show a "sense of the community" (Gemeinsinn), genuine moral and civic solidarity, but that means judgment of right and wrong, and a concern for the "common good." This is what makes Vico's reliance on the humanistic tradition so impressive, for against the intellectualization of the concept of the sense of the community, he firmly retains all the wealth of meaning that lived in the Roman tradition of this word (and to this day is characteristic of the Latin race). Similarly, when Shaftesbury took up the concept it was, as we have seen, also linked to the political and social tradition of humanism. The sensus communis is an element of social and moral being. Even when this concept was associated with a polemical attack on metaphysics (as in Pietism and Scottish philosophy), it still retained its original critical function.

By contrast, Kant's version of this idea in his *Critique of Judgment* has quite a different emphasis.[54] There is no longer any systematic place for the concept's basic moral sense. As we know, he developed his moral philosophy in explicit opposition to the doctrine of "moral feeling" that had been worked out in English philosophy. Thus he totally excluded the concept of sensus communis from moral philosophy.

What appears with the unconditionality of a moral imperative cannot be based on feeling, not even if one does not mean an individual's feeling but common moral sensibility. For the imperative immanent in morality totally excludes any comparative reflection about others. The unconditionality of a moral imperative certainly does not mean that the moral consciousness must remain rigid in judging others. Rather, it is morally imperative to detach oneself from the subjective, private conditions of one's own judgment and to assume the standpoint of the other person. But this unconditionality also means that the moral consciousness cannot avoid appealing to the judgment of others. The obligatoriness of the imperative is universal in a stricter sense than the universality of sensibility can ever attain. Applying the moral law to the will is a matter for judgment. But since it is a question of judgment operating under the laws of pure practical reason, its task consists precisely in preserving one from the "empiricism of practical reason, which bases the practical concepts of good and bad merely on empirical consequences."[55] This is done by the "typic" of pure practical reason.

For Kant there is also another question: how to implant the stern law of pure practical reason in the human mind. He deals with this in the "Methodology of Pure, Practical Reason," which "endeavors to provide a brief outline of the method of engendering and cultivating genuine moral attitudes." For this he in fact calls on ordinary human reason and he wants to exercise and cultivate practical judgment; and certainly aesthetic elements play their part also.[56] But that moral feeling can be cultivated is not really part of moral philosophy, and in any case it is not relevant to its foundations. For Kant requires that our will be determined only by motives founded on the self-legislation of pure practical reason. This cannot be based on a mere commonness of sensibility, but only on "an obscure but still securely guiding practical act of will," to clarify and strengthen which is the task of the *Critique of Practical Reason*.

The sensus communis plays no part in Kant—not even in the logical sense. What Kant treats in the transcendental doctrine of judgment—i.e., the doctrine of schematism and the principles—no longer has anything to do with the sensus communis.[57] For here we are concerned with concepts that are supposed to refer to their objects a priori, and not with the subsumption of the particular under the universal. When, however, we are really concerned with the ability to grasp the particular as an instance of the universal, and we speak of sound understanding, then this is, according to Kant, something that is "common" in the truest sense of the word—i.e., it is "something to be found everywhere, but to possess it is by no means any merit or advantage."[58] The only significance of this sound understanding is that it is a preliminary stage of cultivated and enlightened reason. It is active in an obscure kind of judgment called feeling, but it still judges according to concepts, "though commonly only according to obscurely imagined principles,"[59] and it certainly cannot be considered a special "sense of community." The universal logical use of judgment, which goes back to the sensus communis, contains no principle of its own.[60]

Thus from the whole range of what could be called a sense faculty of judgment, for Kant only the judgment of aesthetic taste is left. Here one may speak of a true sense of community. Doubtful though it may be whether one may speak of knowledge in connection with aesthetic taste, and certain though it is that aesthetic judgments are not made according to concepts, it is still the case that aesthetic taste necessarily implies universal agreement, even if it is sensory and not conceptual. Thus the true sense of community, says Kant, is *taste*.

That is a paradoxical formulation when we recall that the eighteenth century enjoyed discussing precisely diversities of human taste. But even if one draws no skeptical, relativistic conclusions from differences of taste, but holds on to the idea of good taste, it sounds paradoxical to call "good taste"—this strange distinction that differentiates the members of a culti-vated society from all other men—a sense of community. Taken as an empirical statement that would, in fact, be absurd, and we shall see how far this description has meaning for Kant's transcendental purpose—i.e., as an a priori justification for undertaking a criticism of taste. But we shall also have to ask how the truth claim implicit in the sense of community is affected by narrowing the concept of the sense of community to a judgment of taste about what is beautiful, and how the Kantian subjective a priori of taste has affected the self-understanding of the human sci-ences.

(iv) Taste

Again we must go back further in time. It is not only a question of narrowing the concept of the sense of community to taste, but of narrowing the concept of taste itself. The long history of this idea before Kant made it the basis of his *Critique of Judgment* shows that *the concept of taste* was originally more a *moral* than an aesthetic idea. It describes an ideal of genuine humanity and receives its character from the effort to take a critical stand against the dogmatism of the "school." It was only later that the use of the idea was limited to the "aesthetic."

Balthasar *Gracian*[61] stands at the beginning of this history. Gracian starts from the view that the sense of taste, this most animal and most inward of our senses, still contains the beginnings of the intellectual differentiation we make in judging things. Thus the sensory differentiation of taste, which accepts or rejects in the most immediate way, is in fact not merely an instinct, but strikes a balance between sensory instinct and intellectual freedom. The sense of taste is able to gain the distance necessary for choosing and judging what is the most urgent necessity of life. Thus Gracian already sees in taste a "spiritualization of animality" and rightly points out that there is cultivation (cultura) not only of the mind (ingenio) but also of taste (gusto). This is true also, of course, of sensory taste. There are men who have "a good tongue," gourmets who cultivate these delights. This idea of "gusto" is the starting point for Gracian's ideal of social cultivation. His ideal of the cultivated man (the discreto) is that, as an "hombre en su punto," he achieves the proper freedom of distance from all the things of life and society, so that he is able to make distinctions and choices consciously and reflectively.

Gracian's ideal of Bildung (cultivation) was supposed to be a completely new departure. It replaced that of the Christian courtier (Castiglione). It is remarkable within the history of Western ideals of Bildung for being independent of class. It sets out the ideal of a society based on Bildung.[62] This ideal of social Bildung seems to emerge everywhere in the wake of absolutism and its suppression of the hereditary aristocracy. Thus the history of the idea of taste follows the history of absolutism from Spain to France and England and is closely bound up with the antecedents of the third estate. Taste is not only the ideal created by a new society, but we see this ideal of "good taste" producing what was subsequently called "good society." It no longer recognizes and legitimates itself on the basis of birth and rank but simply through the shared nature of its judgments or, rather, its capacity to rise above narrow interests and private predilections to the title of judgment.

The concept of taste undoubtedly implies a *mode of knowing*. The mark of good taste is being able to stand back from ourselves and our private preferences. Thus taste, in its essential nature, is not private but a social phenomenon of the first order. It can even counter the private inclinations of the individual like a court of law, in the name of a universality that it intends and represents. One can like something that one's own taste rejects. The verdict of taste is curiously decisive. As we say, de gustibus non disputandum (Kant rightly says that in matters of taste there can be a disagreement but not a disputation),[63] not just because there are no universal conceptual criteria that everyone must accept, but because one does not look for them and would not even think it right if they existed. One must have taste—one cannot learn through demonstration, nor can one replace it by mere imitation. Nevertheless, taste is not a mere private quality, for it always endeavors to be good taste. The decisiveness of the judgment of taste includes its claim to validity. Good taste is always sure of its judgment—i.e., it is essentially sure taste, an acceptance and rejection that involves no hesitation, no surreptitious glances at others, no searching for reasons.

Taste is therefore something like a sense. In its operation it has no knowledge of reasons. If taste registers a negative reaction to something, it is not able to say why. But it experiences it with the greatest certainty. Sureness of taste is therefore safety from the tasteless. It is a remarkable thing that we are especially sensitive to the negative in the decisions taste renders. The corresponding positive is not properly speaking what is tasteful, but what does not offend taste. That, above all, is what taste judges. Taste is defined precisely by the fact that it is offended by what is tasteless and thus avoids it, like anything else that threatens injury. Thus the contrary of "good taste" actually is not "bad taste." Its opposite is rather to have "no taste." Good taste is a sensitivity which so naturally avoids anything blatant that its reaction is quite incomprehensible to someone who has no taste.

A phenomenon closely connected with taste is *fashion*. Here the element of social generalization implicit in the idea of taste becomes a determining reality. But the very distinction from fashion shows that the universality of taste has quite a different basis and is not the same as empirical universality. (This is the essential point for Kant.) The very word "fashion" (Mode) implies that the concept involves a changeable law (modus) within a constant whole of sociable demeanor. What is merely a matter of mode has no other norm than that given by what everybody does. Fashion regulates as it likes only those things that can equally well be one way as another. It is indeed constituted by empirical universality, consideration for others, comparison, and seeing things from the general point of view. Thus fashion creates a social dependence that is difficult to shake off. Kant is quite right when he considers it better to be a fool in fashion than to be against fashion—even though it is foolish to take fashion too seriously.[64]

By contrast, the phenomenon of taste is an intellectual faculty of differentiation. Taste operates in a community, but is not subservient to it. On the contrary, good taste is distinguished by the fact that it is able to adapt itself to the direction of taste represented by fashion or, contrariwise, is able to adapt what is demanded by fashion to its own good taste. Part of the concept of taste, then, is that one observes measure even in fashion, not blindly following its changing dictates but using one's own judgment. One maintains one's own "style"—i.e., one relates the demands of fashion to a whole that one's own taste keeps in view and accepts only what harmonizes with this whole and fits together as it does.

Thus taste not only recognizes this or that as beautiful, but has an eye to the whole, with which everything that is beautiful must harmonize.[65] Thus taste is not a social sense—that is, dependent on an empirical universality, the complete unanimity of the judgments of others. It does not say that everyone will agree with our judgment, but that they should agree with it (as Kant says).[66] Against the tyranny exercised by fashion, sure taste preserves a specific freedom and superiority. This is its special normative power, peculiar to it alone: the knowledge that it is certain of the agreement of an ideal community. In contrast to taste's being governed by fashion, we see here the ideality of good taste. It follows that taste knows something—though admittedly in a way that cannot be separated from the concrete moment in which that object occurs and cannot be reduced to rules and concepts.

Just this is obviously what gives the idea of taste its original breadth: that it constitutes a special way of knowing. Like reflective judgment, it belongs in the realm of that which grasps, in the individual object, the universal under which it is to be subsumed. Both taste and judgment evaluate the object in relation to a whole in order to see whether it fits in with everything else—that is, whether it is "fitting."[67] One must have a "sense" for it—it cannot be demonstrated.

This kind of sense is obviously needed wherever a whole is intended but not given as a whole—that is, conceived in purposive concepts. Thus taste is in no way limited to what is beautiful in nature and art, judging it in respect to its decorative quality, but embraces the whole realm of morality and manners. Even moral concepts are never given as a whole or determined in a normatively univocal way. Rather, the ordering of life by the rules of law and morality is incomplete and needs productive supplementation. Judgment is necessary in order to make a correct evaluation of the concrete instance. We are familiar with this function of judgment especially from jurisprudence, where the supplementary function of "hermeneutics" consists in concretizing the law.

At issue is always something more than the correct application of general principles. Our knowledge of law and morality too is always supplemented by the individual case, even productively determined by it. The judge not only applies the law in concreto, but contributes through his very judgment to developing the law ("judge-made law"). Like law, morality is constantly developed through the fecundity of the individual case. Thus judgment, as the evaluation of the beautiful and sublime, is by no means productive only in the area of nature and art. One cannot even say, with Kant,[68] that the productivity of judgment is to be found "chiefly" in this area. Rather, the beautiful in nature and art is to be supplemented by the whole ocean of the beautiful spread throughout the moral reality of mankind.

It is only with respect to the exercise of pure theoretical and practical reason that one can speak of subsuming the individual under a given universal (Kant's determinant judgment). But in fact even here an aesthetic judgment is involved. Kant indirectly admits this inasmuch as he acknowledges the value of examples for sharpening the judgment. Admittedly, he adds the qualification: "Correctness and precision of intellectual insight, on the other hand, they more usually somewhat impair. For only very seldom do they adequately fulfill the requirements of the rule (as *casus in terminis*)."[69] But the other side of this qualification is obviously that the case which functions as an example is in fact something different from just a case of the rule. Hence to do real justice to it—even if merely in technical or practical judgment—always includes an aesthetic element. To that extent, the distinction between determinant and reflective judgment, on which Kant bases his critique of judgment, is not absolute.[70]

It is clearly not only a matter of logical but of *aesthetic judgment*. The individual case on which judgment works is never simply a case; it is not exhausted by being a particular example of a universal law or concept. Rather, it is always an "individual case," and it is significant that we call it a special case, because the rule does not comprehend it. Every judgment about something intended in its concrete individuality (e.g., the judgment required in a situation that calls for action) is—strictly speaking—a judgment about a special case. That means nothing less than that judging the case involves not merely applying the universal principle according to which it is judged, but co-determining, supplementing, and correcting that principle. From this it ultimately follows that all moral decisions require taste—which does not mean that this most individual balancing of decision is the only thing that governs them, but it is an indispensable element. It is truly an achievement of undemonstrable tact to hit the target and to discipline the application of the universal, the moral law (Kant), in a way that reason itself cannot. Thus taste is not the ground but the supreme consummation of moral judgment. The man who finds that what is bad goes against his taste has the greatest certainty in accepting the good and rejecting the bad—as great as the certainty of that most vital of our senses, which chooses or rejects food.

Thus the emergence of the concept of taste in the seventeenth century, the social and socially cohesive function of which we have indicated above, has connections with moral philosophy that go back to antiquity.

There is a humanistic and thus ultimately Greek component at work in Christian moral philosophy. Greek ethics—the ethics of measure in the Pythagoreans and Plato, the ethics of the mean (mesotes) that Aristotle developed—is in a profound and comprehensive sense an ethics of good taste.[71]

Such a thesis admittedly sounds strange to our ears—in part because we generally fail to recognize the ideal normative element in the concept of taste and are still affected by the relativistic-skeptical argument about differences of taste. But, above all, we are influenced by Kant's achievement in moral philosophy, which purified ethics from all aesthetics and feeling. If we now examine the importance of Kant's *Critique of Judgment* for the history of the human sciences, we must say that his giving aesthetics a transcendental philosophical basis had major consequences and constituted a turning point. It was the end of a tradition but also the beginning of a new development. It restricted the idea of taste to an area in which, as a special principle of judgment, it could claim independent validity—and, by so doing, limited the concept of knowledge to the theoretical and practical use of reason. The limited phenomenon of judgment, restricted to the beautiful (and sublime), was sufficient for his transcendental purpose; but it shifted the more general concept of the experience of taste, and the activity of aesthetic judgment in law and morality, out of the center of philosophy.[72]

The importance of this cannot be easily overestimated, for what was here surrendered was the element in which philological and historical studies lived, and when they sought to ground themselves methodologically under the name of "human sciences" side by side with the natural sciences, it was the only possible source of their full self-understanding. Now Kant's transcendental analysis made it impossible to acknowledge the truth claim of traditionary materials, to the cultivation and study of which they devoted themselves. But this meant that the methodological uniqueness of the human sciences lost its legitimacy.

In his critique of aesthetic judgment what Kant sought to and did legitimate was the subjective universality of aesthetic taste in which there is no longer any knowledge of the object, and in the area of the "fine arts" the superiority of genius to any aesthetics based on rules. Thus romantic hermeneutics and history found a point of contact for their self-understanding only in the concept of genius, validated by Kant's aesthetics. That was the other side of Kant's influence. The transcendental justification of aesthetic judgment was the basis of the autonomy of aesthetic consciousness, and on the same basis historical consciousness was to be legitimized as well. The radical subjectivization involved in Kant's new way of grounding aesthetics was truly epoch-making. In discrediting any kind of theoretical knowledge except that of natural science, it compelled the human sciences to rely on the methodology of the natural sciences in conceptualizing themselves. But it made this reliance easier by offering the "artistic element," "feeling," and "empathy" as subsidiary elements. Helmholtz's description of the human sciences, which I considered above,[73] is in both respects a good example of the Kantian influence.

If we want to show what is inadequate about this kind of self-interpretation on the part of the human sciences and open up more appropriate possibilities, we will have to proceed with the problems of *aesthetics*. The transcendental function that Kant ascribes to the aesthetic judgment is sufficient to distinguish it from conceptual knowledge and hence to determine the phenomena of the beautiful and of art. But is it right to reserve the concept of truth for conceptual knowledge? Must we not also acknowledge that the work of art possesses truth? We shall see that acknowledging this places not only the phenomenon of art but also that of history in a new light.[74]

2 THE SUBJECTIVIZATION OF AESTHETICS THROUGH THE KANTIAN CRITIQUE

(A) KANT'S DOCTRINE OF TASTE AND GENIUS

(i) The Transcendental Distinctness of Taste

In the process of investigating the foundations of taste, Kant himself was surprised to find an a priori element which went beyond empirical universality.[75] This insight gave birth to the *Critique of Judgment*. It is no longer a mere critique of taste in the sense that taste is the object of critical judgment by an observer. It is a critique of critique; that is, it is concerned with the legitimacy of such a critique in matters of taste. The issue is no longer merely empirical principles which are supposed to justify a widespread and dominant taste—such as, for example, in the old chestnut concerning the origin of differences in taste—but it is concerned with a genuine a priori that, in itself, would totally justify the possibility of critique. What could constitute such a justification?

Clearly the validity of an aesthetic judgment cannot be derived and proved from a universal principle. No one supposes that questions of taste can be decided by argument and proof. Just as clear is that good taste will never really attain empirical universality, and thus appealing to the prevailing taste misses the real nature of taste. Inherent in the concept of taste is that it does not blindly submit to popular values and preferred models, and simply imitate them. In the realm of aesthetic taste models and patterns certainly have a privileged function; but, as Kant rightly says, they are not for imitation but for following.[76] The model and example encourage taste to go its own way, but they do not do taste's job for it. "For taste must be one's very own."[77]

On the other hand, our outline of the history of the concept of taste has shown clearly enough that particular preferences are not what decides; but in the case of an aesthetic judgment, a supra-empirical norm is operative. We will see that Kant's grounding of aesthetics on the judgment of taste does justice to both aspects of the phenomenon: its empirical non-universality and its a priori claim to universality.

But the price that he pays for this legitimation of critique in the area of taste is that he denies taste any *significance as knowledge*. He reduces sensus communis to a subjective principle. In taste nothing is known of the objects judged to be beautiful, but it is stated only that there is a feeling of pleasure connected with them a priori in the subjective consciousness. As we know, Kant sees this feeling as based on the fact that the representation of the object is suited (zweckmäßig) to our faculty of knowledge. It is a free play of imagination and understanding, a subjective relationship that is altogether appropriate to knowledge and that exhibits the reason for the pleasure in the object. This suitedness to the subject is in principle the same for all—i.e., it is universally communicable and thus grounds the claim that the judgment of taste possesses universal validity.

This is the *principle* that Kant discovers in aesthetic judgment. It is its own law. Thus it is an a priori effect of the beautiful located halfway between a mere sensory, empirical agreement in matters of taste and the rationalist universality of a rule. Admittedly, if one takes its relationship to Lebensgefühl (lit. "feeling of life") as its only basis, one can no longer call taste a "cognitio sensitiva." It imparts no knowledge of the object, but neither is it simply a question of a subjective reaction, as produced by what is pleasant to the senses. Taste is "reflective."

Thus when Kant calls taste the true common sense,[78] he is no longer considering the great moral and political tradition of the concept of sensus communis that we outlined above. Rather, he sees this idea as comprising two elements: first, the universality of taste inasmuch as it is the result of the free play of all our cognitive powers and is not limited to a specific area like an external sense; second, the communal quality of taste, inasmuch as, according to Kant, it abstracts from all subjective, private conditions such as attractiveness and emotion. Thus in both respects the universality of this "sense" is defined negatively by being contrasted to that from which it is abstracted, and not positively by what grounds commonality and creates community.

Yet it is true that for Kant the old connection between taste and sociability remains valid. But the "culture of taste" is treated only as an appendix under the title "The Methodology of Taste."[79] There the "human-iora," as represented by the Greek model, is defined as the sociability appropriate to humanity, and cultivating moral feeling is designated as the way in which genuine taste assumes a definite unchangeable form.[80] Thus the specific contents of taste are irrelevant to its transcendental function. Kant is interested only insofar as there is a special principle of aesthetic judgment, and that is why he is interested only in the *pure* judgment of taste.

In accord with his transcendental intention, the "Analytic of Taste" takes its examples of aesthetic pleasure quite indifferently from natural beauty, the decorative, and artistic representation. The type of object whose idea pleases does not affect the essence of the aesthetic judgment. The "critique of aesthetic judgment" does not seek to be a philosophy of art—however much art is an object of this judgment. The concept of the "pure aesthetic judgment of taste" is a methodological abstraction only obliquely related to the difference between nature and art. Thus by examining Kant's aesthetics more closely it is necessary to bring back into proportion those interpretations that read his aesthetics as a philosophy of art, interpretations which rely especially on the concept of genius. To this end we will consider Kant's remarkable and controversial doctrine of free and dependent beauty.[81]

(ii) The Doctrine of Free and Dependent Beauty

Kant here discusses the difference between the "pure" and the "intellectualized" judgment of taste, which corresponds to the contrast between "free" and "dependent" beauty (i.e., dependent on a concept). This is a particularly dangerous doctrine for the understanding of art, since the free beauty of nature and—in the sphere of art—the ornament appear as the beauty proper to the pure judgment of taste, for these are beautiful "in themselves." Wherever a concept is brought in—and that is the case not only in the area of poetry, but in all *representational* art—the situation seems the same as in the examples of "dependent" beauty that Kant mentions. His examples—man, animal, building—are natural things as they occur in the world dominated by human ends, or things that have been manufactured for human ends. In each case the fact that the thing serves some end limits the aesthetic pleasure it can give. Thus for Kant tattooing, decorating the human form, is objectionable, even though it can arouse "unmediated" pleasure. Certainly, Kant is here speaking not of art as such (the "beautiful representation of a thing"), but more emphatically of beautiful things (of nature or architecture).

The distinction between natural and artistic beauty, which he himself later discusses (§48), is not important here; but when among the examples of free beauty apart from flowers he also mentions a carpet with arabesque designs and music ("without a theme" or even "without a text"), then that indirectly indicates all the things included as "objects which come under a determinate concept" and hence must be included under conditional, unfree beauty: the whole realm of poetry, of the plastic arts and of architecture, as well as all the objects of nature that we do not look at simply in terms of their beauty, as we do decorative flowers. In all these cases the judgment of taste is obscured and limited. It seems impossible to do justice to art if aesthetics is founded on the "pure judgment of taste"—unless the criterion of taste is made merely a precondition. The introduction of the concept of genius in the later parts of the *Critique of Judgment* may be thus understood. But that would mean a subsequent shifting of emphasis. For this is not at first the issue. Here (in §16) the standpoint of taste is so far from being a mere precondition that, rather, it claims to exhaust the nature of aesthetic judgment and protect it from being limited by "intellectual" criteria. And even though Kant sees the same object can be judged from the two different points of view—of free and of dependent beauty—the ideal arbiter of taste nevertheless seems to be he who judges according to "what he has present to his senses" and not according to "what he has present to his thoughts." True beauty is that of flowers and of ornament, which in our world, dominated by ends, present themselves as beauties immediately and of themselves, and hence do not require that any concept or purpose be consciously disregarded.

If one looks a little closer, however, this conception fits neither Kant's words nor his subject matter. The presumed shift in Kant's standpoint from taste to genius does not occur; one has only to learn to recognize in the beginning the hidden preparation for what is developed later. There is no doubt that Kant does not deplore but rather demands the restrictions that forbid a man to be tattooed or a church to be decorated with a particular ornament; Kant regards the resulting diminution of aesthetic pleasure as, from the moral point of view, a gain. The examples of free beauty are obviously not intended to exhibit beauty proper, but only to insure that pleasure as such is not a judgment of the perfection of the object. And though, at the end of the section (§16), Kant believes that the distinction between the two kinds of beauty—or rather between the two relationships to the beautiful—enables him to settle many critical disputes about beauty, still this possibility of settling disputes of taste is merely, as it were, a consequence of the co-operation of the two approaches. Indeed, most commonly the two approaches will be united in accord.

This unity will always be given where "looking to a concept" does not abrogate the freedom of the imagination. Without contradicting himself, Kant can describe it as a legitimate condition of *aesthetic* pleasure that there is no conflict with purposive elements. And as it was artificial to isolate beauties which exist freely in themselves ("taste," in any case, seems to prove itself most where not only the right thing is chosen, but the right thing for the right place), so also one can and must go beyond the standpoint of the pure judgment of taste by saying that one certainly cannot speak of beauty when a particular concept of the understanding is illustrated schematically through the imagination, but only when imagination is in free harmony with the understanding—i.e., where it can be productive. This imaginative productivity is not richest where it is merely free, however, as in the convolutions of the arabesque, but rather in a field of play where the understanding's desire for unity does not so much confine it as suggest incitements to play.

(iii) The Doctrine of the Ideal of Beauty

These last remarks have stated more than is actually to be found in Kant's text, but the course of his thought (§17) justifies this interpretation. The balance in this section becomes apparent only after careful examination. The normative idea of beauty discussed there at length is not the main thing and does not represent the ideal of beauty towards which taste naturally strives. Rather, there is an ideal of beauty only with regard to the human form, in the "expression of the moral," "*without which the object could not be universally pleasing.*" Judgment according to an ideal of beauty is then, as Kant says, not a mere judgment of taste. The important consequence of this doctrine will prove to be that something must be more than merely tastefully pleasant in order to please as a work of art.[82]

This is truly astounding. Although we have just seen that real beauty seemed to preclude being tied down by ideas of purpose, here the reverse is stated of a beautiful house, a beautiful tree, a beautiful garden, etc.—i.e., that we can imagine no ideal of these things, "because these ends are *not sufficiently* [my italics] determined and fixed by their concept; and consequently their purposiveness (Zweckmäßigkeit) is almost as free as in the case of beauty that is *quite at large*." There is an ideal of beauty only of the human form precisely because it alone is capable of a beauty fixed by a concept of end! This doctrine, propounded by Winckelmann and Lessing,[83] comes to occupy a key position in Kant's foundation of aesthetics. And this thesis shows clearly how little a formal aesthetic of taste (arabesque aesthetic) corresponds to the Kantian idea.

The doctrine of the ideal of beauty is based on the difference between the normative idea and the rational idea or ideal of beauty. The aesthetic normative idea is found in all natural genera. The way that a beautiful animal (e.g., a cow: Myron) should look is the standard by which to judge the individual example. Thus this normative idea is a single intuition of the imagination as "the image of the genus hovering between all singular individuals." The representation of such a normative idea does not arouse pleasure because of its beauty, however, but merely "because it does not contradict any condition under which alone a thing belonging to this genus can be beautiful." It is not the prototype of beauty but merely of correctness.

This is also true of the normative idea of the human form. But there is a true ideal of the beauty of the human form in the "expression of the moral." Expression of the moral: if we combine that with the later doctrine of aesthetic ideas and of beauty as the symbol of morality, then we can see that the doctrine of the ideal of beauty also prepares a place for the essence of art.[84] The application to art theory in the spirit of Winckelmann's classicism is patent.[85] Obviously what Kant means is that in the representation of the human form the object represented coincides with the artistic meaning that speaks to us in the representation. There can be no other meaning in this representation than is already expressed in the form and appearance of what is represented. In Kantian terms, the intellectualized and interested pleasure in this represented ideal of beauty does not distract us from the aesthetic pleasure but is rather one with it. Only in the representation of the human form does the whole content of the work speak to us, at the same time, as an expression of its object.[86]

The nature of all art, as Hegel formulated it, is that it "presents man with himself."[87] Other natural objects—not only the human form—can express moral ideas in artistic presentation. All artistic representation, whether of landscape, still life, or even an inspiring view of nature, achieves this. Here, however, Kant is right: the expression of moral value is then borrowed. But man expresses these ideas in his own being, and because he is what he is. A tree that is stunted because of unfavorable conditions of growth may seem wretched to us, but the tree does not feel wretched or express this wretchedness, and from the point of view of the ideal of the tree, being stunted is not "wretchedness." The wretched man is wretched, however, as measured by the human moral ideal itself (and not only because we demand that he submit to a human ideal that is simply not valid for him, measured by which he would express wretchedness for us without being wretched). Hegel understood that perfectly in his lectures on aesthetics when he described the expression of the moral as the "radiance of the spiritual."[88]

Thus the formalism of "dry pleasure" leads to the decisive breakup not only of rationalism in aesthetics, but of every universal (cosmological) doctrine of beauty. Using precisely that classicist distinction between a normative idea and the ideal of beauty Kant destroys the grounds on which the aesthetics of perfection finds everything's unique, incomparable beauty in its complete presence to the senses. Only now can "art" become an autonomous phenomenon. Its task is no longer to represent the ideals of nature, but to enable man to encounter himself in nature and in the human, historical world. Kant's demonstration that the beautiful pleases without a concept does not gainsay the fact that only the beautiful thing that speaks meaningfully to us evokes our total interest. The very recognition of the non-conceptuality of taste leads beyond an aesthetics of mere taste.[89]

(iv) The Interest Aroused by Natural and Artistic Beauty

When Kant raises the question of the *interest* that is taken in the beautiful not empirically but a priori, this question of the interest in the beautiful, as opposed to what he states about the fundamental disinterestedness of aesthetic pleasure, raises a new problem and completes the transition from the standpoint of taste to the standpoint of genius. It is the same doctrine that is developed in connection with both phenomena. In establishing foundations, it is important to free the "critique of taste" from sensualistic and rationalistic prejudices. It is perfectly appropriate that Kant does not inquire into the mode of existence of the object being aesthetically judged (and thus into the whole question of the relation between the beauty of nature and that of art). But this dimension of the question is necessarily opened up if one thinks the standpoint of taste through—which means going beyond it.[90] The fundamental problem that motivates Kant's aesthetics is that the beautiful engages our interests. It does so differently in nature and art, and the comparison between natural beauty and artistic beauty opens up this problematic.

Here we find Kant's most characteristic convictions.[91] Contrary to what we might expect, it is not for the sake of art that Kant goes beyond "disinterested pleasure" and inquires into the interest in the beautiful. From the doctrine of the ideal of beauty we derived an advantage of art over natural beauty: the advantage of being a more direct expression of the moral. Kant, on the contrary, emphasizes primarily (§42) the advantage of *natural* over artistic beauty. It is not only for the pure aesthetic judgment that natural beauty has an advantage, namely to make it clear that the beautiful depends on the suitability (Zweckmässigkeit) of the thing represented to our cognitive faculty. This is so clearly the case with natural beauty because it possesses no significance of content, and thus manifests the judgment of taste in its unintellectualized purity.

But it does not have only this methodological advantage; according to Kant it also has one of content, and he obviously thinks a great deal of this point of his doctrine. Beautiful nature is able to arouse an immediate interest, namely a moral one. When we find the beautiful forms of nature beautiful, this discovery points beyond itself to the thought "that nature has produced that beauty." Where this thought arouses interest, we have cultivation of the moral sensibility. While Kant, instructed by Rousseau, refuses to make a general argument back from the refinement of taste for the beautiful to moral sensibility, the sense of the beauty of nature is for Kant a special case. That nature is beautiful arouses interest only in someone who "has already set his interest deep in the morally good." Hence the interest in natural beauty is "akin to the moral." By observing the unintentional consonance of nature with our wholly disinterested pleasure—i.e., the wonderful purposiveness (Zweckmäßigkeit) of nature for us, it points to us as to the ultimate purpose of creation, to the "moral side of our being."

Here the rejection of perfection aesthetics fits beautifully with the moral significance of natural beauty. Precisely because in nature we find no *ends in themselves* and yet find beauty—i.e., a suitedness (Zweckmäßigkeit) to the end (Zweck) of our pleasure, nature gives us a "hint" that we are in fact the ultimate end, the final goal of creation. The dissolution of the ancient cosmological thought that assigned man his place in the total structure of being and assigned each entity its goal of perfection gives the world, which ceases to be beautiful as a structure of absolute ends, the new *beauty* of being purposive for us. It becomes "nature," whose innocence consists in the fact that it knows nothing of man or his social vices. Nevertheless, it has something to say to us. As beautiful, nature finds a *language* that brings to *us* an intelligible idea of what mankind is to be.

Naturally the significance of art also depends on the fact that it speaks to us, that it confronts man with himself in his morally determined existence. But the products of art exist only in order to address us in this way —natural objects, however, do not exist to address us in this way. This is the significant interest of the naturally beautiful: that it is still able to present man with himself in respect to his morally determined existence. Art cannot communicate to us this self-discovery of man in a reality that does not intend to do so. When man encounters himself in art, this is not the confirmation of himself by another.[92]

That is right, as far as it goes. The conclusiveness of Kant's argument is impressive, but he does not employ the appropriate criteria for the phenomenon of art. One can make a counter-argument. The advantage of natural beauty over artistic beauty is only the other side of natural beauty's inability to express something specific. Thus, contrariwise, one can see that the advantage of art over natural beauty is that the language of art exerts its claims, and does not offer itself freely and indeterminately for interpretation according to one's mood, but speaks to us in a significant and definite way. And the wonderful and mysterious thing about art is that this definiteness is by no means a fetter for our mind, but in fact opens up room for play, for the free play of our cognitive faculties. Kant is right when he says that art must be capable of "being regarded as nature"[93]—i.e., please without betraying the constraint of rules. We do not consider the intentional agreement between what is represented and the reality we know, we do not look to see what it resembles, we do not measure its claim to significance by a criterion that we already know well, but on the contrary this criterion—the "concept"—becomes, in an unlimited way, "aesthetically expanded."[94]

Kant's definition of art as the "beautiful representation of a thing" takes this into account inasmuch as even the ugly is beautiful in artistic representation. Nevertheless, the nature of art proper emerges badly from the contrast with natural beauty. If the idea of a thing were presented only in a beautiful way, that would be a merely "academic" representation, and would fulfill only the minimum requirement of all beauty. But for Kant art is more than the "beautiful representation of a thing": it is the presentation of *aesthetic ideas*—i.e., of something that lies beyond all concepts. The concept of genius seeks to formulate this insight of Kant's.

It cannot be denied that the doctrine of aesthetic ideas, through whose representation the artist infinitely expands the given concept and encourages the free play of the mental faculties, has something unsatisfactory about it for a modern reader. It looks as if these ideas were being connected to the already dominant concept, like the attributes of a deity to its form. The traditional superiority of the rational concept over the inexponible aesthetic representation is so strong that even with Kant there arises the false appearance that the concept has precedence over the aesthetic idea, whereas it is not at all the understanding, but the imagination that takes the lead among the faculties in play.[95] The aesthetician will find many other statements in the light of which it is difficult for Kant, without claiming the superiority of the concept, to hold on to his leading insight that the beautiful is grasped without a concept and yet at the same time has a binding force.

But the basic lines of his thinking are free from these faults and exhibit an impressive logical consistency, which reaches its climax in his account of genius as the basis of art. Even without going into a more detailed interpretation of this "capacity to represent aesthetic ideas," it may be pointed out that Kant here is not deflected from transcendental inquiry and pushed into the cul-de-sac of a psychology of artistic creation. Rather, the irrationality of genius brings out one element in the creative production of rules evident both in creator and recipient, namely that there is no other way of grasping the content of a work of art than through the unique form of the work and in the mystery of its impression, which can never be fully expressed by any language. Hence the concept of genius corresponds to what Kant sees as the crucial thing about aesthetic taste, namely that it facilitates the play of one's mental powers, increases the vitality that comes from the harmony between imagination and understanding, and invites one to linger before the beautiful. Genius is ultimately a manifestation of this vivifying spirit for, as opposed to the pedant's rigid adherence to rules, genius exhibits a free sweep of invention and thus the originality that creates new models.

(v) The Relation Between Taste and Genius

In this situation the question arises of how Kant sees the mutual relation between taste and genius. Kant preserves the privileged position of taste, inasmuch as works of art (that is, the art of genius) must be viewed from the guiding viewpoint of beauty. One may regret the improvements that taste imposes on the invention of genius, but taste is a necessary discipline for genius. Thus, in cases of conflict, Kant considers that taste should prevail. But this is not an important question, for, basically, taste and genius share common ground. The art of genius serves to make the free play of the mental faculties communicable. This is achieved by the aesthetic ideas that it invents. But the aesthetic pleasure of taste, too, was characterized by the communicability of a state of mind—pleasure. Taste is a faculty of judgment, and hence reflective, but what it reflects about is only that state of mind—the vitalization of the cognitive powers that results as much from natural as from artistic beauty. Thus the systematic significance of the concept of genius is limited by its being a special case of the artistically beautiful, whereas the concept of taste by contrast is universal.

That Kant makes the concept of genius serve his transcendental inquiry completely and does not slip into empirical psychology is clearly shown by his narrowing the concept of genius to artistic creation. When he withholds this name from the great inventors and investigators in the spheres of science and technology,[96] this is, seen in terms of empirical psychology, completely unjustified. Wherever one must "come upon" something that cannot be found through learning and methodical work alone—i.e., wherever there is inventio, where something is due to inspiration and not to methodical calculation—the important thing is ingenium, genius. And yet Kant's intention is correct: only the work of art is immanently so determined that it can be created only by genius. It is only in the case of the artist that his "invention"—the work—remains, of its own nature, related to the spirit—the spirit that creates as well as the one that judges and enjoys. Only such inventions cannot be imitated, and hence it is right—from a transcendental point of view—when Kant speaks (only here) of genius, and defines art as the art of genius. All other achievements and inventions of genius, however much genius such inventions may have, are not determined in their essence by it.

I maintain that for Kant the concept of genius was really only a complement to what was of interest to him "for transcendental reasons" in aesthetic judgment. We should not forget that the second part of the *Critique of Judgment* is concerned only with *nature* (and with its being judged by concepts of purpose) and not at all with art. Thus for the systematic intention of the whole, applying aesthetic judgment to the beautiful and sublime in *nature* is more important than the transcendental foundation of *art*. The "purposiveness of nature for our cognitive faculties" —which, as the transcendental principle of aesthetic judgment, pertains only to natural beauty (and not to art)—at the same time functions to prepare the understanding to apply the concept of purpose to nature.[97] Thus the critique of taste—i.e., aesthetics—is a preparation for teleology. Kant's philosophical intention is to legitimate teleology, whose constitutive claim as a principle of judgment in the knowledge of nature had been destroyed by the *Critique of Pure Reason*. This intention brings the whole of his philosophy to a systematic conclusion. Judgment provides the bridge between understanding and reason. The intelligible towards which taste points, the supersensible substrate in man, contains at the same time the mediation between the concepts of nature and of freedom.[98] This is the systematic significance that the problem of natural beauty has for Kant: *it grounds the central position of teleology*. Natural beauty alone, not art, can assist in legitimating the concept of purpose in judging nature. For this systematic reason alone, the "pure" judgment of taste provides the indispensable basis of the third Critique.

But even within the "critique of aesthetic judgment" there is no question but that the standpoint of genius finally ousts that of taste. One has only to look at how Kant describes genius: the genius is a favorite of nature —just as natural beauty is regarded as a favor of nature. We must be able to regard art as if it were nature. Through genius, nature gives art its rules. In all these phrases[99] the concept of nature is the uncontested criterion.

Thus what the concept of genius achieves is only to place the products of art on a par aesthetically with natural beauty. Art too is looked at aesthetically—i.e., it too calls for reflective judgment. What is intentionally produced, and hence purposive, is not to be related to a concept, but seeks to please simply in being judged—just like natural beauty. "Art is art created by genius" means that for artistic beauty too there is no other principle of judgment, no criterion of concept and knowledge than that of its suitability to promote the feeling of freedom in the play of our cognitive faculties. Whether in nature *or* art[100] beauty has the same a priori principle, which lies entirely within subjectivity. The autonomy of aesthetic judgment does not mean that there is an autonomous sphere of validity for beautiful objects. Kant's transcendental reflection on the a priori of judgment justifies the claim of aesthetic judgment, but basically it does not permit a philosophical aesthetics in the sense of a philosophy of art (Kant himself says that no doctrine or metaphysics here corresponds to the Critique).[101]

(B) THE AESTHETICS OF GENIUS AND THE CONCEPT OF EXPERIENCE (ERLEBNIS)

(i) The Dominance of the Concept of Genius

Basing aesthetic judgment on the a priori of subjectivity was to acquire a quite new significance when the import of transcendental philosophical reflection changed with Kant's successors. If the metaphysical background which is the basis of the primacy of natural beauty in Kant, and which ties the concept of genius back to nature, no longer exists, the problem of art arises in a new way. Even the way Schiller took up Kant's *Critique of Judgment* and put the whole weight of his moral and pedagogic temperament behind the idea of an "aesthetic education" gave *the standpoint of art*—rather than taste and judgment, as with Kant—pride of place.

From the standpoint of art the Kantian ideas of taste and genius completely traded places. Genius had to become the more comprehensive concept and, contrariwise, the phenomenon of taste had to be devalued.

Now, even in Kant himself, there are openings for such a reversal of values. Even according to Kant, it is of some significance for the judging faculty of taste that art is the creation of genius. One of the things taste judges is whether a work of art has spirit or is spiritless. Kant says of artistic beauty that "in judging such an object one must consider the possibility of spirit—and hence of genius—in it,"[102] and in another place he makes the obvious point that without genius not only art but also a correct, independent taste in judging it is not possible.[103] Therefore the standpoint of taste, insofar as it is practiced on its most important object, art, passes inevitably into the standpoint of genius. Genius in understanding corresponds to genius in creation. Kant does not express it this way, but the concept of spirit that he uses here[104] is equally applicable in both instances. On this basis more must be built later.

It is in fact clear that the concept of taste loses its significance if the phenomenon of art steps into the foreground. The standpoint of taste is secondary to the work of art. The sensitivity in selecting that constitutes taste often has a leveling effect in contrast to the originality of the artistic work of genius. Taste avoids the unusual and the monstrous. It is concerned with the surface of things; it does not concern itself with what is original about an artistic production. Even in the beginnings of the idea of genius in the eighteenth century we find a polemical edge against the concept of taste. It was directed against classicist aesthetics, and it demanded that the ideal of taste of French classicism should make room to accommodate Shakespeare (Lessing). To that extent Kant is old-fashioned and adopts an intermediate position inasmuch as, for transcendental purposes, he steadfastly maintained the concept of taste which the Sturm und Drang not only violently dismissed but also violently demolished.

But when Kant passes from laying general foundations to the specific problems of the philosophy of art, he himself points beyond the standpoint of taste and speaks of a *perfection of taste*.[105] But what is that? The normative character of taste implies the possibility of its being cultivated and perfected. Perfect taste, which it is important to achieve, will assume, according to Kant, a definite unchangeable form. That is quite logical, however absurd it may sound to our ears. For if taste is to be good taste, this puts paid to the whole relativism of taste presumed by aesthetic skepticism. It would embrace all works of art that have "quality," and thus of course all those that are created by genius.

Thus we see that the idea of perfect taste which Kant discusses would be more appropriately defined by the concept of genius. Obviously it would be impossible to apply the idea of perfect taste within the sphere of natural beauty. It might be acceptable in the case of horticulture; but consistent with his argument, Kant assigns horticulture to the sphere of the artistically beautiful.[106] But confronted with natural beauty—say, the beauty of a landscape—the idea of a perfect taste is quite out of place. Would it consist in evaluating each natural beauty according to its merits? Can there be choice in this sphere? Is there an order of merit? Is a sunny landscape more beautiful than one shrouded in rain? Is there anything ugly in nature? Or only variously attractive in various moods, differently pleasing for different tastes? Kant may be right when he considers it morally significant that someone can be pleased by nature. But is it meaningful to distinguish between good and bad taste in relation to it? Where this distinction is indisputably appropriate, however—namely in relation to art and artifice—taste is, as we have seen, only a restriction on the beautiful and it contains no principle of its own. Thus the idea of a perfect taste is dubious in relation to nature as well as to art. One does violence to the concept of taste if one does not accept its variability. Taste is, if anything, a testimony to the mutability of all human things and the relativity of all human values.

Kant's grounding aesthetics on the concept of taste is not wholly satisfactory. The concept of genius, which Kant develops as a transcendental principle for artistic beauty, seems much better suited to be a universal aesthetic principle. For it fulfills much better than does the concept of taste the requirement of being immutable in the stream of time. The miracle of art—that enigmatic perfection possessed by successful artistic creations—is visible in all ages. It seems possible to subordinate taste to the transcendental account of art and to understand by taste the sure sense for genius in art. Kant's statement "Fine art is the art of genius" then becomes a transcendental principle for aesthetics in general. Aesthetics is ultimately possible only as the philosophy of art.

German idealism drew this conclusion. Following Kant's doctrine of transcendental imagination in this and other respects, Fichte and Schelling made new use of this idea in their aesthetics. Unlike Kant they considered the *standpoint of art* (as the unconscious production of genius) all-inclusive—embracing even nature, which is understood as a product of spirit.[107]

But now the basis of aesthetics has shifted. Like the concept of taste, the concept of natural beauty is also devalued, or differently understood. The moral interest in natural beauty that Kant had portrayed so enthusiastically now retreats behind the self-encounter of man in works of art. In Hegel's magnificent *Aesthetics* natural beauty exists only as a "reflection of spirit." There is in fact no longer any independent element in the systematic whole of aesthetics.[108]

Obviously the indeterminacy with which natural beauty presents itself to the interpreting and understanding spirit justifies our saying with Hegel that "its substance [is] contained in the spirit."[109] Aesthetically speaking, Hegel here draws an absolutely correct inference; I approached it above when I spoke of the inappropriateness of applying the idea of taste to nature. For judgments on the beauty of a landscape undoubtedly depend on the artistic taste of the time. One has only to think of the Alpine landscape being described as ugly, which we still find in the eighteenth century—the effect, as we know, of the spirit of artificial symmetry that dominates the century of absolutism. Thus Hegel's aesthetics is based squarely on the standpoint of art. In art man encounters himself, spirit meets spirit.

It is decisive for the development of modern aesthetics that here too, as in the whole sphere of systematic philosophy, speculative idealism had an effect which far exceeds its recognized importance. The violent rejection of the dogmatic schematism of the Hegelian school in the mid-nineteenth century led to the demand for a renewal of criticism under the banner "back to Kant." The same was true in aesthetics. However brilliantly art was used for writing the history of worldviews, like that in Hegel's *Aesthetics*, this method of a priori history writing, which was frequently employed by the Hegelian school (Rosenkranz, Schosler, etc.), was quickly discredited. The call for a return to Kant which arose in opposition to this could not now, however, be a real return and recovery of the horizon of Kant's critiques. Rather, the phenomenon of art and the concept of genius remained at the center of aesthetics; the problem of natural beauty and the concept of taste were marginalized.

This appears in linguistic usage as well. Kant's limiting the concept of genius to the artist (which I have examined above) did not prevail; on the contrary, in the nineteenth century the concept of genius rose to the status of a universal concept of value and—together with the concept of the creative—achieved a true apotheosis. The romantic and idealistic concept of unconscious production lay behind this development and, through Schopenhauer and the philosophy of the unconscious, it acquired enormous popular influence. I have shown that this kind of systematic predominance of the concept of genius over the concept of taste is not Kantian. Kant's main concern, however, was to give aesthetics an autonomous basis freed from the criterion of the concept, and not to raise the question of truth in the sphere of art, but to base aesthetic judgment on the subjective a priori of our feeling of life, the harmony of our capacity for "knowledge in general," which is the essence of both taste and genius. All of this was of a piece with nineteenth-century irrationalism and the cult of genius. Kant's doctrine of the "heightening of the feeling of life" (Lebensgefühl) in aesthetic pleasure helped the idea of "genius" to develop into a comprehensive concept of life (Leben), especially after Fichte had elevated genius and what genius created to a universal transcendental position. Hence, by trying to derive all objective validity from transcendental subjectivity, neo-Kantianism declared the concept of Erlebnis to be the very stuff of consciousness.[110]

(ii) On the History of the Word Erlebnis

It is surprising to find that, unlike the verb erleben, the noun Erlebnis became common only in the 1870s. In the eighteenth century it is not to be found at all, and even Schiller and Goethe do not know it.[111] Its first appearance, seemingly, is in one of Hegel's letters.[112] But even in the thirties and forties I know of only occasional instances (in Tieck, Alexis, and Gutzkow). The word appears equally seldom in the fifties and sixties, and appears suddenly with some frequency in the seventies.[113] Apparently the word enters general usage at the same time as it begins to be used in biographical writing.

Since Erlebnis is a secondary formation from the verb erleben, which is older and appears often in the age of Goethe, we must analyze the meaning of erleben in order to determine why the new word was coined. Erleben means primarily "to be still alive when something happens." Thus the word suggests the immediacy with which something real is grasped —unlike something which one presumes to know but which is unattested by one's own experience, whether because it is taken over from others or comes from hearsay, or whether it is inferred, surmised, or imagined. What is experienced is always what one has experienced oneself.

But at the same time the form "das Erlebte" is used to mean the permanent content of what is experienced. This content is like a yield or result that achieves permanence, weight, and significance from out of the transience of experiencing. Both meanings obviously lie behind the coinage Erlebnis: both the immediacy, which precedes all interpretation, reworking, and communication, and merely offers a starting point for interpretation—material to be shaped—and its discovered yield, its lasting result.

Corresponding to the double meaning of the word erleben is the fact that it is through biographical literature that the word Erlebnis takes root. The essence of biography, especially nineteenth-century biographies of artists and poets, is to understand the works from the life. Their achievement consists precisely in mediating between the two meanings that we have distinguished in the word "Erlebnis" and in seeing these meanings as a productive union: something becomes an "experience" not only insofar as it is experienced, but insofar as its being experienced makes a special impression that gives it lasting importance. An "experience" of this kind acquires a wholly new status when it is expressed in art. Dilthey's famous title *Das Erlebnis und die Dichtung* (Experience and Poetry) succinctly formulates the association. In fact, Dilthey was the first to give the word a conceptual function that soon became so fashionable, designating a concept of value so self-evident, that many European languages took it over as a loan word. But it is reasonable to assume that Dilthey's use of the term merely underlined what actually happened in the life of the language.

In Dilthey we can easily isolate the diverse elements operative in the linguistically and conceptually new word Erlebnis. The title *Das Erlebnis und die Dichtung* is late enough (1905). The first version of the essay on Goethe it contains, which Dilthey published in 1877, uses the word Erlebnis to a certain extent, but exhibits nothing of the concept's later terminological definiteness. The earlier forms of the later, conceptually established meaning of Erlebnis are worth examining more closely. It seems more than mere chance that it is in a biography of Goethe (and in an essay on that topic) that the word suddenly appears with any frequency. Goethe more than anyone else tempts one to coin this word, since in quite a new sense his poetry acquires intelligibility from what he experienced. He said himself that all his poetry had the character of a vast confession.[114] Hermann Grimm's biography of Goethe takes this statement as its methodological principle, and consequently it uses the plural, Erlebnisse, frequently.

Dilthey's essay on Goethe lets us glance back at the unconscious prehistory of the word, since this essay precedes the version of 1877 and its later reworking in *Das Erlebnis und die Dichtung* (1905).[115] In this essay Dilthey compares Goethe with Rousseau, and in order to describe the new kind of writing that Rousseau based on the world of his inner experiences, he employs the expression das Erleben. In his paraphrase of Rousseau we also find the expression "die Erlebnisse früher Tage" (the experiences of early days).[116]

However, even in the early Dilthey the meaning of the word Erlebnis is still rather uncertain. This appears clearly in a passage from which Dilthey cut the word Erlebnis in later editions: "Corresponding both to what he had experienced and what, given his ignorance of the world, he had imagined and treated as experience (Erlebnis). ... "[117] Again he is speaking of Rousseau. But an imaginary experience does not fit the original meaning of erleben, nor even Dilthey's own later technical usage, where Erlebnis means what is directly given, the ultimate material for all imaginative creation.[118] The coined word Erlebnis, of course, expresses the criticism of Enlightenment rationalism, which, following Rousseau, emphasized the concept of life (Leben). It was probably Rousseau's influence on German classicism that introduced the criterion of Erlebtsein (being experienced) and hence made possible the formation of the word Erlebnis.[119] But the concept of life also forms the metaphysical background for German speculative idealism, and plays a fundamental role in Fichte, Hegel, and even Schleiermacher. In contrast to the abstractness of understanding and the particularity of perception or representation, this concept implies a connection with totality, with infinity. This is clearly audible in the tone that the word Erlebnis has even today.

Schleiermacher's appeal to living feeling against the cold rationalism of the Enlightenment, Schiller's call for aesthetic freedom against mechanistic society, Hegel's contrast between life (later, spirit) and "positivity," were the forerunners of the protest against modern industrial society, which at the beginning of our century caused the words Erlebnis and Erleben to become almost sacred clarion calls. The rebellion of the Jugend Bewegung (Youth Movement) against bourgeois culture and its institutions was inspired by these ideas, the influence of Friedrich Nietzsche and Henri Bergson played its part, but also a "spiritual movement" like that around Stefan George and, not least, the seismographical accuracy with which the philosophy of Georg Simmel reacted to these events, are all part of the same thing. The life philosophy of our own day follows on its romantic predecessors. The rejection of the mechanization of life in contemporary mass society makes the word seem so self-evident that its conceptual implications remain totally hidden.[120]

Thus we must understand Dilthey's coining of the concept in the light of the previous history of the word among the romantics and remember that Dilthey was Schleiermacher's biographer. It is true that we do not yet find the word Erlebnis in Schleiermacher, and apparently not even the verb erleben. But there is no lack of synonyms that cover the range of meaning of Erlebnis,[121] and the pantheistic background is always clearly in evidence. Every act, as an element of life, remains connected with the infinity of life that manifests itself in it. Everything finite is an expression, a representation of the infinite.

In fact we find in Dilthey's biography of Schleiermacher, in the description of religious contemplation, a particularly pregnant use of the word Erlebnis, which already intimates its conceptual content: "Each one of his experiences (Erlebnisse) existing by itself is a separate picture of the universe taken out of the explanatory context."[122]

(iii) The Concept of Erlebnis

Having considered the history of the word, let us now examine the history of the concept Erlebnis. We know from the foregoing that Dilthey's concept of Erlebnis clearly contains two elements, the pantheistic and the positivist, the experience (Erlebnis) and still more its result (Erlebnis). This is not an accident, but a result of his own intermediate position between speculation and empiricism, which we shall have to consider later. Since he is concerned to legitimate the work of the human sciences epistemologically, he is dominated throughout by the question of what is truly *given*. Thus his concepts are motivated by this epistemological purpose or rather by the needs of epistemology itself—needs reflected in the linguistic process analyzed above. Just as the remoteness from and hunger for experience, caused by distress over the complicated workings of civilization transformed by the Industrial Revolution, brought the word Erlebnis into general usage, so also the new, distanced attitude that historical consciousness takes to tradition gives the concept of Erlebnis its epistemological function. Characteristic of the development of the human sciences in the nineteenth century is that they not only acknowledge the natural sciences as an extrinsic model but that, coming from the same background as modern science, they develop the same feeling for experiment and research. Just as the age of mechanics felt alienated from nature conceived as the natural world and expressed this feeling epistemologically in the concept of self-consciousness and in the rule, developed into a method, that only "clear and distinct perceptions" are certain, so also the human sciences of the nineteenth century felt a similar alienation from the world of history. The spiritual creations of the past, art and history, no longer belong self-evidently to the present; rather, they are given up to research, they are data or givens (Gegebenheiten) from which a past can be made present. Thus the concept of the given is also important in Dilthey's formulation of the concept of Erlebnis.

What Dilthey tries to grasp with the concept of "experience" is the special nature of the given in the human sciences. Following Descartes' formulation of the res cogitans, he defines the concept of experience by reflexivity, by interiority, and on the basis of this special mode of being given he tries to construct an epistemological justification for knowledge of the historical world. The primary data, to which the interpretation of historical objects goes back, are not data of experiment and measurement but unities of meaning. That is what the concept of experience states: the structures of meaning we meet in the human sciences, however strange and incomprehensible they may seem to us, can be traced back to ultimate units of what is given in consciousness, unities which themselves no longer contain anything alien, objective, or in need of interpretation. These units of experience are themselves units of meaning.

We shall see how crucial it is for Dilthey's thought that the ultimate unit of consciousness is named "Erlebnis," not "sensation," as was automatic in Kantianism and in the positivist epistemology of the nineteenth century up to Ernst Mach. Thus Dilthey circumscribes the ideal of constructing knowledge from atoms of sensation and offers instead a more sharply defined version of the concept of the given. The unity of experience (and not the psychic elements into which it can be analyzed) represents the true unit of what is given. Thus in the epistemology of the human sciences we find a concept of life that restricts the mechanistic model.

This concept of life is conceived teleologically; life, for Dilthey, is productivity. Since life objectifies itself in structures of meaning, all understanding of meaning consists in "translating the objectifications of life back into the spiritual life from which they emerged." Thus the concept of experience is the epistemological basis for all knowledge of the objective.

The epistemological function of the concept of experience in Husserl's phenomenology is equally universal. In the fifth of the *Logical Investigations* (Chapter 2), the phenomenological concept of experience is expressly distinguished from the popular one. The unit of experience is not understood as a piece of the actual flow of experience of an "I," but as an intentional relation. Here too Erlebnis, as a unit of meaning, is teleological. Experiences exist only insofar as something is experienced and intended in them. It is true that Husserl also recognizes non-intentional experiences, but these are merely material for units of meaning, intentional experiences. Thus for Husserl experience becomes the comprehensive name for all acts of consciousness whose essence is intentionality.[123]

Thus both in Dilthey and in Husserl, both in life philosophy and in phenomenology, the concept of Erlebnis is primarily purely epistemological. Its teleological meaning is taken into account, but it is not conceptually determined. That life (Leben) manifests itself in experience (Erlebnis) means simply that life is the ultimate foundation. The history of the word provided a certain justification for conceiving it as an achievement (Leistung). For we have seen that the coinage Erlebnis has a condensing, intensifying meaning. If something is called or considered an

Erlebnis, that means it is rounded into the unity of a significant whole. An experience is as much distinguished from other experiences—in which other things are experienced—as it is from the rest of life in which "nothing" is experienced. An experience is no longer just something that flows past quickly in the stream of conscious life; it is meant as a unity and thus attains a new mode of being *one*. Thus it is quite understandable that the word emerges in biographical literature and ultimately stems from its use in autobiography. What can be called an experience constitutes itself in memory. By calling it such, we are referring to the lasting meaning that an experience has for the person who has it. This is the reason for talking about an intentional experience and the teleological structure of consciousness. On the other hand, however, the notion of experience also implies a contrast between life and mere concept. Experience has a definite immediacy which eludes every opinion about its meaning. Everything that is experienced is experienced by oneself, and part of its meaning is that it belongs to the unity of this self and thus contains an unmistakable and irreplaceable relation to the whole of this one life. Thus, essential to an experience is that it cannot be exhausted in what can be said of it or grasped as its meaning. As determined through autobiographical or biographical reflection, its meaning remains fused with the whole movement of life and constantly accompanies it. The mode of being of experience is precisely to be so determinative that one is never finished with it. Nietzsche says, "all experiences last a long time in profound people."[124] He means that they are not soon forgotten, it takes a long time to assimilate them, and this (rather than their original content as such) constitutes their specific being and significance. What we call an Erlebnis in this emphatic sense thus means something unforgettable and irreplaceable, something whose meaning cannot be exhausted by conceptual determination.[125]

Seen philosophically, the ambiguity we have noted in the concept of Erlebnis means that this concept is not wholly exhausted by its being the ultimate datum and basis of all knowledge. There is something else quite different that needs to be recognized in the concept of "experience," and it reveals a set of problems that have still to be dealt with: its inner relation to life.[126]

There were two starting points for this far-reaching theme—the relationship between life and experience—and we will see below how Dilthey, and more especially Husserl, became caught up in this set of problems. Here we see the crucial importance of Kant's critique of any substantialist doctrine of the soul and, different from it, the importance of the transcendental unity of self-consciousness, the synthetic unity of apperception. This critique of rationalist psychology gave rise to the idea of a psychology based on Kant's critical method, such as Paul Natorp[127] undertook in 1888 and on which Richard Hönigswald later based the concept of Denkpsychologie.[128] Natorp designated Bewußtheit, which expresses the immediacy of experience, as the object of critical psychology, and he developed universal subjectivization as the research method of reconstructive psychology. Natorp later supported and further elaborated his basic idea by a thorough criticism of the concepts of contemporary psychological research, but as early as 1888 the basic idea was already there: the concreteness of primal experience—i.e., the totality of consciousness—represents an undifferentiated unity, which is differentiated and determined by the objectivizing method of knowledge. "But consciousness means life—i.e., an indecomposable interrelationship." This is seen particularly in the relationship between consciousness and time: "Consciousness is not given as an event in time, but time as a form of consciousness."[129]

In the same year, 1888, in which Natorp thus opposed the dominant psychology, Henri Bergson's first book appeared, *Les données immédiates de la conscience*, a critical attack on contemporary psychophysics, which used the idea of life just as firmly as Natorp did against the objectivizing and spatializing tendency of psychological concepts. Here we find statements about "consciousness" and its undivided concretion just like those in Natorp. Bergson coined for it the now famous name durée, which expresses the absolute continuity of the psychic. Bergson understands this as "organization"—i.e., he defines it by appeal to the mode of being of living beings (être vivant), a mode in which every element is representative of the whole (représentatif du tout). He compares the inner interpenetration of all elements in consciousness to the way all the notes intermingle when we listen to a melody. Bergson too, then, defends the anti-Cartesian element of the concept of life against objectivizing science.[130]

If we look more closely at what is here called "life" and which of its aspects affect the concept of experience, we see that the relationship of life to experience is not that of a universal to a particular. Rather, the unity of experience as determined by its intentional content stands in an immediate relationship to the whole, to the totality of life. Bergson speaks of the representation of the whole, and similarly Natorp's concept of interrelationship is an expression of the "organic" relationship of part and whole that takes place here. It was primarily Georg Simmel who analyzed the concept of life in this respect as "life's reaching out beyond itself."[131]

The representation of the whole in the momentary Erlebnis obviously goes far beyond the fact of its being determined by its object. Every experience is, in Schleiermacher's words, "an element of infinite life."[132] Georg Simmel, who was largely responsible for the word Erlebnis becoming so fashionable, considers the important thing about the concept of experience as this: "the objective not only becomes an image and idea, as in knowing, but an element in the life process itself."[133] He even says that every experience has something of an adventure about it.[134] But what is an adventure? An adventure is by no means just an episode. Episodes are a succession of details which have no inner coherence and for that very reason have no permanent significance. An adventure, however, interrupts the customary course of events, but is positively and significantly related to the context which it interrupts. Thus an adventure lets life be felt as a whole, in its breadth and in its strength. Here lies the fascination of an adventure. It removes the conditions and obligations of everyday life. It ventures out into the uncertain.

But at the same time it knows that, as an adventure, it is exceptional and thus remains related to the return of the everyday, into which the adventure cannot be taken. Thus the adventure is "undergone," like a test or trial from which one emerges enriched and more mature.

There is an element of this, in fact, in every Erlebnis. Every experience is taken out of the continuity of life and at the same time related to the whole of one's life. It is not simply that an experience remains vital only as long as it has not been fully integrated into the context of one's life consciousness, but the very way it is "preserved and dissolved" (aufgehoben) by being worked into the whole of life consciousness goes far beyond any "significance" it might be thought to have. Because it is itself within the whole of life, the whole of life is present in it too.

Thus at the end of our conceptual analysis of experience we can see the affinity between the structure of Erlebnis as such and the mode of being of the aesthetic. Aesthetic experience is not just one kind of experience among others, but represents the essence of experience per se. As the work of art as such is a world for itself, so also what is experienced aesthetically is, as an Erlebnis, removed from all connections with actuality. The work of art would seem almost by definition to be an aesthetic experience: that means, however, that the power of the work of art suddenly tears the person experiencing it out of the context of his life, and yet relates him back to the whole of his existence. In the experience of art is present a fullness of meaning that belongs not only to this particular content or object but rather stands for the meaningful whole of life. An aesthetic Erlebnis always contains the experience of an infinite whole. Precisely because it does not combine with other experiences to make one open experiential flow, but immediately represents the whole, its significance is infinite.

Since aesthetic experience, as was said above, is an exemplary instance of the meaning of the concept Erlebnis, it is clear that the concept of Erlebnis is a determining feature of the foundation of art. The work of art is understood as the consummation of the symbolic representation of life, and towards this consummation every experience already tends. Hence it is itself marked out as the object of aesthetic experience. For aesthetics the conclusion follows that so-called Erlebniskunst (art based on experience) is art per se.

(iv) The Limits of Erlebniskunst and the Rehabilitation of Allegory

The concept of *Erlebniskunst* contains an important ambiguity. Originally Erlebniskunst obviously meant that art comes *from* experience and is an expression of experience. But in a derived sense the concept of Erlebniskunst is then used for art that is intended *to be* aesthetically experienced. Both are obviously connected. The significance of that whose being consists in expressing an experience cannot be grasped except through an experience.

As always in such a case, the concept of Erlebniskunst is affected by the experience of the limits set to it. Only when it is no longer self-evident that a work of art consists in the transformation of experiences—and when it is no longer self-evident that this transformation is based on the experience of an inspired genius which, with the assuredness of a somnambulist, creates the work of art, which then becomes an experience for the person exposed to it—does one become conscious of the concept of Erlebniskunst in its outline. The century of Goethe seems remarkable to us for the self-evidence of these assumptions, a century that is a whole age, an epoch. Only because it is self-contained for us and we can see beyond it are we able to see it within its own limits and have a concept of it.

Slowly we realize that this period is only an episode in the total history of art and literature. Curtius' monumental work on medieval literary aesthetics gives us a good idea of this.[135] If we start to look beyond the limits of Erlebniskunst and have recourse to other criteria, new vistas open up within European art: we discover that from the classical period up to the age of the baroque art was dominated by quite other standards of value than that of being experienced, and thus our eyes are opened to totally unfamiliar artistic worlds.

Of course, these too can become "experiences" for us. Such an aesthetic self-understanding is always available. But it cannot be denied that the work of art which becomes an experience for us in this way was not itself meant to be understood thus. Genius and being experienced, our criteria of value, are not adequate here. We may also remember quite different criteria and say, for example, that it is not the genuineness of the experience or the intensity of its expression, but the ingenious manipulation of fixed forms and modes of statement that makes something a work of art. This difference in criteria is true of all kinds of art, but is particularly noticeable in the literary arts.[136] As late as the eighteenth century we find poetry and rhetoric side by side in a way that is surprising to modern consciousness. Kant sees in both "a free play of the imagination and a serious business of the understanding."[137] For him both poetry and rhetoric are fine arts and are "free" insofar as both exhibit the undesigned harmony of both cognitive faculties, the senses and the understanding. Against this tradition, the criteria of being experienced and of the inspired genius inevitably introduced a quite different conception of "free" art, to which poetry belongs only insofar as it eliminates everything merely occasional and banishes rhetoric entirely.

Thus the devaluation of rhetoric in the nineteenth century follows necessarily from the doctrine that genius creates unconsciously. We shall pursue one particular example of this devaluation: the history of the concepts of *symbol* and *allegory*, and the changing relationship between them in the modern period.

Even scholars interested in linguistic history often take insufficient account of the fact that the aesthetic opposition between allegory and symbol—which seems self-evident to us—has been philosophically elaborated only during the last two centuries, and is so little to be expected before then that the question to be asked is rather how the need for this distinction and opposition arose. It cannot be forgotten that Winckelmann, whose influence on the aesthetics and philosophy of history of the time was very great, used both concepts synonymously; and the same is true of eighteenth-century aesthetics as a whole. The meanings of the two words have in fact something in common. Both words refer to something whose meaning does not consist in its external appearance or sound but in a significance that lies beyond it. Common to both is that, in both, one thing stands for another. This relation of meaning whereby the non-sensory is made apparent to the senses is found in the field of poetry and the plastic arts, as well as in that of the religious and sacramental.

A more detailed investigation would be required to discover to what extent the classical use of the words "symbol" and "allegory" paved the way for the later contrast between the two with which we are familiar. Here we can sketch out only a few of the basic outlines. Of course the two words originally had nothing to do with each other. "Allegory" originally belonged to the sphere of talk, of the logos, and is therefore a rhetorical or hermeneutical figure. Instead of what is actually meant, something else, more tangible, is said, but in such a way that the former is understood.[138] "Symbol," however, is not limited to the sphere of the logos, for a symbol is not related by its meaning to another meaning, but its own sensory existence has "meaning." As something shown, it enables one to recognize something else, as with the tessera hospitalis and the like. Obviously a symbol is something which has value not only because of its content, but because it can be "produced"—i.e., because it is a document[139] by means of which the members of a community recognize one another; whether it is a religious symbol or appears in a secular context—as a badge or a pass or a password—in every case the meaning of the symbolon depends on its physical presence and acquires a representational function only by being shown or spoken.

Although the two concepts, allegory and symbol, belong to different spheres, they are close to one another not only because of their common structure, representing one thing by means of another, but also because both find their chief application in the religious sphere. Allegory arises from the theological need to eliminate offensive material from a religious text—originally from Homer—and to recognize valid truths behind it. It acquires a correlative function in rhetoric wherever circumlocution and indirect statement appear more appropriate. The concept of symbol now approaches this rhetorical-hermeneutical concept of allegory (symbol, in the sense of allegory, seems to appear for the first time in Chrysippus),[140] especially through the Christian transformation of Neoplatonism. Pseudo-Dionysius at the very beginning of his magnum opus defends the need to proceed symbolically (symbolikos) by referring to the incommensurability of the suprasensory being of God with our minds, which are accustomed to the world of the senses. Thus symbolon here acquires an anagogic function[141]; it leads to the knowledge of the divine—just as allegorical speech leads to a "higher" meaning. The allegorical procedure of interpretation and the symbolical procedure of knowledge are both necessary for the same reason: it is possible to know the divine in no other way than by starting from the world of the senses.

But the concept of symbol has a metaphysical background that is entirely lacking in the rhetorical use of allegory. It is possible to be led beyond the sensible to the divine. For the world of the senses is not mere nothingness and darkness but the outflowing and reflection of truth. The modern concept of symbol cannot be understood apart from this gnostic function and its metaphysical background. The only reason that the word "symbol" can be raised from its original usage (as a document, sign, or pass) to the philosophical idea of a mysterious sign, and thus become similar to a hieroglyph interpretable only by an initiate, is that the symbol is not an arbitrarily chosen or created sign, but presupposes a metaphysical connection between visible and invisible. The inseparability of visible appearance and invisible significance, this "coincidence" of two spheres, underlies all forms of religious worship. It is easy to see how the term came to be extended to the aesthetic sphere. According to Solger[142] the symbolic refers to an "existent in which the idea is recognized in some way or other"—i.e., the inward unity of ideal and appearance that is specific to the work of art. Allegory, however, creates this meaningful unity only by pointing to something else.

But the concept of allegory too has undergone a considerable expansion, inasmuch as allegory refers not only to the figure of speech and the interpreted sense (sensus allegoricus) but correlatively to abstract concepts artistically represented in images. Obviously the concepts of rhetoric and poetics served as models for developing aesthetic concepts in the sphere of the plastic arts.[143] The rhetorical element in the concept of allegory contributes to this development in meaning insofar as allegory assumes not the kind of original metaphysical affinity that a symbol claims but rather a co-ordination created by convention and dogmatic agreement, which enables one to present in images something that is imageless.

Thus, in sum, the semantic trends at the end of the eighteenth century led to contrasting the symbolic (conceived as something inherently and essentially significant) with the allegorical, which has external and artificial significance. The symbol is the coincidence of the sensible and the non-sensible; allegory, the meaningful relation of the sensible to the non-sensible.

Now, under the influence of the concept of genius and the subjectivization of "expression," this difference of meanings became a contrast of values. The symbol (which can be interpreted inexhaustibly because it is indeterminate) is opposed to allegory (understood as standing in a more exact relation to meaning and exhausted by it) as art is opposed to non-art. The very indeterminateness of its meaning is what gave the victory to the word and *concept of the symbolic* when the rationalist aesthetic of the age of Enlightenment succumbed to critical philosophy and the aesthetics of genius. This connection is worth reviewing in detail.

Kant's logical analysis of the concept of symbol in §59 of the *Critique of Judgment* threw the clearest light on this point and was decisive: he contrasts symbolic and schematic representation. The symbolic is representation (and not just notation, as in so-called logical "symbolism"); but symbolic representation does not present a concept directly (as does transcendental schematism in Kant's philosophy) but only in an indirect manner, "through which the expression does not contain the proper schema for the concept, but merely a symbol for reflection." This concept of symbolic representation is one of the most brilliant results of Kantian thought. He thus does justice to the theological truth that had found its scholastic form in the analogia entis and keeps human concepts separate from God. Beyond this he discovers—referring specifically to the fact that this "business requires a more profound investigation"—the symbolic way that language works (its consistent metaphoricity); and finally he uses the concept of analogy, in particular, to describe the relationship of the beautiful to the morally good, a relationship that can be neither subordination nor equivalence. "The beautiful is the symbol of the morally good." In this formula, as cautious as it is pregnant, Kant combines the demand for full freedom of reflection in aesthetic judgment with its humane significance—an idea which was to be of the greatest historical consequence. Schiller followed him in this respect.[144] When he based the idea of an aesthetic education of humankind on the analogy of beauty and morality that Kant had formulated, Schiller was able to pursue a line explicitly laid down by Kant: "Taste makes possible the transition from sensory attractiveness to habitual moral interest without, as it were, too violent a leap."[145]

The question is, how did symbol and allegory come into the now familiar opposition? At first, we can find nothing of this opposition in Schiller, even though he shares the criticism of the cold and artificial allegory which Klopstock, Lessing, the young Goethe, Karl-Philipp Moritz, and others

directed at the time against Winckelmann.[146] It is only in the correspondence between Schiller and Goethe that we find the beginnings of the new
concept of symbol. In his well-known letter of August 17, 1797, Goethe
describes the sentimental mood brought about by his impressions of
Frankfurt, and says of the objects that induce it "that they are properly
symbolic—i.e., as I hardly need to say, they are eminent examples which
stand in a characteristic multiplicity, as representatives of many others, and
embrace a certain totality. . . . " He attaches importance to this experience
because it is intended to help him escape the "million-headed hydra of
empiricism." Schiller supports him in this and finds this sentimental mode
of feeling wholly in accord with "what we have agreed on in this sphere."
But with Goethe it is, as we know, *not so much an aesthetic experience as an
experience of reality,* and to describe it he apparently draws the concept of the
symbolic from early Protestant usage.

Schiller raises idealist objections to conceiving reality as symbolic, and
thus pushes the meaning of "symbol" towards the aesthetic. Goethe's art-
loving friend, Meyer, also applies the concept of the symbol to the aesthetic
in order to distinguish the true work of art from allegory. But for Goethe
himself the contrast between symbol and allegory in art theory is only a
special instance of the general tendency towards meaning that he seeks in
all phenomena. Thus he applies the concept of the symbol to colors
because there too "the true relationship at the same time expresses the
meaning." Here the influence of the traditional hermeneutical schema of
allegorice, symbolice, mystice is so clear[147] that he finally writes the
sentence, so typical of him: "Everything that happens is a symbol, and, in
fully representing itself, it points towards everything else."[148]

In philosophical aesthetics this usage of the word symbol must have
established itself via the Greek "religion of art." This is shown clearly by
Schelling's developing the philosophy of art out of mythology. In his
Götterlehre Karl-Philipp Moritz, to whom Schelling refers, had rejected
"dissolving" mythological poetry "into mere allegory," but still he did not
use the word "symbol" for this "language of fantasy." However, Schelling
writes, "Mythology in general and any piece of mythological literature in
particular is not to be understood schematically or allegorically, but
symbolically. For the demand of absolute artistic representation is: representation with *complete indifference,* so that the universal *is* wholly the
particular, and the particular is at the same time wholly the universal, and
does not simply mean it."[149] When in his criticism of Heine's view of
Homer Schelling thus establishes the true relationship between mythology

and allegory, he is at the same time giving the concept of symbol a central position within the philosophy of art. Similarly, we find Solger saying that all art is symbolic.[150] Solger opines that the work of art is the existence of the "idea" itself—its meaning is not an "idea sought apart from the actual work of art." For this is what is characteristic of the work of art, the creation of genius: that its meaning lies in the phenomenon itself and is not arbitrarily read into it. Referring to the German translation of the word "symbol" as Sinnbild (meaning image), Schelling describes it "as concrete, resembling only itself, like an image, and yet as universal and full of meaning as a concept."[151] In fact, what distinguishes the symbol even as Goethe conceives it is that in it the idea itself gives itself existence. Only because the concept of symbol implies the inner unity of symbol and what is symbolized, was it possible for the symbol to become a basic concept universal to aesthetics. A symbol is the coincidence of sensible appearance and suprasensible meaning, and this coincidence is, like the original significance of the Greek symbolon and its continuance in the terminology of various religious denominations, not a subsequent co-ordination, as in the use of signs, but the union of two things that belong to each other: all symbolism, through which "the priesthood reflects higher knowledge," rests, rather, on the "original connection" between gods and men, writes Friedrich Creuzer,[152] whose *Symbolik* took on the controversial task of interpreting the enigmatic symbolism of antiquity.

But the concept of symbol was not expanded into a universal aesthetic principle without difficulty. For the inner unity of image and significance that constitutes the symbol is not simple. The symbol does not simply dissolve the tension between the world of ideas and the world of the senses: it points up a disproportion between form and essence, expression and content. In particular the religious function of the symbol lives from this tension. The possibility of the instantaneous and total coincidence of the apparent with the infinite in a religious ceremony assumes that what fills the symbol with meaning is that the finite and infinite genuinely belong together. Thus the religious form of the symbol corresponds exactly to the original nature of "symbolon," the dividing of what is one and reuniting it again.

The disproportion of form and essence is essential to the symbol inasmuch as the meaning of symbols points beyond their sensory appearance. This is the origin of that vacillation, that undecidedness between form and essence that is peculiar to the symbol. This disproportion is obviously greater, the more obscure and more meaningful the symbol is—and less, the more the meaning penetrates the form: that was Creuzer's idea.[153] Hegel limits the term "symbolic" to the symbolic art of the East because of this disproportion of image and meaning. For him, excess of meaning is characteristic of a particular art form,[154] which differs from classical art in that the latter has progressed beyond this disproportion. But to say this is obviously to consciously fix and artificially narrow the concept—a concept which, as we saw, seeks to express less the disproportion than the coincidence of image and meaning. It must also be admitted that when Hegel limits the concept of the symbolic (despite its many followers), he is running counter to the tendency of modern aesthetics, which (since Schelling) has sought to emphasize precisely the unity of appearance and meaning in the symbolic in order thereby to justify aesthetic autonomy against the claims of the concept.[155]

Let us now pursue the corresponding *devaluation of allegory*. At the outset, one factor may have been the abandonment of French classicism in German aesthetics from the time of Lessing and Herder.[156] Still, Solger employs the term "allegorical" in an elevated sense for the whole of Christian art, and Friedrich Schlegel goes even further. He says: all beauty is allegory ("Gespräch über Poesie"). Hegel's use of the concept "symbolic" (like Creuzer's) is still very close to this concept of the allegorical. But the philosophers' usage, based on a romantic conception of the relation of the ineffable to language and on the discovery of the allegorical poetry of the East, was not retained by nineteenth-century cultural humanism. An appeal was made to Weimar classicism, and in fact the demotion of allegory was the dominant concern of German classicism; that concern inevitably resulted from the emergence of the concept of genius and from art's being freed from the fetters of rationalism. Allegory is certainly not the product of genius alone. It rests on firm traditions and always has a fixed, statable meaning which does not resist rational comprehension through the concept—on the contrary, the concept of allegory is closely bound up with dogmatics: with the rationalization of the mythical (as in the Greek Enlightenment), or with the Christian interpretation of Scripture in terms of doctrinal unity (as in patristics), and finally with the reconciliation of the Christian tradition and classical culture, which is the basis of the art and literature of modern Europe and whose last universal form was the baroque. With the breakup of this tradition allegory too was finished. For the moment art freed itself from all dogmatic bonds and could be defined as the unconscious production of genius, allegory inevitably became aesthetically suspect.

Thus Goethe's work in aesthetics has a strong influence in making the symbolic a positive, and the allegorical a negative, artistic concept. His own poetry, especially, had the same effect, for it was seen as the confession of his life, a poetic formation of experience (Erlebnis). In the nineteenth century the criterion of experience, which he himself set up, became the highest standard of value. In accordance with the realistic spirit of the century, whatever in Goethe's work did not conform to this criterion—such as the poetry of his old age—was dismissed as allegorically "overladen."

Ultimately, this also affects the development of philosophical aesthetics, which accepts the concept of the symbol in the universal, Goethean sense; but its thought is based on the opposition between reality and art—i.e., it views things from the "standpoint of art" and of the nineteenth-century aesthetic religion of culture. F. T. Vischer is typical of this view; the further he departs from Hegel, the more he extends Hegel's concept of symbol and sees the symbol as one of the fundamental achievements of subjectivity. The "dark symbolism of the mind" gives soul and significance to what in itself lacks a soul (nature or phenomenal appearances). Since the aesthetic consciousness—as opposed to the mythical-religious—knows that it is free, the symbolism it imparts to everything is also "free." However ambiguous and indeterminate the symbol still remains, it can no longer be characterized by its privative relation to the concept. Rather, it has its own positivity as a creation of the human mind. It is the perfect consonance of appearance and idea which is now—with Schelling—emphasized in the concept of symbol, whereas dissonance is reserved for allegory or mythical consciousness.[157] Similarly, as late as Cassirer we find that aesthetic symbolism is distinguished from mythical symbolism by the fact that in the aesthetic symbol the tension between image and meaning has been equilibrated—a last echo of the classicist concept of the "religion of art."[158]

From this survey of the linguistic history of symbol and allegory I draw a factual inference. The fixed contrast between the two concepts—the symbol that has emerged "organically," and cold, rational allegory—becomes less compelling when we see its connection with the aesthetics of genius and of experience (Erlebnis). If the rediscovery of baroque art (which can be clearly seen in the antique market) and, especially in recent decades, the rediscovery of baroque poetry, together with modern aesthetic research, has led to a certain rehabilitation of allegory, we can now see the theoretical reason for this. Nineteenth-century aesthetics was founded on the freedom of the symbol-making activity of the mind. But is that a sufficient foundation? Is not this symbol-making activity also in fact limited by the continued existence of a mythical, allegorical tradition? Once this is recognized, however, the contrast between symbol and allegory again becomes relative, whereas the prejudice of the aesthetics of Erlebnis made it appear absolute. Likewise, the difference between aesthetic consciousness and mythical consciousness can hardly be considered absolute.

We need to recognize that raising such questions necessitates fundamentally revising the basic concepts of aesthetics. Obviously we are concerned here with more than yet another change in taste and aesthetic values. Rather, the concept of aesthetic consciousness itself becomes dubious, and thus also the standpoint of art to which it belongs. Is the aesthetic approach to a work of art the appropriate one? Or is what we call "aesthetic consciousness" an abstraction? The revaluation of allegory that we have been describing indicates that there is a dogmatic element in aesthetic consciousness too. And if the difference between mythical and aesthetic consciousness is not absolute, does not the concept of art itself become questionable? For it is, as we have seen, a product of aesthetic consciousness. At any rate, it cannot be doubted that the great ages in the history of art were those in which people without any aesthetic consciousness and without our concept of "art" surrounded themselves with creations whose function in religious or secular life could be understood by everyone and which gave no one solely aesthetic pleasure. Can the concept of the aesthetic Erlebnis be applied to these creations without truncating their true being?

3 RETRIEVING THE QUESTION OF ARTISTIC TRUTH

(A) THE DUBIOUSNESS OF THE CONCEPT OF AESTHETIC CULTIVATION (BILDUNG)

In order to gauge the extent of this question correctly, we will first undertake an historical inquiry to discover the specific, historically developed meaning of the concept of "aesthetic consciousness." Obviously today we no longer mean by "aesthetic" what Kant still associated with the word when he called the doctrine of space and time "transcendental aesthetics" and called the doctrine of the beautiful and sublime in nature and art a "critique of aesthetic judgment." The turning point seems to have been Schiller, who transformed the transcendental idea of taste into a moral demand and formulated it as an imperative: Live aesthetically![159] In his aesthetic writings Schiller took the radical subjectivization through which Kant had justified transcendentally the judgment of taste and its claim to universal validity, and changed it from a methodological presupposition to one of content.

It is true that he was able to follow Kant himself, inasmuch as Kant had already accorded taste the significance of a transition from sensory pleasure to moral feeling.[160] But when Schiller proclaimed that art is the practice of freedom, he was referring more to Fichte than to Kant. Kant based the a priori of taste and genius on the free play of the faculties of knowledge. Schiller reinterpreted this anthropologically in terms of Fichte's theory of impulses: the play impulse was to harmonize the form impulse and the matter impulse. Cultivating the play impulse is the end of aesthetic education.

This had far reaching consequences. For now art, as the art of beautiful appearance, was contrasted with practical reality and understood in terms of this contrast. Instead of art and nature complementing each other, as had long seemed to be the case, they were contrasted as appearance and reality. Traditionally the purpose of "art," which also includes all conscious transformation of nature for human use, was to supplement and fill the gaps left open by nature.[161] And "the fine arts," as long as they are seen in this framework, are a perfecting of reality, not appearances that mask, veil, or transfigure it. But if the concept of art is defined as appearance in contrast to reality, then nature no longer represents a comprehensive framework. Art becomes a standpoint of its own and establishes its own autonomous claim to supremacy.

Where art rules, the laws of beauty are in force and the frontiers of reality are transcended. This "ideal kingdom" is to be defended against all encroachment, even against the moralistic guardianship of state and society. It is probably part of the inner shift in the ontological basis of Schiller's aesthetics that his great plan in the *Letters on Aesthetic Education* changes in being worked out. As we know, an education by art becomes an education to art. Instead of art's preparing us for true moral and political freedom, we have the culture of an "aesthetic state," a cultured society (Bildungsgesellschaft) that takes an interest in art.[162] But this raises a new obstacle to overcoming the Kantian dualism of the world of the senses and the world of morality, as they are overcome in the freedom of aesthetic play and the harmony of the work of art. Art's reconciliation of ideal and life is merely a local and temporary reconciliation. Beauty and art give reality only a fleeting and transfiguring sheen. The freedom of spirit to which they raise one up is freedom merely in an aesthetic state and not in reality. Thus beneath the dualism of "is" and "ought" that Kant reconciles aesthetically, a more profound, unresolved dualism opens up. The poetry of aesthetic reconciliation must seek its own self-consciousness against the prose of alienated reality.

The concept of reality to which Schiller opposes poetry is undoubtedly no longer Kantian. For Kant always starts, as we have seen, from natural beauty. But since, for the purpose of criticizing dogmatic metaphysics, Kant limited his concept of knowledge wholly to the possibility of "pure natural science," and thus did not contest the validity of the nominalist concept of reality, the ontological difficulty in which nineteenth-century aesthetics found itself goes back ultimately to Kant himself. Under the domination of nominalist prejudices, aesthetic being can be only inadequately and imperfectly understood.

Basically it is to the phenomenological criticism of nineteenth-century psychology and epistemology that we owe our liberation from the concepts that prevented an appropriate understanding of aesthetic being. This critique has shown the erroneousness of all attempts to conceive the mode of being of the aesthetic in terms of the experience of reality, and as a modification of it.[163] All such ideas as imitation, appearance, irreality, illusion, magic, dream, assume that art is related to something different from itself: real being. But the phenomenological return to aesthetic experience (Erfahrung) teaches us that the latter does not think in terms of this relationship but, rather, regards what it experiences as genuine truth. Correlatively, the nature of aesthetic experience is such that it cannot be disappointed by any more genuine experience of reality. By contrast, an experience of disappointment does necessarily correspond to all of the above-mentioned modifications of the experience of reality. What was only appearance reveals itself, what lacked reality acquires it, what was magical loses its magic, what was illusion is seen through, and from what was a dream we awaken. If the aesthetic were mere appearance in this sense, then its force—like the terror of dreams—could last only as long as there was no doubt about its reality, and it would lose its truth on waking.

The shift in the ontological definition of the aesthetic toward the concept of aesthetic appearance has its theoretical basis in the fact that the domination of the scientific model of epistemology leads to discrediting all the possibilities of knowing that lie outside this new methodology ["fiction"!].

Let us recall that in the well-known quotation from which we started, Helmholtz knew no better way to characterize the quality that distinguishes work in the human sciences from that in the natural sciences than by describing it as "artistic." Corresponding positively to this theoretical relationship is what we may call "aesthetic consciousness." It is given with the "standpoint of art," which Schiller first founded. For just as the art of "beautiful appearance" is opposed to reality, so aesthetic consciousness includes an alienation from reality—it is a form of the "alienated spirit," which is how Hegel understood *culture* (Bildung). The ability to adopt an aesthetic stance is part of cultured (gebildete) consciousness.[164] For in aesthetic consciousness we find the features that distinguish cultured consciousness: rising to the universal, distancing from the particularity of immediate acceptance or rejection, respecting what does not correspond to one's own expectation or preference.

We have discussed above the meaning of the concept of *taste* in this context. However, the unity of an ideal of taste that distinguishes a society and bonds its members together differs from that which constitutes the figure of aesthetic culture. Taste still obeys a criterion of content. What is considered valid in a society, its ruling taste, receives its stamp from the commonalities of social life. Such a society chooses and knows what belongs to it and what does not. Even its artistic interests are not arbitrary or in principle universal, but what artists create and what the society values belong together in the unity of a style of life and an ideal of taste.

In contrast, the idea of aesthetic cultivation—as we derived it from Schiller—consists precisely in precluding any criterion of content and in dissociating the work of art from its world. One expression of this dissociation is that the domain to which the aesthetically cultivated consciousness lays claim is expanded to become universal. Everything to which it ascribes "quality" belongs to it. It no longer chooses, because it is itself nothing, nor does it seek to be anything, on which choice could be based. Through reflection, aesthetic consciousness has passed beyond any determining and determinate taste, and itself represents a total lack of determinacy. It no longer admits that the work of art and its world belong to each other, but on the contrary, aesthetic consciousness is the experiencing (erlebende) center from which everything considered art is measured.

What we call a work of art and experience (erleben) aesthetically depends on a process of abstraction. By disregarding everything in which a work is rooted (its original context of life, and the religious or secular function that gave it significance), it becomes visible as the "pure work of art." In performing this abstraction, aesthetic consciousness performs a task that is positive in itself. It shows what a pure work of art is, and allows it to exist in its own right. I call this "aesthetic differentiation."

Whereas a definite taste differentiates—i.e., selects and rejects—on the basis of some content, aesthetic differentiation is an abstraction that selects only on the basis of aesthetic quality as such. It is performed in the self-consciousness of "aesthetic experiences." Aesthetic experience (Erlebnis) is directed towards what is supposed to be the work proper—what it ignores are the extra-aesthetic elements that cling to it, such as purpose, function, the significance of its content. These elements may be significant enough inasmuch as they situate the work in its world and thus determine the whole meaningfulness that it originally possessed. But as art the work must be distinguished from all that. It practically defines aesthetic consciousness to say that it differentiates what is aesthetically intended from everything that is outside the aesthetic sphere. It abstracts from all the conditions of a work's accessibility. Thus this is a specifically aesthetic kind of differentiation. It distinguishes the aesthetic quality of a work from all the elements of content that induce us to take up a moral or religious stance towards it, and presents it solely by itself in its aesthetic being. Similarly, in the performing arts it differentiates between the original (play or musical composition) and its performance, and in such a way that both the original (in contrast to the reproduction) and the reproduction in itself (in contrast to the original or other possible interpretations) can be posited as what is aesthetic. The sovereignty of aesthetic consciousness consists in its capacity to make this aesthetic differentiation everywhere and to see everything "aesthetically."

Since aesthetic consciousness claims to embrace everything of artistic value, it has the character of simultaneity. As aesthetic, its form of reflection in which it moves is therefore not only present. For inasmuch as aesthetic consciousness makes everything it values simultaneous, it constitutes itself as historical at the same time. It is not just that it includes historical knowledge and uses it as a distinguishing mark:[165] rather, the dissolution of all taste determined by content, as proper to aesthetic taste, is also seen explicitly in the creative work of artists who turn to the historical. The historical picture which does not originate in a contemporary need to depict but is a representation in historical retrospection, the historical novel, and above all the historicizing forms of nineteenth-century architecture that indulged in continual stylistic reminiscence, show how closely the aesthetic and the historical belong together in a cultured consciousness.

It might be objected that simultaneity does not originate with aesthetic differentiation but has always resulted from the integrating process of historical life. The great works of architecture, at least, continue to exist in the life of the present as living witnesses of the past; and all preservation of inherited manners and behavior, images and decoration, does the same thing, for it too mediates an older way of life to that of the present. But aesthetically cultured consciousness is different from this. It does not see itself as this kind of integration of the ages; the simultaneity peculiar to it is based on the consciousness of historical relativity of taste. De facto contemporaneity (Gleichzeitigkeit) becomes simultaneity (Simultaneität) in principle only when one is fundamentally prepared to resist denigrating any taste that differs from one's own "good" taste. In place of the unity of a taste we now have a mobile sense of quality.[166]

The "aesthetic differentiation" performed by aesthetic consciousness also creates an external existence for itself. It proves its productivity by reserving special sites for simultaneity: the "universal library" in the sphere of literature, the museum, the theater, the concert hall, etc. It is important to see how this differs from what came before. The museum, for example, is not simply a collection that has been made public. Rather, the older collections (of courts no less than of towns) reflected the choice of a particular taste and contained primarily the works of the same "school," which was considered exemplary. A museum, however, is a collection of such collections and characteristically finds its perfection in concealing the fact that it grew out of such collections, either by historically rearranging the whole or by expanding it to be as comprehensive as possible. Similarly in the case of permanently established theaters or concert halls over the last century, one could show how the programs have moved further and further away from contemporary work and have adapted themselves to the need for self-confirmation characteristic of the cultured society that supports these institutions. Even art forms such as architecture that seem opposed to it are drawn into the simultaneity of aesthetic experience, either through the modern techniques of reproduction, which turn buildings into pictures, or through modern tourism, which turns travelling into browsing through picture books.[167]

Thus through "aesthetic differentiation" the work loses its place and the world to which it belongs insofar as it belongs instead to aesthetic consciousness. Correlatively, the artist too loses his place in the world. This is seen in the discrediting of what is called commissioned art. In an era when public consciousness is dominated by the idea that art is based on experience (Erlebnis), it is necessary to recall that creation out of a free inspiration—without a commission, a given theme, and a given occasion—was formerly the exception rather than the rule in artistic work, whereas today we feel that an architect is someone sui generis because, unlike the poet, painter, or composer, he is not independent of commission and occasion. The free artist creates without a commission. He seems distinguished by the complete independence of his creativity and thus acquires the characteristic social features of an outsider whose style of life cannot be measured by the standards of public morality. The concept of the bohemian which arose in the nineteenth century reflects this process. The home of the Gypsies became the generic word for the artist's way of life.

But at the same time the artist, who is as "free as a bird or a fish," bears the burden of a vocation that makes him an ambiguous figure. For a cultured society that has fallen away from its religious traditions expects more from art than aesthetic consciousness and the "standpoint of art" can deliver. The romantic demand for a new mythology—as expressed by F. Schlegel, Schelling, Hölderlin, and the young Hegel,[168] but as found also in the paintings and reflections of Runge—gives the artist and his task in the world the consciousness of a new consecration. He is something like a "secular savior" (Immermann), for his creations are expected to achieve on a small scale the propitiation of disaster for which an unsaved world hopes. This claim has since defined the tragedy of the artist in the world, for any fulfillment of it is always only a local one, and in fact that means it is refuted. The experimental search for new symbols or a new myth that will unite everyone may certainly gather a public and create a community, but since every artist finds his own community, the particularity of such communities merely testifies to the disintegration that is taking place. What unites everyone is merely the universal form of aesthetic culture.

Here the actual process of cultivation—i.e., the elevation to the universal—is, as it were, disintegrated in itself. "The readiness of intellectual reflection to move in generalities, to consider anything at all from whatever point of view it adopts, and thus to clothe it with ideas" is, according to Hegel, the way not to get involved with the real content of ideas. Immermann calls this free self-overflowing of the spirit within itself "extravagantly self-indulgent."[169] He thus describes the situation produced by the classical literature and philosophy of the age of Goethe, when the epigones found all forms of the spirit already existing and hence substituted the enjoyment of culture for its genuine achievement, the refining away of the alien and the crude. It had become *easy* to write a good poem, and, for that very reason, hard to be a poet.

(B) CRITIQUE OF THE ABSTRACTION INHERENT IN AESTHETIC CONSCIOUSNESS

Having described the form it took as cultivation (Bildung), let us now consider the concept of aesthetic differentiation, and discuss the theoretical difficulties involved in *the concept of the aesthetic*. Abstracting down to the "purely aesthetic" obviously eliminates it. This is most evident in Hamann's attempt to develop a systematic aesthetics on the basis of Kant's distinctions.[170] Hamann's work is notable for the fact that he really does go back to Kant's transcendental intention and thus demolishes the one-sided use of Erlebnis as the sole criterion of art. By following out the implications of the aesthetic element wherever it is to be found, he does justice even to those particular forms of the aesthetic that are tied to a purpose, such as the art of monuments and posters. But even here Hamann keeps to the task of aesthetic differentiation. For in these forms too he distinguishes the aesthetic from the non-aesthetic relationships in which it stands, just as we can say outside the experience of art that someone behaves aesthetically. Thus the problem of aesthetics is once more accorded its full breadth, and the transcendental inquiry reinstated that had been abandoned through the standpoint of art and its distinction between beautiful appearance and harsh reality. Aesthetic experience is indifferent to whether or not its object is real, whether the scene is the stage or whether it is real life. Aesthetic consciousness has unlimited sovereignty over everything.

But Hamann's attempt fails at the opposite end: in the concept of art, which, with perfect consistency, he impels so far beyond the realm of the aesthetic that it coincides with virtuosity.[171] Here "aesthetic differentiation" is pushed to its furthest extreme. It even abstracts from art.

The basic aesthetic concept from which Hamann starts is that "perception is significant in itself" (Eigenbedeutsamkeit der Wahrnehmung). This concept obviously means the same as Kant's theory of purposive con-sonance with the state of our cognitive faculty. As for Kant, so for Hamann the criterion of the concept or of meaning, which is essential for knowl-edge, is thus suspended. Linguistically considered, the word Bedeutsam-keit (the quality of possessing meaning or significance) is a secondary formation from Bedeutung and significantly transposes the association with a particular meaning into the sphere of the uncertain. Something is bedeutsam if its meaning (Bedeutung) is unstated or unknown. Eigenbe-deutsamkeit, however, goes even beyond that. If a thing is eigenbedeutsam (significant in itself) rather than fremdbedeutsam (significant in relation to something else), it dissociates itself from everything that could determine its meaning. Can such a concept be a solid ground for aesthetics? Can one use the concept "significant in itself" for a perception at all? Must we not also allow of aesthetic "experience" what we say of perception, namely that it perceives truth—i.e., remains related to knowledge?

It is worthwhile to recall Aristotle here. He showed that all aisthesis tends toward a universal, even if every sense has its own specific field and thus what is immediately given in it is not universal. But the specific sensory perception of something as such is an abstraction. The fact is that we see sensory particulars in relation to something universal. For example, we recognize a white phenomenon as a man.[172]

Now, "aesthetic" vision is certainly characterized by not hurrying to relate what one sees to a universal, the known significance, the intended purpose, etc., but by dwelling on it as something aesthetic. But that still does not stop us from seeing relationships—e.g., recognizing that this white phenomenon which we admire aesthetically is in fact a man. Thus our perception is never a simple reflection of what is given to the senses.

On the contrary, we have learned from modern psychology—especially from the trenchant criticism that Scheler, as well as W. Koehler, E. Strauss, M. Wertheimer and others, made of the conception of pure perception as a "response to a stimulus"—that this conception owes its origin to an epistemological dogmatism.[173] Its true sense is merely a normative one: "response to a stimulus" is the ideal end result of the destruction of all instinct fantasies, the consequence of a great sobering-up process that finally enables one to see what is there, instead of the imaginings of the instinct fantasy. But that means that pure perception, defined as the adequacy of response to stimulus, is merely an ideal limiting case.

There is a second point, however. Even perception conceived as an adequate response to a stimulus would never be a mere mirroring of what is there. For it would always remain an understanding of something as something. All understanding-as is an articulation of what is there, in that it looks-away-from, looks-at, sees-together-as. All of this can occupy the center of an observation or can merely "accompany" seeing, at its edge or in the background. Thus there is no doubt that, as an articulating reading of what is there, vision disregards much of what is there, so that for sight, it is simply not there anymore. So too expectations lead it to "read in" what is not there at all. Let us also remember the tendency to invariance operative within vision itself, so that as far as possible one always sees things in the same way.

This criticism of the theory of pure perception, undertaken on the basis of pragmatic experience, was then pursued to its foundation by Heidegger. This means, however, that this criticism also applies to aesthetic consciousness, although here one does not simply "look beyond" what one sees—e.g., to its general use for some end—but dwells on it. Lingering vision and assimilation is not a simple perception of what is there, but is itself understanding-as. The mode of being of what is observed "aesthetically" is not presence-at-hand. In the case of significant representation—e.g., in works of plastic art, providing that they are not non-representational and abstract—the fact of their significance obviously directs the way what is seen is read. Only if we "recognize" what is represented are we able to "read" a picture; in fact, that is what ultimately makes it a picture. Seeing means articulating. While we are still trying various ways of organizing what we see or hesitating between them, as with certain trick pictures, we don't yet see what is there. The trick picture is, as it were, the artificial perpetuation of this hesitation, the "agony" of seeing. The same is true of the literary work. Only when we understand a text—that is, are at least in command of its language—can it be a work of literary art for us. Even in listening to absolute music we must "understand" it. And only when we understand it, when it is "clear" to us, does it exist as an artistic creation for us. Thus, although absolute music is a pure movement of form as such, a kind of auditory mathematics where there is no content with an objective meaning that we can discern, understanding it nevertheless involves entering into a relation with what is meaningful. It is the indefiniteness of this relation that marks such music's specific relation to meaning.[174]

Pure seeing and pure hearing are dogmatic abstractions that artificially reduce phenomena. Perception always includes meaning. Thus to seek the unity of the work of art solely in its form as opposed to its content is a perverse formalism, which moreover cannot invoke the name of Kant. Kant had something quite different in mind with his concept of form. For him the concept of form refers to the structure of the aesthetic object,[175] not as opposed to the meaningful content of a work of art, but to the purely sensuous attractiveness of the material. The so-called objective content is not material waiting for subsequent formation, but is already bound up with the unity of form and meaning in the work of art.

The word "motif," common in the language of painters, illustrates this. It can be representational as well as abstract; but in either case, as a motif it is, seen ontologically, non-material (aneu hules). That in no way means it is without content. Rather, what makes a motif is that it has unity in a convincing way and that the artist has carried through this unity as the unity of a meaning, just as the viewer understands it as a unity. In this connection Kant speaks of "aesthetic ideas," to which "much that is unnameable" is added.[176] That is his way of going beyond the transcendental purity of the aesthetic and recognizing the mode of being of art. As we have shown above, he was far from seeking to avoid the "intellectualization" of pure aesthetic pleasure. The arabesque is by no means his aesthetic ideal, but merely a favorite methodological example. In order to do justice to art, aesthetics must go beyond itself and surrender the "purity" of the aesthetic.[177] But would this really give it a firm position? In Kant the concept of genius had a transcendental function, and the concept of art was grounded through it. We saw how this concept of genius was extended by his successors to become the universal basis of aesthetics. But is the concept of genius really suited to this?

Modern artistic consciousness seems to suggest it is not. A kind of "twilight of genius" seems to have set in. The idea of the somnambulatory unconsciousness with which genius creates—an idea that can, however, be legitimated by Goethe's description of his own manner of writing poetry—today appears to be false romanticism. A poet like Paul Valéry has opposed to it the criterion of an artist and engineer such as Leonardo da Vinci, in whose total genius craftsmanship, mechanical invention, and artistic genius were still undifferentiably one.[178] Popular consciousness, however, is still affected by the eighteenth-century cult of genius and the sacralization of art that we have found to be characteristic of bourgeois society in the nineteenth century. This is confirmed by the fact that the concept of genius is now fundamentally conceived from the point of view of the observer. This ancient concept seems cogent not to the creative, but to the critical mind. The fact that to the observer the work seems to be a miracle, something inconceivable for anyone to make, is reflected as a miraculousness of creation by inspired genius. Those who create then use these same categories in regard to themselves, and thus the genius cult of the eighteenth century was certainly nourished by artists too.[179] But they have never gone as far in self-apotheosis as bourgeois society would have allowed them to. The self-knowledge of the artist remains far more down to earth. He sees possibilities of making and doing, and questions of "technique," where the observer seeks inspiration, mystery, and deeper meaning.[180]

If one wants to take account of this criticism of the theory of the unconscious productivity of genius, one is again faced with the problem that Kant solved by the transcendental function he assigned to the concept of genius. What is a work of art and how does it differ from the product of a craftsman or even from some "potboiler"—i.e., something of inferior aesthetic value? For Kant and idealism the work of art was, by definition, the work of genius. Its distinctiveness—its being completely successful and exemplary—was proved by the fact that it offered to pleasure and contemplation an inexhaustible object of lingering attention and interpretation. That the genius of creation is matched by genius in appreciating was already part of Kant's theory of taste and genius, and K. P. Moritz and Goethe taught it even more explicitly.

But how can the nature of artistic pleasure and the difference between what a craftsman makes and what an artist creates be understood without the concept of genius?

How can even the completeness of a work of art, its being finished, be conceived? The completeness of everything else that is made or produced is measured by the criterion of its purpose—i.e., it is determined by the use that is to be made of it. The work is finished if it answers the purpose for which it is intended.[181] But how is one to conceive of the criterion for measuring the completeness of a work of art? However rationally and soberly one may consider artistic "production," much that we call art is not intended to be used, and none derives the standard of its completeness from such a purpose. Does not the work's existence, then, appear to be the breaking-off of a creative process that actually points beyond it? Perhaps in itself it cannot be completed at all?

Paul Valéry, in fact, thought this was the case. But he did not work out the consequence that followed for someone who encounters a work of art and endeavors to understand it. If it is true that a work of art is not, in itself, completable, what is the criterion for appropriate reception and understanding? A creative process randomly and arbitrarily broken off cannot imply anything obligatory.[182] From this it follows that it must be left to the recipient to make something of the work. One way of understanding a work, then, is no less legitimate than another. There is no criterion of appropriate reaction. Not only does the artist himself possess none—the aesthetics of genius would agree here; every encounter with the work has the rank and rights of a new production. This seems to me an untenable hermeneutic nihilism. If Valéry sometimes drew such conclusions for his work[183] in order to avoid the myth of the unconscious productivity of genius, he has, in my view, become entangled in it, for now he transfers to reader and interpreter the authority of absolute creation that he himself no longer desires to exert. But genius in understanding is, in fact, of no more help than genius in creation.

The same aporia arises if one starts from the concept of aesthetic experience rather than that of genius. On this topic the fundamental essay by Georg von Lukács, "The Subject-Object Relation in Aesthetics,"[184] reveals the problem. He ascribes a Heraclitean structure to the aesthetic sphere, by which he means that the unity of the aesthetic object is not actually given. The work of art is only an empty form, a mere nodal point in the possible variety of aesthetic experiences (Erlebnisse), and the aesthetic object exists in these experiences alone. As is evident, absolute discontinuity—i.e., the disintegration of the unity of the aesthetic object into the multiplicity of experiences—is the necessary consequence of an aesthetics of Erlebnis. Following Lukács' ideas, Oskar Becker has stated outright that "in terms of time the work exists only in a moment (i.e., now); it is 'now' this work and now it is this work no longer!"[185] Actually, that is logical. Basing aesthetics on experience leads to an absolute series of points, which annihilates the unity of the work of art, the identity of the artist with himself, and the identity of the person understanding or enjoying the work of art.[186]

By acknowledging the destructive consequences of subjectivism and describing the self-annihilation of aesthetic immediacy, Kierkegaard seems to me to have been the first to show the untenability of this position. His doctrine of the aesthetic stage of existence is developed from the standpoint of the moralist who has seen how desperate and untenable is existence in pure immediacy and discontinuity. Hence his criticism of aesthetic consciousness is of fundamental importance because he shows the inner contradictions of aesthetic existence, so that it is forced to go beyond itself. Since the aesthetic stage of existence proves itself untenable, we recognize that even the phenomenon of art imposes an ineluctable task on existence, namely to achieve that continuity of self-understanding which alone can support human existence, despite the demands of the absorbing presence of the momentary aesthetic impression.[187]

If one still wanted to define the nature of aesthetic existence in a way that constructed it outside the hermeneutic continuity of human existence, then I think one would have missed the point of Kierkegaard's criticism. Admittedly, the natural, as a joint condition of our mental life, limits our self-understanding and does so by projecting itself into the mental in many forms—as myth, as dream, as the unconscious preformation of conscious life. And one must admit that aesthetic phenomena similarly manifest the limits of Dasein's historical self-understanding. But we are given no vantage point that would allow us to see these limits and conditions in themselves or to see ourselves "from the outside" as limited and conditioned in this way. Even what is closed to our understanding we ourselves experience as limiting, and consequently it still belongs to the continuity of self-understanding in which human existence moves. We recognize "the fragility of the beautiful and the adventurousness of the artist." But that does not constitute being situated outside a "hermeneutic phenomenology" of Dasein. Rather, it sets the task of preserving the hermeneutic continuity which constitutes our being, despite the discontinuity intrinsic to aesthetic being and aesthetic experience.[188]

The pantheon of art is not a timeless present that presents itself to a pure aesthetic consciousness, but the act of a mind and spirit that has collected and gathered itself historically. Our experience of the aesthetic too is a mode of self-understanding. Self-understanding always occurs through understanding something other than the self, and includes the unity and integrity of the other. Since we meet the artwork in the world and encounter a world in the individual artwork, the work of art is not some alien universe into which we are magically transported for a time. Rather, we learn to understand ourselves in and through it, and this means that we sublate (aufheben) the discontinuity and atomism of isolated experiences in the continuity of our own existence. For this reason, we must adopt a standpoint in relation to art and the beautiful that does not pretend to immediacy but corresponds to the historical nature of the human condition. The appeal to immediacy, to the instantaneous flash of genius, to the significance of "experiences" (Erlebnisse), cannot withstand the claim of human existence to continuity and unity of self-understanding. The binding quality of the experience (Erfahrung) of art must not be disintegrated by aesthetic consciousness.

This negative insight, positively expressed, is that art is knowledge and experiencing an artwork means sharing in that knowledge.

This raises the question of how one can do justice to the truth of aesthetic experience (Erfahrung) and overcome the radical subjectivization of the aesthetic that began with Kant's *Critique of Aesthetic Judgment*. We have shown that it was a methodological abstraction corresponding to a quite particular transcendental task of laying foundations which led Kant to relate aesthetic judgment entirely to the condition of the subject. If, however, this aesthetic abstraction was subsequently understood as a content and was changed into the demand that art be understood "purely aesthetically," we can now see how this demand for abstraction ran into indissoluble contradiction with the true experience of art.

Is there to be no knowledge in art? Does not the experience of art contain a claim to truth which is certainly different from that of science, but just as certainly is not inferior to it? And is not the task of aesthetics precisely to ground the fact that the experience (Erfahrung) of art is a mode of knowledge of a unique kind, certainly different from that sensory knowledge which provides science with the ultimate data from which it constructs the knowledge of nature, and certainly different from all moral rational knowledge, and indeed from all conceptual knowledge—but still knowledge, i.e., conveying truth?

This can hardly be recognized if, with Kant, one measures the truth of knowledge by the scientific concept of knowledge and the scientific concept of reality. It is necessary to take the concept of experience (Erfahrung) more broadly than Kant did, so that the experience of the work of art can be understood as experience. For this we can appeal to Hegel's admirable lectures on aesthetics. Here the truth that lies in every artistic experience is recognized and at the same time mediated with historical consciousness. Hence aesthetics becomes a history of worldviews—i.e., a history of truth, as it is manifested in the mirror of art. It is also a fundamental recognition of the task that I formulated thus: to legitimate the knowledge of truth that occurs in the experience of art itself.

The familiar concept of worldview—which first appears in Hegel in the *Phenomenology of Mind*[189] as a term for Kant's and Fichte's postulatory amplification of the basic moral experience into a moral world order —acquires its special stamp only in aesthetics. It is the multiplicity and the possible change of worldviews that has given the concept of worldview its familiar ring.[190] But the history of art is the best example of this, because this historical multiplicity cannot be superseded through progress towards the one, true art. Admittedly, Hegel was able to recognize the truth of art only by subordinating it to philosophy's comprehensive knowledge and by constructing the history of worldviews, like world history and the history of philosophy, from the viewpoint of the present's complete self-consciousness. But this cannot be regarded simply as a wrong turn, for the sphere of subjective mind has been far exceeded. Hegel's move beyond it remains a lasting element of truth in his thought. Certainly, inasmuch as it makes conceptual truth omnipotent, since the concept supersedes all experience, Hegel's philosophy at the same time disavows the way of truth it has recognized in the experience of art. If we want to justify art as a way of truth in its own right, then we must fully realize what truth means here. It is in the human sciences as a whole that an answer to this question must be found. For they seek not to surpass but to understand the variety of experiences—whether of aesthetic, historical, religious, or political consciousness—but that means they expect to find truth in them. We will have to go into the relationship between Hegel and the self-understanding of the human sciences represented by the "historical school" and also into the way the two differ about what makes it possible to understand aright what truth means in the human sciences. At any rate, we will not be able to do justice to the problem of art from the point of view of aesthetic consciousness but only within this wider framework.

We made only one step in this direction in seeking to correct the self-interpretation of aesthetic consciousness and in retrieving the question of the truth of art, to which the aesthetic experience bears witness. Thus our concern is to view the experience of art in such a way that it is understood as experience (Erfahrung). The experience of art should not be falsified by being turned into a possession of aesthetic culture, thus neutralizing its special claim. We will see that this involves a far-reaching hermeneutical consequence, for *all encounter with the language of art is an encounter with an unfinished event and is itself part of this event*. This is what must be emphasized against aesthetic consciousness and its neutralization of the question of truth.

If speculative idealism sought to overcome the aesthetic subjectivism and agnosticism based on Kant by elevating itself to the standpoint of infinite knowledge, then, as we have seen, this gnostic self-redemption of finitude involved art's being superseded by philosophy. We, instead, will have to hold firmly to the standpoint of finiteness. It seems to me that the productive thing about Heidegger's criticism of modern subjectivism is that his temporal interpretation of being has opened up new possibilities. Interpreting being from the horizon of time does not mean, as it is constantly misunderstood to mean, that Dasein is radically temporal, so that it can no longer be considered as everlasting or eternal but is understandable only in relation to its own time and future. If this were its meaning, it would not be a critique and an overcoming of subjectivism but an "existentialist" radicalization of it, which one could easily foresee would have a collectivist future. The philosophical question involved here, however, is directed precisely at this subjectivism itself. The latter is driven to its furthest point only in order to question it. The philosophical question asks, what is the being of self-understanding? With this question it fundamentally transcends the horizon of this self-understanding. In disclosing time as the ground hidden from self-understanding, it does not preach blind commitment out of nihilistic despair, but opens itself to a hitherto concealed experience that transcends thinking from the position of subjectivity, an experience that Heidegger calls *being*.

In order to do justice to the experience (Erfahrung) of art we began with a critique of aesthetic consciousness. The experience of art acknowledges that it cannot present the full truth of what it experiences in terms of definitive knowledge. There is no absolute progress and no final exhaustion of what lies in a work of art. The experience of art knows this of itself. At the same time we cannot simply accept what aesthetic consciousness considers its experience to be. For as we saw, it ultimately considers its experience to be the discontinuity of experiences (Erlebnisse). But we have found this conclusion unacceptable.

We do not ask the experience of art to tell us how it conceives of itself, then, but what it truly is and what its truth is, even if it does not know what it is and cannot say what it knows—just as Heidegger has asked what metaphysics is, by contrast to what it thinks itself to be. In the experience of art we see a genuine experience (Erfahrung) induced by the work, which does not leave him who has it unchanged, and we inquire into the mode of being of what is experienced in this way. So we hope to better understand what kind of truth it is that encounters us there.

We will see that this opens up the dimension in which, in the "understanding" practiced by the human sciences, the question of truth is raised in a new way.[191]

If we want to know what truth is in the field of the human sciences, we will have to ask the philosophical question of the whole procedure of the human sciences in the same way that Heidegger asked it of metaphysics and we have asked it of aesthetic consciousness. But we shall not be able simply to accept the human sciences' own understanding of themselves, but must ask what their mode of understanding in truth is. The question of the truth of art in particular can serve to prepare the way for this more wide-ranging question, because the experience of the work of art includes understanding, and thus itself represents a hermeneutical phenomenon—but not at all in the sense of a scientific method. Rather, understanding belongs to the encounter with the work of art itself, and so this belonging can be illuminated only on the basis of the *mode of being of the work of art itself.*

Notes

1 John Stuart Mill, *System der deduktiven und induktiven Logik*, tr. Schiel, book 6 (2nd ed., 1863), "Von der Logik der Geisteswissenschaften oder moralischen Wissenschaften."

2 David Hume, *Treatise on Human Nature*, Introduction.

3 H. Helmholtz, "Über das Verhältnis der Naturwissenschaften zur Gesamtheit der Wissenschaften," *Vorträge und Reden*, 4th ed., I, 167ff. ["The Relation of the Natural Sciences to Science in General" (1862), tr. N. W. Eve, rev. Russell Kahl, in *Selected Writings of Hermann von Helmholtz*, ed. Russell Kahl (Middletown, Conn.: Wesleyan University Press, 1971), pp. 122–43.]

4 Especially since P. Duhem, whose great book *Études sur Léonard de Vinci* (3 vols.; 1907ff.), has since been supplemented by his posthumous work, which grew to ten volumes, *Le système du monde. Histoire des doctrines cosmologiques de Platon à Copernic* (1913ff.). [But see also Anneliese Maier and A. Koyré, among others.]

5 J. G. Droysen, *Historik*, ed. Erich Rothacker (1925), p.97.

6 W. Dilthey, *Gesammelte Schriften*, V, lxxiv.

7 Op. cit., XI, 244.

8 Op. cit., I, 4.

9 Op. cit., I, 20. [Francis Bacon, *Novum Organon*, bk. 1, Aphorism 3.]

10 Helmholtz, op. cit., p.178.

11 [See my essay "Herder und die geschichtliche Welt," *Kleine Schriften*, III, 101–17 (*GW*, IV).]

12 [One may now consult for political and social history the lexicon *Geschichtliche Grundbegriffe*, ed. Otto Brunner, Werner Conze, and Reinhart Kosellek, and for philosophy, the *Historisches Wörterbuch der Philosophie*, ed. J. Ritter.]

13 I. Schaarschmidt, *Der Bedeutungswandel der Worte Bilden und Bildung* (unpub. diss., Königsberg, 1931).

14 Immanuel Kant, *Metaphysic of Morals*, § 19.

15 G. W. F. Hegel, *Werke* (1832ff.), XVIII, *Philosophische Propädeutik, Erster Cursus*, § 41ff.

16 Wilhelm von Humboldt, *Gesammelte Schriften*, Akadamie ed., VII, part 1, 30.

17 Hegel, *Philosophische Propädeutik*, § 41–45. [See now the anthology by J. E. Pleines, *Bildungstheorien. Probleme und Positionen* (Freiburg, 1978). He also refers to further work by Buck, Pleines, Schaaf.]

18 Hegel, *Phänomenologie des Geistes (Phenomenology of Spirit)*, ed. Hoffmeister, pp. 148ff. [See my essay "Hegel's Dialectic of Self-Consciousness," in *Hegel's Dialectic: Five Hermeneutical Studies*, tr. P. Christopher Smith (New Haven: Yale University Press, 1976), pp. 54–74 and L. Siep, *Anerkennung als Prinzip der praktischen Philosophie: Untersuchungen zu Hegels Jenaer Philosophie des Geistes* (Freiburg, 1979).]

19 Hegel, XVIII, 62.

20 Hegel, *Nürnberger Schriften*, ed. J. Hoffmeister, p.312 (1809 Address).

21 Helmholtz, op. cit., p.178.

22 Friedrich Nietzsche, *Unseasonable Meditations*, 2nd essay, "On the Use and Abuse of History for Life," 1.

23 The history of memory is not the history of the use of it. Mnemotechnics certainly make up a part of this history, but the pragmatic perspective in which the phenomenon of *memoria* appears under that rubric diminishes it. Rather, it should be Augustine who stands at the center of the history of this phenomenon, for he totally transformed the Pythagorean-Platonic tradition that he received. We shall return later to the function of *mneme* in the question of induction. (Cf. in *Umanesimo e Simbolismo*, ed. Castelli [Rome, 1958], the essays of P. Rossi, "La costruzione delli imagini nei trattati di memoria artificiale del Rinascimento," and C. Vasoli, "Umanesimo e simbologia nei primi scritti lulliani e mnemotecnici del Bruno.")

24 *Port Royal Logic*, 4th part, ch. 13ff.

25 G. B. Vico, *On the Study Methods of Our Time*, tr. Elio Gianturco (Library of Liberal Arts; Indianapolis: Bobbs-Merrill, 1965).

26 Werner Jaeger, *Über Ursprung und Kreislauf des philosophischen Lebensideals*, Sitzungsberichte der Preussischen Akademie der Wissenschaften (Berlin, 1928).

27 F. Wieacker, *Vom römischen Recht* (1945).

28 Cf. Nicholas of Cusa, who presents four dialogues, *De sapientia I, II, De mente, De staticis experimentis*, as the writing of an *idiota*.

29 Aristotle, *Nicomachean Ethics*, VI, 9, 1141 b 33: knowing what is good for oneself is one kind of knowledge.

30 Aristotle, *On the Soul*, 425 a 14ff.

31 St. Thomas, *Summa Theologica*, I, ques. 1, 3 ad 2 and ques. 78, 4 ad 1.

32 Tetens, *Philosophische Versuche* (1777), published by the Kant-Gesellschaft, p.515.

33 *Discours préliminaire de l'Encyclopédie*, ed. Köhler (Meiner, 1955), p.80.

34 Cicero, *De oratore*, II, 9, 36.

35 Cf. Leo Strauss, *The Political Philosophy of Hobbes*, ch. 6.

36 Castiglione obviously played an important part in the transmission of this Aristotelian theme; cf. Erich Loos, *Baldassare Castigliones* Libro del cortegiano (Frankfurt, 1955).

37 Shaftesbury, *Characteristics*, Treatise II, esp. part III, sect I.

38 Marcus Aurelius, I, 16.

39 Hutcheson calls the *sensus communis* simply "sympathy."

40 Thomas Reid, *The Philosophical Works*, ed. Hamilton (8th ed., 1895). In II, 774ff., we find a detailed note by Hamilton on the *sensus communis*, which treats the large amount of material in a classificatory rather than historical way. Guenther Pflug informs me that *sensus communis* is found exercising a systematic function in philosophy for the first time in Buffier (1704). That the knowledge of the world through the senses transcends all theoretical problems and is pragmatically justified is, in fact, an old motif of the Skeptics. But Buffier raises the *sensus communis* to the level of an axiom that is to be as much a basis for the knowledge of the external world, the *res extra nos*, as the Cartesian *cogito* is for the world of consciousness. Buffier influenced Reid.

41 Henri Bergson, *Écrits et paroles*, ed. R.–M. Mossé–Bastide, I (Paris: Presses Universitaires de France, 1957), 84–94.

42 I am quoting from *Die Wahrheit des sensus communis oder des allgemeinen Sinnes, in den nach dem Grundtext erklärten Sprüchen und Prediger Salomo oder das beste Haus– und Sittenbuch für Gelehrte und Ungelehrte* by M. Friedrich Christoph Oetinger (new ed. Ehmann, 1861). For his generative method, Oetinger appeals to the rhetorical tradition and further quotes Shaftesbury, Fénelon, and Fleury. According to Fleury, *Discours sur Platon*, the good thing about the method of orators is that it "removes prejudices," and Oetinger says that Fleury is right when he maintains that orators have this method in common with the philosophers (p. 125). According to Oetinger, the Enlightenment is mistaken if it thinks that it is above this method. Our investigation will lead us to confirm this view of Oetinger's. For even though he is attacking a form of the *mos geometricus*, i.e., the Enlightenment ideal of demonstration—something that is no longer of interest today, or is just starting to be so again—the same thing is true of the modern human sciences and their relationship to "logic."

43 F. C. Oetinger, *Inquisitio in sensum communem et rationem* . . . (1753; repr. Stuttgart-Bad Cannstatt, 1964). The following quotations are from this work. See my "Oetinger als Philosoph," *Kleine Schriften* III, 89–100 (*GW*, IV).

44 radicatae tendentia ... Habent vim dictatoriam divinam, irresistibilem.

45 in investigandis ideis usum habet insignem.

46 sunt foecundiores et defaecatiores, quo magis intelliguntur singulae in omnibus et omnes in singulis.

47 Just at this point Oetinger remembers Aristotle's skepticism about having too youthful listeners present during the discussions of moral philosophy. Even this is a sign of how much he is aware of the problem of application. Cf. pp. 290f. below.

48 I refer to Morus, *Hermeneutica*, I, II, II, XXIII.

49 Tetens, *Philosophische Versuche über die menschliche Natur und ihre Entwicklung* (Leipzig, 1777), I, 520.

50 Kant, *Kritik der Urteilskraft*, 1799, 2nd ed., p.VII. *Critique of Judgement*, tr. James Meredith (Oxford, 1952), p.5. Hereafter abbreviated *KdU*.

51 Baumgarten, *Metaphysica* § 606: perfectionem imperfectionemque rerum percipio, i.e., diiudicio.

52 *Eine Vorlesung Kants über Ethik*, ed. Menzer (1924), p.34.

53 Cf. p.35 below.

54 *Critique of Judgement*, § 40.

55 *Kritik der praktischen Vernunft*, 1787, p.124. Hereafter abbreviated *KpV.*

56 Op. cit., 1787, p.272; *Critique of Judgement*, § 60.

57 *Critique of Pure Reason*, B 171ff.

58 *KdU*, 1799, 3rd ed., p.157 (*Critique of Judgement*, p.40).

59 Ibid., p.64.

60 Cf. Kant's recognition of the importance of examples (and thus of history) as "leading strings" for judgment (B 173).

61 The basic work on Gracian and his influence, especially in Germany, is Karl Borinski, *Balthasar Gracian und die Hofliteratur in Deutschland* (1894). This has been supplemented more recently by F. Schummer's *Die Entwicklung des Geschmacksbegriffs in der Philosophie des 17. und 18. Jahrhunderts, Archiv für Begriffsgeschichte*, 1 (1955). [See also W. Krauss, *Studien zur deutschen und französischen Aufklärung* (Berlin, 1963).]

62 F. Heer is, I think, correct in discerning the origin of the modern concept of *Bildung* in the pedagogic culture of the Renaissance, Reformation, and Counter-reformation. Cf. *Der Aufgang Europas*, pp. 82 and 570.

63 Kant, *KdU*, 1799, 3rd ed., p.233.

64 *Anthropologie in pragmatischer Hinsicht*, § 71.

65 Cf. A. Baeumler, *Einleitung in die Kritik der Urteilskraft*, pp. 280ff., esp. 285.

66 *KdU*, 1799, 3rd ed., p.67.

67 This is where the idea of "style" belongs. As a historical category, it comes from the fact that the decorative is to be distinguished from the "beautiful." See pp. 28, 285ff., and Appendix I below [and my essay "The Universality of the

Hermeneutic Problem," in *Philosophical Hermeneutics*, tr. David E. Linge (Berkeley: University of California Press, 1976), pp. 3–17].

68 *KdU*, 1799, p.vii.

69 *Critique of Pure Reason*, B 173 (tr. Kemp Smith).

70 It was obviously this consideration which gave Hegel grounds for going beyond Kant's distinction between determinative and reflective judgment. He acknowledges the speculative meaning in Kant's doctrine of judgment, insofar as in it the universal is conceived as concretely existing in itself, but at the same time makes the reservation that in Kant the relation between the universal and the particular is still not treated as truth, but as something subjective (*Enzyklopädie* § 55ff. and similarly *Logik*, ed. Lasson, II, 19). Kuno Fischer even says that in the philosophy of identity the distinction between the universal that is given and that which has to be found is removed (*Logik und Wissenschaftslehre*, p.148).

71 Aristotle's last word in the detailed description of the virtues and right behavior is therefore always *hos dei* or *hos ho orthos logos*. What can be taught in the practice of ethics is *logos* also, but it is not *akribes* (precise) beyond a general outline. The decisive thing is finding the right nuance. The *phronesis* that does this is a *hexis tou aletheuein*, a state of being in which something hidden is made manifest, i.e., in which something is known. N. Hartmann, in the attempt to understand all the normative elements of ethics in relation to "values," made this into the "value of the situation," a strange extension of the table of the Aristotelian concepts of virtue. [See N. Hartmann, *Ethik* (Berlin, 1926), pp. 330–31 and my "Wertethik und praktische Philosophie," in *Nicolai Hartmann 1882–1982, Gedenkschrift*, ed. A. J. Buch (Bonn, 1982), pp. 113–22 (*GW*, IV)].

72 Of course Kant does not fail to see that taste is decisive for proper behavior as "morality in the world of external appearances" (cf. *Anthropologie*, § 69), but he excludes it from the determination of the will by pure reason.

73 Pp. 5ff. above.

74 Alfred Baeumler's excellent book, *Kants Kritik der Urteilskraft*, informatively examined the positive aspect of the connection between Kant's aesthetics and the problem of history. But we must also reckon up the losses.

75 Cf. Paul Menzer, *Kants Ästhetik in ihrer Entwicklung* (1952).

76 *KdU*, 1799, p.139, cf. p.200 (tr. Meredith, pp. 77, 169, 171, 179, 181).

77 Ibid., § 17, p.54 (tr. Meredith, p.75).

78 Ibid., § 20ff., p.64 (tr. Meredith, pp. 82ff.).

79 Ibid., § 60.

80 Ibid., § 60, p.264 (tr. Meredith, p.227). Nevertheless, despite his critique of the English philosophy of moral feeling, he could not fail to see that this phenomenon of moral feeling is related to the aesthetic. In any case, when he says that pleasure in the beauty of nature is "related to the moral," he is also

able to say that moral feeling, this effect of practical judgment, is a priori a delight (ibid., p.169; tr. Meredith, §42, p.159).

81 Ibid., §16f.

82 [Unfortunately, Kant's analysis of the judgment of taste has again been misapplied in aesthetic theory by T. W. Adorno, *Ästhetische Theorie* (*Schriften*, VII, 22ff.) and H. R. Jauss, *Ästhetische Erfahrung und literarische Hermeneutik* (Frankfurt, 1982), pp. 29f.]

83 Lessing, *Entwürfe zum Laokoon*, no. 20b, in Lessing, *Sämtliche Schriften*, ed. Lachmann (1886ff.), XIV, 415.

84 Note that from here on Kant is obviously thinking of the work of art and no longer chiefly of natural beauty [as he already was in the case of the "normative idea" and its academically correct representation and completely in the case of the ideal: "all the more for one who wants to *represent* it" (*KdU*, §17, p.60).]

85 Cf. Lessing, op. cit., on the "painter of flowers and landscape": "He imitates beauties which are not capable of any ideal," and in positive terms this accords with the pre-eminent position of sculpture within the plastic arts.

86 Here Kant follows Sulzer, who accords a similar distinction to the human form in the article "Beauty" in his *Allgemeine Theorie der schönen Künste*. For the human body is "nothing but the soul made visible." Undoubtedly Schiller in his treatise "Über Matthissons Gedichte" writes in the same sense: "The realm of particular forms does not go beyond the animal body and the human heart, therefore only in the case of these two [he means, as the context shows, the unity of these two, animal corporeality and heart, which comprise the dual nature of man] can an ideal be set up." But Schiller's work is virtually a justification of landscape painting and landscape poetry with the help of the concept of symbol and thus is a prelude to the later aesthetics of art.

87 *Vorlesungen über die Ästhetik*, ed. Lasson, p.57: "Hence the universal need of the work of art is to be sought for within human thought, in that it is a way of showing man what he is."

88 Ibid., p.213.

89 [Kant expressly says that "judgment according to an ideal of beauty is no mere judgment of taste" (*KdU*, p.61). Cf. my essay "Die Stellung der Poesie im Hegel'schen System der Künste," *Hegel-Studien*, 21 (1986).]

90 Rudolf Odebrecht, *Form und Geist: Der Aufstieg des dialektischen Gedankens in Kants Ästhetik* (Berlin, 1930), recognized these connections. [See my "Intuition and Vividness," tr. Dan Tate, in *The Relevance of the Beautiful and Other Essays*, tr. Nicholas Walker (Cambridge: Cambridge University Press, 1986), pp. 157–70.]

91 Schiller rightly felt this when he wrote: "If one has learned to admire the writer only as a great thinker, one will rejoice to discover here a trace of his heart." "Über naive und sentimentalische Dichtung," *Sämmtliche Werke*, ed. Güntter and Witkowski (Leipzig, 1910–), part 17, p.480.

92 [Here the analysis of the sublime in its compulsory functioning would have been particularly important. Cf. J. H. Trede, *Die Differenz von theoretischem und praktischem Vernunftgebrauch und dessen Einheit innerhalb der Kritik der Urteilskraft* (Heidelberg, 1969), and my "Intuition and Vividness," tr. Dan Tate, in *The Relevance of the Beautiful and Other Essays*, tr. Nicholas Walker (Cambridge: Cambridge University Press, 1986), pp. 157–70.]

93 *KdU*, 1799, 3rd ed., pp. 179f. (§45, tr. Meredith, pp. 166f.).

94 Ibid., p.194 (§49, tr. Meredith, p.177).

95 Ibid., p.161 (§35, tr. Meredith, p.143), "Where imagination in its freedom arouses the understanding"; also p.194: "thus the imagination is creative here and sets in motion the faculty of intellectual ideas (reason)" (§49, tr. Meredith, p.177).

96 Ibid., pp. 183f. (§47, tr. Meredith, pp. 169ff.).

97 Ibid., p.li (§vii).

98 Ibid., p.lv ff. (§ix, tr. Meredith, pp. 38ff.).

99 Ibid., p.181 (§§45–6, tr. Meredith, pp. 166–68).

100 Kant characteristically prefers "or" to "and."

101 Ibid., pp. x and lii (tr. Meredith, Preface p.7 and §viii, p.36).

102 Ibid., §48 ["soul" and "soulless" from Meredith for Kant and Gadamer's *geist* and *geistlos*].

103 Ibid., §60.

104 Ibid., §49.

105 Ibid., p.264 (§60).

106 Seeing it, strangely, as a branch of painting and not of architecture (ibid., p.205, §51, tr. Meredith, p.187), a classification that assumes the change of taste from the French to the English ideal of the garden. Cf. Schiller's treatise "Über den Gartenkalender auf das Jahr 1795." Schleiermacher, however, in his *Ästhetik*, ed. Odebrecht, p.204, assigns English gardening to architecture, calling it "horizontal architecture." (Cf. below, n. 78, p.170.)

107 Friedrich Schlegel's first *Lyceum Fragment* (1797) shows to what extent the universal phenomenon of the beautiful was obscured by the development that took place between Kant and his successors and which I call "the standpoint of art": "Many are called artists who are properly works of art produced by nature." In this expression we hear the influence of Kant's explanation of the concept of genius as based on the favor of nature, but it is by then so little valued that on the contrary it becomes an objection against a lack of self-consciousness in artists.

108 Hotho's version of the lectures on aesthetics has given to natural beauty a somewhat too independent position, as is shown by Hegel's original arrangement, reconstructed by Lasson on the basis of lecture notes. Cf. Hegel, *Sämtliche Werke*, ed. Lasson, Xa, 1st half vol. (*Die Idee und das Ideal*), pp. xii ff. [Cf. now the studies preparatory to a new edition by A. Gethmann-Siefert, *Hegel-Studien*, supp. vol. 25 (1985) and my "Die Stellung der Poesie im Hegel'schen System der Künste," *Hegel-Studien*, 21 (1986).]

109 *Vorlesungen über die Ästhetik*, ed. Lasson.

110 It was Luigi Pareyson, in his *L'estetica del idealismo tedesco* (1952), who brought out the importance of Fichte for idealist aesthetics. Similarly, the secret influence of Fichte and Hegel is observable within the whole neo-Kantian movement.

111 According to information from the Deutsche Akademie in Berlin, which had not, however, completed its compilation of examples of the word *Erlebnis*. [See now Konrad Cramer, "Erlebnis," in *Historisches Wörterbuch der Philosophie*, ed. J. Ritter, II, 702–11.]

112 In describing a journey, Hegel writes "my whole experience" (*Erlebnis*), (*Briefe*, ed. Hoffmeister, III, 179). One should note that this is a letter, in which one does not hesitate to use unusual expressions, especially colloquial ones, if no more customary word can be found. Thus Hegel also uses a similar expression (*Briefe*, III, 55), "now about my way of life [*Lebwesen*, a made-up word] in Vienna." He was obviously looking for a generic term that did not yet exist (as is indicated also by his using *Erlebnis* in the feminine gender).

113 In Dilthey's biography of Schleiermacher (1870), in Justi's biography of Winckelmann (1872), in Hermann Grimm's *Goethe* (1877), and presumably frequently elsewhere.

114 *Dichtung und Wahrheit*, part II, book 7 (*Werke*, Sophienausgabe, XXVII, 110).

115 *Zeitschrift für Völkerpsychologie*, X; cf. Dilthey's note on "Goethe und die dichterische Phantasie," *Das Erlebnis und die Dichtung*, pp. 468ff.

116 *Das Erlebnis und die Dichtung*, 6th ed., p.219; cf. Rousseau, *Confessions*, part II, book 9. An exactly corresponding passage cannot be found. Obviously it is not a translation, but a paraphrase of Rousseau's description.

117 *Zeitschrift für Völkerpsychologie*, op. cit.

118 Cf. in the later version of the Goethe essay in *Das Erlebnis und die Dichtung*, p.177: "Poetry is the representation and expression of life. It expresses experience (*Erlebnis*) and represents the external reality of life."

119 Goethe's language was undoubtedly the decisive influence here: "Only ask of a poem whether it contains something experienced (*ein Erlebtes*)" (Jubiläumsausgabe, XXXVIII, 326); or "Books too have their experience (*ihr Erlebtes*)" (ibid., p.257). If the world of culture and of books is measured with this yardstick, then it also is seen as the object of an experience. It is certainly

not accidental that in a more recent Goethe biography, Friedrich Gundolf's, the idea of *Erlebnis* underwent a further terminological development. Gundolf's distinction between *Ur-Erlebnis* (primordial experience) and *Bildungserlebnisse* (cultural experiences) is a logical development of the biographical concept from which the word *Erlebnis* came.

120 Cf., for example, Rothacker's surprise at Heidegger's critique of *Erleben*, directed entirely against the conceptual implications of Cartesianism: *Die dogmatische Denkform in den Geisteswissenschaften und das Problem des Historismus* (1954), p.431.

121 *Akt des Lebens* ("act of life"), *Akt des gemeinschaftlichen Seins* ("act of communal being"), *Moment* ("initial element"), *eigenes Gefühl* ("one's own feeling"), *Empfindung* ("feeling"), *Einwirkung* ("influence"), *Regung als freie Selbstbestimmung des Gemüts* ("feeling as the free self-determination of the heart"), *das ursprünglich Innerliche* ("the original inwardness"), *Erregung* ("excitement"), etc.

122 Dilthey, *Das Leben Schleiermachers*, 2nd ed., p.341. It is interesting that the reading *Erlebnisse* (which I consider the right one) is a correction given in the second ed. (1922, by Mulert) for *Ergebnisse* in the original ed. of 1870 (1st ed., p.305). If this is a misprint in the first edition, it results from the closeness of meaning between *Erlebnis* and *Ergebnis* that we saw above. This can be elucidated by a further example. We read in Hotho, *Vorstudien für Leben und Kunst* (1835): "And yet this kind of imagination depends more on the memory of situations encountered (*erlebter Zustände*), on experiences, rather than being itself originative. Memory preserves and renews the individuality and external type of action of these results (*Ergebnisse*) with all their circumstances and does not allow the universal to emerge for itself." No reader would be surprised at a text which had *Erlebnisse* here rather than *Ergebnisse*. [In the introduction he finally wrote to his biography of Schleiermacher, Dilthey often uses *Erlebnis*. See *Gesammelte Schriften*, XIII, part I, pp. xxxv–xlv.]

123 Cf. Edmund Husserl, *Logische Untersuchungen* II, 365n.; *Ideen zu einer reinen Phänomenologie und phänomenologischen Philosophie*, I, 65.

124 *Gesammelte Werke*, Musarion ed., XIV, 50.

125 Cf. Dilthey, VII, 29ff.

126 This is why Dilthey later limits his own definition of *Erlebnis* when he writes: "*Erlebnis* is a qualitative being, i.e., a reality that cannot be defined through one's inward being, but also reaches down into what is not possessed in a differentiated state." (VII, 230) He does not consciously realize the inadequacy of starting from subjectivity, but he expresses it in his linguistic hesitation: "can one say: is possessed?"

127 *Einleitung in die Psychologie nach kritischer Methode* (1888); *Allgemeine Psychologie nach kritischer Methode* (new ed., 1912).

128 *Die Grundlagen der Denkpsychologie* (1921; 2nd ed., 1925).

129 *Einleitung in die Psychologie nach kritischer Methode*, p.32.

130 Henri Bergson, *Les données immédiates de la conscience*, pp. 76f.

131 Georg Simmel, *Lebensanschauung* (2nd ed., 1922), p.13. We shall see later how Heidegger took the decisive step that made the dialectical play with the concept of life ontologically important (cf. pp. 234ff. below).

132 Friedrich Schleiermacher, *On Religion: Speeches to Its Cultured Despisers*, section II.

133 Georg Simmel, *Brücke und Tür*, ed. Landmann (1957), p.8.

134 Cf. Simmel, *Philosophische Kultur, Gesammelte Essays* (1911), pp. 11–28.

135 Ernst Curtius, *European Literature and the Latin Middle Ages*, tr. Willard Trask (London, 1953).

136 Cf. also the contrast between symbolic and expressive language, on which Paul Böckmann based his *Formgeschichte der deutschen Dichtung*.

137 *KdU*, § 51.

138 *Allegoria* replaces the original *hyponoia*: Plutarch, *Quomodo adolescens poetas audire debeat* ("How a Young Man Ought to Study Poetry," in *Essays on the Study and Use of Poetry*, tr. F. M. Padelford [Yale Studies in English, 15; New York: Holt, 1902]).

139 I leave undecided whether the meaning of *symbolon* as "contract" depends on the character of the agreement itself or on its documentation.

140 *Stoicorum Veterum Fragmenta*, ed. H. von Arnim, II, 257f.

141 *Symbolikos kai anagogikos*, On the Celestial Hierarchy, I, 2.

142 *Vorlesungen über Ästhetik*, ed. Heyse (1829), p.127.

143 It would be worth investigating when the word "allegory" was transferred from the sphere of language to that of the plastic arts. Was it only in the wake of emblematics? (Cf. P. Mesnard, "Symbolisme et Humanisme," in *Umanesimo e Simbolismo*, ed. Castelli [Rome, 1958].) In the eighteenth century, however, people always thought first of the plastic arts when speaking of allegories; and the liberation of poetry from allegory, as undertaken by Lessing, meant in the first place its liberation from the model of the plastic arts. Incidentally, Winckelmann's positive attitude to the idea of allegory is by no means in accord with contemporary taste or with the views of such contemporary theoreticians as du Bos and Algarotti. He seems, rather, to be influenced by Wolff and Baumgarten when he demands that the painter's brush "should be dipped in understanding." Thus he does not dismiss allegory entirely, but refers to classical antiquity in order to evaluate modern allegories against them. How little the general stigmatization of allegory in the nineteenth century—like the way in which the concept of the symbolic is automatically opposed to it—is able to do justice to Winckelmann, we can see from the example of Justi (I, 430ff.).

144 He says, for example, in *Anmut und Würde* that the beautiful object serves as a "symbol" for an idea. *Werke*, ed. Güntter and Witkowski (1910ff.), part 17, p.322.

145 Kant, *KdU*, 3rd ed., p.260 (§59, tr. Meredith, p.225).

146 Careful research by philologists on the use of the word "symbol" in Goethe (Curt Müller, *Die geschichtlichen Voraussetzungen des Symbolbegriffs in Goethes Kunstanschauung* [1933]) shows how important the debate concerning Winckelmann's allegory-aesthetics was for his contemporaries and the significance that Goethe's view of art acquired. In their edition of Winckelmann, Fernow (I, 219) and Heinrich Meyer (II, 675ff.) automatically accept the concept of the symbol as worked out in Weimar classicism. However quickly the influence of Schiller's and Goethe's usage spread, the word does not appear to have had any aesthetic meaning before Goethe. His contribution to the conceptual overtones of "symbol" obviously originates elsewhere, namely in Protestant hermeneutics and sacramental theory, as Looff, *Der Symbolbegriff*, p.195, plausibly suggests by his reference to Gerhard. Karl-Philipp Moritz is a particularly good example of this. Although his view of art is filled entirely with the spirit of Goethe, he can still write in his criticism of allegory that allegory "approaches mere symbol, in which beauty is no longer important" (cited by Müller, p.201). [For extensive additional discussion, see *Formen und Funktionen der Allegorie*, ed. W. Haug (Wolfenbüttel Symposium, 1978; Stuttgart: Metzler, 1979).]

147 *Farbenlehre*, 1st vol. of the 1st, didactic part, no. 916.

148 Letter of April 3, 1818, to Schubart. The young Friedrich Schlegel says similarly (*Neue philosophische Schriften*, ed. J. Körner [1935], p.123): "All knowledge is symbolic."

149 Schelling, *Philosophie der Kunst* (1802), *Sämmtliche Werke*, part I, V, 411.

150 Erwin, *Vier Gespräche über das Schöne und die Kunst*, II, 41.

151 Op. cit., V, 412.

152 F. Creuzer, *Symbolik*, I.

153 Ibid., §30.

154 *Ästhetik*, 1, (*Werke* [1832ff.], X, 1), pp. 403f. [See my "Hegel und die Heidelberger Romantik," *Hegels Dialektik*, pp. 87–98 (*GW*, III).]

155 Nevertheless, we have the example of Schopenhauer to show that a usage which in 1818 conceived the symbol as the special case of a purely conventional allegory was still possible in 1859: *World as Will and Idea*, §50.

156 Here even Winckelmann appears in a false dependency, in the opinion of Klopstock (X, 254ff.): "The two chief mistakes of most allegorical paintings are that they often cannot be understood at all, or only with great difficulty, and that they are, by nature, uninteresting. . . . True sacred and secular history is what the greatest masters prefer to occupy themselves with. . . .

Let the others treat the history of their own country. However interesting it may be, what has even the history of the Greeks and Romans to do with me?" For explicit resistance to the inferior sense of allegory (allegory aimed at the understanding), especially among the French of the period, see Solger, *Vorlesungen zur Ästhetik*, pp. 133ff. Similarly, Erwin II, 49, and *Nachlass*, I, 525.

157 F. T. Vischer, *Kritische Gänge: Das Symbol*. Cf. the fine analysis in E. Volhard, *Zwischen Hegel und Nietzsche* (1932), pp. 157ff., and the genetic account by W. Oelmüller, *F. Th. Vischer und das Problem der nachhegelschen Ästhetik* (1959).

158 Ernst Cassirer, *Der Begriff der symbolischen Form in Aufbau der Geisteswissenschaften*, p.29. [The same point had already been made by Benedetto Croce, *Aesthetic as Science of Expression and General Linguistic* (1902).]

159 In this way one can sum up what is said in his *Letters on the Aesthetic Education of Mankind*, e.g., in the 15th letter: "There should be a harmony between the form instinct and the content instinct, i.e., a play instinct."

160 *KdU*, p.164.

161 *KdU*, p.164.

162 *Letters on the Aesthetic Education of Mankind*, 27th letter. Cf. the excellent account of this process in H. Kuhn, *Die Vollendung der klassischen deutschen Ästhetik durch Hegel* (Berlin, 1931).

163 Cf. Eugen Fink, "Vergegenwärtigung und Bild," *Jahrbuch für Philosophie und phänomenologische Forschung*, 11 (1930).

164 Cf. above pp. 11ff.

165 The pleasure derived from quotations as a social game is typical of this.

166 Cf. also the masterly account of this development in W. Weidlé, *Die Sterblichkeit der Musen*. [Cf. n. 167.]

167 Cf. André Malraux, *La musée imaginaire*, and W. Weidlé, *Les abeilles d'Aristée* (Paris, 1954). And yet in the latter the real consequence that follows from our hermeneutical investigation is missed, in that Weidlé still—in his criticism of the purely aesthetic—holds on to the act of creation as a norm, an act "that precedes the work, but passes into the work itself and that I comprehend, that I look at, when I look at and comprehend the work." (Quoted from the German translation, *Die Sterblichkeit der Musen*, p.181.)

168 Cf. F. Rosenzweig, *Das älteste Systemprogramm des deutschen Idealismus* (1917), p.7. [Cf. the more recent editions by R. Bubner, *Hegel-Studien*, supp. vol. 9 (1973), 261–65, and C. Jamme and H. Schneider, *Mythologie der Vernunft* (Frankfurt, 1984), pp. 11–14.]

169 E.g., in the *Epigonen*. [See my "Zu Immermanns Epigonen-Roman," *Kleine Schriften*, II, 148–60 (*GW*, IX).]

170 Richard Hamann, *Ästhetik* (2nd ed., 1921).

171 "Kunst und Können," *Logos* (1933).

172 Aristotle, *De anima*, 425 *a* 25.

173 Max Scheler in *Die Wissensformen und die Gesellschaft* (1926), pp. 397ff. [Now in *Gesammelte Werke*, VIII, 315ff.]

174 Georgiades' investigations (*Musik und Sprache* [1954]) on the relationship between vocal music and absolute music seem to confirm this connection. [See also Georgiades' posthumous *Nennen und Erklingen* (Göttingen, 1985).] Contemporary discussion about abstract art is, in my view, about to run itself into an abstract opposition of "representational" and "non-representational." Actually, the idea of abstraction strikes a polemical note; but polemics always presupposes something in common. Thus, abstract art does not simply detach itself from the relation to "objectivity," but maintains it in the form of a privation. Beyond this it cannot go, insofar as our seeing is always seeing of objects. Only by disregarding the habits of the practically directed seeing of "objects" can such a thing as aesthetic vision exist—and what one disregards, one cannot help seeing; one must even keep one's eye on it. Bernard Berenson says the same thing: "What we generally call 'seeing' is a practical agreement. . . . " "The plastic arts are a compromise between what we see and what we know" ("Sehen und Wissen," *Neue Rundschau*, 70 [1959], 55–77).

175 Cf. Rudolf Odebrecht, op. cit. (n. 90 above). That Kant, in accordance with the classicist prejudice, opposed color to form and considered it part of sensuous attraction, will not mislead anyone who is familiar with modern painting, in which colors are used structurally.

176 *KdU*, p.197.

177 One day someone should write the history of "purity." H. Sedlmayr, *Die Revolution in der modernen Kunst* (1955), p.100, refers to Calvinistic purism and the deism of the Enlightenment. Kant, who strongly influenced the philosophical terminology of the nineteenth century, also linked himself directly with the classical Pythagorean and Platonic doctrine of purity (cf. G. Mollowitz, "Kants Platoauffassung," *Kantstudien*, [1935]). Is Platonism the common root of all modern "purism"? On catharsis in Plato, cf. Werner Schmitz, *Elenktik und Dialektik als Katharsis* (unpub. diss., Heidelberg, 1953).

178 Paul Valéry, "Introduction à la méthode de Léonard de Vinci et son annotation marginale," *Variété* 1.

179 Cf. my studies on the Prometheus symbol, *Vom geistigen Lauf des Menschen* (1949). [*Kleine Schriften*, II, 105–35 (*GW*, IX).]

180 The methodological justification of the "artist's aesthetics" demanded by Dessoir and others is based on this point.

181 Cf. Plato's remark on the superior knowledge of the user over the producer, *Republic* X, 601c.

182 It was my interest in this question that guided me in my Goethe studies. Cf. *Vom geistigen Lauf des Menschen* (1949); also my lecture in Venice in 1958, "Zur

Fragwürdigkeit des ästhetischen Bewusstseins," *Rivista di Estetica*, III–AIII, 374–83. [Repr. in *Theorien der Kunst*, ed. D. Henrich and W. Iser (Frankfurt, 1982), pp. 59–69.]

183 *Variété* III, "Commentaires de Charmes": "My verses have whatever meaning is given them."

184 In *Logos*, 7 (1917–18). Valéry compares the work of art with a chemical catalyst (op. cit., p.83).

185 Oskar Becker, "Die Hinfälligkeit des Schönen und die Abenteuerlichkeit des Künstler," *Husserl-Festschrift* (1928), p.51. [Repr. Becker, *Dasein und Dawesen* (Pfullingen, 1963), pp. 11–40.]

186 Already in Karl-Philip Moritz we read, "The work has already reached its highest goal in its formation, in its coming to be" (*Von der bildenden Nachahmung des Schönen* [1788], p.26).

187 Cf. Hans Sedlmayr, "Kierkegaard über Picasso," in *Wort und Wahrheit*, V, 356ff.

188 The brilliant ideas of Oskar Becker on "paraontology" seem to regard the "hermeneutic phenomenology" of Heidegger too much as a statement of content and too little as one of methodology. In its content, this para-ontology, which Oskar Becker himself attempts, thinking his way through the problems, comes back to the very point which Heidegger had fixed methodologically. This repeats the quarrel over "nature," in which Schelling remained inferior to the methodological rigor of Fichte's theory of science. If the attempt at paraontology is to acknowledge its complementary character, then it must transcend itself in the direction of something that includes both, a dialectic statement of the actual dimension of the question of being, which Heidegger has raised and which Becker does not appear to recognize as such when he points out the "hyperontological" dimension of the aesthetic problem in order thus to determine ontologically the subjectivity of the artistic genius (see also his essay "Künstler und Philosoph," in *Konkrete Vernunft: Festschrift für Erich Rothacker*) [and see Becker's *Dasein und Dawesen* (Pfullingen, 1963), esp. pp. 67–102].

189 Ed. Hoffmeister, pp. 424ff.

190 The word *Weltanschauung* (cf. A. Götze in *Euphorion* [1924]) at first retains the relationship to the *mundus sensibilis*, even in Hegel, inasmuch as it is art, to the ideas of which the main worldviews belong (*Aesthetik*, II, 131). But since according to Hegel the definiteness of a worldview is for the contemporary artist a thing of the past, the variety and relativity of worldview has become the subject matter for reflection and interiority.

191 [Cf. "Wahrheit in den Geisteswissenschaften," *Kleine Schriften*, I, 39–45 (*GW*, II, 37–43).]

2

The Ontology of the Work of Art and Its Hermeneutic Significance

1 PLAY AS THE CLUE TO ONTOLOGICAL EXPLANATION

(A) THE CONCEPT OF PLAY

For my starting point I select an idea that has played a major role in aesthetics: the concept of *play*. I wish to free this concept of the subjective meaning that it has in Kant and Schiller and that dominates the whole of modern aesthetics and philosophy of man. When we speak of play in reference to the experience of art, this means neither the orientation nor even the state of mind of the creator or of those enjoying the work of art, nor the freedom of a subjectivity engaged in play, but the mode of being of the work of art itself. In analyzing aesthetic consciousness we recognized that conceiving aesthetic consciousness as something that confronts an object does not do justice to the real situation. This is why the concept of play is important in my exposition.

We can certainly distinguish between play and the behavior of the player, which, as such, belongs with the other kinds of subjective behavior. Thus it can be said that for the player play is not serious: that is why he plays. We can try to define the concept of play from this point of view. What is merely play is not serious. Play has a special relation to what is serious. It is not only that the latter gives it its "purpose": we play "for the sake of recreation," as Aristotle says.[1] More important, play itself contains its own, even sacred, seriousness. Yet, in playing, all those purposive relations that determine active and caring existence have not simply disappeared, but are curiously suspended. The player himself knows that play is only play and that it exists in a world determined by the seriousness of purposes. But he does not know this in such a way that, as a player, he actually *intends* this relation to seriousness. Play fulfills its purpose only if the player loses himself in play. Seriousness is not merely something that calls us away from play; rather, seriousness in playing is necessary to make the play wholly play. Someone who doesn't take the game seriously is a spoilsport. The mode of being of play does not allow the player to behave toward play as if toward an object. The player knows very well what play is, and that what he is doing is "only a game"; but he does not know what exactly he "knows" in knowing that.

Our question concerning the nature of play itself cannot, therefore, find an answer if we look for it in the player's subjective reflection.[2] Instead, we are inquiring into the mode of being of play as such. We have seen that it is not aesthetic consciousness but the experience (Erfahrung) of art and thus the question of the mode of being of the work of art that must be the object of our examination. But this was precisely the experience of the work of art that I maintained in opposition to the leveling process of aesthetic consciousness: namely that the work of art is not an object that stands over against a subject for itself. Instead the work of art has its true being in the fact that it becomes an experience that changes the person who experiences it. The "subject" of the experience of art, that which remains and endures, is not the subjectivity of the person who experiences it but the work itself. This is the point at which the mode of being of play becomes significant. For play has its own essence, independent of the consciousness of those who play. Play—indeed, play proper—also exists when the thematic horizon is not limited by any being-for-itself of subjectivity, and where there are no subjects who are behaving "play-fully."

The players are not the subjects of play; instead play merely reaches presentation (Darstellung) through the players. We can already see this from the use of the word, especially from its many metaphorical usages, which Buytendijk in particular has noted.[3]

Here as always the metaphorical usage has methodological priority. If a word is applied to a sphere to which it did not originally belong, the actual "original" meaning emerges quite clearly. Language has performed in advance the abstraction that is, as such, the task of conceptual analysis. Now thinking need only make use of this advance achievement.

The same is also true of etymologies. They are admittedly far less reliable because they are abstractions achieved not by language but by linguistic science, and can never be wholly verified by language itself: that is, by actual usage. Hence even when etymologies are right, they are not proofs but achievements preparatory to conceptual analysis, and only in such analysis do they obtain a firm foundation.[4]

If we examine how the word "play" is used and concentrate on its so-called metaphorical senses, we find talk of the play of light, the play of the waves, the play of gears or parts of machinery, the interplay of limbs, the play of forces, the play of gnats, even a play on words. In each case what is intended is to-and-fro movement that is not tied to any goal that would bring it to an end. Correlatively, the word "Spiel" originally meant "dance," and is still found in many word forms (e.g., in Spielmann, jongleur).[5] The movement of playing has no goal that brings it to an end; rather, it renews itself in constant repetition. The movement backward and forward is obviously so central to the definition of play that it makes no difference who or what performs this movement. The movement of play as such has, as it were, no substrate. It is the game that is played—it is irrelevant whether or not there is a subject who plays it. The play is the occurrence of the movement as such. Thus we speak of the play of colors and do not mean only that one color plays against another, but that there is one process or sight displaying a changing variety of colors.

Hence the mode of being of play is not such that, for the game to be played, there must be a subject who is behaving playfully. Rather, the primordial sense of playing is the medial one. Thus we say that something is "playing" (spielt) somewhere or at some time, that something is going on (im Spiele ist) or that something is happening (sich abspielt).[6]

This linguistic observation seems to me an indirect indication that play is not to be understood as something a person does. As far as language is concerned, the actual subject of play is obviously not the subjectivity of an individual who, among other activities, also plays but is instead the play itself. But we are so accustomed to relating phenomena such as playing to the sphere of subjectivity and the ways it acts that we remain closed to these indications from the spirit of language.

However, modern anthropological research has conceived the nature of play so broadly that it has almost gone beyond viewing play as subjectivity. Huizinga has investigated the element of play in all cultures and most important has worked out the connection of children's and animal's play to "holy play." That led him to recognize the curious indecisiveness of the playing consciousness, which makes it absolutely impossible to decide between belief and non-belief. "The savage himself knows no conceptual distinction between being and playing; he knows nothing of identity, of image or symbol. And that is why it may be asked whether the mental condition of the savage in his sacred observances is not best understood by retaining play as the primary term. In our concept of play the difference between belief and pretense is dissolved."[7]

Here the *primacy of play over the consciousness of the player* is fundamentally acknowledged and, in fact, even the experiences of play that psychologists and anthropologists describe are illuminated afresh if one starts from the medial sense of the word "playing." Play clearly represents an order in which the to-and-fro motion of play follows of itself. It is part of play that the movement is not only without goal or purpose but also without effort. It happens, as it were, by itself. The ease of play—which naturally does not mean that there is any real absence of effort but refers phenomenologically only to the absence of strain[8]—is experienced subjectively as relaxation. The structure of play absorbs the player into itself, and thus frees him from the burden of taking the initiative, which constitutes the actual strain of existence. This is also seen in the spontaneous tendency to repetition that emerges in the player and in the constant self-renewal of play, which affects its form (e.g., the refrain).

The fact that the mode of being of play is so close to the mobile form of nature permits us to draw an important methodological conclusion. It is obviously not correct to say that animals *too* play, nor is it correct to say that, metaphorically speaking, water and light play *as well*. Rather, on the contrary, we can say that *man* too plays. His playing too is a natural process. The meaning of his play too, precisely because—and insofar as—he is part of nature, is a pure self-presentation. Thus in this sphere it becomes finally meaningless to distinguish between literal and metaphorical usage.

But most important the being of the work of art is connected with the medial sense of play (Spiel: also, game and drama). Inasmuch as nature is without purpose and intention, just as it is without exertion, it is a constantly self-renewing play, and can therefore appear as a model for art. Thus Friedrich Schlegel writes, "All the sacred games of art are only remote imitations of the infinite play of the world, the eternally self-creating work of art."[9]

Another question that Huizinga discusses is also clarified through the fundamental role of the to-and-fro movement of play: namely the playful character of the contest. It is true that the contestant does not consider himself to be playing. But through the contest arises the tense to-and-fro movement from which the victor emerges, and thus the whole becomes a game. The movement to-and-fro obviously belongs so essentially to the game that there is an ultimate sense in which you cannot have a game by yourself. In order for there to be a game, there always has to be, not necessarily literally another player, but something else with which the player plays and which automatically responds to his move with a countermove. Thus the cat at play chooses the ball of wool because it responds to play, and ball games will be with us forever because the ball is freely mobile in every direction, appearing to do surprising things of its own accord.

In cases where human subjectivity is what is playing, the primacy of the game over the players engaged in it is experienced by the players themselves in a special way. Once more it is the improper, metaphorical uses of the word that offer most information about its proper essence. Thus we say of someone that he plays with possibilities or with plans. What we mean is clear. He still has not committed himself to the possibilities as to serious aims. He still has the freedom to decide one way or the other, for one or the other possibility. On the other hand, this freedom is not without danger. Rather, the game itself is a risk for the player. One can play only with serious possibilities. Obviously this means that one may become so engrossed in them that they outplay one, as it were, and prevail over one. The attraction that the game exercises on the player lies in this risk. One enjoys a freedom of decision which at the same time is endangered and irrevocably limited. One has only to think of jig-saw puzzles, games of patience, etc. But the same is true in serious matters. If, for the sake of enjoying his own freedom of decision, someone avoids making pressing decisions or plays with possibilities that he is not seriously envisaging and which, therefore, offer no risk that he will choose them and thereby limit himself, we say he is only "playing with life" (verspielt).

This suggests a general characteristic of the nature of play that is reflected in playing: all playing is a being-played. The attraction of a game, the fascination it exerts, consists precisely in the fact that the game masters the players. Even in the case of games in which one tries to perform tasks that one has set oneself, there is a risk that they will not "work," "succeed," or "succeed again," which is the attraction of the game. Whoever "tries" is in fact the one who is tried. The real subject of the game (this is shown in precisely those experiences in which there is only a single player) is not the player but instead the game itself. What holds the player in its spell, draws him into play, and keeps him there is the game itself.

This is shown also by the fact that every game has its own proper spirit.[10] But even this does not refer to the mood or the mental state of those who play the game. Rather, the variety of mental attitudes exhibited in playing various games, and in the desire to play them, is the result and not the cause of the differences among the games themselves. Games differ from one another in their spirit. The reason for this is that the to-and-fro movement that constitutes the game is patterned in various ways. The particular nature of a game lies in the rules and regulations that prescribe the way the field of the game is filled. This is true universally, whenever there is a game. It is true, for example, of the play of fountains and of playing animals. The playing field on which the game is played is, as it were, set by the nature of the game itself and is defined far more by the structure that determines the movement of the game from within than by what it comes up against—i.e., the boundaries of the open space—limiting movement from without.

Apart from these general determining factors, it seems to me characteristic of human play that it plays *something*. That means that the structure of movement to which it submits has a definite quality which the player "chooses." First, he expressly separates his playing behavior from his other behavior by *wanting* to play. But even within his readiness to play he makes a choice. He chooses this game rather than that. Correlatively, the space in which the game's movement takes place is not simply the open space in which one "plays oneself out," but one that is specially marked out and reserved for the movement of the game. Human play requires a playing field. Setting off the playing field—just like setting off sacred precincts, as Huizinga rightly points out[11]—sets off the sphere of play as a closed world, one without transition and mediation to the world of aims. That all play is playing something is true here, where the ordered to-and-fro movement of the game is determined as one kind of *comportment* (Verhalten) among others. A person playing is, even in his play, still someone who comports himself, even if the proper essence of the game consists in his disburdening himself of the tension he feels in his purposive comportment. This determines more exactly why playing is always a playing of something. Every game presents the man who plays it with a task. He cannot enjoy the freedom of playing himself out without transforming the aims of his purposive behavior into mere tasks of the game. Thus the child gives itself a task in playing with a ball, and such tasks are playful ones because the purpose of the game is not really solving the task, but ordering and shaping the movement of the game itself.

Obviously the characteristic lightness and sense of relief we find in playing depends on the particular character of the task set by the game and comes from solving it.

One can say that performing a task successfully "presents it" (stellt sie dar). This phrasing especially suggests itself in the case of a game, for here fulfilling the task does not point to any purposive context. Play is really limited to presenting itself. Thus its mode of being is self-presentation. But self-presentation is a universal ontological characteristic of nature. We know today how inadequate are conceptions of biological purpose when it comes to understanding the form of living things.[12] So too it is an inadequate approach to ask what the life function and biological purpose of play is. First and foremost, play is self-presentation.

As we have seen, the self-presentation of human play depends on the player's conduct being tied to the make-believe goals of the game, but the "meaning" of these goals does not in fact depend on their being achieved. Rather, in spending oneself on the task of the game, one is in fact playing oneself out. The self-presentation of the game involves the player's achieving, as it were, his own self-presentation by playing—i.e., presenting—something. Only because play is always presentation is human play able to make representation itself the task of a game. Thus there are games which must be called representation games, either because, in their use of meaningful allusion, they have something about them of representation (say "Tinker, Tailor, Soldier, Sailor") or because the game itself consists in representing something (e.g., when children play cars).

All presentation is potentially a representation for someone. That this possibility is intended is the characteristic feature of art as play. The closed world of play lets down one of its walls, as it were.[13] A religious rite and a play in a theater obviously do not represent in the same sense as a child playing. Their being is not exhausted by the fact that they present themselves, for at the same time they point beyond themselves to the audience which participates by watching. Play here is no longer the mere self-presentation of an ordered movement, nor mere representation in which the child playing is totally absorbed, but it is "representing for someone." The directedness proper to all representation comes to the fore here and is constitutive of the being of art.

In general, however much games are in essence representations and however much the players represent themselves in them, games are not presented for anyone—i.e., they are not aimed at an audience. Children play for themselves, even when they represent. And not even those games (e.g., sports) that are played before spectators are aimed at them. Indeed, contests are in danger of losing their real play character precisely by becoming shows. A procession as part of a religious rite is more than a spectacle, since its real meaning is to embrace the whole religious community. And yet a religious act is a genuine representation for the community; and likewise, a drama is a kind of playing that, by its nature, calls for an audience. The presentation of a god in a religious rite, the presentation of a myth in a play, are play not only in the sense that the participating players are wholly absorbed in the presentational play and find in it their heightened self-representation, but also in that the players represent a meaningful whole for an audience. Thus it is not really the absence of a fourth wall that turns the play into a show. Rather, openness toward the spectator is part of the closedness of the play. The audience only completes what the play as such is.[14]

This point shows the importance of defining play as a process that takes place "in between." We have seen that play does not have its being in the player's consciousness or attitude, but on the contrary play draws him into its dominion and fills him with its spirit. The player experiences the game as a reality that surpasses him. This is all the more the case where the game is itself "intended" as such a reality—for instance, the play which appears as *presentation for an audience.*

Even a play remains a game—i.e., it has the structure of a game, which is that of a closed world. But however much a religious or profane play represents a world wholly closed within itself, it is as if open toward the spectator, in whom it achieves its whole significance. The players play their roles as in any game, and thus the play is represented, but the play itself is the whole, comprising players and spectators. In fact, it is experienced properly by, and presents itself (as it is "meant") to, one who is not acting in the play but watching it. In him the game is raised, as it were, to its ideality.

For the players this means that they do not simply fulfill their roles as in any game—rather, they play their roles, they represent them for the audience. The way they participate in the game is no longer determined by the fact that they are completely absorbed in it, but by the fact that they play their role in relation and regard to the whole of the play, in which not they but the audience is to become absorbed. A complete change takes place when play as such becomes a play. It puts the spectator in the place of the player. He—and not the player—is the person for and in whom the play is played. Of course this does not mean that the player is not able to experience the significance of the whole in which he plays his representing role. The spectator has only methodological precedence: in that the play is presented for him, it becomes apparent that the play bears within itself a meaning to be understood and that can therefore be detached from the behavior of the player. Basically the difference between the player and the spectator is here superseded. The requirement that the play itself be intended in its meaningfulness is the same for both.

This is still the case even when the play community is sealed off against all spectators, either because it opposes the social institutionalization of artistic life, as in so-called chamber music, which seeks to be more authentic music-making in being performed for the players themselves and not for an audience. If someone performs music in this way, he is also in fact trying to make the music "sound good," but that means that it would really be there for any listener. Artistic presentation, by its nature, exists for someone, even if there is no one there who merely listens or watches.

(B) TRANSFORMATION INTO STRUCTURE AND TOTAL MEDIATION

I call this change, in which human play comes to its true consummation in being art, *transformation into structure*. Only through this change does play achieve ideality, so that it can be intended and understood as play. Only now does it emerge as detached from the representing activity of the players and consist in the pure appearance (Erscheinung) of what they are playing. As such, the play—even the unforeseen elements of improvisation—is in principle repeatable and hence permanent. It has the character of a work, of an ergon and not only of energeia.[15] In this sense I call it a structure (Gebilde).

What can be thus dissociated from the representing activity of the player is still linked to representation. This linkage does not mean dependence in the sense that the play acquires a definite meaning only through the particular persons representing it, nor even through the originator of the work, its real creator, the artist. Rather, in relation to them all, the play has an absolute autonomy, and that is what is suggested by the concept of transformation.

What this implies about defining the nature of art emerges when one takes the sense of transformation seriously. Transformation is not alteration, even an alteration that is especially far-reaching. Alteration always means that what is altered also remains the same and is maintained.

However totally it may change, something changes in it. In terms of the categories, all alteration (alloiosis) belongs in the sphere of quality—i.e., of an accident of substance. But transformation means that something is suddenly and as a whole something else, that this other transformed thing that it has become is its true being, in comparison with which its earlier being is nil. When we find someone transformed we mean precisely this, that he has become another person, as it were. There cannot here be any gradual transition leading from one to the other, since the one is the denial of the other. Thus transformation into structure means that what existed previously exists no longer. But also that what now exists, what represents itself in the play of art, is the lasting and true.

It is clear that to start from subjectivity here is to miss the point. What no longer exists is the players—with the poet or the composer being considered as one of the players. None of them has his own existence for himself, which he retains so that his acting would mean that he "is only acting." If we describe from the point of view of the actor what his acting is, then obviously it is not transformation but disguise. A man who is disguised does not want to be recognized, but instead to appear as someone else and be taken for him. In the eyes of others he no longer wants to be himself, but to be taken for someone else. Thus he does not want to be discovered or recognized. He plays another person, but in the way that we play something in our daily intercourse with other people—i.e., that we merely pretend, act a part, and create an impression. A person who plays such a game denies, to all appearances, continuity with himself. But in truth that means that he holds on to this continuity with himself for himself and only withholds it from those before whom he is acting.

According to all that we have observed concerning the nature of play, this subjective distinction between oneself and the play implicit in putting up a show is not the true nature of play. Rather, play itself is a transformation of such a kind that the identity of the player does not continue to exist for anybody. Everybody asks instead what is supposed to be represented, what is "meant." The players (or playwright) no longer exist, only what they are playing.

But, above all, what no longer exists is the world in which we live as our own. Transformation into structure is not simply transposition into another world. Certainly the play takes place in another, closed world. But inasmuch as it is a structure, it is, so to speak, its own measure and measures itself by nothing outside it. Thus the action of a drama—in this respect it still entirely resembles the religious act—exists as something that rests absolutely within itself. It no longer permits of any comparison with reality as the secret measure of all verisimilitude. It is raised above all such comparisons—and hence also above the question of whether it is all real—because a superior truth speaks from it. Even Plato, the most radical critic of the high estimation of art in the history of philosophy, speaks of the comedy and tragedy of life on the one hand and of the stage on the other without differentiating between them.[16] For this difference is superseded if one knows how to see the meaning of the play that unfolds before one. The pleasure of drama is the same in both cases: it is the joy of knowledge.

This gives what we called transformation into structure its full meaning. The transformation is a transformation into the true. It is not enchantment in the sense of a bewitchment that waits for the redeeming word that will transform things back to what they were; rather, it is itself redemption and transformation back into true being. In being presented in play, what is emerges. It produces and brings to light what is otherwise constantly hidden and withdrawn. Someone who can perceive the comedy and tragedy of life can resist the temptation to think in terms of purposes, which conceals the game that is played with us.

"Reality" always stands in a horizon of desired or feared or, at any rate, still undecided future possibilities. Hence it is always the case that mutually exclusive expectations are aroused, not all of which can be fulfilled. The undecidedness of the future permits such a superfluity of expectations that reality necessarily lags behind them. Now if, in a particular case, a context of meaning closes and completes itself in reality, such that no lines of meaning scatter in the void, then this reality is itself like a drama. Likewise, someone who can see the whole of reality as a closed circle of meaning in which everything is fulfilled will speak of the comedy and tragedy of life. In these cases, where reality is understood as a play, emerges the reality of play, which we call the play of art. The being of all play is always self-realization, sheer fulfillment, energeia which has its telos within itself. The world of the work of art, in which play expresses itself fully in the unity of its course, is in fact a wholly transformed world. In and through it everyone recognizes that that is how things are.

Thus the concept of transformation characterizes the independent and superior mode of being of what we called structure. From this viewpoint "reality" is defined as what is untransformed, and art as the raising up (Aufhebung) of this reality into its truth. The classical theory of art too, which bases all art on the idea of mimesis, *imitation*, obviously starts from play in the form of dancing, which is the representation of the divine.[17]

But the concept of imitation can be used to describe the play of art only if one keeps in mind the cognitive import in imitation. The thing presented is there (Das Dargestellte ist da). That is the situation basic to imitation. When a person imitates something, he allows what he knows to exist and to exist in the way that he knows it. A child begins to play by imitation, affirming what he knows and affirming his own being in the process. Also, when children enjoy dressing up, as Aristotle remarks, they are not trying to hide themselves, pretending to be something else in order to be discovered and recognized behind it; but, on the contrary, they intend a representation of such a kind that only what is represented exists. The child wants at any cost to avoid being discovered behind his disguise. He intends that what he represents should exist, and if something is to be guessed, then this is it. We are supposed to recognize what it "is."[18]

We have established that the cognitive import of imitation lies in recognition. But what is recognition? A more exact analysis of the phenomenon will make quite clear to us the ontological import of representation, which is what we are concerned with. As we know, Aristotle emphasizes that artistic presentation even makes the unpleasant appear pleasant,[19] and for this reason Kant defined art as the beautiful representation of something, because it can make even the ugly appear beautiful.[20] But this obviously does not refer to artifice and artistic technique. One does not admire the skill with which something is done, as in the case of a highwire artist. This has only secondary interest, as Aristotle explicitly says.[21] Rather, what we experience in a work of art and what invites our attention is how true it is—i.e., to what extent one knows and recognizes something and oneself.

But we do not understand what recognition is in its profoundest nature if we only regard it as knowing something again that we know already—i.e., what is familiar is recognized again. The joy of recognition is rather the joy of knowing *more* than is already familiar. In recognition what we know emerges, as if illuminated, from all the contingent and variable circumstances that condition it; it is grasped in its essence. It is known as something.

This is the central motif of Platonism. In his theory of anamnesis Plato combined the mythical idea of remembrance with his dialectic, which sought the truth of being in the logoi—i.e., the ideality of language.[22] In fact this kind of idealism of being is already suggested in the phenomenon of recognition. The "known" enters into its true being and manifests itself as what it is only when it is recognized. As recognized, it is grasped in its essence, detached from its accidental aspects. This applies especially to the kind of recognition that takes place in a play. This kind of representation leaves behind it everything that is accidental and unessential—e.g., the private, particular being of the actor. He disappears entirely in the recognition of what he is representing. But even what is represented, a well-known event of mythological tradition, is—by being represented—raised, as it were, to its own validity and truth. With regard to knowledge of the true, the being of the representation is more than the being of the thing represented, Homer's Achilles more than the original.[23]

Thus the situation basic to imitation that we are discussing not only implies that what is represented is there (das Dargestellte da ist), but also that it has come into the There more authentically (eigentlicher ins Da gekommen ist). Imitation and representation are not merely a repetition, a copy, but knowledge of the essence. Because they are not merely repetition, but a "bringing forth," they imply a spectator as well. They contain in themselves an essential relation to everyone for whom the representation exists.

Indeed, one can say even more: the presentation of the essence, far from being a mere imitation, is necessarily revelatory. In imitating, one has to leave out and to heighten. Because he is pointing to something, he has to exaggerate, whether he likes it or not [aphairein and synhoran also belong together in Plato's doctrine of ideas]. Hence there exists an insuperable ontological difference between the one thing that is a likeness and the other that it seeks to resemble. As we know, Plato insisted on this ontological distance, on the greater or lesser difference between the copy and the original; and for this reason he placed imitation and presentation in the play of art as an imitation of an imitation, in the third rank.[24] Nevertheless, operative in artistic presentation is recognition, which has the character of genuine knowledge of essence; and since Plato considers all knowledge of essence to be recognition, this is the ground of Aristotle's remark that poetry is more philosophical than history.[25]

Thus imitation, as representation, has a special cognitive function. For this reason, the concept of imitation sufficed for the theory of art as long as the cognitive significance of art went unquestioned. But that was the case only as long as knowledge of the true was considered to be knowledge of the essence,[26] for art supports this kind of knowledge in a convincing way. By contrast, for nominalistic modern science and its idea of reality, from which Kant drew agnostic consequences for aesthetics, the concept of mimesis has lost its aesthetic force.

Once the aporias of this subjective turn in aesthetics have become evident to us, we are forced to return to the older tradition. If art is not the variety of changing experiences (Erlebnisse) whose object is filled subjectively with meaning like an empty mold, we must recognize that "presentation" (Darstellung) is the mode of being of the work of art. This was prepared for by deriving the concept of presentation from the concept of play, for self-presentation is the true nature of play—and hence of the work of art also. In being played the play speaks to the spectator through its presentation; and it does so in such a way that, despite the distance between it and himself, the spectator still belongs to play.

This is seen most clearly in one type of representation, a religious rite. Here the relation to the community is obvious. An aesthetic consciousness, however reflective, can no longer suppose that only aesthetic differentiation, which views the aesthetic object in its own right, discovers the true meaning of the religious image or the play. No one will be able to suppose that for religious truth the performance of the ritual is inessential.

The same is true for drama generally, even considered as literature. The performance of a play, like that of a ritual, cannot simply be detached from the play itself, as if it were something that is not part of its essential being, but is as subjective and fluid as the aesthetic experiences in which it is experienced. Rather, it is in the performance and only in it—as we see most clearly in the case of music—that we encounter the work itself, as the divine is encountered in the religious rite. Here it becomes clear why starting from the concept of play is methodologically advantageous. The work of art cannot simply be isolated from the "contingency" of the chance conditions in which it appears, and where this kind of isolation occurs, the result is an abstraction that reduces the actual being of the work. It itself belongs to the world to which it represents itself. A drama really exists only when it is played, and ultimately music must resound.

My thesis, then, is that the being of art cannot be defined as an object of an aesthetic consciousness because, on the contrary, the aesthetic attitude is more than it knows of itself. It is a part of the *event of being that occurs in presentation*, and belongs essentially to play as play.

What ontological consequences does this have? If we start in this way from the play character of play, what follows for defining the mode of being of art more exactly? This much is clear: drama, and the work of art understood as a drama, is not a mere schema of rules or prescribed approaches within which play can freely realize itself. The playing of the drama does not ask to be understood as satisfying a need to play, but as the coming-into-existence of the work itself. And so there arises the question of what such a work properly *is*, given that it exists only in being played and in its presentation as a play, though it is nevertheless its own being that is thereby presented.

Let us recall the phrase used above, "transformation into structure." Play is structure—this means that despite its dependence on being played it is a meaningful whole which can be repeatedly presented as such and the significance of which can be understood. But structure is also play, because—despite this theoretical unity—it achieves its full being only each time it is played. That both sides of the question belong together is what we have to emphasize against the abstraction of aesthetic differentiation.

We may now formulate this by opposing *aesthetic non-differentiation* to aesthetic differentiation, which is the properly constitutive element of aesthetic consciousness. It has become clear that what is imitated in imitation, what is formed by the poet, represented by the actor, and recognized by the spectator is to such an extent what is meant—that in which the significance of the representation lies—that the poet's creativity or the actor's prowess as such are not foregrounded from it. When a distinction is made, it is between the material and what the poet makes of it, between the poem and the "conception." But these distinctions are of a secondary nature. What the actor plays and the spectator recognizes are the forms and the action itself, as they are formed by the poet. Thus we have here a *double mimesis*: the writer represents and the actor represents. But even this double mimesis is *one*: it is the same thing that comes to existence in each case.

More exactly, one can say that the mimetic representation (Darstellung), the performance, brings into existence (zum Dasein) what the play itself requires. The double distinction between a play and its subject matter and a play and its performance corresponds to a double non-distinction as the unity of the truth which one recognizes in the play of art. To investigate the origin of the plot on which it is based is to move out of the real experience of a piece of literature, and likewise it is to move out of the real experience of the play if the spectator reflects about the conception behind a performance or about the proficiency of the actors. Already implicit in this kind of reflection is the aesthetic differentiation of the work itself from its representation. But for the content of the experience as such, as we have seen, it is not even important whether the tragic or comic scene playing before one is taking place on the stage or in life—when one is only a spectator. What we have called a structure is one insofar as it presents itself as a meaningful whole. It does not exist in itself, nor is it encountered in a mediation (Vermittlung) accidental to it; rather, it acquires its proper being in being mediated.

No matter how much the variety of the performances or realizations of such a structure can be traced back to the conception of the players—it also does not remain enclosed in the subjectivity of what they think, but it is embodied there. Thus it is not at all a question of a mere subjective variety of conceptions, but of the work's own possibilities of being that emerge as the work explicates itself, as it were, in the variety of its aspects.

This is not to deny that here there is a possible starting point for aesthetic reflection. In various performances of the same play, say, one can distinguish between one kind of mediation and another, just as one can conceive the conditions of access for different works of art in different ways—e.g., when one regards a building from the viewpoint of how it would look on its own or how its surroundings ought to look; or when one is faced with the problem of restoring a painting. In all such cases the work itself is distinguished from its "presentation."[27] But one fails to appreciate the obligatoriness of the work of art if one regards the variations possible in the presentation as free and arbitrary. In fact they are all subject to the supreme criterion of "right" representation.[28]

We know this in the modern theater as the tradition that stems from a production, the creation of a role, or the practice of a musical performance. Here there is no random succession, a mere variety of conceptions; rather, by constantly following models and developing them, a tradition is formed with which every new attempt must come to terms. The performing artist too has a certain consciousness of this. The way that he approaches a work or a role is always in some way related to models that approached it in the same way. But this has nothing to do with blind imitation. Although the tradition created by a great actor, director, or musician remains effective as a model, it is not a brake on free creation, but has become so fused with the work that concern with this model stimulates an artist's creative interpretive powers no less than does concern with the work itself. The performing arts have this special quality: that the works they deal with are explicitly left open to such re-creation and thus visibly hold the identity and continuity of the work of art open towards its future.[29]

Perhaps in such a case the criterion that determines whether something is "a correct presentation" (Darstellung) is a highly flexible and relative one. But the fact that the representation is bound to the work is not lessened by the fact that this bond can have no fixed criterion. Thus we do not allow the interpretation of a piece of music or a drama the freedom to take the fixed "text" as a basis for arbitrary, ad-lib effects, and yet we would regard the canonization of a particular interpretation—e.g., in a recorded performance conducted by the composer, or the detailed notes on performance which come from the canonized first performance—as a failure to appreciate the real task of interpretation. A "correctness" striven for in this way would not do justice to the true binding nature of the work, which imposes itself on every interpreter immediately, in its own way, and does not allow him to make things easy for himself by simply imitating a model.

As we know, it is also mistaken to limit the "freedom" of interpretive choice to externals and marginal phenomena rather than think of the whole performance in a way that is both bound and free. In a certain sense interpretation probably is re-creation, but this is a re-creation not of the creative act but of the created work, which has to be brought to representation in accord with the meaning the interpreter finds in it. Thus, for example, historicizing presentations—e.g., of music played on old instruments—are not as faithful as they seem. Rather, they are an imitation of an imitation and are thus in danger "of standing at a third remove from the truth" (Plato).

In view of the finitude of our historical existence, it would seem that there is something absurd about the whole idea of a unique, correct interpretation. We will return to this subject in another context.[30] Here the obvious fact that every interpretation tries to be correct serves only to confirm that the non-differentiation of the mediation (Vermittlung) from the work itself is the actual experience of the work. This accords with the fact that aesthetic consciousness is generally able to make the aesthetic distinction between the work and its mediation only in a critical way—i.e., where the interpretation breaks down. The mediation that communicates the work is, in principle, total.

Total mediation means that the medium as such is superseded (aufhebt). In other words, the performance (in the case of drama and music, but also in the recitation of epics or lyrics) does not become, as such, thematic, but the work presents itself through it and in it. We will see that the same is true of the way buildings and statues present themselves to be approached and encountered. Here too the approach as such is not thematic, but neither is it true that one would have to abstract from the work's relations to the life world in order to grasp the work itself. Rather, it exists within them. The fact that works stretch out of a past into the present as enduring monuments still does not mean that their being is an object of aesthetic or historical consciousness. As long as they still fulfill their function, they are contemporaneous with every age. Even if their place is only in museums as works of art, they are not entirely alienated from themselves. Not only does a work of art never completely lose the trace of its original function which enables an expert to reconstruct it, but the work of art that has its place next to others in a gallery is still its own origin. It affirms itself, and the way it does so—by "killing" other things or using them to complement itself—is still part of itself.

We ask what this identity is that presents itself so differently in the changing course of ages and circumstances. It does not disintegrate into the changing aspects of itself so that it would lose all identity, but it is there in them all. They all belong to it. They are all *contemporaneous* (gleichzeitig) with it. Thus we have the task of interpreting the work of art in terms of time (Zeit).

(C) THE TEMPORALITY OF THE AESTHETIC

What kind of contemporaneity is this? What kind of temporality belongs to aesthetic being? This contemporaneity and presentness of aesthetic being is generally called its timelessness. But this timelessness has to be thought of together with the temporality to which it essentially belongs. Timelessness is primarily only a dialectical feature which arises out of temporality and in contrast with it. Even if one tries to define the temporality of the work of art by speaking of two kinds of temporality, a historical and a suprahistorical one, as does Sedlmayr, for example, following Baader and with reference to Bollnow,[31] one cannot move beyond a dialectical antithesis between the two. The suprahistorical, "sacred" time, in which the "present" is not the fleeting moment but the fullness of time, is described from the point of view of "existential" temporality, characterized by its being solemn, leisurely, innocent, or whatever. The inadequacy of this kind of antithesis emerges when one inevitably discovers that "true time" projects into historical existential "appearance time." This kind of projection would obviously have the character of an epiphany, but this means that for the experiencing consciousness it would be without continuity.

This reintroduces all the aporias of aesthetic consciousness that we pointed out above. For it is precisely continuity that every understanding of time has to achieve, even when it is a question of the temporality of a work of art. Here the misunderstanding of Heidegger's ontological exposition of the time horizon takes its revenge. Instead of holding on to the methodological significance of the existential analytic of Dasein, people treat Dasein's existential, historical temporality, determined by care and the movement towards death—i.e., radical finitude—as one among many possible ways of understanding existence, and they forget that it is the mode of being of understanding itself which is here revealed as temporality. To define the proper temporality of the work of art as "sacred time" and distinguish it from transient, historical time remains, in fact, a mere mirroring of the human and finite experience of art. Only a biblical theology of time, starting not from the standpoint of human self-understanding but of divine revelation, would be able to speak of a "sacred time" and theologically legitimate the analogy between the timelessness of the work of art and this "sacred time." Without this kind of theological justification, to speak of "sacred time" obscures the real problem, which does not lie in the artwork's being removed from time but in its temporality.

Thus we take up our question again: what kind of temporality is this?[32]

We started from the position that the work of art is play—i.e., that its actual being cannot be detached from its presentation and that in this presentation the unity and identity of a structure emerge. To be dependent on self-presentation belongs to what it is. This means that however much it is transformed and distorted in being presented, it still remains itself. This constitutes the obligation of every presentation: that it contain a relation to the structure itself and submit itself to the criterion of correctness that derives from it. Even the extreme of a completely distortive presentation confirms this. It is known as a distortion inasmuch as the presentation is intended and judged to be the presentation of the structure. Inescapably, the presentation has the character of a repetition of the same. Here "repetition" does not mean that something is literally repeated—i.e., can be reduced to something original. Rather, every repetition is as original as the work itself.

We are familiar with this kind of highly puzzling temporal structure from festivals.[33] It is in the nature of periodic festivals, at least, to be repeated. We call that the return of the festival. But the festival that comes round again is neither another festival nor a mere remembrance of the one that was originally celebrated. The originally sacral character of all festivals obviously excludes the familiar distinction in time experience between present, memory, and expectation. The time experience of the festival is rather its *celebration*, a present time sui generis.

The temporal character of celebration is difficult to grasp on the basis of the usual experience of temporal succession. If the return of the festival is related to the usual experience of time and its dimensions, it appears as historical temporality. The festival changes from one time to the next. For there are always other things going on at the same time. Nevertheless from this historical perspective it would still remain one and the same festival that undergoes this change. It was originally of such and such a nature and was celebrated in such and such a way, then differently, and then differently again.

However, this perspective does not cover the characteristic of festival time that comes from its being celebrated. For the essence of the festival, its historical connections are secondary. As a festival it is not an identity like a historical event, but neither is it determined by its origin so that there was once the "real" festival—as distinct from the way in which it later came to be celebrated. From its inception—whether instituted in a single act or introduced gradually—the nature of a festival is to be celebrated regularly. Thus its own original essence is always to be something different (even when celebrated in exactly the same way). An entity that exists only by always being something different is temporal in a more radical sense than everything that belongs to history. It has its being only in becoming and return.[34]

A festival exists only in being celebrated. This is not to say that it is of a subjective character and has its being only in the subjectivity of those celebrating it. Rather, the festival is celebrated because it is there. The same is true of drama: it must be presented for the spectator, and yet its being is by no means just the point of intersection of the spectators' experiences. Rather, the contrary is true: the being of the spectator is determined by his "being there present" (Dabeisein). Being present does not simply mean being there along with something else that is there at the same time. To be present means to participate. If someone was present at something, he knows all about how it really was. It is only in a derived sense that presence at something means also a kind of subjective act, that of paying attention to something (Bei-der-Sachesein). Thus watching something is a genuine mode of participating. Here we can recall the concept of sacral communion that lies behind the original Greek concept of theoria. Theoros means someone who takes part in a delegation to a festival. Such a person has no other distinction or function than to be there. Thus the theoros is a spectator in the proper sense of the word, since he participates in the solemn act through his presence at it and thus sacred law accords him a distinction: for example, inviolability.

In the same way, Greek metaphysics still conceives the essence of theoria[35] and of nous as being purely present to what is truly real,[36] and for us too the ability to act theoretically is defined by the fact that in attending to something one is able to forget one's own purposes.[37] But theoria is not to be conceived primarily as subjective conduct, as a self-determination of the subject, but in terms of what it is contemplating. Theoria is a true participation, not something active but something passive (pathos), namely being totally involved in and carried away by what one sees. Gerhard Krüger has tried to explain the religious background of the Greek concept of reason from this point of view.[38]

We started by saying that the true being of the spectator, who belongs to the play of art, cannot be adequately understood in terms of subjectivity, as a way that aesthetic consciousness conducts itself. But this does not mean that the nature of the spectator cannot be described in terms of being present at something, in the way that we pointed out. Considered as a subjective accomplishment in human conduct, being present has the character of being outside oneself. In the *Phaedrus* Plato already described the blunder of those who take the viewpoint of rational reasonableness and tend to misinterpret the ecstatic condition of being outside oneself, seeing it as a mere negation of being composed within oneself and hence as a kind of madness. In fact, being outside oneself is the positive possibility of being wholly with something else. This kind of being present is a self-forgetfulness, and to be a spectator consists in giving oneself in self-forgetfulness to what one is watching. Here self-forgetfulness is anything but a privative condition, for it arises from devoting one's full attention to the matter at hand, and this is the spectator's own positive accomplishment.[39]

Obviously there is an essential difference between a spectator who gives himself entirely to the play of art and someone who merely gapes at something out of curiosity. It is characteristic of curiosity that it too is as if drawn away by what it looks at, that it forgets itself entirely in it, and cannot tear itself away from it. But the important thing about an object of curiosity is that it is basically of no concern to the spectator; it has no significance for him. There is nothing in it which he would really be able to come back to and which would focus his attention. For it is the formal quality of novelty—i.e., abstract difference—that makes up the charm of what one looks at. This is seen in the fact that its dialectical complement is becoming bored and jaded, whereas that which presents itself to the spectator as the play of art does not simply exhaust itself in momentary transport, but has a claim to permanence and the permanence of a claim.

The word "claim" does not occur here by chance. In the theological reflection that began with Kierkegaard and which we call "dialectical theology," it is no accident that this concept has made possible a theological explanation of what Kierkegaard meant by contemporaneity. A claim is something lasting. Its justification (or pretended justification) is the primary thing. Because a claim lasts, it can be enforced at any time. A claim exists against someone and must therefore be enforced against him; but the concept of a claim also implies that it is not itself a fixed demand, the fulfillment of which is agreed on by both sides, but is rather the ground for such. A claim is the legal basis for an unspecified demand. If it is to be answered in such a way as to be settled, then to be enforced it must first take the form of a demand. It belongs to the permanence of a claim that it is concretized in a demand.

The application to Lutheran theology is that the claim of faith began with the proclamation of the gospel and is continually reinforced in preaching. The words of the sermon perform this total mediation, which otherwise is the work of the religious rite—of the mass, for example. We shall see that in other ways too the word is called on to mediate between past and present, and that it therefore comes to play a leading role in the problem of hermeneutics.

In any case, "contemporaneity" belongs to the being of the work of art. It constitutes the essence of "being present." This is not the simultaneity of aesthetic consciousness, for that simply means that several objects of aesthetic experience (Erlebnis) are all held in consciousness at the same time—all indifferently, with the same claim to validity. "Contemporaneity," on the other hand, means that in its presentation this particular thing that presents itself to us achieves full presence, however remote its origin may be. Thus contemporaneity is not a mode of givenness in consciousness, but a task for consciousness and an achievement that is demanded of it. It consists in holding on to the thing in such a way that it becomes "contemporaneous," which is to say, however, that all mediation is superseded in total presence.

This concept of contemporaneity, we know, stems from Kierkegaard, who gave it a particular theological stamp.[40] For Kierkegaard, "contemporaneity" does not mean "existing at the same time." Rather, it names the task that confronts the believer: to bring together two moments that are not concurrent, namely one's own present and the redeeming act of Christ, and yet so totally to mediate them that the latter is experienced and taken seriously as present (and not as something in a distant past). The simultaneity of aesthetic consciousness, by contrast, is just the opposite of this and indeed is based on covering up and concealing the task set by contemporaneity.

Contemporaneity in this sense is found especially in religious rituals and in the proclamation of the Word in preaching. Here, "being present" means genuine participation in the redemptive event itself. No one can doubt that aesthetic differentiation—attending to how "beautiful" the ceremony was or how "well preached" the sermon—is out of place, given the kind of claim that is made on us. Now, I maintain that the same thing is basically true when we experience art. Here too the mediation must be thought of as total. Neither the being that the creating artist is for himself—call it his biography—nor that of whoever is performing the work, nor that of the spectator watching the play, has any legitimacy of its own in the face of the being of the artwork itself.

What unfolds before us is so much lifted out of the ongoing course of the ordinary world and so much enclosed in its own autonomous circle of meaning that no one is prompted to seek some other future or reality behind it. The spectator is set at an absolute distance, a distance that precludes practical or goal-oriented participation. But this distance is aesthetic distance in a true sense, for it signifies the distance necessary for seeing, and thus makes possible a genuine and comprehensive participation in what is presented before us. A spectator's ecstatic self-forgetfulness corresponds to his continuity with himself. Precisely that in which one loses oneself as a spectator demands that one grasp the continuity of meaning. For it is the truth of our own world—the religious and moral world in which we live—that is presented before us and in which we recognize ourselves. Just as the ontological mode of aesthetic being is marked by parousia, absolute presence, and just as an artwork is nevertheless self-identical in every moment where it achieves such a presence, so also the absolute moment in which a spectator stands is both one of self-forgetfulness and of mediation with himself. What rends him from himself at the same time gives him back the whole of his being.

The fact that aesthetic being depends on being presented, then, does not imply some deficiency, some lack of autonomous meaning. Rather, it belongs to its very essence. The spectator is an essential element in the kind of play we call aesthetic. I want to turn now to the famous definition of tragedy in Aristotle's *Poetics*. There the spectator's frame of mind figures expressly in the definition of tragedy's essential nature.

(D) THE EXAMPLE OF THE TRAGIC

Aristotle's theory of tragedy may serve to exemplify the structure of aesthetic being as a whole. To be sure, it is situated in the context of a poetics and seems to apply only to dramatic poetry. However, the tragic is a fundamental phenomenon, a structure of meaning that does not exist only in tragedy, the tragic work of art in the narrower sense, but also in other artistic genres, especially epic. Indeed, it is not even a specifically artistic phenomenon, for it is also found in life. For this reason, modern scholars (Richard Hamann, Max Scheler[41]) see the tragic as something extra-aesthetic, an ethical and metaphysical phenomenon that enters into the sphere of aesthetic problems only from outside.

But now that we have seen how questionable the concept of the aesthetic is, we must now ask, conversely, whether the tragic is not indeed a phenomenon basic to the aesthetic in general. The being of the aesthetic has emerged for us as play and presentation. Thus we may also consult the theory of the tragic play—i.e., the poetics of tragedy—to get at the essence of the tragic.

What we find reflected in thought about the tragic, from Aristotle down to the present, is certainly no unchanging essence. There is no doubt that the essence of tragedy is presented in Attic tragedy in a unique way; and differently for Aristotle, for whom Euripides was the "most tragic,"[42] differently again for someone to whom Aeschylus reveals the true depth of the tragic phenomenon, and very differently for someone who is thinking of Shakespeare. But this variety does not simply mean that the question about the unity of the tragic would be without an object, but rather, on the contrary, that the phenomenon presents itself in an outline drawn together in a historical unity. Modern thought about tragedy is always aware of the fact that, as Kierkegaard has remarked,[43] what is now considered tragic reflects classical thought on the topic. If we begin with Aristotle, we will see the whole scope of the tragic phenomenon. In his famous definition of tragedy Aristotle made a decisive contribution to the problem of the aesthetic: in defining tragedy he included its *effect* (Wirkung) *on the spectator.*

I cannot hope to treat his famous and much discussed definition fully here. But the mere fact that the spectator is included in Aristotle's definition of the essence of tragedy makes quite clear what we have said above: that the spectator belongs essentially to the playing of the play. The way the spectator belongs to it makes apparent why it is meaningful to figure art as play. Thus the spectator's distance from the drama is not an arbitrary posture, but the essential relation whose ground lies in the play's unity of meaning. Tragedy is the unity of a tragic course of events that is experienced as such. But what is experienced as a tragic course of events—even if it is not a play that is shown on the stage but a tragedy in "life"—is a closed circle of meaning that of itself resists all penetration and interference. What is understood as tragic must simply be accepted. Hence it is, in fact, a phenomenon basic to the "aesthetic."

We learn from Aristotle that the representation of the tragic action has a specific effect on the spectator. The representation works through eleos and phobos. The traditional translation of these emotions as "pity" and "fear" gives them a far too subjective tinge. Aristotle is not at all concerned with pity or with the changing valuations of pity over the centuries,[44] and similarly fear is not to be understood as an inner state of mind. Rather, both are events that overwhelm man and sweep him away. Eleos is the misery that comes over us in the face of what we call miserable. Thus we commiserate with the fate of Oedipus (the example that Aristotle always returns to). The German word "Jammer" (misery) is a good equivalent because it too refers not merely to an inner state but to its manifestation. Likewise, phobos is not just a state of mind but, as Aristotle says, a cold shudder[45] that makes one's blood run cold, that makes one shiver. In the particular sense in which phobos is connected to eleos in this definition of tragedy, phobos means the shivers of apprehension that come over us for someone whom we see rushing to his destruction and for whom we fear. Commiseration and apprehension are modes of ekstasis, being outside oneself, which testify to the power of what is being played out before us.

Now, Aristotle says that the play effects the purification of these emotions. As is well known, this translation is problematical, especially the sense of the genitive.[46] But what Aristotle means seems to me to be quite independent of this, and this must ultimately show why two conceptions so different grammatically can confront each other so tenaciously. It seems clear to me that Aristotle is thinking of the tragic pensiveness that comes over the spectator at a tragedy. But pensiveness is a kind of relief and resolution, in which pain and pleasure are peculiarly mixed. How can Aristotle call this condition a purification? What is the impure element in feeling, and how is it removed in the tragic emotion? It seems to me that the answer is as follows: being overcome by misery and horror involves a painful division. There is a disjunction from what is happening, a refusal to accept that rebels against the agonizing events. But the effect of the tragic catastrophe is precisely to dissolve this disjunction from what is. It effects the total liberation of the constrained heart. We are freed not only from the spell in which the misery and horror of the tragic fate had bound us, but at the same time we are free from everything that divides us from what is.

Thus tragic pensiveness reflects a kind of affirmation, a return to ourselves; and if, as is often the case in modern tragedy, the hero's own consciousness is affected by this tragic pensiveness, he himself shares a little in this affirmation, in that he accepts his fate.

But what is the real object of this affirmation? What is affirmed? Certainly not the justice of a moral world order. The notorious theory of the tragic flaw, which plays scarcely any role in Aristotle, is not an explanation suitable even for modern tragedy. For tragedy does not exist where guilt and expiation balance each other out, where a moral bill of guilt is paid in full. Nor in modern tragedy can there be a full subjectivization of guilt and of fate. Rather, the excess of tragic consequences is characteristic of the essence of the tragic. Despite all the subjectivization of guilt in modern tragedy, it still retains an element of the classical sense of the power of destiny that, in the very disproportion between guilt and fate, reveals itself as the same for all. Hebbel seems to occupy the borderline of what can still be called tragedy, so exactly is subjective guilt fitted into the course of the tragic action. For the same reason the idea of Christian tragedy presents a special problem, since in the light of divine salvation the values of happiness and haplessness that constitute tragic action no longer determine human destiny. Even Kierkegaard's[47] brilliant contrast between the classical suffering that followed from a curse laid on a family and the suffering that rends the conflicted consciousness that is not at one with itself only verges on the tragic. His rewritten *Antigone*[48] would no longer be a tragedy.

So we must repeat the question: what does the spectator affirm here? Obviously it is the disproportionate, terrible immensity of the consequences that flow from a guilty deed that is the real claim made on the spectator. The tragic affirmation is the fulfillment of this claim. It has the character of a genuine communion. What is experienced in such an excess of tragic suffering is something truly common. The spectator recognizes himself and his own finiteness in the face of the power of fate. What happens to the great ones of the earth has an exemplary significance. Tragic pensiveness does not affirm the tragic course of events as such, or the justice of the fate that overtakes the hero but rather a metaphysical order of being that is true for all. To see that "this is how it is" is a kind of self-knowledge for the spectator, who emerges with new insight from the illusions in which he, like everyone else, lives. The tragic affirmation is an insight that the spectator has by virtue of the continuity of meaning in which he places himself.

From this analysis it follows that the tragic is not only a concept fundamental to the aesthetic—inasmuch as the distance of the spectator is part of the essence of the tragic—but, more important, the distance inherent in being a spectator, which determines the mode of being of the aesthetic, does not include the "aesthetic differentiation" which we found to be a feature of "aesthetic consciousness." The spectator does not hold himself aloof at the distance characteristic of an aesthetic consciousness enjoying the art with which something is represented,[49] but rather participates in the communion of being present. The real emphasis of the tragic phenomenon lies ultimately on what is presented and recognized, and to participate in it is not a matter of choice. However much the tragic play performed solemnly in the theater presents an exceptional situation in everyone's life, it is not an experience of an adventure producing a temporary intoxication from which one reawakens to one's true being; instead, the elevation and strong emotion that seize the spectator in fact deepen his *continuity with himself.* Tragic pensiveness flows from the self-knowledge that the spectator acquires. He finds himself again in the tragic action because what he encounters is his own story, familiar to him from religious or historical tradition; and even if this tradition is no longer binding for a later consciousness—as was already the case with Aristotle, and was certainly true of Seneca and Corneille—there is more in the continuing effect of such tragic works and themes than merely the continuing influence of a literary model. This effect presumes not only that the spectator is still familiar with the story, but also that its language still really reaches him. Only then can the spectator's encounter with the tragic theme and tragic work become a self-encounter.

What is true of the tragic, however, is true in a far wider context. For the writer, free invention is always only one side of a mediation conditioned by values already given. He does not freely invent his plot, however much he imagines that he does. Rather, even today the mimesis theory still retains something of its old validity. The writer's free invention is the presentation of a common truth that is binding on the writer also.

It is the same with the other arts, especially the plastic arts. The aesthetic myth of freely creative imagination that transforms experience into literature, and the cult of genius belonging to that myth, proves only that in the nineteenth century mythical and historical tradition was no longer a self-evident heritage. But even so the aesthetic myth of imagination and the invention of genius is still an exaggeration that does not stand up to reality. Now as before, the choice of material and the forming of it still do not proceed from the free discretion of the artist and are not the mere expression of his inner life. Rather, the artist addresses people whose minds are prepared and chooses what promises to have an effect on them. He himself stands in the same tradition as the public that he is addressing and which he gathers around him. In this sense it is true that as an individual, a thinking consciousness, he does not need to know explicitly what he is doing and what his work says. The player, sculptor, or viewer is never simply swept away into a strange world of magic, of intoxication, of dream; rather, it is always his own world, and he comes to belong to it more fully by recognizing himself more profoundly in it. There remains a continuity of meaning which links the work of art with the existing world and from which even the alienated consciousness of a cultured society never quite detaches itself.

Let us sum up. What is aesthetic being? We have sought to show something about the concept of play in general and about the transformation into structure characteristic of the play of art: namely that the presentation or performance of a work of literature or music is something essential, and not incidental to it, for it merely completes what the works of art already are—the being there of what is presented in them. The specific temporality of aesthetic being, its having its being in the process of being presented, comes to exist in reproduction as a distinct, independent phenomenon.

Now we can ask whether this is really true generally, whether aesthetic being can be defined on this basis. Does this apply to works of sculptural and architectural art as well? Let us first ask this question of the plastic arts. We will find that the most plastic of the arts, architecture, is especially instructive.

2 AESTHETIC AND HERMENEUTIC CONSEQUENCES

(A) THE ONTOLOGICAL VALENCE OF THE PICTURE[50]

In the plastic arts it first seems as if the work has such a clear identity that there is no variability of presentation. What varies does not seem to belong to the side of the work itself and so seems to be subjective. Thus one might say that certain subjective limitations prevent one's experiencing the work fully, but these subjective limitations can ultimately be overcome. We can experience every work of plastic art "immediately" as itself—i.e., without its needing further mediation to us. In the case of reproductions of statues, these mediations certainly do not belong to the work of art itself. But inasmuch as certain subjective conditions pertain whenever a work of sculpture is accessible, we must obviously abstract from them if we want to experience the work itself. Thus aesthetic differentiation seems to have its full legitimacy here.

It can appeal, in particular, to what general usage calls a "picture." By this we understand, above all, the modern framed picture that is not tied to a particular place but offers itself entirely by itself by virtue of the frame that encloses it. This makes it possible for such pictures to be put side by side in any order, as we see in modern galleries. Such pictures apparently have nothing about them of the objective dependence on mediation that we emphasized in the case of drama and music. And pictures painted for an exhibition or a gallery, which is becoming the rule as commissioned art declines, conform visibly to the abstraction that characterizes aesthetic consciousness and to the theory of inspiration formulated in the aesthetics of genius. The "picture" thus appears to confirm the immediacy of aesthetic consciousness and its claim to universality. It is obviously no coincidence that aesthetic consciousness, which develops the concept of art and the artistic as a way of understanding traditional structures and so performs aesthetic differentiation, is simultaneous with the creation of museum collections that gather together everything we look at in this way. Thus we make every work of art, as it were, into a picture. By detaching all art from its connections with life and the particular conditions of our approach to it, we frame it like a picture and hang it up.

Thus it is necessary to investigate more closely the mode of being of a picture and to ask whether the aesthetic mode of being, which I described in terms of play, also applies to pictures.

The question that I pose here about the mode of being of a picture is an inquiry into what is common to all the different forms of picture. This involves a task of abstraction, but this abstraction is not an arbitrary abstraction undertaken by philosophical reflection; rather, it is performed by aesthetic consciousness itself, since for it everything is a picture that can be subjected to the pictorial techniques of the present. There is certainly no historical truth in this use of the concept of the picture. Contemporary research into the history of art gives us ample evidence that what we call a "picture" has a varied history.[51] The full "sovereignty of a picture" (Theodor Hetzer) was not reached until the stage of Western painting that we call the high Renaissance. Here for the first time we have pictures that stand entirely by themselves and, even without a frame and a setting, are in themselves unified and closed structures. For example, in the con-cinnitas that L. B. Alberti requires of a "picture," we can see a good theoretical expression of the new artistic ideal that governs Renaissance painting.

The interesting thing, however, is that what the theoretician of the "picture" presents here are the classical definitions of the beautiful. That the beautiful is such that nothing can be taken from it and nothing added without destroying it was familiar to Aristotle, for whom there was certainly no such thing as a picture in Alberti's sense.[52] This shows that the concept of the "picture" still has a general sense and that it cannot be limited simply to a particular phase of the history of painting. Even the Ottonian miniature or the Byzantine icon is a picture in an extended sense, though the form of these paintings follows quite different principles and they are to be conceived rather as "picture signs."[53] In the same way the aesthetic concept of a picture will always inevitably include sculpture, which is one of the plastic arts. This is no arbitrary generalization but corresponds to a historical problem of philosophical aesthetics, which ultimately goes back to the role of the image in Platonism and is expressed in the usage of the word Bild (image or picture).[54]

The concept of the picture prevalent in recent centuries cannot automatically be taken as a starting point. Our present investigation seeks to rid itself of that assumption. It tries to find a way of understanding the mode of being of a picture that detaches it both from aesthetic consciousness and from the concept of the picture to which the modern gallery has accustomed us, and it tries to recuperate the concept of the "decorative," discredited by the aesthetics of experience. And if in doing so we find that we share common ground with recent work in art history—which has also sought to free itself from the naive concepts of picture and sculpture that not only dominated aesthetic consciousness in the era of Erlebnis art but also that era's thinking about art history—this convergence of views is certainly no accident. Rather, underlying aesthetic research and philosophical reflection is the same crisis of the picture that the existence of the modern industrial and administrative state and its functionalized public spaces has produced. Only since we no longer have any room for pictures do we know that pictures are not just images but need space.[55]

The intention of the present conceptual analysis, however, has to do not with theory of art but with ontology. Its first task, the criticism of traditional aesthetics, is only a stage on the way to acquiring a horizon that embraces both art and history. In our analysis of the concept of a picture we are concerned with two questions only. We are asking in what respect the picture (Bild: also, image) is different from a *copy* (Abbild)—that is, we are raising the problem of the original (Ur-bild: also, ur-picture). Further, we are asking in what way the picture's relation to its *world* follows from this.

Thus the concept of the picture goes beyond the concept of presentation (Darstellung) used hitherto, because a picture has an essential relation to its original.

To take the first question, here the concept of presentation becomes involved with the concept of the picture that is related to its original. In the temporal or performing arts from which we started, we spoke of presentation but not of a picture. Presentation there seemed doubled, as it were. Both the literary work and its reproduction, say on the stage, are presentations. And it was of key importance for us that the actual experience of art passes through this double presentation without differentiating them. The world that appears in the play of presentation does not stand like a copy next to the real world, but is that world in the heightened truth of its being. And certainly reproduction—e.g., performance on the stage—is not a copy beside which the original performance of the drama itself retains a separate existence. The concept of mimesis, applied to both kinds of presentation, did not mean a copy so much as the appearance of what is presented. Without being imitated in the work, the world does not exist as it exists in the work. It is not there as it is there in the work, and without being reproduced, the work is not there. Hence, in presentation, the presence of what is presented reaches its consummation. The ontological interwovenness of original and reproduced being, and the methodological priority we have accorded the performing arts, will be legitimated if the insight that we have gained from them proves to be true of the plastic arts as well. With respect to these arts, admittedly, one cannot say that reproduction is the real being of the work. On the contrary, as an original the picture resists being reproduced. It seems equally clear that the thing copied has a being that is independent of the copy of it—so much so that the picture seems ontologically inferior to what it represents. Thus we are involved in the ontological problems of original and copy.

We start from the view that the mode of being of the work of art is *presentation* (Darstellung) and ask ourselves how the meaning of presentation can be verified by what we call a *picture*. Here presenting cannot mean copying. We will have to define the mode of being of the picture more exactly by distinguishing the way in which a representation is related to an original from the way a copy is related to an original.

For this we need to make a more exact analysis—one that accords the old priority to what is living, the zoon, and especially to the person.[56] The essence of a copy is to have no other task but to resemble the original. The measure of its success is that one recognizes the original in the copy. This means that its nature is to lose its own independent existence and serve entirely to mediate what is copied. Thus the ideal copy would be a mirror image, for its being really does disappear; it exists only for someone looking into the mirror, and is nothing beyond its mere appearance. But in fact it is not a picture or a copy at all, for it has no separate existence. The mirror reflects the image—i.e., a mirror makes what it reflects visible to someone only for as long as he looks in it and sees his own image or whatever else is reflected in it. It is not accidental, however, that in this instance we still speak of an image (Bild), and not of a copy (Abbild) or illustration (Abbildung). For in the mirror image the entity itself appears in the image so that we have the thing itself in the mirror image. But a copy must always be regarded in relation to the thing it means. A copy tries to be nothing but the reproduction of something and has its only function in identifying it (e.g., as a passport photo or a picture in a sales catalogue). A copy effaces itself in the sense that it functions as a means and, like all means, loses its function when it achieves its end. It exists by itself in order to efface itself in this way. The copy's self-effacement is an intentional element in the being of the copy itself. If there is a change in intention—e.g., if the copy is compared with the original and judgment is passed on the resemblance, i.e., if the copy is distinguished from the original—then its own appearance returns to the fore, like any other means or tool that is being not used but examined. But it has its real function not in the reflective activity of comparison and distinction, but in pointing, through the similarity, to what is copied. Thus it fulfills itself in its self-effacement.

A picture, by contrast, is not destined to be self-effacing, for it is not a means to an end. Here the picture itself is what is meant insofar as the important thing is how the thing represented is presented in it. This means first of all that one is not simply directed away from the picture to what is represented. Rather, the presentation remains essentially connected with what is represented—indeed, belongs to it. This is the reason why the mirror throws back an image and not a copy: what is in the mirror is the image of what is represented and is inseparable from its presence. The mirror can give a distorted image, of course, but that is merely an imperfection: it does not perform its function properly. Thus the mirror confirms the basic point that, unlike a picture, the intention is the original unity and non-differentiation of presentation and what is represented. It is the image of what is represented—it is "its" image, and not that of the mirror, that is seen in the mirror.

Though it is only at the beginning of the history of the picture—in its prehistory, as it were—that we find picture magic, which depends on the identity and non-differentiation of picture and pictured, still this does not mean that a consciousness of the picture that increasingly differentiates and departs further and further from magical identity can ever detach itself entirely from it.[57] Rather, non-differentiation remains essential to all experience of pictures. The irreplaceability of the picture, its fragility, its "sacredness" are all explained in the ontology of the picture here presented. Even the sacralization of "art" in the nineteenth century, described earlier, rests on this basis.

The aesthetic conception of the picture, however, is not fully covered by the model of the mirror image. It only shows the ontological inseparability of the picture from "what is represented." But this is important enough, since it makes clear that the primary intention in the case of a picture is not to differentiate between what is represented and the presentation. That special intention of differentiation that we called "aesthetic" differentiation is only a secondary structure based on this. It distinguishes the representation as such from what is represented. It does not do so by treating the copy of what is represented in the representation the way one usually treats copies. It does not desire the picture to cancel itself, so that what is depicted can exist by itself. On the contrary, it is by affirming its own being that the picture enables what is depicted to exist.

At this point the mirror image can guide us no further as a model. The mirror image is a mere appearance—i.e., it has no real being and is understood in its fleeting existence as something that depends on being reflected. But the picture has its own being. This being as presentation, as precisely that in which it is not the same as what is represented, gives it the positive distinction of being a picture as opposed to a mere reflected image. Even today's mechanical techniques can be used in an artistic way, when they bring out something that is not to be found simply by looking. This kind of picture is not a copy, for it presents something which, without it, would not present itself in this way. It says something about the original [e.g., a good photo portrait].

Hence presentation remains essentially tied to the original represented in it. But it is more than a copy. That the representation is a picture—and not the original itself—does not mean anything negative, any mere diminution of being, but rather an autonomous reality. So the relation of the picture to the original is basically quite different than in the case of a copy. *It is no longer a one-sided relationship*. That the picture has its own reality means the reverse for what is pictured, namely that it comes to presentation in the representation. It presents itself there. It does not follow that it is dependent on this particular presentation in order to appear. It can also present itself as what it is in other ways. But if it presents itself in this way, this is no longer any incidental event but belongs to its own being. Every such presentation is an ontological event and occupies the same ontological level as what is represented. By being presented it experiences, as it were, an *increase in being*. The content of the picture itself is ontologically defined as an emanation of the original.

Essential to an emanation is that what emanates is an overflow. What it flows from does not thereby become less. The development of this concept by Neoplatonic philosophy, which uses it to get beyond Greek substance ontology, is the basis of the positive ontological status of the picture. For if the original One is not diminished by the outflow of the many from it, this means that being increases.

It seems that the Greek fathers used this kind of Neoplatonic thinking in overcoming the Old Testament's hatred of images when it came to christology. They regarded the incarnation of God as a fundamental acknowledgment of the worth of visible appearance, and thus they legitimated works of art. In their overcoming the ban on images we can see the decisive event that enabled the development of the plastic arts in the Christian West.[58]

Thus the ontological relationship between original and copy is the basis of the ontological reality of the picture. But it is important to see that the Platonic conception of the relationship between copy and original does not exhaust the ontological valence of what we call a picture. It seems to me that its mode of being cannot be better characterized than by a concept of canon law: *representation* (Repräsentation).[59]

Obviously the concept of legal representation does not appear by accident when we want to determine the ontological status of the picture in contrast to that of the copy. An essential modification, almost a reversal of the ontological relationship of original and copy, must occur if the picture is an element of "representation" and thus has its own ontological valence. The picture then has an autonomy that also affects the original. For strictly speaking, it is only through the picture (Bild) that the original (Urbild) becomes the original (Ur-bild: also, ur-picture)—e.g., it is only by being pictured that a landscape becomes picturesque.

This can be shown simply in the special case of the representational picture. The way the ruler, the statesman, the hero shows and presents himself—this is brought to presentation in the picture. What does this mean? Not that the person represented acquires a new, more authentic mode of appearance through the picture. Rather, it is the other way around: it is *because* the ruler, the statesman, or the hero must show and present himself to his followers, because he must represent, that the *picture* acquires its own reality. Nevertheless, here there is a reversal. When he shows himself, he must fulfill the expectations that his picture arouses. Only because he thus has his being in showing himself is he represented in the picture. First, then, there is undoubtedly self-presentation, and secondly the representation in the picture of this self-presentation. Pictorial presentation is a special case of public presentation. But the second has an effect on the first. If someone's being necessarily and essentially includes showing himself, he no longer belongs to himself.[60] For example, he can no longer avoid being represented by the picture and, because these representations determine the picture that people have of him, he must ultimately show himself as his picture prescribes. Paradoxical as it may sound, the original acquires an image only by being imaged, and yet the image is nothing but the appearance of the original.[61]

So far we have verified this "ontology" of the picture by secular examples. But, as we know, only the *religious* picture (Bild: also, image) displays the full ontological power of the picture.[62] For it is really true that the divine becomes picturable only through the word and image. Thus the religious picture has an exemplary significance. In it we can see without any doubt that a picture is not a copy of a copied being, but is in ontological communion with what is copied. It is clear from this example that art, as a whole and in a universal sense, increases the picturability of being. Word and image are not mere imitative illustrations, but allow what they present to be for the first time fully what it is.

In the history of art we see the ontological aspect of the picture in the special problem of the rise and change of types. The uniqueness of these relations seems to derive from the fact that here there is a dual creation of pictures, inasmuch as plastic art does to the poetic and religious tradition what the latter already does itself. Herodotus' notorious statement that Homer and Hesiod created the Greek gods means that they introduced the theological system of a family of gods into the varied religious tradition of the Greeks, and thus created distinct forms, both in form and function (in Greek, "eidos" and "time").[63] Here poetry did the work of theology. By articulating the gods' relations to one another it set up a systematic whole.

It made possible the creation of fixed types, and gave plastic art the task of forming and transforming them. As the poetic word goes beyond local cults and unifies religious consciousness, it presents plastic art with a new task. For the poetic always retains a curiously indeterminate quality, in that through the intellectual universality of language it presents something that remains open to all kinds of imaginative elaboration. It is plastic art that fixes and, to that extent, creates the types. This is true even when one does not confuse creating an "image" of the divine with inventing gods and refuses Feuerbach's reversal of the imago dei thesis of Genesis.[64] This anthropological reversal and reinterpretation of religious experience, which became current in the nineteenth century, arises from the same subjectivism that lies at the basis of modern aesthetic thought.

In countering this subjectivist attitude of modern aesthetics I developed the concept of *play* as the event of art proper. This approach has now proved its value, in that the picture—and with it the whole of art that is not dependent on being reproduced and performed—is an event of being and therefore cannot be properly understood as an object of aesthetic consciousness; rather, it is to be grasped in its ontological structure by starting from such phenomena as that of presentation. The picture is an event of being—in it being appears, meaningfully and visibly. The quality of being an original is thus not limited to the "copying" function of the picture, and thus not to "representational" painting and sculpture in particular, architecture being completely excluded. The quality of being an original, rather, is an essential element founded in the fact that art is by nature presentational. The "ideality" of the work of art does not consist in its imitating and reproducing an idea but, as with Hegel, in the "appearing" of the idea itself. On the basis of such an ontology of the picture, the primacy which aesthetic consciousness accords the framed picture that belongs in a collection of paintings can be shown to fail. The picture contains an indissoluble connection with its world.

(B) THE ONTOLOGICAL FOUNDATION OF THE OCCASIONAL AND THE DECORATIVE

If we begin with the fact that the work of art cannot be understood in terms of "aesthetic consciousness," then many phenomena of marginal importance to modern aesthetics become less problematical and, indeed, even move into the center of an "aesthetic" questioning that is not artificially truncated.

I refer to such things as portraits, poems dedicated to someone, or even references to contemporary events in comedy. The aesthetic concepts of the portrait, the dedicated poem, the contemporary allusion are, of course, themselves constructed from the point of view of aesthetic consciousness. For aesthetic consciousness what is common to all of these is the *occasionality* that characterizes such art forms. Occasionality means that their meaning and contents are determined by the occasion for which they are intended, so that they contain more than they would without this occasion.[65] Hence the portrait is related to the man represented, a relation that is not just dragged in but is expressly intended in the representation itself and indeed makes it a portrait.

The important thing is that this occasionality belongs to the work's own claim and is not something forced on it by its interpreter. This is why such art forms as the portrait, where such occasionality is patent, have no real place in an aesthetics based on the concept of experience (Erlebnis). By way of its own pictorial content, a portrait contains a relation to its original. This does not simply mean that the picture is like the original, but rather that it is a picture of the original.

This becomes clear when we distinguish it from the way a painter uses a model in a genre picture or a figure composition. In a portrait the individuality of the person portrayed is represented. If, however, in a genre picture the model appears to be an individual, an interesting type whom the painter has got to sit for him, then this is an objection to the picture; for one then no longer sees *what* the painter presents in the picture, but its untransformed material. Hence it destroys the meaning of the picture of a figure if we recognize the painter's usual model in it. For a model is a disappearing schema. The relation to the original that served the painter must be effaced in the picture.

We also call a "model" something that enables something else that cannot be perceived to become visible—e.g., the model of a house or an atom. Painters' models are not meant as themselves; they serve only to wear a costume or to make gestures clear—like dressed-up dolls. Contrariwise, someone represented in a portrait is so much himself that he does not appear to be dressed up, even if the splendid costume he is wearing attracts attention: for splendor of appearance is part of him. He is the person who he is for others.[66] The interpreter who reads works of literature in terms of their biographical or historical sources is sometimes no better than the art historian who examines the works of a painter in terms of his models.

The difference between the model and the portrait shows us what occasionality means here. Occasionality in the sense intended clearly lies in what the work itself claims to mean, in contradistinction from whatever is discovered in it or can be deduced from it that goes against this claim. A portrait asks to be understood as a portrait, even when the relation to the original is practically crushed by the pictorial content specific to the picture. This is particularly clear in the case of pictures that are not portraits but contain elements of portraiture, so to speak. They too cause one to inquire into the originals recognizable behind the picture, and therefore they are more than a mere model, simply a disappearing schema. It is the same with works of literature, which can contain portraits without therefore necessarily falling a victim to the indiscretion of being a pseudo-artistic roman à clef.[67]

However fluid and controversial the borderline between an intentional allusion referring to something specific and other documentary aspects of a work, there is still the basic question whether one accepts the work's claim to meaning or simply regards it as a historical document that one merely interrogates. The historian will seek out every element that can tell him something of the past, even if it counters the work's claim to meaning. He will examine works of art in order to discover the models: that is, the connections with their own age that are woven into them, even if they remained invisible to contemporary observers and are not important for the meaning of the whole. This is not occasionality in the sense intended here, which pertains rather to those instances in which alluding to a particular original is part of a work's own claim to meaning. It is not, then, left to the observer's whim to decide whether or not a work has such occasional elements. A portrait really *is* a portrait, and does not become one just through and for those who recognize the person portrayed. Although the relation to the original resides in the work itself, it is still right to call it occasional. For the portrait does not say who the person portrayed is, but only that it is a particular individual (and not a type). We can "recognize" who it is only when the person portrayed is known to us, and be sure only when there is a title or some other information to go on. At any rate there resides in the picture an undetermined but still fundamentally determinable reference to something, which constitutes its significance. This occasionality belongs essentially to the import of the "picture," regardless of whether one knows what it refers to.

We can see this in the fact that a portrait looks to us like a portrait (and the representation of a particular person in a picture appears portraitlike) even if we do not know the person portrayed. In this case there is something in the picture that cannot be figured out, namely its occasional aspect. But what cannot be figured out is not therefore not there; it is there in a quite unambiguous way. The same thing is true of many poetic phenomena. Pindar's poems of victory, a comedy that is critical of its age, but also such literary phenomena as the odes and satires of Horace are thoroughly occasional in nature. The occasional in such works has acquired so permanent a form that, even without being figured out or understood, it is still part of the total meaning. Someone might explain to us the particular historical context, but this would be only secondary for the poem as a whole. He would be only filling out the meaning that exists in the poem itself.

It is important to recognize that what I call occasionality here in no way diminishes the claim of such works to be artistic and to be unambiguous. For that which presents itself to aesthetic subjectivity as "the eruption of time into play,"[68] and which in the age of Erlebnis art appeared to diminish a work's aesthetic significance, is in fact only a subjective reflection of the ontological relationship that has been developed above. A work of art belongs so closely to what it is related to that it enriches the being of that as if through a new event of being. To be fixed in a picture, addressed in a poem, to be the object of an allusion from the stage, are not incidental and remote from what the thing essentially is; they are presentations of the essence itself. What was said in general about the ontological valence of the picture includes these occasional elements. With respect to the element of occasionality, these phenomena represent particular cases of a general relationship that obtains for the being of the work of art: namely that it experiences a continued determination of its meaning from the "occasion" of its coming-to-presentation.

This is seen most clearly in the performing arts, especially theater and music, which wait for the occasion in order to exist and define themselves only through that occasion.

Hence the stage is a political institution par excellence because only the performance brings out everything that is in the play, its allusions and its echoes. No one knows beforehand what will "hit home" and what will have no impact. Every performance is an event, but not one in any way separate from the work—the work itself is what "takes place" (ereignet: also, comes into its own) in the event (Ereignis) of performance. To be occasional is essential to it: the occasion of the performance makes it speak and brings out what is in it. The director who stages the play displays his skill in being able to make use of the occasion. But he acts according to the directions of the writer, whose whole work is a stage direction. This is quite clearly the case with a musical work—the score is really only a set of directions. Aesthetic differentiation may judge the performance against the inner structure of sound read in the score, but no one believes that reading music is the same as listening to it.[69]

Essential to dramatic or musical works, then, is that their performance at different times and on different occasions is, and must be, different. Now it is important to see that, mutatis mutandis, the same is true of the plastic arts. But in them too it is not the case that the work exists "an sich" and only the effect varies: it is the work of art itself that displays itself under various conditions. The viewer of today not only sees things in a different

141

way, he sees different things. We have only to recall how the idea of the pale marble of antiquity has governed our taste since the Renaissance and even our attitude to preservation, or how the purist spirituality of Gothic cathedrals reflects the classicist feeling of the romantic north.

But specifically occasional art forms—such as the parabasis in classical comedy or caricature in politics, which are intended for a quite specific "occasion," and finally the portrait as well—are fundamentally forms of the universal occasionality characteristic of the work of art inasmuch as it determines itself anew from occasion to occasion. The uniqueness of an element occasional in this narrower sense is fulfilled in a work of art, but is fulfilled in such a way that through the being of the work this uniqueness comes to participate in a universality that makes it capable of yet further fulfillment. Thus the work's unique relation to the occasion can never be finally determined, but though indeterminable this relation remains present and effective in the work itself. In this sense the portrait too is independent of its unique relation to the original, and contains the latter even in transcending it.

The portrait is only an intensification of what constitutes the essence of all pictures. Every picture is an increase of being and is essentially definable as representation, as coming-to-presentation. In the special case of the portrait this representation acquires a personal significance, in that here an individual is presented in a representative way. For this means that the person represented represents himself in his portrait and is represented by his portrait. The picture is not just an image and certainly not just a copy; it belongs to the present or to the present memory of the man represented. This is its real nature. To that extent the portrait is a special case of the general ontological valence that we have assigned to the picture as such. What comes into being in it is not contained in what acquaintances can already see in the person portrayed. The best judges of a portrait are never the nearest relatives nor even the person himself. For a portrait never tries to reproduce the individual it represents as he appears in the eyes of people close to him. Of necessity, what it shows is an idealization, which can run through an infinite number of stages from the representative to the most intimate. This kind of idealization does not alter the fact that a portrait represents an individual, and not a type, however much the portrait may transform the person portrayed from the incidental and the private into the essential, the true appearance.

Religious or secular monuments display the universal ontological valence of pictures more clearly than do intimate portraits. For their public function depends on it. A monument makes present what it represents in a way that is obviously quite different from the way aesthetic consciousness does so.[70] The monument does not live only through the autonomous expressive power of the images on it. This is clear from the fact that things other than works of art—e.g., symbols or inscriptions—can have the same function. The familiarity—the potential presence, as it were—of what the monument memorializes is always assumed. The figure of a god, the picture of a king, the memorial to someone, assume that the god, the king, the hero, the event—the victory or peace treaty—already possess a presence affecting everyone. The statue that represents them thus adds nothing other than, say, an inscription: it holds them present in their general significance. Nevertheless, if the statue is a work of art, then it not only recalls something whose meaning is already familiar, but it can also say something of its own, and thus it becomes independent of the prior knowledge that it conveys.

Despite all aesthetic differentiation, it remains the case that an image is a manifestation of what it represents—even if it brings it to appearance through its autonomous expressive power. This is obvious in the case of the religious image; but the difference between the sacred and the secular is relative in a work of art. Even an individual portrait, if it is a work of art, shares in the mysterious radiation of being that flows from the being of what is represented, what comes to presence there (was da zur Darstellung kommt).

We can illustrate this by an example: Justi[71] once described Velazquez's *The Surrender of Breda* as a "military sacrament." He meant that the picture was not a group portrait, nor simply a historical picture. What is caught in this picture is not just a solemn event as such. The solemnity of this ceremony is present in the picture because the ceremony itself has a pictorial quality and is performed like a sacrament. There are things that need to be and are suitable for being depicted; their being is, as it were, consummated in being represented in a picture.

It is not accidental that religious concepts come to mind when one is defending the special ontological status of works of fine art against aesthetic leveling.

It is quite in order that the opposition between profane and sacred proves to be only relative. We need only recall the meaning and history of the word "profane": the "profane" is the place in front of the sanctuary. The concept of the profane and its cognate, profanation, always presuppose the sacred. Actually, the difference between profane and sacred could only be relative in classical antiquity, when it originated, since the whole sphere of life was sacrally ordered and determined. Only with Christianity does profaneness come to be understood in a stricter sense. The New Testament undemonized the world to such an extent that an absolute contrast between the profane and the religious became possible. The church's promise of salvation means that the world is always only "this world." The fact that this claim was special to the church also creates the tension between it and the state, which coincides with the end of the classical world; and thus the concept of the profane acquires special currency. The entire history of the Middle Ages is dominated by the tension between church and state. What ultimately opens a place for the secular state is the spiritualistic deepening of the idea of the Christian church. The historical significance of the high Middle Ages is that they created the profane world and gave the concept of the profane its broad modern meaning.[72] But that does not alter the fact that the profane has remained a concept related to sacred law and can be defined by reference to it alone. There is no such thing as profaneness in itself.[73]

The relativity of profane and sacred is not only part of the dialectic of concepts, but can be seen as a reality in the phenomenon of the picture. A work of art always has something sacred about it. True, religious art or a monument on exhibit in a museum can no longer be desecrated in the same sense as one still in its original place. But this only means that it has in fact already suffered an injury in having become a museum piece. Obviously this is not true only of religious works of art. We sometimes have the same feeling in an antique shop when the old pieces on sale still have some trace of intimate life about them; it seems somehow scandalous to us, a kind of offense to piety, a profanation. Ultimately every work of art has something about it that protests against profanation.

This seems decisively proved by the fact that even pure aesthetic consciousness is acquainted with the idea of profanation. It always perceives the destruction of works of art as a sacrilege. (The German word Frevel is now rarely used except in the phrase Kunst-Frevel.) There is plenty of evidence that this feature is characteristic of the modern aesthetic religion of culture. For example, the word "vandalism," which goes back to medieval times, only became popular in reaction to the Jacobins' destructiveness during the French Revolution. To destroy works of art is to violate a world protected by its holiness. Even an autonomous aesthetic consciousness cannot deny that art is more than such consciousness would admit.

All these considerations justify characterizing the mode of being of art in general in terms of *presentation* (Darstellung); this includes *play* (Spiel) and *picture* (Bild), *communion* (Kommunion), and *representation* (Repräsentation). The work of art is conceived as an event of being (Seinsvorgang), and the abstraction performed by aesthetic differentiation is dissolved. A picture is an event of presentation. Its being related to the original is so far from lessening its ontological autonomy that, on the contrary, I had to speak, in regard to the picture, of an increase of being. Using religious concepts thus proved appropriate.

Now, it is important not to confuse the special sense of presentation proper to the work of art with the sacred representation performed by, say, the *symbol*. Not all forms of "representation" have the character of "art." Symbols and badges are also forms of representation. They too indicate something, and this makes them representations.

In the logical analysis of the nature of expression and meaning undertaken during the last few decades, the structure of indicating, common to all these forms of representation, has been investigated in unusually great detail.[74] I mention this work here for another reason. We are primarily concerned not with the problem of meaning but with the nature of a picture. We want to grasp its distinctive nature without being confused by the abstraction performed by aesthetic consciousness. And so to discover both similarities and difference, we need to examine the nature of indicating.

The essence of the picture is situated, as it were, halfway between two extremes: these extremes of representation are *pure indication* (Verweisung: also, reference), which is the essence of the sign, and *pure substitution* (Vertreten), which is the essence of the symbol. There is something of both in a picture. Its representing includes indicating what is represented in it. We saw that this emerges most clearly in specific forms such as the portrait, for which the relation to the original is essential. At the same time a picture is not a *sign* (Zeichen). For a sign is nothing but what its function requires; and that is to point away from itself. In order to fulfill this function, of course, it must first draw attention to itself. It must be striking: that is, it must clearly foreground itself and present itself as an indicator, like a poster. But neither a sign nor a poster is a picture. It should not attract attention to itself in such a way that one lingers over it, for it is there only to make present something that is absent and to do so in such a way that the absent thing, and that alone, comes to mind.[75] It should not invite the viewer to pause over its own intrinsic pictorial interest. The same is true of all signs: for instance, traffic signs, bookmarks, and the like. There is something schematic and abstract about them, because they point not to themselves but to what is not present—e.g., to the curve ahead or to one's page. (Even natural signs—e.g., indications of the weather, function as signs only by way of an abstraction. If we look at the sky and are filled with the beauty of what we see there and linger over it, we experience a shift in attention that causes its sign character to retreat into the background.)

Of all signs, the memento most seems to have a reality of its own. It refers to the past and so is effectively a sign, but it is also precious in itself since, as a bit of the past that has not disappeared, it keeps the past present for us. But it is clear that this characteristic is not grounded in the being of the object itself. A memento has value as a memento only for someone who already—i.e., still—recalls the past. Mementos lose their value when the past of which they remind one no longer has any meaning. Furthermore, someone who not only uses mementos to remind him but makes a cult of them and lives in the past as if it were the present has a disturbed relation to reality.

Hence a picture is certainly not a sign. Even a memento does not cause us to linger over it but over the past that it represents for us. But a picture points to what it represents only through its own content. By concentrating on it, we too come into contact with what is represented. The picture points by causing us to linger over it, for as I emphasized, its ontological valence consists in not being absolutely different from what it represents but sharing in its being. We saw that what is represented comes into its own in the picture. It experiences an increase in being. But that means it is there in the picture itself. To abstract from the presence of the original in the picture is merely an aesthetic reflection—I called it "aesthetic differentiation."

The difference between a picture and a sign has an ontological basis. The picture does not disappear in pointing to something else but, in its own being, shares in what it represents.

This ontological sharing pertains not only to a picture but to what we call a *symbol*. Neither symbol nor picture indicates anything that is not at the same time present in them themselves. Hence the problem arises of differentiating between the mode of being of pictures and the mode of being of symbols.[76]

There is an obvious distinction between a symbol and a sign, for the symbol is more like a picture. The representational function of a symbol is not merely to point to something that is not present. Instead, a symbol manifests the presence of something that really is present. This is seen in the original meaning of "symbol." When a symbol is used as a sign of recognition between separated friends or the scattered members of a religious community to show that they belong together, such a symbol undoubtedly functions as a sign. But it is more than a sign. It not only points to the fact that people belong together, but demonstrates and visibly presents that fact. The "tessera hospitalis" is a relic of past life, and its existence attests to what it indicates: it makes the past itself present again and causes it to be recognized as valid. It is especially true of religious symbols that they not only function as distinguishing marks, but that the meaning of these symbols is understood by everyone, unites everyone, and can therefore assume a sign function. Hence what is symbolized is undoubtedly in need of representation, inasmuch as it is itself non-sensible, infinite, and unrepresentable, but also capable of it. It is only because what is symbolized is present itself that it can be present in the symbol.

A symbol not only points to something; it represents it by taking its place. But to take the place of something means to make something present that is not present. Thus in representing, the symbol takes the place of something: that is, it makes something immediately present. Only because it thus presents the presence of what it represents is the symbol itself treated with the reverence due to the symbolized. Such symbols as a crucifix, a flag, a uniform have so fully taken the place of what is revered that the latter is present in them.

That the concept of representation (Repräsentation) we used above to describe the picture essentially belongs here shows the proximity between pictorial representation and symbolic representation. In both cases, what they represent is itself present. Yet a picture as such is not a symbol, and not only because symbols need not be pictorial. Through their mere existence and manifesting of themselves, symbols function as substitutes; but of themselves they say nothing about what they symbolize. One must be familiar with them in the same way as one must be familiar with a sign, if one is to understand what they refer to. Hence they do not mean an increase of being for what is represented. It is true that making itself present in symbols belongs to the being of what is represented. But its own being is not further determined by the fact that the symbols exist and are shown. It does not exist any *more* fully when they exist. They merely take its place. Hence their own significance (if they have any) is of no importance. They are representatives and receive their ontological function of representing from what they are supposed to represent. The picture also represents, but through itself, through the increment of meaning that it brings. But this means that in it what is represented—the "original"—is there more fully, more genuinely, just as it truly is.

Hence a picture is situated halfway between a sign and a symbol. Its representing is neither a pure pointing-to-something nor a pure taking-the-place-of-something. It is this intermediate position that raises it to a unique ontological status. Artificial signs and symbols alike do not—like the picture—acquire their signifying function from their own content, but must be taken as signs or as symbols. We call the origin of their signifying function their "institution" (Stiftung). In determining the ontological valence of a picture (which is what we are concerned with), it is decisive that in regard to a picture there is no such thing as "institution" in the same sense.

By "institution" we mean the origin of something's being taken as a sign or functioning symbolically. In this fundamental sense, even so-called "natural" signs—e.g., all the indications and presages of an event in nature—are instituted. They function as signs only when they are taken as signs. But they are taken as signs only because the linkage between the sign and the signified has previously been established. This is also true of all artificial signs. Here the sign is established by convention, and the originating act by which it is established is called its "institution." What a sign indicates depends primarily on its institution; for example, the significance of traffic signs depends on the decision of the Ministry of Transport, that of souvenirs on the meaning given to their preservation, etc. So too the symbol has to be instituted, for only this gives it its representational character. For what gives it its significance is not its own ontological content but an act of institution, an installation, a consecration that gives significance to what is, in itself, without significance: for example, the sign of sovereignty, the flag, the crucifix.

It is important to see that a work of art, on the other hand, does not owe its real meaning to such an act of institution, even if it is a religious picture or a secular memorial. The public act of consecration or unveiling that assigns its purpose does not give it its significance. Rather, it is already a structure with a signifying function of its own, as a pictorial or non-pictorial representation, before it is assigned a function as a memorial. Erecting and dedicating a memorial—and it is not by accident that, after a certain historical distance has consecrated them, we speak of religious and secular works of architecture as architectural monuments—therefore only actualizes a function already implicit in the work's own content.

This is why works of art can assume certain real functions and resist others: for instance, religious or secular, public or private ones. They are instituted and erected as memorials of reverence, honor, or piety only because they themselves prescribe and help fashion this kind of functional context. They themselves lay claim to their place, and even if they are displaced—e.g., by being housed in a modern collection—the trace of their original purpose cannot be effaced. It is part of their being because their being is presentation.

If one considers these special forms as possessing exemplary significance, one sees that certain forms of art become central which, from the point of view of Erlebnis art, are peripheral: namely all those whose own content points beyond them to the whole of a context determined by them and for them. The greatest and most distinguished of these forms is *architecture*.[77]

A work of architecture extends beyond itself in two ways. It is as much determined by the aim it is to serve as by the place it is to take up in a total spatial context. Every architect has to consider both these things. His plan is determined by the fact that the building has to serve a particular way of life and adapt itself to particular architectural circumstances. We call a successful building a "happy solution," and mean by this both that it perfectly fulfills its purpose and that its construction has added something new to the spatial dimensions of a town or landscape. Through this dual ordering the building presents a true increase of being: it is a work of art.

A building is not a work of art if it stands just anywhere, as a blot on the landscape, but only if it represents the solution of an "architectural problem." Aesthetics acknowledges only those works of art that are in some way worth thinking about and calls them "architectural monuments." If a building is a work of art, then it is not only the artistic solution to a building problem posed by the contexts of purpose and life to which it originally belongs, but somehow preserves them, so that they are visibly present even though the building's present appearance is completely alienated from its original purpose. Something in it points back to the original. Where the original intention becomes completely unrecognizable, or its unity is destroyed by too many subsequent alterations, then the building itself becomes incomprehensible. Thus architecture, this most statuary of all art forms, shows how secondary "aesthetic differentiation" is. A building is never only a work of art. Its purpose, through which it belongs in the context of life, cannot be separated from it without its losing some of its reality. If it has become merely an object of aesthetic consciousness, then it has merely a shadowy reality and lives a distorted life only in the degenerate form of a tourist attraction or a subject for photography. The "work of art in itself" proves to be a pure abstraction.

In fact the presence of great architectural monuments of the past among the buildings erected by the modern world of commerce poses the task of integrating past and present. Works of architecture do not stand motionless on the shore of the stream of history, but are borne along by it. Even if historically-minded ages try to reconstruct the architecture of an earlier age, they cannot turn back the wheel of history, but must mediate in a new and better way between the past and the present. Even the restorer or the preserver of ancient monuments remains an artist of his time.

The special importance of architecture for our inquiry is that it too displays the element of mediation without which a work of art has no real "presence." Thus even where the work is presented in a way other than through performance (which everyone knows belongs to its own present time), past and present are brought together in a work of art. That every work of art has its own world does not mean that when its original world is altered it has its reality in an alienated aesthetic consciousness. Architecture teaches us this, for it belongs inalienably to its world.

But this involves a further point. Architecture gives shape to space. Space is what surrounds everything that exists in space. That is why architecture embraces all the other forms of representation: all works of plastic art, all ornament. Moreover, it gives a place to the representational arts of poetry, music, acting, and dancing. By embracing all the arts, it asserts its own perspective everywhere. That perspective is *decoration*. Architecture safeguards it even against those forms of art whose works are not decorative but are rather gathered within themselves through the closure of their circle of meaning. Modern research has begun to recall that this is true of all works of plastic art, which had a place assigned them when they were commissioned. Even the free-standing statue on a pedestal is not really removed from the decorative context, but serves to heighten representationally a context of life with which it is decoratively consonant.[78] Even poetry and music, which have the freest mobility and can be read or performed anywhere, are not suited to any space whatever but to one that is appropriate: a theater, concert hall, or church. Here too it is not a question of subsequently finding an external setting for a work that is complete in itself but of obeying the space-creating potentiality of the work itself, which has to adapt to what is given as well as to create its own conditions. (Think only of the problem of acoustics, which is not only technical but architectural.)

Hence, given its comprehensiveness in relation to all the arts, architecture involves a twofold mediation. As the art which creates space, it both shapes it and leaves it free. It not only embraces all decorative shaping of space, including ornament, but is itself decorative in nature. The nature of decoration consists in performing that two-sided mediation: namely to draw the viewer's attention to itself, to satisfy·his taste, and then to redirect it away from itself to the greater whole of the life context which it accompanies.

This is true of the whole span of the decorative, from municipal architecture to the individual ornament. A building should certainly be the solution to an artistic problem and thus attract the viewer's wonder and admiration. At the same time it should fit into a way of life and not be an end in itself. It tries to fit into this way of life by providing ornament, a background of mood, or a framework. The same is true for each individual piece of work that the architect carries out, including ornament, which should not draw attention to itself but function as a decorative accompaniment. But even the extreme case of ornament still has something of the duality of decorative mediation about it. Certainly it should not invite us to linger and notice it as a decorative motif, but should have a merely accompanying effect. Thus in general it will not have any representational content, or will so iron it out through stylization or repetition that one's eye glides across it. It is not intended that the forms of nature used in an ornament should be "recognized." If a repetitive pattern is seen as what it actually is, then its repetition becomes unbearably monotonous. But on the other hand it should not have a dead or monotonous effect, for as an accompaniment it should have an enlivening effect and must, to some extent, draw attention to itself.

On surveying the full extent of the architect's decorative tasks, it is clear that architecture explodes that prejudice of the aesthetic consciousness according to which the actual work of art is what is outside all space and all time, the object of an aesthetic experience. One also sees that the usual distinction between a work of art proper and mere decoration demands revision.

The antithesis of the decorative to a real work of art is obviously based on the idea that the latter originates in "the inspiration of genius." The argument was more or less that what is only decorative is not the art of genius but mere craftsmanship. It is only a means, subordinated to what it is supposed to decorate, and can therefore be replaced, like any other means subordinated to an end, by another appropriate means. It has no share in the uniqueness of the work of art.

The truth is that the concept of decoration needs to be freed from this antithetical relationship to the concept of art as based on experience (Erlebnis); rather, it needs to be grounded in the ontological structure of representation, which we have shown to be the mode of being of the work of art. We have only to remember that the ornamental and the decorative originally meant the beautiful as such. It is necessary to recover this ancient insight. Ornament or decoration is determined by its relation to what it decorates, to what carries it. It has no aesthetic import of its own that is thereafter limited by its relation to what it is decorating. Even Kant, who endorsed this opinion, admits in his famous judgment on tattooing that ornament is ornament only when it suits the wearer.[79] It is part of taste not only to judge something to be beautiful per se but also to know where it belongs and where not. Ornament is not primarily something by itself that is then applied to something else but belongs to the self-presentation of its wearer. Ornament too belongs to presentation. But presentation is an event of being; it is representation. An ornament, a decoration, a piece of sculpture set up in a chosen place are representative in the same sense that, say, the church where they are found is itself representative.

Hence the concept of the decorative serves to complete our inquiry into the mode of being of the aesthetic. Later we will see other reasons for reinstating the old, transcendental meaning of the beautiful. What we mean by "representation" is, at any rate, a universal ontological structural element of the aesthetic, an event of being—not an experiential event that occurs at the moment of artistic creation and is merely repeated each time in the mind of the viewer. Starting from the universal significance of play, we saw that the ontological significance of representation lies in the fact that "reproduction" is the original mode of being of the original artwork itself. Now we have confirmed that painting and the plastic arts generally have, ontologically speaking, the same mode of being. The specific mode of the work of art's presence is the coming-to-presentation of being.

(C) THE BORDERLINE POSITION OF LITERATURE

Now we must test whether the ontological perspective I have developed for art applies to the mode of being of *literature* (Literatur). Here there does not appear to be any presentation that could claim an ontological valence of its own. Reading is a purely interior mental process. It seems to exhibit a complete detachment from the occasional and contingent—by contrast to public reading and performance, for example. The only condition to which literature is subject is being handed down in language and taken up in reading. Is not aesthetic differentiation—by means of which aesthetic consciousness claims to establish itself over against the artwork—legitimated by the autonomy of reading consciousness? Literature, the written word, seems to be poetry alienated from its ontological valence. It could be said of every book—not just the famous one[80] that makes this claim—that it is for everyone and no one.

[But is this a correct conception of literature? Or does it not ultimately originate in a back-projection performed by the alienated cultured consciousness? No doubt the idea that literature is an object to be read silently appears late. But it is no accident that the word literature points not to reading but to writing. Recent research (Parry and others), which has obliged me to revise the views I expressed in earlier editions, has now revived the romantic idea that pre-Homeric epic poetry was oral by showing how long orality sustained Albanian epic poetry. Where script comes into use, however, it forces epic to be fixed in writing. "Literature" arises to serve the reciter—not yet indeed as material to be read silently but to be recited. Still, there is nothing utterly new when silent reading is promoted in opposition to recitation, as occurs in later eras. (Think, for instance, of Aristotle's aversion to theatrical performance.)]

This is immediately obvious as long as reading means reading aloud. But there is obviously no sharp differentiation between reciting and silent reading. Reading with understanding is always a kind of reproduction, performance, and interpretation. Emphasis, rhythmic ordering, and the like are part of wholly silent reading too. Meaning and the understanding of it are so closely connected with the corporeality of language that understanding always involves an inner speaking as well.

If so, then it is just as true that literature—say in its proper art form, the novel—has its original existence in being read, as that the epic has it in being declaimed by the rhapsodist or the picture in being looked at by the spectator. Thus the reading of a book would still remain an event in which the content comes to presentation. True, literature and the reading of it have the maximum degree of freedom and mobility.[81] This is seen simply in the fact that one does not need to read a book at one sitting, so that, if one wants to go on with it, one has to take it up again; this has no analogy in listening to music or looking at a picture, yet it shows that "reading" is related to the unity of the text.

Literary art can be understood only from the ontology of the work of art, and not from the aesthetic experiences that occur in the course of the reading. Like a public reading or performance, being read belongs to literature by its nature. They are stages of what is generally called "reproduction" but which in fact is the *original* mode of being of all performing arts, and that mode of being has proved exemplary for defining the mode of being of all art.

But this has a further consequence. The concept of literature is not unrelated to the reader. Literature does not exist as the dead remnant of an alienated being, left over for a later time as simultaneous with its experiential reality. Literature is a function of being intellectually preserved and handed down, and therefore brings its hidden history into every age. Beginning with the establishment of the canon of classical literature by the Alexandrian philologists, copying and preserving the "classics" is a living cultural tradition that does not simply preserve what exists but acknowledges it as a model and passes it on as an example to be followed. Through all changes of taste, the effective grandeur that we call "classical literature" remains a model for all later writers, up to the time of the ambiguous "battle of the ancients and moderns," and beyond.

Only with the development of historical consciousness is this living unity of world literature transformed from the immediacy of a normative claim to unity into a question of literary history. But this process is unfinished and perhaps never can be finished. It was Goethe who gave the idea of world literature its first formulation in the German language,[82] but for Goethe the normative force of that idea was still self-evident. Even today it has not died out, for we still say of a work of lasting importance that it belongs to world literature.

What belongs to world literature has its place in the consciousness of all. It belongs to the "world." Now, the world which considers a given work to belong to world literature may be far removed from the original world in which that work was born. It is at any rate no longer the same "world." But even then the normative sense implied in the concept of world literature means that works that belong to world literature remain eloquent although the world to which they speak is quite different. Similarly, the existence of literature in translation shows that something is presented in such works that is true and valid for all time. Thus it is by no means the case that world literature is an alienated form of what originally constituted a given work's mode of being. Rather, the historical mode of being of literature is what makes it possible for something to belong to world literature.

The qualitative distinction accorded a work by the fact that it belongs to world literature places the phenomenon of literature in a new perspective. Even though only literature that has value of its own as art is declared to belong to world literature, the concept of literature is far wider than that of the literary work of art. All written texts share in the mode of being of literature—not only religious, legal, economic, public and private texts of all kinds, but also scholarly writings that edit and interpret these texts: namely the human sciences as a whole. Moreover, all scholarly research takes the form of literature insofar as it is essentially bound to language. Literature in the broadest sense is bounded only by what can be said, for everything that can be said can be written.

We may ask ourselves, then, whether what we have discovered about the mode of being of art still applies to literature in this broad sense. Must we confine the normative sense of literature which we elaborated above to literary works that can be considered works of art, and must we say that they alone share in the ontological valence of art? Do the other forms of literature have no share in it?

Or is there no such sharp division here? There are works of scholarship whose literary merit has caused them to be considered works of art and part of world literature. This is clear from the point of view of aesthetic consciousness, inasmuch as the latter does not consider the significance of such works' contents but only the quality of their form as important. But since our criticism of aesthetic consciousness has shown the limited validity of that point of view, this principle dividing literary art from other written texts becomes dubious for us. We have seen that aesthetic consciousness is unable to grasp the essential truth even of literary art. For literary art has in common with all other texts the fact that it speaks to us in terms of the significance of its contents. Our understanding is not specifically concerned with its formal achievement as a work of art but with what it says to us.

The difference between a literary work of art and any other text is not so fundamental. It is true that there is a difference between the language of poetry and the language of prose, and again between the language of poetic prose and that of "scientific" or "scholarly" prose. These differences can certainly also be considered from the point of view of literary form. But the essential difference between these various "languages" obviously lies elsewhere: namely in the distinction between the claims to truth that each makes. All written works have a profound community in that language is what makes the contents meaningful. In this light, when texts are understood by, say, a historian, that is not so very different from their being experienced as art. And it is not mere chance that the concept of literature embraces not only works of literary art but everything passed down in writing.

At any rate, it is not by chance that literature is the place where art and science merge. The mode of being of a text has something unique and incomparable about it. It presents a specific problem of translation to the understanding. Nothing is so strange, and at the same time so demanding, as the written word. Not even meeting speakers of a foreign language can be compared with this strangeness, since the language of gesture and of sound is always in part immediately intelligible. The written word and what partakes of it—literature—is the intelligibility of mind transferred to the most alien medium. Nothing is so purely the trace of the mind as writing, but nothing is so dependent on the understanding mind either. In deciphering and interpreting it, a miracle takes place: the transformation of something alien and dead into total contemporaneity and familiarity. This is like nothing else that comes down to us from the past. The remnants of past life—what is left of buildings, tools, the contents of graves—are weather-beaten by the storms of time that have swept over them, whereas a written tradition, once deciphered and read, is to such an extent pure mind that it speaks to us as if in the present. That is why the capacity to read, to understand what is written, is like a secret art, even a magic that frees and binds us. In it time and space seem to be superseded. People who can read what has been handed down in writing produce and achieve the sheer presence of the past.

Hence we can see that in our context, despite all aesthetic distinctions, the concept of literature is as broad as possible. Just as we were able to show that the being of the work of art is play and that it must be perceived by the spectator in order to be actualized (vollendet), so also it is universally true of texts that only in the process of understanding them is the dead trace of meaning transformed back into living meaning. We must ask whether what we found to be true of the experience of art is also true of texts as a whole, including those that are not works of art. We saw that the work of art is actualized only when it is "presented," and we were drawn to the conclusion that all literary works of art are actualized only when they are read. Is this true also of the understanding of any text? Is the meaning of all texts actualized only when they are understood? In other words, does being understood belong (gehört) to the meaning of a text just as being heard (Zu-Gehör-Bringen) belongs to the meaning of music? Can we still talk of understanding if we are as free with the meaning of the text as the performing artist with his score?

(D) RECONSTRUCTION AND INTEGRATION AS HERMENEUTIC TASKS

The classical discipline concerned with the art of understanding texts is hermeneutics. If my argument is correct, however, the real problem of hermeneutics is quite different from what one might expect. It points in the same direction in which my criticism of aesthetic consciousness has moved the problem of aesthetics. In fact, hermeneutics would then have to be understood in so comprehensive a sense as to embrace the whole sphere of art and its complex of questions. Every work of art, not only literature, must be understood like any other text that requires understanding, and this kind of understanding has to be acquired. This gives hermeneutical consciousness a comprehensiveness that surpasses even that of aesthetic consciousness. *Aesthetics has to be absorbed into hermeneutics.* This statement not only reveals the breadth of the problem but is substantially accurate. Conversely, hermeneutics must be so determined as a whole that it does justice to the experience of art. Understanding must be conceived as a part of the event in which meaning occurs, the event in which the meaning of all statements—those of art and all other kinds of tradition—is formed and actualized.

In the nineteenth century, the hermeneutics that was once merely ancillary to theology and philology was developed into a system and made the basis of all the human sciences. It wholly transcended its original pragmatic purpose of making it possible, or easier, to understand written texts. It is not only the written tradition that is estranged and in need of new and more vital assimilation; everything that is no longer immediately situated in a world—that is, all tradition, whether art or the other spiritual creations of the past: law, religion, philosophy, and so forth—is estranged from its original meaning and depends on the unlocking and mediating spirit that we, like the Greeks, name after Hermes: the messenger of the gods. It is to the *rise of historical consciousness* that hermeneutics owes its centrality within the human sciences. But we may ask whether the whole extent of the problem that hermeneutics poses can be adequately grasped on the basis of the premises of historical consciousness.

Previous work in this field—primarily Wilhelm Dilthey's hermeneutical grounding of the human sciences[83] and his research into the rise of hermeneutics[84]—determined in its way the dimensions of the hermeneutical problem. Today's task could be to free ourselves from the dominant influence of Dilthey's approach to the question and from the prejudices of the discipline that he founded: namely "Geistesgeschichte" (intellectual history).

To give a preliminary sketch of what is involved and to combine the systematic result of my argument so far with the new extension of the problem, let us consider first the hermeneutical task set by the phenomenon of art. However clearly I showed that "aesthetic differentiation" was an abstraction that could not supersede the artwork's belonging to its world, it remains irrefutable that art is never simply past but is able to overcome temporal distance by virtue of its own meaningful presence. Hence art offers an excellent example of understanding in both respects. Even though it is no mere object of historical consciousness, understanding art always includes historical mediation. What, then, is the task of hermeneutics in relation to it?

Schleiermacher and Hegel suggest two very different ways of answering this question. They might be described as *reconstruction* and *integration*. The primary point for both Schleiermacher and Hegel is the consciousness of loss and estrangement in relation to tradition, which rouses them to hermeneutical reflection. Nevertheless, they define the task of hermeneutics very differently.

Schleiermacher (whose theory of hermeneutics will be considered later) is wholly concerned to reconstruct the work, in the understanding, as originally constituted. For art and written texts handed down to us from the past are wrenched from their original world. As my analysis has revealed, this is true of all art, including literature, but it is especially evident in the plastic arts. Schleiermacher writes, "when works of art come into general circulation," they are no longer what they were naturally and originally. "Part of the intelligibility of each one derives from its original constitution." "Hence the work of art loses some of its significance if it is torn from its original context, unless this happens to be historically preserved." He even says, "Hence a work of art, too, is really rooted in its own soil, its own environment. It loses its meaning when it is wrenched from this environment and enters into general circulation; it is like something that has been saved from the fire but still bears the burn marks upon it."[85]

Does it not follow, then, that the work of art enjoys its true significance only where it originally belongs? Does grasping its significance, then, mean somehow reconstructing this original world? If we acknowledge that the work of art is not a timeless object of aesthetic experience but belongs to a "world" that alone determines its full significance, it would seem to follow that the true significance of the work of art can be understood only in terms of its origin and genesis within that "world." Hence all the various means of historical reconstruction—re-establishing the "world" to which it belongs, re-establishing the original situation which the creative artist "had in mind," performing in the original style, and so on—can claim to reveal the true meaning of a work of art and guard against misunderstanding and anachronistic interpretation. This is, in fact, Schleiermacher's conception and the tacit premise of his entire hermeneutics. According to Schleiermacher, historical knowledge opens the possibility of replacing what is lost and reconstructing tradition, inasmuch as it restores the original occasion and circumstances. Hermeneutics endeavors to rediscover the nodal point in the artist's mind that will render the significance of his work fully intelligible, just as in the case of other texts it tries to reproduce the writer's original process of production.

Reconstructing the conditions in which a work passed down to us from the past was originally constituted is undoubtedly an important aid to understanding it. But we may ask whether what we obtain is really the *meaning* of the work of art that we are looking for, and whether it is correct to see understanding as a second creation, the reproduction of the original production. Ultimately, this view of hermeneutics is as nonsensical as all restitution and restoration of past life. Reconstructing the original circumstances, like all restoration, is a futile undertaking in view of the historicity of our being. What is reconstructed, a life brought back from the lost past, is not the original. In its continuance in an estranged state it acquires only a derivative, cultural existence. The recent tendency to take works of art out of museums and put them back in the place for which they were originally intended, or to restore architectural monuments to their original form, merely confirms this judgment. Even a painting taken from the museum and replaced in a church or building restored to its original condition are not what they once were—they become simply tourist attractions. Similarly, a hermeneutics that regarded understanding as reconstructing the original would be no more than handing on a dead meaning.

Hegel, in contrast, exemplifies another way of balancing out the profit and loss of the hermeneutical enterprise. He exhibits a clear grasp of the futility of restoration when he writes as follows of the decline of the classical world and its "religion of art": the works of the Muses "are now what they are for us—beautiful fruits torn from the tree. A friendly fate presents them to us as a girl might offer those fruits. We have not the real life of their being—the tree that bore them, the earth and elements, the climate that constituted their substance, the seasonal changes that governed their growth. Nor does fate give us, with those works of art, their world, the spring and summer of the moral life in which they bloomed and ripened but only the veiled memory of this reality."[86] And he calls the relationship of posterity to those works of art that have been handed down an "external activity" that "wipes spots of rain or dust from this fruit and instead of the internal elements of the surrounding, productive, and lifegiving reality of the moral world, it substitutes the elaborate structure of the dead elements of its external existence, of language, of its historical features and so forth. And this not in order to live within that reality but merely to represent it within oneself."[87] What Hegel is describing here is precisely what is involved in Schleiermacher's prescription for historical preservation, except that with Hegel there is a negative emphasis. The search for the occasional circumstances that would fill out the significance of works of art cannot succeed in reconstructing them. They remain fruit torn from the tree. Putting them back in their historical context does not give us a living relationship with them but rather a merely ideative representation (Vorstellung). Hegel does not deny the legitimacy of adopting a historical approach to the art of the past. On the contrary, he affirms the principle of art-historical research—but this, like any "historical" approach, is, in Hegel's eyes, an external activity.

In regard to history, including the history of art, the authentic task of the thinking mind is not, according to Hegel, an external one, inasmuch as the mind would see itself represented in history in a higher way. Developing his image of the girl who offers the fruit torn from the tree, he writes: "But just as the girl who presents the plucked fruit is more than Nature that presented it in the first place with all its conditions and elements—trees, air, light, and so on—insofar as she combines all these in a higher way in the light of self-consciousness in her eyes and in her gestures, so also the spirit of destiny which gives us these works of art is greater than the ethical life and reality of a particular people, for it is the *interiorizing recollection* (Er-innerung) of the still *externalized* spirit manifest in them. It is the spirit of tragic fate that gathers all these individual gods and attributes of substance within one Pantheon, into spirit conscious of itself as spirit."

Here Hegel points beyond the entire dimension in which Schleiermacher conceived the problem of understanding. Hegel raises it to the level on which he has established philosophy as the highest form of absolute Mind. The self-consciousness of spirit that, as the text has it, comprehends the truth of art within itself "in a higher way," culminates in philosophy as absolute knowledge. For Hegel, then, it is philosophy, the historical self-penetration of spirit, that carries out the hermeneutical task. This is the most extreme counterposition to the self-forgetfulness of historical consciousness. In it the historical approach of ideative reconstruction is transformed into a thinking relation to the past. Here Hegel states a definite truth, inasmuch as the essential nature of the historical spirit consists not in the restoration of the past but in *thoughtful mediation with contemporary life*. Hegel is right when he does not conceive of such thoughtful mediation as an external relationship established after the fact but places it on the same level as the truth of art itself. In this way his idea of hermeneutics is fundamentally superior to Schleiermacher's. The question of the truth of art forces us, too, to undertake a critique of both aesthetic and historical consciousness, inasmuch as we are inquiring into the *truth* that manifests itself in art and history.

Notes

1 Aristotle, *Politics*, VIII, 3, 1337 b 39 and passim. Cf. *Nicomachean Ethics*, X, 6, 1176 b 33: *paizein hopos spoudaze kat' Anacharsin orthos echein dokei.*

2 Kurt Riezler, in his brilliant *Traktat vom Schönen*, started with the subjectivity of the player and hence preserved the antithesis of play and seriousness, so that the concept of play becomes too restricted for him and he has to say: "We doubt whether the play of children is only play" and "The play of art is not only play" (p. 189).

3 F. J. J. Buytendijk, *Wesen und Sinn des Spiels* (1933).

4 This obvious point must be made against those who seek to criticize the truth of Heidegger's statements because of his etymological manner of proceeding.

5 Cf. J. Trier, *Beiträge zur Geschichte der deutschen Sprache und Literatur*, 67 (1947).

6 Johann Huizinga (*Homo Ludens: Vom Ursprung der Kultur im Spiel*, rev. German tr., p.43) points out the following linguistic facts: "One can certainly say in German *ein Spiel treiben* ['to play a game'] and in Dutch *een spelletje doen*, but the appropriate verb is really *spielen* ['to play'] itself. *Man spielt ein Spiel* ['one plays a game']. In other words, in order to express the kind of activity, the idea contained in the noun must be repeated in the verb. That means, it seems, that the action is of such a particular and independent kind that it is different from the usual kinds of activity. Playing is not an activity in the usual sense." Similarly, the phrase *ein Spielchen machen* ["to take a hand"] describes a use of one's time that is by no means play.

7 Huizinga, op. cit., p.32. [See also my "On the Problem of Self-Understanding" (1962), in *Philosophical Hermeneutics*, tr. David E. Linge (Berkeley: University of California Press, 1976), pp. 44–58; and "Man and Language," in the same vol.,

pp. 59–68, esp. pp. 66ff.]

8 Rilke writes in the fifth Duino Elegy: "wo sich das reine Zuwenig unbegreiflich verwandelt—urnspringt in jenes leere Zuviel" ("where the sheer dearth is incomprehensibly transformed—switches into that void excess").

9 Friedrich Schlegel, "Gespräch über die Poesie," *Friedrich Schlegels Jugend- schriften*, ed. J. Minor (1882), II, 364. [In the new critical edition of Schlegel, ed. E. Behler, see Part I, vol. 2, ed. Hans Eichner, pp. 284–351, and p.324 for this citation.]

10 F. G. Jünger, *Die Spiele*.

11 Huizinga, op. cit., p.17.

12 In numerous writings, Adolf Portmann has made this criticism and given a new basis to the legitimacy of the morphological approach.

13 Cf. Rudolf Kassner, *Zahl und Gesicht*, pp. 161f. Kassner states that "the extraordinary unity and duality of child and doll" is connected with the fact that the fourth "open wall of the audience" (as in a religious rite) is missing. I am arguing the other way around—that it is precisely this fourth wall of the audience that closes the play world of the *work of art*.

14 See preceding n.

15 I am making use here of the classical distinction by which Aristotle separates *poiesis* from *praxis* (*Eudemian Ethics*, II, 1; *Nicomachean Ethics*, I, 1).

16 Plato, *Philebus*, 50b.

17 Cf. Koller, *Mimesis* (1954), which proves the original connection between *mimesis* and dance.

18 Aristotle, *Poetics*, 4, esp. 1448 b 16: "inferring what each thing is, for example that this is so-and-so."

19 Ibid., 1448 b 10.

20 Kant, *KdU*, §8.

21 [Aristotle, *Poetics*, 4, 1448 b 10f.]

22 Plato, *Phaedo*, 73ff.

23 [See H. Kuhn, *Sokrates: Versuch über den Ursprung der Metaphysik* (Berlin, 1934).]

24 Plato, *Republic*, X. [See my "Plato and the Poets" (1934), in *Dialogue and Dialectic: Eight Hermeneutical Studies on Plato*, tr. P. Christopher Smith (New Haven: Yale University Press, 1980), pp. 39–72.]

25 Aristotle, *Poetics*, 9, 1451 b 6.

26 Anna Tumarkin has been able to show very clearly in the aesthetics of the eighteenth century the transition from "imitation" to "expression." See her contribution to the *Festschrift für Samuel Singer* (1930). [See W. Beierwaltes on Marsilio Ficino in the *Sitzungsberichte der Heidelberger Akademie der Wissenschaft*, 11 (1980). The Neoplatonic concept of *ektyposis* led into the notion of "self- expression," for instance, in Petrarch. See below pp. 330, 462, and Appendix VI.]

27 It is a problem of a special kind whether the formative process itself should not be seen as already constituting an aesthetic reflection on the work. It is undeniable that when he considers the idea of his work the creator can ponder and critically compare and judge various possibilities of carrying it out. But this sober clarity which is part of creation itself seems to be something very different from the aesthetic reflection and aesthetic criticism, which the work itself is capable of stimulating. It may be that what was the object of the creator's reflection, i.e., the possibilities of form, can also be the starting point of aesthetic criticism. But even in the case of this kind of agreement in content between creative and critical reflection, the criterion is different. Aesthetic criticism is based on the disturbance of unified understanding, whereas the aesthetic reflection of the creator is directed toward establishing precisely this unity of the work. Later, we shall see the hermeneutical consequences of this point.

It still seems to me a vestige of the false psychologism that stems from the aesthetics of taste and genius if one makes the processes of production and reproduction coincide in the idea. This is to fail to appreciate that the success of a work has the character of an event, which goes beyond the subjectivity both of the creator and of the spectator or listener.

28 Although I think his analyses on the "schematism" of the literary work of art have been too little noted, I cannot agree when Roman Ingarden (in his "Bemerkungen zum Problem des ästhetischen Werturteils," *Rivista di Estetica* [1959]) sees in the process of the concretization of an "aesthetic object" the area of the aesthetic evaluation of the work of art. The aesthetic object is not constituted in the aesthetic experience of grasping it, but the work of art itself is experienced in its aesthetic quality through the process of its concretization and creation. In this I agree fully with Luigi Pareyson's aesthetics of *"formativita."*

29 This is not limited to the interpretive arts, but includes any work of art—in fact any meaningful structure—that is raised to a new understanding, as we shall see further on. [Pp. 161ff. discuss the borderline position of literature and thereby bring out the universal significance of "reading" as the temporal constitution of meaning. See my "Zwischen Phänomenologie und Dialektik: Versuch einer Selbstkritik," *GW*, II, 3ff.]

30 [Hans Robert Jauss' "aesthetics of reception" has seized on this point of view, but so overemphasized it that he comes close to Derrida's "deconstruction," contrary to his own wish. See my "Text and Interpretation," tr. Dennis Schmidt, and *"Destruktion* and Deconstruction," tr. Geoff Waite, in *The Gadamer-Derrida Encounter: Texts and Comments*, ed. Diane Michelfelder and Richard Palmer (Albany: SUNY Press, 1988), to which I also refer in "Zwischen Phänomenologie und Dialektik: Versuch einer Selbstkritik," *GW*, II, 3ff.]

31 Hans Sedlmayr, *Kunst und Wahrheit* (rev. ed., 1958), pp. 140ff.

32 For the following, compare the fine analyses by R. and G. Koebner, *Vom Schönen und seiner Wahrheit* (1957), which I came across only when my own work was completed. Cf. the review in the *Philosophische Rundschau*, 7 (1963), 79. [Now see my "Concerning Empty and Ful-filled Time," tr. R. P. O'Hara, in *Martin Heidegger in Europe and America*, ed. E. G. Ballard and C. E. Scott (The Hague: Martinus Nijhoff, 1973), pp. 77–89; "Die Zeitanschauung des Abendlandes," *Kleine Schriften*, IV, 17–33 (*GW*, IV; an earlier version of this essay was translated as "The Western View of the Inner Experience of Time and the Limits of Thought," in *Time and the Philosophies* (Paris: UNESCO, 1977), pp. 33–48); "Die Kunst des Feierns," in *Was der Mensch braucht*, ed. J. Schultz (Stuttgart, 1977), pp. 61–70; and "The Relevance of the Beautiful," in *The Relevance of the Beautiful and Other Essays*, tr. Nicholas Walker (Cambridge: Cambridge University Press, 1986), pp. 3–53.]

33 Walter F. Otto and Karl Kerényi have noted the importance of the festival for the history of religions and anthropology (cf. Karl Kerényi, "Vom Wesen des Festes," *Paideuma* [1938]). [Now see my "The Relevance of the Beautiful" and "Die Kunst des Feierns," cited in n. 321 preceding.]

34 Aristotle refers to the characteristic mode of being of the *apeiron*, for instance in his discussion with reference to Anaximander of the mode of being of the day and of Olympic games, and hence of the festival (*Physics*, III, 6, 206 a 20). Had Anaximander already sought to define the fact that the *apeiron* never came to an end in relation to such pure time phenomena? Did he perhaps have in mind more than can be comprised in the Aristotelian concepts of becoming and being? For the image of the day recurs with a key function in another context: in Plato's *Parmenides*, 131b, Socrates seeks to demonstrate the relation of the idea to things in terms of the presence of the *day*, which exists for all. Here by means of the nature of the day, there is demonstrated not what exists only as it passes away, but the indivisible presence and *parousia* of something that remains the *same*, despite the fact that the day is everywhere different. When the early thinkers thought of being, i.e., presence, did that which was present for them appear in the light of a sacral communion in which the divine shows itself? For Aristotle, the *parousia* of the divine is still the most authentic being, *energeia* which is limited by no *dunamei* (*Metaphysics*, XII, 7). The character of this time cannot be grasped in terms of the usual temporal experience of succession. The dimension of time and its experience permit us to see the return of the festival only as something historical: something that is one and the same changes from time to time. But in fact a festival is not one and the same thing; it exists by being always something different. An entity that exists only in always being something else is temporal in a radical sense; it has its being in becoming. On the ontological character of the "while" (*Weile*), see Martin Heidegger, *Holzwege*, pp. 322ff. [On this same

problem, I have discussed the connection of Heraclitus with Plato in "Vom Anfang bei Heraklit," *GW*, VI, 232–41, and "Heraklit-Studien," *GW*, VII.]

35 [On the concept of "theory," see my "Lob der Theorie," in *Lob der Theorie* (Frankfurt: Suhrkamp, 1983), pp. 26–50.]

36 On the relationship between "*Sein*" and "*Denken*" in Parmenides, see my "Zur Vorgeschichte der Metaphysik," in *Anteile: Martin Heidegger zum 60. Geburtstag* (Frankfurt: Vittorio Klostermann, 1950), pp. 51–79. [*GW*, VI, 9–29.]

37 Cf. what was said above on pp. 8ff. about culture, formation (*Bildung*).

38 Cf. Gerhard Krüger, *Einsicht und Leidenschaft: Das Wesen des platonischen Denkens* (1st ed., 1940). The "Introduction" in particular contains important insights. Since then a published lecture by Krüger, "Grundfragen der Philosophie" (1958), has made his systematic intentions even clearer. Hence we may offer a few observations on what he says. His criticism of modern thinking and its emancipation from all connections with "ontic truth" seems to me without foundation. That modern science, however it may proceed as something constructed, has never abandoned and never can abandon its fundamental connection with experiment and hence with experience, modern philosophy has never been able to forget. One only has to think of Kant's question of how a pure natural science would be possible. But one is also very unfair to speculative idealism if one understands it in the one-sided way that Krüger does. Its construction of the totality of all determinants of thought is by no means the thinking out of some arbitrary view of the world, but desires to bring into thinking the absolute *a posteriori* character of experience, including experiment. This is the exact sense of transcendental reflection. The example of Hegel can teach us that even the renewal of classical conceptual realism can be attempted by its aid. Krüger's view of modern thought is based entirely on the desperate extremism of Nietzsche. However, the perspectivism of the latter's "will-to-power" is not in agreement with idealistic philosophy but, on the contrary, has grown up on the soil which nineteenth century historicism had prepared after the collapse of idealist philosophy. Hence I am not able to give the same value as Krüger to Dilthey's theory of knowledge in the human sciences. Rather, the important thing, in my view, is to correct the philosophical interpretation of the modern human sciences, which even in Dilthey proves to be too dominated by the one-sided methodological thinking of the exact natural sciences. [See my "Wilhelm Dilthey nach 150 Jahren," *Phänomenologische Forschungen*, 16 (1984), 157–82 (*GW*, IV); my lecture to the Dilthey congress (Madrid, 1983), "Dilthey und Ortega: Ein Kapitel europäischer Geistesgeschichte," *GW*, IV; and my lecture to the Dilthey congress (Rome, 1983), "Zwischen Romantik und Positivismus," *GW*, IV.] I certainly agree with Krüger when he appeals to the experience of life and the experience of the artist. But the continuing validity of these for our thinking

seems to show that the contrast between classical thought and modern thought, which Krüger draws very sharply, is itself a modern construction.

If we are reflecting on the experience of art—as opposed to the subjectivization of philosophical aesthetics—we are not aiming simply at a question of aesthetics, but at an adequate self-interpretation of modern thought in general, which has more in it than the modern concept of method recognizes.

39 Eugen Fink has tried to clarify the meaning of man's being outside himself in enthusiasm by making a distinction which is obviously inspired by Plato's *Phaedrus*. But whereas in Plato the counterideal of pure rationality makes his distinction into one between good and bad madness, Fink lacks a corresponding criterion when he contrasts "purely human rapture" with that enthusiasm by which man is in God. For ultimately "purely human rapture" is also a being away from oneself and an involvement with something else of which man is "incapable," but which comes over him, and thus seems to me indistinguishable from enthusiasm. That there is a kind of rapture which it is in man's power to induce and that by contrast enthusiasm is the experience of a superior power which simply overwhelms us: these distinctions of control over oneself and of being overwhelmed are themselves conceived in terms of power and therefore do not do justice to the interpenetration of being outside oneself and being involved with something, which is the case in every form of rapture and enthusiasm. The forms of "purely human rapture" described by Fink are themselves, if only they are not narcissistically and psychologically misinterpreted, modes of the "finite self-transcendence of finiteness" (cf. Eugen Fink, *Vom Wesen des Enthusiasmus*, esp. pp. 22–25).

40 Kierkegaard, *Philosophical Fragments*, ch. 4, and elsewhere.

41 Richard Hamann, *Ästhetik*, p.97: "Hence the tragic has nothing to do with aesthetics"; Max Scheler, *Vom Umsturz der Werte*, "Zum Phänomen des Tragischen": "It is even doubtful whether the tragic is an essentially 'aesthetic' phenomenon." For the meaning of the word "tragedy," see Emil Staiger, *Die Kunst der Interpretation*, pp. 132ff.

42 Aristotle, *Poetics*, 13, 1453 a 29.

43 Kierkegaard, *Either-Or*, 1.

44 Max Kommerell, *Lessing und Aristoteles*, has described this history of pity, but not distinguished it sufficiently from the original sense of *eleos*. Cf. also W. Schadewaldt, "Furcht und Mitleid?" *Hermes*, 83 (1955), 129ff., and the supplementary article by H. Flashar, *Hermes*, 84 (1956), 12–48.

45 Aristotle, *Rhetoric*, II, 13, 1389 b 32.

46 Cf. Max Kommerell, who gives an account of the older interpretations: op. cit., pp. 262–72. There have also been those who defend the objective genitive, e.g., K. H. Volkmann-Schluck in "Varia Variorum," in *Festschrift* for Karl Reinhardt (1952).

47 Kierkegaard, *Either-Or*, I (German tr. Diederichs), p.133. [See the new edition by E. Hirsch, I, part I, 1, pp. 157ff.]

48 Ibid., pp. 139ff.

49 Aristotle, *Poetics* 4, 1448 b 18: " . . . but by virtue of its workmanship or its finish or some other cause of that kind" (tr. Else)—in opposition to the "recognition" of what is imitated (*mimema*).

50 [See now G. Boehm, "Zu einer Hermeneutik des Bildes," in *Die Hermeneutik und die Wissenschaften*, ed. H.–G. Gadamer and G. Boehm (Frankfurt, 1978), pp. 444–71, and my "Von Bauten und Bildern," in the *Festschrift* for Imdahl (1986).]

51 I acknowledge the valuable confirmation and help I received from a discussion that I had with Wolfgang Schöne at the conference of art historians of the evangelical academies (Christophorus-Stift) in Münster in 1956.

52 Cf. *Nicomachean Ethics*, II, 5, 1106 b 10.

53 Dagobert Frey uses this expression in his essay in the *Festschrift* for Jantzen.

54 Cf. W. Paatz, "Von den Gattungen und vom Sinn der gotischen Rundfigur," *Abhandlungen der Heidelberger Akademie der Wissenschaften* (1951), pp. 24f.

55 Cf. W. Weischedel, *Wirklichkeit und Wirklichkeiten* (1960), pp. 158ff.

56 It is not without reason that *zoon* also means simply "picture." We shall later have to test our results to see whether they have lost the connection with this model. Similarly, Bauch (see following n.) says of *imago*: "At any rate it is still a question of the picture in human form. This is the sole theme of medieval art!" (p. 132, n.)

57 Cf. the history of the concept of *imago* in the transition from antiquity to the Middle Ages, in Kurt Bauch, *Beiträge zur Philosophie und Wissenschaft: W. Szilasi zum 70. Geburtstag*, pp. 9–28.

58 Cf. John Damascene, according to Campenhausen, *Zeitschrift für Theologie und Kirche* (1952), pp. 54f., and Hubert Schrade, *Der Verborgene Gott* (1949), p.23.

59 The history of this word is very informative. The Romans used it, but in the light of the Christian idea of the incarnation and the mystical body it acquired a completely new meaning. Representation now no longer means "copy" or "representation in a picture," or "rendering" in the business sense of paying the price of something, but "replacement," as when someone "represents" another person. The word can obviously have this meaning because what is represented is present in the copy. *Repraesentare* means "to make present." Canon law used this word in the sense of legal representation. Nicholas of Cusa used it in this sense and gave both to it and the concept of the image a new systematic account. Cf. G. Kallen, "Die politische Theorie im philosophischen System des Nikolaus von Cues," *Historische Zeitschrift*, 165 (1942), 275ff., and his notes on *De auctoritate presidendi, Sitzungsberichte der Heidelberger Akademie, phil.–hist. Klasse* (1935/36), no. 3, 64ff. The important thing about

the legal idea of representation is that the *persona repraesentata* is only the person represented, and yet the representative, who is exercising the former's rights, is *dependent* on him. It is curious that this legal sense of *repraesentatio* does not appear to have played any part in the prehistory of Leibniz's concept of representation. Rather, Leibniz's profound metaphysical theory of the *repraesentatio universi* which exists in every monad obviously follows the mathematical use of the idea. Thus *repraesentatio* here obviously means the mathematical "expression" for something, the unambiguous orientation toward something else. The development into the subjective sphere, which is obvious in our concept of *Vorstellung*, originated in the subjectivization of the concept of "idea" in the seventeenth century, with Malebranche influencing Leibniz. Cf. Dietrich Mahnke, *Jahrbuch für Philosophie und phänomenologische Forschung*, 7 (1925), 519ff., 589ff. *Repraesentatio* in the sense of "representation" on the stage—which in the Middle Ages can only mean in a religious play—can already be found in the thirteenth and fourteenth centuries, as E. Wolf shows in his "Die Terminologie des mittelalterlichen Dramas," *Anglia*, 78 (1960), 1–27. But this does not mean that *repraesentatio* signifies "performance," but up until the seventeenth century, it means the represented presence of the divine itself, which takes place in the liturgical performance. Thus here also, as with its use in canon and secular law, the recasting of the classical Latin word is based on the new theological understanding of church and ritual. The application of the word to the play itself—instead of what is represented in it—is an entirely secondary event, which presupposes the detachment of the theater from its liturgical function.

[Meanwhile, for the history of the concept of "representation" in the law, see the comprehensive work of Hasso Hofmann, *Repräsentation: Studien zur Wortund Begriffsgeschichte von der Antike bis ins 19. Jahrhundert* (Berlin, 1974).]

60 The constitutional concept of representation here receives a special inflection. It is clear that the meaning of representation determined by it always refers basically to a representative presence. It is only because the bearer of a public function—the ruler, the official, etc.—does not appear as a private individual when he makes an official appearance, but in his function, which he thus brings to representation, that one can say of him that he is representing.

61 On the productive variety of meanings that the word *Bild* has and on its historical background, cf. the observation on pp. 10f. above. That we no longer use the word *Urbild* ("original," "model") to mean "picture" is the late result of a nominalist understanding of being—as our analysis shows, this is an essential aspect of the "dialectic" of the image.

62 It seems to be established that *bilidi* in Old High German always has the primary meaning of "power" (cf. Kluge-Goetze s.v.).

63 Herodotus, *History*, II, 53.

64 Cf. Karl Barth, "Ludwig Feuerbach," in *Zwischen den Zeiten*, 5 (1927), 17ff.

65 I begin with this sense of occasionality, which has become customary in modern logic. A good example of how the aesthetics of experience discredited occasionality is the mutilation of Hölderlin's hymn "The Rhein" in the edition of 1826. The dedication to Sinclair seemed so alien that the last two stanzas were omitted and the whole described as a fragment.

66 Plato speaks of the proximity of the seemly (*prepon*) to the beautiful (*kalon*). *Greater Hippias*, 293e.

67 J. Bruns' valuable book *Das literarische Porträt bei den Griechen* suffers from lack of clarity on this point.

68 Cf. Appendix II below.

69 [On "reading," see my "Zwischen Phänomenologie und Dialektik: Versuch einer Selbstkritik," *GW*, II, 3ff. and my essays there cited.]

70 Cf. p.65 above.

71 Carl Justi, *Diego Velasquez und sein Jahrhundert*, I (1888), 366.

72 Cf. Friedrich Heer, *Der Aufgang Europas* (Vienna, 1949).

73 W. Kamlah in *Der Mensch in der Profanität* (1948) has tried to give the concept of the profane this meaning in order to characterize the nature of modern science, but also sees this concept as determined by its counterconcept, the "acceptance of the beautiful."

74 Above all in the first of Edmund Husserl's *Logical Investigations*, in Dilthey's studies on the *Aufbau der geschichtlichen Welt* (*Gesammelte Schriften*, VII) which are influenced by Husserl, and in Martin Heidegger's analysis of the "world-hood" of the world in *Being and Time* §§17 and 18.

75 I said above (p. 130) that the concept of a picture used here finds its historical fulfillment in the modern easel picture. Nevertheless, its "transcendental" application seems unobjectionable. If for historical purposes medieval representations have been distinguished from the later "picture" by being called *Bildzeichen* ("picture signs," Dagobert Frey), much that is said in the text of the "sign" is true of such representations, but still the difference between them and the mere sign is obvious. Picture signs are not a kind of sign, but a kind of picture.

76 Cf. above pp. 62–70, the distinction, in terms of the history of the two concepts, between "symbol" and "allegory."

77 [See my "Vom Lesen von Bauten und Bildern," in the *Festschrift* for H. Imdahl, ed. G. Boehm (Wurzburg, 1986).]

78 In his *Ästhetik*, p.201, Schleiermacher rightly stresses (as against Kant) that the art of gardening is not part of painting but of architecture. [On the topic of landscape vs. gardening, see J. Ritter, *Landschaft: Zur Funktion des Ästhetischen in der modernen Gesellschaft* (Münster, 1963), especially the erudite n. 61 to pp. 52ff.]

79 Kant, *KdU*, 1799, p.50 (§16, tr. Meredith, p.73).

80 Friedrich Nietzsche, *Also sprach Zarathustra: Ein Buch für alle und keinen* (A book for everyone and no one).

81 Roman Ingarden, in his *The Literary Work of Art* (1931), has given excellent analyses of the linguistic levels of literature and the mobility of intuitions that fill it out. But cf. n. 28 above. [Meanwhile, a series of studies on this topic has appeared. Cf. "Zwischen Phänomenologie und Dialektik: Versuch einer Selbstkritik," *GW*, II, and esp. "Text and Interpretation" in *The Gadamer-Derrida Encounter* (cited n. 30 above), as well as the essays forthcoming in *GW*, VIII.]

82 Goethe, "Kunst und Altertum," *Jubiläumsausgabe*, XXXVIII, 97, and the conversation with Eckermann of January 31, 1827.

83 Wilhelm Dilthey, *Gesammelte Schriften*, VII and VIII.

84 Ibid., V.

85 Schleiermacher, *Ästhetik*, ed. R. Odebrecht, pp. 84ff.

86 G. W. F. Hegel, *Phänomenologie des Geistes*, ed. Hoffmeister, p.524.

87 A remark in the *Aesthetik* (ed. Hotho, II, 233) indicates that merely to "accustom oneself gradually" to some outmoded state would not have been a solution for Hegel: "It is useless to appropriate substantially, as it were, the worldviews of the past, i.e., to attempt to settle within one of those views by, for instance, becoming a Catholic, as many have done in modern times for the sake of art and to achieve peace of mind. . . . "

PART TWO

The Extension of the Question of Truth to Understanding in the Human Sciences

---

*Qui non intelligit res, non potest
ex verbis sensum elicere.*

M. Luther

3
Historical Preparation

1 THE QUESTIONABLENESS OF ROMANTIC HERMENEUTICS AND ITS APPLICATION TO THE STUDY OF HISTORY

(A) THE CHANGE IN HERMENEUTICS FROM THE ENLIGHTENMENT TO ROMANTICISM

If we are to follow Hegel rather than Schleiermacher, the history of hermeneutics must place its emphases quite differently. Its culmination will no longer consist in historical understanding being liberated from all dogmatic bias, and we will no longer be able to view the rise of hermeneutics as Dilthey, following Schleiermacher, presented it. Rather, we must retrace Dilthey's steps and look out for goals other than those of Dilthey's historical self-consciousness. We will entirely disregard the dogmatic interest in the hermeneutical problem that the Old Testament already presented to the early church[1] and will be content to pursue the development of the hermeneutical method in the modern period, which culminates in the rise of historical consciousness.

(i) The Prehistory of Romantic Hermeneutics

The art or technique of understanding and interpretation developed from analogous impulses along two paths—theological and philological. Theological hermeneutics, as Dilthey showed,[2] developed from the reformers' defense of their own understanding of Scripture against the attack of the Tridentine theologians and their appeal to the indispensability of tradition; philological hermeneutics developed as instrumental to the humanist claim to revive classical literature. Both involve a rediscovery: a rediscovery of something that was not absolutely unknown, but whose meaning had become alien and inaccessible. Classical literature, though constantly present as material for humanistic education, had been completely absorbed within the Christian world. Similarly, the Bible was the church's sacred book and as such was constantly read, but the understanding of it was determined, and—as the reformers insisted—obscured, by the dogmatic tradition of the church. Both traditions are dealing with a foreign language and not with the scholar's universal language of the Latin Middle Ages, so studying the tradition in the original made it necessary to learn Greek and Hebrew as well as to purify Latin. By applying specialized techniques, hermeneutics claimed to reveal the original meaning of the texts in both traditions—humanistic literature and the Bible. It is of decisive importance that through Luther and Melanchthon the humanistic tradition was united with the reform.

Insofar as scriptural hermeneutics is regarded as the prehistory of the hermeneutics of the modern human sciences, it is based on the scriptural principle of the Reformation. Luther's position is more or less the following: Scripture is sui ipsius interpres.[3] We do not need tradition to achieve the proper understanding of Scripture, nor do we need an art of interpretation in the style of the ancient doctrine of the fourfold meaning of Scripture, but the Scripture has a univocal sense that can be derived from the text: the sensus literalis. The allegorical method in particular, which had formerly seemed indispensable for the dogmatic unity of scriptural doctrine, is now legitimate only where the allegorical intention is given in Scripture itself. Thus it is appropriate when dealing with the parables. The Old Testament, however, should not acquire its specifically Christian relevance through an allegorical interpretation. We must take it literally, and precisely by its being understood literally, and seen as the expression of the law superseded by the grace of Christ, the Old Testament acquires a Christian significance.

The literal meaning of Scripture, however, is not univocally intelligible in every place and at every moment. For the whole of Scripture guides the understanding of individual passages: and again this whole can be reached only through the cumulative understanding of individual passages. This circular relationship between the whole and the parts is not new. It was already known to classical rhetoric, which compares perfect speech with the organic body, with the relationship between head and limbs. Luther and his successors[4] transferred this image, familiar from classical rhetoric, to the process of understanding; and they developed the universal principle of textual interpretation that all the details of a text were to be understood from the contextus and from the scopus, the unified sense at which the whole aims.[5]

Insofar as Reformation theology relies on this principle in interpreting Scripture, it remains bound to a postulate that is itself based on a dogma, namely that the Bible is itself a unity. Judged from the eighteenth century's historical point of view, reformed theology is also dogmatic and excludes any sound individual interpretation of Scripture that takes account of the relative context of a text, its specific purpose, and its composition.

Indeed, reformed theology does not even seem to be consistent. By ultimately asserting the Protestant credal formulae as guides to the understanding of the unity of the Bible, it too supersedes the scriptural principle in favor of a rather brief Reformation tradition. This was the judgment not only of counter-Reformation theology but of Dilthey.[6] He glosses these contradictions in Protestant hermeneutics from the viewpoint of the full self-awareness of the historical sciences. We in turn will have to inquire whether this self-consciousness, precisely in regard to the theological meaning of scriptural exegesis, is really justified or whether the literary and hermeneutical principle of understanding texts in their own terms is not itself unsatisfactory and always in need of support from a generally unacknowledged dogmatic guideline.

We can ask this question today, however, after historical enlightenment has reached the full extent of its possibilities: Dilthey's studies on the origin of hermeneutics manifest a convincing logical coherence, given the modern concept of science. Hermeneutics had to rid itself one day of all its dogmatic limitations and become free to be itself, so that it could rise to the significance of a universal historical organon. This took place in the eighteenth century, when men like Semler and Ernesti realized that to understand Scripture properly it was necessary to recognize that it had various authors—i.e., to abandon the idea of the dogmatic unity of the canon. With this "liberation of interpretation from dogma" (Dilthey), the collection of the sacred Christian writings came to be seen as a collection of historical sources that, as written works, had to be subjected not only to grammatical but also to historical interpretation.[7] Understanding them in terms of their total context now necessarily also required the historical restitution of the living context to which the documents belong. The old interpretive principle of understanding the part in terms of the whole was no longer bound and limited to the dogmatic unity of the canon; it was concerned with the totality of the historical reality to which each individual historical document belonged.

And since there is no longer any difference between interpreting sacred or secular writings, and since there is therefore only *one* hermeneutics, this hermeneutics has ultimately not only the propaedeutic function of all historical research—as the art of the correct interpretation of literary sources—but involves the whole business of historical research itself. For what is true of the written sources, that every sentence in them can be understood only on the basis of its context, is also true of their content. Its meaning is not fixed. The context of world history—in which appears the true meaning of the individual objects, large or small, of historical research—is itself a whole, in terms of which the meaning of every particular is to be fully understood, and which in turn can be fully understood only in terms of these particulars. World history is, as it were, the great dark book, the collected work of the human spirit, written in the languages of the past, whose texts it is our task to understand. Historical research conceives itself on the model of philology. We will see that this is, in fact, the model on which Dilthey founded the historical view of the world.

In Dilthey's eyes, then, hermeneutics comes into its own only when it ceases serving a dogmatic purpose—which, for the Christian theologian, is the right proclamation of the gospel—and begins functioning as a historical organon. If, however, the ideal of the historical enlightenment that Dilthey pursued should prove to be an illusion, then the prehistory of hermeneutics that he outlined will also acquire a quite different significance. Its evolution to historical consciousness would not then be its liberation from the chains of dogma but a transformation of its nature. Precisely the same thing is true of philological hermeneutics. For the ars critica of philology unreflectively presupposed the exemplariness of classical antiquity, which it helped to hand down. It, too, had to change its nature when there was no longer any clear relation of model to copy between classical antiquity and the present. That this is the case is shown by the querelle des anciens et des modernes, which sounds the general theme for the whole period from French classicism to the German classical period. This problem resulted in the development of historical reflection, which finally demolished classical antiquity's claim to be normative. In the case of both literary criticism and theology, then, the same process led ultimately to the conception of a universal hermeneutics for which the special exemplariness of tradition is no longer a presupposition of the hermeneutical task.

Thus the science of hermeneutics—as developed by Schleiermacher in his debate with the philologists F. A. Wolf and F. Ast, and further elaborated in Ernesti's theological hermeneutics—is not, then, just one more stage in the history of the art of understanding. Actually, the history of understanding has been accompanied, since the days of classical philology, by theoretical reflection. But these reflections have the character of a "technique"—i.e., they try to serve the art of understanding, just as rhetoric tries to serve the art of speaking, and "poetics" the art and appreciation of poetry. In this sense both the theological hermeneutics of the fathers and that of the Reformation were techniques. But now understanding as such becomes a problem. The universality of this problem shows that understanding has become a task in a new sense, and hence theoretical reflection acquires a new significance. It is no longer a set of techniques guiding the practice of philologist or theologian. Schleiermacher, it is true, calls his hermeneutics a technique, but in a quite different, systematic sense. He seeks the theoretical foundation of the procedure common to theologians and philologists by reaching back beyond the concerns of each to the more fundamental relation—the understanding of thoughts.

It was different for the philologists who were his immediate predecessors. For them, hermeneutics was determined by the content of what was to be understood—and this was the self-evident unity of classical and Christian literature. Ast's goal for all hermeneutics, "to demonstrate the unity of Greek and Christian life," expresses what, basically, all "Christian humanists" think.[8] Schleiermacher, on the other hand, *no longer* seeks the unity of hermeneutics in the *unity of the content of tradition* to which understanding is applied, but rather he seeks it, apart from any particular content, in the unity of a procedure that is not differentiated even by the way the ideas are transmitted—whether in writing or orally, in a foreign language or in one's own. The effort to understand is needed wherever there is no immediate understanding—i.e., whenever the possibility of misunderstanding has to be reckoned with.

Schleiermacher's idea of a universal hermeneutics starts from this: that the experience of the alien and the possibility of misunderstanding is universal. It is true that this alienation is greater, and misunderstanding easier, in artistic than in non-artistic utterance, and it is greater with written than with oral utterance, which is, as it were, continuously interpreted by the living voice. But precisely Schleiermacher's extending the hermeneutical task to "meaningful dialogue," which is especially

179

characteristic of him, shows how fundamentally the meaning of alienation, which hermeneutics is supposed to overcome, has changed in
comparison to the task of hermeneutics as hitherto conceived. In a new
and universal sense, alienation is inextricably given with the individuality
of the Thou.

However we should not take the lively, even brilliant sense of human
individuality that characterizes Schleiermacher as an individual idiosyncrasy influencing his theory. Rather, through critique he rejected everything that, under the rubric of "rational ideas" (vernünftige Gedanken),
the Enlightenment regarded as the common nature of humanity, and this
rejection necessitated completely redefining our relation to tradition.[9] The
art of understanding came under fundamental theoretical examination
and universal cultivation because neither scripturally nor rationally
founded agreement could any longer constitute the dogmatic guideline of
textual understanding. Thus it was necessary for Schleiermacher to
provide a fundamental motivation for hermeneutical reflection and so
place the problem of hermeneutics within a hitherto unknown horizon.

To provide the right background for the genuine change that Schleiermacher makes in the history of hermeneutics, let us consider a point which
Schleiermacher himself does not and which, since Schleiermacher, has
totally disappeared from the sphere of hermeneutics (its absence curiously
narrows Dilthey's historical interest in the history of hermeneutics);
nevertheless, it in fact dominates the problem of hermeneutics and must
be taken into account if we are to understand Schleiermacher's place in its
history. We begin with this proposition: "to understand means to come to
an understanding with each other" (sich miteinander verstehen). Understanding is, primarily, agreement (Verständnis ist zunächst Einverständnis). Thus people usually understand (verstehen) each other immediately,
or they make themselves understood (verständigen sich) with a view
toward reaching agreement (Einverständnis). Coming to an understanding
(Verständigung), then, is always coming to an understanding about
something. Understanding each other (sich verstehen) is always understanding each other with respect to something. From language we learn
that the subject matter (Sache) is not merely an arbitrary object of
discussion, independent of the process of mutual understanding (Sichverstehen), but rather is the path and goal of mutual understanding itself. And
if two people understand each other independently of any topic, then this
means that they understand each other not only in this or that respect, but
in all the essential things that unite human beings. Understanding becomes

a special task only when natural life, this joint meaning of the meant where both intend a common *subject matter*, is disturbed. Where misunderstandings have arisen or where an expression of opinion alienates us because it is unintelligible, there natural life in the subject matter intended is impeded in such a way that the meaning is given as the opinion of another, the opinion of the Thou or of the text, or in general as a fixed datum. And even then in general one attempts to reach a substantive agreement—not just sympathetic understanding of the other person—and this in such a way that again one proceeds via the subject matter. Only if all these movements comprising the art of conversation—argument, question and answer, objection and refutation, which are undertaken in regard to a text as an inner dialogue of the soul seeking understanding —are in vain is the inquiry detoured. Only then does the effort of understanding become aware of the individuality of the Thou and take account of his *uniqueness*. If we are dealing with a foreign language, the text will already be the object of a grammatical, linguistic interpretation, but that is only a preliminary condition. The real problem of understanding obviously arises when, in the endeavor to understand the content of what is said, the reflective question arises: how did he come to such an opinion? For this kind of question reveals an alienness that is clearly of a quite different kind and ultimately signifies a renunciation of shared meaning.

Spinoza's critique of the Bible is a good example of this (and at the same time one of the earliest). In Chapter 7 of the *Tractatus theologico-politicus* Spinoza elaborates his method of interpreting Scripture by analogy to the interpretation of nature: we have to derive the meaning (mens) of the authors from historical data, since things are related in these books (stories of miracles and revelations) that cannot be derived from the principles known to us by natural reason. Independently of the fact that Scripture on the whole undoubtedly has a moral significance, in these matters which are, in themselves, incomprehensible (imperceptibiles), everything important can be understood if only we understand the mind of the author "historically"—i.e., overcome our prejudices and think of nothing but what the author could have had in mind.

Historical interpretation "in the spirit of the writer" is necessary, then, because of the hieroglyphic and incomprehensible nature of the contents. In interpreting Euclid, says Spinoza, no one pays any heed to the life, studies, and habits (vita, studium et mores) of that author,[10] and this is true also for the spirit of the Bible in moral matters (circa documenta moralia). Only because there are incomprehensible things (res imperceptibiles) in the stories of the Bible does our understanding of them depend on our being able to derive the author's meaning from the whole of his work (ut mentem auctoris percipiamus). And here, in fact, it does not matter whether what is meant corresponds to our insight since we want to know only the meaning of the statements (sensus orationum) but not their truth (veritas). For this we need to exclude all prepossessions, even those of reason (and, of course, especially those generated by our prejudices).

Thus the "naturalness" of the understanding of Scripture depends on the fact that what makes sense can be understood at sight, and what does not can be understood "historically." The breakdown of the immediate understanding of things in their truth is the motive for the detour into history. What this formulation of the interpretative principle means for Spinoza's own relationship to scriptural tradition is a separate question. In any case, for Spinoza, the *extent* of what can be understood only in this historical way is very great, even if the spirit of the whole (quod ipsa veram virtutem doceat—it teaches true virtue) is clear and what is clear is of overwhelming *significance*.

If we go back to the prehistory of historical hermeneutics in this way, the first thing to be noted is that there is a close correspondence between philology and natural science in their early visions of themselves. That has two implications. On the one hand, "natural" scientific procedure is supposed to apply to one's approach to scriptural tradition as well, and is supported by the historical method. But on the other hand, just as naturalness in the art of philology means understanding from a context, so naturalness in the investigation of nature means deciphering the "book of nature."[11] To this extent scientific method is based on the model of *philology*.

This is reflected in the fact that the enemy against which the new science of nature has to assert itself is the knowledge gained from Scripture and authorities. By contrast, the essence of the new science consists in its special methodology, which leads through mathematics and reason to an insight into what is intelligible in itself.

The historical critique of Scripture that emerges fully in the eighteenth century has its dogmatic basis, as our brief look at Spinoza has shown, in the Enlightenment's faith in reason. In a similar way other forerunners of historical thinking—among whom there were, in the eighteenth century, many now long forgotten names—have tried to give guidelines for understanding and interpreting historical books. Among them *Chladenius*[12] has been singled out as a precursor of romantic hermeneutics,[13] and in fact we find in him the interesting concept of "point of view," which explains "why we see a thing in one way and not in another," a concept from optics, which the author explicitly borrows from Leibniz.

However, as we learn from the title of his work, Chladenius is basically put in a false light if we see his hermeneutics as an early form of historical methodology. It is not just that for him "interpreting historical books" is not at all most important—in every case the substantive content of the writings is the important thing—but basically the whole problem of interpretation appears to him as pedagogical and *occasional*. Interpretation is explicitly concerned with "rational discourses and writings." For him, interpretation means "adducing those ideas that are necessary for the perfect understanding of a passage." Thus interpretation does not serve "to indicate the true understanding of a passage"; rather, it is expressly intended to remove obscurities in texts that hinder the student from achieving "full understanding" (preface). In interpretation one must accommodate oneself to the insight of the student (§102).

Thus, for Chladenius, understanding and interpretation are not the same thing (§648). Clearly it is quite exceptional for a passage to require interpretation; in general, a passage is immediately understood when one is familiar with the subject matter it deals with, whether one is reminded of it by the passage or one comes to know it only through the passage (§682). Undoubtedly the important thing for *understanding* here is still understanding the subject matter, the substantive insight. It is neither a historical nor a psychological genetic procedure.

Nevertheless, the author is quite certain that the art of interpretation has acquired a new and special urgency, inasmuch as the art of interpretation is what legitimates the interpretation. Such an art is obviously not necessary as long as "the student has the same knowledge as the interpreter" (so that "what is to be understood" is clear without needing to be demonstrated) or "because of the trust he places in the interpreter." Neither condition seems to Chladenius to be fulfilled in his own time; the latter insofar as (in the spirit of the Enlightenment) "the students want to see with their own eyes," the former insofar as with the growth of knowledge—i.e., with the advance of science—the obscurity of the passages to be understood grows ever greater (§668f.). Thus the need for a hermeneutics is given precisely with the decline of self-evident understanding.

In this way the fact that interpretation is impelled by the occasion finally exhibits its fundamental significance. Chladenius reaches a highly interesting conclusion. He sees that to understand an author perfectly is not the same thing as to understand speech or writing perfectly (§86). The norm for understanding a book is not the author's meaning. For, "since men cannot be aware of everything, their words, speech and writing can mean something that they themselves did not intend to say or write," and consequently "when trying to understand their writings, one can rightly think of things that had not occurred to the writers."

Even if the reverse is the case, "that an author meant more than one has been able to understand," for Chladenius the real task of hermeneutics is not to understand this "more," but to understand the true meaning of the books themselves (i.e., their content). Because "all men's books and speech have something incomprehensible about them"—namely obscurities due to our insufficient knowledge about the subject matter—correct interpretation is necessary: "unfruitful passages can become fruitful for us," since they "give rise to many thoughts."

It should be noted that in making all these observations Chladenius is not considering edifying exegesis of Scripture; he explicitly disregards the "sacred writings," for which the "philosophical art of interpretation" is only a preliminary. Nor is he attempting to legitimize everything that can be thought (every "application") as part of the meaning of a book, but only what corresponds to the intentions of the writer. But for him this clearly does not imply a historical or psychological limitation; it refers to a correspondence with respect to the subject matter, which, as he states explicitly, exegetically takes account of recent theology.[14]

(ii) Schleiermacher's Project of a Universal Hermeneutics

As we see, the prehistory of nineteenth-century hermeneutics looks very different if we no longer view it with Dilthey's preconceptions. What a gulf lies between Spinoza and Chladenius on the one hand and Schleiermacher on the other! Unintelligibility, which for Spinoza motivates the detour via the historical and for Chladenius involves the art of interpretation in the sense of being directed entirely towards the subject matter, has for Schleiermacher a completely different, universal significance.

The first interesting difference, as I see it, is that Schleiermacher speaks not so much of lack of understanding as of misunderstanding. What he has in mind is no longer the pedagogical function of interpretation as an aid to the other's (the student's) understanding; for him interpretation and understanding are closely interwoven, like the outer and the inner word, and every problem of interpretation is, in fact, a problem of understanding.[15] He is concerned solely with the subtilitas intelligendi, not with the subtilitas explicandi[16] (let alone applicatio).[17] But, most important, Schleiermacher explicitly distinguishes between a looser hermeneutical praxis, in which understanding follows automatically, and a stricter one that begins with the premise that what follows automatically is misunderstanding.[18] His particular achievement—which was to develop a real art of understanding instead of an "aggregate of observations"—is based on this distinction. This is something fundamentally new. For from now on we no longer consider the difficulties and failures of understanding as occasional but as integral elements that have to be prevented in advance. Thus Schleiermacher even defines hermeneutics as "the art of avoiding misunderstandings." It rises above the pedagogical occasionality of interpretation and acquires the independence of a method, inasmuch as "misunderstanding follows automatically and understanding must be desired and sought at every point."[19] The avoidance of misunderstanding: "all tasks are contained in this negative expression." Schleiermacher sees their positive solution as a canon of grammatical and psychological rules of interpretation, which even in the interpreter's consciousness are quite distinct from obligation to a dogmatic content.

Now Schleiermacher was undoubtedly not the first to limit the scope of hermeneutics to making intelligible what others have said in speech and text. The art of hermeneutics has never been the organon of the study of things. This distinguishes it at the outset from what Schleiermacher calls dialectic. But indirectly, wherever an attempt is made to understand something (e.g., Scripture or the classics), there is reference to the truth that lies hidden in the text and must be brought to light. What is to be understood is, in fact, not a thought considered as part of another's life, but as a truth. Precisely for this reason hermeneutics has an ancillary function and remains subordinate to the study of things. Schleiermacher takes account of this, insofar as he relates hermeneutics, within the system of sciences, to dialectics.

Nevertheless, the task he sets himself is precisely that of isolating the procedure of understanding. He endeavors to make it an independent method of its own. For Schleiermacher this also involves freeing himself from the limited tasks that constitute the nature of hermeneutics for his predecessors, Wolf and Ast. He does not accept its being restricted to foreign languages, or to the written word, "as if the same thing could not happen in conversation and in listening to a speech."[20]

This is more than an extension of the hermeneutical problem from understanding what is written to understanding discourse in general; it suggests a fundamental shift. What is to be understood is now not only the exact words and their objective meaning, but also the individuality of the speaker or author. Schleiermacher holds that the author can really be understood only by going back to the origin of the thought. What is for Spinoza a limiting case of intelligibility, and hence requires a detour via the historical, is for Schleiermacher the norm and the presupposition from which he develops his theory of understanding. What he finds "most neglected, and even largely ignored" is "understanding a succession of thoughts as an emerging element of life, as an act that is connected with many others, even of another kind."[21]

Thus beside grammatical interpretation he places psychological (technical) interpretation. This is his most characteristic contribution.[22] We will pass over Schleiermacher's brilliant comments on grammatical interpretation. They contain remarks on the role that the pre-given totality of language plays for the writer—and hence also for his interpreter—as well as remarks on the significance of the whole of a literature for an individual work. It may be, as seems probable from a recent investigation of Schleiermacher's unpublished texts,[23] that psychological interpretation only gradually came to dominate the development of his thought. At any rate, psychological interpretation became the main influence on the theorists of the nineteenth century—Savigny, Boeckh, Steinthal and, above all, Dilthey.

Even in the case of the Bible, where interpreting each writer in terms of his individual psychology is of less moment than the significance of what is dogmatically uniform and common to them,[24] Schleiermacher still regards the methodological distinction between philology and dogmatics as essential.[25] Hermeneutics includes grammatical and psychological interpretation. But Schleiermacher's particular contribution is psychological interpretation. It is ultimately a divinatory process, a placing of oneself within the whole framework of the author, an apprehension of the "inner origin" of the composition of a work,[26] a re-creation of the creative act. Thus understanding is a reproduction of an original production, a knowing of what has been known (Boeckh),[27] a reconstruction that starts from the vital moment of conception, the "germinal decision" as the composition's organizing center.[28]

Isolating understanding in this way, however, means that the structure of thought we are trying to understand as an utterance or as a text is not to be understood in terms of its subject matter but as an aesthetic construct, as a work of art or "artistic thought." If we keep this in mind, we will understand why what is at issue is not a relation to the subject matter (Schleiermacher's "being"). Schleiermacher is following Kant's definitions of the aesthetic when he says that "artistic thought can be differentiated only by greater or lesser pleasure" and is "properly only the momentaneous act of the subject."[29] Now, the precondition of there being an understanding at all is that this "artistic thought" is not a mere momentaneous act but expresses itself. Schleiermacher sees "artistic thoughts" as life moments that contain so much pleasure that they burst into utterance, but—however much pleasure they evoke in the "originals of artistic works"—even then they remain individual thought, a free construct that is not tied to being. This is precisely what distinguishes poetic from scientific texts.[30] By this, Schleiermacher undoubtedly means that poetic utterance is not subject to the already described criterion of agreement concerning the thing meant, because what is said in poetry cannot be separated from the way it is said. The Trojan War, for example, *exists* in Homer's poem—a person who is concerned with historical fact is no longer reading Homer as poetic discourse. No one would maintain that Homer's poem gained in artistic reality as a result of archaeologists' excavations. What is to be understood here is not a shared thought about some subject matter, but individual thought that by its very nature is a free construct and the free expression of an individual being.

But it is characteristic of Schleiermacher that he seeks this element of free production everywhere. He even differentiates kinds of dialogue in the same way when—in addition to "dialogue proper," which is concerned with the common search for meaning and is the original form of dialectics—he speaks of "free dialogue," which he ascribes to artistic thought. In free dialogue the content of the thoughts "is virtually ignored." Dialogue is nothing but the mutual stimulation of thought ("and has no other natural end than the gradual exhaustion of the process described"),[31] a kind of artistic creation in the reciprocation of communication.

Insofar as utterance is not merely an inner product of thought but also communication and has, as such, an external form, it is not simply the immediate manifestation of the thought but presupposes reflection. This is primarily true, of course, of what is fixed in writing and hence of all texts. They are always presentation through art.[32] But where speaking is an art, so is understanding. Thus all speech and all texts are basically related to the art of understanding, hermeneutics, and this explains the connection between rhetoric (which is a part of aesthetics) and hermeneutics; every act of understanding is for Schleiermacher the inverse of an act of speech, the reconstruction of a construction. Thus hermeneutics is a kind of inversion of rhetoric and poetics.

We may be somewhat surprised to find poetry linked in this way with the art of speaking,[33] for it seems to us precisely the distinction and dignity of poetry that in it language is not rhetoric—i.e., that it possesses a unity of meaning and form that is independent of any connection with rhetoric in the sense of addressing or persuading. However, Schleiermacher's conception of "artistic thought" (in which he includes poetry and rhetoric) is concerned not with the product but with the orientation of the subject. Thus eloquence is here regarded purely as art—i.e., disregarding any reference to purpose or fact—as an expression of a creative productivity. Of course the borderline between the artistic and the non-artistic is fluid, like that between artless (immediate) understanding and the understanding reached through an artful procedure. Insofar as this production takes place mechanically according to laws and rules and not through unconscious genius, the process of composition will be consciously reperformed by the interpreter; but if it is an individual, truly creative product of genius, then there can be no such re-creation according to rules. Genius itself creates models and rules. It creates new ways of using language, new literary forms. Schleiermacher is fully cognizant of this difference. In hermeneutics, what corresponds to the production of genius is divination, the immediate solution, which ultimately presupposes a kind of con-geniality. But the frontier between artless and artful, mechanical and genial production, is fluid insofar as an individuality is always being expressed and hence an element of rule-free genius is always at work—as with children, who grow into a language; it follows that the ultimate ground of all understanding must always be a divinatory act of con-geniality, the possibility of which depends on a pre-existing bond between all individuals.

This is, in fact, Schleiermacher's presupposition, namely that all individuality is a manifestation of universal life and hence "everyone carries a tiny bit of everyone else within him, so that divination is stimulated by comparison with oneself." Thus he can say that the individuality of the author can be directly grasped "by, as it were, transforming oneself into the other." Since Schleiermacher focuses understanding on the problem of individuality, the task of hermeneutics presents itself to him as universal.

For the extremes of alienness and familiarity are both given with the relative difference of all individuality. The "method" of understanding will be concerned equally with what is common, by comparison, and with what is unique, by intuition; it will be both comparative and divinatory. But in both respects it remains "art," because it cannot be turned into a mechanical application of rules. The divinatory remains indispensable.[34]

On the basis of this aesthetic metaphysics of individuality, the hermeneutical principles used by the philologist and the theologian undergo an important change. Schleiermacher follows Friedrich Ast and the whole hermeneutical and rhetorical tradition when he regards it as a fundamental principle of understanding that the meaning of the part can be discovered only from the context—i.e., ultimately from the whole. This is, of course, true of understanding any sentence grammatically as well as setting it within the context of the whole work, even of the whole of that literature or literary form concerned; but *Schleiermacher applies it to psychological understanding*, which necessarily understands every structure of thought as an element in the total context of a man's life.

It has always been known that this is a logically circular argument, insofar as the whole, in terms of which the part is to be understood, is not given before the part, unless in the manner of a dogmatic canon (as governs the Catholic and, as we saw, to some degree the Protestant understanding of Scripture) or of some analogous preconception of the spirit of an age (as, for example, when Ast presumes that retribution characterizes the spirit of the ancient world).

But Schleiermacher says that these dogmatic guidelines cannot claim any prior validity and hence are only relative limitations of the circularity. Fundamentally, understanding is always a movement in this kind of circle, which is why the repeated return from the whole to the parts, and vice versa, is essential. Moreover, this circle is constantly expanding, since the concept of the whole is relative, and being integrated in ever larger contexts always affects the understanding of the individual part. Schleiermacher applies his usual procedure of a polar dialectical description to hermeneutics, and thus he takes account of the fact that understanding is provisional and unending by elaborating it on the basis of the old hermeneutical principle of the whole and the parts. But he intends this characteristic speculative relativization more as a schema describing the process of understanding than as a fundamental principle. This is shown by the fact that he assumes something like complete understanding when

189

divinatory transposition takes place, "when all the individual elements at last suddenly seem to receive full illumination."

We might ask whether such phrases (which we also find in Boeckh with the same meaning) are to be taken strictly or as describing only a relative completeness of understanding. It is true that Schleiermacher saw individuality as a secret that can never be fully unlocked—as Wilhelm von Humboldt even more definitely did; but even this statement needs to be taken only in a relative way: the barrier to reason and understanding that remains here is not entirely insuperable. It is to be overcome by *feeling*, by an immediate, sympathetic, and con-genial understanding. Hermeneutics is an *art* and not a mechanical process. Thus it brings its work, understanding, to completion like a work of art.

Now, the limitation of this hermeneutics based on the concept of individuality can be seen in the fact that Schleiermacher does not find the task of literary or scriptural exegesis—i.e., of understanding a text written in a foreign language and coming from a past age—fundamentally more problematical than any other kind of understanding. It is true that, even according to Schleiermacher, there is a special task when a temporal distance has to be bridged. Schleiermacher calls it "identifying with the original reader." But this "process of identifying, the linguistic and historical production of sameness, is for him only an ideal precondition for the actual act of understanding, which for him does not consist in identifying with the original reader but in putting oneself on the same level as the author, whereby the text is revealed as a unique manifestation of the author's life. Schleiermacher's problem is not historical obscurity, but the obscurity of the Thou.

We may wonder, however, whether it is possible to distinguish in this way between identifying with the original reader and the process of understanding. Actually this ideal precondition of understanding—identifying with the original reader—cannot be fulfilled prior to the effort of understanding proper but rather is inextricable from it. Even in the case of a contemporary text with whose language or content we are unfamiliar, the meaning is revealed only in the manner described, in the oscillating movement between whole and part. Schleiermacher recognizes this. It is always in this movement that we learn to understand an unfamiliar meaning, a foreign language or a strange past. The circular movement is necessary because "nothing that needs interpretation can be understood at once."[35] For even within one's own language it is still true that the reader must completely assimilate both the author's vocabulary and, even more, the uniqueness of what he says. From these statements, which are found in Schleiermacher himself, it follows that identifying with the original reader is not a preliminary operation that can be detached from the actual effort of understanding, which Schleiermacher sees as identifying with the writer.

Let us examine more closely what Schleiermacher means by identification, for of course it cannot mean mere equation. Production and reproduction remain essentially distinct operations. Thus Schleiermacher asserts that the aim is *to understand a writer better than he understood himself,* a formula that has been repeated ever since; and in its changing interpretation the whole history of modern hermeneutics can be read. Indeed, this statement contains the whole problem of hermeneutics. It would be valuable, therefore, to go further into its meaning.

What it means for Schleiermacher is clear. He sees the act of understanding as the reconstruction of the production. This inevitably renders many things conscious of which the writer may be unconscious. It is obvious that here Schleiermacher is applying the aesthetics of genius to his universal hermeneutics. Creation by artistic genius is the model on which this theory of unconscious production and necessarily conscious reproduction is based.[36]

In fact the formula, understood in this way, can be regarded as a principle of all philology, insofar as the latter is regarded as the understanding of artful discourse. The better understanding that distinguishes the interpreter from the writer does not refer to the understanding of the text's subject matter but simply to the understanding of the text—i.e., of what the author meant and expressed. This understanding can be called "better" insofar as the explicit, thematized understanding of an opinion as opposed to actualizing its contents implies an increased knowledge. Thus the sentence says something almost self-evident. A person who learns to understand a text in a foreign language will make explicitly conscious the grammatical rules and literary forms which the author followed without noticing, because he lived in the language and in its means of artistic expression. The same is true of all production by artistic genius and its reception by others. We must remember this especially in regard to the interpretation of poetry. There too it is necessary to understand a poet better than he understood himself, for he did not "understand himself" at all when the structure of his text took shape within him.

From this also follows the point—which hermeneutics ought never to forget—that the artist who creates something is not the appointed interpreter of it. As an interpreter he has no automatic authority over the person who is simply receiving his work. Insofar as he reflects on his own work, he is his own reader. The meaning that he, as reader, gives his own work does not set the standard. The only standard of interpretation is the sense of his creation, what it "means."[37] Thus the idea of production by genius performs an important theoretical task, in that it collapses the distinction between interpreter and author. It legitimizes identification insofar as it is not the author's reflective self-interpretation but the unconscious meaning of the author that is to be understood. This is what Schleiermacher means by his paradoxical formula.

Since Schleiermacher others, including August Boeckh, Steinthal, and Dilthey, have repeated his formula in the same sense: "The philologist understands the speaker and poet better than he understands himself and better than his contemporaries understood him, for he brings clearly into consciousness what was actually, but only unconsciously, present in the other."[38] Through the "knowledge of psychological laws" the philologist, according to Steinthal, can deepen his understanding by grasping the causality, the genesis of the work of literature, and the mechanics of the writer's mind.

Steinthal's repetition of Schleiermacher's statement already betrays the effect of psychological research which takes research into nature as its model. Dilthey is freer here, because he more firmly preserves the connection with the aesthetics of genius. In particular, he applies the formula to the interpretation of poetry. To understand the "idea" of a poem from its "inner form" can of course be called "understanding it better." Dilthey regards this as the "highest triumph of hermeneutics,"[39] for the philosophical import of great poetry is revealed when it is understood as free creation. Free creation is not restricted by external conditions or by conditions of subject matter, and can therefore be grasped only as "inner form."

But we might ask whether this ideal case of "free creation" can really be taken as paradigmatic of the problem of hermeneutics; indeed, whether even the understanding of works of art can be satisfactorily conceived by this criterion. We must also ask whether the statement that the aim is to understand an author better than he understood himself still retains its original meaning when taken in conjunction with the presupposition of the aesthetics of genius, or whether it has not changed into something completely new.

In fact, Schleiermacher's formula is not new with him. Bollnow, who has investigated the subject,[40] quotes two places where this statement can be found before Schleiermacher, namely in Fichte[41] and in Kant.[42] He could not find any earlier instances. For this reason, Bollnow surmises that it was an oral tradition, a kind of philologist's rule of thumb that people passed on and Schleiermacher took up.

For both external and internal reasons this seems to me highly unlikely.[43] This sophisticated methodological formula, which is still often used today as a license for arbitrary interpretations and is accordingly attacked, does not seem consistent with the philological mind. As "humanists," they take pride in recognizing the absolute exemplariness of classical texts. For the true humanist, the classic author is certainly not such that the interpreter would claim to understand the work better than did the author himself. We must not forget that the highest aim of the humanist was not originally to "understand" his models, but to imitate or even surpass them. Hence he was originally obligated to his models, not only as an expositor but also as an imitator—if not a rival. Like the dogmatic bond to the Bible, the humanist's bond to the classics had to give way to a looser relationship, if the work of the interpreter was to reach the extreme self-conscious assurance expressed in the formula we are considering.

Hence it is likely that not until Schleiermacher—with whom hermeneutics became an independent method, detached from all content—could the interpreter claim superiority over his object. On closer examination, this accords with Kant and Fichte's use of the formula, for the context in which this alleged "philologist's rule of thumb" is employed shows that Fichte and Kant meant something quite different by it. With them it is not a principle of philology, but a philosophical claim to move beyond the contradictions of a given theory by achieving greater conceptual clarity. Thus it is a principle entirely in the spirit of rationalism; it claims, solely through thought, through elaborating the implications of an author's ideas, to achieve insights into the real intention of the author—insights he would have shared if his thinking had been clear enough. Even the hermeneutically impossible thesis in which Fichte involves himself in the polemic against the dominant interpretation of Kant—that "the inventor of a system is one thing, its expositors and followers another"[44]—as well as his claim to "interpret Kant according to the *spirit*"[45] are justified by the claim to critique the subject matter. Thus the disputed formula makes no claim beyond that of philosophic critique of the subject matter. Someone who is better able to think his way through what an author is talking about will be able to see what the author says in the light of a truth hidden from the author. In this sense the principle that one must understand an author better than he understands himself is a very old one, as old as scientific critique itself,[46] but it acquires its special pertinence to philosophical critique from the spirit of rationalism. As such it has a sense completely different from Schleiermacher's philological rule. It is likely that Schleiermacher reinterpreted this principle of philosophical critique and made it a principle of philological interpretation.[47] This would clearly indicate the position of Schleiermacher and the romantics. In creating a universal hermeneutics they expel critique based on understanding the subject matter from the sphere of scholarly interpretation.

Schleiermacher's formula, as he understands it, no longer pertains to the subject matter under discussion; rather, he views the statement a text makes as a free production, and disregards its content as knowledge. Accordingly he organizes hermeneutics, which for him is concerned with understanding everything cast in language, according to the normative example of language itself. The discourse of the individual is in fact a free creative activity, however much its possibilities are limited by the fixed forms that language has taken. Language is an expressive field, and its primacy in the field of hermeneutics means, for Schleiermacher, that as an interpreter he regards the texts, independently of their claim to truth, as purely expressive phenomena.

For him even history is simply the display of this free creation, that of a divine productivity, and he regards the historian's posture as the observation and enjoyment of this mighty spectacle. The entry in Schleiermacher's diary that Dilthey quotes[48] describes beautifully this romantic reflective enjoyment of history: "True historical significance rises above history. Phenomena exist, like miracles, only to direct our attention towards the Spirit that playfully generates them."

When we read this, we can see how tremendous was the step that led from Schleiermacher's hermeneutics to a universal understanding of the historical sciences. But however universal the hermeneutics that Schleiermacher evolved, it was a universality with very perceptible limits. His hermeneutics, in fact, had in mind texts whose authority was undisputed. Undoubtedly it is an important step in the development of historical consciousness that understanding and interpretation—of both the Bible and the literature of classical antiquity—was now completely detached from all dogmatic interest. Neither the saving truth of Scripture nor the exemplariness of the classics was to influence a procedure that was able to grasp every text as an expression of life and ignore the truth of what was said.

However, the interest that motivated Schleiermacher's methodological abstraction was not that of the historian but the theologian. He sought to teach how speech and a written tradition were to be understood, because theology was concerned with one particular tradition, the biblical. For this reason his hermeneutical theory was still a long way from a historiology that could serve as a methodological organon for the human sciences. Its goal was the exact understanding of particular texts, which was to be aided by the universality of historical contexts. This is Schleiermacher's limitation, and the historical worldview had to move beyond it.

(B) THE CONNECTION BETWEEN THE HISTORICAL SCHOOL AND ROMANTIC HERMENEUTICS

(i) The Dilemma Involved in the Ideal of Universal History

We must ask how historians understood their work in terms of their own hermeneutical theory. Their subject is not the individual text but *universal history*. It falls to the historian to understand the history of mankind as a whole. The individual text has no value in itself but serves only as a source—i.e., only as material conveying knowledge of the historical context, just like the other silent relics of the past. Hence the historical school could not really build on Schleiermacher's hermeneutics.[49]

But the historical worldview, which pursues the great goal of understanding universal history, had been based on the romantic theory of individuality and the corresponding hermeneutics. This can be put negatively by saying that what tradition represents for the present, namely the priority of history to life, had not yet been subjected to methodological reflection. Rather, historians saw their task as investigating tradition, and thus making the past available to the present. The basic scheme according to which the historical school conceives the methodology of universal history is therefore really the same methodology that applies to every text: the schema of whole and part. It certainly makes a difference whether one is trying to understand a text's intention and form as a literary structure or whether one is trying to use it as a document in investigating a larger historical context, concerning which it gives information that is to be examined critically. Nevertheless both literary and historical inquiry stress now the one and now the other approach. Historical interpretation, for example, can serve as a means to understand a given text even when, from another perspective, it sees the text simply as a source which is part of the totality of the historical tradition.

We find this expressed in clear methodological terms neither in Ranke nor in the acute methodologist Droysen, but for the first time in Dilthey, who consciously takes up romantic hermeneutics and expands it into a historical method—indeed into an epistemology of the human sciences. Dilthey's logical analysis of the concept of context and coherence in history, in fact, consists in applying to history the hermeneutical principle that we can understand a detail only in terms of the whole text, and the whole only in terms of the detail. It is not just that sources are texts, but historical reality itself is a text that has to be understood. But in thus *transposing hermeneutics to the study of history,* Dilthey is only the interpreter of the historical school. He is formulating what Ranke and Droysen really think.

So we see that romantic hermeneutics and its background, the pantheistic metaphysics of individuality, was a decisive influence on the theory of historical research in the nineteenth century. This was fatal for the human sciences and for the worldview of the historical school. We will see that Hegel's philosophy of world history, against which the historical school rebelled, recognized far more profoundly the importance of history for the being of spirit and the knowledge of truth than did the great historians, who would not admit that they were dependent on him. Schleiermacher's concept of individuality—which accorded so well with the concerns of theology, aesthetics, and literary criticism—was not only a means of critiquing the aprioristic construction of the philosophy of history; it also provided the historical sciences with a methodological orientation that directed them, no less than the natural sciences, toward research—i.e., to the only basis for progressive experience. Thus resistance to the philosophy of world history drove history into the wake of philology. Its pride was to conceive the continuity of world history not teleologically, nor in the style of pre– or postromantic enlightenment, in terms of a final state which would be the end of history, a day of judgment for world history, as it were. But for the historical school there exists neither an end of history nor anything outside it. Hence the whole continuity of universal history can be understood only from historical tradition itself. But this is precisely the claim of literary hermeneutics, namely that the meaning of a text can be understood from itself. *Thus the foundation for the study of history is hermeneutics.*

However, the ideal of universal history necessarily becomes a special problem for the historical worldview, since the book of history is a fragment that, so far as any particular present time is concerned, breaks off in the dark. The universal context of history lacks the self-containedness that a text has for the critic and that, for the historian, seems to make a biography—or the history of a nation that has exited from the stage of world history, or even the history of a period that is over and now lies behind us—into a complete unit of meaning, a text intelligible within itself.

We will see that Dilthey too thought in terms of these relative wholes and hence built his work entirely upon the basis of romantic hermeneutics. What has to be understood in both cases is a totality of meaning which, also in both cases, has the same detachment from the person understanding it. It is always an alien individuality that must be judged according to its own concepts and criteria of value, but can nevertheless be understood because I and Thou are of the same life.

The hermeneutical basis can support us thus far. But neither this detachment of the object from its interpreter nor the self-containedness of content in a totality of meaning can possibly support the task *specific* to the historian, universal history. For history is not only not at its end, but we its interpreters are situated within it, as a conditioned and finite link in a continuing chain. Given this problematical situation in regard to universal history, it would be reasonable to doubt that hermeneutics can really be the foundation for the study of history. Universal history is not a merely marginal and vestigial problem of historical investigation, but its very heart. Even the "historical school" knew that fundamentally there can be no other history than universal history, because the unique significance of the detail can be determined only from the whole. But since the whole can never be given to the empirical researcher, how can he maintain his ground against the philosopher and his a priori arbitrariness?

Let us consider first how the "historical school" tries to deal with this problem of universal history. For this we have to start further afield, although within the theoretical context presented by the historical school we are pursuing only the problem of universal history and hence are restricting ourselves to Ranke and Droysen.

We remember how the historical school distinguished itself from Hegel. Its birth certificate, as it were, is its rejection of the aprioristic construction of world history. Its new claim is that not speculative philosophy but only historical research can lead to a universal view of history.

It was Herder's critique of the Enlightenment's schema of the philosophy of history that made this development possible. Herder's attack on the Enlightenment's pride in reason had its most effective weapon in the exemplary character of classical antiquity, which Winckelmann, in particular, had proclaimed. The *History of Ancient Art* was obviously more than a historical account. It was a critique of the present and a program. But because of the ambiguity of any critique of the present, the proclamation of the exemplary character of Greek art, which was supposed to erect a new ideal for one's own present, was still a genuine step towards historical knowledge. The past, which is here offered as a model for the present, proves to be something that is unique and unrepeatable precisely because he is investigating the reasons for its peculiarity.

Herder went only a little beyond Winckelmann when he saw that in everything past there is a dialectical relationship between what is exemplary and what is unrepeatable. He could then set a universal historical worldview against the Enlightenment's teleological view of history. To think historically now means to acknowledge that each period has its own right to exist, its own perfection. Herder took this step. The historical worldview could not reach full development as long as classicist prejudices accorded a special, paradigmatic place to classical antiquity. For not only a teleology in the style of the Enlightenment's belief in reason, but also a reverse teleology that situates perfection in a past era or at the beginning of history, still posits a criterion that is beyond history.

There are many ways of conceiving history in terms of a criterion that lies beyond it. Wilhelm von Humboldt's classicism views history as the decline and fall of the perfection of Greek life. The gnostic theology of history of Goethe's time, whose influence on the young Ranke has been recently demonstrated,[50] conceives the future as the re-establishment of a lost perfection of some primal time. Hegel reconciled the aesthetic exemplariness of classical antiquity with the self-conscious assurance of the present, by describing the Greek religion of art as a form of the spirit that had been superseded and by proclaiming the perfect fulfillment of history in the present in the universal self-consciousness of freedom. All these are ways of conceiving history that invoke a criterion that lies outside history.

However, the denial of this kind of a priori, unhistorical criterion, which comes at the beginning of the historical inquiry of the nineteenth century, is not as free from metaphysical assumptions as it believes itself to be when it regards itself as scientific research. This can be seen by analyzing the leading concepts of the historical worldview. It is true that the purpose of these concepts is to avoid the preconceptions of an a priori historical construction; but although they are directed polemically against the idealistic concept of spirit, they remain related to it. This emerges very clearly in Dilthey's philosophical analysis of the historical worldview.

Its starting point is entirely determined by its antithesis to "philosophy of history." The basic assumption common to all these representatives of the historical worldview—Ranke, Droysen, and Dilthey—is that idea, essence, and freedom do not find any full or even sufficient expression in historical reality. This must not be regarded as a mere deficiency or shortcoming. Rather, they find the constitutive principle of history in the fact that the idea is only imperfectly represented in history. For this reason philosophy must be replaced by historical research to inform man about himself and his place in this world. The idea of a history that would be the pure representation of the idea would mean renouncing history as an independent way to truth.

But on the other hand historical reality is not merely a heavy, opaque medium, mindless matter, rigid necessity against which the spirit beats in vain and in whose bonds it suffocates. This kind of gnostic, Neoplatonic view of historical events as emergence into the external world of appearance does not do justice to the metaphysical value of history and hence to the status of historical science as knowledge. The unfolding of human life in time has its own productivity. The plenitude and variety of the human is increasingly realized in the unending vicissitudes of human destinies: this is a reasonable formulation of the basic assumption of the historical school. Its connection with the classicism of the age of Goethe is unmistakable.

The guiding thought here is, basically, a humanist ideal. Wilhelm von Humboldt attributed the specific perfection of Greece to the rich variety of great individual forms that it manifests. Of course the great historians were not to be limited to this kind of classicist ideal; instead they followed Herder. But now that it no longer acknowledges the pre-eminence of a classical age, what can the historical worldview that starts with Herder do, other than to view the whole of world history in terms of the same criterion that Wilhelm von Humboldt used to justify the pre-eminence of classical antiquity? A rich variety of individual phenomena is distinctive not only of Greek life; it is distinctive of historical life in general, and that

199

is what constitutes the value and meaning of history. This is supposed to provide an answer to the anxious question about the meaning of the spectacle of brilliant victories and terrible defeats that troubles the human heart.

The advantage of this answer is that the humanistic ideal implies no particular content, but is based on the formal idea of the greatest variety. This kind of ideal is truly universal, for it cannot be shaken by any historical experience, any disturbing evidence of the transience of human things. History has a meaning in itself. What seems to speak against it—the transience of all that is earthly—is in fact its real basis. In impermanence itself lies the mystery of an inexhaustible productivity of historical life.

The question is only how to conceive the unity of world history in terms of the formal ideal of history, and how to justify the claim that we can have knowledge of world history. First, Ranke: "Every act which is truly part of world history, which never consists solely of negation, but rather is able to engender in the fleeting present moment something for the future, includes within itself a full and immediate sense of its own indestructible value."[51]

Neither the pre-eminent position of classical antiquity nor that of the present or future to which it leads, neither decline nor progress—those traditional basic categories of universal history—can be reconciled with genuine historical thought. On the other hand, the celebrated immediacy of the relationship between all periods and God can very easily be combined with this idea of the continuity (Zusammenhang: also, coherence) of world history. For continuity—Herder calls it "order in the succession of events"—is the manifestation of historical reality itself. What is historically real emerges "according to strict laws of succession: subsequent events place the nature and effect of what has just preceded in a bright, public light."[52] The first statement, then, concerning the formal structure of history—namely that it comes into being in its very passing away—is that, throughout the changing destinies of men, the continuity of life persists unbroken.

From this, however, it is possible to see what Ranke considers an "event that is truly part of world history" and what the continuity of world history is really based on. It has no fixed goal that can be discovered outside itself. To this extent there is no necessity, knowable a priori, at work in history. But the structure of historical continuity is still teleological, and its criterion is success. We saw that successive events indicate the importance of those preceding them. Ranke may have meant that this is a mere condition of historical knowledge. In fact it is also the basis of the peculiar importance accorded to the meaning of history. Whether or not something is successful not only determines the meaning of a single event and accounts for the fact that it produces a lasting effect or passes unnoticed; success or failure causes a whole series of actions and events to be meaningful or meaningless. The ontological structure of history itself, then, is teleological, although without a telos.[53] This defines Ranke's concept of an event that is truly part of world history. It is such if it makes history—i.e., if it has an effect (Wirkung) that lends it a continuing historical significance. Hence the elements of historical coherence, in fact, are determined by an unconscious teleology that connects them and excludes the insignificant from this coherence.

(ii) Ranke's Historical Worldview

This kind of teleology cannot, of course, be demonstrated in terms of a philosophical concept. It does not make world history into an a priori system in which the actors are placed, as within a mechanism that is unconsciously directing them. It is, rather, compatible with freedom of action. Ranke is able to say that the links that create historical continuity are "scenes of freedom."[54] This expression means that in the infinite web of events there are particularly significant incidents in which historical decisions are, as it were, concentrated. Decisions are made wherever actions are performed in freedom, but that this decision really decides *something*—i.e., that a decision makes history and through its effect reveals its full and lasting significance—is the mark of truly historic moments. They articulate the historical whole. We call such moments, in which a freely chosen action has a decisive effect on history, epoch-making moments or crises, and the individuals whose actions have this effect can be called, to use Hegel's phrase, "historic individuals." Ranke calls them "original minds which intervene independently in the battle of ideas and world forces and gather together the most powerful ones, those on which the future depends." This is absolutely Hegelian thinking.

We have a highly informative reflection of Ranke's on how the historical whole follows from such free decisions: "Let us admit that history can never have the unity of a philosophical system; but it is not without inner coherence. Before us we see a range of successive events that condition one another. When I say 'condition' I do not mean with absolute necessity.

Rather, the important thing is that human freedom is involved everywhere. The writing of history follows the scenes of freedom. This is its greatest attraction. But freedom involves power, germinal power. Without the latter the former disappears, both in world events and in the sphere of ideas. At every moment something new can begin, something whose sole origin is the primary and common source of all human activity. Nothing exists entirely for the sake of something else, nothing is entirely identical with the reality of something else. But still a deep inner coherence penetrates everywhere, and no one is entirely independent of it. Beside freedom stands necessity. It consists in what has already been formed and cannot be destroyed, which is the basis of all new activity. What has already come into being coheres with what is coming into being. But even this continuity itself is not something arbitrary to be merely accepted, but it has come into existence in one particular way, and not another. It is, likewise, an object of knowledge. A long series of events—succeeding and simultaneous to one another—linked together in this way constitute a century, an epoch. . . . "[55]

The significant thing about this account is the way the concept of freedom is linked to the concept of power. Power is obviously the central category of the historical worldview. Herder had already used it to escape from the Enlightenment's schema of progress and especially from the concept of reason that underlay it.[56] The concept of power has such a central place within the historical worldview because in it interiority and exteriority are held in a peculiarly tense unity. All power exists only in its expression. Expression is not only the manifestation of power but its reality. Hegel was quite right when he explicated the intrinsic relationship between power and expression dialectically. But this dialectic also shows that power is more than its expression. It possesses potentiality also—i.e., it is not only the cause of a particular effect but the capacity, wherever it is used, to have that effect. Thus its mode of being is different from that of an effect. It has the mode of "suspension" (Anstellen)—a word that suggests itself because it expresses precisely the independent existence of power as against the indefiniteness of whatever it may express itself in. It follows that power cannot be known or measured in terms of its expressions, but only experienced as an indwelling. The observation of an effect always shows only the cause, and not the power, if the power is an inner surplus over and above the cause of a given effect. This surplus, of which we are aware in the cause, can certainly be understood also in terms of the effect, in the resistance it offers, in that offering resistance is itself an expression of power. But even then it is through an awareness that power is experienced. Interiority is the mode of experiencing power because power, of its nature, is related to itself alone. In his *Phenomenology of Mind* Hegel has convincingly demonstrated how the concept of power is dialectically superseded in the infinity of life, which is related to itself alone and dwells in itself.[57]

Thus Ranke's formulation takes on a world-historical character, one within the world history of thought and philosophy. Plato was the first to remark the reflexive structure of dunamis in this connection,[58] and this made it possible to apply it to the nature of the soul; this Aristotle did in his doctrine of the dunameis, the powers of the soul. Ontologically, power is "inwardness." Thus it is quite correct for Ranke to write: "Freedom is combined with power." For power that is more than its expression is always freedom. This is of decisive importance for the historian. He knows that everything could have been different, and every acting individual could have acted differently. The power that makes history is not mechanical power. Ranke excludes this specifically by calling it "germinal power" and speaking of "the primary and common source of all human activity" —for Ranke this is freedom.

It is not a contradiction for freedom to be limited. We can see this from the nature of power when it expresses itself. That is why Ranke can say, "Beside freedom stands necessity." For necessity does not mean here a cause that excludes freedom, but the resistance that free power encounters. Here the truth of the dialectic of power that Hegel revealed is made manifest.[59] The resistance that free power encounters is itself freedom. The necessity we are concerned with here is the power of what has been transmitted and of those who are acting against one, which is prior to any operation of free activity. By excluding many things as impossible, it limits action to the possible. Necessity itself comes from freedom and is itself qualified by the freedom that reckons with it. In terms of logic it is a question of hypothetical necessity (the ex hupotheseos anankaion); in terms of content, we are concerned not with nature but with historical being: what has come into being cannot simply be destroyed. Hence it is "the basis of all new activity," as Ranke says, and yet it is something that has come about through actions. In that what has come into existence persists as a foundation for the new, it sets the new action within a unified context. Ranke says, "What has already come into being coheres with what is coming into being." This very obscure sentence is clearly trying to express the nature of historical reality: that what comes into being is free, but the freedom from which it comes is always limited by what has come into being—i.e., by the situation into which it comes. The concepts that historians use—such as power, force, determining tendency—all seek to reveal the essence of historical being, in that they imply that the idea never attains full representation in history. It is not the plans and views of those who act that constitute the meaning of the event, but historical effects that reveal the historical powers. The historical powers, not the monadic subjectivity of the individual, are the real basis of historical development. In fact, all individuation is itself already partly characterized by the reality that stands over against it, and that is why individuality is not subjectivity but living power. Even states are such living powers for Ranke. He explicitly said of them that they are not "divisions of the universal," but individualities, "real spiritual beings."[60] Ranke calls them "thoughts of God" in order to indicate that what brings them into being is their own living power and not some human creation or desire, or some plan that people project.

The use of the category of power now makes it possible to think of the coherence of history as a primary given. Power is real always only as an interplay of powers, and history is this interplay of powers that produces a continuity. Both Ranke and Droysen say in this regard that history is a "growing sum." Thus they reject all claim to an a priori construction of world history, and they consider this view to be based wholly on experience.[61] The question is, however, whether more is not assumed here than they know. That universal history is a growing sum means that it is a whole—though an unfinished one. But this is by no means obvious. Items that are qualitatively different cannot be added up. Adding up, rather, presupposes that the unity in terms of which they are grouped is already the criterion of that grouping. But this presupposition is an assertion. The idea of unity in history is, in fact, not so formal and independent from understanding the contents of history as it appears to be.[62]

The world of history has not always been conceived in terms of the unity of world history. As with Herodotus, for example, it can also be considered a moral phenomenon. As such it offers a large number of exempla but no unity. What justifies talk of the unity of world history? This question used to be answered easily when it was assumed that there was a unity of goal, and hence of a plan, in history. But what is the common denominator that allows historical events to be grouped together if this kind of goal and plan in history is not accepted?

If the reality of history is conceived as an interplay of forces, this concept is obviously not enough to make its unity necessary. What guided Herder and Humboldt, the ideal of the rich variety of the manifestations of human life, does not as such ground any true unity. In the continuity of events there must be the *something* that emerges as a goal giving an orientation to the whole. In fact, the place that is occupied in the eschatologies of the philosophy of history, both of religious origin and in their secularized versions, is here empty.[63] No preconceived idea concerning the significance of history should prejudice historical research. However, the self-evident assumption of historical research is that history constitutes a unity. Thus Droysen can explicitly acknowledge that the unity of world history is a regulative idea, even if it is not a concept of a providential plan.

However, in this postulate lies a further assumption that determines its content. The idea of the unity of world history implies the uninterrupted continuity of the development of world history. This idea of coherence or continuity is primarily formal in nature and does not imply any actual contents. It too is like an a priori of research that invites one to penetrate ever more deeply into the complexities of historical continuity. To this extent it is only methodological naivete on Ranke's part when he speaks of the "amazing steadiness" of historical development.[64] What he actually means by this is not the structure of this steadiness itself, but the contents that emerge in this steady development. That something unique finally emerges from the vast and multifarious whole of historical development—namely the unity of Western civilization which, produced by the Germanic and Romance peoples, spreads over the whole earth—is what arouses his admiration.

Admittedly, even if we acknowledge the significance of Ranke's admiration of "steadiness" in terms of content, his naivete is still there. That world history has produced Western culture in a continuous development is again not a mere fact of experience that historical consciousness acknowledges but a condition of historical consciousness itself—i.e., something that need not have happened or could be canceled out by new experience. Only because history has taken this course can the question of its meaning be raised by a world-historical consciousness and the unity of its continuity be meant.

For this we can cite Ranke himself. As he sees it, the main difference between the Eastern and the Western system is that in the West historical continuity constitutes the form of cultural existence.[65] Nor is it by chance that the unity of history depends on the unity of Western civilization, to which belong Western science in general and history as science, in particular. And it is also not by chance that Western civilization is characterized by Christianity, which has its absolute temporal moment in the unique redemptive event. Ranke recognized something of this when he viewed the Christian religion as the restoration of man to "immediacy to God," which, in romantic fashion, he set at the primeval beginning of all history.[66] But we will see below that the fundamental significance of this situation has not been fully acknowledged in the philosophical reflection of the proponents of the historical worldview.

Thus the empirical orientation of the historical sciences is not without philosophical assumptions. It was the acute methodologist Droysen who freed history from its empirical disguise and recognized its fundamental significance. His basic viewpoint is that continuity is the essence of history, because history, unlike nature, includes the element of time. Droysen constantly quotes Aristotle's statement about the soul—that it increases within itself (epidosis eis hauto). Unlike the mere repetitiveness of nature, history is characterized by this increase within itself. But this involves preservation and at the same time surpassing what is preserved. Self-knowledge embraces both. Thus history is not only an object of knowledge; self-knowledge determines its being. "Knowledge of it is itself" (*Historik* §15). The amazing steadiness of historical development of which Ranke spoke is based on the consciousness of continuity, a consciousness that makes history history (*Historik* §48).

It would be quite wrong to regard this as only an idealist prejudice. Rather, this a priori of historical thought is itself a historical reality. Jakob Burckhardt is quite right to view the continuity of Western cultural tradition as the very condition of the existence of Western culture.[67] The collapse of this tradition, the rise of a new barbarism, which Burckhardt prophesied, would not, for the historical worldview, be a catastrophe within history but the end of world history itself, at least insofar as it tries to understand itself as a world-historical unity. It is important to recognize this presupposition in the historical school's inquiry into universal history precisely because its existence is fundamentally denied.

Thus as we saw in Ranke and Droysen, the historical school's hermeneutical self-understanding has its ultimate foundation in the idea of universal history. The historical school, however, could not accept Hegel's explanation of the unity of world history through the concept of spirit. That spirit reaches its culmination in the perfect self-consciousness of the historical present, which constitutes the significance of history, is an eschatological self-interpretation which basically supersedes history by turning it into a speculative concept. The historical school was, instead, forced into a theological understanding of itself. If it was not to undermine its own disposition to think of itself as progressive research, it had to relate its own finite and limited knowledge to a divine spirit, to which things are known in their perfection. It is the old ideal of infinite understanding applied to the knowledge of history. Ranke writes, "I imagine the Deity—if I may allow myself this observation—as seeing the whole of historical humanity in its totality (since no time lies before the Deity), and finding it all equally valuable."[68]

Here the idea of an infinite understanding (intellectus infinitus) for which everything exists simultaneously (omnia simul) is transformed into the original image of historical impartiality. The historian who knows that all epochs and all historical phenomena are equally justified before God approximates that image. Thus the historian's consciousness represents the perfect culmination of human self-consciousness. The more he is able to recognize the unique, indestructible value of every phenomenon—that is, to think historically—the more his thought is God-like.[69] That is why Ranke compares the office of historian to that of priest. "Immediacy to God" is for the Lutheran Ranke the real content of the Christian gospel. The re-establishment of the immediacy that existed before the fall does not take place through the church's means of grace alone. The historian has a share in it too, in that he makes mankind, which has fallen into history, the object of his study, and knows mankind in the immediacy to God which it has never entirely lost.

Universal history, world history, are not, in fact, epitomes of a formal kind, referring to the totality of events; rather, in historical thinking, the universe, as the divine creation, is raised to a consciousness of itself. True, this is not a conceptual consciousness; the ultimate result of the study of history is "sympathy, co-knowledge of the universe."[70] It is against this pantheistic background that Ranke's famous remark that he would like to extinguish himself is to be understood. Of course, as Dilthey objected,[71] this self-extinction is in fact the expansion of the self to make a universe within. But it is not by chance that Ranke does not take this further mental step, a step that leads Dilthey to ground the human sciences in psychology. For Ranke, self-extinction is still a form of real sharing. We must not understand this concept of sharing in a psychological and subjective way but in terms of the underlying concept of life. Because all historical phenomena are manifestations of universal life, to share in them is to share in life.

This gives the word "understanding" its almost religious tone. To understand is to participate immediately in life, without any mediation through concepts. Just this is what the historian is concerned with: not relating reality to ideas, but everywhere reaching the point where "life thinks and thought lives." In being understood, the phenomena of historical life are seen as manifestations of universal life, of the divinity. Understanding and penetration mean, indeed, more than a human cognitive achievement and more than merely the creation of an inner universe—as Dilthey, contradicting Ranke, reformulated the ideal of the historian. It is a metaphysical statement, which brings Ranke very close to Fichte and Hegel, when he says: "The clear, full, lived insight is the very pith of being made visible and transparent to itself."[72] It is quite obvious from such a remark that fundamentally Ranke remained close to German idealism. The full self-transparency of being, which Hegel saw as realized in the absolute knowledge of philosophy, is the basis of Ranke's consciousness of himself as a historian, however much he rejects speculative philosophy. That is why the image of the poet is so close to him, and he feels no need to distinguish himself as an historian from the poet. For what the historian has in common with the poet is that, like the poet, he depicts the element in which everyone lives "as something that lies outside him."[73] The complete surrender to the contemplation of things, the epic attitude of a man who is trying to tell the tale of world history,[74] may in fact be called poetic, since for the historian God is present in all things, not as a concept but as an "outward idea." We cannot describe Ranke's view of himself better than by these terms of Hegel. The historian, as Ranke sees him, belongs to that form of absolute spirit Hegel called religion of art.

(iii) The Relation Between Historical Study and Hermeneutics in J. G. Droysen

A historian whose thinking was more acute inevitably realized the problems of this self-conception. The philosophical significance of Droysen's *Historik* is that he tries to free the concept of understanding from the indefiniteness of the aesthetic-pantheistic communion that it has in Ranke, and formulate its conceptual presuppositions. The first of these is "expression."[75] Understanding is the understanding of expression. In expression something interior is immediately present. But this inward thing, "the inner essence," is the first and true reality. Here Droysen is entirely Cartesian, and he stands in the tradition of Kant and Wilhelm von Humboldt. The individual ego is like a lonely point in the world of appearances. But in its utterances, above all in language and in all the forms in which it expresses itself, it is no longer a lonely point. It belongs to the world of the intelligible. Understanding history is not, however, fundamentally different from understanding language. Like language, the world of history does not possess the character of a purely spiritual being: "to want to understand the ethical and the historical world means above all that one recognizes that it is neither merely docetic nor merely metabolism."[76] He asserts this against the empiricism of Buckle, but it is also valid against the spiritualism of, say, Hegel's philosophy of history. Droysen sees the dual nature of history as founded in the "curious charism of human nature, which is so happily imperfect that both mentally and physically it has to behave ethically."[77]

With these ideas borrowed from Wilhelm von Humboldt, Droysen is not trying to say anything other than what Ranke meant when he emphasized power. He, too, regards the reality of history as something other than pure spirit. To behave ethically implies, rather, seeing that the world of history is not merely the impress of the will on wholly malleable material. Its reality consists in the mind's constantly renewed effort to grasp and form the "ever-changing finite systems" to which every person belongs. From this dual nature of history Droysen can now draw conclusions about the historical approach.

Modeling it on the way poets work, as Ranke did, is no longer sufficient for him. Self-extinction in contemplation or narration does not lead us to historical reality, for the poets "compose a psychological interpretation of the events they describe. But in real life there are elements at work quite other than personalities" (*Historik* §41). The poets treat historical reality as if it were intended and planned by the persons engaged in it; but the reality of history does not consist in being "meant" in this way. Hence the real desires and plans of the actors are not the specific object of historical understanding. Psychological interpretation of particular individuals cannot exhaust the significance of historical events. "Neither is the person's will fully realized in this particular situation, nor is what has come about simply the result of his strength of will and intelligence. It is neither the pure, nor the whole expression of his personality" (§41). Hence psychological interpretation is only a subordinate element in historical understanding, and that not only because it does not really attain its goal. It is not just that it meets impediments. The interiority of the person, the sanctum of conscience, is not only unattainable by the historian, but what can be reached only by sympathy and love is not the goal and object of his research. He does not have to penetrate the mysteries of individual people. What he investigates is not individuals as such, but what they mean as elements in the movement of moral powers.

The concept of moral powers occupies a central place in Droysen (§55ff.). It is the basis of both history's mode of being and the possibility of knowing it. Ranke's vague reflections on freedom, power, and necessity now acquire their substantive content. Similarly, Ranke's use of the concept of historical fact is corrected by Droysen. The individual, in the contingency of his particular drives and purposes, is not an element in history, but only insofar as he raises himself to the sphere of moral commonality and participates in it. The movement of these moral powers, which is achieved through the common work of humankind, constitutes the course of things. It is perfectly true that what is possible is thereby limited; but to speak of a conflict between freedom and necessity would be to reflect oneself out of one's own historical finiteness. The actor is inextricably situated under the postulate of freedom. The course of things is not an extrinsic barrier to freedom, for it depends not on rigid necessity but on the movement of the moral powers, to which one is always related. It sets the task in performing which the moral energy of the actor proves itself.[78] Hence Droysen establishes a far more adequate relationship between freedom and necessity in history when he sees it entirely in terms of the historical actor. He relates necessity to the unconditional moral imperative, and, freedom to the unconditional will; both are expressions of the moral power by which the individual belongs to the moral sphere (§76).

For Droysen too it is the concept of power that reveals the limits of all speculative metaphysics of history. Accordingly, like Ranke, he criticizes Hegel's concept of development, in that there is no germ that simply grows in the course of history. But he defines more sharply what power means here: "Powers grow with work." The moral power of the individual becomes a historical power insofar as it is at work on the great common goals. It becomes a historical power in that the moral sphere is what is lasting and powerful in the movement of history. Hence power is no longer an original and direct manifestation of universal life, as with Ranke, but exists only in this mediation and only through mediation does it achieve historical reality.

The mediate moral world moves in such a way that everyone participates in it, but in different ways. Some preserve existing conditions by continuing to do the customary thing, while others have new ideas and express them. The continuity of the historical process consists in this constant overcoming of what is, through criticism based on what ought to be (§77f.). Thus Droysen would not speak of mere "scenes of freedom," for freedom is the fundamental pulse of historical life and does not exist only in exceptional cases. The great personalities of history are only one element in the forward progress of the moral world, which is as a whole and in every detail a world of freedom.

He agrees with Ranke, against historical apriorism, that we cannot see the end but only the direction of the movement. The final goal of all our aims, toward which the restless activity of mankind is drawn, cannot be discerned through historical knowledge. It is only something we sense dimly, something we believe (§80–86).

The place he assigns historical knowledge accords with this image of history. It, too, cannot be understood as Ranke understood it—as aesthetic self-forgetfulness and self-extinction in the manner of great epic poets. The pantheistic element in Ranke was responsible for the claim to a universal and yet immediate participation in, a co-knowledge of, the universe. Droysen, on the other hand, thinks of the intermediaries in which understanding moves. The moral powers are the actual reality of history, and to them not only the individual rises in his acts; the historian also rises to them, transcending his own particularity. The historian is defined and limited by belonging to particular moral spheres: his native land, and his political and religious persuasions. But his participation depends precisely on this insuperable one-sidedness. Within the concrete conditions of his own historical existence—not from some position suspended above things—he sets himself the task of being fair. "This is his fairness, namely that he tries to understand" (§91).

Hence Droysen's formula for historical knowledge is "understanding through research" (§8). This process implies both an infinite mediation and an ultimate immediacy. The concept of research, which Droysen links here so significantly with that of understanding, is intended to designate the infinite nature of the task that distinguishes the historian from the completeness of an artistic creation just as fundamentally as from the complete harmony produced by the sympathy and love between I and Thou. Only in "ceaseless" research into the tradition, in opening up new sources and in ever new interpretations of them, does research move progressively toward the "idea." This sounds as if it were based on the procedure of the natural sciences and were an anticipation of the neo-Kantian interpretation of the "thing-in-itself" as the infinite task. But on closer examination we see that something more is also involved. Droysen's formulation distinguishes the activity of the historian not only from the ideal completeness of art and the intimate communion of souls but also, it seems, from the procedure of the natural sciences.

At the end of the lecture of 1882[79] we find the words " . . . that we, unlike the natural sciences, cannot make use of experiment, that we only do research and can do nothing but research." Thus there must be another element in the concept of research that is important for Droysen, and not just the fact that the task of historical research is infinite, like the infinite progress of research into nature—an element which, in contrast to the "science" of the eighteenth century and the "doctrina" of earlier centuries, contributed to the rise of the concept of research in the nineteenth century. Starting probably from the image of a studious traveler penetrating into unknown regions, this conception of "research" embraces the knowledge of both nature and the historical world. The more the theological and philosophical background of the knowledge of the world fades away, the more science is conceived as an advance into unknown regions and hence is called "research."

But this is not enough to explain how Droysen distinguishes historical method from the experimental method of the natural sciences when he says that historical work is "research, nothing but research." There must be another infinity, different from that of the unknown world, which in Droysen's eyes distinguishes historical knowledge from research. His thought seems as follows: research possesses a different, as it were qualitative infiniteness, if what is studied can never itself come into view. This is, in fact, the case with the historical past, in contrast to the self-givenness of experiment in the study of nature. In order to know, historical research investigates something that is always different, namely tradition, which is always new. Unlike the experiment, its answer never has the clear unambiguity of what has been seen with one's own eyes.

If we now ask what is the origin of this element in the concept of research, which Droysen follows in the surprising antithesis of experiment and research, then we are brought, it seems to me, to the concept of the study of conscience. The world of history depends on freedom, and this on the mystery of the person that is ultimately unfathomable by research.[80] Only the self-research of one's own conscience can approach it, and only

God can know the truth here. For this reason historical research does not seek knowledge of laws and cannot appeal to the decisiveness of experiment. For the historian is separated from his object by the infinite mediation of tradition.

But on the other hand this distance is also proximity. This historian does not investigate his "object" by establishing it unequivocally in an experiment; rather, through the intelligibility and familiarity of the moral world, he is integrated with his object in a way completely different from the way a natural scientist is bound to his. "Hearsay" is here not bad evidence, but the only evidence possible.

"Every ego enclosed within itself, each one revealing itself to every other one in its utterances" (§91). What is known is, accordingly, totally different in both cases: what laws are to the study of nature, moral powers are to the historian (§16). In them he finds his truth.

Through ceaseless research into tradition, understanding is, in the end, always possible. Despite all mediation, for Droysen the concept of understanding is still characterized by an ultimate immediacy. "The possibility of understanding consists in the fact that the utterances presented to us as historical material are congenial to us." "With respect to men, human utterances, and forms, we are, and feel ourselves to be, essentially similar and in a condition of mutuality" (§9). Just as understanding connects the individual ego with the moral commonalities to which it belongs, so also these moral commonalities themselves—family, people, state, and religion—can be understood as expressions.

Thus, by means of the concept of *expression*, historical reality rises into the sphere of meaning, and hence *in Droysen's deliberations on method too hermeneutics becomes the master key to the study of history*. "The detail is understood within the whole, and the whole from the detail" (§10). This is the old rhetorico-hermeneutic rule, now turned inward: "The man understanding, because he is an ego, a totality in himself, like those whom he is trying to understand, completes this totality with the individual utterance, and the individual utterance with this totality." This is Schleiermacher's formula. In applying it, Droysen shares its premise—namely that history, which he sees as acts of freedom, is nevertheless as profoundly intelligible and meaningful as a text. Understanding history, like understanding a text, culminates in "spiritual presence." Thus we see that Droysen determines more exactly than Ranke what mediate elements are involved in research and understanding, but ultimately even he can conceive the task of historical research only in aesthetic-hermeneutic categories. For Droysen too the aim of historical research is to reconstruct the great text of history from the fragments of tradition.

2 DILTHEY'S ENTANGLEMENT IN THE APORIAS OF HISTORICISM[81]

(A) FROM THE EPISTEMOLOGICAL PROBLEM OF HISTORY TO THE HERMENEUTIC FOUNDATION OF THE HUMAN SCIENCES[82]

The tension between aesthetic hermeneutics and philosophy of history comes to a climax with *Wilhelm Dilthey*. Dilthey owes his importance to the fact that he really recognizes the epistemological problem that the historical view implies with respect to idealism. As Schleiermacher's biographer, as a historian who, with the romantic theory of understanding, asks the historical question about the rise and the nature of hermeneutics and writes the history of Western metaphysics, he moves within the horizon of problems implicit in German idealism; but as a student of Ranke and of that century's new empiricism, his thinking is so different that neither the aesthetic-pantheistic identity philosophy of Schleiermacher nor Hegel's metaphysics, integrated with the philosophy of history, remain valid for him. It is true that in Ranke and Droysen we found minds similarly torn between idealism and empiricism, but in Dilthey this dichotomy becomes particularly acute. For in him it is no longer the mere continuation of the classic-romantic spirit together with an empirical conception of research, but this continuing tradition is overlaid by his conscious adoption of the ideas first of Schleiermacher and later of Hegel.

Even when we exclude the early and great influence of British empiricism and of the epistemology of the natural sciences on Dilthey as being a distortion of his real intentions, it is still not so easy to understand what these intentions were. Georg Misch has taken an important step in this direction.[83] But since Misch wanted to confront Dilthey's position with Husserl's phenomenology and the fundamental ontology of Heidegger, he described the inner conflict in Dilthey's "life philosophy" in terms of these contemporary contrasting positions. The same may be said of O. F. Bollnow.[84]

The root of the conflict in Dilthey lies in the historical school's intermediate position between philosophy and experience. Far from being obviated by Dilthey's attempt to provide an epistemological foundation, it is rendered more acute. Dilthey's attempt to provide a philosophical foundation for the human sciences endeavors to draw the epistemological consequences of what Ranke and Droysen asserted against German idealism. Dilthey himself was fully aware of this. He viewed the weakness of the historical school as a lack of logical consistency in its thinking: "Instead of going back to the epistemological postulates of the historical school and those of idealism from Kant to Hegel and thus recognizing the incompatibility of these postulates, they have uncritically combined these two points of view."[85] Thus he set himself the task of constructing a new and more viable epistemological basis between historical experience and the idealistic heritage of the historical school. This is the meaning of his intention to complement Kant's *Critique of Pure Reason* with a critique of historical reason.

This aim in itself exhibits his withdrawal from speculative idealism. It sets up an analogy that has to be understood in a quite literal way. Dilthey wants to say that historical reason calls for the same kind of justification as pure reason. The epoch-making result of the *Critique of Pure Reason* was not only that it destroyed metaphysics as a purely rational science of the world, the soul, and God, but that, at the same time, it revealed an area within which the use of a priori concepts is justified and which makes knowledge possible. The *Critique of Pure Reason* not merely destroyed the dreams of a seer; it also answered the question of how pure science is possible. Meanwhile, speculative idealism had integrated the world of history into the self-analysis of reason and, moreover, especially through Hegel, had performed remarkable feats, precisely in the historical field. Thus the claim of the pure science of reason was extended to historical knowledge. It was a part of the encyclopedia of mind.

But in the eyes of the historical school, speculative philosophy of history was a dogmatism no less crass than rational metaphysics. So that school had to provide a philosophical grounding for historical knowledge of the same kind that Kant achieved for the knowledge of nature.

This demand was not to be fulfilled by simply going back to Kant, as it might have seemed from the aberrations of "nature philosophy." Kant had brought to conclusion the work on the problem of knowledge as it was posed by the emergence of the new science in the seventeenth century. Kant provided the mathematico-scientific mode of construction, used by the new science, with the epistemological justification it needed because its ideas had no claim to existence other than as entia rationis. The old representationalist theory was clearly no longer adequate.[86] Thus, because of the incommensurability of thought and being, the problem of knowledge was posed in a new way. Dilthey saw this clearly, and in his correspondence with Count Yorck he speaks of the nominalist background of seventeenth-century epistemology, which has been brilliantly verified by modern research since Duhem.[87]

The problem of epistemology acquires a new urgency through the historical sciences. We learn this from linguistic history, for the word Erkenntnistheorie (epistemology) arose only in the period after Hegel. It came into use when empirical research had discredited the Hegelian system. The nineteenth century became the century of epistemology because, with the dissolution of Hegelian philosophy, the correspondence between logos and being was finally destroyed.[88] In that Hegel taught reason in everything, even in history, he was the last and most universal representative of ancient logos philosophy. Now, in view of the critique of the a priori philosophy of history, people were drawn again under the spell of Kant's critique, whose problem was now posed for the historical world as well, since the claim to provide a purely rational construction of world history had been rejected and historical knowledge was likewise limited to experience. If history is considered to be no more a manifestation of mind than is nature, then how the human mind can know history becomes just as problematic as how nature can be known through mathematical constructs had been for Kant. Thus, just as Kant had answered the question of how pure science was possible, Dilthey had to answer the question of how historical experience can become a science. Hence, in a clear analogy to the Kantian question he sought to discover the categories of the historical world that would be able to support the human sciences.

What constitutes Dilthey's special importance and distinguishes him from the neo-Kantians, who tried to involve the human sciences in the renewal of critical philosophy, is that he does not forget that in this instance experience is something quite different from what it is in the investigation of nature. In the latter, all that matters are verifiable discoveries arising from experience—i.e., that which detaches itself from an individual's experience and constitutes part of the reliable stock of experimental knowledge. For the neo-Kantians, the categorial analysis of this "object of knowledge" had been the positive achievement of transcendental philosophy.[89]

Simply to adapt Kant's construction and apply it to the field of historical knowledge, as neo-Kantianism did in the form of the philosophy of value, could not satisfy Dilthey. He considered neo-Kantian critical philosophy itself to be dogmatic, and he was equally correct in calling British empiricism dogmatic. For the structure of the historical world is not based on facts taken from experience which then acquire a value relation, but rather on the inner historicity that belongs to experience itself. What we call experience (Erfahrung) and acquire through experience is a living historical process; and its paradigm is not the discovery of facts but the peculiar fusion of memory and expectation into a whole. Thus what preshapes the special mode of knowing in the historical sciences is the suffering and instruction that the person who is growing in insight receives from the painful experience of reality. The historical sciences only advance and broaden the thought already implicit in the experience of life.[90]

Thus epistemological inquiry here begins with a different starting point. In some ways its task is easier. It does not need to investigate the grounds of the possibility of the fact that our ideas accord with the "external world." We are concerned here with knowledge of the historical world, and that is always a world constituted and formed by the human mind. For this reason Dilthey does not regard the universally valid synthetic judgments of history as any problem.[91] Here he finds support in Vico. We recall that, in reaction against Cartesian doubt and the certainty of the mathematical knowledge of nature based on it, Vico asserted the epistemological primacy of the man-made historical world. Dilthey repeats the same argument and writes, "The first condition of possibility of a science of history is that I myself am a historical being, that the person studying history is the person making history."[92] What makes historical knowledge possible is the homogeneity of subject and object.

This, however, is no solution to the epistemological problem that Dilthey posed. Rather, positing homogeneity as its condition conceals the real epistemological problem of history. The question is how the individual's experience and the knowledge of it come to be historical experience. In history we are no longer concerned with coherent wholes that are experienced as such by the individual or are re-experienced as such by others. Dilthey's argument applies only to the experiencing and re-experiencing done by the individual, and this is the starting point for his epistemological theory. By elaborating the way an individual's life acquires continuity, Dilthey hopes to obtain constitutive concepts that will serve to ground both historical continuity and the knowledge of it.

Unlike the categories of the study of nature, these concepts are concepts drawn from life. For Dilthey the ultimate presupposition for knowledge of the historical world is experience (Erlebnis). In it the identity between consciousness and object—that postulate of speculative idealism—is still demonstrable reality. This is where immediate certitude is to be found, for experience is no longer divided into an act (a becoming conscious) and a content (that of which one is conscious).[93] It is, rather, indivisible consciousness. Even to say that experience is *of* something is to make too great a division. Dilthey now investigates how continuity is created from the element of the world of the mind that is immediately certain and how the knowledge of this continuity is possible.

Even in his ideas on "descriptive and analytical psychology," Dilthey was trying to explain "how one's inner life is woven into continuity" (Zusammenhang) in a way that is different from explaining the knowledge of nature by appeal to the categories.[94] He used the concept of structure to distinguish the experiential character of psychological continuity from the causal continuity of natural processes. Logically "structure" is distinguished by its referring to a totality of relationships that do not depend on a temporal, causal succession but on intrinsic connections.

In structure Dilthey thought he had found a valid starting point and had overcome the shortcomings of Ranke and Droysen's methodological reflections. But he conceded that the historical school was right on one point: there was no such thing as a universal subject, only historical individuals. The ideality of meaning was not to be located in a transcendental subject, but emerged from the historical reality of life. It is life itself that unfolds and forms itself in intelligible unities, and it is in terms of the single individual that these unities are understood. This is the self-evident starting point for Dilthey's analysis. The continuity of life as it appears to the individual (and is re-experienced and understood by others through biographical knowledge) is created through the significance of particular experiences (Erlebnisse). Around them, as around an organizing center, the unity of a life is created in the same way that a melody acquires its form—not from the mere succession of notes but from the musical motifs that determine its formal unity.

It is clear that here also, as with Droysen, the method of romantic hermeneutics is being expanded into universality. Like the coherence of a text, the structural coherence of life is defined as a relation between the whole and the parts. Every part expresses something of the whole of life—i.e., has significance for the whole—just as its own significance is determined by the whole. It is the old hermeneutical principle of textual interpretation, and it applies to the coherence of life insofar as life presupposes a unity of meaning that is expressed in all its parts.

The decisive step for Dilthey's epistemological grounding of the human sciences is the transition from the structure of coherence in an individual's experience to *historical coherence*, which is *not experienced by any individual at all*. Here—despite all the critique of speculation—it is necessary to put "logical subjects" instead of "real subjects." Dilthey is aware of this difficulty, but he considers it permissible, since the way individuals belong together—as in the solidarity of one generation or one nation—represents a spiritual reality that must be recognized as such precisely because it is not possible to get behind it in order to explain it. True, this is not a real subject; that is clear enough from the fluidity of its boundaries. Moreover, individuals are involved in it with a part of their being only. But for Dilthey there is no question but that statements can be made about this kind of subject. The historian does it constantly when he speaks of the deeds and the destinies of peoples.[95] The question is simply how such statements can be justified epistemologically.

It cannot be said that Dilthey's thinking on this point, which he himself sees as the key problem, reached perfect clarity. The decisive problem here is making the transition from a *psychological* to a *hermeneutical* grounding of the human sciences. Dilthey never got beyond mere sketches of it. So it is that the two completed parts of the *Aufbau*,[96] autobiography and biography, which are both special cases of historical experience and knowledge, retain an undue preponderance. For the real historical problem, as we have seen, is less how coherence is generally experienced and known than how a coherence that no one has experienced can be known. Still, there can be no doubt about the way Dilthey would have clarified the problem of understanding. To understand is to understand an expression. What is expressed is present in the expression in a different way than the cause is present in the effect. It is present in the expression itself and will be understood when the expression is understood.

From the outset Dilthey's efforts were directed toward distinguishing relationships in the historical world from the causal relationships of the natural order, and so the concepts of understanding standing and expression were always central for him. The methodological clarity he achieved through Husserl's influence allowed him in the end to integrate the concept of significance—a concept that arises from the continuity of effect—with the latter's *Logical Investigations*. Dilthey's concept of the structural quality of the life of spirit corresponds to the theory of the intentionality of consciousness in that structure is not merely a psychological fact but the phenomenological description of an essential quality of consciousness. Every consciousness is consciousness of something; every relation is a relation to something. According to Husserl, the correlative of this intentionality—the intentional object—is not a psychic component but an ideal unity, and meant as such. Thus Husserl's first "Logical Investigation" defended the concept of the one ideal significance against the prejudices of logical psychologism. This demonstration came to assume key importance for Dilthey. For it was only as a result of Husserl's analysis that he was able to say what distinguished "structure" from causal continuity.

An example will make this clear: a psychic structure, say an individual, acquires his individuality by developing his talents and at the same time experiencing the conditioning effect of circumstances. What emerges, the actual "individuality"—i.e., the character of the individual—is not a mere consequence of the causal factors nor to be understood only in terms of these causes, but it constitutes a unity that is intelligible in itself, a unity of life that is expressed in every one of its manifestations and hence can be understood in each of them. Something becomes fused here to form a unique configuration, independently of the system of cause and effect. This is what Dilthey meant by "structural continuity" and what, with Husserl, he now calls "significance."

Dilthey can now also say to what extent structural coherence is *given*—his chief bone of contention with Ebbinghaus. It is not given in the immediacy of an experience, but neither is it simply constructed on the basis of the "mechanism" of the psyche as the result of causal factors. Rather, the theory of the intentionality of consciousness provides a new foundation for the idea of givenness. Now one can no longer derive coherence from atoms of experience (Erlebnis) or explain it in this way. Consciousness, rather, is always already involved in coherence and has its own being in intending it. Thus Dilthey considered Husserl's *Logical Investigations* epoch-making[97] because he had legitimized such concepts as structure and significance, although they were not derivable from elements. They were now shown to be more fundamental than the elements from and upon which they were supposed to be built.

True, Husserl's demonstration of the ideality of significance was the result of purely *logical* investigations. What Dilthey makes of it is something quite different. For him significance is not a logical concept, but is to be understood as an expression of *life*. Life itself, flowing temporality, is ordered toward the formation of enduring units of significance. Life interprets itself. Life itself has a hermeneutical structure. Thus life constitutes the real ground of the human sciences. Hermeneutics is not a romantic heritage in Dilthey's thinking, but follows from the fact that philosophy is grounded in "life." Dilthey believes that here he has risen entirely above the "intellectualism" of Hegel. Nor could the romantic and pantheistic concept of individuality that derived from Leibniz satisfy him. Grounding philosophy in life defends it against the metaphysics of individuality and consciously distances it from the viewpoint of Leibniz's windowless monads that develop their own law. Individuality now is not a primordial idea rooted in phenomena. Rather, Dilthey insists that all "psychological life" is subject to the force of circumstances.[98] There is no such thing as the originating power of individuality. It becomes what it is by carrying itself out. Essential to the idea of individuality, as of all historical ideas, is that it is limited by the course of its effect. Even concepts like purpose and significance are not, for Dilthey, ideas in the Platonic or scholastic sense. They too are historical ideas, for they are limited by the course of their effect: they must be concepts of energy. Dilthey here relies on Fichte,[99] who also had an important influence on Ranke. Thus Dilthey's hermeneutics of life fundamentally seeks to retain the historical worldview.[100] Philosophy gives him only the conceptual tools to declare the latter's truth.

Despite these qualifications, however, it is still not clear whether Dilthey's grounding of hermeneutics in "life" really avoided the *implicit* consequences of idealistic metaphysics.[101] He sees the question as follows. How is the power of the individual related to what exists beyond and prior to him: objective spirit? What is the relation between power and significance, between forces and ideas, between the facticity and the ideality of life? This question must ultimately decide how knowledge of history is possible. For man in history is similarly wholly defined by the relation between individuality and objective spirit.

Now this relationship is clearly not unambiguous. It is, on the one hand, the experience of limitation, pressure, and resistance, through which the individual becomes aware of his own power. But it is not only the solid walls of actuality that he experiences. Rather, as a historical being he experiences historical realities which support the individual and in which he at once expresses and rediscovers himself. As such they are not "solid walls," but objectifications of life. (Droysen spoke of "moral forces.")

This is of great methodological importance for specifying the nature of the human sciences. Here the concept of the given has a basically different structure. Characteristic of the given in the human, unlike the natural, sciences is "that one has to discard all ideas of anything fixed or alien, which are appropriate to images of the physical world."[102] Here, the given is something made. Dilthey regards the old superiority that Vico attributed to historical objects as the ground of the universality with which understanding grasps the historical world.

The question is, however, whether the transition from the psychological to the hermeneutical standpoint can really succeed on this basis or whether Dilthey is ensnared in problems that bring him into undesired and unacknowledged proximity to speculative idealism.

For not only Fichte but Hegel can be heard in the passage referred to—even in the very words. His critique of "positivity,"[103] the concept of self-alienation, the definition of mind as recognition of oneself in other being can easily be derived from Dilthey's statement, and we may ask wherein lies the difference that the historical worldview asserted against idealism and that Dilthey undertook to validate epistemologically.

This question becomes more pressing when we consider the central phrase with which Dilthey characterizes life, this basic fact of history. He speaks of the "thought-forming work of life."[104] It is not easy to say how this phrase differs from Hegel. However "unfathomable a countenance"[105] life may present, and however much Dilthey may mock the over-optimistic view that regards life as only the progress of civilization, insofar as it is understood in terms of the thoughts that it forms, a teleological interpretative schema is imposed on life and it is conceived as *spirit*. Accordingly, we find that in his later years Dilthey draws closer and closer to Hegel and speaks of *spirit* where he used to say "life." He is simply repeating a conceptual development that Hegel himself underwent. In light of this fact it is interesting to note that we owe to Dilthey the knowledge of the early, so-called "theological," writings of Hegel. It emerges quite clearly from this material, which helps us to understand the evolution of Hegel's thinking, that his concept of spirit was based on a spiritual concept of life.[106]

Dilthey himself tried to give an account of what he has in common with Hegel and what separates them.[107] But what does his critique of Hegel's belief in reason, his speculative construction of world history, and his aprioristic deduction of all ideas from the dialectical self-unfolding of the absolute, amount to, if he himself still gives the concept of "objective mind" such a central place? It is true that Dilthey opposes Hegel's abstract construction of this concept: "today we must start from the reality of life." He writes, "We are seeking to understand the latter and present it in suitable concepts. Freed from the idealist construction and from being based one-sidedly on universal reason as expressing the essence of world spirit, a new concept of objective mind becomes possible: it comprises language, customs, every form of life, as well as the family, civil society, state, and law. And what Hegel calls absolute spirit as distinct from objective—namely, art, religion, and philosophy—also come under this concept . . . " (*Ges. Schr.* VII, 150).

Without a doubt this is an adaptation of Hegel. What does it mean? How far does it take account of the "reality of life"? The most significant thing is obviously Dilthey's extending the concept of objective spirit to art, religion, and philosophy. For this means that Dilthey does not regard them as immediate truth but as forms in which life expresses itself. In putting art and religion on the same level as philosophy he is likewise rejecting the claim of the speculative concept. At the same time, Dilthey is not denying that these forms take precedence over the other forms of objective spirit, for "precisely in their powerful forms" spirit objectifies itself and is known. This priority of a perfect self-knowledge of spirit was what caused Hegel to view these as forms of absolute spirit. There was no longer anything alien in them and hence spirit was entirely at home with itself. For Dilthey too, as we have seen, the objectifications of art represented the real triumph of hermeneutics. Thus he differs from Hegel ultimately on one thing only, that according to Hegel the homecoming of the spirit takes place in the philosophical concept whereas, for Dilthey, the philosophical concept is significant not as knowledge but as expression.

Thus we must ask whether there is not also for Dilthey a form of the spirit that is truly "absolute spirit"—i.e., transparency, the complete dissolution of all alienness, of all difference. For Dilthey there is no question that it exists and that what corresponds to this ideal is historical consciousness, not speculative philosophy. It sees all the phenomena of the human, historical world only as objects by means of which the spirit knows itself more fully. Understanding them as objectifications of spirit, it translates them back "into the mental life whence they came."[108] Thus for historical consciousness the forms that objective spirit takes are objects of this spirit's self-knowledge. Historical consciousness expands to universality, for it sees all the data of history as manifestations of the life from which they stem: "Here life is understood by life."[109] Hence, for historical consciousness the whole of tradition becomes the self-encounter of the human mind. Historical consciousness appropriates what seemed specially reserved to art, religion, and philosophy. *It is not in the speculative knowledge of the concept, but in historical consciousness that spirit's knowledge of itself is consummated.* Historical consciousness discerns historical spirit in all things. Even philosophy is to be regarded only as an expression of life. Insofar as philosophy is aware of this, it will give up its old claim to be knowledge through concepts. It becomes the philosophy of philosophy, a philosophical account of why there is philosophy in life, side by side with science. In his later writings Dilthey outlined this kind of philosophy of philosophy, and there he attributed the various types of worldviews to the variousness of the life that interprets itself.[110]

This historical overcoming of metaphysics is linked to the interpretation of great literature, which Dilthey regarded as the triumph of hermeneutics. But philosophy and art retain only a relative importance for the consciousness that understands historically. They assume a special place because mind does not have to be separated out of them by interpretation, since they are "sheer expression" and do not seek to be anything other than that. But even as such they are not immediate truth, but serve only as an organ for understanding life. Just as certain high points of a civilization more readily reveal the "spirit" of that civilization, and just as the really significant historical decisions appear in the plans and deeds of great men, so too philosophy and art are especially open to interpretive understanding. Here intellectual history avails itself of *form*, the pure development of meaningful wholes that have freed themselves from the stream of becoming. In the introduction to his biography of Schleiermacher Dilthey writes: "The history of intellectual movements has the advantage of possessing truthful monuments. One can be wrong about the intention, but not about the content of the actual inner self that is expressed in these works."[111] It is no accident that Dilthey has passed on to us this note of Schleiermacher's: "The blossom is the real maturity. The fruit is only the chaotic covering for what no longer belongs to the organic plant."[112] Dilthey obviously shares this aesthetic metaphysics. It is at the basis of his relation to history.

This corresponds to the transformed concept of objective mind with which historical consciousness replaces metaphysics. But we may ask whether historical consciousness is really able to fill the place vacated by Hegel's absolute knowledge, in which spirit comprehends itself in the speculative concept. Dilthey himself has pointed out that we understand historically because we are ourselves historical beings. This is supposed to make things easier epistemologically. But does it? Is Vico's oft repeated formula correct? Does it not transpose an experience of the human artistic spirit to the historical world, where, in the face of the course of events, one can no longer speak of "making"—i.e., of planning and carrying out? How are things made easier epistemologically? Are they not, in fact, made more difficult? Is not the fact that consciousness is historically conditioned inevitably an insuperable barrier to its reaching perfect fulfillment in historical knowledge? Hegel could regard this barrier as overcome by virtue of history's being superseded by absolute knowledge. But if life is the inexhaustible, creative reality that Dilthey thinks it, then must not the constant alteration of historical context preclude any knowledge from attaining to objectivity? Is it not the case, then, that historical consciousness is ultimately a utopian ideal, containing an internal contradiction?

(B) THE CONFLICT BETWEEN SCIENCE AND LIFE-PHILOSOPHY IN DILTHEY'S ANALYSIS OF HISTORICAL CONSCIOUSNESS

Dilthey thought about this problem tirelessly. He was always attempting to legitimate the knowledge of what was historically conditioned as an achievement of objective science, despite the fact that the knower is himself conditioned. It was to be legitimated by the theory of structure, which builds up its unity out of its own center. That a structured whole could be understood in terms of its own center corresponded to the old principle of hermeneutics and to the insistence of historical thinking that an age should be understood in terms of itself and not according to the criterion of some alien present. Dilthey thought[113] that the knowledge of increasingly large historical units could be conceived according to this schema and expanded to constitute knowledge of universal history, just as a word can be understood only in terms of the whole sentence, and the sentence fully understood only within the context of the whole text, indeed of the whole of literature.

Applying this schema presumes, of course, that one can overcome the fact that the historical observer is tied to time and place. But this is precisely the claim of historical consciousness, namely to have a truly historical viewpoint on everything. It sees this as its culminating achievement. Hence it is concerned to develop the "historical sense" in order to transcend the prejudices of one's own time. Thus Dilthey considered himself the true perfecter of the historical worldview because he sought to justify the rise of consciousness to historical consciousness. What his epistemological thinking tried to justify was fundamentally nothing other than the epic self-forgetfulness of Ranke. But in place of aesthetic self-forgetfulness there was the sovereignty of an infinite understanding. Basing historical study on a psychology of understanding, as Dilthey hoped to do, transports the historian to the ideative contemporaneity with his object that we call aesthetic and that we admire in Ranke.

Yet the important question remains how such infinite understanding is possible for finite human nature. Can this really have been Dilthey's meaning? For did he not insist against Hegel that one must preserve the consciousness of one's own *finitude?*

Let us examine this more closely. Dilthey's critique of Hegel's rational idealism was concerned only with the apriorism of his conceptual speculation. Fundamentally, he did not hesitate about the inner infinity of the mind, for he saw it as positively fulfilled in the ideal of a historically enlightened reason that has matured into a genius who understands everything. For Dilthey the awareness of finitude does not mean that consciousness was made finite or limited in any way; rather, that awareness bears witness to the capacity of life to rise in energy and activity above all limitations. Thus it represents precisely the potential infinity of the mind—though it is not in speculation, but in historical reason that this infinity is realized. Historical understanding expands to embrace all historical data and is truly universal, because it has a firm foundation in the inner totality and infinity of mind. Here Dilthey is following the old theory that understanding is possible because of the homogeneity of human nature. He sees the individual's private world of experience as the starting point for an expansion that, in a living transposition, fills out the narrowness and fortuitousness of his private experience with the infinity of what is available by re-experiencing the historical world.

Thus to him the limits on the universality of understanding that are due to the historical finitude of our being are only of a subjective nature. It is true that he still sees something positive in these limits that is fruitful for knowledge; thus he declares that only sympathy makes true understanding possible.[114] But we may ask whether this has any fundamental significance. First, let us establish one thing: he regards sympathy only as a condition of knowledge. With Droysen, we can ask whether sympathy (which is a form of love) is not something more than an emotive condition of knowledge. It is one of the forms of relationship between I and Thou. Certainly there is knowledge involved in this real moral relationship, and so it is that love gives insight.[115] But sympathy is much more than simply a condition of knowledge. Through it another person is transformed at the same time. Droysen makes the profound remark: "You must be like that, for that is the way I love you: the secret of all education."[116]

When Dilthey speaks about universal sympathy and thinks of the ripe, detached wisdom of old age, he certainly does not mean this moral phenomenon of sympathy; he is thinking of an ideal historical consciousness which fundamentally transcends the limitations of understanding that are due to the subjective accidents of preference and affinity for an object. Here Dilthey follows Ranke, who regarded universal sympathy as comprising the historian's dignity.[117] True, he seems to restrict his meaning when he says that the optimal conditions for historical understanding occur where there is a "continuing conditioning of one's own life by the great object," and when he regards this as the greatest possibility of understanding.[118] But it would be wrong to understand this conditioning of one's own life as anything but a subjective condition of knowledge.

We can see this from examples. When Dilthey talks of Thucidydes' relationship to Pericles or Ranke's to Luther, he means a con-genial intuitive bond that spontaneously evokes in the historian an understanding that would otherwise be difficult to achieve. But fundamentally he regards this kind of understanding, which succeeds brilliantly in exceptional cases, as always obtainable through scientific method. He explicitly justifies the human sciences' use of comparative methods by saying that their task is to overcome the accidental limits imposed by one's own range of experience and "to rise to truths of greater universality."[119]

This is one of the most questionable points of his theory. Comparison essentially presupposes that the knowing subjectivity has the freedom to have both members of the comparison at its disposal. It openly makes both things contemporary. Hence we must doubt whether the method of comparison really satisfies the idea of historical knowledge. Is it not the case that this procedure—adopted in some areas of the natural sciences and very successful in many fields of the human sciences, e.g., linguistics, law, aesthetics[120]—is being promoted from a subordinate tool to central importance for defining historical knowledge, and that it often gives false legitimacy to superficial and arbitrary reflection? We must agree with Count Yorck here when he writes: "Comparison is always aesthetic; it is always concerned with the form,"[121] and we recall that before him Hegel brilliantly criticized the comparative method.[122]

At any rate, it is clear that Dilthey did not regard the fact that finite, historical man is tied to a particular time and place as any fundamental impairment of the possibility of knowledge in the human sciences. Historical consciousness was supposed to rise above its own relativity in a way that made objectivity in the human sciences possible. We may ask how this claim can be justified without implying a concept of absolute, philosophical knowledge beyond all historical consciousness. What is the special virtue of historical consciousness—by contrast to all other forms of consciousness in history—that its own relativity does not endanger the fundamental claim to objective knowledge?

This virtue cannot consist in its really being "absolute knowledge" in Hegel's sense—i.e., in its uniting the whole history of mind in a present self-consciousness. The claim of philosophical consciousness to contain within itself the whole truth of the history of mind is contested precisely by the historical worldview. That impossibility is, rather, the reason historical experience is necessary; human consciousness is not an infinite intellect for which everything exists, simultaneous and co-present. The absolute identity of consciousness and object simply cannot be achieved by finite, historical consciousness. It always remains entangled in the context of historical effect. What, then, accounts for its nevertheless being able to transcend itself and thus achieve objective historical knowledge?

We will not find any explicit answer to this question in Dilthey. But all his work as a scholar gives an indirect answer. We might say that historical consciousness is not so much self-extinction as the intensified possession of itself, which distinguishes it from all other forms of mental life. However indissoluble the ground of historical life from which it emerges, historical consciousness can still understand historically its own capacity to take up a historical orientation. Hence, unlike consciousness before its victorious development into historical consciousness, it is not the immediate expression of a living reality. Historical consciousness no longer simply applies its own criteria of understanding to the tradition in which it is situated, nor does it naively assimilate tradition and simply carry it on. Rather, it adopts a reflective posture toward both itself and the tradition in which it is situated. It understands itself in terms of its own history. *Historical consciousness is a mode of self-knowledge.*

This kind of answer shows the need for a fuller account of the nature of self-knowledge. And, in fact, Dilthey's efforts—unsuccessful, as we shall see—were directed toward explaining "in terms of life" how self-knowledge gives birth to scientific consciousness.

Dilthey starts from life: life itself is ordered toward reflection. We are indebted to Georg Misch for a rigorous account of the influence of life philosophy in Dilthey's thought. It rests on the fact that there is knowledge in life itself. Even the interiority that characterizes experience (Erlebnis) contains a kind of return of life to itself. "Knowledge is there; it is unreflectively connected with experience" (VI, 18). For Dilthey the same immanent reflexivity of life, however, also determines the way significance emerges from a life context. For significance is experienced only in our stepping outside the "pursuit of goals." This kind of reflection is possible when we distance ourselves from the context of our own activity. Dilthey emphasizes—and he is undoubtedly correct—that life's natural view of itself is developed prior to any scientific objectification. It objectifies itself in the wisdom of proverb and legend, but above all in great works of art, where "something of the mind detaches itself from its creator."[123] Art is a special organ for understanding life because in its "confines between knowledge and act" life reveals itself at a depth that is inaccessible to observation, reflection, and theory.

If life itself is ordered towards reflection, then the pure expression of experience in great art has a special value. But this is not to deny that knowledge is already operative and hence truth can be recognized in every expression of life. For the forms of expression that dominate human life are all forms of objective mind. In language, customs, and legal forms the individual has always already risen above his particularity. The great shared moral world in which he lives represents a fixed point through which he can understand himself in the face of the fluid contingency of his subjective emotions. In being devoted to common aims, in being absorbed in activity for the community, a person is "freed from particularity and transience."

Droysen could have said the same thing, but in Dilthey it has its own tone. According to Dilthey the same life tendency is seen both in contemplation and in practical reflection: a "striving towards stability."[124] This shows why he was able to regard the objectivity of scientific knowledge and philosophical self-analysis as the culmination of a natural tendency of life. In Dilthey's thinking there is no merely extrinsic accommodation between the method of the human sciences and the procedure of the natural sciences; rather, he sees a genuine community between them. The essence of the experimental method consists in rising above the subjective fortuitousness of observation and with the help of method attaining knowledge of natural laws. Similarly, the human sciences endeavor to rise methodologically above the subjective fortuitousness of their own standpoint in history through the tradition accessible to them, and thus attain objective historical knowledge. Philosophical self-analysis also moves in the same direction insofar as it "objectifies itself as a human, historical fact" and gives up the claim to pure knowledge through concepts.

Hence for Dilthey the connection between life and knowledge is an original datum. This makes Dilthey's position invulnerable to all the objections of philosophy, especially the arguments of idealistic reflective philosophy against historical "relativism." His basing philosophy on the original fact of life does not require a collection of noncontradictory propositions to replace the system of thought of earlier philosophies. Rather, what Dilthey showed was true of the role of reflection in life is likewise true of philosophical self-reflection. It "thinks life itself to the end" by understanding philosophy as an objectification of life. It becomes philosophy of philosophy, but not in the idealistic sense. It does not try to base the one possible philosophy on the unity of a speculative principle, but continues along the path of historical self-reflection. Hence it is not open to the objection of relativism.

Dilthey himself constantly pondered this objection and sought to determine how objectivity is possible in relativity and how we are to conceive the relation of the finite to the absolute. "The task is to show how the values relative to an age have expanded into something absolute."[125] But we will not find in Dilthey a real answer to the problem of relativism, not because he never found the right answer, but because this was not properly his question. He knew, rather, that in the evolution of historical self-reflection leading him from relativity to relativity, he was on the way toward the absolute. Thus Ernst Troeltsch quite rightly summed up Dilthey's life's work in the words: "from relativity to totality." Dilthey's formulation of the same thing was "to be conscious that one is relative"[126]—a formulation openly directed against the claim of reflective philosophy to leave behind all the limitations of finitude, in soaring toward absoluteness and infinity of spirit, in the climax and truth of self-awareness. But that he was always reflecting on the charge of "relativism" shows that he was not really able to steadfastly follow out the logical consequences of his life philosophy against the reflective philosophy of idealism. Otherwise, he could not have avoided viewing the charge of relativism as an instance of the "intellectualism" that he had sought to undermine by beginning from the immanence of knowledge in life.

This ambiguity has its ultimate foundation in an inner disunity of his thought, the unresolved Cartesianism from which he starts. His epistemological reflections on the basis of the human sciences are not really compatible with his starting from life philosophy. We have eloquent proof of this in his last writings. There Dilthey calls for a philosophical foundation that would extend to every area in which "consciousness has shaken off authority and is trying to attain valid knowledge through reflection and doubt."[127] This statement seems a harmless pronouncement on the nature of science and modern philosophy in general. The Cartesian echoes cannot be missed. But in fact the statement is applied in a completely different sense when Dilthey goes on: "Everywhere life leads to reflection on what is given in it, and reflection leads to doubt. If life is able to maintain itself against doubt, then thought can finally attain valid knowledge."[128] Here it is no longer philosophical prejudices that are to be overcome through an epistemological grounding in the style of Descartes, but it is the realities of life, the tradition of morals, religion, and positive law that are being destroyed by reflection and need a new order. When Dilthey speaks here of knowledge and reflection, he does not mean the general immanence of knowledge in life, but *a movement that is directed against life*. Tradition in the form of morals, religion, and law rests, by contrast, on a knowledge that life has of itself. Indeed, we have seen that in consciously surrendering to tradition, the individual is raised to objective mind. We will readily grant Dilthey that the influence of thought on life "comes from the inner need to find something firm in the ceaseless change of sense impressions, desires, and feelings, something that enables one's life to be steady and unified."[129] But this achievement of thought is something immanent in life itself. It takes place in morals, law, and religion—objectifications of mind that support the individual insofar as he surrenders himself to the objectivity of society. The fact that it is necessary to adopt the "standpoint of reflection and doubt" and that this is what happens "in all forms of scientific reflection" (and not elsewhere) is simply incompatible with Dilthey's life philosophy.[130] This is, rather, a description of the special ideal of scientific enlightenment, which is as little compatible with a reflection immanent in life as was the "intellectualism" of the Enlightenment, against which Dilthey's grounding in philosophy of life was directed.

In fact, there are various kinds of certainty. The kind of certainty afforded by a verification that has passed through doubt is different from the immediate living certainty that all ends and values have when they appear in human consciousness with an absolute claim. But the certainty of science is very different from the certainty acquired in life. Scientific certainty always has something Cartesian about it. It is the result of a critical method that admits only the validity of what cannot be doubted. This certainty, then, does not proceed from doubts arising and being overcome, but is always anterior to doubt's occurring to anyone. Just as when in his famous meditation on doubt Descartes set up an artificial and hyperbolical doubt like an experiment, which led to the fundamentum inconcussum of self-consciousness, so methodical science fundamentally doubts everything that can be doubted in order to guarantee the certainty of its results.

It is characteristic of the problem involved in Dilthey's attempt to ground the human sciences that he does not distinguish between this methodological doubt and the doubts that come "of their own accord." The certainty of science is, for him, the culminating form of the certainty of life. That does not mean he did not experience the uncertainty of life in the full weight of historical concreteness. On the contrary, the more he grew into modern science, the more strongly he experienced the tension between the Christian tradition of his origin and the historical forces liberated by modern life. Dilthey's need for something firm is explicitly the need for protection from the frightful realities of life. But he expects the uncertainty and unsureness of life to be overcome not so much by the stability that the experience of life provides as by science.

For Dilthey, a child of the Enlightenment, the Cartesian way of proceeding via doubt to the certain is immediately self-evident. The shaking off of the authoritative, of which he speaks, corresponds not only to the need to ground the natural sciences epistemologically, but has to do as well with the knowledge of values and ends. For him they too are no longer an indubitable whole consisting of tradition, morals, religion, and law, but "the spirit must, here also, produce out of itself valid knowledge."[131]

The private secularization process that brings Dilthey, the theological student, to philosophy is of a piece with the historical development of modern science. Just as modern science does not view nature as an intelligible whole but as a process that has nothing to do with human beings, a process on which scientific research throws a limited, but reliable light, thus making it possible to control it, so the human mind, seeking protection and certainty, sets scientific understanding against the "incomprehensibility of life," this "frightful countenance." It is supposed to reveal the social, historical reality of life so fully that, despite the ultimate incomprehensibility of life, such knowledge will impart protection and certainty. *The Enlightenment reaches its consummation as historical enlightenment.*

We can thus understand why Dilthey starts from romantic hermeneutics.[132] With its aid he succeeds in concealing the difference between the nature of historical experience and science's mode of knowledge or, better, he succeeds in harmonizing the human sciences' mode of knowledge with the methodological criteria of the natural sciences. We saw above[133] that no extrinsic accommodation led him to do so. We can now see that he was able to harmonize them only by neglecting the essential historicity of the human sciences. This can be seen clearly in the kind of objectivity he attributed to them; as sciences they are supposed to have the same objectivity as the natural sciences. So Dilthey loves the term "results,"[134] and in describing the methodology of the human sciences, he is at pains to show them as the equals of the natural sciences. Romantic hermeneutics here came to his assistance since, as we saw, it took no account whatsoever of the historical nature of experience. It assumed that the object of understanding is the text to be deciphered and its meaning understood. Thus for romanitic hermeneutics every encounter with a text is an encounter of the spirit with itself. Every text is strange enough to present a problem, and yet familiar enough to be fundamentally intelligible even when we know nothing about it except that it is text, writing, an expression of mind.

As we saw, Schleiermacher's model of hermeneutics is the congenial understanding that can be achieved in the relation between I and Thou. Texts are just as susceptible of being fully understood as is the Thou. The author's meaning can be divined directly from his text. The interpreter is absolutely contemporaneous with his author. This is the triumph of philological method, understanding the mind of the past as present, the strange as familiar. Dilthey has a profound sense of this triumph. He uses it to justify the equality of the human sciences. Just as natural science always examines some present thing for the information it can yield, so the human scientist interrogates texts.

Dilthey thought he was legitimating the human sciences epistemologically by conceiving the historical world as a text to be deciphered. He drew a consequence which the historical school, as we have seen, was never quite able to accept. True, Ranke viewed the sacred task of the historian as deciphering the hieroglyphs of history. But the idea that historical reality is such a pure thread of meaning that it need only be deciphered like a text did not really accord with the deeper tendency of the historical school. Yet Dilthey, the interpreter of this historical worldview, was driven to this conclusion (as Ranke and Droysen had basically been) to the extent that hermeneutics was his model. The result was that history was ultimately reduced to intellectual history, a reduction which Dilthey accepts in his half-negation, half-affirmation of Hegel's philosophy of mind. Schleiermacher's hermeneutics rested on an artificial methodical abstraction which tried to establish a universal instrument of the mind, but tried to use this instrument to express the saving power of the Christian faith; but in Dilthey's grounding of the human sciences hermeneutics is more than a means. It is the universal medium of the historical consciousness, for which there no longer exists any knowledge of truth other than the understanding of expression and, through expression, life. Everything in history is intelligible, for everything is text. "Life and history make sense like the letters of a word."[135] Thus Dilthey ultimately conceives inquiring into the historical past *as deciphering and not as historical experience* (Erfahrung).

Undoubtedly this did not do justice to the truth of the historical school. Romantic hermeneutics and the philosophical method on which it is based are not adequate as the basis of historical study. Similarly, Dilthey's concept of inductive procedure, borrowed from the natural sciences, is inadequate. Fundamentally, historical experience, as he means it, is not a procedure and does not have the anonymity of a method. Admittedly, one can derive general rules of experience from it, but their methodological value is not that of laws under which all cases could be clearly subsumed. Rather, rules of experience require experience in order to use them and are basically what they are only in this use. In view of this situation it must be admitted that knowledge in the human sciences is not the same as in the inductive sciences, but has quite a different kind of objectivity and is acquired in a quite different way. Dilthey's grounding of the human sciences in life philosophy and his critique of all dogmatism, including even empiricism, had attempted to show just this. But the epistemological Cartesianism that dominated him proved stronger, so that in Dilthey the historicity of historical experience is never truly integrated in his thought. It is true that Dilthey did not overlook the significance that the individual and universal experience of life have for the human sciences, but he defines both merely privatively. Such experience (Erfahrung) is an unmethodical and unverifiable induction that already points to the methodological induction of science.

If we now recall the self-understanding of the human sciences from which we started, we can see that Dilthey's contribution to it was especially characteristic. The conflict that he tried to resolve shows clearly what pressure the methodology of modern science exerts and what our task must be: namely to describe more adequately the experience of the human sciences and the objectivity they are able to achieve.

3 OVERCOMING THE EPISTEMOLOGICAL PROBLEM THROUGH PHENOMENOLOGICAL RESEARCH

(A) THE CONCEPT OF LIFE IN HUSSERL AND COUNT YORCK

It belongs to the nature of the case that speculative idealism offers greater possibilities for performing our task than did Schleiermacher and the hermeneutics emanating from him. For in speculative idealism the concept of the given, of positivity, had been subjected to a fundamental critique —and it is to this that Dilthey ultimately tried to appeal in support of his own tendency toward life philosophy. He writes, "How does Fichte characterize the beginning of something new? He starts from the intellectual intuition of the 'I,' but does not conceive the latter as a substance, as a being, as something given but—precisely because of this intuition, i.e. this deepening of the 'I' in itself—as life, activity, and energy; and, accordingly, he shows that it contains energy concepts such as antithesis."[136] Similarly, Dilthey ultimately came to regard Hegel's concept of mind as a genuine living historical concept.[137] As we found in our analysis of the concept of experience, some of his contemporaries worked in the same direction: Nietzsche, Bergson—that late successor of the romantic critique of the mode of thinking embodied in mechanics—and Georg Simmel. But the concept of substance is in fact inadequate for historical being and knowledge; *Heidegger* was the first to make generally known the radical challenge of thought implicit in this inadequacy.[138] He was the first to liberate Dilthey's philosophical intention. His work built on research in intentionality carried out by *the phenomenology of Husserl*, which was a decisive breakthrough in that it was not at all the extreme Platonism that Dilthey believed it to be.[139]

Rather, the more insight into the slow growth of Husserl's ideas we gain from working through the great edition of his works, the clearer it becomes that with intentionality we get a more and more radical critique of the "objectivism" of previous philosophy, Dilthey included.[140] This was to culminate in the claim "that intentional phenomenology has made the mind, as mind, into a field of systematic experience and science, and thus has totally transformed the task of knowledge. The universality of absolute mind embraces all beings in an absolute historicity in which nature as a construct of the mind also finds its place."[141] It is not by accident that mind as the only absolute, i.e. non-relative, thing is here distinguished from the relativity of everything that appears before it. Even Husserl himself recognizes that his phenomenology continues the transcendental inquiry of Kant and Fichte: "In justice, however, it must be added that the German idealism originating in Kant was already passionately concerned to overcome the naivete [of objectivism] that had already become quite perceptible."[142]

These statements in the later Husserl might be motivated by the debate with *Being and Time*, but they are preceded by so many other attempts to formulate his position that it is clear that Husserl had always intended to apply his ideas to the problems of the historical sciences. Thus what we have here is not an extrinsic association with the work of Dilthey (or, later, with that of Heidegger), but the consequence of his own critique of objectivist psychology and of the pseudo-Platonism of previous philosophy of consciousness. After the publication of *Ideas II* this is quite clear.[143]

In view of this, we need to make room in our discussion for Husserl's phenomenology.[144]

When Dilthey linked his reflections to Husserl's *Logical Investigations*, he grasped what had been the salient point throughout. According to Husserl himself[145] the a priori correlation of the object of experience with modes of givenness dominated his life's work after the *Logical Investigations*. In the fifth "Logical Investigation" he elaborated the nature of intentional experiences and distinguished consciousness "as an intentional experience" (this is the title of the second chapter) from the real unity of consciousness in experience and from the inner perception of it. Here already consciousness was not an "object," but an essential co-ordination—the point that was so illuminating for Dilthey. What investigating this co-ordination revealed was a starting point for overcoming "objectivism," insofar as the meaning of words could no longer be confused with the actual psychic content of consciousness—e.g., the associative images that a word evokes. The intention and fulfillment of meaning belong essentially to the unity of meaning, and like the meanings of the words that we use, every existing thing that has validity for me possesses correlatively and by virtue of its nature an "ideal universality of actual and potential experiencing modes of givenness."[146]

Thus was born the idea of "phenomenology"—i.e. bracketing all positing of being and investigating the subjective modes of givenness. This became a universal program, the aim of which was to make intelligible all objectivity, all being-sense. But human subjectivity also possesses being-value. Thus it too can be regarded as a "phenomenon" and can be explored in its various modes of givenness. This exploration of the "I" as phenomenon is not exploring the "inner perception" of a real "I," nor is it the mere reconstruction of "consciousness"—i.e., the relation of the contents of consciousness to a transcendental "I" pole (Natorp),[147] but it is a highly differentiated theme of transcendental reflection. In contrast to the mere givenness of the phenomena of objective consciousness, a givenness in intentional experiences, this reflection constitutes a new dimension of research. For there is such a thing as givenness that is not itself the object of intentional acts. Every experience has implicit horizons of before and after, and finally fuses with the continuum of the experiences present in the before and after to form a unified flow of experience.

Husserl's investigations of the constitution of time consciousness come from the need to grasp the mode of being of this flow and hence to draw subjectivity into research on intentional correlation. From now on all other phenomenological research sees itself as an inquiry into the constitution of the unities of time consciousness and in time consciousness, which themselves again presuppose the constitution of time consciousness itself. This shows that the discreteness of experience (Erlebnis)—however much it may retain its methodological significance as the intentional correlate of a constituted meaning value—is not an ultimate phenomenological datum. Rather, every such intentional experience always implies a twofold empty horizon of what is not actually meant in it, but toward which an actual meaning can, of its nature, be directed; and the unity of the flow of experience obviously includes the whole of all experiences that can be thematized in this way. Hence the constitution of the temporality of consciousness underlies all the problems of constitution. The flow of experience has the character of a universal horizon consciousness, and only from it is the discrete experience given as an experience at all.

Undoubtedly the concept and phenomenon of the *horizon* is of crucial importance for Husserl's phenomenological research. With this concept, which we too shall have occasion to use, Husserl is obviously seeking to capture the way all limited intentionality of meaning merges into the fundamental continuity of the whole. A horizon is not a rigid boundary but something that moves with one and invites one to advance further. Thus the horizon intentionality which constitutes the unity of the flow of experience is paralleled by an equally comprehensive horizon intentionality on the objective side. For everything that is given as existent is given in terms of a world and hence brings the world horizon with it. In explicit self-criticism of *Ideas I*, Husserl emphasized that he had not at the time (1923) been sufficiently aware of the importance of the phenomenon of world.[148] The theory of transcendental reduction that he had laid out in his *Ideas* was inevitably made more and more complicated by this. Merely superseding the validity of the objective sciences was no longer enough, for even in a perfect "epoche"—bracketing the being posited by scientific knowledge—the world still remains valid as something pregiven. Hence epistemological self-questioning which inquires only into the a priori, eidetic truths of science is not radical enough.

On this point Husserl could regard himself as in a certain agreement with Dilthey's intentions. In similar fashion Dilthey had opposed neo-Kantian critical philosophy for only going back to the epistemological subject. "No real blood runs in the veins of the cognitive subject that Locke, Hume, and Kant constructed."[149] Dilthey himself went back to the unity of life, to the "standpoint of life"; and similarly Husserl's "conscious life," a word that he apparently took over from Natorp, already indicates the subsequent strong tendency to study not only individual experiences, but the concealed, anonymously implicit intentionalities of consciousness, and in this way to make all objective validity of being intelligible. Subsequently this is called illuminating the achievements (Leistungen) of "productive life" (leistenden Lebens).

That Husserl is everywhere concerned with the "achievements" of transcendental subjectivity is simply in agreement with phenomenology's task of studying constitution. It is characteristic of his own intention, however, that he no longer says "consciousness," or even "subjectivity," but "life." He is trying to penetrate behind the actuality of the sense-giving consciousness, and even behind the potentiality of shared meaning, to the universality of an achievement that is alone able to measure the universality of what is achieved—i.e., constituted in its validity. The all-embracing world horizon is constituted by a fundamentally *anonymous* intentionality—i.e., not achieved by anyone by name. Using a concept consciously formulated in contrast to a concept of the world that includes the universe of what can be made objective by science, Husserl calls this phenomeno-logical concept of the world "life-world"—i.e., the world in which we are immersed in the natural attitude that never becomes an object as such for us, but that represents the pregiven basis of all experience. This world horizon is a presupposition of all science as well and is, therefore, more fundamental. As a horizon phenomenon "world" is essentially related to subjectivity, and this relation means also that it "exists in transiency."[150] The life-world exists in a constant movement of relative validity.

The concept of the *life-world*[151] is the antithesis of all objectivism. It is an essentially historical concept, which does not refer to a universe of being, to an "existent world." In fact, not even the infinite idea of a true world can be meaningfully created out of the infinite progress of human historical worlds in historical experience (Erfahrung). Certainly one can inquire into the structure embracing all the worlds that man has ever experienced, which is simply the experience of the possibility of world, and in this sense we can indeed speak of an ontology of the world. But this ontology of the world would still remain something quite different from what the natural sciences could even ideally achieve. It would present a philosophical task whose object was the essential structure of the world. But the *life-world* means something else, namely the whole in which we live as historical creatures. And here we cannot avoid the consequence that, given the historicity of experience implied in it, the idea of a universe of possible historical life-worlds simply does not make sense. The infiniteness of the past, and above all the openness of the historical future, is incompatible with the idea of a historical universe. Husserl has explicitly drawn this conclusion, without being frightened by the "specter" of relativism.[152]

It is clear that the life-world is always at the same time a communal world that involves being with other people as well. It is a world of persons, and in the natural attitude the validity of this personal world is always assumed. But how can its validity be based on an achievement of subjectivity? For phenomenological analysis of constitution, this presents the most difficult task of all, and Husserl never tires of examining its paradoxes. How can something that has no validity as an object, but itself seeks to be an "I," originate in the "pure I"?

The principle of "radical" idealism—namely of always going back to the constitutive acts of transcendental subjectivity—must obviously illuminate the universal horizon of consciousness that is the "world" and, above all, the intersubjectivity of this world—although what is constituted in this way, the world as what is common to many individuals, itself includes subjectivity. Though it is supposed to bracket all the validity of the world and all the pregivenness of anything else, transcendental reflection must regard itself too as included in the life-world. The reflective "I" sees itself as living in the context of ends for which the life-world is the basis. Thus, constituting the life-world (as well as intersubjectivity) is a paradoxical task. But Husserl regards all these as only apparent paradoxes. He is convinced that they are resolved if we consistently maintain the transcendental meaning of the phenomenological reduction and don't fear the bogey of a transcendental solipsism. Given this clear tendency of Husserl's thought, it seems to me wrong to accuse him of any ambiguity in the concept of constitution, regarding it as something intermediate between definition and creation.[153] He himself maintains that his thinking has entirely overcome the fear of generative idealism. His theory of phenomenological reduction seeks, rather, to display the true meaning of this idealism for the first time. Transcendental subjectivity is the Ur-Ich ("the primal I") and not "an I." For it the basis of the pregiven world is superseded. It is the absolute irrelative to which all relativity, including that of the inquiring "I," is related.

There is one element in Husserl's thinking, however, that constantly threatens to burst this framework asunder. His position, in fact, is more than simply a radicalization of transcendental idealism, and this "more" is indicated by the function that the concept of "life" performs in his thought. "Life" is not just the unreflective living characteristic of the natural attitude. "Life" is also, and no less, the transcendentally reduced subjectivity that is the source of all objectifications. "Life" is what Husserl emphasizes as his own achievement in his critique of the objectivist naivete of all previous philosophy. In his eyes, it consists in having revealed the unreality of the long-standing epistemological controversy between idealism and realism and, instead, in having thematized the inner co-ordination between subjectivity and objectivity.[154] This is the reason for his phrase "productive life." "The radical contemplation of the world is the systematic and pure interior contemplation of subjectivity, which externalizes itself in the 'exterior.'[155] As with the unity of a living organism, we can certainly examine and analyze it from outside, but can understand only if we go back to its hidden roots. . . . "[156] Thus, too, the intelligibility of the subject's comportment to the world does not reside in conscious experiences and their intentionality but in the anonymous "productions" of life. The metaphor of the organism that Husserl employs here is more than a metaphor. As he expressly states, he wants to be taken literally.

If we follow up these and similar linguistic and conceptual hints that we find here and there in Husserl, we find ourselves moving closer to the speculative concept of life held by German idealism. What Husserl means, however, is that we cannot conceive subjectivity as the opposite of objectivity, because this concept of subjectivity would itself be conceived in objective terms. Instead, his transcendental phenomenology seeks to be "correlation research." But this means that the relation is the primary thing, and the "poles" into which it unfolds itself are contained within it,[157] just as what is alive contains all its expressions of life in the unity of its organic being. "The naivete of talk about 'objectivity' which completely ignores experiencing, knowing subjectivity, subjectivity which performs real, concrete achievements, the naivete of the scientist concerned with nature, with the world in general, who is blind to the fact that all the truths that he acquires as objective, and the objective world itself that is the substratum in his formulas is his own *life construct* that has grown within him, is, of course, no longer possible, when *life* comes on the scene," writes Husserl with regard to Hume.[158]

Here the concept of life clearly plays the same role as the concept of the coherence of experience (Erlebnis) in Dilthey's investigations. Just as Dilthey begins with experience only in order to reach the concept of psychic coherence, so Husserl shows that the unity of the flow of experience is prior to the discreteness of experiences and essentially necessary to it. As in Dilthey, the thematic investigation of conscious life must overcome the tendency to base itself on individual experiences. To this extent there is a genuine parallel between the two thinkers. They both go back to the concreteness of life.

Yet the question arises whether or not they do justice to the speculative demands implied by the concept of life. Dilthey endeavors to derive the structure of the historical world from the reflexivity inherent in life, and Husserl attempts to derive the constitution of the historical world from "conscious life." We might ask whether, in both cases, the genuine content of the concept of life does not become alienated when it is articulated in terms of the epistemological schema: deriving it from the ultimate data of consciousness. The problem of intersubjectivity and the understanding of the other "I" evokes this question. We have the same difficulty in both Husserl and Dilthey. The immanent data of reflectively examined consciousness do not include the "Thou" in an immediate and primary way. Husserl is quite right when he emphasizes that the "Thou" does not possess the kind of immanent transcendence that belongs to the objects of experience (Erfahrung) in the external world; for every "Thou" is an alter ego, i.e. it is understood in terms of the ego and, at the same, as detached from it and, like the ego itself, as independent. Through the most painstaking investigations, Husserl tried to illuminate the analogy between the "I" and the "Thou"—which Dilthey interprets purely psychologically through the analogy of empathy—by way of the intersubjectivity of the communal world. He was sufficiently rigorous not to limit the epistemological priority of transcendental subjectivity in any way. But his ontological prejudice is the same as Dilthey's. The other person is first apprehended as an object of perception which then, through empathy, becomes a "Thou." In Husserl the concept of empathy has a purely transcendental meaning no doubt,[159] but it is still oriented to the interiority of self-consciousness and fails to orient itself toward the functional circle[160] of life, which goes far beyond consciousness, to which, however, it claims to return.

Thus, in fact, the speculative import of the concept of life remained undeveloped in both men. Dilthey simply tries to play off the viewpoint of life polemically against metaphysical thinking, and Husserl has absolutely no idea of the connection between this concept and the metaphysical tradition in general and speculative idealism in particular.

At this point the posthumous papers of *Count Yorck*, though unfortunately very fragmentary, are of surprising contemporary importance.[161] Although reference had been made to the brilliant insights of this major figure by Heidegger, who regarded Yorck's ideas as even more important than Dilthey's, the fact still remained that Dilthey completed a great life's work, whereas the letters of Yorck were never developed into a larger systematic whole. The posthumous papers from the last years, however, have now thoroughly changed this situation. Even though they are only fragments, his systematic intention is still sufficiently developed to leave no doubt about the place of his work in the history of thought.

It achieves precisely what we failed to find above in Dilthey and Husserl. It makes a bridge between speculative idealism and the century's new experimental standpoint, for the concept of life is presented as comprehending both. However speculative it sounds, the analysis of being alive, which is for Yorck the starting point, still embraces the scientific mode of thinking of the century—explicitly the concept of life held by Darwin. Life is self-assertion; this is the basis. The structure of being-alive consists in being primordial division (Urteilung)—i.e., in still continuing to assert itself as a unity in division and articulation. But judgment (Urteilung) is also viewed as the essence of self-consciousness, for even if it always distinguishes itself into what is itself and what is other, it still consists—as a living thing—in the play and interplay of the factors that constitute it. Like all life it is a test, an experiment. "Spontaneity and dependence are the basic characteristics of consciousness, constitutive in the area both of somatic and of psychic articulation, just as neither seeing, physical sensation, imagining, willing, nor feeling would exist without the existence of objects."[162] Consciousness too is to be understood as a life comportment. This is the fundamental methodological demand that Yorck makes of philosophy, and in this he considers himself at one with Dilthey. Thought must be brought back to this hidden foundation (Husserl would say: to this hidden achievement). To do so, the effort of philosophical reflection is necessary, for philosophy acts against the tendency of life. Yorck writes, "Now our thinking moves in the sphere of conscious results" (i.e., it is not aware of the real relation of the "results" to the life comportment on which the results depend). "The achieved diremption is its presupposition."[163] Yorck means that the results of thinking are results only because they have become detached from the life comportment and can be so detached. From this Yorck concludes that philosophy must reverse this process of detachment. It must repeat the experiment of life in reverse, "in order to know the conditions which govern the results of life."[164] This is admittedly formulated in a very objectivist and scientific way, and Husserl's theory of reduction would appeal, against it, to its own purely transcendental mode of thinking. In fact, however, Yorck's bold and assured thinking not only shows the influence of Dilthey and Husserl, but proves to be superior to them both. For here thought truly develops at the level of the identity philosophy of speculative idealism and thus reveals the hidden origin of the concept of life at which Dilthey and Husserl are aiming.

If we pursue Yorck's thought further, the persistence of idealist motifs becomes quite clear. What Yorck is presenting here is the structural *correlation between life and self-consciousness* already developed in Hegel's *Phenomenology*. In the manuscript fragments that have been preserved, we can see the central importance that the concept of life had for Hegel as early as his last years in Frankfurt. In his *Phenomenology* the phenomenon of life makes the decisive transition from consciousness to self-consciousness. This is, in fact, no artificial connection, for life and self-consciousness really are analogous. Life is defined by the fact that what is alive differentiates itself from the world in which it lives and with which it remains connected, and preserves itself in this differentiation. What is alive preserves itself by drawing into itself everything that is outside it. Everything that is alive nourishes itself on what is alien to it. The fundamental fact of being alive is assimilation. Differentiation, then, is at the same time non-differentiation. The alien is appropriated.

As Hegel had already shown and Yorck continues to hold, this structure of being alive has its correlative in the nature of self-consciousness. Its being consists in its ability to make everything the object of its knowledge, and yet in everything that it knows, it knows itself. Thus as knowledge it differentiates itself from itself and, at the same time, as self-consciousness, it folds back on and returns to itself.

Obviously we are concerned here with more than a mere structural correspondence between life and self-consciousness. Hegel quite rightly derives self-consciousness dialectically from life. What is alive can never be really known by objective consciousness, by the effort of understanding which seeks to penetrate the law of appearances. What is alive is not such that a person could ever grasp it from outside, in its living quality. The only way to grasp life is, rather, to become inwardly aware of it. Hegel refers to the story of the veiled image of Sais when describing the inner self-objectification of life and self-consciousness: "here the inner contemplates the inner."[165] Life is experienced only in the awareness of oneself, the inner consciousness of one's own living. Hegel shows how this experience flares up in desire and is extinguished in the satisfaction of desire. This self-awareness in which being alive becomes aware of itself is a false preform, the lowest form of self-consciousness, for becoming conscious of oneself in desire is also annihilated by the satisfaction of desire. However untrue it is when compared with objective truth, the consciousness of something alien, still, as "the feeling of life," it is the first truth of self-consciousness.

This seems to me where Yorck's work becomes most fruitful. From the correspondence between life and self-awareness, it derives a methodological standard by means of which it defines the nature and task of philosophy. Its leading concepts are projection and abstraction. Projection and abstraction constitute the primary life comportment; but they apply equally to recapitulatory historical comportment. Only insofar as philosophical reflection corresponds to the structure of being alive does it acquire its own legitimacy. Its task is to understand the achievements of consciousness in terms of their origin, understanding them as results—i.e., as the projection of the original being-alive and its original division.

Yorck thus raises to a methodological principle what Husserl was later to develop more broadly in his phenomenology. This makes it clear how thinkers as different as Husserl and Dilthey could ever come together. Both go back behind the abstraction of neo-Kantianism, and Yorck agrees with them, though in fact he achieves even more. For he goes back to life not only with an epistemological intention, but maintains the metaphysical connection between life and self-consciousness worked out by Hegel. In this he is superior to both Dilthey and Husserl.

As we saw, Dilthey's epistemological reflections went wrong in that he derived the objectivity of science too easily from life comportment and its drive toward something fixed. Husserl entirely lacked any more exact definition of what life is, although the central core of phenomenology—correlation research—in fact follows the structural model of life comportment. Yorck, however, is the missing link between Hegel's *Phenomenology of Mind* and Husserl's *Phenomenology of Transcendental Subjectivity*.[166] Regrettably, the fragmentariness of his posthumous papers prevents us from knowing how he intended to avoid the dialectical metaphysicizing of life of which he accuses Hegel.

(B) HEIDEGGER'S PROJECT OF A HERMENEUTIC PHENOMENOLOGY[167]

The tendency which Dilthey and Yorck formulated as common to them, of "understanding in terms of life," and which was expressed in Husserl's going back behind the objectivity of science to the life-world, was characteristic of Heidegger's own first approach. But he was no longer dependent on the epistemological requirement that the return to life (Dilthey) and the transcendental reduction (Husserl's way of absolutely radical self-reflection) be based methodologically on the self-givenness of experience. On the contrary, all this became the object of Heidegger's critique. Under the rubric of a "hermeneutics of facticity," Heidegger confronted Husserl's eidetic phenomenology, as well as the distinction between fact and essence on which it depended, with a paradoxical demand. Phenomenology should be ontologically based on the facticity of Dasein, existence, which cannot be based on or derived from anything else, and not on the pure cogito as the essential constitution of typical universality—a bold idea, but difficult to carry through.

The critical side of this idea was certainly not something entirely new. The neo-Hegelians had already conceived of it as a critique of idealism, and so it is no accident that Heidegger and the other critics of neo-Kantian idealism seized on Kierkegaard, who emerged out of the spiritual crisis of Hegelianism. On the other hand, however, this critique of idealism was faced then, as now, with the comprehensive claim of transcendental inquiry. Since transcendental reflection left no possible area of thought unconsidered in explicating the content of the mind—and, since Fichte, this was the claim of transcendental philosophy—it had already included every possible objection within the total reflection of the mind. This is true also of the transcendental position from which Husserl gives phenomenology the universal task of discovering how all being-value is constituted. It obviously had to include the facticity asserted by Heidegger. Thus Husserl was able to acknowledge being-in-the-world as a problem of the horizon intentionality of transcendental consciousness, for the absolute historicity of transcendental subjectivity had to be able to demonstrate the meaning of facticity. Hence Husserl, holding consistently to his central idea of the proto-I, had been able to argue against Heidegger that the meaning of facticity is itself an eidos, and that it therefore belongs essentially to the eidetic sphere of "universality of essence." If we examine the sketches for Husserl's later writings, especially those gathered together in vol. 7 on the *Crisis*, we find numerous analyses of "absolute historicity" that follow logically from the problems of the *Ideas*, and that correspond to Heidegger's revolutionary and polemical beginning.[168]

Let us remember that Husserl himself faced the problem of the paradoxes that followed from carrying through his transcendental solipsism. Hence it is not at all easy to fix the point from which Heidegger could confront the phenomenological idealism of Husserl. We must even admit that Heidegger's project in *Being and Time* does not completely escape the problematic of transcendental reflection. The idea of fundamental ontology, its foundation in Dasein, which is concerned "with being," and the analysis of Dasein seemed first simply to mark a new dimension within transcendental phenomenology.[169] The view that the whole meaning of being and objectivity can be made intelligible and demonstrated solely in terms of the temporality and historicity of Dasein—a possible way of describing the main tendency of *Being and Time*—Husserl would have claimed in his own way—i.e., on the ground of the absolute historicity of the Ur-I. And if Heidegger's methodological program was directed toward criticizing the concept of transcendental subjectivity, to which Husserl related all ultimate foundation, Husserl would have said that this was a failure to recognize the radicality of the transcendental reduction. He would undoubtedly have said that transcendental subjectivity itself had already overcome and done away with all the implications of a substance ontology and hence with the objectivism of tradition. *Husserl, too, regarded himself as opposed to the whole of metaphysics.*

Yet it is notable that Husserl was least opposed to the transcendental inquiry undertaken by Kant, and his predecessors, and successors. Here Husserl recognized his own real predecessors and forerunners. The radical self-reflection that was his deepest concern and that he regarded as the essence of modern philosophy led him back to Descartes and the British and to the methodological model of the Kantian critique. But his "constitutive" phenomenology was marked by a universality foreign to Kant and which surpassed the neo-Kantianism that did not question the "fact of science."

But Husserl's appeal to his forerunners makes clear his difference from Heidegger. Husserl's critique of the objectivism of all earlier philosophies was a methodological extension of modern tendencies, and he regarded it as such. Heidegger's aim, however, was from the beginning more that of a teleology in reverse. He regarded his own work not so much as the fulfillment of a long prepared development but, rather, as a return to the beginnings of Western philosophy and a revival of the long forgotten Greek argument about "being." Of course, when *Being and Time* appeared, it was already clear that this return to the beginnings was also an advance beyond the position of contemporary philosophy, and it was no arbitrary accident that Heidegger made the researches of Dilthey and the ideas of Yorck part of the development of phenomenological philosophy.[170] After all, the problem of facticity was also the central problem of historicism, at least in the form of the critique of Hegel's dialectical assumption that there is "reason in history."

Thus it was clear that Heidegger's project of a fundamental ontology had to place the problem of history in the foreground. But it soon emerged that what constituted the significance of Heidegger's *fundamental ontology* was not that is was the solution to the problem of historicism, and certainly not a more original grounding of science, nor even, as with Husserl, philosophy's ultimate radical grounding of itself; rather, *the whole idea of grounding itself underwent a total reversal.* It was no longer with the same intention as Husserl that Heidegger undertook to interpret being, truth, and history in terms of absolute temporality. For this temporality was not that of "consciousness" nor of the transcendental Ur-I. True, as the ideas of *Being and Time* unfolded, it seemed at first simply an intensification of transcendental reflection, the reaching of a higher stage of reflection, where the horizon of being was shown to be time. It was, after all, the ontological groundlessness of transcendental subjectivity, of which Heidegger accused Husserl's phenomenology, that seemed to be overcome by reviving the question of being. What being is was to be determined from within the horizon of time. Thus the structure of temporality appeared as ontologically definitive of subjectivity. But it was more than that. Heidegger's thesis was that being itself is time. This burst asunder the whole subjectivism of modern philosophy—and, in fact, as was soon to appear, the whole horizon of questions asked by metaphysics, which tended to define being as what is present. The fact that being is an issue for Dasein, that it is distinguished from all other beings by its understanding of being, does not constitute the ultimate basis from which a transcendental approach has to start, as seems to be the case in *Being and Time*. Rather, there is a quite different reason why the understanding of being is possible at all, namely that there is a "there," a clearing in being—i.e., a distinction between being and beings. Inquiry into the fundamental fact that this "exists" is, in fact, inquiry into being, but in a direction that necessarily remained unconsidered in all previous inquiry into the being of beings—that was indeed concealed by metaphysical inquiry into being. Heidegger revealed the essential forgetfulness of being that had dominated Western thought since Greek metaphysics because of the embarrassing problem of nothingness. By showing that the question of being included the question of nothingness, he joined the beginning to the end of metaphysics. That the question of being could represent itself as the question of nothingness postulated a thinking of nothingness impossible for metaphysics.

In raising the question of being and thus reversing the whole direction of Western metaphysics, the true predecessor of Heidegger was neither Dilthey nor Husserl, then, but rather *Nietzsche*. Heidegger may have realized this only later; but in retrospect we can see that the aims already implicit in *Being and Time* were to raise Nietzsche's radical critique of "Platonism" to the level of the tradition he criticizes, to confront Western metaphysics on its own level, and to recognize that transcendental inquiry is a consequence of modern subjectivism, and so overcome it.

What Heidegger called "the turn" was not a new departure in the development of transcendental reflection, but the making possible and carrying out of the above aims. Although *Being and Time* criticized the lack of ontological determinacy in Husserl's concept of transcendental subjectivity, it still formulated its own account of the question of being in terms of transcendental philosophy. In fact, however, renewing the question of being, the task that Heidegger set himself, meant that within the "positivism" of phenomenology he recognized *the unresolved problem of metaphysics*, concealed in its ultimate culmination: the concept of mind or *spirit* as conceived by speculative idealism. In grounding the "hermeneutics of facticity" he went beyond both the concept of mind developed by classical idealism and the thematic of transcendental consciousness purified by phenomenological reduction.

Heidegger's hermeneutical phenomenology and his analysis of Dasein's historicity had as their aim renewing the question of being in general and not producing a theory of the human sciences or overcoming the aporias of historicism. These were merely particular contemporary problems in which he was able to demonstrate the consequences of his radical renewal of the question of being. But precisely because of the radicality of his approach he was able to move beyond the complications on which Dilthey's and Husserl's investigations into the fundamental concepts of the human sciences had foundered.

Dilthey's attempt to explicate the human sciences in terms of life, and to start from the experience of life, was never really reconciled with his firmly held Cartesian conception of science. However much he might over-emphasize the contemplative tendency of life and its immanent "drive towards stability," the objectivity of science, understood as an objectivity of results, had a different origin. For this reason Dilthey was unable to accomplish the task that he had himself chosen, which was to justify epistemologically the special methodological character of the human sciences and hence make them the equals of the natural sciences.

Heidegger, however, was able to make a completely fresh beginning because, as we have seen, Husserl had made it an absolutely universal working method to go back to life and hence had abandoned for good the narrow approach of simply inquiring into the methods of the human sciences. His analysis of the life-world and of the anonymous creation of meaning that forms the ground of all experience, gave the question of objectivity in the human sciences a completely new background by making science's concept of objectivity appear to be a special case. Science is anything but a fact from which to start. Rather, the constitution of the scientific world presents a special task, namely of clarifying the idealization that is endemic to science. But this is not the most fundamental task. When we go back to "productive life," the antithesis between nature and spirit does not prove to be of ultimate validity. Both the human and the natural sciences are to be understood as achievements of the intentionality of universal life—i.e., of absolute historicity. Only this kind of under-standing satisfies the self-reflection of philosophy.

Heidegger gave this matter a new and radical turn in light of the question of being which he revived. In legitimating the special methodo-logical nature of the historical sciences, he follows Husserl in that historical being is not to be distinguished from natural being, as Dilthey does. On the contrary, the natural sciences' mode of knowledge appears, rather, as a subspecies of understanding "that has strayed into the legitimate task of grasping the present-at-hand in its essential unintelligibility."[171] *Understanding* is not a resigned ideal of human experience adopted in the old age of the spirit, as with Dilthey; nor is it, as with Husserl, a last methodological ideal of philosophy in contrast to the naivete of unreflecting life; it is, on the contrary, the *original form of the realization of Dasein*, which is being-in-the-world. Before any differentiation of understanding into the various directions of pragmatic or theoretical interest, understanding is Dasein's mode of being, insofar as it is potentiality-for-being and "possibility."

Against the background of this existential analysis of Dasein, with all its far-reaching consequences for metaphysics, the problems of a herme-neutics of the human sciences suddenly look very different. The present work is devoted to this new aspect of the hermeneutical problem. In reviving the question of being and thus moving beyond all previous metaphysics—and not just its climax in the Cartesianism of modern science and transcendental philosophy—Heidegger attained a fundamen-tally new position with regard to the aporias of historicism. The concept of understanding is no longer a methodological concept, as with Droysen. Nor, as in Dilthey's attempt to provide a hermeneutical ground for the human sciences, is the process of understanding an inverse operation that simply traces backward life's tendency toward ideality. Understanding is the original characteristic of the being of human life itself. Starting from Dilthey, Misch had recognized "free distance toward oneself" as the basic structure of human life on which all understanding depended; Heidegger's radical ontological reflection was concerned to clarify this structure of Dasein through a "transcendental analytic of Dasein." He revealed the projective character of all understanding and conceived the act of under-standing itself as the movement of transcendence, of moving beyond the existent.

This asks quite a lot of traditional hermeneutics.[172] It is true that the German language uses the word for "understanding" (Verstehen) also in the sense of a practical ability (e.g., er versteht nicht zu lesen, "he can't read"). But this seems essentially different from the understanding that takes place in science and that is concerned with knowledge. If we examine the two senses more closely, we can see that they have something in common: both senses contain the element of recognition, of being well versed in something. Similarly, a person who "understands" a text (or even a law) has not only projected himself understandingly toward a meaning—in the effort of understanding—but the accomplished understanding constitutes a state of new intellectual freedom. It implies the general possibility of interpreting, of seeing connections, of drawing conclusions, which constitutes being well versed in textual interpretation. Someone who knows his way around a machine, who understands how to use it, or who knows a trade—granted that there are different norms for purpose-oriented rationality and for understanding the expressions of life or of texts—it still remains true that *all such understanding is ultimately self-understanding* (Sichverstehen: knowing one's way around). Even understanding an expression means, ultimately, not only immediately grasping what lies in the expression, but disclosing what is enclosed in it, so that one now knows this hidden part also. But this means that one knows one's way around in it (sich auskennt). Thus it is true in every case that a person who understands, understands himself (sich versteht), projecting himself upon his possibilities.[173] Traditional hermeneutics has inappropriately narrowed the horizon to which understanding belongs. That is why Heidegger's advance over Dilthey is valuable for the problem of hermeneutics also. True, Dilthey had already rejected applying the methods of the natural sciences to the human sciences, and Husserl had called applying the natural sciences' concept of objectivity to the human sciences "nonsense" and established the essential relativity of all historical worlds and all historical knowledge.[174] But now, as a result of the existential futurality of human Dasein, the structure of historical understanding appears with its full ontological background.

Even though historical knowledge receives its justification from the fore-structure of Dasein, this is no reason for anyone to interfere with the immanent criteria of what is called knowledge. For Heidegger too historical knowledge is not a projection in the sense of a plan, the extrapolation of aims of the will, an ordering of things according to the wishes, prejudices, or promptings of the powerful; rather, it remains something adapted to the object, a mensuratio ad rem. Yet this thing is not a factum brutum, not something that is merely at hand, something that can simply be established and measured, but it itself ultimately has the same mode of being as Dasein.

The important thing, however, is to understand this oft-repeated statement correctly. It does not mean simply that there is a "homogeneity" between the knower and the known, on which it would be possible to base psychic transposition as the special "method" of the human sciences. This would make historical hermeneutics a branch of psychology (which was what Dilthey had in mind). In fact, however, the coordination of all knowing activity with what is known is not based on the fact that they have the same mode of being but draws its significance from the *particular nature* of the mode of being that is common to them. It consists in the fact that neither the knower nor the known is "present-at-hand" in an "ontic" way, but in a "historical" one—i.e., they both have the *mode of being of historicity.* Hence, as Yorck says, everything depends on "the generic difference between the ontic and the historical."[175] The fact that Yorck contrasts "homogeneity" with "belonging" reveals the problem[176] that Heidegger was the first to unfold in its full radicality: that we study history only insofar as we are ourselves "historical" means that the historicity of human Dasein in its expectancy and its forgetting is the condition of our being able to re-present the past. What first seemed simply a barrier, according to the traditional concept of science and method, or a subjective condition of access to historical knowledge, now becomes the center of a fundamental inquiry. "Belonging" is a condition of the original meaning of historical interest not because the choice of theme and inquiry is subject to extrascientific, subjective motivations (then belonging would be no more than a special case of emotional dependence, of the same type as sympathy), but because belonging to traditions belongs just as originally and essentially to the historical finitude of Dasein as does its projectedness toward future possibilities of itself. Heidegger was right to insist that what he called "thrownness" belongs together with projection.[177] Thus there is no understanding or interpretation in which the totality of this existential structure does not function, even if the intention of the knower is simply to read "what is there" and to discover from his sources "how it really was."[178]

We will try to determine whether Heidegger's ontological radicalization can contribute to the construction of a historical hermeneutics. Heidegger's intention was undoubtedly a different one, and we must beware of drawing overhasty conclusions from his existential analysis of the historicity of Dasein. For Heidegger, the existential analytic of Dasein implies no particular historical ideal of existence. Hence with regard to any theological statement about man and his existence in faith it claims an a priori, neutral validity. This may be a problematical claim for the self-understanding of faith, as the controversy surrounding Bultmann shows.[179] On the other hand, this by no means excludes the fact that both Christian theology and the historical sciences are subject to content-specific (existential) presuppositions. But precisely for this reason we are forced to acknowledge that the existential analytic itself does not, with respect to its own intention, contain any existential ideal and therefore cannot be criticized as one (however many attempts may have been made to do so).

It is sheer misunderstanding to regard the temporality structure of care as a particular ideal of existence, which could be countered with more attractive modes (Bollnow),[180] such as the ideal of being free from care or, with Nietzsche, the natural innocence of animals and birds. It cannot be denied that this too is an ideal of existence; but it is also true that its structure is the existential one that Heidegger has revealed.

It is nonetheless true that the being of children or indeed of animals—in contrast to that ideal of "innocence"—remains an ontological problem.[181] Their mode of being is not, at any rate, "existence" and historicity such as Heidegger claims for human Dasein. We may also ask what it means for human existence to be based on something outside history—i.e., on nature. If we really want to break out of the spell of idealistic speculation, then we must obviously not conceive the mode of being of "life" in terms of self-consciousness. When Heidegger set about revising the transcendental self-conception of *Being and Time*, it followed that he would have to come to grips afresh with the problem of *life*. Thus in his letter on humanism he spoke of the great gulf between man and animal.[182] It is quite clear that Heidegger's own transcendental grounding of fundamental ontology in the analytic of Dasein did not yet permit a positive account of the mode of being of life. There are still open questions; but none of this alters the fact that it would be completely to mistake the significance of what Heidegger calls existential were it thought possible to counter the existential of "care" with another specific ideal of existence, whatever it might be. To do so is to miss the dimension of inquiry that *Being and Time* opened up. In defending himself against such superficially argued polemics, Heidegger could quite legitimately refer to the transcendental intention of his own work, in the same sense that Kant's inquiry was transcendental. From the start his inquiry transcended all empirical differences and hence all ideals based on content. [Whether it fulfilled its intention to rekindle the question of "being" is another matter.]

Hence we too are beginning with the *transcendental* significance of Heidegger's problematic.[183] The problem of hermeneutics becomes universal in scope, even attaining a new dimension, through his transcendental interpretation of understanding. The interpreter's belonging to his object, which the historical school was unable to offer any convincing account of, now acquires a concretely demonstrable significance, and it is the task of hermeneutics to demonstrate it. That the structure of Dasein is thrown projection, that in realizing its own being Dasein is understanding, must also be true of the act of understanding in the human sciences. The general structure of understanding is concretized in historical understanding, in that the concrete bonds of custom and tradition and the corresponding possibilities of one's own future become effective in understanding itself. Dasein that projects itself on its own potentiality-for-being has always already "been." This is the meaning of the existential of "thrownness." The main point of the hermeneutics of facticity and its contrast with the transcendental constitution research of Husserl's phenomenology was that no freely chosen relation toward one's own being can get behind the facticity of this being. Everything that makes possible and limits Dasein's projection ineluctably precedes it. This existential structure of Dasein must be expressed in the understanding of historical tradition as well, and so we will start by following Heidegger.[184]

Notes

1 E.g., Augustine's *De doctrina christiana*. Cf. Gerhard Ebeling's article "Herme-neutik" in *Religion in Geschichte und Gegenwart*, 3rd ed.

2 Dilthey, "Die Entstehung der Hermeneutik," *Gesammelte Schriften*, V, 317–38. [Meanwhile, Dilthey's very learned original version has appeared as vol. 2, part 2 of his biography of Schleiermacher. See my appreciation in the "Afterword" below, p.566–7]

3 The hermeneutical principles of Luther's explanation of the Bible have been investigated in detail, following K. Holl's work, chiefly by Gerhard Ebeling, *Evangelische Evangelienauslegung: Eine Untersuchung zu Luthers Hermeneutik* (1942) and "Die Anfänge von Luthers Hermeneutik," *Zeitschrift für Theologie und Kirche*, 48 (1951), 172–230, and more recently, "Wort Gottes und Hermeneutik," *ZThK*, 56 (1959). Here we must make do with a summary account that serves simply to make the necessary distinctions and clarify the move of hermeneutics into the historical sphere that came with the eighteenth century. For the actual problems of the *sola scriptura* position, cf. Ebeling's article "Hermeneutik" (cited n. 1 above). [See Ebeling, *Wort und Glaube*, II (Tübingen, 1969), 99–120. See also my "Klassische und philosophische Hermeneutik," *GW*, II, 92–117, and *Philosophische Hermeneutik*, ed. H. G. Gadamer and G. Boehm (Frankfurt: Suhrkamp, 1976).]

4 The simile of *caput* and *membra* is found also in Flacius.

5 The origin of the concept of system is obviously based on the same theological situation as hermeneutics. O. Ritschl's inquiry *System und systematische Methode in der Geschichte des wissenschaftlichen Sprachgebrauchs und in der philosophischen Methodologie* (Bonn, 1906) is very instructive. It shows that because the theology of the Reformation no longer desired to be an encyclopedic assimila-tion of dogmatic tradition, but sought to reorganize Christian teaching on the

basis of key passages in the Bible (*loci communes*), it tended toward system-atization—a statement that is doubly instructive when we consider the later emergence of the term "system" in the philosophy of the seventeenth century. There too something new broke into the traditional structure of the total science of Scholasticism: the new natural sciences. This new element forced philosophy into systematization, i.e., the harmonization of old and new. The concept of system, which has since become a methodologically essential requisite of philosophy, thus has its historical root in the divergence of philosophy and science at the beginning of the modern period, and it appears as something obviously to be required of philosophy only because this divergence between philosophy and science has since presented philosophy with its constant task. [On the history of the word: one should begin with *Epinomis*, 991e, where the word *systema* appears connected with *arithmos* and *harmonia*. It thus appears to be carried over from the relations of numbers and tones in the ordering of the heavens. (See *Stoicorum Veterum Fragmenta*, ed. Arnim, II, 168, fr. 527, 11 passim.) One thinks also of Heraclitus' concept of *harmonia* (*Vorsokratische Schriften*, ed. Diels-Kranz, 12 B 54): dissonances appear to be "overcome" in harmonic intervals. That contrary elements are unified forms part of the astronomical as well as philosophical concept of "system."]

6 Cf. Dilthey II, 126, n. 3, dealing with Richard Simon's critique of Flacius.

7 Semler, who calls for this, still thinks that he is serving the redemptive meaning of the Bible, insofar as the man who understands it historically "is now also able to speak of these objects in a way dictated by the changed times and the other circumstances of the men around us" (quoted from Ebeling, "Hermeneutik," cited n. 1 above)—i.e., this is historical research in the service of *applicatio*.

8 Dilthey, who notes this but evaluates it differently, writes as early as 1859: "it should be noted that philology, theology, history, and philosophy . . . were not yet nearly so distinct as we are accustomed to think them. Heyne was the first to set up philology as a separate discipline, and Wolf was the first to call himself a student of it." *Der junge Dilthey*, p.88.

9 Christian Wolff and his school logically considered the "general art of interpretation" as part of philosophy, since "ultimately everything is directed towards our recognizing and testing the truths of others when we understand what they say" (Walch, p.165). It is the same for Bentley, when he calls for the critic "to have as his sole guides reason—the light of the author's ideas and their compelling power" (quoted from Wegner, *Altertumskunde*, p.94).

10 It is symptomatic of the triumph of historical thought that in his hermeneutics Schleiermacher still considers the possibility of interpreting Euclid sub-jectively, i.e., considering the genesis of his ideas (p. 151).

11 Thus Bacon understands his new method as an *interpretatio naturae*. Cf. p.342 below. [See also Ernst Curtius, *Europäische Literatur und lateinisches Mittelalter*

(Bern, 1948), pp. 116ff. and Erich Rothacker, *Das 'Buch der Natur': Materialien und Grundsätzliches zur Metapherngeschichte*, ed. W. Perpeet (Bonn, 1979).]

12 *Einleitung zur richtigen Auslegung vernünftiger Reden und Schriften* (1742).

13 Joachim Wach, whose three-volume work *Das Verstehen* remains entirely within the horizon of Dilthey's ideas.

14 That would certainly apply to Semler, whose statement, quoted above in n. 7, shows the theological dimension of his demand for historical interpretation.

15 [This fusing of understanding and interpretation, of which I am accused by writers like E. D. Hirsch, I derived from Schleiermacher. See his *Sämtliche Werke*, III, part 3, 384 (repr. in *Philosophische Hermeneutik*, ed. Gadamer and Boehm (Frankfurt: Suhrkamp, 1976), p.163): "Interpretation differs from understanding only as speaking aloud from speaking silently to oneself." This view has important consequences for the linguisticality of thinking.]

16 Which Ernesti places beside it, *Institutio interpretis NT* (1761), p.7.

17 J. J. Rambach, *Institutiones hermeneuticae sacrae* (1723), p.2.

18 *Hermeneutik*, §§15 and 16, *Werke*, I, part 7, 29f.

19 Ibid., p.27.

20 Friedrich Schleiermacher, *Werke*, III, part 3, 390.

21 [Ibid., p.392 (*Philosophische Hermeneutik*), pp. 177f.]

22 [See Manfred Frank's critique of my view and my reply in "Zwischen Phänomenologie und Dialektik: Versuch einer Selbstkritik," *GW*, II, 13ff.]

23 Hitherto our knowledge of Schleiermacher's hermeneutics rested on his "Academy Lectures" of 1829 and on the lecture on hermeneutics published by Lücke. The latter was reconstructed on the basis of a manuscript of 1819 and lecture notes from Schleiermacher's last ten years. Even this external fact shows that it is to the late phase of Schleiermacher's thought—and not the period of his fruitful beginnings with Friedrich Schlegel—that the hermeneutic theory we know belongs. This is what, primarily through Dilthey, has been influential. The above discussion also starts from these texts and seeks to draw out their essential tendencies. However, Lücke's version is not quite free of elements that point to a development of Schleiermacher's hermeneutical thought and are deserving of attention. At my suggestion, Heinz Kimmerle has worked through the unpublished material in the hands of the Deutsche Akademie in Berlin and has published a critical revised text in the *Abhandlungen der Heidelberger Akademie der Wissenschaften* (1959), 2nd *Abhandlung*. In his thesis, quoted there, Kimmerle attempts to determine the direction of Schleiermacher's development. Cf. his essay in *Kantstudien*, 51, no. 4, 410ff. [Kimmerle's new edition is more authentic, but less readable than Lücke's, which is now again accessible as F. D. E. Schleiermacher, *Hermeneutik und Kritik*, ed. Manfred Frank (Frankfurt, 1977).]

24 Op.Cit. I, part 7, 262: "Even though we shall never be able to achieve the complete understanding of every personal idiosyncrasy of the writers of the

New Testament, the supreme achievement is still possible, namely of grasping ever more perfectly . . . the life that is common to them."

25 *Werke*, I, part 7, 83.

26 *Werke*, III, part 3, 355, 358, 364.

27 *Enzyklopädie und Methodologie der philologischen Wissenschaften*, ed. Bratuschek (2nd ed., 1886), p.10.

28 In the context of his studies on poetic imagination, Dilthey coined the term "point of impression" and explicitly transferred its application from artist to historian (VI, 283). We shall discuss later the significance of this application from the point of view of intellectual history. Its basis is Schleiermacher's concept of *life*: "Where life exists, we have functions and parts held together." The expression "germinal decision" is found in his *Werke*, I, part 7, 168.

29 Schleiermacher, *Dialektik*, ed. Odebrecht, pp. 569f.

30 *Dialektik*, p.470.

31 *Dialektik*, p.572.

32 *Ästhetik*, ed. Odebrecht, p.269.

33 *Ästhetik*, p.384.

34 Schleiermacher, *Werke*, I, part 7, 146f.

35 *Werke*, I, part 7, 33.

36 H. Patsch has now clarified more precisely the early history of romantic hermeneutics. See his "Friedrich Schlegels 'Philosophie der Philologie' und Schleiermachers frühe Entwürfe zur Hermeneutik," *Zeitschrift für Theologie und Kirche* (1966), pp. 434–472.

37 The modern habit of applying a writer's interpretation of himself as a canon of interpretation is a product of a false psychologism. On the other hand, however, the "theory," e.g., of music or poetics and rhetoric, can well be a legitimate canon of interpretation. [See my "Zwischen Phänomenologie und Dialektik: Versuch einer Selbstkritik," *GW*, II, 3ff.]

38 Steinthal, *Einleitung in die Psychologie und Sprachwissenschaft* (Berlin, 1881).

39 V, 335.

40 O. F. Bollnow, *Das Verstehen*.

41 *Werke*, VI, 337.

42 *Critique of Pure Reason*, B 370.

43 [In his new edition of Dilthey's *Schleiermachers Leben*, II, part 1, liv, M. Redeker includes the contemporary testimony of Herder (*Briefe, das Studium der Theologie betreffend*, 5. Teil, 1781) and refers to the formula of the early Luther (Clemen V, 416), which I cite in n. 46 below.]

44 "Zweite Einleitung in die Wissenschaftslehre," *Werke*, I, 485.

45 Ibid., 479n.

46 I owe to H. Bornkamm a neat example of how this formula, alleged to belong to the tools of philology, presents itself automatically when one is indulging in polemical criticism. After applying Aristotle's idea of motion to the Trinity,

Luther says (Sermon of December 25, 1514, Weimar edition, I, 28): *Vide quam apte serviat Aristoteles in philosophia sua theologiae, si non ut ipse voluit, sed melius intellegitur et applicatur. Nam res vere est elocutus et credo quod aliunde furatus sit, quae tanta pompa profert et jactat.* I cannot imagine that the philological guild would recognize itself in this formulation of its "rule."

47 The way Schleiermacher introduces it suggests this: "Yes, if the formula has something true about it . . . then all it can mean is this . . . " In his "Address to the Academy" (*Werke*, III, part 3, 362) he avoids the paradox by writing: "then he can give an account of himself to himself." In the lecture manuscript of the same period (1828) we find also, "to understand words first as well, and then better than the one who wrote them" (*Abhandlung der Heidelberger Akademie*, [1959], 2nd *Abhandlung*, p.87). The aphorisms of Friedrich Schlegel from his *Philosophische Lehrjahre* present a confirmation of the above conjecture. Precisely at the time of his closest connection with Schleiermacher, Schlegel made the following note: "To understand someone one must first be cleverer than he, then just as clever, and then just as stupid. It is not enough to understand the actual meaning of a confused work better than the author understood it. One must also be able to know, characterize, and construct the principles of the confusion itself" (*Schriften und Fragmente*, ed. Ernst Behler, p.158).

This passage proves again that "understanding better" is still seen as entirely directed toward the object: "better" means "not confused." But inasmuch as confusion is then made into an object of understanding and of "construction," we see here the development that led to Schleiermacher's new hermeneutical principle. We have reached here the precise point of transition between the universal significance of the statement as understood by the Enlightenment, and the new romantic interpretation of it. [Heinrich Nüsse, *Die Sprachtheorie F. Schlegels*, pp. 92ff., argues persuasively that Schlegel's formula is that of a historically faithful philologist: he must "distinguish" the author in his meaning (even when he only "half" understands himself, *Athenaeum* fragment, 401). Ultimately Schleiermacher sees the real accomplishment not in that, but in a romantically reinterpreted "understanding better."] There is a similar transitional point in Schelling's *System des transzendentalen Idealismus* (*Werke*, III, 623), where we find, "if a person says and maintains things, the meaning of which it was impossible for him to realize fully, either because of the age in which he lived or because of his other pronouncements, i.e., when he apparently expressed consciously what he could not really have been fully conscious of . . . " Cf. Chladenius' distinction quoted on p.182 above, between "understanding an author" and "understanding a text." As evidence that the formula's original sense derived from the Enlightenment we offer a recent approximation to it [though parallel to one in Arthur Schopenhauer, *Die Welt als Wille und Vorstellung*, *Sämtliche Werke*, ed. Paul Deussen, II, 299] by a quite unromantic thinker who undoubtedly combines with it the criterion of criticism of the object: cf. *Husserliana*, VI, 74.

48 *Das Leben Schleiermachers*, 1st ed., Appendix, p.117.

49 [See my "Zum sachlichen Problem der Kontinuität der Geschichte," *Kleine Schriften*, I, 149–60, esp. pp. 158ff. (*GW*, II, 133ff.).]

50 C. Hinrichs, *Ranke und die Geschichtstheologie der Goethezeit* (1954). Cf. my review in the *Philosophische Rundschau*, IV, 123ff.

51 Ranke, *Weltgeschichte*, IX, part 1, 270.

52 Ranke, *Lutherfragmente*, I.

53 Cf. Gerhard Masur, *Rankes Begriff der Weltgeschichte* (1926).

54 Ranke, *Weltgeschichte*, IX, part 2, xiv.

55 Ranke, *Weltgeschichte*, IX, part 2, xiii f.

56 In my "Volk und Geschichte im Denken Herders" (1942) [*Kleine Schriften*, III, 101–17; *GW*, IV], I have shown that Herder applied Leibniz's concept of power to the historical world.

57 Hegel, *Phänomenologie des Geistes*, ed. Hoffmeister, pp. 120ff.

58 Plato, *Charmides*, 169 a. [See also my "Vorgestalten der Reflexion," *Kleine Schriften*, III, 1–13 (*GW*, VI, 116–28).]

59 Hegel, *Enzyklopädie*, §§136f., and his *Phänomenologie*, ed. Hoffmeister, pp. 105ff; *Logik*, ed. Lasson, pp. 144ff.

60 Ranke, *Das politische Gespräch*, ed. Rothacker, pp. 19, 22, 25.

61 Ibid., p.163; Droysen, *Historik*, ed. Rothacker, p.72.

62 It is highly indicative of the hidden spirit of the historical school that Ranke (and he is not alone in this) thinks and writes the word *subsumieren* ("subsume") as *summieren* ("sum up," "aggregate"), e.g., ibid. (n. 60 above), p.63.

63 Cf. Karl Löwith, *Weltgeschichte und Heilsgeschehen* (Stuttgart, 1953), and my article "Geschichtsphilosophie" in *Religion in Geschichte und Gegenwart*, 3rd ed.

64 Ranke, *Weltgeschichte*, IX, part 2, xiii.

65 Ranke, *Weltgeschichte*, IX, part 1, 270f.

66 Cf. Hinrichs, *Ranke und die Geschichtstheologie der Goethezeit*, pp. 239f.

67 Cf. Löwith, *Weltgeschichte und Heilsgeschehen*, ch. 1.

68 Ranke, *Weltgeschichte*, IX, part 2, 5, 7.

69 "For this is, as it were, a share in divine knowledge." Ranke, *Das politische Gespräch*, ed. Rothacker, p.43, also p.52.

70 Ibid., p.5.

71 *Gesammelte Schriften*, V, 281.

72 *Lutherfragmente*, 13.

73 *Lutherfragmente*, 1.

74 To Heinrich Ranke, November, 1828 (*Zur eigenen Lebensgeschichte*, p.162).

75 [See also pp. 330f. and 462f. below and Appendix VI.]

76 Droysen, *Historik*, ed. Rothacker, p.65.

77 Ibid., p.65.

78 See Droysen's *Auseinandersetzung mit Buckle*, newly ed. Rothacker, p.61. ("The Elevation of History to the Rank of a Science: Being a Review of the *History of Civilization in England* by H. T. Buckle," in *Outline of the Principles of History*, tr. E. Benjamin Andrews [Boston: Ginn, 1897], pp. 61–89.)

79 Johann Gustav Droysen, *Historik*, ed. R. Hübner (1935), p.316, based on notes taken by Friedrich Meinecke.

80 [The theological element in the concept of "research" lies not only in the relation to the *person* and its freedom, which cannot be fathomed by research, but also in the relation to the hidden "meaning" of history, to what is "intended" in God's providence, which we can never entirely decipher. To that degree "Historik" is never entirely estranged from hermeneutics, as is fitting for Droysen, the discoverer of "Hellenism." See my *GW*, II, 123f. and my "Heideggers Wege," *Die Marburger Theologie*, pp. 35ff. (*GW*, III).]

81 [See my "Das Problem der Geschichte in der neueren deutschen Philosophie" (1943), *Kleine Schriften*, I, 1–10 (*GW*, II, 27ff.).]

82 [See my "The Problem of Historical Consciousness," tr. J. L. Close, *Graduate Faculty Philosophy Journal* (New School for Social Research), 5 (1975), 1–51, and my more recent contributions on the occasion of the Dilthey jubilee in 1983 (*GW*, IV). Dilthey studies have been given a new impetus especially by the edition of the preparatory materials for the continuation of the *Einleitung in die Geisteswissenschaften* (*Gesammelte Schriften*, XVIII and XIX).]

83 Both through his long introduction to vol. V of Dilthey's collected works and his account of Dilthey in his book *Lebensphilosophie und Phänomenologie* (1st ed., 1930).

84 O. F. Bollnow, *Dilthey* (1936).

85 *Gesammelte Schriften*, VII, 281.

86 The early form of the problem of knowledge which we find in classical antiquity with, say, Democritus, and which the neo-Kantian historians also read into Plato, had another basis. The discussion of the problem of knowledge, which began with Democritus, in fact came to an end with the Skeptics (see Paul Natorp, *Studien zum Erkenntnisproblem im Altertum* [1892] and my "Antike Atomtheorie," *GW*, V, 263–82).

87 P. Duhem, *Études sur Léonard de Vinci* (3 vols.; Paris, 1955); *Le système du monde*, X (Paris, 1959). [See Part One, n. 4, above.]

88 [See E. Zeller, "Über Bedeutung und Aufgabe der Erkenntnistheorie" (1862), *Vorträge und Abhandlungen* (Leipzig, 1875–84), II, 446–78, and my "E. Zeller: Der Weg eines Liberalen von der Theologie zur Philosophie," in *Semper Apertus: 600 Jahre Ruprecht-Karls-Universität Heidelberg, 1386–1986*, ed. W. Doerr (6 vols.; Heidelberg, 1985), II.]

89 Cf. H. Rickert, *Der Gegenstand der Erkenntnis* (Freiburg, 1892).

90 Cf. the analysis of the historicity of experience, pp. 340ff. below.

91 *Gesammelte Schriften*, VII, 278.

92 Loc. cit. [But who, properly speaking, "makes" history?]

93 VII, 27f., 230.

94 VII, 177.

95 Dilthey, VII, 282ff. Georg Simmel tries to solve the same problem by the dialectic of the subjectivity of the experience and the continuity of the object—i.e., ultimately psychologically. Cf. *Brücke und Tor*, pp. 82f.

96 Dilthey, *Der Aufbau der geschichtlichen Welt in den Geisteswissenschaften, Gesammelte Schriften*, VII.

97 VII, 13a.

98 V, 266.

99 VII, 157, 280, 333.

100 VII, 280.

101 O. F. Bollnow, *Dilthey*, pp. 168f., saw correctly that in Dilthey the concept of power was pushed too much into the background. This is a sign of the victory of romantic hermeneutics over Dilthey's thinking.

102 VII, 148.

103 *Hegels theologische Jugendschriften*, ed. Nohl, pp. 139f.

104 VII, 136.

105 VIII, 224.

106 Dilthey's ground-breaking work, *Die Jugendgeschichte Hegels*, which appeared first in 1906 and was supplemented by posthumous manuscripts in vol. IV of the *Gesammelte Schriften* (1921), opened up a new epoch in Hegel studies, less because of its results than because of the task it had set itself. It was soon joined by the publication of the *Theologische Jugendschriften* by Hermann Nohl in 1911, writings which Theodor Haering's penetrating commentary (*Hegel*, I [1928]) opened up. Cf. my "Hegel und die geschichtliche Geist" together with my book *Hegel's Dialectic* (both now in *GW*, III) and Herbert Marcuse, *Hegels Ontologie und die Grundlegung einer Theorie der Geschichtlichkeit* (1932), which showed the exemplary function of the concept of life for the *Phenomenology of Mind*.

107 In detail in the posthumous notes on his *Jugendgeschichte Hegels, Gesammelte Schriften*, IV, 217–58, and more profoundly in his *Aufbau*, ch. 3, pp. 146ff.

108 V, 265.

109 VII, 136.

110 V, 339ff. and VIII.

111 *Leben Schleiermachers*, ed. Mulert (1922), p.xxxi.

112 *Leben Schleiermachers* (1st ed., 1870); *Denkmale der inneren Entwicklung Schleiermachers*, p.118. See Schleiermacher, *Monologen*, p.417.

113 VII, 291: "Life and history have a meaning just like the letters of a word."

114 V, 277.

115 Cf., in particular, what Max Scheler says concerning this in *Zur Phänomenologie und Theorie der Sympathiegefühle und von Liebe und Hass* (1913).

116 *Historik*, §1.

117 He also follows Schleiermacher, who sees old age as a model only in a very qualified sense. Cf. the following note on Schleiermacher (in Dilthey's *Leben Schleiermachers* [1st ed., p.417]): "The dissatisfaction of age over the real world in particular is a misunderstanding of youth and its joy, which was also not concerned with the real world. Old men's dislike of new times is concomitant with elegy. So the historical sense is highly necessary in order to attain eternal youth, which is not a gift of nature, but something acquired through freedom."

118 V, 278.

119 VII, 99.

120 An eloquent exponent of this "method" is Eric Rothacker, whose own contributions to the subject actually testify effectively to the opposite, namely, the non-methodical character of his brilliant ideas and bold syntheses.

121 Paul Graf Yorck von Wartenburg, *Briefwechsel* (1923), p.193.

122 *Wissenschaft der Logik*, ed. Lasson (1934), II, 36f.

123 VII, 207.

124 VII, 347.

125 VII, 290.

126 V, 364.

127 VII, 6.

128 VII, 6.

129 VII, 3.

130 This has also been pointed out by Misch, *Lebensphilosophie und Phänomenologie*, p.295, and esp. 312ff. Misch distinguishes between becoming conscious and making conscious. Philosophical reflection may be both at once. But Dilthey, he says, wrongly seeks an unbroken transition from the one to the other. "The essentially *theoretical* orientation towards objectivity cannot be derived solely from the idea of the objectification of life" (p. 298). The present work gives this criticism by Misch another facet, in that it reveals in romantic hermeneutics the Cartesianism that makes Dilthey's thought here ambiguous.

131 VII, 6.

132 An original Schleiermacher text has crept into the material from Dilthey's posthumous papers for the *Aufbau* (*Gesammelte Schriften*, VII, 225, "Hermeneutik"), which Dilthey had already printed in the appendix to his Schleiermacher biography—an indirect proof that Dilthey never really got over his romantic beginnings. It is often hard to distinguish his own writing from his citations.

133 Pp. 229f.

134 See the nice misprint cited above, n. 122 to Part One.

135 VII, 291.

136 VII, 333.

137 VII, 148.

138 As early as 1923, Heidegger spoke to me with admiration of the late writings of Georg Simmel. This was not just a general acknowledgment of Simmel as a philosophical personality. The specific stimulus that Heidegger had received from his work will be apparent to anyone who today reads, in the first of the four "Metaphysical Chapters" gathered together under the title *Lebensanschauung*, what the dying Simmel conceived as his philosophical task. There we read: "Life is effectually past and future." He calls "the transcendence of life the true absolute," and the essay concludes: "I know very well what logical obstacles there are to the conceptual expression of this way of seeing life. I have tried to formulate them, in full awareness of the logical danger, since it is *possible* that we have reached here the level at which logical difficulties do not simply command us to be silent—because it is the same level as that from which is nourished the metaphysical root of logic itself."

139 Cf. Natorp's critique of Husserl's *Ideas* (1914) in *Logos*, (1917), and Husserl himself in a private letter to Natorp of June 29, 1918: "—and I may perhaps point out that I overcame the stage of static Platonism more than ten years ago and established the idea of transcendental genesis as the main theme of phenomenology." O. Becker's note in the Husserl *Festschrift*, p.39, says more or less the same thing.

140 *Husserliana*, VI, 344.

141 *Husserliana*, VI, 346.

142 *Husserliana*, VI, 339 and VI, 271.

143 *Husserliana*, IV (1952).

144 [On what follows, see my "The Phenomenological Movement," in *Philosophical Hermeneutics*, tr. David E. Linge (Berkeley: University of California Press, 1976), pp. 130–81, and "Die Wissenschaft von der Lebenswelt," *Kleine Schriften*, III, 190–201 (*GW*, III).]

145 *Husserliana*, VI, 169, n. 1.

146 *Husserliana*, VI, 169.

147 *Einleitung in die Psychologie nach kritischer Methode* (1888); *Allgemeine Psychologie nach kritischer Methode* (1911).

148 *Husserliana*, III, 390: "The great mistake of starting from the natural world (without characterizing it as world)" (1922) and the more detailed self-criticism of III, 399 (1929). According to *Husserliana*, VI, 267, the concepts of "horizon" and of "horizon consciousness" were in part suggested by William James' idea of "fringes." [On the importance of Richard Avenarius, *Der menschliche Weltbegriff* (Leipzig, 1912) for Husserl's critical turning against the

"scientific world," see H. Lübbe's "Positivismus und Phänomenologie (Mach und Husserl)," in the *Festschrift* for W. Szilasi (Munich, 1960), pp. 161–84, esp. pp. 171f.]

149 *Gesammelte Schriften*, I, xviii.

150 *Husserliana*, VI, 148.

151 [On the problem of the "life-world," besides my own work collected in *GW*, III (see the essays cited in n. 144 above), and the similar line of thought by Ludwig Landgrebe, much new work has appeared by A. Schütz, G. Brand, U. Claesgens, K. Düsing, P. Janssen, and others.]

152 *Husserliana*, VI, 501.

153 As does Eugen Fink in "L'analyse intentionelle et le problème de la pensée spéculative," in *Problèmes actuels de la phénoménologie* (1952).

154 *Husserliana*, VI, §34, 265f.

155 *Husserliana*, VI, 116.

156 It is hard to see how the recent attempts to play off the being of "nature" against historicity are tenable in the face of this *methodologically* intended verdict.

157 [See C. Wolzogen, *Die autonome Relation: Zum Problem der Beziehung im Spätwerk Paul Natorps. Ein Beitrag zur Geschichte der Theorien der Relation* (1984) and my review, *Philosophische Rundschau*, 32 (1985), 160.]

158 *Husserliana*, VI, 99.

159 D. Sinn, *Die transzendentale Intersubjektivität mit ihren Seinshorizonten bei E. Husserl* (unpub. diss., Heidelberg, 1958), saw the methodological-transcendental significance of the concept of "empathy" behind the constitution of intersubjectivity, which escaped Alfred Schütz in his "Das Problem der transzendentalen Intersubjektivität bei Husserl," *Philosophische Rundschau*, 5 (1957). [For an excellent summary of the intention of the late Heidegger, see also D. Sinn's essay in *Philosophische Rundschau*, 14 (1967), 81–182.]

160 I am referring here to the broad perspectives opened by Viktor von Weizsäcker's concept of the *Gestaltkreis*.

161 *Bewusstseinsstellung und Geschichte* (Tübingen, 1956).

162 Op. cit., p.39.

163 Loc. cit.

164 Loc. cit.

165 *Phänomenologie des Geistes*, ed. Hoffmeister, p.128.

166 Cf. on this subject the important observations of A. de Waelhens, *Existence et signification* (Louvain, 1957), pp. 7–29.

167 [On what follows, see my *Heideggers Wege: Studien zum Spätwerk* (Tübingen, 1983) (*GW*, III).]

168 It is notable that in all the *Husserliana* to date there has hardly been any confrontation with Heidegger by name. There are, undoubtedly, more than mere biographical reasons for this. Rather, Husserl may have seen that he

was constantly caught up in the ambiguity that made Heidegger's starting point in *Being and Time* sometimes appear like transcendental phenomenology and sometimes like its critique. He recognized his own ideas in it, and yet they appeared in quite a different light; in, as it seemed to him, a polemical distortion.

169 As O. Becker was quick to point out in the Husserl *Festschrift*, p.39.

170 *Being and Time*, §77.

171 *Sein und Zeit*, p.153.

172 Cf. Emilio Betti's almost angry polemic in his scholarly and brilliant treatise *Zur Grundlegung einer allgemeinen Auslegungslehre*, p.91, n. 14b.

173 Even the history of the meaning of the word *Verstehen* ("understanding") points in this direction. The original meaning seems to have been the legal sense of the word, i.e., representing a case before a court. That the word then developed an intellectual sense is obviously due to the fact that to represent a case in court involves understanding it, i.e., mastering it to such an extent that one can cope with all the possible moves of the opposing party and assert one's own legal standpoint. [That this meaning, which Heidegger introduced, namely "understanding" (*verstehen*) as "standing up for" (*stehen für* . . .), takes on its true force as directed against another person, making it possible to "answer" and compel him to come *with* one to "judgment": these are the elements of "conflict," which authentic "dialogue" includes, and they are expressly emphasized against Hegel's "dialectic" in Part Three of this work. See also my "On the Problem of Self-Understanding," *Philosophical Hermeneutics*, tr. David E. Linge (Berkeley: University of California Press, 1976), pp. 44–58.]

174 [Edmund Husserl, *Die Krisis der europäischen Wissenschaften und transzendentale Phänomenologie, Husserliana*, VI, 91 (219).]

175 *Briefwechsel mit Dilthey*, p.191.

176 Cf. F. Kaufmann, "Die Philosophie des Grafen Paul Yorck von Wartenburg," *Jahrbuch für Philosophie und phänomenologische Forschung*, 9 (1928), 50ff. [The significance of Dilthey has now been newly assessed in the *Dilthey Jahrbuch* for 1983. See also my own contributions in *GW*, IV.]

177 *Sein und Zeit*, pp. 181, 192 and passim.

178 O. Vossler has shown in *Rankes historisches Problem* that this phrase of Ranke's is not as naive as it sounds, but is directed against the "superior attitude" of a moralistic school of historiography. [See my "The Universality of the Hermeneutical Problem," *Philosophical Hermeneutics*, tr. David E. Linge (Berkeley: University of California Press, 1976), pp. 3–17.]

179 Cf. pp. 331ff. below.

180 O. F. Bollnow, *Das Wesen der Stimmungen* (Freiburg, 1943).

181 [This was the question raised by O. Becker, *Dasein und Dawesen* (Pfullingen, 1963), pp. 67ff.]

182 *Über den Humanismus* (Berne, 1947), p.69.

183 [See the criticism of Emilio Betti in "Hermeneutics and Historicism," Supplement I below.]

184 Cf. Appendix III below.

4
Elements of a Theory of Hermeneutic Experience

1 THE ELEVATION OF THE HISTORICITY OF UNDERSTANDING TO THE STATUS OF A HERMENEUTIC PRINCIPLE

(A) THE HERMENEUTIC CIRCLE AND THE PROBLEM OF PREJUDICES

(i) Heidegger's Disclosure of the Fore-Structure of Understanding

Heidegger entered into the problems of historical hermeneutics and critique only in order to explicate the fore-structure of understanding for the purposes of ontology.[1] Our question, by contrast, is how hermeneutics, once freed from the ontological obstructions of the scientific concept of objectivity, can do justice to the historicity of understanding. Hermeneutics has traditionally understood itself as an art or technique.[2] This is true even of Dilthey's expansion of hermeneutics into an organon of the human sciences. One might wonder whether there is such an art or technique of understanding—we shall come back to the point. But at any rate we can inquire into the consequences for the hermeneutics of the human sciences of the fact that Heidegger derives the circular structure of understanding from the temporality of Dasein. These consequences do not need to be such that a theory is applied to practice so that the latter is performed differently—i.e., in a way that is technically correct. They could also consist in correcting (and refining) the way in which constantly exercised understanding understands itself—a process that would benefit the art of understanding at most only indirectly.

Hence we will once more examine Heidegger's description of the hermeneutical circle in order to make its new fundamental significance fruitful for our purposes. Heidegger writes, "It is not to be reduced to the level of a vicious circle, or even of a circle which is merely tolerated. In the circle is hidden a positive possibility of the most primordial kind of knowing, and we genuinely grasp this possibility only when we have understood that our first, last, and constant task in interpreting is never to allow our fore-having, fore-sight, and fore-conception to be presented to us by fancies and popular conceptions, but rather to make the scientific theme secure by working out these fore-structures in terms of the things themselves" (*Being and Time*, p.153).

What Heidegger is working out here is not primarily a prescription for the practice of understanding, but a description of the way interpretive understanding is achieved. The point of Heidegger's hermeneutical reflection is not so much to prove that there is a circle as to show that this circle possesses an ontologically positive significance. The description as such will be obvious to every interpreter who knows what he is about.[3] All correct interpretation must be on guard against arbitrary fancies and the limitations imposed by imperceptible habits of thought, and it must direct its gaze "on the things themselves" (which, in the case of the literary critic, are meaningful texts, which themselves are again concerned with objects). For the interpreter to let himself be guided by the things themselves is obviously not a matter of a single, "conscientious" decision, but is "the first, last, and constant task." For it is necessary to keep one's gaze fixed on the thing throughout all the constant distractions that originate in the interpreter himself. A person who is trying to understand a text is always projecting. He projects a meaning for the text as a whole as soon as some initial meaning emerges in the text. Again, the initial meaning emerges only because he is reading the text with particular expectations in regard to a certain meaning. Working out this fore-projection, which is constantly revised in terms of what emerges as he penetrates into the meaning, is understanding what is there.

This description is, of course, a rough abbreviation of the whole. The process that Heidegger describes is that every revision of the fore-projection is capable of projecting before itself a new projection of meaning; rival projects can emerge side by side until it becomes clearer what the unity of meaning is; interpretation begins with fore-conceptions that are replaced by more suitable ones. This constant process of new projection constitutes the movement of understanding and interpretation.

A person who is trying to understand is exposed to distraction from fore-meanings that are not borne out by the things themselves. Working out appropriate projections, anticipatory in nature, to be confirmed "by the things" themselves, is the constant task of understanding. The only "objectivity" here is the confirmation of a fore-meaning in its being worked out. Indeed, what characterizes the arbitrariness of inappropriate fore-meanings if not that they come to nothing in being worked out? But understanding realizes its full potential only when the fore-meanings that it begins with are not arbitrary. Thus it is quite right for the interpreter not to approach the text directly, relying solely on the fore-meaning already available to him, but rather explicitly to examine the legitimacy—i.e., the origin and validity—of the fore-meanings dwelling within him.

This basic requirement must be seen as the radicalization of a procedure that we in fact exercise whenever we understand anything. Every text presents the task of not simply leaving our own linguistic usage unexamined—or in the case of a foreign language the usage that we are familiar with from writers or from daily intercourse. Rather, we regard our task as deriving our understanding of the text from the linguistic usage of the time or of the author. The question is, of course, how this general requirement can be fulfilled. Especially in the field of semantics we are confronted with the problem that our own use of language is unconscious. How do we discover that there is a difference between our own customary usage and that of the text?

I think we must say that generally we do so in the experience of being pulled up short by the text. Either it does not yield any meaning at all or its meaning is not compatible with what we had expected. This is what brings us up short and alerts us to a possible difference in usage. Someone who speaks the same language as I do uses the words in the sense familiar to me—this is a general presupposition that can be questioned only in particular cases. The same thing is true in the case of a foreign language: we all think we have a standard knowledge of it and assume this standard usage when we are reading a text.

What is true of fore-meanings that stem from usage, however, is equally true of the fore-meanings concerning content with which we read texts, and which make up our fore-understanding. Here too we may ask how we can break the spell of our own fore-meanings. There can, of course, be a general expectation that what the text says will fit perfectly with my own meanings and expectations. But what another person tells me, whether in conversation, letter, book, or whatever, is generally supposed to be his own and not my opinion; and this is what I am to take note of without necessarily having to share it. Yet this presupposition is not something that makes understanding easier, but harder, since the fore-meanings that determine my own understanding can go entirely unnoticed. If they give rise to misunderstandings, how can our misunderstandings of a text be perceived at all if there is nothing to contradict them? How can a text be protected against misunderstanding from the start?

If we examine the situation more closely, however, we find that meanings cannot be understood in an arbitrary way. Just as we cannot continually misunderstand the use of a word without its affecting the meaning of the whole, so we cannot stick blindly to our own fore-meaning about the thing if we want to understand the meaning of another. Of course this does not mean that when we listen to someone or read a book we must forget all our fore-meanings concerning the content and all our own ideas. All that is asked is that we remain open to the meaning of the other person or text. But this openness always includes our situating the other meaning in relation to the whole of our own meanings or ourselves in relation to it. Now, the fact is that meanings represent a fluid multiplicity of possibilities (in comparison to the agreement presented by a language and a vocabulary), but within this multiplicity of what can be thought—i.e., of what a reader can find meaningful and hence expect to find—not everything is possible; and if a person fails to hear what the other person is really saying, he will not be able to fit what he has misunderstood into the range of his own various expectations of meaning. Thus there is a criterion here also. *The hermeneutical task becomes of itself a questioning of things* and is always in part so defined. This places hermeneutical work on a firm basis. A person trying to understand something will not resign himself from the start to relying on his own accidental fore-meanings, ignoring as consistently and stubbornly as possible the actual meaning of the text until the latter becomes so persistently audible that it breaks through what the interpreter imagines it to be. Rather, a person trying to understand a text is prepared for it to tell him something. That is why a hermeneutically trained consciousness must be, from the start, sensitive to the text's alterity. But this kind of sensitivity involves neither "neutrality" with respect to content nor the extinction of one's self, but the foregrounding and appropriation of one's own fore-meanings and prejudices. The important thing is to be aware of one's own bias, so that the text can present itself in all its otherness and thus assert its own truth against one's own fore-meanings.

When Heidegger disclosed the fore-structure of understanding in what is considered merely "reading what is there," this was a completely correct phenomenological description. He also exemplified the task that follows from this. In *Being and Time* he gave the general hermeneutical problem a concrete form in the question of being.[4] In order to explain the hermeneutical situation of the question of being in terms of fore-having, foresight, and fore-conception, he critically tested his question, directed at metaphysics, on important turning points in the history of metaphysics. Here he was only doing what historical-hermeneutical consciousness requires in every case. Methodologically conscious understanding will be concerned not merely to form anticipatory ideas, but to make them conscious, so as to check them and thus acquire right understanding from the things themselves. This is what Heidegger means when he talks about making our scientific theme "secure" by deriving our fore-having, foresight and fore-conception from the things themselves.

It is not at all a matter of securing ourselves against the tradition that speaks out of the text then, but, on the contrary, of excluding everything that could hinder us from understanding it in terms of the subject matter. It is the tyranny of hidden prejudices that makes us deaf to what speaks to us in tradition. Heidegger's demonstration that the concept of consciousness in Descartes and of spirit in Hegel is still influenced by Greek substance ontology, which sees being in terms of what is present, undoubtedly surpasses the self-understanding of modern metaphysics, yet not in an arbitrary, willful way, but on the basis of a "fore-having" that in fact makes this tradition intelligible by revealing the ontological premises of the concept of subjectivity. On the other hand, Heidegger discovers in Kant's critique of "dogmatic" metaphysics the idea of a metaphysics of finitude which is a challenge to his own ontological scheme. Thus he "secures" the scientific theme by framing it within the understanding of tradition and so putting it, in a sense, at risk. All of this is a concretization of the historical consciousness involved in understanding.

The recognition that all understanding inevitably involves some prejudice gives the hermeneutical problem its real thrust. In light of this insight it appears that *historicism, despite its critique of rationalism and of natural law philosophy, is based on the modern Enlightenment and unwittingly shares its prejudices*. And there is one prejudice of the Enlightenment that defines its essence: the fundamental prejudice of the Enlightenment is the prejudice against prejudice itself, which denies tradition its power.

The history of ideas shows that not until the Enlightenment does *the concept of prejudice* acquire the negative connotation familiar today. Actually "prejudice" means a judgment that is rendered before all the elements that determine a situation have been finally examined. In German legal terminology a "prejudice" is a provisional legal verdict before the final verdict is reached. For someone involved in a legal dispute, this kind of judgment against him affects his chances adversely. Accordingly, the French préjudice, as well as the Latin praejudicium, means simply "adverse effect," "disadvantage," "harm." But this negative sense is only derivative. The negative consequence depends precisely on the positive validity, the value of the provisional decision as a prejudgment, like that of any precedent.

Thus "prejudice" certainly does not necessarily mean a false judgment, but part of the idea is that it can have either a positive or a negative value. This is clearly due to the influence of the Latin praejudicium. There are such things as préjugés légitimes. This seems a long way from our current use of the word. The German Vorurteil, like the English "prejudice" and even more than the French préjugé, seems to have been limited in its meaning by the Enlightenment critique of religion simply to the sense of an "unfounded judgment."[5] The only thing that gives a judgment dignity is its having a basis, a methodological justification (and not the fact that it may actually be correct). For the Enlightenment the absence of such a basis does not mean that there might be other kinds of certainty, but rather that the judgment has no foundation in the things themselves—i.e., that it is "unfounded." This conclusion follows only in the spirit of rationalism. It is the reason for discrediting prejudices and the reason scientific knowledge claims to exclude them completely.

In adopting this principle, modern science is following the rule of Cartesian doubt, accepting nothing as certain that can in any way be doubted, and adopting the idea of method that follows from this rule. In our introductory observations we have already pointed out how difficult it is to harmonize the historical knowledge that helps to shape our historical consciousness with this ideal and how difficult it is, for that reason, to comprehend its true nature on the basis of the modern conception of method. This is the place to turn those negative statements into positive ones. The concept of "prejudice" is where we can start.

(ii) The Discrediting of Prejudice by the Enlightenment

If we consider the Enlightenment doctrine of prejudice, we find that it makes the following division: we must make a basic distinction between the prejudice due to human authority and that due to overhastiness.[6] This distinction is based on the origin of prejudices in the persons who have them. Either the respect we have for others and their authority leads us into error, or else an overhastiness in ourselves. That authority is a source of prejudices accords with the well-known principle of the Enlightenment that Kant formulated: Have the courage to make use of your *own* understanding.[7] Although this distinction is certainly not limited to the role that prejudices play in understanding texts, its chief application is still in the sphere of hermeneutics, for Enlightenment critique is primarily directed against the religious tradition of Christianity—i.e., the Bible. By treating the Bible as a historical document, biblical criticism endangers its own dogmatic claims. This is the real radicality of the modern Enlightenment compared to all other movements of enlightenment: it must assert itself against the Bible and dogmatic interpretation of it.[8] It is therefore particularly concerned with the hermeneutical problem. It wants to understand tradition correctly—i.e., rationally and without prejudice. But there is a special difficulty about this, since the sheer fact that something is written down gives it special authority. It is not altogether easy to realize that what is written down can be untrue. The written word has the tangible quality of something that can be demonstrated and is like a proof. It requires a special critical effort to free oneself from the prejudice in favor of what is written down and to distinguish here also, no less than in the case of oral assertions, between opinion and truth.[9] In general, the Enlightenment tends to accept no authority and to decide everything before the judgment seat of reason. Thus the written tradition of Scripture, like any other historical document, can claim no absolute validity; the possible truth of the tradition depends on the credibility that reason accords it. It is not tradition but reason that constitutes the ultimate source of all authority. What is written down is not necessarily true. We can know better: this is the maxim with which the modern Enlightenment approaches tradition and which ultimately leads it to undertake historical research.[10] It takes tradition as an object of critique, just as the natural sciences do with the evidence of the senses. This does not necessarily mean that the "prejudice against prejudices" was everywhere taken to the extremes of free thinking and atheism, as in England and France. On the contrary, the German Enlightenment recognized the "true prejudices" of the Christian religion. Since the human intellect is too weak to manage without prejudices, it is at least fortunate to have been educated with true prejudices.

It would be valuable to investigate to what extent this kind of modification and moderation of the Enlightenment[11] prepared the way for the rise of the romantic movement in Germany, as undoubtedly did the critique of the Enlightenment and the revolution by Edmund Burke. But none of this alters the fundamental fact. True prejudices must still finally be justified by rational knowledge, even though the task can never be fully completed.

Thus the criteria of the modern Enlightenment still determine the self-understanding of historicism. They do so not directly, but through a curious refraction caused by romanticism. This can be seen with particular clarity in the fundamental schema of the philosophy of history that romanticism shares with the Enlightenment and that precisely through the romantic reaction to the Enlightenment became an unshakable premise: the schema of the conquest of mythos by logos. What gives this schema its validity is the presupposition of the progressive retreat of magic in the world. It is supposed to represent progress in the history of the mind, and precisely because romanticism disparages this development, it takes over the schema itself as a self-evident truth. It shares the presupposition of the Enlightenment and only reverses its values, seeking to establish the validity of what is old simply on the fact that it is old: the "gothic" Middle Ages, the Christian European community of states, the permanent structure of society, but also the simplicity of peasant life and closeness to nature.

In contrast to the Enlightenment's faith in perfection, which thinks in terms of complete freedom from "superstition" and the prejudices of the past, we now find that olden times—the world of myth, unreflective life, not yet analyzed away by consciousness, in a "society close to nature," the world of Christian chivalry—all these acquire a romantic magic, even a priority over truth.[12] Reversing the Enlightenment's presupposition results in the paradoxical tendency toward restoration—i.e., the tendency to reconstruct the old because it is old, the conscious return to the unconscious, culminating in the recognition of the superior wisdom of the primeval age of myth. But the romantic reversal of the Enlightenment's criteria of value actually perpetuates the abstract contrast between myth and reason. All criticism of the Enlightenment now proceeds via this romantic mirror image of the Enlightenment. Belief in the perfectibility of

reason suddenly changes into the perfection of the "mythical" consciousness and finds itself reflected in a paradisiacal primal state before the "fall"
of thought.[13]

In fact the presupposition of a mysterious darkness in which there was
a mythical collective consciousness that preceded all thought is just as
dogmatic and abstract as that of a state of perfect enlightenment or of
absolute knowledge. Primeval wisdom is only the counterimage of "primeval stupidity." All mythical consciousness is still knowledge, and if it knows
about divine powers, then it has progressed beyond mere trembling before
power (if this is to be regarded as the primeval state), but also beyond a
collective life contained in magic rituals (as we find in the early Orient). It
knows about itself, and in this knowledge it is no longer simply outside
itself.[14]

There is the related point that even the contrast between genuine
mythical thinking and pseudomythical poetic thinking is a romantic
illusion based on a prejudice of the Enlightenment: namely that the poetic
act no longer shares the binding quality of myth because it is a creation of
the free imagination. It is the old quarrel between the poets and the
philosophers in the modern garb appropriate to the age of belief in science.
It is now said, not that poets tell lies, but that they are incapable of saying
anything true; they have only an aesthetic effect and, through their
imaginative creations, they merely seek to stimulate the imagination and
vitality of their hearers or readers.

Another case of romantic refraction is probably to be found in the
concept of an "organic society," which Ladendorf says was introduced by
H. Leo.[15] In Karl Marx it appears as a kind of relic of natural law that limits
the validity of his socio-economic theory of the class struggle.[16] Does the
idea go back to Rousseau's description of society before the division of
labor and the introduction of property?[17] At any rate, Plato had already
demonstrated the illusory nature of this political theory in his ironical
account of a state of nature in the third book of the *Republic*.[18]

These romantic revaluations give rise to historical science in the nineteenth century. It no longer measures the past by the standards of the
present, as if they were an absolute, but it ascribes to past ages a value of
their own and can even acknowledge their superiority in one respect or
another. The great achievements of romanticism—the revival of the past,
the discovery of the voices of the peoples in their songs, the collecting of
fairy tales and legends, the cultivation of ancient customs, the discovery of
the worldviews implicit in languages, the study of the "religion and

wisdom of India"—all contributed to the rise of historical research, which was slowly, step by step, transformed from intuitive revival into detached historical knowledge. The fact that it was romanticism that gave birth to the historical school confirms that the romantic retrieval of origins is itself based on the Enlightenment. Nineteenth-century historiography is its finest fruit and sees itself precisely as the fulfillment of the Enlightenment, as the last step in the liberation of the mind from the trammels of dogma, the step to objective knowledge of the historical world, which stands on a par with the knowledge of nature achieved by modern science.

The fact that the restorative tendency of romanticism could combine with the fundamental concerns of the Enlightenment to create the historical sciences simply indicates that the same break with the continuity of meaning in tradition lies behind both. If the Enlightenment considers it an established fact that all tradition that reason shows to be impossible (i.e., nonsense) can only be understood historically—i.e., by going back to the past's way of looking at things—then the historical consciousness that emerges in romanticism involves a radicalization of the Enlightenment. For nonsensical tradition, which had been the exception, has become the general rule for historical consciousness. Meaning that is generally accessible through reason is so little believed that the whole of the past—even, ultimately, all the thinking of one's contemporaries—is understood only "historically." Thus the romantic critique of the Enlightenment itself ends in Enlightenment, for it evolves as historical science and draws everything into the orbit of historicism. The basic discreditation of all prejudices, which unites the experimental fervor of the new natural sciences during the Enlightenment, is universalized and radicalized in the historical Enlightenment.

This is the point at which the attempt to critique historical hermeneutics has to start. The overcoming of all prejudices, this global demand of the Enlightenment, will itself prove to be a prejudice, and removing it opens the way to an appropriate understanding of the finitude which dominates not only our humanity but also our historical consciousness.

Does being situated within traditions really mean being subject to prejudices and limited in one's freedom? Is not, rather, all human existence, even the freest, limited and qualified in various ways? If this is true, the idea of an absolute reason is not a possibility for historical humanity. Reason exists for us only in concrete, historical terms—i.e., it is not its own master but remains constantly dependent on the given circumstances in which it operates. This is true not only in the sense in which Kant, under the influence of the skeptical critique of Hume, limited the claims of rationalism to the a priori element in the knowledge of nature; it is still truer of historical consciousness and the possibility of historical knowledge. For that man is concerned here with himself and his own creations (Vico) is only an apparent solution of the problem posed by historical knowledge. Man is alien to himself and his historical fate in a way quite different from the way nature, which knows nothing of him, is alien to him.

The epistemological question must be asked here in a fundamentally different way. We have shown above that Dilthey probably saw this, but he was not able to escape his entanglement in traditional epistemology. Since he started from the awareness of "experiences" (Erlebnisse), he was unable to build a bridge to the historical realities, because the great historical realities of society and state always have a predeterminate influence on any "experience." Self-reflection and autobiography—Dilthey's starting points—are not primary and are therefore not an adequate basis for the hermeneutical problem, because through them history is made private once more. In fact history does not belong to us; we belong to it. Long before we understand ourselves through the process of self-examination, we understand ourselves in a self-evident way in the family, society, and state in which we live. The focus of subjectivity is a distorting mirror. The self-awareness of the individual is only a flickering in the closed circuits of historical life. *That is why the prejudices of the individual, far more than his judgments, constitute the historical reality of his being.*

(B) PREJUDICES AS CONDITIONS OF UNDERSTANDING

(i) The Rehabilitation of Authority and Tradition

Here is the point of departure for the hermeneutical problem. This is why we examined the Enlightenment's discreditation of the concept of "prejudice." What appears to be a limiting prejudice from the viewpoint of the absolute self-construction of reason in fact belongs to historical reality itself. If we want to do justice to man's finite, historical mode of being, it is necessary to fundamentally rehabilitate the concept of prejudice and acknowledge the fact that there are legitimate prejudices. Thus we can formulate the fundamental epistemological question for a truly historical hermeneutics as follows: what is the ground of the legitimacy of prejudices? What distinguishes legitimate prejudices from the countless others which it is the undeniable task of critical reason to overcome?

We can approach this question by taking the Enlightenment's critical theory of prejudices, as set out above, and giving it a positive value. The division of prejudices into those of "authority" and those of "overhastiness" is obviously based on the fundamental presupposition of the Enlightenment, namely that methodologically disciplined use of reason can safeguard us from all error. This was Descartes' idea of method. Overhastiness is the source of errors that arise in the use of one's own reason. Authority, however, is responsible for one's not using one's own reason at all. Thus the division is based on a mutually exclusive antithesis between authority and reason. The false prepossession in favor of what is old, in favor of authorities, is what has to be fought. Thus the Enlightenment attributes to Luther's reforms the fact that "the prejudice of human prestige, especially that of the philosophical [he means Aristotle] and the Roman pope, was greatly weakened."[19] The Reformation, then, gives rise to a flourishing hermeneutics which teaches the right use of reason in understanding traditionary texts. Neither the doctrinal authority of the pope nor the appeal to tradition can obviate the work of hermeneutics, which can safeguard the reasonable meaning of a text against all imposition.

This kind of hermeneutics need not lead to the radical critique of religion that we found, for example, in Spinoza. Rather, the possibility of supernatural truth can remain entirely open. Thus especially in the field of German popular philosophy, the Enlightenment limited the claims of reason and acknowledged the authority of Bible and church. We read in Walch, for example, that he distinguishes between the two classes of prejudice—authority and overhastiness—but considers them two extremes, between which it is necessary to find the right middle path, namely a mediation between reason and biblical authority. Accordingly, he regards prejudices deriving from overhastiness as prejudices in favor of the new, a predisposition to the overhasty rejection of truths simply because they are old and attested by authorities.[20] Thus he disputes the British free thinkers (such as Collins and others) and defends the historical faith against the norm of reason. Here the meaning of prejudice deriving from overhastiness is given a conservative reinterpretation.

There can be no doubt, however, that the real consequence of the Enlightenment is different: namely the subjection of all authority to reason. Accordingly, prejudice from overhastiness is to be understood as Descartes understood it—i.e., as the source of all error in the use of reason. This fits in with the fact that after the victory of the Enlightenment, when hermeneutics was freed from all dogmatic ties, the old division returns in a new guise. Thus Schleiermacher distinguishes between partiality and overhastiness as the causes of misunderstanding.[21] To the lasting prejudices due to partiality he contrasts the momentary ones due to overhastiness, but only the former are of interest to those concerned with scientific method. It no longer even occurs to Schleiermacher that among the prejudices in favor of authorities there might be some that are true—yet this was implied in the concept of authority in the first place. His alteration of the traditional division of prejudices documents the victory of the Enlightenment. Partiality now means only an individual limitation of understanding: "The one-sided preference for what is close to one's own sphere of ideas."

In fact, however, the decisive question is concealed behind the concept of partiality. That the prejudices determining what I think are due to my own partiality is a judgment based on the standpoint of their having been dissolved and enlightened, and it holds only for unjustified prejudices. If, on the other hand, there are justified prejudices productive of knowledge, then we are back to the problem of authority. Hence the radical consequences of the Enlightenment, which are still to be found in Schleiermacher's faith in method, are not tenable.

The Enlightenment's distinction between faith in authority and using one's own reason is, in itself, legitimate. If the prestige of authority displaces one's own judgment, then authority is in fact a source of prejudices. But this does not preclude its being a source of truth, and that is what the Enlightenment failed to see when it denigrated all authority. To be convinced of this, we need only consider one of the greatest forerunners of the European Enlightenment, namely Descartes. Despite the radicalness of his methodological thinking, we know that Descartes excluded morality from the total reconstruction of all truths by reason. This was what he meant by his provisional morality. It seems to me symptomatic that he did not in fact elaborate his definitive morality and that its principles, as far as we can judge from his letters to Elizabeth, contain hardly anything new. It is obviously unthinkable to defer morality until modern science has progressed enough to provide a new basis for it. In fact the denigration of authority is not the only prejudice established by the Enlightenment. It also distorted the very concept of authority. Based on the Enlightenment conception of reason and freedom, the concept of authority could be viewed as diametrically opposed to reason and freedom: to be, in fact, blind obedience. This is the meaning that we find in the language critical of modern dictatorships.

But this is not the essence of authority. Admittedly, it is primarily persons that have authority; but the authority of persons is ultimately based not on the subjection and abdication of reason but on an act of acknowledgment and knowledge—the knowledge, namely, that the other is superior to oneself in judgment and insight and that for this reason his judgment takes precedence—i.e., it has priority over one's own. This is connected with the fact that authority cannot actually be bestowed but is earned, and must be earned if someone is to lay claim to it. It rests on acknowledgment and hence on an act of reason itself which, aware of its own limitations, trusts to the better insight of others. Authority in this sense, properly understood, has nothing to do with blind obedience to commands. Indeed, authority has to do not with obedience but rather with knowledge. It is true that authority implies the capacity to command and be obeyed. But this proceeds only from the authority that a person has. Even the anonymous and impersonal authority of a superior which derives from his office is not ultimately based on this hierarchy, but is what makes it possible. Here also its true basis is an act of freedom and reason that grants the authority of a superior fundamentally because he has a wider view of things or is better informed—i.e., once again, because he knows more.[22] Thus, acknowledging authority is always connected with the idea that what the authority says is not irrational and arbitrary but can, in principle, be discovered to be true. This is the essence of the authority claimed by the teacher, the superior, the expert. The prejudices that they implant are legitimized by the person who presents them. But in this way they become prejudices not just in favor of a person but a content, since they effect the same disposition to believe something that can be brought about in other ways—e.g., by good reasons. Thus the essence of authority belongs in the context of a theory of prejudices free from the extremism of the Enlightenment.

Here we can find support in the romantic criticism of the Enlightenment; for there is one form of authority particularly defended by romanticism, namely tradition. That which has been sanctioned by tradition and custom has an authority that is nameless, and our finite historical being is marked by the fact that the authority of what has been handed down to us—and not just what is clearly grounded—always has power over our attitudes and behavior. All education depends on this, and even though, in the case of education, the educator loses his function when his charge comes of age and sets his own insight and decisions in the place of the authority of the educator, becoming mature does not mean that a person becomes his own master in the sense that he is freed from all tradition. The real force of morals, for example, is based on tradition. They are freely taken over but by no means created by a free insight or grounded on reasons. This is precisely what we call tradition: the ground of their validity. And in fact it is to romanticism that we owe this correction of the Enlightenment: that tradition has a justification that lies beyond rational grounding and in large measure determines our institutions and attitudes. What makes classical ethics superior to modern moral philosophy is that it grounds the transition from ethics to "politics," the art of right legislation, on the indispensability of tradition.[23] By comparison, the modern Enlightenment is abstract and revolutionary.

The concept of tradition, however, has become no less ambiguous than that of authority, and for the same reason—namely that what determines the romantic understanding of tradition is its abstract opposition to the principle of enlightenment. Romanticism conceives of tradition as an antithesis to the freedom of reason and regards it as something historically given, like nature. And whether one wants to be revolutionary and oppose it or preserve it, tradition is still viewed as the abstract opposite of free self-determination, since its validity does not require any reasons but conditions us without our questioning it. Of course, the romantic critique of the Enlightenment is not an instance of tradition's automatic dominance of tradition, of its persisting unaffected by doubt and criticism. Rather, a particular critical attitude again addresses itself to the truth of tradition and seeks to renew it. We can call it "traditionalism."

It seems to me, however, that there is no such unconditional antithesis between tradition and reason. However problematical the conscious restoration of old or the creation of new traditions may be, the romantic faith in the "growth of tradition," before which all reason must remain silent, is fundamentally like the Enlightenment, and just as prejudiced. The fact is that in tradition there is always an element of freedom and of history itself. Even the most genuine and pure tradition does not persist because of the inertia of what once existed. It needs to be affirmed, embraced, cultivated. It is, essentially, preservation, and it is active in all historical change. But preservation is an act of reason, though an inconspicuous one. For this reason, only innovation and planning appear to be the result of reason. But this is an illusion. Even where life changes violently, as in ages of revolution, far more of the old is preserved in the supposed transformation of everything than anyone knows, and it combines with the new to create a new value. At any rate, preservation is as much a freely chosen action as are revolution and renewal. That is why both the Enlightenment's critique of tradition and the romantic rehabilitation of it lag behind their true historical being.

These thoughts raise the question of whether in the hermeneutics of the human sciences the element of tradition should not be given its full value. Research in the human sciences cannot regard itself as in an absolute antithesis to the way in which we, as historical beings, relate to the past. At any rate, our usual relationship to the past is not characterized by distancing and freeing ourselves from tradition. Rather, we are always situated within traditions, and this is no objectifying process—i.e., we do not conceive of what tradition says as something other, something alien. It is always part of us, a model or exemplar, a kind of cognizance that our later historical judgment would hardly regard as a kind of knowledge but as the most ingenuous affinity with tradition.

Hence in regard to the dominant epistemological methodologism we must ask: has the rise of historical consciousness really divorced our scholarship from this natural relation to the past? Does understanding in the human sciences understand itself correctly when it relegates the whole of its own historicality to the position of prejudices from which we must free ourselves? Or does "unprejudiced scholarship" share more than it realizes with that naive openness and reflection in which traditions live and the past is present?

In any case, understanding in the human sciences shares one fundamental condition with the life of tradition: it lets itself be *addressed* by tradition. Is it not true of the objects that the human sciences investigate, just as for the contents of tradition, that what they are really about can be experienced only when one is addressed by them? However mediated this significance may be, and though it may proceed from a historical interest that appears to bear no relation to the present—even in the extreme case of "objective" historical research—the real fulfillment of the historical task is to determine anew the significance of what is examined. But the significance exists at the beginning of any such research as well as at the end: in choosing the theme to be investigated, awakening the desire to investigate, gaining a new problematic.

At the beginning of all historical hermeneutics, then, *the abstract antithesis between tradition and historical research, between history and the knowledge of it,* _must be discarded_. The effect (Wirkung) of a living tradition and the effect of historical study must constitute a unity of effect, the analysis of which would reveal only a texture of reciprocal effects.[24] Hence we would do well not to regard historical consciousness as something radically new—as it seems at first—but as a new element in what has always constituted the human relation to the past. In other words, we have to recognize the element of tradition in historical research and inquire into its hermeneutic productivity.

That an element of tradition affects the human sciences despite the methodological purity of their procedures, an element that constitutes their real nature and distinguishing mark, is immediately clear if we examine the history of research and note the difference between the human and natural sciences with regard to their history. Of course none of man's finite historical endeavors can completely erase the traces of this finitude. The history of mathematics or of the natural sciences is also a part of the history of the human spirit and reflects its destinies. Nevertheless, it is not just historical naivete when the natural scientist writes the history of his subject in terms of the present state of knowledge. For him errors and wrong turnings are of historical interest only, because the progress of research is the self-evident standard of examination. Thus it is only of secondary interest to see how advances in the natural sciences or in mathematics belong to the moment in history at which they took place. This interest does not affect the epistemic value of discoveries in those fields.

There is, then, no need to deny that elements of tradition can also affect the natural sciences—e.g., particular lines of research are preferred at particular places. But scientific research as such derives the law of its development not from these circumstances but from the law of the object it is investigating, which conceals its methodical efforts.[25]

It is clear that the human sciences cannot be adequately described in terms of this conception of research and progress. Of course it is possible to write a history of the solution of a problem—e.g., the deciphering of barely legible inscriptions—in which the only interest is in ultimately reaching the final result. Were this not so, it would have been impossible for the human sciences to have borrowed the methodology of the natural ones, as happened in the last century. But what the human sciences share with the natural is only a subordinate element of the work done in the human sciences.

This is shown by the fact that the great achievements in the human sciences almost never become outdated. A modern reader can easily make allowances for the fact that, a hundred years ago, less knowledge was available to a historian, and he therefore made judgments that were incorrect in some details. On the whole, he would still rather read Droysen or Mommsen than the latest account of the subject from the pen of a historian living today. What is the criterion here? Obviously the value and importance of research cannot be measured by a criterion based in the subject matter. Rather, the subject matter appears truly significant only when it is properly portrayed for us. Thus we are certainly interested in the subject matter, but it acquires its life only from the light in which it is presented to us. We accept the fact that the subject presents different aspects of itself at different times or from different standpoints. We accept the fact that these aspects do not simply cancel one another out as research proceeds, but are like mutually exclusive conditions that exist by themselves and combine only in us. Our historical consciousness is always filled with a variety of voices in which the echo of the past is heard. Only in the multifariousness of such voices does it exist: this constitutes the nature of the tradition in which we want to share and have a part. Modern historical research itself is not only research, but the handing down of tradition. We do not see it only in terms of progress and verified results; in it we have, as it were, a new experience of history whenever the past resounds in a new voice.

Why is this so? Obviously, in the human sciences we cannot speak of an object of research in the same sense as in the natural sciences, where research penetrates more and more deeply into nature. Rather, in the human sciences the particular research questions concerning tradition that we are interested in pursuing are motivated in a special way by the present and its interests. The theme and object of research are actually constituted by the motivation of the inquiry.[26] Hence historical research is carried along by the historical movement of life itself and cannot be understood teleologically in terms of the object into which it is inquiring. Such an "object in itself" clearly does not exist at all. This is precisely what distinguishes the human sciences from the natural sciences. Whereas the object of the natural sciences can be described idealiter as what would be known in the perfect knowledge of nature, it is senseless to speak of a perfect knowledge of history, and for this reason it is not possible to speak of an "object in itself" toward which its research is directed.[27]

(ii) The Example of the Classical[28]

Of course it is a lot to ask that the self-understanding of the human sciences detach itself, in the whole of its activity, from the model of the natural sciences and regard the historical movement of the things they are concerned with not simply as an impairment of their objectivity, but as something of positive value. In the recent development of the human sciences, however, there are starting points for a reflection that would really do justice to the problem. The naive schema of history-as-research no longer dominates the way the human sciences conceive of themselves. The advancement of inquiry is no longer universally conceived of as an expansion or penetration into new fields or material, but instead as raising the inquiry to a higher stage of reflection. But even where this happens, one is still thinking teleologically, from the viewpoint of progressive research, in a way appropriate to a research scientist. But a hermeneutical consciousness is gradually growing that is infusing research with a spirit of self-reflection; this is true, above all, in those human sciences that have the oldest tradition. Thus the study of classical antiquity, after it had worked over the whole extent of the available transmitted texts, continually applied itself again, with more subtle questions, to its favorite objects of study. This introduced something of an element of self-criticism by inviting reflection on what constituted the real merit of its favorite objects. The concept of the classical, which since Droysen's discovery of Hellenism had been reduced by historical thinking to a mere stylistic concept, now acquired a new scholarly legitimacy.

It requires hermeneutical reflection of some sophistication to discover how it is possible for a normative concept such as the classical to acquire or regain its scholarly legitimacy. For it follows from the self-understanding of historical consciousness that all of the past's normative significance has been finally dissolved by sovereign historical reason. Only at the beginnings of historicism, as for example in Winckelmann's epoch-making work, had the normative element been a real motive of historical research.

The concept of classical antiquity and of the classical—which dominated pedagogical thought in particular since the days of German classicism —combined both a normative and a historical side. A particular stage in the historical development of humanity was thought to have produced a mature and perfect form of the human. This mediation between the normative and historical senses of the concept goes back to Herder. But

Hegel still preserved this mediation, even though he gave it a different emphasis, namely in terms of the history of philosophy. For him classical art retained its special distinction by being regarded as the "religion of art." Since this form of spirit is past, it is exemplary only in a qualified sense. The fact that it is a past art testifies to the "past" character of art in general. In this way Hegel systematically justified the historicization of the concept of the classical, and he began the process of development that finally changed the classical into a descriptive stylistic concept—one that describes the short lived harmony of measure and fullness that comes between archaic rigidity and baroque dissolution. Since it became part of the aesthetic vocabulary of historical studies, the concept of the classical retains the sense of a normative content only in an unacknowledged way.[29]

Symptomatic of renewed historical self-criticism was that after the First World War classical philology started to examine itself under the banner of a new humanism, and hesitantly again acknowledged the combination of normative and historical elements in "the classical."[30] In so doing, it proved impossible (however one tried) to interpret the concept of the classical —which arose in antiquity and canonized certain writers—as if it expressed the unity of a stylistic ideal.[31] On the contrary, as a stylistic term the ancient concept was wholly ambiguous. Today when we use classical as a historical stylistic concept whose clear meaning is defined by its being set against what came before and after, this concept has become quite detached from the ancient one. The concept of the classical now signifies a period of time, a phase of historical development but not a suprahistorical value.

In fact, however, the normative element in the concept of the classical has never completely disappeared. Even today it is still the basis of the idea of liberal education. The philologist is rightly dissatisfied with simply applying to his texts the historical stylistic concept that developed through the history of the plastic arts. The question whether Homer too is "classical" shatters the notion that the classical is merely a historical category of style analogous to categories of style used in the history of art—an instance of the fact that historical consciousness always includes more than it admits of itself.

If we try to see what this implies, we might say that the classical is a truly historical category, precisely because it is more than a concept of a period or of a historical style, and yet it nevertheless does not try to be the concept of a suprahistorical value. It does not refer to a quality that we ascribe to particular historical phenomena but to a notable mode of being historical:

the historical process of preservation (Bewahrung) that, through constantly proving itself (Bewährung), allows something true (ein Wahres) to come into being. It is not at all the case, as the historical mode of thought would have us believe, that the value judgment which accords something the status of a classic was in fact destroyed by historical reflection and its criticism of all teleological construals of the process of history. Rather, through this criticism the value judgment implicit in the concept of the classical acquires a new, special legitimacy. The classical is something that resists historical criticism because its historical dominion, the binding power of the validity that is preserved and handed down, precedes all historical reflection and continues in it.

To take the key example of the blanket concept of "classical antiquity," it is, of course, unhistorical to devalue Hellenism as an age of the decline and fall of classicism, and Droysen has rightly emphasized its place in the continuity of world history and stressed the importance of Hellenism for the birth and spread of Christianity. But he would not have needed to undertake this historical theodicy if there had not always been a prejudice in favor of the classical and if the culture of "humanism" had not held on to "classical antiquity" and preserved it within Western culture as the heritage of the past. The classical is fundamentally something quite different from a descriptive concept used by an objectivizing historical consciousness. It is a historical reality to which historical consciousness belongs and is subordinate. The "classical" is something raised above the vicissitudes of changing times and changing tastes. It is immediately accessible, not through that shock of recognition, as it were, that sometimes characterizes a work of art for its contemporaries and in which the beholder experiences a fulfilled apprehension of meaning that surpasses all conscious expectations. Rather, when we call something classical, there is a consciousness of something enduring, of significance that cannot be lost and that is independent of all the circumstances of time—a kind of timeless present that is contemporaneous with every other present.

So the most important thing about the concept of the classical (and this is wholly true of both the ancient and the modern use of the word) is the normative sense. But insofar as this norm is related retrospectively to a past greatness that fulfilled and embodied it, it always contains a temporal quality that articulates it historically. So it is not surprising that, with the rise of historical reflection in Germany which took Winckelmann's classicism as its standard, a historical concept of a time or period detached itself from what was regarded as classical in Winckelmann's sense. It denoted a quite specific stylistic ideal and, in a historically descriptive way, also a time or period that fulfilled this ideal. From the distance of the epigones who set up the criterion, this stylistic ideal seemed to designate a historic moment that belonged to the past. Accordingly, the concept of the classical came to be used in modern thought to describe the whole of "classical antiquity" when humanism again proclaimed the exemplarity of this antiquity. It was reviving an ancient usage, and with some justification, for those ancient authors who were "discovered" by humanism were the same ones who in late antiquity comprised the canon of classics.

They were preserved in the history of Western culture precisely because they became canonical as the writers of the "school." But it is easy to see how the historical stylistic concept was able to adopt this usage. For although there is a normative consciousness behind this concept, there is still a retrospective element. What gives birth to the classical norm is an awareness of decline and distance. It is not by accident that the concept of the classical and of classical style emerges in late periods. Callimachus and Tacitus' *Dialogue on Oratory* played a decisive role in this connection.[32] But there is something else. The authors regarded as classical are, as we know, always the representatives of particular literary genres. They were considered the culmination of the norm of that literary genre, an ideal that literary criticism makes plain in retrospect. If we now examine these generic norms historically—i.e., if we consider their history—then the classical is seen as a stylistic phase, a climax that articulates the history of the genre in terms of before and after. Insofar as the climactic points in the history of genres belong largely within the same brief period of time, within the totality of the historical development of classical antiquity, the classical refers to such a period and thus also becomes a concept denoting a period and fuses with a concept of style.

As such a historical stylistic concept, the concept of the classical is capable of being extended to any "development" to which an immanent telos gives unity. And in fact all cultures have high periods, when a particular civilization is marked by special achievements in all fields. Thus, via its particular historical fulfillment, the classical as a general concept of value again becomes a general historical stylistic concept.

Although this is an understandable development, the historicization of the concept also involves its uprooting, and that is why when historical consciousness started to engage in self-criticism, it reinstated the normative element in the concept of the classical as well as the historical uniqueness of its fulfillment. Every "new humanism" shares with the first and oldest the consciousness of belonging in an immediate way and being bound to its model—which, as something past, is unattainable and yet present. Thus the classical epitomizes a general characteristic of historical being: preservation amid the ruins of time. The general nature of tradition is such that only the part of the past that is not past offers the possibility of historical knowledge. The classical, however, as Hegel says, is "that which is self-significant (selbst bedeutende) and hence also self-interpretive (selber Deutende)."[33] But that ultimately means that the classical preserves itself precisely *because* it is significant in itself and interprets itself; i.e., it speaks in such a way that it is not a statement about what is past—documentary evidence that still needs to be interpreted—rather, it says something to the present as if it were said specifically to it. What we call "classical" does not first require the overcoming of historical distance, for in its own constant mediation it overcomes this distance by itself. The classical, then, is certainly "timeless," but this timelessness is a mode of historical being.

Of course this is not to deny that works regarded as classical present tasks of historical understanding to a developed historical consciousness, one that is aware of historical distance. The aim of historical consciousness is not to use the classical model in the direct way, like Palladio or Corneille, but to know it as a historical phenomenon that can be understood solely in terms of its own time. But understanding it will always involve *more* than merely historically reconstructing the past "world" to which the work belongs. Our understanding will always retain the consciousness that we too belong to that world, and correlatively, that the work too belongs to our world.

This is just what the word "classical" means: that the duration of a work's power to speak directly is fundamentally unlimited.[34] However much the concept of the classical expresses distance and unattainability and is part of cultural consciousness, the phrase "classical culture" still implies something of the continuing validity of the classical. Cultural consciousness manifests an ultimate community and sharing with the world from which a classical work speaks.

This discussion of the concept of the classical claims no independent significance, but serves only to evoke a general question, namely: Does the kind of historical mediation between the past and the present that characterizes the classical ultimately underlie all historical activity as its effective substratum? Whereas romantic hermeneutics had taken homogeneous human nature as the unhistorical substratum of its theory of

understanding and hence had freed the con-genial interprete
historical conditions, the self-criticism of historical consciou:
finally to recognizing historical movement not only in events but also in
understanding itself. *Understanding is to be thought of less as a subjective act*
than as participating in an event of tradition, a process of transmission in
which past and present are constantly mediated. This is what must be
validated by hermeneutic theory, which is far too dominated by the idea of
a procedure, a method.

(iii) The Hermeneutic Significance of Temporal Distance[35]

Let us next consider how hermeneutics goes about its work. What
consequences for understanding follow from the fact that belonging to a
tradition is a condition of hermeneutics? We recall the hermeneutical rule
that we must understand the whole in terms of the detail and the detail in
terms of the whole. This principle stems from ancient rhetoric, and modern
hermeneutics has transferred it to the art of understanding. It is a circular
relationship in both cases. The anticipation of meaning in which the whole
is envisaged becomes actual understanding when the parts that are
determined by the whole themselves also determine this whole.

We know this from learning ancient languages. We learn that we must
"construe" a sentence before we attempt to understand the linguistic
meaning of the individual parts of the sentence. But the process of
construal is itself already governed by an expectation of meaning that
follows from the context of what has gone before. It is of course necessary
for this expectation to be adjusted if the text calls for it. This means, then,
that the expectation changes and that the text unifies its meaning around
another expectation. Thus the movement of understanding is constantly
from the whole to the part and back to the whole. Our task is to expand the
unity of the understood meaning centrifugally. The harmony of all the
details with the whole is the criterion of correct understanding. The failure
to achieve this harmony means that understanding has failed.

Schleiermacher elaborated this hermeneutic circle of part and whole in
both its objective and its subjective aspects. As the single word belongs in
the total context of the sentence, so the single text belongs in the total
context of a writer's work, and the latter in the whole of the literary genre
or of literature. At the same time, however, the same text, as a manifestation of a creative moment, belongs to the whole of its author's inner life.
Full understanding can take place only within this objective and subjective

whole. Following this theory, Dilthey speaks of "structure" and of the "centering in a mid-point," which permits one to understand the whole. In this (as we have already said above[36]) he is applying to the historical world what has always been a principle of all textual interpretation: namely that a text must be understood in its own terms.

The question is, however, whether this is an adequate account of the circular movement of understanding. Here we must return to what we concluded from our analysis of Schleiermacher's hermeneutics. We can set aside Schleiermacher's ideas on subjective interpretation. When we try to understand a text, we do not try to transpose ourselves into the author's mind but, if one wants to use this terminology, we try to transpose ourselves into the perspective within which he has formed his views. But this simply means that we try to understand how what he is saying could be right. If we want to understand, we will try to make his arguments even stronger. This happens even in conversation, and it is a fortiori true of understanding what is written down that we are moving in a dimension of meaning that is intelligible in itself and as such offers no reason for going back to the subjectivity of the author. The task of hermeneutics is to clarify this miracle of understanding, which is not a mysterious communion of souls, but sharing in a common meaning.

But even Schleiermacher's description of the objective side of this circle does not get to the heart of the matter. We have seen that the goal of all attempts to reach an understanding is agreement concerning the subject matter. Hence the task of hermeneutics has always been to establish agreement where there was none or where it had been disturbed in some way. The history of hermeneutics confirms this if, for example, we think of Augustine, who sought to mediate the Gospel with the Old Testament[37]; or early Protestantism, which faced the same problem;[38] or, finally, the Enlightenment, when (almost as if renouncing the possibility of agreement) it was supposed that a text could be "fully understood" only by means of historical interpretation. It is something qualitatively new when romanticism and Schleiermacher universalize historical consciousness by denying that the binding form of the tradition from which they come and in which they are situated provides a solid basis for all hermeneutic endeavor.

One of the immediate predecessors of Schleiermacher, the philologist Friedrich Ast, still had a view of hermeneutical work that was markedly concerned with content, since for him its purpose was to establish harmony between the worlds of classical antiquity and Christianity, between a newly discovered genuine antiquity and the Christian tradition. This is something new. In contrast to the Enlightenment, this hermeneutics no longer evaluates and rejects tradition according to the criterion of natural reason. But in its attempt to bring about a meaningful agreement between the two traditions to which it sees itself as belonging, this kind of hermeneutics is still pursuing the task of all preceding hermeneutics, namely to bring about agreement *in content*.

In going beyond the "particularity" of this reconciliation of the ancient classical world and Christianity, Schleiermacher and, following him, nineteenth-century science conceive the task of hermeneutics in a way that is *formally* universal. They were able to harmonize it with the natural sciences' ideal of objectivity, but only by ignoring the concretion of historical consciousness in hermeneutical theory.

Heidegger's description and existential grounding of the hermeneutic circle, by contrast, constitute a decisive turning point. Nineteenth-century hermeneutic theory often discussed the circular structure of understanding, but always within the framework of a formal relation between part and whole—or its subjective reflex, the intuitive anticipation of the whole and its subsequent articulation in the parts. According to this theory, the circular movement of understanding runs backward and forward along the text, and ceases when the text is perfectly understood. This view of understanding came to its logical culmination in Schleiermacher's theory of the divinatory act, by means of which one places oneself entirely within the writer's mind and from there resolves all that is strange and alien about the text. In contrast to this approach, Heidegger describes the circle in such a way that the understanding of the text remains permanently determined by the anticipatory movement of fore-understanding. The circle of whole and part is not dissolved in perfect understanding but, on the contrary, is most fully realized.

The circle, then, is not formal in nature. It is neither subjective nor objective, but describes understanding as the interplay of the movement of tradition and the movement of the interpreter. The anticipation of meaning that governs our understanding of a text is not an act of subjectivity, but proceeds from the commonality that binds us to the tradition. But this commonality is constantly being formed in our relation to tradition. Tradition is not simply a permanent precondition; rather, we produce it ourselves inasmuch as we understand, participate in the evolution of tradition, and hence further determine it ourselves. Thus the circle of understanding is not a "methodological" circle, but describes an element of the ontological structure of understanding.

The circle, which is fundamental to all understanding, has a further hermeneutic implication which I call the "fore-conception of completeness." But this, too, is obviously a formal condition of all understanding. It states that only what really constitutes a unity of meaning is intelligible. So when we read a text we always assume its completeness, and only when this assumption proves mistaken—i.e., the text is not intelligible—do we begin to suspect the text and try to discover how it can be remedied. The rules of such textual criticism can be left aside, for the important thing to note is that applying them properly depends on understanding the content.

The fore-conception of completeness that guides all our understanding is, then, always determined by the specific content. Not only does the reader assume an immanent unity of meaning, but his understanding is likewise guided by the constant transcendent expectations of meaning that proceed from the relation to the truth of what is being said. Just as the recipient of a letter understands the news that it contains and first sees things with the eyes of the person who wrote the letter—i.e., considers what he writes as true, and is not trying to understand the writer's peculiar opinions as such—so also do we understand traditionary texts on the basis of expectations of meaning drawn from our own prior relation to the subject matter. And just as we believe the news reported by a correspondent because he was present or is better informed, so too are we fundamentally open to the possibility that the writer of a transmitted text is better informed than we are, with our prior opinion. It is only when the attempt to accept what is said as true fails that we try to "understand" the text, psychologically or historically, as another's opinion.[39] The prejudice of completeness, then, implies not only this formal element—that a text should completely express its meaning—but also that what it says should be the complete truth.

Here again we see that understanding means, primarily, to understand the content of what is said, and only secondarily to isolate and understand another's meaning as such. Hence the most basic of all hermeneutic preconditions remains one's own fore-understanding, which comes from being concerned with the same subject. This is what determines what can be realized as unified meaning and thus determines how the fore-conception of completeness is applied.[40]

Thus the meaning of "belonging"—i.e., the element of tradition in our historical-hermeneutical activity—is fulfilled in the commonality of fundamental, enabling prejudices. Hermeneutics must start from the position that a person seeking to understand something has a bond to the subject matter that comes into language through the traditionary text and has, or acquires, a connection with the tradition from which the text speaks. On the other hand, hermeneutical consciousness is aware that its bond to this subject matter does not consist in some self-evident, unquestioned unanimity, as is the case with the unbroken stream of tradition. Hermeneutic work is based on a polarity of familiarity and strangeness; but this polarity is not to be regarded psychologically, with Schleiermacher, as the range that covers the mystery of individuality, but truly hermeneutically—i.e., in regard to what has been said: the language in which the text addresses us, the story that it tells us. Here too there is a tension. It is in the play between the traditionary text's strangeness and familiarity to us, between being a historically intended, distanced object and belonging to a tradition. *The true locus of hermeneutics is this in-between.*

Given the intermediate position in which hermeneutics operates, it follows that its work is not to develop a procedure of understanding, but to clarify the conditions in which understanding takes place. But these conditions do not amount to a "procedure" or method which the interpreter must of himself bring to bear on the text; rather, they must be given. The prejudices and fore-meanings that occupy the interpreter's consciousness are not at his free disposal. He cannot separate in advance the productive prejudices that enable understanding from the prejudices that hinder it and lead to misunderstandings.

Rather, this separation must take place in the process of understanding itself, and hence hermeneutics must ask how that happens. But that means it must foreground what has remained entirely peripheral in previous hermeneutics: temporal distance and its significance for understanding.

This point can be clarified by comparing it with the hermeneutic theory of romanticism. We recall that the latter conceived of understanding as the reproduction of an original production. Hence it was possible to say that one should be able to understand an author better than he understood himself. We examined the origin of this statement and its connection with the aesthetics of genius, but must now come back to it, since our present inquiry lends it a new importance.

That subsequent understanding is superior to the original production and hence can be described as superior understanding does not depend so much on the conscious realization that places the interpreter on the same level as the author (as Schleiermacher said) but instead denotes an insuperable difference between the interpreter and the author that is created by historical distance. Every age has to understand a transmitted text in its own way, for the text belongs to the whole tradition whose content interests the age and in which it seeks to understand itself. The real meaning of a text, as it speaks to the interpreter, does not depend on the contingencies of the author and his original audience. It certainly is not identical with them, for it is always co-determined also by the historical situation of the interpreter and hence by the totality of the objective course of history. A writer like Chladenius,[41] who does not yet view understanding in terms of history, is saying the same thing in a naive, ingenuous way when he says that an author does not need to know the real meaning of what he has written; and hence the interpreter can, and must, often understand more than he. But this is of fundamental importance. Not just occasionally but always, the meaning of a text goes beyond its author. That is why understanding is not merely a reproductive but always a productive activity as well. Perhaps it is not correct to refer to this productive element in understanding as "better understanding." For this phrase is, as we have shown, a principle of criticism taken from the Enlightenment and revised on the basis of the aesthetics of genius. Understanding is not, in fact, understanding better, either in the sense of superior knowledge of the subject because of clearer ideas or in the sense of fundamental superiority of conscious over unconscious production. It is enough to say that we understand in a *different* way, *if we understand at all*.

Such a conception of understanding breaks right through the circle drawn by romantic hermeneutics. Since we are now concerned not with individuality and what it thinks but with the truth of what is said, a text is not understood as a mere expression of life but is taken seriously in its claim to truth. That this is what is meant by "understanding" was once self-evident (we need only recall Chladenius).[42] But this dimension of the hermeneutical problem was discredited by historical consciousness and the psychological turn that Schleiermacher gave to hermeneutics, and could only be regained when the aporias of historicism came to light and led finally to the fundamentally new development to which Heidegger, in my view, gave the decisive impetus. For the hermeneutic productivity of temporal distance could be understood only when Heidegger gave understanding an ontological orientation by interpreting it as an "existential" and when he interpreted Dasein's mode of being in terms of time.

Time is no longer primarily a gulf to be bridged because it separates; it is actually the supportive ground of the course of events in which the present is rooted. Hence temporal distance is not something that must be overcome. This was, rather, the naive assumption of historicism, namely that we must transpose ourselves into the spirit of the age, think with its ideas and its thoughts, not with our own, and thus advance toward historical objectivity. In fact the important thing is to recognize temporal distance as a positive and productive condition enabling understanding. It is not a yawning abyss but is filled with the continuity of custom and tradition, in the light of which everything handed down presents itself to us. Here it is not too much to speak of the genuine productivity of the course of events. Everyone is familiar with the curious impotence of our judgment where temporal distance has not given us sure criteria. Thus the judgment of contemporary works of art is desperately uncertain for the scholarly consciousness. Obviously we approach such creations with unverifiable prejudices, presuppositions that have too great an influence over us for us to know about them; these can give contemporary creations an extra resonance that does not correspond to their true content and significance. Only when all their relations to the present time have faded away can their real nature appear, so that the understanding of what is said in them can claim to be authoritative and universal.

In historical studies this experience has led to the idea that objective knowledge can be achieved only if there has been a certain historical distance. It is true that what a thing has to say, its intrinsic content, first appears only after it is divorced from the fleeting circumstances that gave rise to it. The positive conditions of historical understanding include the relative closure of a historical event, which allows us to view it as a whole, and its distance from contemporary opinions concerning its import. The implicit presupposition of historical method, then, is that the permanent significance of something can first be known objectively only when it belongs to a closed context—in other words, when it is dead enough to have only historical interest. Only then does it seem possible to exclude the subjective involvement of the observer. This is, in fact, a paradox, the epistemological counterpart to the old moral problem of whether anyone can be called happy before his death. Just as Aristotle showed how this kind of problem can serve to sharpen the powers of human judgment,[43] so hermeneutical reflection cannot fail to find here a sharpening of the methodological self-consciousness of science. It is true that certain hermeneutic requirements are automatically fulfilled when a historical context has come to be of only historical interest. Certain sources of error are automatically excluded. But it is questionable whether this is the end of the hermeneutical problem. Temporal distance obviously means something other than the extinction of our interest in the object. It lets the true meaning of the object emerge fully. But the discovery of the true meaning of a text or a work of art is never finished; it is in fact an infinite process. Not only are fresh sources of error constantly excluded, so that all kinds of things are filtered out that obscure the true meaning; but new sources of understanding are continually emerging that reveal unsuspected elements of meaning. The temporal distance that performs the filtering process is not fixed, but is itself undergoing constant movement and extension. And along with the negative side of the filtering process brought about by temporal distance there is also the positive side, namely the value it has for understanding. It not only lets local and limited prejudices die away, but allows those that bring about genuine understanding to emerge clearly as such.

Often temporal distance[44] can solve question of critique in hermeneutics, namely how to distinguish the true prejudices, by which we *understand,* from the *false* ones, by which we *misunderstand.* Hence the hermeneutically trained mind will also include historical consciousness. It will make conscious the prejudices governing our own understanding, so that the text, as another's meaning, can be isolated and valued on its own. Foregrounding (abheben) a prejudice clearly requires suspending its validity for us. For as long as our mind is influenced by a prejudice, we do not consider it a judgment. How then can we foreground it? It is impossible to make ourselves aware of a prejudice while it is constantly operating unnoticed, but only when it is, so to speak, provoked. The encounter with a traditionary text can provide this provocation. For what leads to understanding must be something that has already asserted itself in its own separate validity. Understanding begins, as we have already said above,[45] when something addresses us. This is the first condition of hermeneutics. We now know what this requires, namely the fundamental suspension of our own prejudices. But all suspension of judgments and hence, a fortiori, of prejudices, has the logical structure of a *question.*

The essence of the *question* is to open up possibilities and keep them open. If a prejudice becomes questionable in view of what another person or a text says to us, this does not mean that it is simply set aside and the text or the other person accepted as valid in its place. Rather, historical objectivism shows its naivete in accepting this disregarding of ourselves as what actually happens. In fact our own prejudice is properly brought into play by being put at risk. Only by being given full play is it able to experience the other's claim to truth and make it possible for him to have full play himself.

The naivete of so-called historicism consists in the fact that it does not undertake this reflection, and in trusting to the fact that its procedure is methodical, it forgets its own historicity. We must here appeal from a badly understood historical thinking to one that can better perform the task of understanding. Real historical thinking must take account of its own historicity. Only then will it cease to chase the phantom of a historical object that is the object of progressive research, and learn to view the object as the counterpart of itself and hence understand both. The true historical object is not an object at all, but the unity of the one and the other, a relationship that constitutes both the reality of history and the reality of historical understanding.[46] A hermeneutics adequate to the subject matter would have to demonstrate the reality and efficacy of history within understanding itself. I shall refer to this as "history of effect." *Understanding is, essentially, a historically effected event.*

(iv) The Principle of History of Effect (Wirkungsgeschichte)

Historical interest is directed not only toward the historical phenomenon and the traditionary work but also, secondarily, toward their effect in history (which also includes the history of research); the history of effect is generally regarded as a mere supplement to historical inquiry, from Hermann Grimm's *Raffael* to Gundolf and beyond—though it has occasioned many valuable insights. To this extent, history of effect is not new. But to require an inquiry into history of effect every time a work of art or an aspect of the tradition is led out of the twilight region between tradition and history so that it can be seen clearly and openly in terms of its own meaning—this is a new demand (addressed not to research, but to its methodological consciousness) that proceeds inevitably from thinking historical consciousness through.

It is not, of course, a hermeneutical requirement in the sense of the traditional conception of hermeneutics. I am not saying that historical inquiry should develop inquiry into the history of effect as a kind of inquiry separate from understanding the work itself. The requirement is of a more theoretical kind. Historical consciousness must become conscious that in the apparent immediacy with which it approaches a work of art or a traditionary text, there is also another kind of inquiry in play, albeit unrecognized and unregulated. If we are trying to understand a historical phenomenon from the historical distance that is characteristic of our hermeneutical situation, we are always already affected by history. It determines in advance both what seems to us worth inquiring about and what will appear as an object of investigation, and we more or less forget half of what is really there—in fact, we miss the whole truth of the phenomenon—when we take its immediate appearance as the whole truth.

In our understanding, which we imagine is so innocent because its results seem so self-evident, the other presents itself so much in terms of our own selves that there is no longer a question of self and other. In relying on its critical method, historical objectivism conceals the fact that historical consciousness is itself situated in the web of historical effects. By means of methodical critique it does away with the arbitrariness of "relevant" appropriations of the past, but it preserves its good conscience by failing to recognize the presuppositions—certainly not arbitrary, but still fundamental—that govern its own understanding, and hence falls short of reaching that truth which, despite the finite nature of our understanding, could be reached. In this respect, historical objectivism resembles statistics, which are such excellent means of propaganda because they let the "facts" speak and hence simulate an objectivity that in reality depends on the legitimacy of the questions asked.

We are not saying, then, that history of effect must be developed as a new independent discipline ancillary to the human sciences, but that we should learn to understand ourselves better and recognize that in all understanding, whether we are expressly aware of it or not, the efficacy of history is at work. When a naive faith in scientific method denies the existence of effective history, there can be an actual deformation of knowledge. We are familiar with this from the history of science, where it appears as the irrefutable proof of something that is obviously false. But on the whole the power of effective history does not depend on its being recognized. This, precisely, is the power of history over finite human consciousness, namely that it prevails even where faith in method leads one to deny one's own historicity. Our need to become conscious of effective history is urgent because it is necessary for scientific consciousness. But this does not mean it can ever be absolutely fulfilled. That we should become completely aware of effective history is just as hybrid a statement as when Hegel speaks of absolute knowledge, in which history would become completely transparent to itself and hence be raised to the level of a concept. Rather, historically effected consciousness (wirkungs-geschichtliches Bewußtsein) is an element in the act of understanding itself and, as we shall see, is already effectual in *finding the right questions to ask*.

Consciousness of being affected by history (wirkungsgeschichtliches Bewußtsein) is primarily consciousness of the hermeneutical *situation*. To acquire an awareness of a situation is, however, always a task of peculiar difficulty. The very idea of a situation means that we are not standing outside it and hence are unable to have any objective knowledge of it.[47] We always find ourselves within a situation, and throwing light on it is a task that is never entirely finished. This is also true of the hermeneutic situation—i.e., the situation in which we find ourselves with regard to the tradition that we are trying to understand. The illumination of this situation—reflection on effective history—can never be completely achieved; yet the fact that it cannot be completed is due not to a deficiency in reflection but to the essence of the historical being that we are. *To be historically means that knowledge of oneself can never be complete*. All self-knowledge arises from what is historically pregiven, what with Hegel we call "substance," because it underlies all subjective intentions and actions, and hence both prescribes and limits every possibility for understanding any tradition whatsoever in its historical alterity. This almost defines the aim of philosophical hermeneutics: its task is to retrace the path of Hegel's phenomenology of mind until we discover in all that is subjective the substantiality that determines it.

Every finite present has its limitations. We define the concept of "situation" by saying that it represents a standpoint that limits the possibility of vision. Hence essential to the concept of situation is the concept of "*horizon*." The horizon is the range of vision that includes everything that can be seen from a particular vantage point. Applying this to the thinking mind, we speak of narrowness of horizon, of the possible expansion of horizon, of the opening up of new horizons, and so forth. Since Nietzsche and Husserl,[48] the word has been used in philosophy to characterize the way in which thought is tied to its finite determinacy, and the way one's range of vision is gradually expanded. A person who has no horizon does not see far enough and hence over-values what is nearest to him. On the other hand, "to have a horizon" means not being limited to what is nearby but being able to see beyond it. A person who has an horizon knows the relative significance of everything within this horizon, whether it is near or far, great or small. Similarly, working out the hermeneutical situation means acquiring the right horizon of inquiry for the questions evoked by the encounter with tradition.

In the sphere of historical understanding, too, we speak of horizons, especially when referring to the claim of historical consciousness to see the past in its own terms, not in terms of our contemporary criteria and prejudices but within its own historical horizon. The task of historical understanding also involves acquiring an appropriate historical horizon, so that what we are trying to understand can be seen in its true dimensions. If we fail to transpose ourselves into the historical horizon from which the traditionary text speaks, we will misunderstand the significance of what it has to say to us. To that extent this seems a legitimate hermeneutical requirement: we must place ourselves in the other situation in order to understand it. We may wonder, however, whether this phrase is adequate to describe the understanding that is required of us. The same is true of a conversation that we have with someone simply in order to get to know him—i.e., to discover where he is coming from and his horizon. This is not a true conversation—that is, we are not seeking agreement on some subject—because the specific contents of the conversation are only a means to get to know the horizon of the other person. Examples are oral examinations and certain kinds of conversation between doctor and patient. Historical consciousness is clearly doing something similar when it transposes itself into the situation of the past and thereby claims to have acquired the right historical horizon. In a conversation, when we have discovered the other person's standpoint and horizon, his ideas become intelligible without our necessarily having to agree with him; so also when someone thinks historically, he comes to understand the meaning of what has been handed down without necessarily agreeing with it or seeing himself in it.

In both cases, the person understanding has, as it were, stopped trying to reach an agreement. He himself cannot be reached. By factoring the other person's standpoint into what he is claiming to say, we are making our own standpoint safely unattainable.[49] In considering the origin of historical thinking, we have seen that in fact it makes this ambiguous transition from means to ends—i.e., it makes an end of what is only a means. The text that is understood historically is forced to abandon its claim to be saying something true. We think we understand when we see the past from a historical standpoint—i.e., transpose ourselves into the historical situation and try to reconstruct the historical horizon. In fact, however, we have given up the claim to find in the past any truth that is valid and intelligible for ourselves. Acknowledging the otherness of the other in this way, making him the object of objective knowledge, involves the fundamental suspension of his claim to truth.

However, the question is whether this description really fits the hermeneutical phenomenon. Are there really two different horizons here—the horizon in which the person seeking to understand lives and the historical horizon within which he places himself? Is it a correct description of the art of historical understanding to say that we learn to transpose ourselves into alien horizons? Are there such things as closed horizons, in this sense? We recall Nietzsche's complaint against historicism that it destroyed the horizon bounded by myth in which alone a culture is able to live.[50] Is the horizon of one's own present time ever closed in this way, and can a historical situation be imagined that has this kind of closed horizon?

Or is this a romantic refraction, a kind of Robinson Crusoe dream of historical enlightenment, the fiction of an unattainable island, as artificial as Crusoe himself—i.e., as the alleged primacy of the solus ipse? Just as the individual is never simply an individual because he is always in understanding with others, so too the closed horizon that is supposed to enclose a culture is an abstraction. The historical movement of human life consists in the fact that it is never absolutely bound to any one standpoint, and hence can never have a truly closed horizon. The horizon is, rather, something into which we move and that moves with us. Horizons change for a person who is moving. Thus the horizon of the past, out of which all human life lives and which exists in the form of tradition, is always in motion. The surrounding horizon is not set in motion by historical consciousness. But in it this motion becomes aware of itself.

When our historical consciousness transposes itself into historical horizons, this does not entail passing into alien worlds unconnected in any way with our own; instead, they together constitute the one great horizon that moves from within and that, beyond the frontiers of the present, embraces the historical depths of our self-consciousness. Everything contained in historical consciousness is in fact embraced by a single historical horizon. Our own past and that other past toward which our historical consciousness is directed help to shape this moving horizon out of which human life always lives and which determines it as heritage and tradition.

Understanding tradition undoubtedly requires a historical horizon, then. But it is not the case that we acquire this horizon by transposing ourselves into a historical situation. Rather, we must always already have a horizon in order to be able to transpose ourselves into a situation. For what do we mean by "transposing ourselves"? Certainly not just disregarding ourselves. This is necessary, of course, insofar as we must imagine the other situation. But into this other situation we must bring, precisely, ourselves. Only this is the full meaning of "transposing ourselves." If we put ourselves in someone else's shoes, for example, then we will understand him—i.e., become aware of the otherness, the indissoluble individuality of the other person—by putting *ourselves* in his position.

Transposing ourselves consists neither in the empathy of one individual for another nor in subordinating another person to our own standards; rather, it always involves rising to a higher universality that overcomes not only our own particularity but also that of the other. The concept of "horizon" suggests itself because it expresses the superior breadth of vision that the person who is trying to understand must have. To acquire a horizon means that one learns to look beyond what is close at hand—not in order to look away from it but to see it better, within a larger whole and in truer proportion. To speak, with Nietzsche, of the many changing horizons into which historical consciousness teaches us to place ourselves is not a correct description. If we disregard ourselves in this way, we have no historical horizon. Nietzsche's view that historical study is deleterious to life is not, in fact, directed against historical consciousness as such, but against the self-alienation it undergoes when it regards the method of modern historical science as its own true nature. We have already pointed out that a truly historical consciousness always sees its own present in such a way that it sees itself, as well as the historically other, within the right relationships. It requires a special effort to acquire a historical horizon. We are always affected, in hope and fear, by what is nearest to us, and hence we approach the testimony of the past under its influence. Thus it is constantly necessary to guard against overhastily assimilating the past to our own expectations of meaning. Only then can we listen to tradition in a way that permits it to make its own meaning heard.

We have shown above that this is a process of foregrounding (abheben). Let us consider what this idea of foregrounding involves. It is always reciprocal. Whatever is being foregrounded must be foregrounded from something else, which, in turn, must be foregrounded from it. Thus all foregrounding also makes visible that from which something is foregrounded. We have described this above as the way prejudices are brought into play. We started by saying that a hermeneutical situation is determined by the prejudices that we bring with us. They constitute, then, the horizon of a particular present, for they represent that beyond which it is impossible to see. But now it is important to avoid the error of thinking that the horizon of the present consists of a fixed set of opinions and valuations, and that the otherness of the past can be foregrounded from it as from a fixed ground.

In fact the horizon of the present is continually in the process of being formed because we are continually having to test all our prejudices. An important part of this testing occurs in encountering the past and in understanding the tradition from which we come. Hence the horizon of the present cannot be formed without the past. There is no more an isolated horizon of the present in itself than there are historical horizons which have to be acquired. *Rather, understanding is always the fusion of these horizons supposedly existing by themselves.* We are familiar with the power of this kind of fusion chiefly from earlier times and their naivete about themselves and their heritage. In a tradition this process of fusion is continually going on, for there old and new are always combining into something of living value, without either being explicitly foregrounded from the other.

If, however, there is no such thing as these distinct horizons, why do we speak of the fusion of horizons and not simply of the formation of the one horizon, whose bounds are set in the depths of tradition? To ask the question means that we are recognizing that understanding becomes a scholarly task only under special circumstances and that it is necessary to work out these circumstances as a hermeneutical situation. Every encounter with tradition that takes place within historical consciousness involves the experience of a tension between the text and the present. The hermeneutic task consists in not covering up this tension by attempting a naive assimilation of the two but in consciously bringing it out. This is why it is part of the hermeneutic approach to project a historical horizon that is different from the horizon of the present. Historical consciousness is aware of its own otherness and hence foregrounds the horizon of the past from its own. On the other hand, it is itself, as we are trying to show, only something superimposed upon continuing tradition, and hence it immediately recombines with what it has foregrounded itself from in order to become one with itself again in the unity of the historical horizon that it thus acquires.

Projecting a historical horizon, then, is only one phase in the process of understanding; it does not become solidified into the self-alienation of a past consciousness, but is overtaken by our own present horizon of understanding. In the process of understanding, a real fusing of horizons occurs—which means that as the historical horizon is projected, it is simultaneously superseded. To bring about this fusion in a regulated way is the task of what we called historically effected consciousness. Although this task was obscured by aesthetic-historical positivism following on the heels of romantic hermeneutics, it is, in fact, the central problem of hermeneutics. It is the problem of *application*, which is to be found in all understanding.

2 THE RECOVERY OF THE FUNDAMENTAL HERMENEUTIC PROBLEM

(A) THE HERMENEUTIC PROBLEM OF APPLICATION

In the early tradition of hermeneutics, which was completely invisible to the historical self-consciousness of post-romantic scientific epistemology, this problem had its systematic place. Hermeneutics was subdivided as follows: there was a distinction between subtilitas intelligendi (understanding) and subtilitas explicandi (interpretation); and pietism added a third element, subtilitas applicandi (application), as in J. J. Rambach. The process of understanding was regarded as consisting of these three elements. It is notable that all three are called subtilitas—i.e., they are considered less as methods that we have at our disposal than as talents requiring particular finesse of mind.[51] As we have seen, the hermeneutic problem acquired systematic importance because the romantics recognized the inner unity of intelligere and explicare. Interpretation is not an occasional, post facto supplement to understanding; rather, understanding is always interpretation, and hence interpretation is the explicit form of understanding. In accordance with this insight, interpretive language and concepts were recognized as belonging to the inner structure of understanding. This moves the whole problem of language from its peripheral and incidental position into the center of philosophy. We will return to this point.

The inner fusion of understanding and interpretation led to the third element in the hermeneutical problem, *application*, becoming wholly excluded from any connection with hermeneutics. The edifying application of Scripture in Christian preaching, for example, now seemed very different from the historical and theological understanding of it. In the course of our reflections we have come to see that understanding always involves something like applying the text to be understood to the interpreter's present situation. Thus we are forced to go one step beyond romantic hermeneutics, as it were, by regarding not only understanding and interpretation, but also application as comprising one unified process. This is not to return to the pietist tradition of the three separate "subtleties," for, on the contrary, we consider application to be just as integral a part of the hermeneutical process as are understanding and interpretation.[52]

The current state of the hermeneutical discussion is what occasions my emphasizing the fundamental importance of this point. We can appeal first to the forgotten history of hermeneutics. Formerly it was considered obvious that the task of hermeneutics was to adapt the text's meaning to the concrete situation to which the text is speaking. The interpreter of the divine will who can interpret the oracle's language is the original model for this. But even today it is still the case that an interpreter's task is not simply to repeat what one of the partners says in the discussion he is translating, but to express what is said in the way that seems most appropriate to him, considering the real situation of the dialogue, which only he knows, since he alone knows both languages being used in the discussion.

Similarly, the history of hermeneutics teaches us that besides literary hermeneutics, there is also a theological and a legal hermeneutics, and together they make up the full concept of hermeneutics. As a result of the emergence of historical consciousness in the eighteenth and nineteenth centuries, philological hermeneutics and historical studies cut their ties with the other hermeneutical disciplines and established themselves as models of methodology for research in the human sciences.

The fact that *philological, legal, and theological* hermeneutics originally belonged closely together depended on recognizing application as an integral element of all understanding. In both legal and theological hermeneutics there is an essential tension between the fixed text—the law or the gospel—on the one hand and, on the other, the sense arrived at by applying it at the concrete moment of interpretation, either in judgment or in preaching. A law does not exist in order to be understood historically, but to be concretized in its legal validity by being interpreted. Similarly, the gospel does not exist in order to be understood as a merely historical document, but to be taken in such a way that it exercises its saving effect. This implies that the text, whether law or gospel, if it is to be understood properly—i.e., according to the claim it makes—must be understood at every moment, in every concrete situation, in a new and different way. Understanding here is always application.

We began by showing that understanding, as it occurs in the human sciences, is essentially historical—i.e., that in them a text is understood only if it is understood in a different way as the occasion requires. Precisely this indicates the task of a historical hermeneutics: to consider the tension that exists between the identity of the common object and the changing situation in which it must be understood. We began by saying that the historical movement of understanding, which romantic hermeneutics pushed to the periphery, is the true center of hermeneutical inquiry appropriate to historical consciousness. Our consideration of the significance of tradition in historical consciousness started from Heidegger's analysis of the hermeneutics of facticity and sought to apply it to a hermeneutics of the human sciences. We showed that understanding is not a method which the inquiring consciousness applies to an object it chooses and so turns it into objective knowledge; rather, being situated within an event of tradition, a process of handing down, is a prior condition of understanding. *Understanding proves to be an event*, and the task of hermeneutics, seen philosophically, consists in asking what kind of understanding, what kind of science it is, that is itself advanced by historical change.

We are quite aware that we are asking something unusual of the self-understanding of modern science. All of our considerations thus far have been directed toward making this task easier by showing that it results from the convergence of a large number of problems. In fact, hermeneutical theory hitherto falls apart into distinctions that it cannot itself maintain. This is seen clearly in the attempt to construct a general theory of interpretation. When a distinction is made between cognitive, normative, and reproductive interpretation, as in Betti's *General Theory of Interpretation*,[53] which is based on a remarkable knowledge and survey of the subject, difficulties arise in categorizing phenomena according to this division. This is especially true of scholarly interpretation. If we put theological interpretation together with legal interpretation and assign them a normative function, then we must remember Schleiermacher who, on the contrary, closely connected theological interpretation with general interpretation, which was for him the philological-historical one. In fact, the split between the cognitive and the normative function runs right through theological hermeneutics and can hardly be overcome by distinguishing scientific knowledge from the subsequent edifying application.

The split runs through legal interpretation also, in that discovering the meaning of a legal text and discovering how to apply it in a particular legal instance are not two separate actions, but one unitary process.

But even the kind of interpretation that seems furthest from the kinds we have been considering, namely performative interpretation, as in the cases of music and drama—and they acquire their real existence only in being played[54]—is scarcely an independent mode of interpretation. In it too there is a split between the cognitive and the normative function. No one can stage a play, read a poem, or perform a piece of music without understanding the original meaning of the text and presenting it in his reproduction and interpretation. But, similarly, no one will be able to make a performative interpretation without taking account of that other normative element—the stylistic values of one's own day—which, whenever a text is brought to sensory appearance, sets limits to the demand for a stylistically correct reproduction. When we consider that translating texts in a foreign language, imitating them, or even reading texts aloud correctly, involves the same explanatory achievement as philological interpretation, so that the two things become as one, then we cannot avoid the conclusion that the suggested distinction between cognitive, normative, and reproductive interpretation has no fundamental validity, but all three constitute one unitary phenomenon.

If this is the case, then we have the task of *redefining the hermeneutics of the human sciences in terms of legal and theological hermeneutics*. For this we must remember the insight gained from our investigation into romantic hermeneutics, namely that both it and its culmination in psychological interpretation—i.e., deciphering and explaining the individuality of the other—treat the problem of understanding in a way that is far too one-sided. Our line of thought prevents us from dividing the hermeneutic problem in terms of the subjectivity of the interpreter and the objectivity of the meaning to be understood. This would be starting from a false antithesis that cannot be resolved even by recognizing the dialectic of subjective and objective. To distinguish between a normative function and a cognitive one is to separate what clearly belong together. The meaning of a law that emerges in its normative application is fundamentally no different from the meaning reached in understanding a text. It is quite mistaken to base the possibility of understanding a text on the postulate of a "con-geniality" that supposedly unites the creator and the interpreter of a work. If this were really the case, then the human sciences would be in a bad way. But the miracle of understanding consists in the fact that no like-mindedness is necessary to recognize what is really significant and fundamentally meaningful in tradition. We have the ability to open ourselves to the superior claim the text makes and to respond to what it has to tell us. Hermeneutics in the sphere of philology and the historical sciences is not "knowledge as domination"[55]—i.e., an appropriation as taking possession; rather, it consists in subordinating ourselves to the text's claim to dominate our minds. Of this, however, legal and theological hermeneutics are the true model. To interpret the law's will or the promises of God is clearly not a form of domination but of service. They are interpretations—which includes application—in the service of what is considered valid. Our thesis is that historical hermeneutics too has a task of application to perform, because it too serves applicable meaning, in that it explicitly and consciously bridges the temporal distance that separates the interpreter from the text and overcomes the alienation of meaning that the text has undergone.[56]

(B) THE HERMENEUTIC RELEVANCE OF ARISTOTLE[57]

At this point a problem arises that we have touched on several times. If the heart of the hermeneutical problem is that one and the same tradition must time and again be understood in a different way, the problem, logically speaking, concerns the relationship between the universal and the particular. Understanding, then, is a special case of applying something universal to a particular situation. This makes *Aristotelian ethics* especially important for us—we touched on it in the introductory remarks on the theory of the human sciences.[58] It is true that Aristotle is not concerned with the hermeneutical problem and certainly not with its historical dimension, but with the right estimation of the role that reason has to play in moral action. But what interests us here is precisely that he is concerned with reason and with knowledge, not detached from a being that is becoming, but determined by it and determinative of it. By circumscribing the intellectualism of Socrates and Plato in his inquiry into the good, Aristotle became the founder of ethics as a discipline independent of metaphysics. Criticizing the Platonic idea of the good as an empty generality, he asks instead the question of what is humanly good, what is good in terms of human action.[59] His critique demonstrates that the equation of virtue and knowledge, arete and logos, which is the basis of Plato's and Socrates' theory of virtue, is an exaggeration. Aristotle restores the balance by showing that the basis of moral knowledge in man is orexis, striving, and its development into a fixed demeanor (hexis). The very name "ethics" indicates that Aristotle bases arete on practice and "ethos."

Human civilization differs essentially from nature in that it is not simply a place where capacities and powers work themselves out; man becomes what he is through what he does and how he behaves—i.e., he behaves in a certain way because of what he has become. Thus Aristotle sees ethos as differing from physis in being a sphere in which the laws of nature do not operate, yet not a sphere of lawlessness but of human institutions and human modes of behavior which are mutable, and like rules only to a limited degree.

The question is whether there can be any such thing as philosophical knowledge of the moral being of man and what role knowledge (i.e., logos) plays in the moral being of man. If man always encounters the good in the form of the particular practical situation in which he finds himself, the task of moral knowledge is to determine what the concrete situation asks of him—or, to put it another way, the person acting must view the concrete situation in light of what is asked of him in general. But—negatively put—this means that knowledge that cannot be applied to the concrete situation remains meaningless and even risks obscuring what the situation calls for. This state of affairs, which represents the nature of moral reflection, not only makes philosophical ethics a methodologically difficult problem, but *also gives the problem of method a moral relevance*. In contrast to the theory of the good based on Plato's doctrine of ideas, Aristotle emphasizes that it is impossible for ethics to achieve the extreme exactitude of mathematics. Indeed, to demand this kind of exactitude would be inappropriate. What needs to be done is simply to make an outline and by means of this sketch give some help to moral consciousness.[60] But how such help can be possible is already a moral problem. For obviously it is characteristic of the moral phenomenon that the person acting must himself know and decide, and he cannot let anything take this responsibility from him. Thus it is essential that philosophical ethics have the right approach, so that it does not usurp the place of moral consciousness and yet does not seek a purely theoretical and "historical" knowledge either but, by outlining phenomena, helps moral consciousness to attain clarity concerning itself. This asks a lot of the person who is to receive this help, namely the person listening to Aristotle's lecture. He must be mature enough not to ask that his instruction provide anything other than it can and may give. To put it positively, through education and practice he must himself already have developed a demeanor that he is constantly concerned to preserve in the concrete situations of his life and prove through right behavior.[61]

As we see, the problem of method is entirely determined by the object—a general Aristotelian principle—and the important thing for us is to examine more closely the curious relation between moral being and moral consciousness that Aristotle sets out in his *Ethics*. Aristotle remains Socratic in that he retains knowledge as an essential component of moral being, and it is precisely the balance between the heritage of Socrates and Plato and Aristotle's point concerning ethos that interests us. *For the hermeneutical problem too is clearly distinct from "pure" knowledge detached from any particular kind of being*. We spoke of the interpreter's belonging to the tradition he is interpreting, and we saw that understanding itself is a historical event. The alienation of the interpreter from the interpreted by the objectifying methods of modern science, characteristic of the hermeneutics and historiography of the nineteenth century, appeared as the consequence of a false objectification. My purpose in returning to the example of Aristotelian ethics is to help us realize and avoid this. For moral knowledge, as Aristotle describes it, is clearly not objective knowledge—i.e., the knower is not standing over against a situation that he merely observes; he is directly confronted with what he sees. It is something that he has to do.[62]

Obviously this is not what we mean by knowing in the realm of science. Thus the distinction that Aristotle makes between moral knowledge (phronesis) and theoretical knowledge (episteme) is a simple one, especially when we remember that science, for the Greeks, is represented by the model of mathematics, a knowledge of what is unchangeable, a knowledge that depends on proof and that can therefore be learned by anybody. A hermeneutics of the human sciences certainly has nothing to learn from mathematical as distinguished from moral knowledge. The human sciences stand closer to moral knowledge than to that kind of "theoretical" knowledge. They are "moral sciences." Their object is man and what he knows of himself. But he knows himself as an acting being, and this kind of knowledge of himself does not seek to establish what is. An active being, rather, is concerned with what is not always the same but can also be different. In it he can discover the point at which he has to act. The purpose of his knowledge is to govern his *action*.

Here lies the real problem of moral knowledge that occupies Aristotle in his *Ethics*. For we find action governed by knowledge in an exemplary form where the Greeks speak of techne. This is the skill, the knowledge of the craftsman who knows how to make some specific thing. The question is whether moral knowledge is knowledge of this kind. This would mean that it was knowledge of how to make oneself. Does man learn to make himself what he ought to be, in the same way that the craftsman learns to make things according to his plan and will? Does man project himself on an eidos of himself in the same way that the craftsman carries within himself an eidos of what he is trying to make and embody in his material? We know that Socrates and Plato did apply the concept of techne to the concept of man's being, and it is undeniable that they did discover something true here. In the political sphere, at any rate, the model of techne has an eminently critical function, in that it reveals the untenability of what is called the art of politics, in which everyone involved in politics—i.e., every citizen—regards himself as an expert. Characteristically, the knowledge of the craftsman is the only one that Socrates, in his famous account of his experience of his fellow-countrymen, recognizes as real knowledge within its own sphere.[63] But even the craftsmen disappoint him. Their knowledge is not the true knowledge that constitutes a man and a citizen as such. But it is real knowledge. It is a real art and skill, and not simply a high degree of experience. In this respect it is clearly one with the true moral knowledge that Socrates is seeking. Both are practical knowledge—i.e., their purpose is to determine and guide action. Consequently, they must include the application of knowledge to the particular task.

This is the point at which we can relate Aristotle's analysis of moral knowledge to the hermeneutical problem of the modern human sciences. Admittedly, hermeneutical consciousness is involved neither with technical nor moral knowledge, but these two types of knowledge still include *the same task of application* that we have recognized as the central problem of hermeneutics. Certainly application does not mean the same thing in each case. There is a curious tension between a techne that can be taught and one acquired through experience. The prior knowledge that a person has who has been taught a craft is not, in practice, necessarily superior to the kind of knowledge that someone has who is untrained but has had extensive experience. Although this is the case, the prior knowledge involved in a techne cannot be called "theoretical," especially since experience is automatically acquired in using this knowledge. For, as knowledge, it is always related to practical application, and even if the recalcitrant material does not always obey the person who has learned his craft, Aristotle can still rightly quote the words of the poet: "Techne loves tyche (luck) and tyche loves techne." This means that the person who has been taught his trade is will have the most luck. A genuine mastery of the matter is acquired practically in the techne, and just this provides a model for moral knowledge. For in moral knowledge too it is clear that experience can never be sufficient for making right moral decisions. Here too moral consciousness itself calls for prior direction to guide action; indeed, we cannot be content here with the uncertain relation between prior knowledge and success in the present case that obtains in the case of a techne. There is, no doubt, a real analogy between the fully developed moral consciousness and the capacity to make something—i.e., a techne —but they are certainly not the same.

On the contrary, the differences are patent. It is obvious that man is not at his own disposal in the same way that the craftsman's material is at his disposal. Clearly he cannot make himself in the same way that he can make something else. Thus it will have to be another kind of knowledge that he has of himself in his moral being, a knowledge that is distinct from the knowledge that guides the making of something. Aristotle captures this difference in a bold and unique way when he calls this kind of knowledge self-knowledge—i.e., knowledge for oneself.[64] This distinguishes the self-knowledge of moral consciousness from *theoretical* knowledge in a way that seems immediately evident. But it also distinguishes it from *technical* knowledge, and to make this double distinction Aristotle ventures the odd expression "self-knowledge."

It is the distinction from technical knowledge that is the more difficult task if, with Aristotle, we define the "object" of this knowledge onto-logically not as something general that always is as it is, but as something individual that can also be different. For at first sight the tasks seem wholly analogous. A person who knows how to make something knows some-thing good, and he knows it "for himself," so that, where there is the possibility of doing so, he is really able to make it. He takes the right material and chooses the right means to do the work. Thus he must know how to apply what has been learned in a general way to the concrete situation. Is the same not true of moral consciousness? A person who has to make moral decisions has always already learned something. He has been so formed by education and custom that he knows in general what is right. The task of making a moral decision is that of doing the right thing in a particular situation—i.e., seeing what is right within the situation and grasping it. He too has to act, choosing the right means, and his conduct must be governed just as carefully as that of the craftsman. How then is it nevertheless a knowledge of a quite different kind?

From Aristotle's analysis of phronesis one can derive a variety of answers to this question, for Aristotle's ability to describe phenomena from every aspect constitutes his real genius. "The empirical, comprehended in its synthesis, is the speculative concept" (Hegel).[65] Let us consider here a few points that are important for our discussion.

1. We learn a techne and can also forget it. But we do not learn moral knowledge, nor can we forget it. We do not stand over against it, as if it were something that we can acquire or not, as we can choose to acquire an objective skill, a techne. Rather, we are always already in the situation of having to act (disregarding the special position of children, for whom obedience to the person educating them replaces their own decision), and hence we must already possess and be able to apply moral knowledge. That is why the concept of application is highly problematical. For we can only apply something that we already have; but we do not possess moral knowledge in such a way that we already have it and then apply it to specific situations. The image that a man has of what he ought to be—i.e., his ideas of right and wrong, of decency, courage, dignity, loyalty, and so forth (all concepts that have their equivalents in Aristotle's catalogue of virtues)—are certainly in some sense images that he uses to guide his conduct. But there is still a basic difference between this and the guiding image the craftsman uses: the plan of the object he is going to make. What is right, for example, cannot be fully determined independently of the situation that requires a right action from me, whereas the eidos of what a craftsman wants to make is fully determined by the use for which it is intended.

It is true that what is right seems equally determinate in an absolute sense. For what is right is formulated in laws and contained in general rules of conduct that, although uncodified, can be very exactly determined and are universally binding. Thus, administering justice is a special task that requires both knowledge and skill. Is it not a techne, then? Does it not also consist in applying laws and rules to the concrete case? Do we not speak of the "art" of the judge? Why is what Aristotle describes as the judge's form of phronesis (dikastike phronesis) not a techne?[66]

If we think about it, we shall see that applying laws involves a curious legal ambiguity. The situation of the craftsman is quite different. With the design of the object and the rules for executing it, the craftsman proceeds to carry it out. He may be forced to adapt himself to particular circumstances; he may have to resign himself to executing his design in a way other than he originally intended. But this resignation does not mean that his knowledge of what he wants is improved. Rather, he simply omits certain things in the execution. What we have here is the painful imperfection associated with applying one's knowledge.

By comparison, the situation of the person "applying" law is quite different. In a certain instance he will have to refrain from applying the full rigor of the law. But if he does, it is not because he has no alternative, but because to do otherwise would not be right. In restraining the law, he is not diminishing it but, on the contrary, finding the better law. Aristotle[67] expresses this very clearly in his analysis of epieikeia (equity): epieikeia is the correction of the law.[68] Aristotle shows that every law is in a necessary tension with concrete action, in that it is general and hence cannot contain practical reality in its full concreteness. We have already touched on this problem near the beginning of the present volume when we were considering the faculty of judgment.[69] Clearly legal hermeneutics finds its proper place here.[70] The law is always deficient, not because it is imperfect in itself but because human reality is necessarily imperfect in comparison to the ordered world of law, and hence allows of no simple application of the law.

From what we have said it is clear that Aristotle's position on the problem of *natural law* is highly subtle and certainly not to be equated with the later natural-law tradition. I will briefly outline the way the idea of natural law is related to the hermeneutical problem.[71] It follows from our discussion so far that Aristotle does not simply dismiss the question of natural law. He does not regard a system of laws as true law in an absolute sense, but considers the concept of equity as a necessary supplement to law. Thus he opposes an extreme conventionalism or legal positivism by explicitly distinguishing between what is naturally right and what is legally right.[72] The distinction he has in mind is not simply that between the unchangeability of natural law and the changeability of positive law. It is true that Aristotle has generally been understood as meaning this. But the true profundity of his insight has been missed. Certainly he accepts the idea of an absolutely unchangeable law, but he limits it explicitly to the gods and says that among men not only statutory law but also natural law is changeable. For Aristotle, this changeability is wholly compatible with the fact that it is "natural" law. The sense of this assertion seems to me to be the following: some laws are entirely a matter of mere agreement (e.g., traffic regulations), but there are also things that do not admit of regulation by mere human convention because the "nature of the thing" constantly asserts itself. Thus it is quite legitimate to call such things "natural law."[73] In that the nature of the thing still allows some room for play, natural law is still changeable. This is clearly evidenced by the examples that Aristotle adduces from other spheres. The right hand is naturally the stronger one, but there is nothing to stop us from training the left one so that it becomes as strong as the right (Aristotle obviously uses this example because it was a favorite of Plato's). A second example is even more illuminating because it already belongs in the legal sphere: one and the same measure always proves smaller when we buy wine in it than when we sell wine in it. Aristotle is not saying that people in the wine trade are constantly trying to trick their customers, but rather that this behavior corresponds to the area of free play permitted within the set limits of what is right. And he quite clearly explains that the best state "is everywhere one and the same," but it is the same in a different way that "fire burns everywhere in the same way, whether in Greece or in Persia."

Despite this clear statement by Aristotle, later thinkers on natural law quoted this passage as if he were comparing the unchangeability of human law with the unchangeability of natural laws.[74] The opposite is the case. In fact, as his very distinction shows, for Aristotle the idea of natural law has only a critical function. No dogmatic use can be made of it—i.e., we cannot invest particular laws with the dignity and inviolability of natural law. In view of the necessary imperfection of all human laws, the idea of natural law is indispensable for Aristotle; and it becomes particularly important in the question of what is equitable, which is what first really decides the law. But its function is a critical one in that the appeal to natural law is legitimate only where a discrepancy emerges between one law and another.

The special question of natural law, which Aristotle answers in extenso, does not as such interest us here, except by reason of its fundamental significance. For what Aristotle shows here is true of all man's ideas of what he ought to be, and not only of the problem of law. All these concepts are not just arbitrary ideals conditioned by convention, but despite all the variety of moral ideas in the most different times and peoples, in this sphere there is still something like the nature of the thing. This is not to say that the nature of the thing—e.g., the ideal of bravery—is a fixed standard that we could recognize and apply by ourselves. Rather, Aristotle affirms as true of the teacher of ethics precisely what is true, in his view, of all men:

that he too is always already involved in a moral and political context and acquires his image of the thing from that standpoint. He does not himself regard the guiding principles that he describes as knowledge that can be taught. They are valid only as schemata. They are concretized only in the concrete situation of the person acting. Thus they are not norms to be found in the stars, nor do they have an unchanging place in a natural moral universe, so that all that would be necessary would be to perceive them. Nor are they mere conventions, but really do correspond to the nature of the thing—except that the latter is always itself determined in each case by the use the moral consciousness makes of them.

2. Here we see a fundamental modification of the conceptual relation between means and end, one that distinguishes moral from technical knowledge. It is not only that moral knowledge has no merely particular end but pertains to right living in general, whereas all technical knowledge is particular and serves particular ends. Nor is it the case simply that moral knowledge must take over where technical knowledge would be desirable but is unavailable. Certainly if technical knowledge were available, it would always make it unnecessary to deliberate with oneself about the subject. Where there is a techne, we must learn it and then we are able to find the right means. We see that moral knowledge, however, always requires this kind of self-deliberation. Even if we conceive this knowledge in ideal perfection, it is perfect deliberation with oneself (euboulia) and not knowledge in the manner of a techne.

Thus we are dealing here with a fundamental relationship. It is not the case that extending technical knowledge would obviate the need for moral knowledge, this deliberating with oneself. Moral knowledge can never be knowable in advance like knowledge that can be taught. The relation between means and ends here is not such that one can know the right means in advance, and that is because the right end is not a mere object of knowledge either. There can be no anterior certainty concerning what the good life is directed toward as a whole. Hence Aristotle's definitions of phronesis have a marked uncertainty about them, in that this knowledge is sometimes related more to the end, and sometimes more to the means to the end.[75] In fact this means that the end toward which our life as a whole tends and its elaboration in the moral principles of action described in Aristotle's *Ethics* cannot be the object of a knowledge that can be taught. No more can ethics be used dogmatically than can natural law. Rather, Aristotle's theory of virtue describes typical forms of the true mean to be observed in human life and behavior; but the moral knowledge that is oriented by these guiding images is the same knowledge that has to respond to the demands of the situation of the moment.

Hence also mere expediency cannot enter considerations about what might further moral ends; rather, the consideration of the means is itself a moral consideration and it is this that concretizes the moral rightness of the end. The self-knowledge of which Aristotle speaks is characterized by the fact that it includes perfect application and employs its knowledge in the immediacy of the given situation. Thus a knowledge of the particular situation (which is nevertheless not a perceptual seeing) is a necessary supplement to moral knowledge. For although it is necessary to see what a situation is asking of us, this seeing does not mean that we perceive in the situation what is visible as such, but that we learn to see it as the situation of action and hence in the light of what is right. Just as we "see" from the geometrical analysis of plane surfaces that the triangle is the simplest two-dimensional plane figure, so that we can go no further with our subdivisions, but must stop here, so also in moral deliberation, seeing what is immediately to be done is not a mere seeing but nous. This is also confirmed by what constitutes the opposite of this kind of seeing.[76] The opposite of seeing what is right is not error or deception but blindness. A person who is overwhelmed by his passions suddenly no longer sees what is right to do in a given situation. He has lost his self-mastery and hence his own rightness—i.e., the right orientation within himself—so that, driven by the dialectic of passion, whatever his passion tells him is right seems so. Moral knowledge is really knowledge of a special kind. In a curious way it embraces both means and end, and hence differs from technical knowledge. That is why it is pointless to distinguish here between knowledge and experience, as can be done in the case of a techne. For moral knowledge contains a kind of experience in itself, and in fact we shall see that this is perhaps the fundamental form of experience (Erfahrung), compared with which all other experience represents an alienation, not to say a denaturing.[77]

3. The self-knowledge of moral reflection has, in fact, a unique relation to itself. We can see this from the modifications that Aristotle presents in the context of his analysis of phronesis. Beside phronesis, the virtue of thoughtful reflection, stands "sympathetic understanding."[78] "Being understanding" is introduced as a modification of the virtue of moral knowledge since in this case it is not I who must act. Accordingly synesis means simply the capacity for moral judgment. Someone's sympathetic understanding is praised, of course, when in order to judge he transposes

himself fully into the concrete situation of the person who has to act.[79] The question here, then, is not about knowledge in general but its concretion at a particular moment. This knowledge also is not in any sense technical knowledge or the application of such. The man of the world, the man who knows all the tricks and dodges and is experienced in everything there is, does not really have sympathetic understanding for the person acting: he has it only if he satisfies one requirement, namely that he too is seeking what is right—i.e., that he is united with the other person in this commonality. The concrete example of this is the phenomenon of advice in "questions of conscience." Both the person asking for advice and the person giving it assume that they are bound together in friendship. Only friends can advise each other or, to put it another way, only a piece of advice that is meant in a friendly way has meaning for the person advised. Once again we discover that the person who is understanding does not know and judge as one who stands apart and unaffected but rather he thinks along with the other from the perspective of a specific bond of belonging, as if he too were affected.

This becomes fully clear when we consider other varieties of moral reflection listed by Aristotle, namely insight and fellow feeling.[80] Insight here means a quality. We say that someone is insightful when they make a fair, correct judgment. An insightful person is prepared to consider the particular situation of the other person, and hence he is also most inclined to be forbearing or to forgive. Here again it is clear that this is not technical knowledge.

Finally, Aristotle makes the special nature of moral knowledge and the virtue of possessing it particularly clear by describing a naturally debased version of this moral knowledge.[81] He says that the deinos is a man who has all the natural prerequisites and gifts for this moral knowledge, a man who is able, with remarkable skill, to get the most out of any situation, who is able to turn everything to his advantage and finds a way out of every situation.[82] But this natural counterpart to phronesis is characterized by the fact that the deinos is "capable of anything"; he uses his skills to any purpose and is without inhibition. He is aneu aretes. And it is more than accidental that such a person is given a name that also means "terrible." Nothing is so terrible, so uncanny, so appalling, as the exercise of brilliant talents for evil.

To summarize, if we relate Aristotle's description of the ethical phenomenon and especially the virtue of moral knowledge to our own investigation, we find that his analysis in fact offers a kind of *model of the problems of hermeneutics*. We too determined that application is neither a subsequent nor merely an occasional part of the phenomenon of understanding, but codetermines it as a whole from the beginning. Here too application did not consist in relating some pregiven universal to the particular situation. The interpreter dealing with a traditionary text tries to apply it to himself. But this does not mean that the text is given for him as something universal, that he first understands it per se, and then afterward uses it for particular applications. Rather, the interpreter seeks no more than to understand this universal, the text—i.e., to understand what it says, what constitutes the text's meaning and significance. In order to understand that, he must not try to disregard himself and his particular hermeneutical situation. He must relate the text to this situation if he wants to understand at all.

(C) THE EXEMPLARY SIGNIFICANCE OF LEGAL HERMENEUTICS

If this is the case, the gap between hermeneutics of the human sciences and legal hermeneutics cannot be as wide as is generally assumed. The dominant view is, of course, that only with the rise of historical consciousness was understanding raised to a method of objective science and that hermeneutics came into its own when it was elaborated into a general theory of the understanding and interpretation of texts. Legal hermeneutics does not belong in this context, for its purpose is not to understand given texts, but to be a practical measure filling a kind of gap in the system of legal dogmatics. It is thought, then, that it has nothing to do with the task of hermeneutics in the human sciences, which is the understanding of traditionary material.

But in that case *theological hermeneutics* cannot claim any independent systematic significance. Schleiermacher consciously placed it wholly within *general hermeneutics* and merely regarded it as a special application of it. Since then, scientific theology's claim to be a discipline on a par with the modern historical sciences seems to depend on the fact that no laws and rules are to be applied in interpreting Scripture other than those used in understanding any other traditionary material. Thus there could no longer be any such thing as a specifically theological hermeneutics.

It is a paradoxical position if we, nevertheless, try to revive the old truth and the old unity of hermeneutical discipline within modern science. It seems that methodology of the human sciences moves into modernity when it detaches itself from all dogmatic ties. Legal hermeneutics was separated from theory of understanding as a whole because it has a dogmatic purpose, just as, by giving up its dogmatic commitment, theological hermeneutics was united with philological-historical method.

In this situation we can take special interest in the divergence between legal and historical hermeneutics and consider those cases in which legal and historical hermeneutics are concerned with the same object—i.e., cases in which legal texts are interpreted legally, in court, and also understood historically. So we will consider the approaches taken by the legal historian and the jurist to the same legal text. We can turn here to the excellent writings of E. Betti[83] and pursue our own thinking from there. Our question is *whether or not there is an unequivocal distinction between dogmatic and historical interest.*

That there is a difference is clear. The jurist understands the meaning of the law from the present case and for the sake of this present case. By contrast, the legal historian has no case from which to start, but he seeks to determine the meaning of the law by constructing the whole range of its applications. It is only in all its applications that the law becomes concrete. Thus the legal historian cannot be content to take the original application of the law as determining its original meaning. As a historian he will, rather, have to take account of the historical change that the law has undergone. In understanding, he will have to mediate between the original application and the present application of the law.

In my view it would not be enough to say that the task of the historian was simply to "reconstruct the original meaning of the legal formula" and that of the jurist to "harmonize that meaning with the present living actuality." This kind of division would mean that the definition of the jurist is more comprehensive and includes the task of the legal historian. Someone who is seeking to understand the correct meaning of a law must first know the original one. Thus he must think in terms of legal history—but here historical understanding serves merely as a means to an end. On the other hand, the historian as such has no dogmatic task. As a historian he approaches the historical object in order to determine its historical value, whereas the jurist, in addition, applies what has been learned in this way to the legal present. This is what Betti says.

We may ask, however, whether he has viewed and described the task of the historian in a sufficiently comprehensive way. In our particular example, where does the historical element come in? In regard to a law still in force we naturally assume that its legal meaning is clear and that the legal practice of the present simply follows the original meaning. If this were always the case, the question about the meaning of a law would be both juridically and historically the same. For the jurist too the hermeneutical task would be just to establish the original meaning of the law and apply it as the right one. Hence as late as 1840, Savigny, in his *System des römischen Rechts*, regarded the task of legal hermeneutics as purely historical. Just as Schleiermacher saw no problem in the interpreter's having to identify himself with the original reader, so Savigny ignores the tension between the original and the present legal sense.[84]

It has emerged clearly enough in the course of time that this is a legally untenable fiction. Ernst Forsthoff has shown in a valuable study that for purely legal reasons it was necessary for an awareness of historical change to develop, which involved distinguishing between the original meaning of a law and that applied in current legal practice.[85] It is true that the jurist is always concerned with the law itself, but he determines its normative content in regard to the given case to which it is to be applied. In order to determine this content exactly, it is necessary to have historical knowledge of the original meaning, and only for this reason does the judge concern himself with the historical value that the law has through the act of legislation. But he cannot let himself be bound by what, say, an account of the parliamentary proceedings tells him about the intentions of those who first passed the law. Rather, he has to take account of the change in circumstances and hence define afresh the normative function of the law.

It is quite different with the legal historian. He is apparently concerned only with the original meaning of the law, the way in which it was meant, and the validity it had when it was first promulgated. But how can he know this? Can he know it without being aware of the change in circumstances that separates his own present time from that past time? Must he not then do exactly the same thing as the judge does—i.e., distinguish between the original meaning of the text of the law and the legal meaning which he as someone who lives in the present automatically assumes? The hermeneutical situation of both the historian and the jurist seems to me to be the same in that, when faced with any text, we have an immediate expectation of meaning. There can be no such thing as a direct access to the historical object that would objectively reveal its historical value. The historian has to undertake the same reflection as the jurist.

Thus the actual content of what is understood in each of the two ways is the same. The above description of the historian's approach, then, is inadequate. Historical knowledge can be gained only by seeing the past in its continuity with the present—which is exactly what the jurist does in his practical, normative work of "ensuring the unbroken continuance of law and preserving the tradition of the legal idea."[86]

We must consider, though, whether the case we have been discussing is really characteristic of the general problem of historical understanding. The model from which we started was the understanding of a law still in force. Here the historian and the dogmatist were concerned with the same object. But is this not a special case? A legal historian who turns to the legal cultures of the past, and certainly any other historian who is seeking to understand a past that no longer has any direct continuity with the present, would not recognize himself in the case we have been considering—namely a law still in force. He would say that legal hermeneutics has a special dogmatic task that is quite foreign to the context of historical hermeneutics.

In fact the situation seems to me just the opposite. Legal hermeneutics serves to remind us what the real procedure of the human sciences is. Here we have the model for the relationship between past and present that we are seeking. The judge who adapts the transmitted law to the needs of the present is undoubtedly seeking to perform a practical task, but his interpretation of the law is by no means merely for that reason an arbitrary revision. Here again, to understand and to interpret means to discover and recognize a valid meaning. The judge seeks to be in accord with the "legal idea" in mediating it with the present. This is, of course, a legal mediation. It is the legal significance of the law—and not the historical significance of the law's promulgation or of particular cases of its application—that he is trying to understand. Thus his orientation is not that of a historian, but he has an orientation to his own history, which is his present. Thus he can always approach as a historian those questions that he has implicitly concluded as a judge.

On the other hand, the historian, who has no juridical task before him but is trying to discover the legal meaning of this law—like anything else that has been handed down in history—cannot disregard the fact that he is concerned with a legal creation that needs to be understood in a legal way. He must be able to think not only historically but also legally. It is true that it is a special case when a historian is examining a legal text that is still valid today. But this special case shows us what determines our relationship to any traditionary text. Trying to understand the law in terms of its historical origin, the historian cannot disregard its continuing effect: it presents him with the questions that he has to ask of historical tradition. Is this not true of every text—i.e., that it must be understood in terms of what it says? Does this not mean that it always needs to be restated? And does not this restatement always take place through its being related to the present? Inasmuch as the actual object of historical understanding is not events but their "significance," it is clearly an incorrect description of this understanding to speak of an object existing in itself and of the subject's approach to it. The truth is that historical understanding always implies that the tradition reaching us speaks into the present and must be understood in this mediation—indeed, *as* this mediation. *In reality then, legal hermeneutics is no special case but is, on the contrary, capable of restoring the hermeneutical problem to its full breadth and so re-establishing the former unity of hermeneutics, in which jurist and theologian meet the philologist.*

We saw above[87] that one of the conditions of understanding in the human sciences is belonging to tradition. Let us now try to verify this by seeing how this structural element of understanding obtains in the case of legal and theological hermeneutics. This condition is clearly not so much a limiting condition as one that makes understanding possible. The way the interpreter belongs to his text is like the way the point from which we are to view a picture belongs to its perspective. It is not a matter of looking for this viewpoint and adopting it as one's standpoint. The interpreter similarly finds his point of view already given, and does not choose it arbitrarily. Thus it is an essential condition of the possibility of legal hermeneutics that the law is binding on all members of the community in the same way. Where this is not the case—for example in an absolutist state, where the will of the absolute ruler is above the law—hermeneutics cannot exist, "since an absolute ruler can explain his words in a sense that abrogates the general rules of interpretation."[88] For in this instance the law is not interpreted in such a way that the particular case is decided justly according to the right sense of the law. On the contrary, the will of a monarch who is not bound by the law can effect whatever seems just to him without regard for the law—that is, without the effort of inter-pretation. The need to understand and interpret arises only when some-thing is enacted in such a way that it is, as enacted, irrevocable and binding.

The work of interpretation is *to concretize* the law in each specific case[89]—i.e., it is a work of *application*. The creative supplementing of the law that is involved is a task reserved to the judge, but he is subject to the law in the same way as is every other member of the community. It is part of the idea of a rule of law that the judge's judgment does not proceed from an arbitrary and unpredictable decision, but from the just weighing up of the whole. Anyone who has immersed himself in the particular situation is capable of undertaking this just weighing-up. This is why in a state governed by law, there is legal certainty—i.e., it is in principle possible to know what the exact situation is. Every lawyer and every counsel is able, in principle, to give correct advice—i.e., he can accurately predict the judge's decision on the basis of the existing laws. Applying the law is not simply a matter of knowing the law. If one has to give a legal judgment on a particular case, of course it is necessary to know the law and all the elements that have determined it. But the only belonging under the law necessary here is that the legal order is recognized as valid for everyone and that no one is exempt from it. Hence it is always possible to grasp the existing legal order as such—i.e., to assimilate dogmatically any past supplement to the law. Consequently there is an essential connection between legal hermeneutics and legal dogmatics, and in it hermeneutics has the more important place. For the idea of a perfect legal dogmatics, which would make every judgment a mere act of subsumption, is untenable.[90]

Let us now consider the case of *theological hermeneutics*, as developed by Protestant theology, as it applies to our question.[91] Here there is a genuine parallel to legal hermeneutics, for here too dogmatics cannot claim any primacy. The proclamation is genuinely concretized in preaching, as is the legal order in judgment. But there is still a big difference between them. Unlike a legal verdict, preaching is not a creative supplement to the text it is interpreting. Hence the gospel acquires no new content in being preached that could be compared with the power of the judge's verdict to supplement the law. It is not the case that the gospel of salvation becomes more clearly determined only through the preacher's thoughts. As a preacher, he does not speak before the community with the same dogmatic authority that a judge does. Certainly preaching too is concerned with interpreting a valid truth, but this truth is proclamation; and whether it is successful or not is not decided by the ideas of the preacher, but by the power of the word itself, which can call men to repentance even though the sermon is a bad one. The proclamation cannot be detached from its fulfillment. The dogmatic establishment of pure doctrine is a secondary matter. Scripture is the word of God, and that means it has an absolute priority over the doctrine of those who interpret it.

Interpretation should never overlook this. Even as the scholarly inter-pretation of the theologian, it must never forget that Scripture is the divine proclamation of salvation. Understanding it, therefore, cannot simply be a scientific or scholarly exploration of its meaning. Bultmann once wrote, "The interpretation of the biblical writings is subject to exactly the same conditions as any other literature."[92] But the meaning of this statement is ambiguous, for the question is whether all literature is not subject to conditions of understanding other than those formal general ones that have to be fulfilled in regard to every text. Bultmann himself points out that all understanding presumes a living relationship between the interpreter and the text, his previous connection with the subject matter it deals with. He calls this hermeneutical requirement *fore-understanding*, because it is clearly not something to be attained through the process of understanding but is already presupposed. Thus Hofmann, whom Bultmann quotes with approval, writes that scriptural hermeneutics presupposes a relationship to the content of the Bible.

We may ask, however, what kind of "presupposition" this is. Is it something that is given with human life itself? Does there exist in every man a prior connection with the truth of divine revelation because man as such is concerned with the question of God? Or must we say that it is first from God—i.e., from faith—that human existence experiences itself as being affected by the question of God? But then the sense of the presupposition implied in the concept of fore-understanding becomes questionable. For then the presupposition would not be valid universally but only from the viewpoint of true faith.

In regard to the Old Testament this is a venerable hermeneutical problem. Which is the right interpretation of it, the Jewish one or the Christian one in light of the New Testament? Or are both legitimate interpretations—i.e., do they have something in common, and is this what is really being understood by the interpreter? The Jew who understands the text of the Old Testament in a different way than the Christian shares with him the presupposition that he too is concerned with the question of God. At the same time, he will hold that a Christian theologian misunderstands the Old Testament if he takes its truths as qualified by the New Testament. Hence the presupposition that one is moved by the question of God already involves a claim to knowledge concerning the true God and his revelation. Even unbelief is defined in terms of the faith that is demanded of one. The existential fore-understanding from which Bultmann starts can only be a Christian one.

We could perhaps try to escape this conclusion by saying that it is enough to *know* that religious texts are to be understood only as texts that answer the question of God. There need be no claim on the religious commitment of the interpreter himself. But what would a Marxist, who understands religious utterances only as the reflection of class interests, say? He will not accept the presupposition that human existence as such is moved by the question of God. This presupposition is obviously held only by someone who already recognizes the alternative of belief or unbelief in the true God. Thus the hermeneutical significance of fore-understanding in theology seems itself theological. After all, the history of hermeneutics shows how the examination of the texts is determined by a very precise fore-understanding. As a Protestant art of interpreting Scripture, modern hermeneutics is clearly related in a polemical way to the dogmatic tradition of the Catholic church. It has itself a dogmatic denominational significance. This does not mean that such theological hermeneutics is dogmatically predisposed, so that it reads out of the text what it has put into it. Rather, it really risks itself. But it assumes that the word of Scripture addresses us and that only the person who allows himself to be addressed—whether he believes or doubts—understands. Hence the primary thing is application.

We can, then, distinguish what is truly common to all forms of hermeneutics: the meaning to be understood is concretized and fully realized only in interpretation, but the interpretive activity considers itself wholly bound by the meaning of the text. Neither jurist nor theologian regards the work of application as making free with the text.

The task of concretizing something universal and applying it to oneself seems, however, to have a very different function in the historical sciences. If we ask what application means here and how it occurs in the kind of understanding undertaken in the human sciences, we can acknowledge that a certain class of traditionary material is applied in the same way the jurist does in regard to the law and the theologian the proclamation. Just as in the one case the judge seeks to dispense justice and in the other the preacher to proclaim salvation, and as, in both, the meaning of what is proclaimed finds its fullest realization in the proclamation of justice and the proclamation of the gospel, so in the case of a philosophical text or a work of literature we can see that these texts require a special activity of the reader and interpreter, and that we do not have the freedom to adopt a historical distance toward them. It will be seen that here understanding always involves applying the meaning understood.

But does application essentially and necessarily belong to understanding? From the point of view of modern science the answer will be that it does not, and it will be said that the kind of application that makes the interpreter the person to whom the text was originally addressed, as it were, is quite unscientific and is to be wholly excluded from the historical sciences. What makes modern scholarship scientific is precisely the fact that it objectifies tradition and methodically eliminates the influence of the interpreter and his time on understanding. It may often be difficult to attain this goal, and it will be difficult to preserve the distinction between historical and dogmatic interest in the case of texts that are addressed to no one in particular and claim to be valid for anyone who receives the tradition. A good example of this is the problem of scientific theology and its relation to the tradition of Scripture. It may seem in this case that the balance between historico-scientific and dogmatic interpretation is to be found in the private world of the person. It may be the same with the philosopher and also with our aesthetic consciousness when it finds itself addressed by a work of art. But according to this view, science claims to remain independent of all subjective applications by reason of its method.

This is the kind of argument that would have to be presented by proponents of the modern theory of science. Those cases in which the interpreter cannot immediately substitute for the original addressee will be considered exemplary—i.e., where a text has a quite specific addressee, such as the partner to an agreement, or the recipient of a bill or an order. Here, to understand the meaning of the text fully, we must, as it were, put ourselves in the place of the addressee, and insofar as this transposition serves to give the text its full concrete form, we can regard this also as an achievement of interpretation. But this transposing of ourselves into the position of the original reader (Schleiermacher) is something quite different from application. It actually skips the task of mediating between then and now, between the Thou and the I, which is what we mean by application and which legal hermeneutics also regards as its task.

Let us take the example of understanding an order. An order exists only where there is someone to obey it. Here, then, understanding belongs to a relationship between persons, one of whom has to give the order. To understand the order means to apply it to the specific situation to which it pertains. It is true that one makes the other repeat the order to make sure it has been understood, but that does not alter the fact that it is given its real meaning when it is carried out and concretized in accordance with its meaning. This is why there is such a thing as an explicit refusal to obey that is not simply disobedience but derives from the meaning of the order and its concretization. A person who refuses to obey an order has understood it, and because he applies it to the situation and knows what obedience would mean in that situation, he refuses. The criterion of understanding is clearly not in the order's actual words, nor in the mind of the person giving the order, but solely in the understanding of the situation and in the responsible behavior of the person who obeys. Even when an order is written down so one can be sure it will be correctly understood and executed, no one assumes that it makes everything explicit. The comic situation in which orders are carried out literally but not according to their meaning is well known. Thus there is no doubt that the recipient of an order must perform a definite creative act in understanding its meaning.

If we now imagine a *historian* who regards a traditionary text as such an order and seeks to understand it, he is, of course, in a situation quite different from that of the original addressee. He is not the person to whom the order is addressed and so cannot relate it to himself. But if he really wants to understand the order, then he must, idealiter, perform *the same act* as that performed by the intended recipient of the order. The latter too, who applies the order to himself, is well able to distinguish between understanding and obeying an order. It is possible for him not to obey even when—indeed, precisely when—he has understood it. It may be difficult for the historian to reconstruct the original situation in which the order arose. But he will understand it fully only when he has thus made the order concrete. This, then, is the clear hermeneutical demand: to understand a text in terms of the specific situation in which it was written.

According to the self-understanding of science, then, it can make no difference to the historian whether a text was addressed to a particular person or was intended "to belong to all ages." The general requirement of hermeneutics is, rather, that every text must be understood according to the aim appropriate to it. But this means that historical scholarship first seeks to understand every text in its own terms and does not accept the content of what it says as true, but leaves it undecided. Understanding is certainly concretization, but one that involves keeping a hermeneutical distance. Understanding is possible only if one keeps oneself out of play. This is the demand of science.

According to this self-interpretation of the methodology of the human sciences, it is generally said that the interpreter imagines an addressee for every text, whether expressly addressed by the text or not. This addressee is in every case the original reader, and the interpreter knows that this is a different person from himself. This is obvious, when thus negatively expressed. A person trying to understand a text, whether literary critic or historian, does not, at any rate, apply what it says to himself. He is simply trying to understand what the author is saying, and if he is simply trying to understand, he is not interested in the objective truth of what is said as such, not even if the text itself claims to teach truth. On this the philologist and the historian are in agreement.

Hermeneutics and historical study, however, are clearly not the same thing. By examining the methodological differences between the two, we will discover that *what they really have in common* is not what they are generally thought to have. The historian has a different orientation to the texts of the past, in that he is trying to discover something about the past through them. He therefore uses other traditionary material to supplement and verify what the texts say. He considers it as more or less of a weakness when the philologist regards his text as a work of art. A work of art is a whole, self-sufficient world. But the interest of the historian knows no such self-sufficiency. Against Schleiermacher, Dilthey once said, "Philology would like to see self-contained existence everywhere."[93] If a work of literature from the past makes an impression on a historian, this will have no hermeneutical significance for him. It is fundamentally impossible for him to regard himself as the addressee of the text and accept its claim on him. Rather, he examines the text to find something it is not, of itself, attempting to provide. This is true even of traditionary material which itself purports to be historical representation. Even the writer of history is subject to historical critique.

Thus the historian goes beyond hermeneutics, and the idea of interpretation acquires a new and more defined meaning. It no longer refers only to the explicit act of understanding a given text, as for the philologist. The concept of historical interpretation corresponds more to the idea of the *expression*, which is not understood by historical hermeneutics in its classical and traditional sense—i.e., as a rhetorical term that refers to the relation of language to thought. What the expression expresses is not merely what is supposed to be expressed in it—what is meant by it— but primarily what is also expressed by the words without its being intended—i.e., what the expression, as it were, "betrays." In this wider sense the word "expression" refers to far more than linguistic expression; rather, it includes everything that we have to get behind, and that at the same time enables us to get behind it. Interpretation here, then, does not refer to the sense intended, but to the sense that is hidden and has to be disclosed. In this sense every text not only presents an intelligible meaning but, in many respects, needs to be interpreted. The text is primarily a phenomenon of expression. It is understandable that the historian is interested in this aspect. For the documentary value of, say, a report depends in part on what the text, as a phenomenon of expression, displays. From this, one can discover what the writer intended without saying, what party he belonged to, with what views he approached things, or even what degree of lack of principle or dishonesty is to be expected of him. These subjective elements affecting the credibility of the witness must be taken into consideration. But, above all, the content of the traditionary material must itself be interpreted, even if its subjective reliability is established—i.e., the text is understood as a document whose true meaning can be discovered only behind its literal meaning, by comparing it with other data that allow us to estimate its historical value.

Thus *for the historian it is a basic principle that tradition is to be interpreted in a sense different than the texts, of themselves, call for.* He will always go back behind them and the meaning they express to inquire into the reality they express involuntarily. Texts must be treated in the same way as other available historical material—i.e., as the so-called relics of the past. Like everything else, they need explication—i.e., to be understood in terms of not only what they say but what they exemplify.

The concept of interpretation reaches its culmination here. Interpretation is necessary where the meaning of a text cannot be immediately understood. It is necessary wherever one is not prepared to trust what a phenomenon immediately presents to us. The psychologist interprets in this way by not accepting the expressions of life in their intended sense but delving back into what was taking place in the unconscious. Similarly, the historian interprets the data of tradition in order to discover the true meaning that is expressed and, at the same time, hidden in them.

Thus there is a natural tension between the historian and the philologist who seeks to understand a text for the sake of its beauty and its truth. The historian's interpretation is concerned with something that is not expressed in the text itself and need have nothing to do with the intended meaning of the text. There is a fundamental conflict here between the historical and the literary consciousness, although this tension scarcely exists now that historical consciousness has also altered the orientation of the critic. He has given up the claim that his texts have a normative validity for him. He no longer regards them as models of the best that has been thought and said, but looks at them in a way that they themselves did not intend to be looked at; he looks at them as a historian. This has made philology and criticism subsidiary disciplines of historical studies. This could be glimpsed already in classical philology when it began to call itself the science of antiquity (Wilamowitz). It is a department of historical research concerned primarily with language and literature. The philologist is a historian, in that he discovers a historical dimension in his literary sources. Understanding, then, is for him a matter of placing a given text in the context of the history of language, literary form, style, and so on, and thus ultimately mediating it with the whole context of historical life. Only occasionally does his own original nature come through. Thus, in judging the ancient historians, he tends to give these great writers more credence than the historian finds justified. This ideological credulity, which makes the philologist overestimate the value of his texts as evidence, is the last vestige of his old claim to be the friend of "eloquence" and the mediator of classical literature.

Let us now inquire whether this description of the procedure of the human sciences, in which the historian and the critic of today are one, is accurate and whether the claim of historical consciousness to be universal is justified. In regard to *philology* it seems questionable.[94] The critic is ultimately mistaking his own nature, as a friend of eloquence, if he bows to the standard of historical studies. If his texts possess an exemplary character for him, this may be primarily in regard to form. The older humanism fervently believed that everything in classical literature was said in an exemplary way; but what is said in such a way is actually more than an exemplar of form. Eloquence (schöne Reden) is not called such simply because what is said is said beautifully, but also because something beautiful is said. It seeks to be more than mere rhetoric. It is particularly true of the national poetic traditions that we admire not only their poetic power, the imagination and art of their expression, but above all the great truth that speaks in them.

If in the work of the critic, then, there is still something of only acknowledging models, he is not in fact relating his texts merely to a reconstructed addressee but also to himself (though he is unwilling to accept this). But in accepting models there is always an understanding that does not leave their exemplarity undecided, but rather has already chosen and considers itself obligated to them. That is why relating oneself to an exemplar is always like following in someone's footsteps. And just as this is more than mere imitation, so this understanding is a continually new form of encounter and has itself the character of an event precisely because it does not simply leave things up in the air but involves application. The literary critic, as it were, weaves a little further on the great tapestry of tradition that supports us.

If we acknowledge this, then criticism and philology can attain their true dignity and proper knowledge of themselves only by being liberated from history. Yet this seems to me to be only half the truth. Rather, we should ask whether the picture of the historical approach, as set out here, is not itself distorted. Perhaps not only the approach of the critic and philologist but *also that of the historian* should be oriented not so much to the methodological ideal of the natural sciences as to the model offered us by legal and theological hermeneutics. It may be that the historical approach to texts differs specifically from the original bond of the critic to his texts. It may be that the historian tries to get behind the texts in order to force them to yield information that they do not intend, and are unable of themselves to give. With regard to the individual text, this would seem to be the case. The historian approaches his texts the way an investigating magistrate approaches his witnesses. But simply establishing facts, elicited from possibly prejudiced witnesses, does not make the historian. What makes the historian is understanding the significance of what he finds. Thus the testimony of history is like that given before a court. It is no accident that in German the same word is used for both, Zeugnis (testimony; witness). In both cases testimony aids in establishing the facts. But the facts are not the real objects of inquiry; they are simply material for the real tasks of the judge and of the historian—that is, respectively, to reach a just decision and to establish the historical significance of an event within the totality of his historical self-consciousness.

Thus the whole difference is possibly only a question of the criteria. One should not choose too nicely if one would reach the essentials. We have already shown that traditional hermeneutics artificially limited the dimensions of the phenomenon, and perhaps the same is true of the historical approach. Is it not the case here too that the really important things precede any application of historical methods? A historical hermeneutics that does not make the *nature of the historical question* the central thing, and does not inquire into a historian's motives in examining historical material, lacks its most important element.

If we accept this, then the relation between literary criticism and historical studies suddenly appears quite different. Although we spoke of the humanities as being under the alien control of historical studies, this is not the last word on the matter. Rather, it seems to me that the *problem of application*, of which we had to remind the critic, *also characterizes the more complicated situation of historical understanding.* All appearances seem to be against this, it is true, for historical understanding seems to fall entirely short of the traditionary text's claim to applicability. We have seen that history does not regard a text in terms of the text's intention but in terms of its own characteristic and different intention—i.e., as a historical source—using it to understand what the text did not at all intend to say but we nevertheless find expressed in it.

On closer examination, however, the question arises whether the historian's understanding is really different in structure from the critic's. It is true that he considers the texts from another point of view, but this difference of intention applies only to the individual text as such. For the historian, however, the individual text makes up, together with other sources and testimonies, the unity of the whole tradition. The whole unified tradition is his true hermeneutical object. It is this that he must understand in the same sense in which the literary critic understands his text in the unity of its meaning. Thus the historian too must perform a task of application. This is the important point: historical understanding proves to be a kind of literary criticism writ large.

But this does not mean that we share the hermeneutical approach of the historical school, the problems of which we outlined above. We spoke of the dominance of the philological schema in historical self-understanding and used Dilthey's foundation of the human sciences to show that the historical school's aim of seeing history as reality and not simply as unfolding complexes of ideas could not be achieved. We, for our part, are not maintaining, with Dilthey, that every event is as perfectly meaningful as a text. When I called history criticism writ large, this did not mean that historical studies are to be understood as part of intellectual history (Geistesgeschichte).

I am saying just the opposite. We have seen, I think more correctly, what is involved in reading a text. Of course the reader before whose eyes the great book of world history simply lies open does not exist. But neither does the reader exist who, when he has his text before him, simply reads what is there. Rather, all reading involves application, so that a person reading a text is himself part of the meaning he apprehends. He belongs to the text that he is reading. The line of meaning that the text manifests to him as he reads it always and necessarily breaks off in an open indeterminacy. He can, indeed he must, accept the fact that future generations will understand differently what he has read in the text. And what is true of every reader is also true of the historian. The historian is concerned with the whole of historical tradition, which he has to mediate with his own present existence if he wants to understand it and which in this way he keeps open for the future.

Thus *we too acknowledge that there is an inner unity between philology and literary criticism on the one hand and historical studies on the other,* but we do not see it in the universality of the historical method, nor in the objectifying replacement of the interpreter by the original reader, nor in historical critique of tradition as such but, on the contrary, in the fact that both perform an act of application that is different only in degree. If the philologist or critic understands the given text—i.e., understands himself in the text in the way we have said—the historian too understands the great text of world history he has himself discovered, in which every text handed down to us is but a fragment of meaning, one letter, as it were, and he understands himself in this great text. Both the critic and the historian thus emerge from the self-forgetfulness to which they had been banished by a thinking for which the only criterion was the methodology of modern science. Both find their true ground in *historically effected consciousness.*

This shows that the model of legal hermeneutics was, in fact, a useful one. When a judge regards himself as entitled to supplement the original meaning of the text of a law, he is doing exactly what takes place in all other understanding. *The old unity of the hermeneutical disciplines comes into its own again if we recognize that historically effected consciousness is at work in all hermeneutical activity, that of philologist as well as of the historian.*

The meaning of the application involved in all forms of understanding is now clear. Application does not mean first understanding a given universal in itself and then afterward applying it to a concrete case. It is the very understanding of the universal—the text—itself. Understanding proves to be a kind of effect and knows itself as such.

3 ANALYSIS OF HISTORICALLY EFFECTED CONSCIOUSNESS

(A) THE LIMITATIONS OF REFLECTIVE PHILOSOPHY[95]

We must now ask how knowledge and effect belong together. I have already pointed out above[96] that historically effected consciousness is something other than inquiry into the history of a particular work's effect—as it were, the trace a work leaves behind. It is, rather, a consciousness of the work itself, and hence itself has an effect. The purpose of the whole account of the formation and fusion of horizons was to show how historically effected consciousness operates. But what sort of consciousness is this? That is the decisive problem. However much we emphasize that historically effected consciousness itself belongs to the effect, what is essential to it as consciousness is that it can rise above that of which it is conscious. The structure of reflexivity is fundamentally given with all consciousness. Thus this must also be the case for historically effected consciousness.

We might also express it thus: when we speak of historically effected consciousness, are we not confined within the immanent laws of reflection, which destroy any immediate effect? Are we not forced to admit that *Hegel* was right and regard the basis of hermeneutics as *the absolute mediation of history and truth?*

We cannot underestimate this point if we think of the historical worldview and its development from Schleiermacher to Dilthey. It was the same everywhere. Everywhere the claim of hermeneutics seems capable of being met only in the infinity of knowledge, in the thoughtful fusion of the whole of tradition with the present. We see it based on the ideal of perfect enlightenment, on the complete limitlessness of our historical horizon, on the abolition of our finiteness in the infinity of knowledge, in short, on the omnipresence of the historically knowing spirit. It is clearly of no fundamental significance that nineteenth-century historicism never expressly acknowledged this consequence. Ultimately it finds its justification in Hegel, even if the historians, filled with enthusiasm for experience, preferred to quote Schleiermacher and Wilhelm von Humboldt. But neither Schleiermacher nor Humboldt really thought through their positions fully. However much they emphasize the individuality, the barrier of alienness, that our understanding has to overcome, understanding ultimately finds its fulfillment only in an infinite consciousness, just as the idea of individuality finds its ground there as well. The fact that all individuality is pantheistically embraced within the absolute is what makes possible the miracle of understanding. Thus here too being and knowledge interpenetrate each other in the absolute. Neither Schleiermacher's nor Humboldt's Kantianism, then, affirms an independent system distinct from the consummation of speculative idealism in the absolute dialectic of Hegel. The critique of reflective philosophy that applies to Hegel applies to them also.

We must ask whether our own attempt at a historical hermeneutics is not subject to the same critique. Have we succeeded in keeping ourselves free from the metaphysical claims of reflective philosophy? Have we legitimated the hermeneutical experience by agreeing with the critique that the young Hegelians leveled at Hegel, a critique that proved historically so important?

To do so we must acknowledge that absolute reflection is powerfully compelling and admit that Hegel's critics never really succeeded in breaking its magic spell. We can detach the problem of a historical hermeneutics from the hybrid consequences of speculative idealism only if we refuse to be satisfied with the irrationalistic reduction of it, but preserve the truth of Hegel's thought. We are concerned with understanding historically effected consciousness in such a way that the immediacy and superiority of the work does not dissolve into a mere reflective reality in the consciousness of the effect—i.e., we are concerned to conceive a reality that limits and exceeds the omnipotence of reflection. This was precisely the point against which the critique of Hegel was directed and where the principle of reflective philosophy actually proved itself superior to all its critics.

This can be exemplified by Hegel's polemic against Kant's "thing-in-itself."[97] Kant's critical delimitation of reason had limited the application of the categories to the objects of possible experience and declared that the thing-in-itself behind appearances was unknowable. Hegel's dialectical argument objected that by making this distinction, and separating the appearance from the thing-in-itself, reason was proving this distinction to be its own. In doing so it by no means comes up against its own limits; rather, reason has itself set this limit, and that means it has already gone beyond that limit. What makes a limit a limit always also includes knowledge of what is on both sides of it. It is the dialectic of the limit to exist only by being superseded. Thus the quality of being-in-itself that distinguishes the thing-in-itself from its appearance is in-itself only for us. What appears in logical generality in the dialectic of the limit becomes specified in consciousness by the experience that the being-in-itself distinguished from consciousness is the other of itself, and is known in its truth when it is known as self—i.e., when it knows itself in full and absolute self-consciousness. We will consider the legitimacy and limitations of this argument below.

The varied critique of this philosophy of absolute reason by Hegel's critics cannot withstand the logical consequences of total dialectical self-mediation that Hegel has described, especially in his *Phenomenology*, the science of phenomenal knowledge. That the other must be experienced not as the other of myself grasped by pure self-consciousness, Thou—this prototype of all objections to the infiniteness of dialectic—does not seriously challenge him. The dialectical process *Phenomenology of Mind* is perhaps determined by nothing so much as by the problem of the recognition of the Thou. To mention only a few stages of this history: our own self-consciousness, for Hegel, attains to the truth of its self-consciousness only by fighting to be recognized by the other person. The immediate relationship between man and woman is the natural knowledge of mutual recognition (p. 325).[98] Beyond this, conscience represents the spiritual side of being recognized, and the mutual self-recognition in which the spirit is absolute can be attained only via confession and forgiveness. It cannot be denied that Feuerbach and Kierkegaard's objections are already anticipated when Hegel describes these forms of spirit.

Polemics against an absolute thinker has itself no starting point. The Archimedean point from which Hegel's philosophy could be toppled can never be found through reflection. The formal superiority of reflective philosophy is precisely that every possible position is drawn into the reflective movement of consciousness coming to itself. The appeal to immediacy—whether of bodily nature, or the Thou making claims on us, or the impenetrable factualness of historical accident, or the reality of the relations of production—has always been self-refuting, in that it is not itself an immediate relation, but a reflective activity. The left-Hegelian critique of merely intellectual reconciliation that fails to take account of the real transformation of the world, the whole doctrine of the transformation of philosophy into politics, is inevitably the self-abolition of philosophy.[99]

Thus the question arises how far the dialectical superiority of reflective philosophy corresponds to a substantive truth and how far it merely creates a formal appearance. For the arguments of reflective philosophy cannot ultimately obscure the fact that there is some truth in the critique of speculative thought based on the standpoint of finite human consciousness. This emerges, in particular, in the epigones of idealism—e.g., the neo-Kantian critics of life philosophy and existentialism. Heinrich Rickert, who attempted in 1920 to destroy life philosophy through argument, was unable to come anywhere near the influence of Nietzsche and Dilthey, which was beginning to grow at that time. However clearly one demonstrates the inner contradictions of all relativist views, it is as Heidegger has said: all these victorious arguments have something of the attempt to bowl one over.[100] However cogent they may seem, they still miss the main point. In making use of them one is proved right, and yet they do not express any superior insight of value. That the thesis of skepticism or relativism refutes itself to the extent that it claims to be true is an irrefutable argument. But what does it achieve? The reflective argument that proves successful here rebounds against the arguer, for it renders the truth value of reflection suspect. It is not the reality of skepticism or of truth-dissolving relativism but the truth claim of all formal argument that is affected.

Thus the formalism of such reflective argument is of specious philosophical legitimacy. In fact it tells us nothing. We are familiar with this kind of thing from the Greek Sophists, whose inner hollowness Plato demonstrated. It was also he who saw clearly that there is no argumentatively adequate criterion by which to distinguish between truly philosophical and sophistic discourse. In particular, he shows in his *Seventh Letter* that the formal refutability of a proposition does not necessarily exclude its being true.[101]

The model of all empty argument is the sophistic question how one can inquire into anything that one does not already know. This sophistical objection, which Plato formulates in the *Meno*, is not, characteristically enough, overcome there through superior argument, but by appealing to the myth of the pre-existence of the soul.[102] This is a very ironic appeal, since the myth of pre-existence and anamnesis, which is supposed to solve the mystery of questioning and seeking, does not present a religious certainty but depends on the certainty of the knowledge-seeking soul, which prevails against the emptiness of formal arguments. Nevertheless, it is characteristic of the weakness that Plato recognizes in the logos that he bases his critique of the Sophists' argument not on logic but myth. Just as true opinion is a divine favor and gift, so the search for and recognition of the true logos is not the free self-possession of the human mind. We will see below that Plato's mythical justification of Socratic dialectic is of fundamental importance. Were not the Sophists refuted—and this cannot be done through argument—their argument would lead to resignation. It is the argument of "lazy reason" and has a truly symbolic importance, since all empty reflection, despite its appearance of victory, leads to the discrediting of all reflective thought.

But however convincing it seems, Plato's mythical refutation of dialectical sophism does not satisfy the modern mind. There is no mythical foundation of philosophy in Hegel; for him myth is part of pedagogy.

Ultimately, reason is its own foundation. By working through the dialectic of reflection as the total self-mediation of reason, Hegel is fundamentally beyond the argumentative formalism that we, like Plato, call "sophistical." Hence his dialectic is no less polemical toward the empty arguments of logic, which he calls "external reflection," than are the arguments of Plato's Socrates. That is why it is of central importance that the hermeneutical problem come to grips with Hegel. For Hegel's whole philosophy of mind claims to achieve the total fusion of history with the present. It is concerned not with a reflective formalism but with the same thing as we are. Hegel has thought through the historical dimension in which the problem of hermeneutics is rooted.

For this reason we will have to define *the structure of historically effected consciousness* with an eye to Hegel, setting it against his own approach. Hegel's spiritualistic interpretation of Christianity, which he uses to define the nature of mind, is not affected by the objection that it leaves no room for the experience of the other and the alterity of history. The life of the mind consists precisely in recognizing oneself in other being. The mind directed toward self-knowledge regards itself as alienated from the "positive" and must learn to reconcile itself with it, seeing it as its own, as its home. By dissolving the hard edge of positivity, it becomes reconciled with itself. In that this kind of reconciliation is the historical work of the mind, the historical activity of the mind is neither self-reflection nor the merely formal dialectical supersession of the self-alienation that it has undergone, but an *experience* that experiences reality and is itself real.

(B) THE CONCEPT OF EXPERIENCE (ERFAHRUNG) AND THE ESSENCE OF THE HERMENEUTIC EXPERIENCE

This is precisely what we have to keep in mind in analyzing historically effected consciousness: it has the structure of *experience* (Erfahrung). However paradoxical it may seem, the concept of experience seems to me one of the most obscure we have. Because it plays an important role in the natural sciences in the logic of induction, it has been subjected to an epistemological schematization that, for me, truncates its original meaning. We may remember that Dilthey accused British empiricism of a lack of historical culture. Considering his unresolved hesitation between life philosophy and philosophy of science, we can regard this as a very half-hearted criticism. In fact, the main deficiency in theory of experience hitherto—and this includes Dilthey himself—is that it is entirely oriented toward science and hence takes no account of the inner historicity of experience. The aim of science is so to objectify experience that it no longer contains any historical element. Scientific experiment does this by its methodical procedure. The historico-critical method, moreover, does something similar in the human sciences. Through the objectivity of their approach, both methods are concerned to guarantee that these basic experiences can be repeated by anyone. Just as in the natural sciences experiments must be verifiable, so also must the whole process be capable of being checked in the human sciences also. Hence there can be no place for the historicity of experience in science.

In its methodology modern science thus simply proceeds further toward a goal that experience has always striven after. Experience is valid only if it is confirmed; hence its dignity depends on its being in principle repeatable. But this means that by its very nature, experience abolishes its history and thus itself. This is true even of everyday experience, and much more so of any scientific version of it. Theory of experience is related exclusively teleologically to the truth that is derived from it, and this is not just an accidental one-sidedness in modern scientific theory but has a foundation in fact.

In recent times *Edmund Husserl*, in particular, has directed his attention to this problem. In a series of many investigations he attempted to throw light on the one-sidedness of the scientific idealization of experience.[103] To this end he gives a genealogy of the experience which, as experience of the living world, precedes its being idealized by science. To me, however, he still seems dominated by the one-sidedness that he criticizes, for he projects the idealized world of exact scientific experience into the original experience of the world, in that he makes perception, as something directed toward merely external physical appearances, the basis of all other experience. To quote him: "Although, because of this sensible presence it also attracts our practical or affective interest, presenting itself to us at once as something useful, attractive, or repulsive, all this is based on the fact that there is a substratum with qualities that can be apprehended simply by the senses, to which there always leads a path of possible explication."[104] [It is easy to see how much the ontological fore-conception of "presence" dominates him.] Husserl's attempt to go back genetically to the origin of experience, and to overcome its idealization by science, obviously has to struggle especially with the difficulty that the pure transcendental sub-jectivity of the ego is not really given as such but always given in the idealization of language; moreover, language is already present in any acquisition of experience, and in it the individual ego comes to belong to a particular linguistic community.

In fact, when we go back to the beginnings of modern scientific theory and logic, we find this same problem: the extent to which there can be such a thing as the pure use of our reason, proceeding according to methodological principles, superior to all prejudices and predispositions, especially "verbalistic" ones. The particular achievement of *Bacon* in this field is that he was not satisfied with the immanent logical task of elaborating the theory of experience as the theory of true induction; instead, he discussed the whole moral difficulty and anthropological questionableness of this kind of experiential product. His method of induction seeks to rise above the irregular and accidental way daily experience occurs and certainly above its dialectical use. In this connection he undermined the theory of induction based on enumeratio simplex, still held by humanist scholasticism, an achievement that foreshadowed the new age of scientific method. The concept of induction makes use of the idea that we generalize on the basis of chance observation and, if we encounter no contrary instance, we pronounce it valid. Against anticipatio, this overhasty generalization of everyday experience, Bacon opposes what he calls interpretatio naturae—i.e., the expert interpretation of the true being of nature.[105] Methodically conducted experiments permit us to progress step by step toward the true and tenable universals, the simple forms of nature. This true method is characterized by the fact that the mind is not left to its own devices;[106] it cannot soar as it would like. Rather, it has to climb gradatim (step by step) from the particular to the universal in order to achieve an ordered experience that avoids all hasty conclusions.[107]

Bacon himself describes the method he calls for as experimental.[108] But it must be remembered that by experiment Bacon does not always mean just the scientist's technical procedure of artificially inducing processes under conditions that isolate them and render them capable of being measured. An experiment is also, and primarily, the careful directing of our mind, preventing it from indulging in overhasty generalizations, consciously confronting it with the most remote and apparently most diverse instances, so that gradually and continuously it can learn to work, via the process of exclusion, toward the axioms.[109]

On the whole, we have to agree with the usual criticism of Bacon and admit that his methodological suggestions are disappointing. As we can see today, they are too vague and general and have produced little, especially when applied to the study of nature. It is true that this opponent of empty dialectical casuistry himself remained profoundly involved in the metaphysical tradition and in the dialectical forms of argument that he attacked. His goal of conquering nature through obedience—the new approach of attacking and forcing nature's secrets from it which makes him the predecessor of modern science—is only the programmatic side of his work, and his contribution has hardly been enduring. His real achievement is, rather, that he undertakes a comprehensive examination of the prejudices that hold the human mind captive and lead it away from the true knowledge of things. He thus carries out a methodical self-purification of the mind that is more a discipline than a method. Bacon's famous doctrine of the "prejudices" first and foremost makes the methodical use of reason possible.[110] This is precisely why he interests us, for he expresses, albeit with a critical and exclusionary intention, elements in experience that are not teleologically related to the goal of science. For example, among the idola tribus, Bacon speaks of the tendency of the human mind always to remember what is positive and forget all instantiae negativae. A case in point is the belief in oracles, which is based on this remarkable forgetfulness, which remembers only the true prophecies and forgets the false ones. Similarly, in Bacon's eyes the relation of the human mind to the conventions of language is a case of knowledge being distracted by empty conventional forms. It is one of the idola fori.

These two examples are enough to indicate that the teleological aspect, which dominates this question for Bacon, is not the only one possible. Whether the positive should always have priority in the memory, or whether the tendency of life to forget the negative is to be criticized in all respects, is a question that needs asking. Ever since the *Prometheus* of Aeschylus, hope has been such a clear mark of human experience that, in view of its human importance, we must regard as one-sided the principle that experience should be evaluated only teleologically, by the degree to which it ends in knowledge. We will probably come to a similar conclusion with regard to language, which precedes experience, and although illusory verbalistic problems can derive from the dominance of linguistic conventions, it is equally certain that language is at the same time a positive condition of, and guide to, experience itself. Even Husserl, like Bacon, noted more the negative than the positive side of language.

In analyzing the concept of experience we will not let ourselves be guided by these models, since we cannot confine ourselves to the teleological perspective, which until now has largely governed considera-tion of the problem. This is not to say that this perspective has not correctly grasped a true element in the structure of experience. The fact that experience is valid so long as it is not contradicted by new experience (ubi non reperitur instantia contradictoria) is clearly characteristic of the general nature of experience, whether we are dealing with scientific procedure in the modern sense or with the experience of daily life that men have always had.

Thus this characterization of experience is entirely in agreement with Aristotle's analysis of the concept of induction in the appendix to his *Posterior Analytics*.[111] There (as in Chapter 1 of his *Metaphysics*) he describes how various perceptions unite to form the unity of experience when many individual perceptions are retained. What sort of unity is this? Clearly it is the unity of a universal. But the universality of experience is not yet the universality of science. Rather, according to Aristotle, it occupies a remark-ably indeterminate intermediate position between the many individual perceptions and the true universality of the concept. Science and technol-ogy start from the universality of the concept. But what is the universality of experience, and how does it evolve into the new universality of the logos? If experience shows us that a particular remedy has a particular effect, this means that something common has been noticed in a number of observations, and it is clear that the actual medical question, the scientific question—i.e., the question about the logos—is possible only on the basis of this kind of observation. Science knows why, for what reason, this remedy has a healing effect. Experience is not science itself, but it is a necessary condition of it. There must already be certainty—i.e., the individual observations must show the same regularity. Only when the universality found in experience has been attained can we look for the reason and hence begin a scientific inquiry. We ask again: what kind of universality is this? It is obviously concerned with the undifferentiated commonality of many single observations. It is because we retain these that we can make certain predictions.

However, the relation among experience, retention, and the resulting unity of experience remains conspicuously vague. Aristotle is obviously basing what he says here on an argument that by his time already had a certain classic stamp. We find it first in Anaxagoras who, according to Plutarch, distinguished man from the beasts through his powers of empeiria, mneme, sophia and techne.[112] We find a similar point in Aeschylus' emphasis on mneme in the *Prometheus*,[113] and although we do not find the corresponding emphasis on mneme in Plato's myth in the Protagoras, both Plato[114] and Aristotle indicate that it was already an established theory. The persistence of important perceptions (mone) is clearly the linking motif through which the knowledge of the universal can emerge from the experience of the individual. All animals that possess mneme in this sense—i.e., a sense of the past, of time—approximate the human in this respect. A separate investigation into this early theory of experience, whose traces we have outlined, would be necessary to discover how influential was the connection between memory (mneme) and language. It is clear that universal concepts are acquired by learning names and speech generally, and Themistius exemplified Aristotle's analysis of induction simply by reference to learning to speak and form words. At any rate, the universality of experience of which Aristotle speaks is not that of the concept or of science. (The problematic which we approach with this theory is undoubtedly that of the Sophists' educational thought, for we find in all the available documents a connection between that distinctiveness of the human that concerns us here and the general arrangement of nature. But this motif—the contrast of men and beasts—was the natural basis for the Sophists' educational ideal.) Experience is always actually present only in the individual observation. It is not known in a previous universality. Here lies the fundamental openness of experience to new experience, not only in the general sense that errors are corrected, but that experience is essentially dependent on constant confirmation and necessarily becomes a different kind of experience where there is no confirmation (ubi reperitur instantia contradictoria).

Aristotle has a very fine image for the logic of this procedure. He compares the many observations someone makes to a fleeing army. They too hurry away—i.e., they do not stand fast. But if in this general flight an observation is confirmed by its being experienced repeatedly, then it does stand fast. At this point the general flight begins to stop. If others join it, then finally the whole fleeing host stops and again obeys a single command. The whole army under unified control is an image of science. The image is intended to show how science—i.e., universal truth—is possible, considering that it must not depend on the contingency of observations, but be valid in a really universal way. How is that possible on the basis of such contingent observations?

The image is important for us because it illustrates the crucial element in the nature of experience. Like all images, it is not entirely perfect; however, the imperfection of a symbol is not a shortcoming but the other side of the work of abstraction that it performs. Aristotle's image of the fleeing army is imperfect because it starts from the wrong assumption, namely that before fleeing the army was standing fast. Of course this is not true of the tenor, namely the way knowledge is born. But this very lack shows clearly the only thing that the image is intended to illustrate: the birth of experience as an event over which no one has control and which is not even determined by the particular weight of this or that observation, but in which everything is co-ordinated in a way that is ultimately incomprehensible. The image captures the curious openness in which experience is acquired, suddenly, through this or that feature, unpredictably, and yet not without preparation, and it is valid from then on until there is a new experience—i.e., it holds not only for this or that instance but everything of the kind. According to Aristotle, it is through this universality of experience that the true universality of the concept and the possibility of science comes about. Thus the image illustrates the way the unprincipled universality of experience (its accretion) eventually leads to the unity of the arche (which means both "command" and "principle").

But if, like Aristotle, we think of the essence of experience only in regard to "science" [which in any case is not "modern" science but "knowledge"], then we are simplifying the process by which it comes about. His image describes this process, but it describes it under oversimplified conditions. As if one could automatically give a straightforward account of experience that contained no contradictions! Aristotle here presupposes that what persists in the flight of observations and emerges as a universal is, in fact, something common to them: for him the universality of the concept is ontologically prior. What concerns Aristotle about experience is merely how it contributes to the formation of concepts.

If we thus regard experience in terms of its result, we have ignored the fact that experience is a process. In fact, this process is essentially negative. It cannot be described simply as the unbroken generation of typical universals. Rather, this generation takes place as false generalizations are continually refuted by experience and what was regarded as typical is shown not to be so.[115] Language shows this when we use the word "experience" in two different senses: the experiences that conform to our expectation and confirm it and the new experiences that occur to us. This latter—"experience" in the genuine sense—is always negative. If a new experience of an object occurs to us, this means that hitherto we have not seen the thing correctly and now know it better. Thus the negativity of experience has a curiously productive meaning. It is not simply that we see through a deception and hence make a correction, but we acquire a comprehensive knowledge. We cannot, therefore, have a new experience of any object at random, but it must be of such a nature that we gain better knowledge through it, not only of itself, but of what we thought we knew before—i.e., of a universal. The negation by means of which it achieves this is a determinate negation. We call this kind of experience *dialectical*.

It is not Aristotle but, most important, *Hegel* who testifies to the dialectical element in experience. With him the element of historicity comes into its own. He conceives experience as skepticism in action. We saw that one's experience changes one's whole knowledge. Strictly speaking, we cannot have the same experience twice. It is true, of course, that part of the nature of experience is to be continually confirmed; it is, as it were, acquired only by being repeated. But it is no longer a new experience when it is repeated and confirmed. When we have had an experience, this means that we possess it. We can now predict what was previously unexpected. The same thing cannot again become a new experience for us; only something different and unexpected can provide someone who has experience with a new one. Thus the experiencing consciousness has reversed its direction—i.e., it has turned back on itself. The experiencer has become aware of his experience; he is "experienced." He has acquired a new horizon within which something can become an experience for him.

This is the point at which Hegel becomes an important witness for us. In his *Phenomenology of Mind* he shows how the consciousness that would be certain of itself has new experiences. For consciousness its object is the in-itself, but what is in-itself can be known only as it presents itself to the experiencing consciousness. Thus the experiencing consciousness has precisely this experience: that the in-itselfness of the object is in-itself "for us."[116]

Hegel here analyzes the concept of experience—an analysis that has drawn the special attention of Heidegger, who was both attracted and repulsed by it.[117] Hegel says, "The dialectical movement that consciousness carries out in regard to itself, both in regard to its knowledge and to its object *inasmuch as its new, true object emerges* from this, is actually what is called *experience*." Remembering what we have said above, let us ask what Hegel means, since he is here clearly trying to say something about the general nature of experience. Heidegger has pointed out, rightly in my opinion, that here Hegel is not interpreting experience dialectically but rather conceiving what is dialectical in terms of the nature of experience.[118] According to Hegel, experience has the structure of a reversal of consciousness and hence it is a dialectical movement. Hegel behaves, of course, as if what is generally meant by experience were something else, in that in general we "experience the falsehood of this first concept through another object" (and not in such a way that the object itself changes). But it is only apparently different. Actually, the philosophical mind realizes what the experiencing mind is really doing when it proceeds from one to the other: it is reversing itself. Thus Hegel declares that the true nature of experience is to reverse itself in this way.

In fact, as we saw, experience is initially always experience of negation: something is not what we supposed it to be. In view of the experience that we have of another object, both things change—our knowledge and its object. We know better now, and that means that the object itself "does not pass the test." The new object contains the truth about the old one.

What Hegel thus describes as experience is the experience that consciousness has of itself. "The principle of experience contains the infinitely important element that in order to accept a content as true, the man himself must be *present* or, more precisely, he must find such content in unity and combined with the *certainty of himself*," writes Hegel in the *Encyclopedia*.[119] The concept of experience means precisely this, that this kind of unity with oneself is first established. This is the reversal that consciousness undergoes when it recognizes itself in what is alien and different. Whether experience moves by expanding into the manifoldness of the contents or as the continual emergence of new forms of mind, the necessity of which is understood by philosophical science, in any case it is a reversal of consciousness. Hegel's dialectical description of experience has some truth.

For Hegel, it is necessary, of course, that conscious experience should lead to a self-knowledge that no longer has anything other than or alien to itself. For him the consummation of experience is "science," the certainty of itself in knowledge. Hence his criterion of experience is self-knowledge. That is why the dialectic of experience must end in that overcoming of all experience which is attained in absolute knowledge—i.e., in the complete identity of consciousness and object. We can now understand why applying Hegel's dialectic to history, insofar as he regarded it as part of the absolute self-consciousness of philosophy, does not do justice to hermeneutical consciousness. The nature of experience is conceived in terms of something that surpasses it; for experience itself can never be science.

Experience stands in an ineluctable opposition to knowledge and to the kind of instruction that follows from general theoretical or technical knowledge. The truth of experience always implies an orientation toward new experience. That is why a person who is called experienced has become so not only *through* experiences but is also open *to* new experiences. The consummation of his experience, the perfection that we call "being experienced," does not consist in the fact that someone already knows everything and knows better than anyone else. Rather, the experienced person proves to be, on the contrary, someone who is radically undogmatic; who, because of the many experiences he has had and the knowledge he has drawn from them, is particularly well equipped to have new experiences and to learn from them. The dialectic of experience has its proper fulfillment not in definitive knowledge but in the openness to experience that is made possible by experience itself.

But then this gives the concept of experience that we are concerned with here a qualitatively new element. It refers not only to experience in the sense of information about this or that. It refers to experience in general. This experience is always to be acquired, and from it no one can be exempt. Experience in this sense belongs to the historical nature of man. Although in bringing up children, for example, parents may try to spare them certain experiences, experience as a whole is not something anyone can be spared. Rather, experience in this sense inevitably involves many disappointments of one's expectations and only thus is experience acquired. That experience refers chiefly to painful and disagreeable experiences does not mean that we are being especially pessimistic, but can be seen directly from its nature. Only through negative instances do we acquire new experiences, as Bacon saw. Every experience worthy of the name thwarts an expectation. Thus the historical nature of man essentially implies a fundamental negativity that emerges in the relation between experience and insight.

Insight is more than the knowledge of this or that situation. It always involves an escape from something that had deceived us and held us captive. Thus insight always involves an element of self-knowledge and constitutes a necessary side of what we called experience in the proper sense. Insight is something we come to. It too is ultimately part of the vocation of man—i.e., to be discerning and insightful.

If we want to quote another witness for this third element in the nature of experience, the best is *Aeschylus*. He found the formula—or, rather, recognized its metaphysical significance as expressing the inner historicality of experience—of "learning though suffering" (pathei mathos). This phrase does not mean only that we become wise through suffering and that our knowledge of things must first be corrected through deception and undeception. Understood in this way, the formula is probably as old as human experience itself. But Aeschylus means more than this.[120] He refers to the reason why this is so. What a man has to learn through suffering is not this or that particular thing, but insight into the limitations of humanity, into the absoluteness of the barrier that separates man from the divine. It is ultimately a religious insight—the kind of insight that gave birth to Greek tragedy.

Thus experience is experience of human finitude. The truly experienced person is one who has taken this to heart, who knows that he is master neither of time nor the future. The experienced man knows that all foresight is limited and all plans uncertain. In him is realized the truth value of experience. If it is characteristic of every phase of the process of experience that the experienced person acquires a new openness to new experiences, this is certainly true of the idea of being perfectly experienced. It does not mean that experience has ceased and a higher form of knowledge is reached (Hegel), but that for the first time experience fully and truly is. In it all dogmatism, which proceeds from the soaring desires of the human heart, reaches an absolute barrier. Experience teaches us to acknowledge the real. The genuine result of experience, then—as of all desire to know—is to know what is. But "what is," here, is not this or that thing, but "what cannot be destroyed" (Ranke).

Real experience is that whereby man becomes aware of his finiteness. In it are discovered the limits of the power and the self-knowledge of his planning reason. The idea that everything can be reversed, that there is always time for everything and that everything somehow returns, proves to be an illusion. Rather, the person who is situated and acts in history continually experiences the fact that nothing returns. To acknowledge what is does not just mean to recognize what is at this moment, but to have insight into the limited degree to which the future is still open to expectation and planning or, even more fundamentally, to have the insight that all the expectation and planning of finite beings is finite and limited. Genuine experience is experience of one's own historicity. Our discussion of the concept of experience thus arrives at a conclusion that is of considerable importance to our inquiry into the nature of historically effected consciousness. As a genuine form of experience it must reflect the general structure of experience. Thus we will have to seek out in *hermeneutical experience* those elements that we have found in our analysis of experience in general.

Hermeneutical experience is concerned with *tradition*. This is what is to be experienced. But tradition is not simply a process that experience teaches us to know and govern; it is *language*—i.e., it expresses itself like a Thou. A Thou is not an object; it relates itself to us. It would be wrong to think that this means that what is experienced in tradition is to be taken as the opinion of another person, a Thou. Rather, I maintain that the understanding of tradition does not take the traditionary text as an expression of another person's life, but as meaning that is detached from the person who means it, from an I or a Thou. Still, the relationship to the Thou and the meaning of experience implicit in that relation must be capable of teaching us something about hermeneutical experience. For tradition is a genuine partner in dialogue, and we belong to it, as does the I with a Thou.

It is clear that the *experience of the Thou* must be special because the Thou is not an object but is in relationship with us. For this reason the elements we have emphasized in the structure of experience will undergo a change. Since here the object of experience is a person, this kind of experience is a moral phenomenon—as is the knowledge acquired through experience, the understanding of the other person. Let us therefore consider the change that occurs in the structure of experience when it is experience of the Thou and when it is hermeneutical experience.

There is a kind of experience of the Thou that tries to discover typical behavior in one's fellowmen and can make predictions about others on the basis of experience. We call this a knowledge of human nature. We understand the other person in the same way that we understand any other typical event in our experiential field—i.e., he is predictable. His behavior is as much a means to our end as any other means. From the moral point of view this orientation toward the Thou is purely self-regarding and contradicts the moral definition of man. As we know, in interpreting the categorical imperative Kant said, inter alia, that the other should never be used as a means but always as an end in himself.

If we relate this form of the I-Thou relation—the kind of understanding of the Thou that constitutes knowledge of human nature—to the hermeneutical problem, the equivalent is naive faith in method and in the objectivity that can be attained through it. Someone who understands tradition in this way makes it an object—i.e., he confronts it in a free and uninvolved way—and by methodically excluding everything subjective, he discovers what it contains. We saw that he thereby detaches himself from the continuing effect of the tradition in which he himself has his historical reality. It is the method of the social sciences, following the methodological ideas of the eighteenth century and their programatic formulation by Hume, ideas that are a clichéd version of scientific method.[121] But this covers only part of the actual procedure of the human sciences, and even that is schematically reduced, since it recognizes only what is typical and regular in behavior. It flattens out the nature of hermeneutical experience in precisely the same way as we have seen in the teleological interpretation of the concept of induction since Aristotle.

A second way in which the Thou is experienced and understood is that the Thou is acknowledged as a person, but despite this acknowledgment the understanding of the Thou is still a form of self-relatedness. Such self-regard derives from the dialectical appearance that the dialectic of the I-Thou relation brings with it. This relation is not immediate but reflective. To every claim there is a counterclaim. This is why it is possible for each of the partners in the relationship reflectively to outdo the other. One claims to know the other's claim from his point of view and even to understand the other better than the other understands himself. In this way the Thou loses the immediacy with which it makes its claim. It is understood, but this means it is co-opted and pre-empted reflectively from the standpoint of the other person. Because it is a mutual relationship, it helps to constitute the reality of the I-Thou relationship itself. The inner historicity of all the relations in the lives of men consists in the fact that there is a constant struggle for mutual recognition. This can have very varied degrees of tension, to the point of the complete domination of one person by the other. But even the most extreme forms of mastery and slavery are a genuine dialectical relationship of the kind that Hegel has elaborated.[122]

The experience of the Thou attained here is more adequate than what we have called the knowledge of human nature, which merely seeks to calculate how the other person will behave. It is an illusion to see another person as a tool that can be absolutely known and used. Even a slave still has a will to power that turns against his master, as Nietzsche rightly said.[123] But the dialectic of reciprocity that governs all I-Thou relationships is inevitably hidden from the consciousness of the individual. The servant who tyrannizes his master by serving him does not believe that he is serving his own aims by doing so. In fact, his own self-consciousness consists precisely in withdrawing from the dialectic of this reciprocity, in reflecting himself out of his relation to the other and so becoming unreachable by him. By understanding the other, by claiming to know him, one robs his claims of their legitimacy. In particular, the dialectic of charitable or welfare work operates in this way, penetrating all relationships between men as a reflective form of the effort to dominate. The claim to understand the other person in advance functions to keep the other person's claim at a distance. We are familiar with this from the teacher-pupil relationship, an authoritative form of welfare work. In these reflective forms the dialectic of the I-Thou relation becomes more clearly defined.

In the hermeneutical sphere the parallel to this experience of the Thou is what we generally call *historical consciousness*. Historical consciousness knows about the otherness of the other, about the past in its otherness, just as the understanding of the Thou knows the Thou as a person. In the otherness of the past it seeks not the instantiation of a general law but something historically unique. By claiming to transcend its own conditionedness completely in knowing the other, it is involved in a false dialectical appearance, since it is actually seeking to master the past, as it were. This need not be accompanied by the speculative claim of a philosophy of world history; as an ideal of perfect enlightenment, it sheds light on the process of experience in the historical sciences, as we find, for example, in Dilthey. In my analysis of hermeneutical consciousness I have shown that the dialectical illusion which historical consciousness creates, and which corresponds to the dialectical illusion of experience perfected and replaced by knowledge, is the unattainable ideal of the Enlightenment. A person who believes he is free of prejudices, relying on the objectivity of his procedures and denying that he is himself conditioned by historical circumstances, experiences the power of the prejudices that unconsciously dominate him as a vis a tergo. A person who does not admit that he is dominated by prejudices will fail to see what manifests itself by their light. It is like the relation between I and Thou. A person who reflects himself out of the mutuality of such a relation changes this relationship and destroys its moral bond. *A person who reflects himself out of a living relationship to tradition destroys the true meaning of this tradition in exactly the same way.* In seeking to understand tradition historical consciousness must not rely on the critical method with which it approaches its sources, as if this preserved it from mixing in its own judgments and prejudices. It must, in fact, think within its own historicity. To be situated within a tradition does not limit the freedom of knowledge but makes it possible.

Knowing and recognizing this constitutes the third, and highest, type of hermeneutical experience: the openness to tradition characteristic of historically effected consciousness. It too has a real analogue in the I's experience of the Thou. In human relations the important thing is, as we have seen, to experience the Thou truly as a Thou—i.e., not to overlook his claim but to let him really say something to us. Here is where openness belongs. But ultimately this openness does not exist only for the person who speaks; rather, anyone who listens is fundamentally open. Without such openness to one another there is no genuine human bond. Belonging together always also means being able to listen to one another. When two people understand each other, this does not mean that one person "understands" the other. Similarly, "to hear and obey someone" (auf jemanden hören) does not mean simply that we do blindly what the other desires. We call such a person slavish (hörig). Openness to the other, then, involves recognizing that I myself must accept some things that are against me, even though no one else forces me to do so.

This is the parallel to the hermeneutical experience. I must allow tradition's claim to validity, not in the sense of simply acknowledging the past in its otherness, but in such a way that it has something to say to me. This too calls for a fundamental sort of openness. Someone who is open to tradition in this way sees that historical consciousness is not really open at all, but rather, when it reads its texts "historically," it has always thoroughly smoothed them out beforehand, so that the criteria of the historian's own knowledge can never be called into question by tradition. Recall the naive mode of comparison that the historical approach generally engages in. The 25th "Lyceum Fragment" by Friedrich Schlegel reads: "The two basic principles of so-called historical criticism are the postulate of the commonplace and the axiom of familiarity. The postulate of the commonplace is that everything that is really great, good, and beautiful is improbable, for it is extraordinary or at least suspicious. The axiom of familiarity is that things must always have been just as they are for us, for things are naturally like this." By contrast, historically effected consciousness rises above such naive comparisons and assimilations by letting itself experience tradition and by keeping itself open to the truth claim encountered in it. The hermeneutical consciousness culminates not in methodological sureness of itself, but in the same readiness for experience that distinguishes the experienced man from the man captivated by dogma. As we can now say more exactly in terms of the concept of experience, this readiness is what distinguishes historically effected consciousness.

(C) THE HERMENEUTIC PRIORITY OF THE QUESTION

(i) The Model of Platonic Dialectic

This indicates the direction our inquiry must take. We will now examine the *logical structure of openness* that characterizes hermeneutical consciousness, recalling the importance of the concept of the *question* to our analysis of the hermeneutical situation. It is clear that the structure of the question is implicit in all experience. We cannot have experiences without asking questions. Recognizing that an object is different, and not as we first thought, obviously presupposes the question whether it was this or that. From a logical point of view, the openness essential to experience is precisely the openness of being either this or that. It has the structure of a question. And just as the dialectical negativity of experience culminates in the idea of being perfectly experienced—i.e., being aware of our finitude and limitedness—so also the logical form of the question and the negativity that is part of it culminate in a radical negativity: the knowledge of not knowing. This is the famous Socratic *docta ignorantia* which, amid the most extreme negativity of doubt, opens up the way to the true superiority of questioning. We will have to consider *the essence of the question* in greater depth if we are to clarify the particular nature of hermeneutical experience.

The essence of the question is to have sense. Now sense involves a sense of direction. Hence the sense of the question is the only direction from which the answer can be given if it is to make sense. A question places what is questioned in a particular perspective. When a question arises, it breaks open the being of the object, as it were. Hence the logos that explicates this opened-up being is an answer. Its sense lies in the sense of the question.

Among the greatest insights that Plato's account of Socrates affords us is that, contrary to the general opinion, it is more difficult to ask questions than to answer them. When the partners in the Socratic dialogue are unable to answer Socrates' awkward questions and try to turn the tables by assuming what they suppose is the preferable role of the questioner, they come to grief.[124] Behind this comic motif in the Platonic dialogues there is the critical distinction between authentic and inauthentic dialogue. To someone who engages in dialogue only to prove himself right and not to gain insight, asking questions will indeed seem easier than answering them. There is no risk that he will be unable to answer a question. In fact, however, the continual failure of the interlocutor shows that people who

think they know better cannot even ask the right questions. ʌ
able to ask, one must want to know, and that means knowι
does not know. In the comic confusion between question aι
knowledge and ignorance that Plato describes, there is a profoun
tion of the *priority of the question* in all knowledge and discourse that really
reveals something of an object. Discourse that is intended to reveal
something requires that that thing be broken open by the question.

For this reason, dialectic proceeds by way of question and answer or,
rather, the path of all knowledge leads through the question. To ask a
question means to bring into the open. The openness of what is in question
consists in the fact that the answer is not settled. It must still be
undetermined, awaiting a decisive answer. The significance of questioning
consists in revealing the questionability of what is questioned. It has to be
brought into this state of indeterminacy, so that there is an equilibrium
between pro and contra. The sense of every question is realized in passing
through this state of indeterminacy, in which it becomes an open question.
Every true question requires this openness. Without it, it is basically no
more than an apparent question. We are familiar with this from the
example of the pedagogical question, whose paradoxical difficulty consists
in the fact that it is a question without a questioner. Or from the rhetorical
question, which not only has no questioner but no object.

The openness of a question is not boundless. It is limited by the horizon
of the question. A question that lacks this horizon is, so to speak, floating.
It becomes a question only when its fluid indeterminacy is concretized in
a specific "this or that." In other words, the question has to be posed.
Posing a question implies openness but also limitation. It implies the
explicit establishing of presuppositions, in terms of which can be seen what
still remains open. Hence a question can be asked rightly or wrongly,
according as it reaches into the sphere of the truly open or fails to do so. We
say that a question has been put wrongly when it does not reach the state
of openness but precludes reaching it by retaining false presuppositions. It
pretends to an openness and susceptibility to decision that it does not have.
But if what is in question is not foregrounded, or not correctly foregrounded, from those presuppositions that are really held, then it is not
brought into the open and nothing can be decided.

This is shown clearly in the case of the slanted question that we are so
familiar with in everyday life. There can be no answer to a slanted question
because it leads us only apparently, and not really, through the open state
of indeterminacy in which a decision is made. We call it slanted rather than

wrongly put because there is a question behind it—i.e., there is an openness intended, but it does not lie in the direction in which the slanted question is pointing. The word "slanted" refers to something that has deviated from the right direction. The slant of a question consists in the fact that it does not give any real direction, and hence no answer to it is possible. Similarly, we say that statements which are not exactly wrong but also not right are "slanted." This too is determined by their sense—i.e., by their relation to the question. We cannot call them wrong, since we detect something true about them, but neither can we properly call them right because they do not correspond to any meaningful question and hence have no correct meaning unless they are themselves corrected. Sense is always sense of direction for a possible question. Correct sense must accord with the direction in which a question points.

Insofar as a question remains open, it always includes both negative and positive judgments. This is the basis of the essential relation between question and knowledge. For it is the essence of knowledge not only to judge something correctly but, at the same time and for the same reason, to exclude what is wrong. Deciding the question is the path to knowledge. What decides a question is the preponderance of reasons for the one and against the other possibility. But this is still not full knowledge. The thing itself is known only when the counterinstances are dissolved, only when the counterarguments are seen to be incorrect.

We are familiar with this especially from medieval dialectic, which lists not only the pro and contra and then its own decision, but finally sets out all the arguments. This form of medieval dialectic is not simply the consequence of an educational system emphasizing disputation, but on the contrary, it depends on the inner connection between knowledge and dialectic—i.e., between answer and question. There is a famous passage in Aristotle's *Metaphysics*[125] that has attracted a great deal of attention and can be explained in terms of what we have been saying. Aristotle says that dialectic is the power to investigate contraries independently of the object, and to see whether one and the same science can be concerned with contraries. Here it seems that a general account of dialectic (which corresponds exactly to what we find, for example, in Plato's *Parmenides*) is linked to a highly specialized "logical" problem which is familiar to us from the *Topics*.[126] It does indeed seem a very curious question whether the same science can be concerned with contraries. Hence the attempt has been made to dismiss this as a gloss.[127] The connection between the two questions becomes clear, however, as soon as we accept the priority of the question over the answer, which is the basis of the concept of knowledge. Knowledge always means, precisely, considering opposites. Its superiority over preconceived opinion consists in the fact that it is able to conceive of possibilities as possibilities. Knowledge is dialectical from the ground up. Only a person who has questions can have knowledge, but questions include the antithesis of yes and no, of being like this and being like that. Only because knowledge is dialectical in this comprehensive sense can there be a "dialectic" that explicitly makes its object the antithesis of yes and no. Thus the apparently over-specialized question of whether or not it is possible to have one and the same science of contraries contains, in fact, the ground of the very possibility of dialectic.

Even Aristotle's views on proof and argument—which, in fact, make dialectic a subordinate element in knowledge—accord the same priority to the question, as has been demonstrated by Ernst Kapp's brilliant work on the origin of Aristotle's syllogistic.[128] The priority of the question in knowledge shows how fundamentally the idea of method is limited for knowledge, which has been the starting point for our argument as a whole. There is no such thing as a method of learning to ask questions, of learning to see what is questionable. On the contrary, the example of Socrates teaches that the important thing is the knowledge that one does not know. Hence the Socratic dialectic—which leads, through its art of confusing the interlocutor, to this knowledge—creates the conditions for the question. All questioning and desire to know presuppose a knowledge that one does not know; so much so, indeed, that a particular lack of knowledge leads to a particular question.

Plato shows in an unforgettable way where the difficulty lies in knowing what one does not know. It is the power of opinion against which it is so hard to obtain an admission of ignorance. It is opinion that suppresses questions. Opinion has a curious tendency to propagate itself. It would always like to be the general opinion, just as the word that the Greeks have for opinion, doxa, also means the decision made by the majority in the council assembly. How, then, can ignorance be admitted and questions arise?

Let us say first of all that it can occur only in the way any idea occurs to us. It is true that we do speak of ideas occurring to us less in regard to questions than to answers—e.g., the solution of problems; and by this we mean to say that there is no methodical way to arrive at the solution. But we also know that such ideas do not occur to us entirely unexpectedly. They always presuppose an orientation toward an area of openness from which the idea can occur—i.e., they presuppose questions. The real nature of the sudden idea is perhaps less that a solution occurs to us like an answer to a riddle than that a question occurs to us that breaks through into the open and thereby makes an answer possible. Every sudden idea has the structure of a question. But the sudden occurrence of the question is already a breach in the smooth front of popular opinion. Hence we say that a question too "occurs" to us, that it "arises" or "presents itself" more than that we raise it or present it.

We have already seen that, logically considered, the negativity of experience implies a question. In fact we have experiences when we are shocked by things that do not accord with our expectations. Thus questioning too is more a passion than an action. A question presses itself on us; we can no longer avoid it and persist in our accustomed opinion.

It seems to conflict with these conclusions, however, that the Socratic-Platonic dialectic raises the art of questioning to a conscious art; but there is something peculiar about this art. We have seen that it is reserved to the person who wants to know—i.e., who already has questions. The art of questioning is not the art of resisting the pressure of opinion; it already presupposes this freedom. It is not an art in the sense that the Greeks speak of techne, not a craft that can be taught or by means of which we could master the discovery of truth. The so-called epistemological digression of the *Seventh Letter* is directed, rather, to distinguishing the unique art of dialectic from everything that can be taught and learned. The art of dialectic is not the art of being able to win every argument. On the contrary, it is possible that someone practicing the art of dialectic—i.e., the art of questioning and of seeking truth—comes off worse in the argument in the eyes of those listening to it. As the art of asking questions, dialectic proves its value because only the person who knows how to ask questions is able to persist in his questioning, which involves being able to preserve his orientation toward openness. The art of questioning is the art of questioning ever further—i.e., the art of thinking. It is called dialectic because it is the art of conducting a real dialogue.

To conduct a dialogue requires first of all that the partners do not talk at cross purposes. Hence it necessarily has the structure of question and answer. The first condition of the art of conversation is ensuring that the other person is with us. We know this only too well from the reiterated 'yes' of the interlocutors in the Platonic dialogues. The positive side of this monotony is the inner logic with which the subject matter is developed in the conversation. To conduct a conversation means to allow oneself to be conducted by the subject matter to which the partners in the dialogue are oriented. It requires that one does not try to argue the other person down but that one really considers the weight of the other's opinion. Hence it is an art of testing.[129] But the art of testing is the art of questioning. For we have seen that to question means to lay open, to place in the open. As against the fixity of opinions, questioning makes the object and all its possibilities fluid. A person skilled in the "art" of questioning is a person who can prevent questions from being suppressed by the dominant opinion. A person who possesses this art will himself search for everything in favor of an opinion. Dialectic consists not in trying to discover the weakness of what is said, but in bringing out its real strength. It is not the art of arguing (which can make a strong case out of a weak one) but the art of thinking (which can strengthen objections by referring to the subject matter).

The unique and continuing relevance of the Platonic dialogues is due to this art of strengthening, for in this process what is said is continually transformed into the uttermost possibilities of its rightness and truth, and overcomes all opposition that tries to limit its validity. Here again it is not simply a matter of leaving the subject undecided. Someone who wants to know something cannot just leave it a matter of mere opinion, which is to say that he cannot hold himself aloof from the opinions that are in question.[130] The speaker (der Redende) is put to the question (zur Rede gestellt) until the truth of what is under discussion (wovon der Rede ist) finally emerges. The maieutic productivity of the Socratic dialogue, the art of using words as a midwife, is certainly directed toward the people who are the partners in the dialogue, but it is concerned merely with the opinions they express, the immanent logic of the subject matter that is unfolded in the dialogue. What emerges in its truth is the logos, which is neither mine nor yours and hence so far transcends the interlocutors' subjective opinions that even the person leading the conversation knows that he does not know. As the art of conducting a conversation, dialectic is also the art of seeing things in the unity of an aspect (sunoran eis hen eidos)—i.e., it is the art of forming concepts through working out the common meaning. What characterizes a dialogue, in contrast with the rigid form of statements that demand to be set down in writing, is precisely this: that in dialogue spoken language—in the process of question and answer, giving and taking, talking at cross purposes and seeing each other's point—performs the communication of meaning that, with respect to the written tradition, is the task of hermeneutics. Hence it is more than a metaphor; it is a memory of what originally was the case, to describe the task of hermeneutics as entering into dialogue with the text. That this interpretation is performed by spoken language does not mean that it is transposed into a foreign medium; rather, being transformed into spoken language represents the restoration of the original communication of meaning. When it is interpreted, written tradition is brought back out of the alienation in which it finds itself and into the living present of conversation, which is always fundamentally realized in question and answer.

Thus we can appeal to Plato if we want to foreground the place of the question in hermeneutics. We can do this all the more readily since Plato himself manifests the hermeneutical phenomenon in a specific way. It would be worth investigating his critique of the written word as evidence that the poetic and philosophical tradition was becoming a literature in Athens. In Plato's dialogues we see how the kind of textual "interpretation" cultivated by the sophists, especially the interpretation of poetry for didactic ends, elicited Plato's opposition. We can see, further, how Plato tries to overcome the weakness of the logoi, especially the written logoi, through his own dialogues. The literary form of the dialogue places language and concept back within the original movement of the conversation. This protects words from all dogmatic abuse.

The primacy of conversation can also be seen in derivative forms in which the relation between question and answer is obscured. Letters, for example, are an interesting intermediate phenomenon: a kind of written conversation that, as it were, stretches out the movement of talking at cross purposes and seeing each other's point. The art of writing letters consists in not letting what one says become a treatise on the subject but in making it acceptable to the correspondent. But on the other hand it also consists in preserving and fulfilling the standard of finality that everything stated in writing has. The time lapse between sending a letter and receiving an answer is not just an external factor, but gives this form of communication its special nature as a particular form of writing. So we note that speeding up the post has not improved this form of communication but, on the contrary, has led to a decline in the art of letter writing.

The primacy of dialogue, the relation of question and answer, can be seen in even so extreme a case as that of Hegel's dialectic as a philosophical method. To elaborate the totality of the determinations of thought, which was the aim of Hegel's logic, is as it were the attempt to comprehend within the great monologue of modern "method" the continuum of meaning that is realized in every particular instance of dialogue. When Hegel sets himself the task of making the abstract determinations of thought fluid and subtle, this means dissolving and remolding logic into concrete language, and transforming the concept into the meaningful power of the word that questions and answers—a magnificent reminder, even if unsuccessful, of what dialectic really was and is. Hegel's dialectic is a monologue of thinking that tries to carry out in advance what matures little by little in every genuine dialogue.

(ii) The Logic of Question and Answer

Thus we return to the conclusion that the hermeneutic phenomenon too implies the primacy of dialogue and the structure of question and answer. That a historical text is made the object of interpretation means that it puts a question to the interpreter. Thus interpretation always involves a relation to the question that is asked of the interpreter. To understand a text means to understand this question. But this takes place, as we showed, by our attaining the hermeneutical horizon. We now recognize this as the *horizon of the question* within which the sense of the text is determined.

Thus a person who wants to understand must question what lies behind what is said. He must understand it as an answer to a question. If we go back *behind* what is said, then we inevitably ask questions *beyond* what is said. We understand the sense of the text only by acquiring the horizon of the question—a horizon that, as such, necessarily includes other possible answers. Thus the meaning of a sentence is relative to the question to which it is a reply, but that implies that its meaning necessarily exceeds what is said in it. As these considerations show, then, the logic of the human sciences is a logic of the question.

Despite Plato we are not very ready for such a logic. Almost the only person I find a link with here is R. G. Collingwood. In a brilliant and telling critique of the Oxford "realist" school, he developed the idea of a logic of question and answer, but unfortunately never elaborated it systematically.[131] He clearly saw what was missing in naive hermeneutics founded on the prevailing philosophical critique. In particular the practice that Collingwood found in English universities of discussing "statements," though perhaps good practice for sharpening one's intelligence, obviously failed to take account of the historicity that is part of all understanding. Collingwood argues thus: We can understand a text only when we have understood the question to which it is an answer. But since this question can be derived solely from the text and accordingly the appropriateness of the reply is the methodological presupposition for the reconstruction of the question, any criticism of this reply from some other quarter is pure shadow boxing. It is like understanding works of art. A work of art can be understood only if we assume its adequacy as an expression of the artistic idea. Here too we have to discover the question which it answers, if we are to understand it as an answer. This is, in fact, an axiom of all hermeneutics: we described it above as the "fore-conception of completeness."[132]

For Collingwood, this is the nerve of all historical knowledge. The historical method requires that the logic of question and answer be applied to historical tradition. We will understand historical events only if we reconstruct the question to which the historical actions of the persons involved were the answer. As an example Collingwood cites the Battle of Trafalgar and Nelson's plan on which it was based. The example is intended to show that the course of the battle helps us to understand Nelson's real plan, because it was successfully carried out. Because his opponent's plan failed, however, it cannot be reconstructed from the events. Thus, understanding the course of the battle and understanding the plan that Nelson carried out in it are one and the same process.[133]

But yet one cannot conceal the fact that the logic of question and answer has to reconstruct two different questions that have two different answers: the question of the meaning of a great event and the question of whether this event went according to plan. Clearly, the two questions coincide only when the plan coincides with the course of events. But we cannot suppose such coincidence as a methodological principle when we are concerned with a historical tradition which deals with men, like ourselves, in history. Tolstoy's celebrated description of the council of war before the battle—in which all the strategic possibilities are calculated and all the plans considered, thoroughly and perceptively, while the general sits there and sleeps, but in the night before the battle goes round all the sentry posts—is obviously a more accurate account of what we call history. Kutusov gets nearer to the reality and the forces that determine it than the strategists of the war council. The conclusion to be drawn from this example is that the interpreter of history always runs the risk of hypostasizing the connectedness of events when he regards their significance as that intended by the actual actors and planners.[134]

This is a legitimate undertaking only if Hegel's conditions hold good—i.e., the philosophy of history is made party to the plans of the world spirit and on the basis of this esoteric knowledge is able to mark out certain individuals as having world-historical importance, since there is a real correlation between their particular ideas and the world-historical meaning of events. But it is impossible to derive a hermeneutical principle for the knowledge of history from such conjunctions of the subjective and objective in history. In regard to historical tradition Hegel's theory clearly has only a limited truth. The infinite web of motivations that constitutes history only occasionally and briefly acquires the clarity of what a single individual has planned. Thus what Hegel describes as an exception proves the rule that there is a disproportion between an individual's subjective thoughts and the meaning of the whole course of history. As a rule we experience the course of events as something that continually changes our plans and expectations. Someone who tries to stick to his plans discovers precisely how powerless his reason is. There are rare occasions when everything happens, as it were, of its own accord—i.e., events seem to be automatically in accord with our plans and wishes. On these occasions we can say that everything is going according to plan. But to apply this experience to the whole of history is to make a great extrapolation that completely contradicts our experience.

Collingwood's use of the logic of question and answer in hermeneutical theory is made ambiguous by this extrapolation. Our understanding of written tradition per se is not such that we can simply presuppose that the meaning we discover in it agrees with what its author intended. Just as the events of history do not in general manifest any agreement with the subjective ideas of the person who stands and acts within history, so the sense of a text in general reaches far beyond what its author originally intended.[135] The task of understanding is concerned above all with the meaning of the text itself.

This is clearly what Collingwood had in mind when he denied that there is any difference between the historical question and the philosophical question to which the text is supposed to be an answer. Nevertheless, we must remember that the question we are concerned to reconstruct has to do not with the mental experiences of the author but simply with the meaning of the text itself. Thus if we have understood the meaning of a sentence—i.e., have reconstructed the question to which it really is the answer—it must be possible to inquire also about the questioner and his intended question, to which the text is perhaps only an imagined answer. Collingwood is wrong when he finds it methodologically unsound to differentiate between the question which the text is intended to answer and the question to which it really is an answer. He is right only insofar as understanding a text does not generally involve such a distinction, if we are concerned with the subject matter of which the text speaks. Reconstructing the author's ideas is quite a different task.

We will have to ask what conditions apply to this different task. For it is undoubtedly true that, compared with the genuine hermeneutical experience that understands the meaning of the text, reconstructing what the author really had in mind is a limited undertaking. Historicism tempts us to regard such reduction as a scientific virtue and to regard understanding as a kind of reconstruction which in effect repeats the process whereby the text came into being. Hence it follows the cognitive ideal familiar to us from the knowledge of nature, where we understand a process only when we are able to reproduce it artificially.

I have shown above[136] how questionable is Vico's statement that this ideal finds its purest culmination in history because there man encounters his own human-historical reality. I have asserted, on the contrary, that every historian and philologist must reckon with the fundamental non-definitiveness of the horizon in which his understanding moves. Historical tradition can be understood only as something always in the process of being defined by the course of events. Similarly, the philologist dealing with poetic or philosophical texts knows that they are inexhaustible. In both cases it is the course of events that brings out new aspects of meaning in historical material. By being re-actualized in understanding, texts are drawn into a genuine course of events in exactly the same way as are events themselves. This is what we described as the history of effect as an element in hermeneutical experience. Every actualization in understanding can be regarded as a historical potential of what is understood. It is part of the historical finitude of our being that we are aware that others after us will understand in a different way. And yet it is equally indubitable that it remains the same work whose fullness of meaning is realized in the changing process of understanding, just as it is the same history whose meaning is constantly in the process of being defined. The hermeneutical reduction to the author's meaning is just as inappropriate as the reduction of historical events to the intentions of their protagonists.

However, we cannot take the reconstruction of the question to which a given text is an answer simply as an achievement of historical method. The most important thing is the question that the text puts to us, our being perplexed by the traditionary word, so that understanding it must already include the task of the historical self-mediation between the present and tradition. Thus the relation of question and answer is, in fact, reversed. The voice that speaks to us from the past—whether text, work, trace—itself poses a question and places our meaning in openness. In order to answer the question put to us, we the interrogated must ourselves begin to ask questions. We must attempt to reconstruct the question to which the traditionary text is the answer. But we will be unable to do so without going beyond the historical horizon it presents us. Reconstructing the question to which the text is presumed to be the answer itself takes place within a process of questioning through which we try to answer the question that the text asks us. A reconstructed question can never stand within its original horizon: for the historical horizon that circumscribed the reconstruction is not a truly comprehensive one. It is, rather, included within the horizon that embraces us as the questioners who have been encountered by the traditionary word.

Hence it is a hermeneutical necessity always to go beyond mere reconstruction. We cannot avoid thinking about what the author accepted unquestioningly and hence did not consider, and bringing it into the openness of the question. This is not to open the door to arbitrariness in interpretation but to reveal what always takes place. Understanding the word of tradition always requires that the reconstructed question be set within the openness of its questionableness—i.e., that it merge with the question that tradition is for us. If the "historical" question emerges by itself, this means that it no longer arises as a question. It results from the cessation of understanding—a detour in which we get stuck.[137] Part of real understanding, however, is that we regain the concepts of a historical past in such a way that they also include our own comprehension of them. Above I called this "the fusion of horizons."[138] With Collingwood, we can say that we understand only when we understand the question to which something is the answer, but the intention of what is understood in this way does not remain foregrounded against our own intention. Rather, reconstructing the question to which the meaning of a text is understood as an answer merges with our own questioning. For the text must be understood as an answer to a real question.

The close relation between questioning and understanding is what gives the hermeneutic experience its true dimension. However much a person trying to understand may leave open the truth of what is said, however much he may dismiss the immediate meaning of the object and consider its deeper significance instead, and take the latter not as true but merely as meaningful, so that the possibility of its truth remains unsettled, this is the real and fundamental nature of a question: namely to make things indeterminate. Questions always bring out the undetermined possibilities of a thing. That is why we cannot understand the questionableness of something without asking real questions, though we can understand a meaning without meaning it. *To understand the questionableness of something is already to be questioning.* There can be no tentative or potential attitude to questioning, for questioning is not the positing but the testing of possibilities. Here the nature of questioning indicates what is demonstrated by the actual operation of the Platonic dialogue.[139] A person who thinks must ask himself questions. Even when a person says that such and such a question might arise, this is already a real questioning that simply masks itself, out of either caution or politeness.

This is the reason why understanding is always more than merely re-creating someone else's meaning. Questioning opens up possibilities of meaning, and thus what is meaningful passes into one's own thinking on the subject. Only in an inauthentic sense can we talk about understanding questions that one does not pose oneself—e.g., questions that are outdated or empty. We understand how certain questions came to be asked in particular historical circumstances. Understanding such questions means, then, understanding the particular presuppositions whose demise makes such questions "dead." An example is perpetual motion. The horizon of meaning of such questions is only apparently still open. They are no longer understood as questions. For what we understand, in such cases, is precisely that there is no question.

To understand a question means to ask it. To understand meaning is to understand it as the answer to a question.

The logic of question and answer that Collingwood elaborated puts an end to talk about permanent *problems*, as in the way the "Oxford realists" approach to the classics of philosophy, and hence also an end to the concept of *history of problems* developed by neo-Kantianism. History of problems would truly be history only if it acknowledged that the identity of the problem is an empty abstraction and permitted itself to be transformed into questioning. There is no such thing, in fact, as a point outside history from which the identity of a problem can be conceived within the vicissitudes of the history of attempts to solve it. The fact is that understanding philosophical texts always requires re-cognizing what is cognized in them. Without this we would understand nothing at all. But this in no way means that we step outside the historical conditions in which we are situated and in which we understand. The problem that we re-cognize is not in fact simply the same if it is to be understood in a genuine act of questioning. We can regard it as the same only because of our historical short-sightedness. The standpoint that is beyond any standpoint, a standpoint from which we could conceive its true identity, is a pure illusion.

We can understand the reason for this now. The concept of the problem is clearly an abstraction, namely the detachment of the content of the question from the question that in fact first reveals it. It refers to the abstract schema to which real and really motivated questions can be reduced and under which they can be subsumed. Such a "problem" has fallen out of the motivated context of questioning, from which it receives the clarity of its sense. Hence it is insoluble, like every question that has no clear, unambiguous sense, because it is not really motivated and asked.

This also confirms the origin of the concept of the problem. It does not belong in the sphere of those "honestly motivated refutations"[140] in which the truth of the subject matter is advanced, but in the sphere of dialectic as a weapon to amaze or make a fool of one's opponent. In Aristotle, the word "problema" refers to those questions that present themselves as open alternatives because there is evidence for both views and we think that they cannot be decided by reasons, since the questions involved are too great.[141] Problems are not real questions that arise of themselves and hence acquire the pattern of their answer from the genesis of their meaning, but are alternatives that can only be accepted as themselves and thus can be treated only in a dialectical way. This dialectical sense of the "problem" has its proper place in rhetoric, not in philosophy. Part of the concept of the problem is that there can be no clear decision on the basis of reasons. That is why Kant sees the rise of the concept of the problem as limited to the dialectic of pure reason. Problems are "tasks that emerge entirely from its own womb"—i.e., products of reason itself, the complete solution of which it cannot hope to achieve.[142] It is interesting that in the nineteenth century, with the collapse of the unbroken tradition of philosophical questioning and the rise of historicism, the concept of the problem acquires a universal validity—a sign of the fact that an immediate relation to the questions of philosophy no longer exists. It is typical of the embarrassment of philosophical consciousness when faced with historicism that it took flight into an abstraction, the concept of the "problem," and saw no problem about the manner in which problems actually "exist." Neo-Kantian history of problems is a bastard of historicism. Critiquing the concept of the problem by appealing to a logic of question and answer must destroy the illusion that problems exist like stars in the sky.[143]

Reflection on the hermeneutical experience transforms problems back to questions that arise and that derive their sense from their motivation.

The dialectic of question and answer disclosed in the structure of hermeneutical experience now permits us to state more exactly what kind of consciousness historically effected consciousness is. For the dialectic of question and answer that we demonstrated makes understanding appear to be a reciprocal relationship of the same kind as conversation. It is true that a text does not speak to us in the same way as does a Thou. We who are attempting to understand must ourselves make it speak. But we found that this kind of understanding, "making the text speak," is not an arbitrary procedure that we undertake on our own initiative but that, as a question, it is related to the answer that is expected in the text. Anticipating an answer itself presupposes that the questioner is part of the tradition and regards himself as addressed by it. This is the truth of historically effected consciousness. It is the historically experienced consciousness that, by renouncing the chimera of perfect enlightenment, is open to the experience of history. We described its realization as the fusion of the horizons of understanding, which is what mediates between the text and its interpreter.

The guiding idea of the following discussion is *that the fusion of horizons that takes place in understanding is actually the achievement of language.* Admittedly, what language is belongs among the most mysterious questions that man ponders. Language is so uncannily near our thinking, and when it functions it is so little an object, that it seems to conceal its own being from us. In our analysis of the thinking of the human sciences, however, we came so close to this universal mystery of language that is prior to everything else, that we can entrust ourselves to what we are investigating to guide us safely in the quest. In other words we are endeavoring to approach the mystery of language from the conversation that we ourselves are.

When we try to examine the hermeneutical phenomenon through the model of conversation between two persons, the chief thing that these apparently so different situations—understanding a text and reaching an understanding in a conversation—have in common is that both are concerned with a subject matter that is placed before them. Just as each interlocutor is trying to reach agreement on some subject with his partner, so also the interpreter is trying to understand what the text is saying. This understanding of the subject matter must take the form of language. It is not that the understanding is subsequently put into words; rather, the way understanding occurs—whether in the case of a text or a dialogue with another person who raises an issue with us—is the coming-into-language of the thing itself. Thus we will first consider the structure of dialogue proper, in order to specify the character of that other form of dialogue that is the understanding of texts. Whereas up to now we have framed the constitutive significance of the *question* for the hermeneutical phenomenon in terms of conversation, we must now demonstrate the linguisticality of dialogue, which is the basis of the question, as an element of hermeneutics.

Our first point is that the language in which something comes to speak is not a possession at the disposal of one or the other of the interlocutors. Every conversation presupposes a common language, or better, creates a common language. Something is placed in the center, as the Greeks say, which the partners in dialogue both share, and concerning which they can exchange ideas with one another. Hence reaching an understanding on the subject matter of a conversation necessarily means that a common language must first be worked out in the conversation. This is not an external matter of simply adjusting our tools; nor is it even right to say that the partners adapt themselves to one another but, rather, in a successful conversation they both come under the influence of the truth of the object and are thus bound to one another in a new community. To reach an understanding in a dialogue is not merely a matter of putting oneself forward and successfully asserting one's own point of view, but being transformed into a communion in which we do not remain what we were.[144]

Notes

1 Heidegger, *Sein und Zeit*, pp. 312ff.

2 Cf. Schleiermacher's *Hermeneutik*, ed. Heinz Kimmerle in *Abhandlungen der Heidelberger Akademie*, (1959), 2nd *Abhandlung*, which is explicitly committed to the old ideal of an art formulated in rules (p. 127, n.: "I . . . hate it when theory does not go beyond nature and the bases of art, whose object it is"). [See above pp. 178f.]

3 Cf. Emil Staiger's description, which accords with that of Heidegger, in *Die Kunst der Interpretation*, pp. 11ff. I do not, however, agree that the work of a literary critic begins only "when we are in the situation of a contemporary reader." This is something we never are, and yet we are capable of understanding, although we can never achieve a definite "personal or temporal identity" with the author. Cf. also Appendix IV below. [See also my "Vom Zirkel des Verstehens," *Kleine Schriften*, IV, 54–61 (*GW*, II, 57–65) and the criticism of W. Stegmüller, *Der sogenannte Zirkel des Verstehens* (Darmstadt, 1974). The objection raised from a logical point of view against talk of the "hermeneutic circle" fails to recognize that this concept makes no claim to scientific proof, but presents a logical metaphor, known to rhetoric ever since Schleiermacher. Rightly opposed to this misunderstanding is Karl-Otto Apel, *Transformationen der Philosophie* (2 vols.; Frankfurt, 1973), II, 83, 89, 216 and passim.]

4 *Sein und Zeit*, pp. 312ff.

5 Cf. Leo Strauss, *Die Religionskritik Spinozas*, p.163: "The word 'prejudice' is the most suitable expression for the great aim of the Enlightenment, the desire for free, untrammeled verification; the *Vorurteil* is the unambiguous polemical correlate of the very ambiguous word 'freedom.'"

6 *Praeiudicium auctoritatis et precipitantiae*, which we find as early as Christian

Thomasius' *Lectiones de praeiudiciis* (1689/90) and his *Einleitung der Vernunft-lehre*, ch. 13, §§39–40. Cf. the article in Walch, *Philosophisches Lexikon* (1726), pp. 2794ff.

7 At the beginning of his essay, "What Is Enlightenment?" (1784).

8 The enlightenment of the classical world, the fruit of which was Greek philosophy and its culmination in sophism, was quite different in nature and hence permitted a thinker like Plato to use philosophical myths to convey the religious tradition and the dialectical method of philosophizing. Cf. Erich Frank, *Philosophische Erkenntnis und religiöse Wahrheit*, pp. 31ff., and my review of it in the *Theologische Rundschau*, (1950), pp. 260–66. And see especially Gerhard Krüger, *Einsicht und Leidenschaft* (2nd ed., 1951).

9 A good example of this is the length of time it has taken for the authority of the historical writing of antiquity to be destroyed in historical studies and how slowly the study of archives and the research into sources have established themselves (cf. R. G. Collingwood, *Autobiography* [Oxford, 1939], ch. 11, where he more or less draws a parallel between turning to the study of sources and the Baconian revolution in the study of nature).

10 Cf. what we said about Spinoza's *Theological-Political Treatise*, pp. 180f. above.

11 As we find, for example, in G. F. Meier's *Beiträge zu der Lehre von den Vorurteilen des menschlichen Geschlechts* (1766).

12 I have analyzed an example of this process in a little study on Immermann's "Chiliastische Sonette," *Kleine Schriften*, II, 136–47 (*GW*, IX).

13 [See my "Mythos und Vernunft," *Kleine Schriften*, IV, 48–53 (*GW*, VIII) and "Mythos und Wissenschaft," *GW*, VIII.]

14 Horkheimer and Adorno seem to me right in their analysis of the "dialectic of the Enlightenment" (although I must regard the application of sociological concepts such as "bourgeois" to Odysseus as a failure of historical reflection, if not, indeed, a confusion of Homer with Johann Heinrich Voss [author of the standard German translation of Homer], who had already been criticized by Goethe.

15 H. Leo, *Studien und Skizzen zu einer Naturlehre des Staates* (1833).

16 Cf. the reflections on this important question by G. von Lukács in his *History and Class Consciousness*, tr. Rodney Livingstone (1923; Cambridge, Mass.: MIT Press, 1971).

17 Rousseau, *Discourse on the Origin of Inequality*.

18 Cf. my "Plato and the Poets," in *Dialogue and Dialectic: Eight Hermeneutical Studies on Plato*, tr. P. Christopher Smith (New Haven: Yale University Press, 1980), pp. 54f.

19 Walch, *Philosophisches Lexicon* (1726), p.1013.

20 Walch, op. cit., pp. 1006ff. under the entry "Freiheit zu gedenken." See p.273 above.

21 Schleiermacher, *Werke*, I, part 7, 31.

22 (It seems to me that the tendency to acknowledge authority, as for instance in Karl Jaspers, *Von der Wahrheit*, pp. 766ff., and Gerhard Krüger, *Freiheit und Weltverwaltung*, pp. 231ff., lacks an intelligible basis so long as this proposition is not acknowledged.) The notorious statement, "The party (or the Leader) is always right" is not wrong because it claims that a certain leadership is superior, but because it serves to shield the leadership, by a dictatorial decree, from any criticism that might be true. True authority does not have to be authoritarian. [This issue has meanwhile been much debated, particularly in my exchange with Jürgen Habermas. See *Hermeneutik und Ideologiekritik*, ed. Jürgen Habermas (Frankfurt, 1977) and my lecture at Solothurn, "Über den Zusammenhang von Autorität und kritischer Freiheit," *Schweizer Archiv für Neurologie, Neurochirurgie und Psychiatrie*, 133 (1983), 11–16. Arnold Gehlen especially has worked out the role of institutions.]

23 Cf. Aristotle, *Nichomachean Ethics*, X, 10.

24 I don't agree with Scheler that the preconscious pressure of tradition decreases as historical study proceeds (*Stellung des Menschen im Kosmos*, p.37). The independence of historical study implied in this view seems to me a liberal fiction of a sort that Scheler is generally able to see through. (Cf. similarly in his *Nachlass*, I, 228ff., where he affirms his faith in enlightenment through historical study or sociology of knowledge.)

25 [The question appears much more complicated since Thomas Kuhn's *The Structure of Scientific Revolutions* (Chicago, 1963) and *The Essential Tension: Selected Studies in Scientific Tradition and Change* (Chicago, 1977).]

26 [That K.–G. Faber in his thorough discussion in *Theorie der Geschichtswissenschaft* (2nd ed., Munich, 1972), p.25, cannot quote this statement without placing an ironic exclamation mark after "constituted" obliges me to ask how else one defines a "historical fact"?]

27 [Now, in the light of the past three decades of work in the philosophy of science, I willingly acknowledge that even this formulation is too undifferentiated.]

28 [See my "Zwischen Phänomenologie und Dialektik: Versuch einer Selbstkritik," *GW*, II.]

29 [On the concept of "style," see Part One, n. 67, and Appendix I below.]

30 The congress at Naumburg on the classical (1930), which was completely dominated by Werner Jaeger, is as much an example of this as the founding of the periodical *Die Antike*. Cf. *Das Problem des Klassischen und die Antike* (1931).

31 Cf. the legitimate criticism that A. Körte made of the Naumburg lecture by J. Stroux, in the *Berichte der Sächsischen Akademie der Wissenschaften*, 86 (1934), and my note in *Gnomon*, 11 (1935), 612f. [repr. in *GW*, V, 350–53].

32 Thus Tacitus' *Dialogue on the Orators* rightly received special attention in the Naumburg discussions on the classical. The reasons for the decline of rhetoric

include the recognition of its former greatness, i.e., a normative awareness. Bruno Snell is correct when he points out that the historical stylistic concepts of "baroque," "archaic," etc. all presuppose a relation to the normative concept of the classical and have only gradually lost their pejorative sense ("Wesen und Wirklichkeit des Menschen," *Festschrift für H. Plessner*, pp. 333ff.).

33 Hegel, *Ästhetik*, II, 3.

34 Friedrich Schlegel, *Fragmente*, ed. Minor, no. 20, draws the hermeneutical consequence: "A classical work of literature is one that can never be completely understood. But it must also be one from which those who are educated and educating themselves must always desire to learn more."

35 [Here especially, see my "Zwischen Phänomenologie und Dialektik: Versuch einer Selbstkritik," *GW*, II, 3ff.]

36 Pp. 195, 232.

37 [See G. Ripanti, *Agostino teoretico del'interpretazione* (Brescia, 1980).]

38 [See M. Flacius, *Clavis Scripturae sacrae seu de Sermone sacrarum literarum*, book II (1676).]

39 In a lecture on aesthetic judgment at a conference in Venice in 1958 I tried to show that it too, like historical judgment, is secondary in character and confirms the "anticipation of completeness." ("On the Problematic Character of Aesthetic Consciousness," tr. E. Kelly, *Graduate Faculty Philosophy Journal* (New School for Social Research), 9 (1982), 31–40.)

40 There is one exception to this anticipation of completeness, namely the case of writing that is presenting something in disguise, e.g., a *roman à clef*. This presents one of the most difficult hermeneutical problems (cf. the interesting remarks by Leo Strauss in *Persecution and the Art of Writing*). This exceptional hermeneutical case is of special significance, in that it goes beyond interpretation of meaning in the same way as when historical source criticism goes back behind the tradition. Although the task here is not a historical, but a hermeneutical one, it can be performed only by using understanding of the subject matter as a key to discover what is behind the disguise—just as in conversation we understand irony to the extent to which we are in agreement with the other person on the subject matter. Thus the apparent exception confirms that understanding involves agreement. [I doubt that Strauss is right in the way he carries out his theory, for instance in his discussion of Spinoza. Dissembling meaning implies a high degree of consciousness. Accommodation, conforming, and so on do not have to occur consciously. In my view, Strauss did not sufficiently see this. See op. cit., pp. 223ff. and my "Hermeneutics and Historicism," Supplement I below. These problems have meanwhile been much disputed, in my view, on too narrowly semantic a basis. See Donald Davidson, *Inquiries into Truth and Interpretation* (Oxford, 1984).]

41 Cf. p.182 above.

42 Cf. p.182 above.

43 *Nicomachean Ethics*, I, 7.

44 [I have here softened the original text ("It is only temporal distance that can solve ... "): it is distance, not only temporal distance, that makes this hermeneutic problem solvable. See also *GW*, II, 64.]

45 Pp. 289 and 293 above.

46 [Here constantly arises the danger of "appropriating" the other person in one's own understanding and thereby failing to recognize his or her otherness.]

47 The structure of the concept of situation has been illuminated chiefly by Karl Jaspers, *Die geistige Situation der Zeit*, and Erich Rothacker. [See my "Was ist Wahrheit," *Kleine Schriften*, I, 46–58, esp. pp. 55ff. (*GW*, II, 44ff.)]

48 [H. Kuhn already referred to this in "The Phenomenological Concept of 'Horizon,'" in *Philosophical Essays in Memory of Husserl*, ed. Martin Farber (Cambridge, 1940), pp. 106–23. See my observations on "horizon" above, pp. 236ff.]

49 [I already discussed the moral aspect of this topic in my 1943 essay "Das Problem der Geschichte in der neueren deutschen Philosophie," *Kleine Schriften*, I, 1–10 (*GW*, II, 27–36). It will also be more emphatically stressed in what follows.]

50 Nietzsche, *Untimely Meditations*, II, at the beginning.

51 Rambach's *Institutiones hermeneuticae sacrae* (1723) are known to me in the compilation by Morus. There we read: *Solemus autem intelligendi explicandique subtilitatem (soliditatem vulgo)*.

52 [Unfortunately, this plain statement is often overlooked by both sides in debates over hermeneutics.]

53 Cf. Emilio Betti's treatise, cited above, n. 172, p. 265 and his monumental work, *Teoria generale dell'interpretazione* (2 vol., Milan, 1955). [See "Hermeneutics and Historicism," Supplement I below and my "Emilio Betti und das idealistische Erbe," *Quaderni Fiorentini*, 7 (1978), 5–11 (*GW*, IV).]

54 Cf. the analysis of the ontology of the work of art in Part One, pp. 102ff. above.

55 Cf. the distinctions in Max Scheler, *Wissen und Bildung* (1927), p.26.

56 [In many respects, the discussion here is much too restricted to the special situation of the historical human sciences and "being that is oriented to a text." Only in Part Three have I succeeded in broadening the issue to language and dialogue, though in fact I have had it constantly in view; and consequently, only there have I grasped in a fundamental way the notions of distance and otherness. See also pp. 296f.]

57 See my "Zwischen Phänomenologie und Dialektik: Versuch einer Selbstkritik," *GW*, II, and its reference on p.12 to my "Praktisches Wissen," *GW*, V, 230–48.]

58 Cf. pp. 13ff. and 28 above.

59 *Nicomachean Ethics*, I, 4. [See my *The Idea of the Good in Platonic-Aristotelian Philosophy*, tr. P. Christopher Smith (New Haven: Yale University Press, 1986).]

60 Cf. *Nicomachean Ethics*, I, 7 and II, 2.

61 The final chapter of the *Nicomachean Ethics* gives the fullest expression to this requirement and thus forms the transition to the *Politics*.

62 Here we shall be following *Nicomachean Ethics*, VI, unless otherwise noted. [An analysis of this book written in 1930 was first published under the title "Praktisches Wissen" in *GW*, V, 230–48.]

63 Plato, *Apology*, 22cd.

64 *Nicomachean Ethics*, VI, 8, 1141 b 33, 1142 a 30; *Eudemean Ethics*, VIII, 2, 1246 b 36. [In my view, one misses the essential methodological unity of ethics and politics in Aristotle if one does not include here *politike phronesis* (as Gauthier fails to do in the new introduction to the 2nd ed. of his commentary on the *Nicomachean Ethics* [Louvain, 1970]). See my review, reprinted in *GW*, VI, 304–06.]

65 *Werke* (1832), XIV, 341.

66 *Nicomachean Ethics*, VI, 8.

67 *Nicomachean Ethics*, V, 14.

68 *Lex superior preferenda est inferiori*, writes Melanchthon in his explanation of the *ratio* of *epieikeia* (in the earliest version of Melanchthon's *Ethics*, ed. H. Heineck [Berlin, 1893], p.29).

69 Above, pp. 34ff.

70 *Ideo adhibenda est ad omnes leges interpretatio quae flectat eas ad humaniorem ac leniorem sententiam* (Melanchthon, 29): "Therefore an interpretation should be applied to every law that would bend it to more humane and lenient decisions."

71 Cf. the excellent critique by H. Kuhn of Leo Strauss' *Naturrecht und Geschichte* (1953), in the *Zeitschrift für Politik*, 3, no. 4 (1956).

72 *Nicomachean Ethics*, V, 10. The distinction itself originates, of course, with the Sophists, but it loses its destructive meaning through Plato's restriction of the *logos*, and its positive meaning in law becomes clear only in Plato's *Statesman*, 294ff., and in Aristotle.

73 The train of thought in the parallel place in the *Magna Moralia*, I, 33, 1194 b 30–95 a 7, cannot be understood unless one does this: "Do not suppose that if things change owing to our use, there is not therefore a natural justice; because there is" (tr. Ross).

74 Cf. Melanchthon, op. cit., p.28.

75 Aristotle says in general that *phronesis* is concerned with the means (*ta pros to telos*) and not with the *telos* itself. It is probably the contrast with the Platonic doctrine of the idea of the good that makes him emphasize that. However, *phronesis* is not simply the capacity to make the right choice of means, but is

itself a moral *hexis* that also sees the *telos* toward which the person acting is aiming with his moral being. This emerges clearly from its place within the system of Aristotle's ethics. Cf. in particular *Nicomachean Ethics*, VI, 10, 1142 b 33, 1140 b 13, 1141 b 15. I was glad to see that H. Kuhn in his essay "Die Gegenwart der Griechen," *Festschrift* for H.–G. Gadamer (1960), pp. 134ff., now does full justice to this situation, although he tries to demonstrate that there is an ultimate "preferential choice" that makes Aristotle lag behind Plato. [The Latin translation of *phronesis* as *prudentia* abetted the failure to see the real state of affairs, a failure which still haunts contemporary "deontic" logic. In my review of recent work in ethics, *Philosophische Rundschau*, 32 (1985), 1–26, the noteworthy exception was T. Engberg-Pederson, *Aristotle's Theory of Moral Insight* (Oxford, 1983).]

76 *Nicomachean Ethics*, VI, 9, 1142 a 25ff.

77 Cf. pp. 350ff. below.

78 *sunesis* ("fellow-feeling, forbearance, forgiveness"), *Nicomachean Ethics*, VI, 11.

79 [I have slightly revised the text here. The phrase *allou legoutos* (1145 a 15) surely means only that it is not a case in which *I* must act. I can listen with understanding when another relates something even if I am not going to offer advice.]

80 *gnome, syngnome*.

81 *Nicomachean Ethics*, VI, 13, 1144 a 23ff.

82 He is a *panourgos*, i.e., he is capable of anything.

83 In addition to the works cited in nn. 172 and 53 above are many shorter articles. [Cf. also Supplement I below, "Hermeneutics and Historicism," and my essay "Emilio Betti und das idealistische Erbe," in *Quaderni Fiorentini*, 7 (1978), 5–11.]

84 Is it just an accident that Schleiermacher's lecture on hermeneutics first appeared in a posthumous edition two years before Savigny's book? It would be worth making a special study of hermeneutical theory in Savigny, an area that Forsthoff left out in his study. On Savigny, see Franz Wieacker's note in *Gründer und Bewahrer*, p.110.

85 "Recht und Sprache," *Abhandlungen der Königsberger Gelehrten Gesellschaft* (1940).

86 Betti, op. cit., n. 62 a.

87 Above, p.251 and passim.

88 Walch, p.158. [Enlightened despotism gives the appearance that the "ruler" interprets his command in such a way that the law is not superseded, but reinterpreted, so that it corresponds with his will without needing to observe any rule of explanation.]

89 The importance of this concretizing of the law is so central to jurisprudence that there is a vast literature on the subject. Cf. Karl Engisch, *Die Idee der Konkretisierung, Abhandlungen der Heidelberger Akademie* (1953). [See also his more recent works, *Methoden der Rechtswissenschaft* (Munich, 1972), pp. 39–80, and *Recht und Sittlichkeit: Hauptthemen der Rechtsphilosophie* (Munich, 1971).]

90 Cf. F. Wieacker, who has investigated the problem of an extralegal order of law from the point of view of the art of giving legal judgment and of the elements that determine it: *Gesetz und Richterkunst* (1957).

91 Over and above the aspect discussed here, the overcoming of the hermeneutics of historicism, which is the general purpose of the present investigation, has positive consequences for theology, which seem to approach the views of the theologians Ernst Fuchs and Gerhard Ebeling (Fuchs, *Hermeneutik* [2nd ed., 1960]; Ebeling, "Hermeneutik," in *Religion in Geschichte und Gegenwart*, 3rd ed.). [See also my "On the Problem of Self-Understanding," in *Philosophical Hermeneutics*, tr. David E. Linge (Berkeley: University of California Press, 1976), pp. 44–58.]

92 *Glauben und Verstehen*, II, 231.

93 *Der junge Dilthey*, p.94.

94 Cf. the essay by H. Patzer, "Der Humanismus als Methodenproblem der klassischen Philologie," *Studium Generale*, 1 (1947), 84–92.

95 [The expression "reflective philosophy" was coined by Hegel against Jacobi, Kant, and Fichte. It is used already in "Glauben und Wissen," but as a "reflective philosophy of subjectivity." Hegel himself counterposes it to the reflection of *reason*.]

96 Cf. p.298 above.

97 Cf. *Encyclopedia*, §60.

98 [I have given a detailed interpretation of the dialectic of recognition (*Phenomenology of Mind*, IV, A: "Independence and Dependence of Self-Consciousness: Lordship and Bondage") in *Hegel's Dialectic: Five Hermeneutical Studies*, tr. P. Christopher Smith (New Haven: Yale University Press, 1976), ch. 3.]

99 This is evident in Marxist literature even today. Cf. the energetic elaboration of this point in Jürgen Habermas' "Zur philosophischen Diskussion um Marx und den Marxismus," *Philosophische Rundschau*, 5, nos. 3/4 (1957), 183ff.

100 Heidegger, *Sein und Zeit*, p.229.

101 This is the meaning of the difficult passage 343cd, for the authorship of which those who deny the authenticity of the *Seventh Letter* have to assume a second, nameless Plato. [See my detailed study, "Dialectic and Sophism in Plato's *Seventh Letter*," in *Dialogue and Dialectic: Eight Hermeneutical Studies on Plato*, tr. P. Christopher Smith (New Haven: Yale University Press, 1980), pp. 93–123.]

102 *Meno*, 80d ff.

103 Cf. his account in *Erfahrung und Urteil*, p.42, and in his great work, *Die Krisis der europäischen Wissenschaften und die transzendentale Phänomenologie*, pp. 48ff., 130ff. [What is said here is based on a quite different concept of "founding." Phenomenologically considered, "pure" perception seems to me a mere construction, which corresponds to the derivative concept of "presence-at-hand"—and consequently appears as a position left over from the latter's idealization in the theory of science.]

104 *Husserliana*, VI, loc. cit. See above pp. 237f.

105 Francis Bacon, *Novum Organum*, I, 26ff.

106 Op. cit., I, 20f., 104.

107 Op. cit., I, 19ff.

108 Op. cit.; cf. in particular the *distributio operis*.

109 Op. cit., I, 22, 28.

110 Op. cit. I, 38ff.

111 *Posterior Analytics*, II, 19, 99ff.

112 Plutarch, *De fortuna*, III, 98 F = Diels, *Fragmente der Vorsokratiker*, Anaxagoras B 21 b.

113 Aeschylus, *Prometheus*, 461.

114 *Phaedo*, 96.

115 [This parallels Karl Popper's paired concepts of "trial and error"—with the restriction that those concepts all too often proceed from the deliberate, and all too rarely from the suffering side of human experience of life. Or at least that is so, insofar as one looks only to the "logic of scientific discovery," but not if one thinks of the logic actually effective in human experience of life.]

116 Hegel, *Phänomenologie*, "Introduction," ed. Hoffmeister, p.73.

117 Heidegger, *Hegel's Concept of Experience* (New York: Harper and Row, 1970).

118 *Holzwege* (Frankfurt, 1950), p.169.

119 Hegel, *Encyclopedia*, §7.

120 In his informative study, "Leid und Erfahrung," *Akademie der Wissenschaften und der Literatur in Mainz*, no. 5 (1956), H. Dörrie investigated the origin of the rhyme *pathos mathos* in proverbial modes of expression. He considers that the original meaning of the proverb was that only the foolish man has to suffer in order to become wise, whereas the wise man is more prudent. The religious element that Aeschylus gives to the phrase is a later development. This is not very convincing in view of the fact that the myth that Aeschylus takes up speaks of the shortsightedness of the human race, and not just of individual fools. Moreover, the limits of human prediction are such an early and human experience and so closely connected with the universal human experience of suffering that we can hardly believe that this insight remained hidden in a simple little proverb until Aeschylus discovered it. [On this

Aschylean motif, see more recently Heinz Neiztel, *Gymnasium*, 87 (1980), 283ff. According to him, what is meant is punishment for *hybris*, as in: "Who refuses to listen, must be made to feel."]

121 Cf. our remarks on this in the "Introduction" above.

122 Cf. the outstanding analysis of this reflective dialectic of I and Thou in Karl Löwith, *Das Individuum in der Rolle des Mitmenschen* (1928) and my review of it in *Logos*, 18 (1929), 436–40 [*GW*, IV].

123 *Thus Spake Zarathustra*, II, "Of self-overcoming."

124 Cf. the argument concerning the form of discourse in the *Protagoras*, 335ff.

125 *Metaphysics*, XIII, 4, 1078 b 25ff.

126 105 b 23.

127 H. Maier, *Syllogistik des Aristoteles*, II, 2, 168.

128 Cf. chiefly his article "Syllogistik" in Pauly-Wissowa, *Real-Encyclopädie für Altertumswissenschaft*.

129 Aristotle, *Metaphysics*, 1004 b 25: *esti de he dialektike peirastike*. Here we can already discern the idiom of being led, which is the real sense of dialectic, in that the testing of an opinion gives it the chance to conquer and hence puts one's own previous opinion at risk.

130 See above pp. 291f., 331f.

131 Cf. Collingwood's *Autobiography*, which at my suggestion was published in German translation as *Denken*, pp. 30ff., as well as Joachim Finkeldei, *Grund und Wesen des Fragens* (unpub. diss., Heidelberg, 1954). A similar position is adopted by Croce (who influenced Collingwood) in his *Logic as Science of the Pure Concept*, tr. Ainsley (London, 1917), German tr., pp. 135ff., where he understands every definition as an answer to a question and hence historical.

132 Cf. pp. 292–93f. above, and my critique of Guardini, *Kleine Schriften*, II, 178–87 (*GW*, IX), where I said: "All criticism of literature is always the self-criticism of interpretation."

133 Collingwood, *An Autobiography* (Oxford: Galaxy ed., 1970), p.70.

134 There are some good observations on this subject in Erich Seeberg's "Zum Problem der pneumatischen Exegese," in *Festschrift* for Sellin, pp. 127ff. [repr. in *Die Hermeneutik und die Wissenschaften*, ed. H.–G. Gadamer and G. Boehm (Frankfurt, 1978), pp. 272–82].

135 See pp. 182, 294 above and passim.

136 Pp. 216f. and 277f. above.

137 See the account of this wrong turning of the historical in my analysis above, pp. 180ff., of Spinoza's *Theologico-Political Treatise*.

138 Cf. pp. 304ff. above.

139 Pp. 355ff. above.

140 Plato, *Seventh Letter*, 344b.

141 Aristotle, *Topics*, I, 11.

142 *Critique of Pure Reason,* A 321ff.

143 Nicolai Hartmann, in his essay "Der philosophische Gedanke und seine Geschichte," *Abhandlungen der preussischen Akademie der Wissenschaften* (1936), no. 5 (repr. in Hartmann, *Kleine Schriften,* II, 1–47), rightly pointed out that the important thing is to realize once more in our own minds what the great thinkers realized. But when, in order to hold something fixed against the inroads of historicism, he distinguished between the constancy of what the "real problems are concerned with" and the changing nature of the way in which they have to be both asked and answered, he failed to see that neither "change," nor "constancy," the antithesis of "problem" and "system," nor the criterion of "achievements" is consonant with the character of philosophy as knowledge. When he wrote that "only when the individual avails himself of the enormous intellectual experience of the centuries, and his own experience is based on what he has recognized and what has been well tried . . . , can that knowledge be sure of its own further progress" (p. 18), he interpreted the "systematic acquaintance with the problems" according to the model of an experimental science and a progress of knowledge that falls far short of the complicated interpenetration of tradition and history that we have seen in hermeneutical consciousness.

144 Cf. my "Was ist Wahrheit?," *Kleine Schriften,* I, 46–58 (*GW,* II, 44–56).

PART THREE
The Ontological Shift of Hermeneutics Guided
by Language

*Everything presupposed in hermeneutics
is but language.*

F. Schleiermacher

5
Language and Hermeneutics

1 LANGUAGE AS THE MEDIUM OF HERMENEUTIC EXPERIENCE

We say that we "conduct" a conversation, but the more genuine a conversation is, the less its conduct lies within the will of either partner. Thus a genuine conversation is never the one that we wanted to conduct. Rather, it is generally more correct to say that we fall into conversation, or even that we become involved in it. The way one word follows another, with the conversation taking its own twists and reaching its own conclusion, may well be conducted in some way, but the partners conversing are far less the leaders of it than the led. No one knows in advance what will "come out" of a conversation. Understanding or its failure is like an event that happens to us. Thus we can say that something was a good conversation or that it was ill fated. All this shows that a conversation has a spirit of its own, and that the language in which it is conducted bears its own truth within it—i.e., that it allows something to "emerge" which henceforth exists.

In our analysis of romantic hermeneutics we have already seen that understanding is not based on transposing oneself into another person, on one person's immediate participation with another. To understand what a person says is, as we saw, to come to an understanding about the subject matter, not to get inside another person and relive his experiences (Erlebnisse). We emphasized that the experience (Erfahrung) of meaning that takes place in understanding always includes application. Now we are to note *that this whole process is verbal*. It is not for nothing that the special problematic of understanding and the attempt to master it as an art—the concern of hermeneutics—belongs traditionally to the sphere of grammar and rhetoric. Language is the medium in which substantive understanding and agreement take place between two people.

In situations where coming to an understanding is disrupted or impeded, we first become conscious of the conditions of all understanding. Thus the verbal process whereby a conversation in two different languages is made possible through translation is especially informative. Here the translator must translate the meaning to be understood into the context in which the other speaker lives. This does not, of course, mean that he is at liberty to falsify the meaning of what the other person says. Rather, the meaning must be preserved, but since it must be understood within a new language world, it must establish its validity within it in a new way. Thus every translation is at the same time an interpretation. We can even say that the translation is the culmination of the interpretation that the translator has made of the words given him.

The example of translation, then, makes us aware that language as the medium of understanding must be consciously created by an explicit mediation. This kind of explicit process is undoubtedly not the norm in a conversation. Nor is translation the norm in the way we approach a foreign language. Rather, having to rely on translation is tantamount to two people giving up their independent authority. Where a translation is necessary, the gap between the spirit of the original words and that of their reproduction must be taken into account. It is a gap that can never be completely closed. But in these cases understanding does not really take place between the partners of the conversation, but between the inter-preters, who can really have an encounter in a common world of understanding. (It is well known that nothing is more difficult than a dialogue in two different languages in which one person speaks one and the other person the other, each understanding the other's language but not speaking it. As if impelled by a higher force, one of the languages always tries to establish itself over the other as the medium of under-standing.)

Where there is understanding, there is not translation but speech. To understand a foreign language means that we do not need to translate it into our own. When we really master a language, then no translation is necessary—in fact, any translation seems impossible. Understanding how to speak is not yet of itself real understanding and does not involve an interpretive process; it is an accomplishment of life. For you understand a language by living in it—a statement that is true, as we know, not only of living but dead languages as well. Thus the hermeneutical problem concerns not the correct mastery of language but coming to a proper understanding about the subject matter, which takes place in the medium of language. Every language can be learned so perfectly that using it no longer means translating from or into one's native tongue, but thinking in the foreign language. Mastering the language is a necessary precondition for coming to an understanding in a conversation. Every conversation obviously presupposes that the two speakers speak the same language. Only when two people can make themselves understood through language by talking together can the problem of understanding and agreement even be raised. Having to depend on an interpreter's translation is an extreme case that doubles the hermeneutical process, namely the conversation: there is one conversation between the interpreter and the other, and a second between the interpreter and oneself.

Conversation is a process of coming to an understanding. Thus it belongs to every true conversation that each person opens himself to the other, truly accepts his point of view as valid and transposes himself into the other to such an extent that he understands not the particular individual but what he says. What is to be grasped is the substantive rightness of his opinion, so that we can be at one with each other on the subject. Thus we do not relate the other's opinion to him but to our own opinions and views. Where a person is concerned with the other as individuality—e.g., in a therapeutic conversation or the interrogation of a man accused of a crime—this is not really a situation in which two people are trying to come to an understanding.[1]

Everything we have said characterizing the situation of two people coming to an understanding in conversation has a genuine application to hermeneutics, which is concerned with *understanding texts*. Let us again start by considering the extreme case of translation from a foreign language. Here no one can doubt that the translation of a text, however much the translator may have dwelt with and empathized with his author, cannot be simply a re-awakening of the original process in the writer's mind; rather, it is necessarily a re-creation of the text guided by the way the translator understands what it says. No one can doubt that what we are dealing with here is interpretation, and not simply reproduction. A new light falls on the text from the other language and for the reader of it. The requirement that a translation be faithful cannot remove the fundamental gulf between the two languages. However faithful we try to be, we have to make difficult decisions. In our translation if we want to emphasize a feature of the original that is important to us, then we can do so only by playing down or entirely suppressing other features. But this is precisely the activity that we call interpretation. Translation, like all interpretation, is a highlighting. A translator must understand that highlighting is part of his task. Obviously he must not leave open whatever is not clear to him. He must show his colors. Yet there are borderline cases in the original (and for the "original reader") where something is in fact unclear. But precisely these hermeneutical borderline cases show the straits in which the translator constantly finds himself. Here he must resign himself. He must state clearly how he understands. But since he is always in the position of not really being able to express all the dimensions of his text, he must make a constant renunciation. Every translation that takes its task seriously is at once clearer and flatter than the original. Even if it is a masterly re-creation, it must lack some of the overtones that vibrate in the original. (In rare cases of masterly re-creation the loss can be made good or even mean a gain—think, for example, of how Baudelaire's *Les fleurs du mal* seems to acquire an odd new vigor in Stefan George's version.)

The translator is often painfully aware of his inevitable distance from the original. His dealing with the text is like the effort to come to an understanding in conversation. But translating is like an especially laborious process of understanding, in which one views the distance between one's own opinion and its contrary as ultimately unbridgeable. And, as in conversation, when there are such unbridgeable differences, a compromise can sometimes be achieved in the to and fro of dialogue, so in the to and fro of weighing and balancing possibilities, the translator will seek the best solution—a solution that can never be more than a compromise. As one tries in conversation to transpose oneself into the other person in order to understand his point of view, so also does the translator try to transpose himself completely into his author. But doing so does not automatically mean that understanding is achieved in a conversation, nor for the translator does such transposition mean success in re-creating the meaning. The structures are clearly analogous. Reaching an understanding in conversation presupposes that both partners are ready for it and are trying to recognize the full value of what is alien and opposed to them. If this happens mutually, and each of the partners, while simultaneously holding on to his own arguments, weighs the counterarguments, it is finally possible to achieve—in an imperceptible but not arbitrary reciprocal translation of the other's position (we call this an exchange of views)—a common diction and a common dictum. Similarly, the translator must preserve the character of his own language, the language into which he is translating, while still recognizing the value of the alien, even antagonistic character of the text and its expression. Perhaps, however, this description of the translator's activity is too truncated. Even in these extreme situations where it is necessary to translate from one language into another, the subject matter can scarcely be separated from the language. Only that translator can truly re-create who brings into language the subject matter that the text points to; but this means finding a language that is not only his but is also proportionate to the original.[2] The situation of the translator and that of the interpreter are fundamentally the same.

In bridging the gulf between languages, the translator clearly exemplifies the reciprocal relationship that exists between interpreter and text, and that corresponds to the reciprocity involved in reaching an understanding in conversation. For every translator is an interpreter. The fact that a foreign language is being translated means that this is simply an extreme case of hermeneutical difficulty—i.e., of alienness and its conquest. In fact all the "objects" with which traditional hermeneutics is concerned are alien in the same unequivocally defined sense. The translator's task of re-creation differs only in degree, not in kind, from the general hermeneutical task that any text presents.

This is not to say, of course, that the hermeneutic situation in regard to texts is exactly the same as that between two people in conversation. Texts are "enduringly fixed expressions of life"[3] that are to be understood; and that means that one partner in the hermeneutical conversation, the text, speaks only through the other partner, the interpreter. Only through him are the written marks changed back into meaning. Nevertheless, in being changed back by understanding, the subject matter of which the text speaks itself finds expression. It is like a real conversation in that the common subject matter is what binds the two partners, the text and the interpreter, to each other. When a translator interprets a conversation, he can make mutual understanding possible only if he participates in the subject under discussion; so also in relation to a text it is indispensable that the interpreter participate in its meaning.

Thus it is perfectly legitimate to speak of a *hermeneutical conversation*. But from this it follows that hermeneutical conversation, like real conversation, finds a common language, and that finding a common language is not, any more than in real conversation, preparing a tool for the purpose of reaching understanding but, rather, coincides with the very act of understanding and reaching agreement. Even between the partners of this "conversation" a communication like that between two people takes place that is more than mere accommodation. The text brings a subject matter into language, but that it does so is ultimately the achievement of the interpreter. Both have a share in it.

Hence the meaning of a text is not to be compared with an immovably and obstinately fixed point of view that suggests only one question to the person trying to understand it, namely how the other person could have arrived at such an absurd opinion. In this sense understanding is certainly not concerned with "understanding historically"—i.e., reconstructing the way the text came into being. Rather, one intends to *understand the text itself*. But this means that the interpreter's own thoughts too have gone into re-awakening the text's meaning. In this the interpreter's own horizon is decisive, yet not as a personal standpoint that he maintains or enforces, but more as an opinion and a possibility that one brings into play and puts at risk, and that helps one truly to make one's own what the text says. I have described this above as a "fusion of horizons." We can now see that this is what takes place in conversation, in which something is expressed that is not only mine or my author's, but common.

We are indebted to German romanticism for disclosing the systematic significance of the verbal nature of conversation for all understanding. It has taught us that understanding and interpretation are ultimately the same thing. As we have seen, this insight elevates the idea of interpretation from the merely occasional and pedagogical significance it had in the eighteenth century to a systematic position, as indicated by the key importance that the problem of language has acquired in philosophical inquiry.

Since the romantic period we can no longer hold the view that, in the absence of immediate understanding, interpretive ideas are drawn, as needed, out of a linguistic storeroom where they are lying ready. *Rather, language is the universal medium in which understanding occurs. Understanding occurs in interpreting.* This statement does not mean that there is no special problem of expression. The difference between the language of a text and the language of the interpreter, or the gulf that separates the translator from the original, is not merely a secondary question. On the contrary, the fact is that the problems of verbal expression are themselves problems of understanding. All understanding is interpretation, and all interpretation takes place in the medium of a language that allows the object to come into words and yet is at the same time the interpreter's own language.

Thus the hermeneutical phenomenon proves to be a special case of the general relationship between thinking and speaking, whose enigmatic intimacy conceals the role of language in thought. Like conversation, interpretation is a circle closed by the dialectic of question and answer. It is a genuine historical life comportment achieved through the medium of language, and we can call it a conversation with respect to the interpretation of texts as well. The linguisticality of understanding is *the concretion of historically effected consciousness*.

The essential relation between language and understanding is seen primarily in the fact that the essence of tradition is to exist in the medium of language, so that the preferred *object* of interpretation is a verbal one.

(A) LANGUAGE AS DETERMINATION OF THE HERMENEUTIC OBJECT

The fact that tradition is essentially verbal in character has consequences for hermeneutics. The understanding of verbal tradition retains special priority over all other tradition. Linguistic tradition may have less perceptual immediacy than monuments of plastic art. Its lack of immediacy, however, is not a defect; rather, this apparent lack, the abstract alienness of all "texts," uniquely expresses the fact that everything in language belongs to the process of understanding. Linguistic tradition is tradition in the proper sense of the word—i.e., something handed down. It is not just something left over, to be investigated and interpreted as a remnant of the past. What has come down to us by way of verbal tradition is not left over but given to us, told us—whether through direct retelling, in which myth, legend, and custom have their life, or through written tradition, whose signs are, as it were, immediately clear to every reader who can read them.

The full hermeneutical significance of the fact that tradition is essentially verbal becomes clear in the case of a *written* tradition. The detachability of language from speaking derives from the fact that it can be written. In the form of writing, all tradition is contemporaneous with each present time. Moreover, it involves a unique co-existence of past and present, insofar as present consciousness has the possibility of a free access to everything handed down in writing. No longer dependent on retelling, which mediates past knowledge with the present, understanding consciousness acquires—through its immediate access to literary tradition—a genuine opportunity to change and widen its horizon, and thus enrich its world by a whole new and deeper dimension. The appropriation of literary tradition

391

even surpasses the experience connected with the adventure of traveling and being immersed in the world of a foreign language. At every moment the reader who studies a foreign language and literature retains the possibility of free movement back to himself, and thus is at once both here and there.

A written tradition is not a fragment of a past world, but has already raised itself beyond this into the sphere of the meaning that it expresses. The ideality of the word is what raises everything linguistic beyond the finitude and transience that characterize other remnants of past existence. It is not this document, as a piece of the past, that is the bearer of tradition but the continuity of memory. Through it tradition becomes part of our own world, and thus what it communicates can be stated immediately. Where we have a written tradition, we are not just told a particular thing; a past humanity itself becomes present to us in its general relation to the world. That is why our understanding remains curiously unsure and fragmentary when we have no written tradition of a culture but only dumb monuments, and we do not call this information about the past "history." Texts, on the other hand, always express a whole. Meaningless strokes that seem strange and incomprehensible prove suddenly intelligible in every detail when they can be interpreted as writing—so much so that even the arbitrariness of a corrupt text can be corrected if the context as a whole is understood.

Thus written texts present the real hermeneutical task. Writing is self-alienation. Overcoming it, reading the text, is thus the highest task of understanding. Even the pure signs of an inscription can be seen properly and articulated correctly only if the text can be transformed back into language. As we have said, however, this transformation always establishes a relationship to what is meant, to the subject matter being discussed. Here the process of understanding moves entirely in a sphere of meaning mediated by the verbal tradition. Thus in the case of an inscription the hermeneutical task starts only after it has been deciphered (presumably correctly). Only in an extended sense do non-literary monuments present a hermeneutical task, for they cannot be understood of themselves. What they mean is a question of their interpretation, not of deciphering and understanding the wording of a text.

In writing, language gains its true ideality, for in encountering a written tradition understanding consciousness acquires its full sovereignty. Its being does not depend on anything. Thus reading consciousness is in potential possession of its history. It is not for nothing that with the emergence of a literary culture the idea of "philology," "love of speech," was transferred entirely to the all-embracing art of reading, losing its original connection with the cultivation of speech and argument. A reading consciousness is necessarily a historical consciousness and communicates freely with historical tradition. Thus it is historically legitimate to say with Hegel that history begins with the emergence of a will to hand things down, "to make memory last."[4] Writing is no mere accident or mere supplement that qualitatively changes nothing in the course of oral tradition. Certainly, there can be a will to make things continue, a will to permanence, without writing. But only a written tradition can detach itself from the mere continuance of the vestiges of past life, remnants from which one human being can by inference piece out another's existence.

The tradition of inscriptions has never shared in the free form of tradition that we call literature, since it depends on the existence of the remains, whether of stone or whatever material. But it is true of everything that has come down to us by being written down that here a will to permanence has created the unique forms of continuance that we call literature. It does not present us with only a stock of memorials and signs. Rather, literature has acquired its own contemporaneity with every present. To understand it does not mean primarily to reason one's way back into the past, but to have a present involvement in what is said. It is not really a relationship between persons, between the reader and the author (who is perhaps quite unknown), but about sharing in what the text shares with us. The meaning of what is said is, when we understand it, quite independent of whether the traditionary text gives us a picture of the author and of whether or not we want to interpret it as a historical source.

Let us here recall that the task of hermeneutics was first and foremost the understanding of texts. Schleiermacher was the first to downplay the importance of writing for the hermeneutical problem because he saw that the problem of understanding was raised—and perhaps in its fullest form—by oral utterance too. We have outlined above[5] how the psychological dimension he gave hermeneutics concealed its historical dimension. In actual fact, writing is central to the hermeneutical phenomenon insofar as its detachment both from the writer or author and from a specifically addressed recipient or reader gives it a life of its own. What is fixed in writing has raised itself into a public sphere of meaning in which everyone who can read has an equal share.

Certainly, in relation to language, writing seems a secondary phenomenon. The sign language of writing refers to the actual language of speech. But that language is capable of being written is by no means incidental to its nature. Rather, this capacity for being written down is based on the fact that speech itself shares in the pure ideality of the meaning that communicates itself in it. In writing, the meaning of what is spoken exists purely for itself, completely detached from all emotional elements of expression and communication. A text is not to be understood as an expression of life but with respect to what it says. Writing is the abstract ideality of language. Hence the meaning of something written is fundamentally identifiable and repeatable. What is identical in the repetition is only what was actually deposited in the written record. This indicates that "repetition" cannot be meant here in its strict sense. It does not mean referring back to the original source where something is said or written. The understanding of something written is not a repetition of something past but the sharing of a present meaning.

Writing has the methodological advantage of presenting the hermeneutical problem in all its purity, detached from everything psychological. However, what is from our point of view and for our purpose a methodological advantage is at the same time the expression of a specific weakness that is even more characteristic of writing than of speaking. The task of understanding is presented with particular clarity when we recognize the weakness of all writing. We need only recall what Plato said, namely that the specific weakness of writing was that no one could come to the aid of the written word if it falls victim to misunderstanding, intentional or unintentional.[6]

In the helplessness of the written word Plato discerned a more serious weakness than the weakness of speech (to asthenes ton logon) and when he calls on dialectic to come to the aid of the weakness of speech, while declaring the condition of the written word beyond hope, this is obviously an ironic exaggeration with which to conceal his own writing and his own art. In fact, writing and speech are in the same plight. Just as in speech there is an art of appearances and a corresponding art of true thought—sophistry and dialectic—so in writing there are two arts, one serving sophistic, the other dialectic. There is, then, an art of writing that comes to the aid of thought, and it is to this that the art of understanding—which affords the same help to what is written—is allied.

As we have said, all writing is a kind of alienated speech, and its signs need to be transformed back into speech and meaning. Because the meaning has undergone a kind of self-alienation through being written down, this transformation back is the real hermeneutical task. The meaning of what has been said is to be stated anew, simply on the basis of the words passed on by means of the written signs. In contrast to the spoken word there is no other aid in interpreting the written word. Thus in a special sense everything depends on the "art" of writing.[7] The spoken word interprets itself to an astonishing degree, by the manner of speaking, the tone of voice, the tempo, and so on, and also by the circumstances in which it is spoken.[8]

But there is also such a thing as writing that, as it were, reads itself. A remarkable debate on the spirit and the letter in philosophy between two great German philosophical writers, Schiller and Fichte,[9] starts from this fact. It is interesting that the dispute cannot be resolved with the aesthetic criteria used by the two men. Fundamentally this is not a question of the aesthetics of good style, but a hermeneutical question. The "art" of writing in such a way that the thoughts of the reader are stimulated and held in productive movement has little to do with the conventional rhetorical or aesthetic means. Rather, it consists entirely in one's being drawn into the course of thought. The "art" of writing does not try to be understood and noticed as such. The art of writing, like the art of speaking, is not an end in itself and therefore not the fundamental object of hermeneutical effort. Understanding is drawn on entirely by the subject matter. Hence unclear thinking and "bad" writing are not exemplary cases where the art of hermeneutics can show itself in its full glory but, on the contrary, limiting cases which undermine the basic presupposition of all hermeneutical success, namely the clear unambiguity of the intended meaning.

All writing claims it can be awakened into spoken language, and this claim to autonomy of meaning goes so far that even an authentic reading—e.g., a poet's reading of his poem—becomes questionable when we are listening to something other than what our understanding should really be directed toward. Because the important thing is communicating the text's true meaning, interpreting it is already subject to the norm of the subject matter. This is the requirement that the Platonic dialectic makes when it tries to bring out the logos as such and in doing so often leaves behind the actual partner in the conversation. In fact, the particular weakness of writing, its greater helplessness as compared to speech, has another side to it, in that it demonstrates with redoubled clarity the dialectical task of understanding. As in conversation, understanding here too must try to strengthen the meaning of what is said. What is stated in the text must be detached from all contingent factors and grasped in its full ideality, in which alone it has validity. Thus, precisely because it entirely detaches the sense of what is said from the person saying it, the written word makes the understanding reader the arbiter of its claim to truth. The reader experiences what is addressed to him and what he understands in all its validity. What he understands is always more than an unfamiliar opinion: it is always possible truth. This is what emerges from detaching what is spoken from the speaker and from the permanence that writing bestows. This is the deeper hermeneutical reason for the fact, mentioned above,[10] that it does not occur to people who are not used to reading that what is written down could be wrong, since to them anything written seems like a self-authenticating document.

Everything written is, in fact, the paradigmatic object of hermeneutics. What we found in the extreme case of a foreign language and in the problems of translation is confirmed here by the autonomy of reading: understanding is not a psychic transposition. The horizon of understanding cannot be limited either by what the writer originally had in mind or by the horizon of the person to whom the text was originally addressed.

It sounds at first like a sensible hermeneutical rule—and is generally recognized as such—that nothing should be put into a text that the writer or the reader could not have intended. But this rule can be applied only in extreme cases. For texts do not ask to be understood as a living expression of the subjectivity of their writers. This, then, cannot define the limits of a text's meaning. However, it is not only limiting a text's meaning to the "actual" thoughts of the *author* that is questionable. Even if one tries to determine the meaning of a text objectively by regarding it as a contemporary document and in relation to its original *reader*, as was Schleiermacher's basic procedure, one does not get beyond an accidental delimitation. The idea of the contemporary addressee can claim only a restricted critical validity. For what is contemporaneity? Listeners of the day before yesterday as well as of the day after tomorrow are always among those to whom one speaks as a contemporary. Where are we to draw the line that excludes a reader from being addressed? What are contemporaries and what is a text's claim to truth in the face of this multifarious mixture of past and future? The idea of the original reader is full of unexamined idealization.

Furthermore, our conception of the nature of literary tradition contains a fundamental objection to the hermeneutical legitimacy of the idea of the original reader. We saw that literature is defined by the will to hand on.

But a person who copies and passes on is doing it for his own contemporaries. Thus the reference to the original reader, like that to the meaning of the author, seems to offer only a very crude historico-hermeneutical criterion that cannot really limit the horizon of a text's meaning. What is fixed in writing has detached itself from the contingency of its origin and its author and made itself free for new relationships. Normative concepts such as the author's meaning or the original reader's understanding in fact represent only an empty space that is filled from time to time in understanding.

(B) LANGUAGE AS DETERMINATION OF THE HERMENEUTIC ACT

This brings us to the second aspect of the relationship between language and understanding. Not only is the special object of understanding, namely tradition, of a verbal nature; understanding itself has a fundamental connection with language. We started from the proposition that understanding is already interpretation because it creates the hermeneutical horizon within which the meaning of a text comes into force. But in order to be able to express a text's meaning and subject matter, we must translate it into our own language. However, this involves relating it to the whole complex of possible meanings in which we linguistically move. We have already investigated the logical structure of this in relation to the special place of the *question* as a hermeneutical phenomenon. In now considering the verbal nature of all understanding, we are expressing from another angle what we already saw in considering the dialectic of question and answer.

Here we are emphasizing a dimension that is generally ignored by the dominant conception that the historical sciences have of themselves. For the historian usually chooses concepts to describe the historical particularity of his objects without expressly reflecting on their origin and justification. He simply follows his interest in the material and takes no account of the fact that the descriptive concepts he chooses can be highly detrimental to his proper purpose if they assimilate what is historically different to what is familiar and thus, despite all impartiality, subordinate the alien being of the object to his own preconceptions. Thus, despite his scientific method, he behaves just like everyone else—as a child of his time who is unquestioningly dominated by the concepts and prejudices of his own age.[11]

Insofar as the historian does not admit this naivete to himself, he fails to reach the level of reflection that the subject matter demands. But his naivete becomes truly abysmal when he starts to become aware of the problems it raises and so demands that in understanding history one must leave one's own concepts aside and think only in the concepts of the epoch one is trying to understand.[12] This demand, which sounds like a logical implementation of historical consciousness is, as will be clear to every thoughtful reader, a naive illusion. The naivete of this claim does not consist in the fact that it goes unfulfilled because the interpreter does not sufficiently attain the ideal of leaving himself aside. This would still mean that it was a legitimate ideal, and one should strive to reach it as far as possible. But what the legitimate demand of the historical consciousness—to understand a period in terms of its own concepts—really means is something quite different. The call to leave aside the concepts of the present does not mean a naive transposition into the past. It is, rather, an essentially relative demand that has meaning only in relation to one's own concepts. Historical consciousness fails to understand its own nature if, in order to understand, it seeks to exclude what alone makes understanding possible. *To think historically* means, in fact, *to perform the transposition that the concepts of the past undergo* when we try to think in them. To think historically always involves mediating between those ideas and one's own thinking. To try to escape from one's own concepts in interpretation is not only impossible but manifestly absurd. To interpret means precisely to bring one's own preconceptions into play so that the text's meaning can really be made to speak for us.

In our analysis of the hermeneutical process we saw that to acquire a horizon of interpretation requires a fusion of horizons. This is now confirmed by the verbal aspect of interpretation. The text is made to speak through interpretation. But no text and no book speaks if it does not speak a language that reaches the other person. Thus interpretation must find the right language if it really wants to make the text speak. There cannot, therefore, be any single interpretation that is correct "in itself," precisely because every interpretation is concerned with the text itself. The historical life of a tradition depends on being constantly assimilated and interpreted. An interpretation that was correct in itself would be a foolish ideal that mistook the nature of tradition. Every interpretation has to adapt itself to the hermeneutical situation to which it belongs.

Being bound by a situation does not mean that the claim to correctness that every interpretation must make is dissolved into the subjective or the occasional. We must not here abandon the insights of the romantics, who purified the problem of hermeneutics from all its occasional elements. Interpretation is not something pedagogical for us either; it is the act of understanding itself, which is realized—not just for the one for whom one is interpreting but also for the interpreter himself—in the explicitness of verbal interpretation. Thanks to the verbal nature of all interpretation, every interpretation includes the possibility of a relationship with others. There can be no speaking that does not bind the speaker and the person spoken to. This is true of the hermeneutic process as well. But this relationship does not determine the interpretative process of understanding—as if interpreting were a conscious adaptation to a pedagogical situation; rather, this process is simply *the concretion of the meaning itself.* Let us recall our emphasis on the element of application, which had completely disappeared from hermeneutics. We saw that to understand a text always means to apply it to ourselves and to know that, even if it must always be understood in different ways, it is still the same text presenting itself to us in these different ways. That this does not in the least relativize the claim to truth of every interpretation is seen from the fact that all interpretation is essentially verbal. The verbal explicitness that understanding achieves through interpretation does not create a second sense apart from that which is understood and interpreted. The interpretive concepts are not, as such, thematic in understanding. Rather, it is their nature to disappear behind what they bring to speech in interpretation. Paradoxically, an interpretation is right when it is capable of disappearing in this way. And yet at the same time it must be expressed as something that is supposed to disappear. The possibility of understanding is dependent on the possibility of this kind of mediating interpretation.

This is also true in those cases when there is immediate understanding and no explicit interpretation is undertaken. For in these cases too interpretation must be possible. But this means that interpretation is contained potentially within the understanding process. It simply makes the understanding explicit. Thus interpretation is not a means through which understanding is achieved; rather, it enters into the content of what is understood. Let us recall that this means not only that the sense of the text can be realized as a unity but that the subject matter of which the text speaks is also expressed. The interpretation places the object, as it were, on the scales of words. There are a few characteristic variations on this general statement that indirectly confirm it. When we are concerned with understanding and interpreting verbal texts, interpretation in the medium of language itself shows what understanding always is: assimilating what is said to the point that it becomes one's own. Verbal interpretation is the form of all interpretation, even when what is to be interpreted is not linguistic in nature—i.e., is not a text but a statue or a musical composition. We must not let ourselves be confused by forms of interpretation that are not verbal but in fact presuppose language. It is possible to demonstrate something by means of contrast—e.g., by placing two pictures alongside each other or reading two poems one after the other, so that one is interpreted by the other. In these cases demonstration seems to obviate verbal interpretation. But in fact this kind of demonstration is a modification of verbal interpretation. In such demonstration we have the reflection of interpretation, and the demonstration is used as a visual shortcut. Demonstration is interpretation in much the same sense as is a translation that embodies an interpretation, or the correct reading aloud of a text that has already decided the questions of interpretation, because one can only read aloud what one has understood. Understanding and interpretation are indissolubly bound together.

Obviously connected with the fact that interpretation and understanding are bound up with each other is that the concept of *interpretation* can be applied not only to scholarly interpretation but to artistic *reproduction*—e.g., musical or dramatic performance. We have shown above that this kind of reproduction is not a second creation re-creating the first; rather, it makes the work of art appear as itself for the first time. It brings to life the signs of the musical or dramatic text. Reading aloud is a similar process, in that it awakens a text and brings it into new immediacy.[13]

From this it follows that the same thing must be true of understanding in silent reading. Reading fundamentally involves interpretation. This is not to say that understanding as one reads is a kind of inner production in which the work of art would acquire an independent existence—as in a production visible to all—although remaining in the intimate sphere of one's own inner life. Rather, we are stating the contrary, namely that a production that takes place in the external world of space and time does not in fact have any existence independent of the work itself and can acquire such only through a secondary aesthetic differentiation. Interpreting music or a play by performing it is not basically different from understanding a text by reading it: understanding always includes interpretation. The work of the philologist too consists in making texts readable and intelligible—i.e., safeguarding a text against misunderstandings. Thus there is no essential difference between the interpretation that a work undergoes in being performed and that which the scholar produces. A performing artist may feel that justifying his interpretation in words is very secondary, rejecting it as inartistic, but he cannot want to deny that such an account can be given of his reproductive interpretation. He too must want his interpretation to be correct and convincing, and it will not occur to him to deny that it is tied to the text he has before him. But this text is the same one that presents the scholarly interpreter with his task. Thus the performing artist will be unable to deny that his own understanding of a work, expressed in his reproductive interpretation, can itself be understood—i.e., interpreted and justified—and this interpretation will take place in verbal form. But even this is not a new creation of meaning. Rather, it too disappears again as an interpretation and preserves its truth in the immediacy of understanding.

This insight into the way interpretation and understanding are bound together will destroy that false romanticism of immediacy that artists and connoisseurs have pursued, and still do pursue, under the banner of the aesthetics of genius. Interpretation does not try to replace the interpreted work. It does not, for example, try to draw attention to itself by the poetic power of its own utterance. Rather, it remains *fundamentally* accidental. This is true not only of the interpreting word but also of performative interpretation. The interpreting word always has something accidental about it insofar as it is motivated by the hermeneutic question, not just for the pedagogical purposes to which it was limited in the Enlightenment but because understanding is always a genuine event.[14] Similarly, performative interpretation is accidental in a fundamental sense—i.e., not just when something is played, imitated, translated, or read aloud for didactic purposes. These cases—where performance is interpretation in a special demonstrative sense, where it includes demonstrative exaggeration and highlighting—in fact differ only in degree, and not in kind, from other sorts of reproductive interpretation. However much it is the literary work or musical composition itself that acquires its mimic presence through the performance, every performance still has its own emphasis. There is little difference between this emphasis and using emphasis for didactic ends. All performance is interpretation. All interpretation is highlighting.

It is only because the performance has no permanent being of its own and disappears in the work which it reproduces that this fact does not emerge clearly. But if we take a comparable example from the plastic arts—e.g., drawings after old masters made by a great artist—we find the same interpretive highlighting in them. The same effect is experienced in watching revivals of old films or seeing for a second time a film that one has just seen and remembers clearly: everything seems overplayed. Thus it is wholly legitimate for us to speak of the interpretation that lies behind every reproduction, and it must be possible to give a fundamental account of it. The interpretation as a whole is made up of a thousand little decisions which all claim to be correct. Argumentative justification and interpretation do not need to be the artist's proper concern. Moreover, an explicit interpretation in language would only approximate correctness and fall short of the rounded concreteness achieved by an "artistic" reproduction. But this precludes neither the fact that all understanding has an intrinsic relation to interpretation nor the basic possibility of an interpretation in words.

We must rightly understand the fundamental priority of language asserted here. Indeed, language often seems ill suited to express what we feel. In the face of the overwhelming presence of works of art, the task of expressing in words what they say to us seems like an infinite and hopeless undertaking. The fact that our desire and capacity to understand always go beyond any statement that we can make seems like a critique of language. But this does not alter the fundamental priority of language. The possibilities of our knowledge seem to be far more individual than the possibilities of expression offered by language. Faced with the socially motivated tendency toward uniformity with which language forces understanding into particular schematic forms which hem us in, our desire for knowledge tries to escape from these schematizations and predecisions. However, the critical superiority which we claim over language pertains not to the conventions of verbal expression but to the conventions of meaning that have become sedimented in language. Thus that superiority says nothing against the essential connection between understanding and language. In fact it confirms this connection. For all critique that rises above the schematism of our statements in order to understand finds its expression in the form of language. Hence language always forestalls any objection to its jurisdiction. Its universality keeps pace with the universality of reason. Hermeneutical consciousness only participates in what constitutes the general relation between language and reason. If all understanding stands in a necessary relation of equivalence to its possible interpretation, and if there are basically no bounds set to understanding, then the verbal form in which this understanding is interpreted must contain within it an infinite dimension that transcends all bounds. Language is the language of reason itself.

One says this, and then one hesitates. For this makes language so close to reason—which means, to the things it names—that one may ask why there should be different languages at all, since all seem to have the same proximity to reason and to objects. When a person lives in a language, he is filled with the sense of the unsurpassable appropriateness of the words he uses for the subject matter he is talking about. It seems impossible that other words in other languages could name the things equally well. The suitable word always seems to be one's own and unique, just as the thing referred to is always unique. The agony of translation consists ultimately in the fact that the original words seem to be inseparable from the things they refer to, so that to make a text intelligible one often has to give an interpretive paraphrase of it rather than translate it. The more sensitively our historical consciousness reacts, the more it seems to be aware of the untranslatability of the unfamiliar. But this makes the intimate unity of word and thing a hermeneutical scandal. How can we possibly understand anything written in a foreign language if we are thus imprisoned in our own?

It is necessary to see the speciousness of this argument. In actual fact the sensitivity of our historical consciousness tells us the opposite. The work of understanding and interpretation always remains meaningful. This shows the superior universality with which reason rises above the limitations of any given language. The hermeneutical experience is the corrective by means of which the thinking reason escapes the prison of language, and it is itself verbally constituted.

From this point of view the problem of language does not present itself in the same way as *philosophy of language* raises it. Certainly the variety of languages in which linguistics is interested presents us with a question. But this question is simply how every language, despite its difference from other languages, can say everything it wants. Linguistics teaches us that every language does this in its own way. But we then ask how, amid the variety of these forms of utterance, there is still the same unity of thought and speech, so that everything that has been transmitted in writing can be understood. Thus we are interested in the opposite of what linguistics tries to investigate.

The intimate unity of language and thought is the premise from which linguistics too starts. It is this alone that has made it a science. For only because this unity exists is it worthwhile for the investigator to make the abstraction which causes language to be the object of his research. Only by breaking with the conventionalist prejudices of theology and rationalism could Herder and Humboldt learn to see languages as views of the world. By acknowledging the unity of thought and language they could envision the task of comparing the various forms of this unity. We are starting from the same insight but going, as it were, in the opposite direction. Despite the multiplicity of ways of speech, we are trying to keep in mind the indissoluble unity of thought and language as we encounter it in the hermeneutical phenomenon, namely as the unity of understanding and interpretation.

Thus the question that concerns us is *the conceptual character* of all understanding. This only appears to be a secondary question. We have seen that conceptual interpretation is the realization of the hermeneutical experience itself. That is why our problem is so difficult. The interpreter does not know that he is bringing himself and his own concepts into the interpretation. The verbal formulation is so much part of the interpreter's mind that he never becomes aware of it as an object. Thus it is understandable that this side of the hermeneutic process has been wholly ignored. But there is the further point that the situation has been confused by incorrect *theories of language*. It is obvious that an instrumentalist theory of signs which sees words and concepts as handy tools has missed the point of the hermeneutical phenomenon. If we stick to what takes place in speech and, above all, in every dialogue with tradition carried on by the human sciences, we cannot fail to see that here concepts are constantly in the process of being formed. This does not mean that the interpreter is using new or unusual words. But the capacity to use familiar words is not based on an act of logical subsumption, through which a particular is placed under a universal concept. Let us remember, rather, that understanding always includes an element of application and thus produces an ongoing process of concept formation. We must consider this now if we want to liberate the verbal nature of understanding from the presuppositions of philosophy of language. The interpreter does not use words and concepts like a craftsman who picks up his tools and then puts them away. Rather, we must recognize that all understanding is interwoven with concepts and reject any theory that does not accept the intimate unity of word and subject matter.

Indeed, the situation is even more difficult. It is doubtful that the *concept of language* that modern linguistics and philosophy of language take as their starting point is adequate to the situation. It has recently been stated by some linguists—and rightly so—that the modern concept of language presumes a verbal consciousness that is itself a product of history and does not apply to the beginning of the historical process, especially to what language was for the Greeks.[15] From the complete unconsciousness of language that we find in classical Greece, the path leads to the instrumentalist devaluation of language that we find in modern times. This process of increasing consciousness, which also involves a change in the attitude to language, makes it possible for "language" as such—i.e., its form, separated from all content—to become an independent object of attention.

We can doubt whether this view's characterization of the relation between language behavior and language theory is correct, but there is no doubt that the science and philosophy of language operate on the premise that their only concern is the *form* of language. Is the idea of form still appropriate here? Is language a symbolic form, as Cassirer calls it? Does this take account of the fact that language is unique in embracing everything—myth, art, law, and so on—that Cassirer also calls symbolic form?[16]

In analyzing the hermeneutical phenomenon we have stumbled upon the universal function of language. In revealing the verbal nature of the hermeneutical phenomenon, we see that it has a universal significance. Understanding and interpretation are related to verbal tradition in a specific way. But at the same time they transcend this relationship not only because all the creations of human culture, including the nonverbal ones, can be understood in this way, but more fundamentally because everything that is intelligible must be accessible to understanding and to interpretation. What is true of understanding is just as true of language. Neither is to be grasped simply as a fact that can be empirically investigated. Neither is ever simply an object but instead comprehends everything that can ever be an object.[17]

If we recognize this basic connection between language and understanding, we will not be able to view the development from unconsciousness of language via consciousness of language to the devaluation of language[18] even as an unequivocally correct description of the historical process. This schema does not seem to me to be adequate even for the history of theories of language, as we shall see, let alone for the life of language. The language that lives in speech—which comprehends all understanding, including that of the interpreter of texts—is so much bound up with thinking and interpretation that we have too little left if we ignore the actual content of what languages hand down to us and try to consider language only as form. Unconsciousness of language has not ceased to be the genuine mode of being of speech. Let us, therefore, turn our attention to the *Greeks*, who did not have a word for what we call language, when the all-embracing unity of word and thing became problematical for them and hence worthy of attention. We will also consider *Christian thought in the Middle Ages*, which, because of its interest in dogmatic theology, rethought the mystery of this unity.

2 THE DEVELOPMENT OF THE CONCEPT OF LANGUAGE IN THE HISTORY OF WESTERN THOUGHT

(A) LANGUAGE AND LOGOS

In the earliest times the intimate unity of word and thing was so obvious that the true name was considered to be part of the bearer of the name, if not indeed to substitute for him. In Greek the expression for "word," onoma, also means "name," and especially "proper name"—i.e., the name by which something is called. The word is understood primarily as a name. But a name is what it is because it is what someone is called and what he answers to. It belongs to its bearer. The rightness of the name is confirmed by the fact that someone answers to it. Thus it seems to belong to his being.

Greek philosophy more or less began with the insight that a word is *only* a name—i.e., that it does not represent true being. This is precisely the breakthrough of philosophical inquiry into the territory over which the name had undisputed rule. Belief in the word and doubt about it constitute the problem that the Greek Enlightenment saw in the relationship between the word and thing. Thereby the word changed from presenting the thing to substituting for it. The name that is given and can be altered raises doubt about the truth of the word. Can we speak of the rightness of names? But must we not speak of the rightness of words—i.e., insist on the unity of word and thing? Did not the most profound of all early thinkers, Heraclitus, discover the depth of meaning contained in the play on words? This is the background of Plato's *Cratylus*—the fundamental statement of Greek thought on language, which covers the whole range of problems so thoroughly that later Greek discussion (of which we have, in any case, only an imperfect knowledge) adds scarcely anything essential.[19]

Two theories discussed in Plato's *Cratylus* try in different ways to describe the relationship between word and thing: the conventionalist theory regards unambiguous linguistic usage, reached by agreement and practice, as the only source of the meaning of words. The opposed theory holds that there is a natural agreement between word and object that is described by the idea of correctness (orthotes). It is clear that both of these positions are extremes and so do not necessarily exclude each other in fact. At any rate, the ordinary speaker knows nothing of the "correctness" of the word that this position presumes.

The mode of being of language that we call "customary usage" sets a limit to both theories: the limit of *conventionalism* is that we cannot arbitrarily change the meaning of words if there is to be *language*. The problem of "special languages" shows the conditions that apply to this kind of renaming. In the *Cratylus* Hermogenes himself gives an example: the renaming of a servant.[20] The dependency of a servant's life world, the coincidence of his person with his function, makes possible the renaming that a free man's claim to independence and the preservation of his honor would make impossible. Children and lovers likewise have "their" language, by which they communicate with each other in a world that belongs to them alone. But even this is not so much because they have arbitrarily agreed on it, but because a verbal custom has grown up between them. Language always presupposes a common world—even if it is only a play world.

The limitation of the *similarity theory* is also clear. We cannot look at the things referred to and criticize the words for not correctly representing them. Language is not a mere tool we use, something we construct in order to communicate and differentiate.[21] Both these interpretations of language start from the existence and instrumentality of words, and regard the subject matter as something we know about previously from an independent source. Thus they start too late. We must then ask if, in showing the two extreme positions to be untenable, Plato is questioning a presupposition common to them both. Plato's intention seems quite clear to me—and this cannot be emphasized sufficiently in view of the fact that the *Cratylus* is constantly misused in discussing the systematic problems of the philosophy of language: in this discussion of contemporary theories of language Plato wants to demonstrate that no truth (aletheia ton onton) can be attained in language—in language's claim to correctness (orthotes ton onomaton)—and that without words (aneu ton onomaton) being must be known purely from itself (auta ex heauton).[22] This radically displaces the problem to another plane. The dialectic which aims to achieve this obviously claims to make thought dependent on itself alone and to open it to its true objects, the "ideas," so that the power of words (dunamis ton onomaton) and their demonic technologization in sophistical argument are overcome. The conquest of the sphere of words (onomata) by dialectic does not of course mean that there really is such a thing as knowledge without words, but only that it is not the *word* that opens up the way to truth. Rather, on the contrary, the adequacy of the word can be judged only from the knowledge of the thing it refers to.

We can grant that this is true and yet feel there is something missing. Plato avoids considering the real relationship between words and things. Here he clarifies the question of how one can know that something is too big; and where he does speak about it, where he does describe the true nature of dialectic, as in the excursus of the *Seventh Letter,*[23] language is regarded only as an external and equivocal element. Like the sensible appearance of things, it is one of those specious things (proteinomena) that insinuate themselves and that the true dialectician must leave behind. The pure thought of ideas, dianoia, is silent, for it is a dialogue of the soul with itself (aneu phones). The logos[24] is the stream that flows from this thought and sounds out through the mouth (rheuma dia tou stomatos meta phthongou). It is obvious that, of itself, audible perceptibility involves no claim that what is said is true. Plato undoubtedly did not consider the fact that the process of thought, if conceived as a dialogue of soul, itself involves a connection with language; and although we find that there is something about this in the *Seventh Letter,* it is in relation to the dialectic of knowledge—i.e., to the orientation of the whole movement of knowing toward the one (auto). Although there is here a fundamental recognition of the connection with language, its significance does not really emerge. It is only one of the elements of knowing, and its dialectical provisionality emerges from the subject matter itself toward which the act of knowing is directed. The net result, then, is that Plato's discovery of the ideas conceals the true nature of language even more than the theories of the Sophists, who developed their own art (techne) in the use and abuse of language.

Even where Plato moves beyond the level of discussion in the *Cratylus* and points forward to his dialectic, we find no other relation to language than that already discussed there: language is a tool, a copy constructed and judged in terms of the original, the things themselves. Thus even when he assigns no independent function to the sphere of words (ono-mata) and calls for transcending it, he stays within the horizon in which the question of the "correctness" of the name presents itself. Even when (as in the context of the *Seventh Letter*) he does not accept a natural correctness of names, he still retains resemblance (homoion) as the criterion: for him the copy and the original constitute the metaphysical model for everything within the noetic sphere. In their various media the craftsman and the divine demiurge, the orator and the philosophical dialectician, copy the true being of ideas. There is always a gap (apechei), even if the true dialectician bridges it for himself. The element of true speech remains the word (onoma and rhema)—the same word in which truth is hidden to the point of unrecognizability and even complete disappearance.[25]

If against this background we consider the dispute about the "correctness of names," as settled by the *Cratylus*, the theories discussed there suddenly acquire an interest that goes beyond Plato and his own particular purpose. For neither of the theories that Plato's Socrates disproves is considered in its full weight. The conventionalist theory bases the idea of the "correctness" of words on giving names to things—christening them, as it were. This theory obviously does not regard names as having any claim to purvey knowledge of the thing. Socrates refutes the exponent of this view by starting from the distinction between the true and the false logos, then making him admit that the constituents of the logos, the words (onomata), are also true or false—thus relating naming, as part of speaking, to the revelation of being (ousia) that takes place in speaking.[26] This is a proposition so incompatible with the conventionalist view that it is easy to see that it implies, on the contrary, a "nature" that is the criterion of the true name and correct naming. Socrates himself admits that understanding the "correctness" of names in this way leads to etymological intoxication, among other absurd consequences. But the same is true of his treatment of the opposed view, according to which words are part of nature (phusei). Although we might expect this view to be refuted by revealing the faultiness of arguing from the truth of discourse to that of the words of which it is made up (the *Sophist* rectifies this), we are disappointed. The discussion stays entirely within the fundamental assumptions of the "nature" theory—i.e., the similarity principle—demolishing it only by progressive limitation. If the "correctness" of names really depends on finding the right name—i.e., the name that is adequate to the thing—then, as with all such adequacy, there are grades and degrees of correctness. If a name with only a small degree of correctness still conveys the outline (tupos) of a thing, then it may still be good enough to be usable.[27] But we must be even more generous: a word can be understood, obviously from habit and convention, if it contains sounds that bear no resemblance to what it names, so that the whole principle of similarity falters and is refuted by such examples as the words for numbers. There can be no similarity at all here, because numbers do not belong to the visible and moved world, so that they obviously come under the principle of convention alone.

The abandonment of the *phusei theory* seems very conciliatory, for the convention principle has to act as a complement when the similarity principle fails. Plato seems to hold that the similarity principle is reasonable, but it needs to be applied in a very liberal way. Convention—which operates in practical usage and alone constitutes the correctness of words—can make use of the similarity principle but is not bound to it.[28] This is a very moderate point of view, but it involves the basic assumption that words have no real cognitive significance of their own, a conclusion that points beyond the whole sphere of words and the question of their correctness to the knowledge of the thing. This is obviously Plato's sole concern.

And yet, by keeping within the framework of finding and giving names, the Socratic argument against Cratylus suppresses a number of insights. To say that the word is a tool we construct in order to deal with things for purposes of instruction and differentiation, and so that it is a being that can be more or less adequate to and in accord with its Being, fixes the nature of the inquiry into the nature of the word in a dubious manner. The specific way of dealing with the thing that we are concerned with here is that of making the thing meant apparent. The word is correct if it brings the thing to presentation (Darstellung)—i.e., if it is a representation (mimesis). What is involved here is certainly not an imitative representation in the sense of a direct copy, depicting the visual or aural appearance of something, but it is the being (ousia)—that which is considered worthy of the attribute "to be" (einai)—that is to be revealed by the word. But we must ask whether the concepts used in the dialogue, the concepts of mimema and of deloma understood as mimema, are correct.

The word that names an object names it as what it is because the word itself has the meaning whereby the object intended is named, but that does not necessarily imply that the two are related as original and copy. Certainly the nature of mimema consists in part in representing something different from what it itself contains. Thus, mere imitation, "being like," always offers a starting point for reflecting on the ontological gap between the imitation and the original. But words name things in a much too intimate and intellectual way for the question of the degree of similarity to be appropriate here. Cratylus is quite right when he resists this notion. He is likewise quite right when he says that inasmuch as a word is a word, it must be "correct," must fit correctly. If not, it has no meaning, and it is merely sounding brass.[29] It makes no sense to speak of wrongness in such a case.

Of course it can also happen that we do not address someone by his right name because we confuse him with someone else, or that we do not use "the right word" for something because we do not recognize the thing. It is not the word that is wrong here but its use. It only seems to fit the thing for which it is used. In fact it is the word for something else and, as such, is correct. Likewise, someone learning a foreign language assumes that words have real meanings that are displayed in usage and conveyed in the dictionary. One can always confuse these meanings, but that always means using the "right" words wrongly. Thus we may speak of an *absolute perfection of the word*, inasmuch as there is no perceptible relationship—i.e., no gap—between its appearance to the senses and its meaning. Hence there is no reason why Cratylus should allow himself to be subjected to the yoke of the schema of original and copy. It is true that a copy, without being a mere duplicate of the original, resembles the original; it is a different thing that, because of its imperfect similarity, points to the other that it represents. But this obviously does not pertain to the relationship between the word and its meaning. Thus it is like the revelation of a wholly obscured truth when Socrates says that words, unlike pictures (zoa), can be not only correct but true (alethe).[30] The "truth" of a word does not depend on its correctness, its correct adequation to the thing. It lies rather in its perfect intellectuality—i.e., the manifestness of the word's meaning in its sound. In this sense all words are "true"—i.e., their being is wholly absorbed in their meaning—whereas a copy is only more or less similar and thus, judged by reference to the appearance of the original, only more or less correct.

But, as always with Plato, there is a reason for Socrates' being so blind to what he refutes. Cratylus is unaware that the meaning of words is not simply identical with the objects named; and still less is he aware—and this is the reason for Socrates' tacit superiority—that logos (discourse and speech) and the manifestation of things that takes place in it, is something different from the act of intending the meanings contained in words, and it is here, in speaking, that the actual capacity of language to communicate what is correct and true has its locus. The Sophists' misuse of speech arises from their failure to recognize its capacity for truth (the contrary capacity of which is falseness, pseudos). If logos is understood as a thing's presentation (deloma), as its manifestation, without making a fundamental distinction between this truth function of speech and the signific character of words, then there opens up a kind of confusion peculiar to language. We can then imagine that in the word we have the thing. The legitimate path to knowledge will seem to be to stick to the word. But the reverse is also true. Where we have knowledge, the truth of an utterance must be built up out of the truth of words, as if out of its elements, and just as we assume the "correctness" of these words—i.e., their natural adequation to what they name—we should be able to interpret even the elements of these words, namely the letters, in terms of their copying function in relation to things. This is the conclusion to which Socrates compels his partner.

But all this misses the point that the truth of things resides in discourse —which means, ultimately, in intending a unitary meaning concerning things—and not in the individual words, not even in a language's entire stock of words. It is this error that enables Socrates to refute the objections of Cratylus, even though they are so apt in relation to the truth of the word—i.e., to its significance. Against him Socrates employs the usage of words—that is speech, logos, with its possibility of being either true or false. The name, the word, seems to be true or false to the extent that it is used rightly or wrongly—i.e., rightly or wrongly associated with some- thing. This association, however, is not that of the word; rather, it is already logos and in such a logos can find its adequate expression. For example, to name someone "Socrates" is to say that this person is called "Socrates."

Thus the relational ordering that is logos is much more than the mere correspondence of words and things, as is ultimately assumed in the Eleatic doctrine of being and in the copy theory. The truth contained in the logos is not that of mere perception (of noein), not just letting being appear; rather, it always places being in a relationship, assigning something to it. For precisely this reason, it is not the word (onoma) but the logos that is the bearer of truth (and also error). From this it necessarily follows that being expressed, and thus being bound to language, is quite secondary to the system of relations within which logos articulates and interprets the thing. We see that it is *not word but number* that is the real paradigm of the noetic: number, whose name is obviously pure convention and whose "exactitude" consists in the fact that every number is defined by its place in the series, so that it is a pure structure of intelligibility, an ens rationis, not in the weak sense of a being-validity but in the strong sense of perfect rationality. This is the real conclusion to which the *Cratylus* is drawn, and it has one very important consequence, which in fact influences all further thinking about language.

If the sphere of the logos represents the sphere of the noetic in the variety of its associations, then the *word*, just like the number, becomes the mere *sign* of a being that is well defined and hence preknown. This is, fundamentally, to turn the question around. Now we are not starting from the thing and inquiring into the being of the word as a means of conveying it. Rather, beginning from the word as a means, we are asking what and how it communicates to the person who uses it. By nature, the *sign* has its being only in application, and so its "self" consists only in pointing to something "other." It must be foregrounded from the context in which it is encountered and taken as a sign, in order for its own being as an object to be superseded and for it to dissolve (disappear) into its meaning. It is the abstraction of pointing itself (Verweisung: also, referring).

A sign, then, is not something that insists on its own content. It does not even need to have any similarity to its referent—and if it has, then it need be only schematic. But this means again that all visible content of its own is reduced to the minimum necessary to assist its pointing function. The more univocally a sign-thing signifies, the more the sign is a pure sign—i.e., it is exhausted in the co-ordination. Thus for example, written signs are co-ordinated with particular sounds, numerical signs with particular numbers, and they are the most ideal signs because their position in the order completely exhausts them. Badges, marks, ciphers, and so on have ideality insofar as they are taken as signs—i.e., are reduced to their referential function. Here a sign-being subsists only in something else, which, as a sign-thing, both exists in itself and has its own meaning on the one hand and on the other has the meaning that it signifies as a sign. In this case the sign acquires meaning as a sign only in relation to the subject who takes it as a sign. "It does not have its absolute significance within itself—i.e., the subject is not superseded in it."[31] It is still an immediate entity (it still subsists in the context of other entities; in a decorative context, for example, even written signs have ornamental value), and only on the basis of its own immediate being is it at the same time something referential, ideal. The difference between what it is and what it means is absolute.

At the other extreme—the *copy*—the situation is quite different. Certainly the copy implies the same contradiction between its being and its meaning, but it does so in such a way that it supersedes this contradiction within itself precisely by means of the resemblance that lies within itself. It does not acquire the function of pointing or representing from the subject who takes it as a sign but from its own content. It is not a mere sign. For in it the thing copied is itself represented, caught, and made present. That is why it can be judged by the standard of resemblance—i.e., by *the extent to which* it makes present in itself what is not present.

The legitimate question whether the word is nothing but a "pure sign" or instead something like a "copy" or an "image" is thoroughly discredited by the *Cratylus*. Since there the argument that the word is a copy is driven ad absurdum, the only alternative seems to be that it is a sign. Although it is not especially emphasized, this consequence results from the negative discussion of the *Cratylus* and is sealed by knowledge being banished to the intelligible sphere. Thus, in all discussion of language ever since, the concept of the image (eikon) has been replaced by that of the sign (semeion or semainon). This is not just a terminological change; it expresses an epoch-making decision about thought concerning language.[32] That the true being of things is to be investigated "without names" means that there is no access to truth in the proper being of words as such—even though, of course, no questioning, answering, instructing, and differentiating can take place without the help of language. This is to say that thought is so independent of the being of words—which thought takes as mere signs through which what is referred to, the idea, the thing, is brought into view—that the word is reduced to a wholly secondary relation to the thing. It is a mere instrument of communication, the bringing forth (ekpherein) and uttering (logos prophorikos) of what is meant in the medium of the voice. It follows that an ideal system of signs, whose sole purpose is to coordinate all signs in an unambiguous system, makes the power of words (dunamis ton onomaton)—the range of variation of the contingent in the historical languages as they have actually developed—appear as a mere flaw in their utility. This is the ideal of a characteristica universalis.

The exclusion of what a language "is" beyond its efficient functioning as sign material—i.e., the self-conquest of language by a system of artificial, unambiguously defined symbols—this ideal of the eighteenth-and twentieth-century Enlightenments, represents the ideal language, because to it would correspond the totality of the knowable: Being as absolutely available objectivity. We cannot object that no such mathematical sign language is conceivable without a language that would introduce its conventions. This problem of a "metalanguage" may be unsolvable because it involves a reiterative regress. But the interminability of this process constitutes no fundamental objection to accepting the ideal it approaches.

It must also be admitted that every development of scientific terminology, however confined its use may be, constitutes a phase of this process. For what is a *technical term?* A word whose meaning is univocally defined, inasmuch as it signifies a defined concept. A technical term is always somewhat artificial insofar as either the word itself is artificially formed or—as is more frequent—a word already in use has the variety and breadth of its meanings excised and is assigned only one particular conceptual meaning. In contrast to the living meaning of the words in spoken language—to which, as Wilhelm von Humboldt rightly showed,[33] a certain range of variation is essential—a technical term is a word that has become ossified. Using a word as a technical term is an act of violence against language. Unlike the pure sign language of symbolic logic, however, the use of technical terminology (even if often in the guise of a foreign word) passes into the spoken language. There is no such thing as purely technical discourse; but the technical term, created artificially and against the spirit of language, returns into its stream (as we can see even from the artificial terms of modern advertising). This is indirectly confirmed by the fact that sometimes a technical distinction does not catch on and is constantly denied in common usage. Obviously this means that it must bow to the demands of language. We need think only of the impotent pedantry with which neo-Kantianism castigated the use of "transcendental" for "transcendent," or the use of "ideology" in a positive, dogmatic sense which has become general despite its being originally coined for polemical and instrumental purposes. Hence, in interpreting scientific texts, one must always count on finding the technical and the freer use of a word juxtaposed.[34] Modern interpreters of classical texts easily underestimate the need to do so because in modern scientific usage a concept is more artificial and hence more fixed than in the ancient world, which had no foreign words and very few artificial ones.

Only through mathematical symbolism would it be possible to rise entirely above the contingency of the historical languages and the vagueness of their concepts. Through the permutations and combinations of such a sign system, Leibniz believed, we would acquire new, mathematically certain truths, because the "ordo" imaged in such a sign system would find an echo in all languages.[35] Leibniz's claim that the characteristica universalis is an ars inveniendi clearly depends on the artificiality of its symbols. This is what makes calculation possible—i.e., the discovery of relations from the formal laws of the system of combinations—independently of whether or not experience presents us with relationships between things corresponding to those combinations. By thinking ahead in this way into the sphere of possibilities, thinking reason is itself brought to its absolute perfection. For human reason there is no more adequate form of knowledge than the notitia numerorum,[36] and all calculation proceeds on its model. But it is a universal truth that human imperfection precludes adequate knowledge a priori, and that experience is indispensable. Knowledge acquired through these symbols is not clear and distinct, for a symbol gives nothing to the senses to perceive; rather, such knowledge is "blind," inasmuch as the symbol is a substitute for a real piece of knowledge, merely indicating that it could be acquired.

Thus the ideal of language that Leibniz is pursuing is a "language" of reason: an "analysis notionum" which, starting from "first" concepts, would develop the whole system of true concepts and so be a copy of the universe of beings, just as is the divine reason.[37] In this way, the world—conceived as the calculation of God, who works out the best among all the possibilities of being—would be recalculated by human reason.

From this ideal it becomes clear that language is something other than a mere sign system denoting the totality of objects. A word is not just a sign. In a sense that is hard to grasp, it is also something almost like a copy or image. We need only think of the other extreme possibility—of a purely artificial language—to see the relative justification of such an archaic theory of language. A word has a mysterious connection with what it "images"; it belongs to its being. This is meant in a fundamental way; it is not just that mimesis has a certain share in creating language, for no one denies that. Plato obviously thought so, as does philology today when it assigns a certain function to onomatopoeia in the history of language. But fundamentally language is taken to be something wholly detached from the being of what is under consideration; it is taken to be an instrument of subjectivity. To say this is to follow a path of abstraction that ultimately leads to the rational construction of an artificial language.

In my view this path leads us away from the nature of language.[38] Language and thinking about things are so bound together that it is an abstraction to conceive of the system of truths as a pregiven system of possibilities of being for which the signifying subject selects corresponding signs. A word is not a sign that one selects, nor is it a sign that one makes or gives to another; it is not an existent thing that one picks up and gives an ideality of meaning in order to make another being visible through it. This is mistaken on both counts. Rather, the ideality of the meaning lies in the word itself. It is meaningful already. But this does not imply, on the other hand, that the word precedes all experience and simply advenes to an experience in an external way, by subjecting itself to it. Experience is not wordless to begin with, subsequently becoming an object of reflection by being named, by being subsumed under the universality of the word. Rather, experience of itself seeks and finds words that express it. We seek the right word—i.e., the word that really belongs to the thing—so that in it the thing comes into language. Even if we keep in mind that this does not imply any simple copying, the word still belongs to the thing insofar as a word is not a sign coordinated to the thing ex post facto. Aristotle's analysis of how concepts are formed by induction, which we considered above, offers an indirect proof of this. Admittedly, Aristotle himself does not explicitly connect the formation of concepts with the problem of the formation of words and the learning of language, but in his paraphrase Themistius exemplifies the formation of concepts by children's learning to speak.[39] So much is the logos bound up with language.

If Greek philosophy does not want to admit this relationship between word and thing, speech and thought, the reason no doubt is that thought had to protect itself against the intimate relationship between word and thing in which the speaker lives. The dominion of this "most speakable of all languages" (Nietzsche) over thought was so great that the chief concern of philosophy was to free itself from it. Thus from early on, the Greek philosophers fought against the "onoma" as the source of the seduction and confusion of thought, and instead embraced the ideality that is constantly created in language. This was already true when Parmenides conceived the truth of the thing from the logos, and certainly after the Platonic turn to "discourse," followed by Aristotle's orienting the forms of being to the forms of assertion (schemata tes kategorias). Because here orientation to the eidos was conceived as determining the logos, the notion that language should have a being of its own could only be regarded as a confusion, and to banish and control it was the purpose of thought. Hence the critique of the correctness of names in the *Cratylus* is the first step toward modern instrumental theory of language and the ideal of a sign system of reason. Wedged in between image and sign, the being of language could only be reduced to the level of pure sign.

There is, however, an idea that is not Greek which does more justice to the being of language, and so prevented the forgetfulness of language in Western thought from being complete. This is the Christian idea of *incarnation*. Incarnation is obviously not embodiment. Neither the idea of the soul nor of God that is connected with embodiment corresponds to the Christian idea of incarnation.

The relation between soul and body as conceived in these theories—for instance, in Platonic and Pythagorean philosophy, and corresponding to the religious idea of the migration of souls—assumes that soul and body are completely different. The soul retains its own separate nature throughout all its embodiments, and the separation from the body is regarded as a purification—i.e., as a restoration of its true and real being. Even the appearance of the divine in human form, which makes Greek religion so human, has nothing to do with incarnation. God does not become man, but rather shows himself to men in human form while wholly retaining his superhuman divinity. By contrast, the fact that God became man, as the Christian religion teaches, implies the sacrifice that the crucified Christ accepts as the Son of Man. But this is a relationship that is strangely different from embodiment and is expressed theologically in the doctrine of the Trinity.

This cornerstone of Christian thought is all the more important for us because for Christian thought too the incarnation is closely connected to the problem of the word. First in the Fathers and then in the systematic elaboration of Augustinianism during the Scholastic period, the interpretation of the *mystery of the Trinity,* the most important task confronting the thinking of the Middle Ages, had to do with the relationship between human speech and thought. Here dogmatic theology relied chiefly on the prologue to the Gospel of John and, although theology was applying Greek ideas to its own theological tasks, philosophy acquired by this very means a dimension foreign to Greek thought. If the Word became flesh and if it is only in the incarnation that spirit is fully realized, then the logos is freed from its spirituality, which means, at the same time, from its cosmic potentiality. The uniqueness of the redemptive event introduces the essence of history into Western thought, brings the phenomenon of language out of its immersion in the ideality of meaning, and offers it to philosophical reflection. For, in contrast to the Greek logos, the word is pure event (verbum proprie dicitur personaliter tantum).[40]

Of course human language thereby only indirectly becomes an object of reflection. The human word is used only as a counterpart to the theological problem of the Word, the verbum dei—i.e., the unity of God the Father and God the Son. But the important thing for us is precisely that the mystery of this unity is reflected in the phenomenon of language.

Even the way the Fathers connect theological speculation about the mystery of the incarnation to Hellenistic thought is interesting because of the new dimension which they envisage. Thus initially they tried to make use of the Stoic antithesis of the inner and the outer logos (logos endiathetos—prophorikos).[41] This distinction was originally intended to distinguish the Stoic world principle of the logos from the externality of merely repeating a word.[42] But now the contrary immediately acquires a positive significance for the Christian doctrine of incarnation. The analogy between the inner and the outer word, speaking the word aloud in the vox, now acquires an exemplary value.

Creation once took place through the word of God. In this way the early Fathers used the miracle of language to explain the un-Greek idea of the creation. But most important the actual redemptive act, the sending of the Son, the mystery of the incarnation, is described in St. John's prologue itself in terms of the word. Exegesis interprets the speaking of the word to be as miraculous as the incarnation of God. In both cases the act of becoming is not the kind of becoming in which something turns into something else. Neither does it consist in separating one thing from the other (kat' apokopen), nor in lessening the inner word by its emergence into exteriority, nor in becoming something different, so that the inner word is used up.[43] Even in the earliest applications of Greek thought we can discern a new orientation toward the mysterious unity of Father and Son, of Spirit and Word. And if direct reference to the act of uttering, to speaking the word aloud, is ultimately rejected in Christian dogmatics—in the rejection of subordinationism—it is still necessary, because of this very decision, to reconsider philosophically the mystery of language and its connection to thought. The greater miracle of language lies not in the fact that the Word becomes flesh and emerges in external being, but that that which emerges and externalizes itself in utterance is always already a word. That the Word is with God from all eternity is the victorious doctrine of the church in its defense against subordinationism, and it situates the problem of language, too, entirely within inner thought.

The external word, and with it the whole problem of the variety of languages, was explicitly devalued by Augustine, though he still discusses it.[44] The external word—just like the word that is reproduced only inwardly—is tied to a particular tongue (lingua). The fact that the verbum is spoken differently in different languages, however, means only that it cannot reveal itself through the human tongue in its true being. In a depreciation of sensible appearance that is entirely Platonic, Augustine says, "We do not say a thing as it is but as it can be seen or heard by our senses." The "true" word, the verbum cordis, is completely independent of such an appearance. It is neither prolativum (brought forth) nor cogitativum in similitudine soni (thought in the likeness of sound). Hence this inner word is the mirror and the image of the divine Word. When Augustine and the Scholastics consider the problem of the verbum in order to attain the conceptual means to elucidate the mystery of the Trinity, they are concerned exclusively with this inner word, the word of the heart, and its relation to the "intelligentia" (Lat.).

Thus it is a quite specific side of the nature of language that comes to light here. The mystery of the Trinity is mirrored in the miracle of language insofar as the word that is true, because it says what the thing is, is nothing by itself and does not seek to be anything: nihil de suo habens, sed totum de illa scientia de qua nascitur. It has its being in its revealing. Exactly the same thing is true of the mystery of the Trinity. Here too the important thing is not the earthly appearance of the Redeemer as such, but rather his complete divinity, his consubstantiality with God. To grasp the independent personal existence of Christ within this sameness of being is the task of theology. Here a human analogue—the mental word, the verbum intellectus—is helpful. This is more than a mere metaphor, for the human relationship between thought and speech corresponds, despite its imperfections, to the divine relationship of the Trinity. The inner mental word is just as consubstantial with thought as is God the Son with God the Father.

One might well ask whether we are not here using the unintelligible to explain the unintelligible. What sort of word is it that remains the inner dialogue of thought and finds no outer form in sound? Does such a thing exist? Does not all our thinking always follow the paths of a particular language, and do we not know perfectly well that one has to think in a language if one really wants to speak it? Even if we remember that our reason preserves its freedom in the face of the bond of our thinking with language, either by inventing and using artificial sign languages or by translating from one language into another—which presume a capacity to rise above bondage to language to attain the sense intended—nevertheless this capacity itself is, as we have seen, linguistic. The "language of reason" is not a special language. So, given that the bond to language cannot be superseded, what sense does it make to talk about an "inner word" that is spoken, as it were, in the pure language of reason? How does the word of reason (if we can translate "intellectus" here by "reason") prove itself a real "word," if it is not a word with a sound nor even the image of one, but that which is signified by a sign—i.e., what is meant and thought itself?

Because the doctrine of the inner word is intended to undergird theological interpretation of the Trinity by analogy, the theological question as such can be of no further help to us. Rather, we must turn our attention to the "inner word" itself and ask what it may be. It cannot be simply the Greek logos, the dialogue that the soul conducts with itself. On the contrary, the mere fact that logos is translated both by ratio and verbum indicates that the phenomenon of language is becoming more important in the Scholastic elaboration of Greek metaphysics than was the case with the Greeks themselves.

The particular difficulty of enlisting the aid of Scholastic thinking for our problem is that the Christian understanding of the word—as we find it in the Fathers, who in part take over and in part extend late classical ideas—once again approximated the classical concept of logos when Aristotelianism entered High Scholasticism. Thus St. Thomas took the Christian doctrine developed from the prologue to the Gospel of John and systematically combined it with Aristotle.[45] With him, significantly, there is hardly any talk of the variety of languages, although Augustine still discusses it, even if only to discard it in favor of the "inner word." For him the doctrine of the "inner word" is the self-evident premise for investigating the connection between forma and verbum.

Nevertheless, even for Thomas logos and verbum do not completely coincide. Certainly the word is not the event of utterance, this irrevocable handing over of one's own thinking to another, but the word still has the ontological character of an event. The inner word remains related to its possible utterance. While it is being conceived by the intellect, the subject matter is at the same time ordered toward being uttered (similitudo rei concepta in intellectu et ordinata ad manifestationem vel ad se vel ad alterum). Thus the inner word is certainly not related to a particular language, nor does it have the character of vaguely imagined words that proceed from the memory; rather, it is the subject matter thought through to the end (forma excogitata). Since a process of thinking through to the end is involved, we have to acknowledge a processual element in it. It proceeds per modum egredientis. It is not utterance but thought; however, what is achieved in this speaking to oneself is the perfection of thought. So the inner word, by expressing thought, images the finiteness of our discursive understanding. Because our understanding does not compre- hend what it knows in one single inclusive glance, it must always draw what it thinks out of itself, and present it to itself as if in an inner dialogue with itself. In this sense all thought is speaking to oneself.

Greek logos philosophy undoubtedly knew this. Plato described thought as an inner dialogue of the soul with itself,[46] and the infiniteness of the dialectical effort that he requires of the philosopher expresses the dis- cursiveness of our finite understanding. However much he called for "pure thought," Plato always recognized too that the medium of onoma and logos remained essential for thought about an object. But if the doctrine of the inner word means nothing more than the discursiveness of human thought and speech, how can the "word" be analogous to the process of the divine persons expressed in the doctrine of the Trinity? Does not the very antithesis between intuition and discursiveness get in the way here? What is common to both "processes"?

It is true that no temporality enters into the relations of the divine persons to one another. But the successiveness characteristic of the discursiveness of human thought is not basically temporal in nature either. When human thought passes from one thing to another—i.e., thinks first this thing and then that—it is still not just a series of one thought after another. It does not think in a simple succession, first one thing and then another, which would mean that it would itself constantly change in the process. If it thinks first of one thing and then of another, that means it knows what it is doing, and knows how to connect the one thing with the next. Hence what is involved is not a temporal relation but a mental process, an emanatio intellectualis.

Thomas uses this Neoplatonic concept to describe both the processual character of the inner word and the process of the Trinity. This brings out a point not implied in Plato's logos philosophy. The idea of emanation in Neoplatonism implies more than the physical movement of flowing out. The primary image, rather, is that of a fountain.[47] In the process of emanation, that from which something flows, the One, is not deprived or depleted. The same is true of the birth of the Son from the Father, who does not use up anything of himself but takes something to himself. And this is likewise true of the mental emergence that takes place in the process of thought, speaking to oneself. This kind of production is at the same time a total remaining within oneself. If it can be said of the divine relationship between word and intellect that the word originates not partially but wholly (totaliter) in the intellect, then it is true also that one word originates totaliter from another—i.e., has its origin in the mind—like the deduction of a conclusion from the premises (ut conclusio ex principiis). Thus the process and emergence of thought is not a process of change (motus), not a transition from potentiality into action, but an emergence ut actus ex actu. The word is not formed only after the act of knowledge has been completed—in Scholastic terms, after the intellect has been informed by the species; it is the act of knowledge itself. Thus the word is simultaneous with this forming (formatio) of the intellect.

Thus we can see how the creation of the word came to be viewed as a true image of the Trinity. It is a true generatio, a true birth, even though, of course, there is no receptive part to go with a generating one. It is precisely the intellectual nature of the generation of the word, however, that is of decisive importance for its function as a theological model. The process of the divine persons and the process of thought really have something in common.

Nevertheless, it is the differences rather than the similarities between the divine and human word that are important to us. This is theologically sound. The mystery of the Trinity, which the analogy with the inner word is supposed to illuminate, must ultimately remain incomprehensible in terms of human thought. If the whole of the divine mind is expressed in the divine Word, then the processual element in this word signifies something for which we basically have no analogy. Insofar as, in knowing itself, the divine mind likewise knows all beings, the word of God is the word of the Spirit that knows and creates everything in one intuition (intuitus). The act of production disappears in the immediacy of divine omniscience. Creation is not a real process, but only interprets the structure of the universe in a temporal scheme.[48] If we want to grasp the processual element in the word more exactly, which is the important thing for our inquiry into the connection between language and understanding, we cannot rest content with the theologians' way of stating this difference; rather, we will have to linger over the imperfection of the human mind and its difference from the divine. Here we can follow Thomas, who specifies three differences.

1. The first thing is that the human word is potential before it is actualized. It is capable of being formed, though it is not yet formed. The

process of thought begins with something coming into our mind from our memory. But even this is an emanation, for the memory is not plundered and does not lose anything. But what comes into our mind in this way is not yet something finished and thought out to its conclusion. Rather, the real movement of thought now begins: the mind hurries from one thing to the other, turns this way and that, considering this and that, and seeks the perfect expression of its thoughts through inquiry (inquisitio) and thoughtfulness (cogitatio). The perfect word, therefore, is formed only in thinking, like a tool, but once it exists as the full perfection of the thought, nothing more is created with it. Rather, the thing is then present in it. Thus it is not a real tool. Thomas found a brilliant metaphor for this: the word is like a mirror in which the thing is seen. The curious thing about this mirror, however, is that it nowhere extends beyond the image of the thing. In it nothing is mirrored except this one thing, so that the whole mirror reflects only the image (similitudo). What is remarkable about this metaphor is that the word is understood here entirely as the perfect reflection of the thing—i.e., as the expression of the thing—and has left behind it the path of the thought to which alone, however, it owes its existence. This does not happen with the divine mind.

2. Unlike the divine word, the human word is essentially incomplete. No human word can express our mind completely. But as the image of the mirror shows, this does not mean that the word as such is incomplete. The word reflects completely what the mind is thinking. Rather, the imperfection of the human mind consists in its never being completely present to itself but in being dispersed into thinking this or that. From this essential imperfection it follows that the human word is not one, like the divine word, but must necessarily be many words. Hence the variety of words does not in any way mean that the individual word has some remediable deficiency, in that it did not completely express what the mind is thinking; but because our intellect is imperfect—i.e., is not completely present to itself in what it knows—it needs the multiplicity of words. It does not really know what it knows.

3. The third difference is connected with this point. Whereas God completely expresses his nature and substance in the Word in pure immediacy, every thought that we think (and therefore every word in which the thought expresses itself) is a mere accident of the mind. The word of human thought is directed toward the thing, but it cannot contain it as a whole within itself. Thus thought constantly proceeds to new

conceptions and is fundamentally incapable of being wholly realized in any. This incapacity for completeness has a positive side: it reveals the true infinity of the mind, which constantly surpasses itself in a new mental process and in doing so also finds the freedom for constantly new projects.

Summing up what we have learned from the theology of the verbum, *first* let us make a point that has hardly come to the fore in the preceding analysis—nor was it expressed in Scholastic thought. Yet it is of particular importance for the hermeneutical phenomenon. The inner unity of thinking and speaking to oneself, which corresponds to the Trinitarian mystery of the incarnation, implies that the inner mental word *is not formed by a reflective act*. A person who thinks something—i.e., says it to himself —means by it the thing that he thinks. His mind is not directed back toward his own thinking when he forms the word. The word is, of course, the product of the work of his mind. It forms the word in itself by thinking the thought through. But unlike other products it remains entirely within the mental sphere. This gives the impression that what is involved is a relationship to itself and that speaking to oneself is a reflexive act. This is not so, in fact, but this structure of thought undoubtedly explains why thought can direct itself reflectively toward itself and can thus become an object to itself. The inwardness of the word, which constitutes the inner unity of thought and speech, is the reason for its being easy to miss the direct and unreflective character of the "word." In thinking, a person does not move from the one thing to the other, from thinking to speaking to himself. The word does not emerge in a sphere of the mind that is still free of thought (in aliquo sui nudo). Hence the appearance is created that the formation of the word arises from the mind's being directed toward itself. In fact there is no reflection when the word is formed, for the word is not expressing the mind but the thing intended. The starting point for the formation of the word is the substantive content (the species) that fills the mind. The thought seeking expression refers not to the mind but to the thing. Thus the word is not the expression of the mind but is concerned with the similitudo rei. The subject matter that is thought (the species) and the word belong as closely together as possible. Their unity is so close that the word does not occupy a second place in the mind beside the "species" (Lat.); rather, the word is that in which knowledge is consummated—i.e., that in which the species is fully thought. Thomas points out that in this respect the word resembles light, which is what makes color visible.

But there is a *second* thing that Scholastic thinking teaches us. The difference between the unity of the divine Word and the multiplicity of human words does not exhaust the matter. Rather, unity and multiplicity are fundamentally in dialectical relationship to each other. The dialectic of this relationship conditions the whole nature of the word. Even the divine Word is not entirely free of the idea of multiplicity. It is true that the divine Word is one unique word that came into the world in the form of the Redeemer; but insofar as it remains an event—and this is the case, despite the rejection of subordinationism, as we have seen—there is an essential connection between the unity of the divine Word and its appearance in the church. The proclamation of salvation, the content of the Christian gospel, is itself an event that takes place in sacrament and preaching, and yet it expresses only what took place in Christ's redemptive act. Hence it is one word that is proclaimed ever anew in preaching. Its character as gospel, then, already points to the multiplicity of its proclamation. The meaning of the word cannot be detached from the event of proclamation. *Quite the contrary, being an event is a characteristic belonging to the meaning itself*. It is like a curse, which obviously cannot be separated from the act of uttering it. What we understand from it is not an abstractable logical sense like that of a statement, but the actual curse that occurs in it.[49] The same holds for the unity and the multiplicity of the word proclaimed by the church. The saving message preached in every sermon is the crucifixion and resurrection of Christ. The Christ of the resurrection and the Christ of the kerygma are one and the same. Modern Protestant theology, in particular, has elaborated the eschatological character of the faith that depends on this dialectical relationship.

The human word puts the dialectical relationship between the multiplicity of words and the unity of the word in a new light. Plato recognized that the human word is essentially discursive—i.e., that the association of a multiplicity of words expresses one meaning; this structure of the logos he developed dialectically. Then Aristotle demonstrated the logical structure of the proposition, the judgment, the syllogism, and the argument. But even this does not exhaust the matter. The unity of the word that explicates itself in the multiplicity of words manifests something that is not covered by the structure of logic and that brings out the *character of language as event*: the *process of concept formation*. In developing the doctrine of the verbum, Scholastic thought is not content with viewing concept formation as simply the reflection of the order of things.

(c) LANGUAGE AND CONCEPT FORMATION

The natural concept formation that keeps pace with language does not always simply follow the order of things, but very often takes place as a result of accidents and relations. This is confirmed by a glance at Plato's analysis of concepts and at Aristotle's definitions. But the precedence of the logical order established by the concepts of substance and accidence makes language's natural concept formation appear only as an imperfection of our finite mind. It is because we know only the accidents that we follow them in forming concepts. Even if this is right, a curious advantage follows from this imperfection, as Thomas seems correctly to have pointed out: the freedom to form an infinite number of concepts and to penetrate what is meant ever more deeply.[50] Because the process of thought is conceived as the process of explication in words, a logical achievement of language becomes apparent that cannot be fully understood in terms of an order of things as they would appear to an infinite mind. The subordination of the natural concept formation that occurs in language to the structure of logic, as taught by Aristotle and, following him, Thomas, thus has only a relative truth. *Rather, when the Greek idea of logic is penetrated by Christian theology, something new is born: the medium of language, in which the mediation of the incarnation event achieves its full truth.* Christology prepares the way for a new philosophy of man, which mediates in a new way between the mind of man in its finitude and the divine infinity. Here what we have called the hermeneutical experience finds its own, special ground.

Thus we turn to the natural formation of concepts that takes place in language. Even if each particular case of speech involves subordinating what is meant to the universality of a pre-established verbal meaning, it is obvious that speaking cannot be thought of as the combination of these acts of subsumption, through which something particular is subordinated to a general concept. A person who speaks—who, that is to say, uses the general meanings of words—is so oriented toward the particularity of what he is perceiving that everything he says acquires a share in the particularity of the circumstances he is considering.[51]

But that means, on the other hand, that the general concept meant by the word is enriched by any given perception of a thing, so that what emerges is a new, more specific word formation which does more justice to the particularity of that act of perception. However certainly speaking implies using pre-established words with general meanings, at the same time, a constant process of concept formation is going on, by means of which the life of a language develops.

The logical schema of induction and abstraction is very misleading here, since in verbal consciousness there is no explicit reflection on what is common to different things, nor does using words in their general meaning regard what they designate as a case subsumed under a universal. The universality of the genus and the formation of classificatory concepts are far removed from verbal consciousness. Even disregarding all formal similarities that have nothing to do with the generic concept, if a person transfers an expression from one thing to the other, he has in mind something that is common to both of them; but this in no way needs to be generic universality. Rather, he is following his widening experience, which looks for similarities, whether in the appearance of things or in their significance for us. The genius of verbal consciousness consists in being able to express these similarities. This is its fundamental metaphorical nature, and it is important to see that to regard the metaphorical use of a word as not its real sense is the prejudice of a theory of logic that is alien to language.[52]

It is obvious that the particularity of an experience finds expression in metaphorical transference, and is not at all the fruit of a concept formed by means of abstraction. But it is equally obvious that knowledge of what is common is obtained in this way. Thus thought can turn for its own instruction[53] to this stock that language has built up. Plato explicitly did so with his "flight into the logoi." But classificatory logic also starts from the logical advance work that language has done for it.[54]

This is confirmed by a look at its *prehistory*, especially at the theory of concept formation in the Platonic Academy. We have seen that Plato's call to rise above names assumes that the cosmos of ideas is fundamentally independent of language. But since rising above names takes place in regard to the idea and is a dialectic—i.e., an insight into the unity of what is observed, seeing what is common to various phenomena—it follows the natural direction in which language itself develops. Rising above names means simply that the truth of the thing is not contained in the name itself. It does not mean that thinking can dispense with the use of name and logos. On the contrary, Plato always recognized that these intermediaries of thought are necessary, even though they must always be regarded as susceptible of improvement. The idea, the true being of the thing, cannot be known in any other way than by passing through these intermediaries.

But is there a knowledge of the idea itself as this particular and individual thing? Is not the nature of things a whole in the same way that language too is a whole? Just as individual words acquire their meaning and relative unambiguity only in the unity of discourse, so the true knowledge of being can be achieved only in the whole of the relational structure of the ideas. This is the thesis of Plato's *Parmenides*. This, however, raises the following question: in order to define a single idea—i.e., to be able to distinguish it from everything else that exists—do we not need to know the whole?

We can hardly escape this consequence if, like Plato, we regard the cosmos of ideas as the true structure of being. We are told that the Platonist Speusippus, Plato's successor as the head of the Academy, did not escape it.[55] We know that he was particularly concerned with discovering what is common (homoia) and that he far exceeded what generic logic called universalization by using analogy—i.e., proportional correspondence—as a method of research. Here the dialectical capacity of discovering similarities and seeing one quality common to many things is still very close to the free universality of language and its principles of word formation. Analogies, which Speusippus sought everywhere—correspondences such as "wings are to birds what fins are to fish"—thus serve the definition of concepts because at the same time these correspondences constitute the most important developmental principles in the formation of words. Transference from one sphere to another not only has a logical function; it corresponds to the fundamental metaphoricity of language. The well-known stylistic figure of metaphor is only the rhetorical form of this universal—both linguistic and logical—generative principle. Thus Aristotle says, "To make a good metaphor means to recognize similarity."[56] Aristotle's *Topics* offers many confirmations of the indissolubility of the connection between concept and language. There, the common genus is derived explicitly from the observation of similarity.[57] Thus at the beginning of generic logic stands the advance work of language itself.

Accordingly Aristotle himself always assigns the greatest importance to the way in which the order of things becomes apparent in speaking about them. (The "categories"—and not only what Aristotle explicitly calls such—are forms of statement.) The formation of concepts by language is not only used by philosophical thought; it is developed further in certain directions. We have already referred above to the fact that Aristotle's theory of concept formation, the theory of the epagoge, could be illustrated by children learning to speak.[58] In fact, however fundamental Plato's demystification of speech was for Aristotle, however great its influence on his own development of "logic," however much he was concerned to reflect the order of things and to detach it from all verbal contingencies by the conscious use of a logic of definition, especially in the classificatory description of nature, nevertheless for him speech and thought remained completely unified.

Hence the few places where he speaks of language as such hardly isolate the sphere of verbal meaning from the world of things it names. When Aristotle says of sounds or written signs that they "describe" when they become a symbolon, this means, certainly, that they do not exist naturally but by convention (kata suntheken). But his is not an instrumental theory of signs. Rather, the convention according to which the sounds of language or the signs of writing mean something is not an agreement on a means of understanding—that would already presuppose language; it is the agreement on which human community, its harmony with respect to what is good and proper, is founded.[59] Agreement in using verbal sounds and signs is only an expression of that fundamental agreement in what is good and proper. It is true that the Greeks liked to consider what was good and proper, what they called the nomoi, as the decree and the achievement of divine men. But for Aristotle this derivation of the nomos characterizes more its value than its actual origin. This is not to say that Aristotle no longer acknowledges the religious tradition, but that this, like every question of origin, is for him a way to the knowledge of being and value. The convention of which Aristotle speaks in regard to language characterizes its mode of being and implies nothing about its origin.

If we recall the analysis of the epagoge, we shall find further evidence of this.[60] There, we saw, Aristotle ingeniously left open the question of how universal concepts are formed. We can see now that he was taking account of the fact that the natural process of concept formation by language is always already going on. Thus even according to Aristotle the formation of concepts by language possesses a perfectly undogmatic freedom, for experiencing similarity among the things one encounters, which then leads to a universal, is merely a preliminary achievement: it stands at the beginning of science but is not yet science. This is what Aristotle emphasizes. If science erects compelling proof as its ideal, then it must advance beyond such modes of procedure. Thus, in accord with this ideal of proof, Aristotle criticized both Speusippus' doctrine of the common and the diairetical dialectic of Plato.

The consequence of accepting the ideal of logical proof as a yardstick, however, is that the Aristotelian critique has robbed the logical achievement of language of its scientific legitimacy. That achievement is recognized only from the point of view of rhetoric and is understood there as the artistic device of metaphor. The logical ideal of the ordered arrangement of concepts takes precedence over the living metaphoricity of language, on which all natural concept formation depends. For only a grammar based on logic will distinguish between the *proper* and the *metaphorical* meaning of a word. What originally constituted the basis of the life of language and its logical productivity, the spontaneous and inventive seeking out of similarities by means of which it is possible to order things, is now marginalized and instrumentalized into a rhetorical figure called metaphor. The struggle between philosophy and rhetoric for the training of Greek youth, which was decided with the victory of Attic philosophy, has also this side to it, namely that thinking about language becomes the matter of a grammar and rhetoric that have already acknowledged scientific concept formation as an ideal. Thus the sphere of verbal meanings begins to become detached from the sphere of things encountered in verbal form. Stoic logic speaks of incorporeal meanings by means of which talk about things occurs (to lekton). It is highly significant that these meanings are put on the same level as topos—i.e., space.[61] Just as empty space is first given to thought only by mentally removing the objects related to each another within it,[62] so "meanings" as such are now conceived by themselves for the first time, and a concept is created for them by mentally removing the things that are named by the meaning of words. Meanings, too, are like a space in which things are related to one another.

Such ideas obviously become possible only when the natural relationship—i.e., the intimate unity of speech and thought—is upset. We can mention the connection between Stoic thought and the grammatical and syntactical structure of the Latin language, which Lohmann has pointed out.[63] Undoubtedly, the fact that two languages were beginning to be used throughout the Hellenistic oikumene had a beneficial influence on thinking about language. But perhaps this development originates far earlier, and it is the birth of science itself that initiates this process. If so, its beginnings go back to the early days of Greek science. That this is so is suggested by the development of scientific concepts in the fields of music, mathematics, and physics, because there a field of rational objectivities is marked out, the construction of which calls into being corresponding terms that can no longer really be called words. It can be stated as a fundamental principle that wherever words assume a mere sign function, the original connection between speaking and thinking, with which we are concerned, has been changed into an instrumental relationship. This changed relationship of word and sign is at the basis of concept formation in science and has become so self-evident to us that it requires a special effort of memory to recall that, alongside the scientific ideal of unambiguous designation, the life of language itself continues unchanged.

There is no lack of reminders, of course, when we consider the history of philosophy. Thus we showed that in medieval thought the problem of language as it pertains to theology constantly points back to the problem of the unity of thinking and speaking, and also brings out an aspect of the problem that classical Greek philosophy was unaware of. That the word is a process in which the unity of what is meant is fully expressed—as in speculation on the verbum—is something new that goes beyond the Platonic dialectic of the one and the many. For Plato sees the logos itself as moving within this dialectic and being nothing but the undergoing of the dialectic of the ideas. There is no real problem of interpretation here, in that its means, word and speech, are constantly being overtaken by the thinking mind. In contrast, we found that in Trinitarian speculation the procession of the divine persons involves the Neoplatonic inquiry into explication, unfolding—i.e., the proceeding from the One, and hence for the first time does justice to the processual character of the Word. But the problem of language could not emerge fully until the Scholastic combination of Christian thought with Aristotelian philosophy was supplemented by a new element that turned the distinction between the divine and the human mind into something positive and was to acquire the greatest importance for modern times. This is the element, common to both, of the *creative*. This, it seems to me, is the real importance of *Nicholas of Cusa*, who has recently been so much discussed.[64]

Of course the analogy between the two modes of creativity has its limits; they correspond to the differences stressed above between the divine and the human word. Certainly, the divine word creates the world, but not in a temporal succession of creative thoughts and creative days. The human mind, on the other hand, possesses the whole of its thoughts only in temporal succession. It is true that this is not a purely temporal relationship, as we have seen already in St. Thomas. Nicholas of Cusa also points this out. It is like the number series, whose production is not really a temporal occurrence either but a movement of reason. Nicholas of Cusa discerns the same movement of reason operating when genera and species are developed from out of the sphere of the sensible and explicated in individual concepts and words. They, too, are entia rationis. However Platonic and Neoplatonic this talk of unfolding may sound, in actual fact Nicholas of Cusa has decisively overcome the emanistic schema of the Neoplatonic doctrine of explication. He opposes to it the Christian doctrine of the verbum.[65] The word is for him no less than the mind itself, not a diminished or weakened manifestation of it. Knowing this constitutes the superiority of the Christian philosopher over the Platonist. Accordingly, the multiplicity in which the human mind unfolds itself is not a mere fall from true unity and not a loss of its home. Rather, there has to be a positive justification for the finitude of the human mind, however much this finitude remains related to the infinite unity of absolute being. This is prepared for in the idea of complicatio, and from this point of view the phenomenon of language also acquires a new aspect. It is the human mind that both complicates and explicates. The unfolding into discursive multiplicity is not only conceptual, but also extends into the verbal sphere. It is the variety of possible appellations—according to the various languages —that potentiates conceptual differentiation.

With the nominalist breakup of the classical logic of essence, the problem of language enters a new stage. Suddenly it is of positive significance that things can be articulated in various ways (though not in any way at all) according to their similarities and their differences. If the relationship of genus and species can be justified not only with regard to the nature of things—on the model of the "genuine" species in the self-construction of living nature—but also in another way with regard to man and his power to give names, then languages as they have grown up historically, with their history of meanings, their grammar and their syntax, can be seen as the varied forms of a logic of experience, of natural—i.e., historical—experience (which even includes supernatural experience). The thing itself is quite clear.[66] The articulation of words and things that each language performs in its own way always constitutes a primary natural way of forming concepts that is much different from the system of scientific concept formation. It exclusively follows the human aspect of things, the system of man's needs and interests. What a linguistic community regards as important about a thing can be given the same name as other things that are perhaps of a quite different nature in other respects, so long as they all have the same quality that is important to the community. A nomenclature (impositio nominis) in no way corresponds to the concepts of science and its classificatory system of genus and species. Rather, compared to the latter, it is often accidental attributes from which the general meaning of a word is derived.

Moreover, we must take account of the fact that science has a certain influence on language. For example, we no longer call whales fish because now everyone knows that whales are mammals. On the other hand, the rich variety of popular names for certain things is being ironed out, partly as a result of modern communications and partly by scientific and technological standardization, just as our vocabulary has generally contracted rather than expanded in such areas. There is said to be an African language that has two hundred different words for camel, according to the camel's particular circumstances and relationships to the desert dwellers. The specific meaning that "camel" has in all these different denominations makes it seem an entirely different creature.[67] In such cases we can say that there is an extreme tension between the genus and the linguistic designation. But we can also say that the tendency toward conceptual universality and that toward pragmatic meaning are never completely harmonized in any living language. That is why it is always artificial and contrary to the nature of language to measure the contingency of natural concept formation against the true order of things and to see the former as purely accidental. This contingency comes about, in fact, through the human mind's necessary and legitimate range of variation in articulating the essential order of things.

Despite the scriptural importance of the confusion of tongues, the fact that the Latin Middle Ages did not really pursue this aspect of the problem of language can be explained chiefly by the unquestioned dominance of Latin among scholars and by the continued influence of the Greek doctrine of the logos. It was only with the Renaissance, when the laity became important and the national languages part of cultivated learning, that people began to think productively about the relation of these languages to the inner—i.e., "natural"—word. But we must be careful not to ascribe the posture of inquiry characteristic of modern linguistic philosophy and its instrumental concept of language to the Renaissance. The significance of the first emergence of the problem of language in the Renaissance lies rather in the fact that the Graeco-Christian heritage was still automatically accepted as valid. This is quite clear in Nicholas of Cusa. As an explication of the unity of the spirit, the concepts expressed in words still retain their connection with a natural word (vocabulum naturale), which is reflected (relucet) in all of them, however arbitrary the individual name may be (impositio nominis fit ad beneplacitum).[68] We may ask ourselves what this connection is and what this natural word is supposed to be. But it makes methodological sense to say that the individual words of each language are in an ultimate harmony with those of every other one, in that all languages are explications of the one unity of the mind.

Nicholas of Cusa, too, does not mean by the *natural word* the word of an original language that preceded the confusion of tongues. This kind of language of Adam, in the sense of the doctrine of a primal state, is far removed from his thinking. He starts, rather, from the fundamental inexactness of all human knowledge. Combining Platonic and nominalist elements, Cusa's theory of knowledge is that all human knowledge is mere conjecture and opinion (coniectura, opinio).[69] It is this doctrine that he now applies to language. Thus he can acknowledge the differences among national languages and the apparent arbitrariness of their vocabularies, without for that reason falling into a purely conventionalist theory of language and an instrumentalist conception of language. Just as human knowledge is essentially "inexact"—i.e., admits of a more or a less—so also is human language. Something for which there is a proper expression in one language (propria vocabula) is expressed in another by a more barbarous and remote word (magis barbara et remotiora vocabula). Thus expressions are more or less proper (propria vocabula). In a certain sense, all actual designations are arbitrary, and yet they have a necessary connection with the natural expression (nomen naturale) that corresponds to the thing itself (forma). Every expression is fitting (congruum), but not every one is exact (precisum).

Such a theory of language presupposes not that the things (formae) to which the words are attached belong to a pre-established order of original models that human knowledge is gradually approaching, but that this order is created by differentiation and combination out of the given nature of things. In this Nicholas of Cusa's thought has been influenced by nominalism. If the genera and species are themselves in this way intelligible being (entia rationis), then it is clear that the words can be in agreement with the perception of the thing to which they give expression, even if different languages use different words. For in this case it is not a question of variations in expression but of variations in the perception of the thing and of the formation of concepts that follows it—i.e., there is an essential inexactness; nevertheless, this variability does not preclude all expressions from being a reflection of the thing itself (forma). This kind of essential inexactness can be overcome only if the mind rises to the infinite.

In the infinite there is, then, only one single thing (forma) and one single word (vocabulum), namely the ineffable Word of God (verbum Dei) that is reflected in everything (relucet).

If we thus regard the human mind as related to the divine as a copy to the original, we can accept the range of variation in human languages. As at the beginning, in the discussion about the search for analogies in the Platonic academy, so also at the end, in the medieval discussion of universals, there is the idea of a real affinity between word and concept. We are still a long way here from the relativity of worldviews that modern thought considers a consequence of the variation of languages. Despite all their differences, Nicholas of Cusa still preserves their concordance, and that is what the Christian Platonist is concerned with. Essential for him is the fact that all human speech is related to the thing, and not so much the fact that human knowledge of things is bound to language. The latter represents only a prismatic refraction in which there shines the one truth.

3 LANGUAGE AS HORIZON OF A HERMENEUTIC ONTOLOGY

(A) LANGUAGE AS EXPERIENCE OF THE WORLD

We have considered in depth some phases of the history of the problem of language in order to present certain points of view that are remote from the modern philosophy and science of language. Since Herder and Humboldt, modern thinking about language has been governed by a quite different interest. It tries to study the way in which natural language unfolds in the range of experience of differences between human languages—an insight painfully won against the forces of rationalism and orthodoxy. Regarding every language as an organism, it undertakes a comparative study of the large variety of means which the human mind has used to exercise its capacity for language. Nicholas of Cusa was still a long way from this kind of empirical comparative inquiry. He remained a Platonist, since for him differences within the inexact imply no truth of their own and hence are deserving of interest only insofar as they are in agreement with the "true." For him the national peculiarities of the emergent national languages are without interest; in this respect he differed from Wilhelm von Humboldt, for example.

If we are to do justice to this founder of the modern philosophy of language, however, we must beware of the overresonance created by comparative linguistics and the psychology of peoples that Humboldt inaugurated. With him the problem of the "truth of the word"[70] is not yet entirely obscured. Humboldt does not examine the empirical variety of the structure of human language merely in order to penetrate the individual peculiarities of different peoples by means of this tangible field of human expression.[71] His interest in individuality, like that of his age, is not to be regarded as a turning away from the universality of the concept. Rather, for him there exists an indissoluble connection between individuality and universal nature. Together with the feeling of individuality, the sense of a totality is given as well,[72] and so the study of the individuality of linguistic phenomena is itself intended as a means of insight into the whole of human language.

He starts from the position that languages are the products of man's "mental power." Wherever there is language, the originary verbal power of the human mind is at work, and every language is capable of attaining the general goal toward which this natural power of man is directed. This does not preclude but rather legitimates the fact that comparing languages calls for a criterion of perfection according to which they are differentiated. For the "effort to realize the idea of the perfect language" is common to all languages, and the business of the linguist is to investigate to what extent and with what means the various languages approximate this idea. For Humboldt, then, there are undoubtedly differences in the perfection of the various languages; but he does not force a preconceived criterion on the variety of phenomena he is studying; rather, he derives this criterion from the inner nature of language itself and its rich variety.

Thus his normative interest in comparing the structure of human languages does not get in the way of acknowledging the individuality—and that means the relative perfection—of each language. It is well known that Humboldt taught that every language should be seen as a particular view of the world, and he investigated the *inner form* in which the originary event of human language formation is, in each instance, differentiated. Behind this view there lies not only idealistic philosophy, which emphasizes the part played by the subject in understanding the world, but also the *metaphysics of individuality* first developed by Leibniz. This is expressed both in the concept of mental power, which is the corollary of the phenomenon of language, and especially in Humboldt's claim that this mental power—that is, the interior sense of language —differentiates not only sounds but also whole languages. He speaks of the "individuality of intimate sense in the phenomenon" and means by this "the energy of the power" by means of which the inner sense acts on the sound.[73] To him it is self-evident that this energy cannot be everywhere the same. Thus, as we see, he shares the principle of the Enlightenment, namely to see the principle of individuation in the approach to the true and the perfect. It is the monadological universe of Leibniz, of which the differences in the structure of human language are a part.

The path of investigation that Humboldt follows is characterized by *abstraction down to form*. Although Humboldt revealed the significance of human languages as mirrors of the individual mentalities of the nations, nevertheless he thereby limited the universality of the connection between language and thought to the formalism of a faculty.

Humboldt sees the main significance of the problem when he says that language is "really situated in relation to an infinite and truly boundless sphere, the epitome of everything that can be thought. Thus it must make an infinite use of finite means and is able to do so through the identity of the faculty that generates thoughts and language."[74] The actual essence of a faculty that is aware of itself is to be able to make infinite use of finite means. It embraces everything on which it can act. Thus the linguistic faculty is also superior to any content to which it can be applied. Hence, as the formalism of a faculty, it can always be detached from the determinate content of what is said. To this Humboldt owes brilliant insights, especially since he does not fail to see that, however limited the power of the individual when compared with the might of language, there is a recipro-cal relationship between the individual and language which allows man a certain freedom with respect to language. That this freedom is limited he is aware, inasmuch as every language has a life of its own vis-à-vis what is said at any given time, so that in it one vividly senses "the way in which the distant past is still connected with the feeling of the present since language has passed through the sensations of earlier generations and has preserved their inspiration."[75] In language conceived as form, Humboldt has still been able to perceive the historical life of the mind. To base the phenomenon of language on the concept of a linguistic faculty gives the concept of inner form a special legitimacy justified by the historical vicissitudes of the life of language.

Nevertheless this concept of language constitutes an abstraction that has to be reversed for our purposes. *Verbal form and traditionary content cannot be separated in the hermeneutic experience.* If every language is a view of the world, it is so not primarily because it is a particular type of language (in the way that linguists view language) but because of what is said or handed down in this language.

An example will illustrate how the problem is shifted—or, rather, comes into the right focus—when the unity between language and tradition is acknowledged. Wilhelm von Humboldt once remarked that to learn a foreign language involves acquiring a new standpoint in regard to one's previous worldview, and he went on to say, "Only because we always more or less totally carry over our own worldview, even our own language-view, into a foreign language, is this achievement not experienced in a pure and perfect way."[76] What is here considered a limitation and a shortcoming (and rightly so, from the point of view of the linguist, who is concerned with his own way of knowledge) is, in fact, the way hermeneutical experience is consummated. It is not learning a foreign language as such but its use, whether in conversation with its speakers or in the study of its literature, that gives one a new standpoint "on one's previous worldview." However thoroughly one may adopt a foreign frame of mind, one still does not forget one's worldview and language-view. Rather, the other world we encounter is not only foreign but is also related to us. It has not only its own truth *in itself* but also its own truth *for us*.

The other world that is experienced here is not simply an object of research and knowledge. Someone who exposes himself to the literary tradition of a foreign language so that it comes to speak to him has no objective relationship to the language as such, any more than has the traveler who uses it. He has quite a different attitude from the philologist, to whom linguistic tradition is material for the history of language and comparative linguistics. We know this only too well from our experience of learning foreign languages and the strange way that the works of literature our teachers used to introduce us to these languages got killed in the process. Obviously we cannot understand a traditionary work if we thematize the language as such. But the other side of the question, which must not be ignored, is that it is impossible to understand what the work has to say if it does not speak into a familiar world that can find a point of contact with what the text says. Thus to learn a language is to increase the extent of what one can learn. Only on the reflective level of the linguist could one imagine saying that this point of contact prevents the achievement of learning a foreign language from being experienced "in a pure and perfect way." The hermeneutical experience is exactly the reverse of this: to have learned a foreign language and to be able to understand it—this formalism of a faculty—means nothing else than to be in a position to accept what is said in it as said to oneself. The exercise of this capacity for understanding always means that what is said has a claim over one, and this is impossible if one's own "worldview and language-view" is not also involved. It would be worth investigating the extent to which Humboldt's own actual familiarity with the literary traditions of different peoples played a part in his abstract concern with language as such.

His real importance for the problem of hermeneutics lies elsewhere, namely in showing that *a language-view is a worldview*. He recognized that the living act of speech, verbal energeia, is the essence of language, and thus overcame the dogmatism of the grammarians. On the basis of the concept of mental power, which dominates all his thinking about language, he was able to correctly formulate the question of the origin of language, which had been weighed down with theological considerations. He showed how mistaken this question is if it implies a human world without language, which subsequently emerged into language somehow at some time in the past. By contrast, Humboldt rightly emphasized that language was human from its very beginning.[77] This not only alters the meaning of the question of the origin of language; it is the basis of a far-reaching anthropological insight.

Language is not just one of man's possessions in the world; rather, on it depends the fact that man has a *world* at all. The world as world exists for man as for no other creature that is in the world. But this world is verbal in nature. This is the real heart of Humboldt's assertion (which he intended quite differently) that languages are worldviews.[78] By this Humboldt means that language maintains a kind of independent life vis-à-vis the individual member of a linguistic community; and as he grows into it, it introduces him to a particular orientation and relationship to the world as well. But the ground of this statement is more important, namely that language has no independent life apart from the world that comes to language within it. Not only is the world world only insofar as it comes into language, but language, too, has its real being only in the fact that the world is presented in it. Thus, that language is originarily human means at the same time that man's being-in-the-world is primordially linguistic. We will have to investigate the relation between *language and world* in order to attain the horizon adequate to the fact that *hermeneutic experience is verbal in nature*.[79]

To have a world means to have an orientation (Verhalten) toward it. To have an orientation toward the world, however, means to keep oneself so free from what one encounters of the world that one can present it to oneself as it is. This capacity is at once to have a world and to have language. The concept of *world* is thus opposed to the concept of *environment*, which all living beings in the world possess.

It is true that the concept of environment was first used for the purely human world, and for it alone. The environment is the "milieu" in which man lives, and its importance consists in its influence on his character and way of life. Man is not independent of the particular aspect that the world shows him. Thus the concept of environment is originally a social concept that tries to express the individual's dependence on society—i.e., it is related only to man. In a broad sense, however, this concept can be used to comprehend all the conditions on which a living creature depends. But it is thus clear that man, unlike all other living creatures, has a "world," for other creatures do not in the same sense have a relationship to the world, but are, as it were, embedded in their environment. Thus extending the concept of environment to all living things has in fact changed its meaning.

Moreover, unlike all other living creatures, man's relationship to the world is characterized by *freedom from environment*. This freedom implies the linguistic constitution of the world. Both belong together. To rise above the pressure of what impinges on us from the world means to have language and to have "world." It is in this form that recent philosophical anthropology, in its confrontation with Nietzsche, has worked out the special position of man and shown that the verbal constitution of the world is far from meaning that man's relationship to the world is imprisoned within a verbally schematized environment.[80] On the contrary, wherever language and men exist, there is not only a freedom from the pressure of the world, but this freedom from the environment is also freedom in relation to the names that we give things, as stated in the profound account in Genesis, according to which God gave Adam the authority to name creatures.

Once we realize the full importance of this, it becomes clear why man has a multiplicity of diverse languages, as well as a general verbal relationship to the world. Man's freedom in relation to the environment is the reason for his free capacity for speech and also for the historical multiplicity of human speech in relation to the one world. When myth speaks of a primal language and the subsequent confusion of languages, this idea meaningfully reflects the genuine riddle that the multiplicity of languages presents for reason; but in what it says this mythical account turns things on their head when it conceives mankind as originally unified in using an original language later sundered in a confusion of languages. The truth is that because man can always rise above the particular environment in which he happens to find himself, and because his speech brings the world into language, he is, from the beginning, free for variety in exercising his capacity for language.

To rise above the environment has from the outset a human—i.e., a verbal—significance. Animals can leave their environment and move over the whole earth without severing their environmental dependence. For man, however, rising above the environment means *rising to "world"* itself, to true environment. This does not mean that he leaves his habitat but that he has another posture toward it—a free, distanced orientation—that is always realized in language. Animals have a language only per aequivocationem, for language is a human possibility that is free and variable in its use. For man language is variable not only in the sense that there are foreign languages that one can learn but also variable in itself, for it contains various possibilities for saying the same thing. Even in exceptional cases like deaf and dumb language, there is not a real, expressive language of gesture but a substitution of an articulated use of gesture that represents articulated vocalized language. Animals do not have this variability when making themselves understood to one another. This means, ontologically, that they make themselves understood, but not about matters of fact, the epitome of which is the world. Aristotle saw this with full clarity. Whereas the call of animals induces particular behavior in the members of the species, men's coming to a linguistic understanding with one another through the logos reveals the existent itself.[81]

From the relation of language to world follows its unique *factualness* (Sachlichkeit). It is matters of fact (Sachverhalte) that come into language. That a thing behaves (eine Sache verhalt sich) in various ways permits one to recognize its independent otherness, which presupposes a real distance between the speaker and the thing. That something can foreground itself as a genuine matter of fact and become the content of an assertion that others can understand depends on this distance. In the structure of a matter of fact that foregrounds itself, there is always a negative aspect as well. To be this and not that constitutes the determinacy of all beings. Fundamentally, therefore, there are also negative matters of fact. This is the aspect of language that Greek philosophy conceived for the first time. Even in the silent monotony of the Eleatic principle of the association of being and noein, Greek thought followed the fundamental factualness of language; and then, in overcoming the Eleatic conception of being, Plato saw the element of non-being in being as what really made it possible to speak of the existent at all. In the elaborate articulation of the logos of the eidos, the question of the real being of language could not be properly developed, since Greek thought was so full of the sense of the factualness of language. By pursuing the natural experience of the world in its linguistic form, it conceives the world as being. Whatever it conceives as existent emerges as logos, as an expressible matter of fact, from the surrounding whole that constitutes the world-horizon of language. What is thus conceived of as existing is not really the *object* of statements, but it "comes to language in statements." It thereby acquires its truth, its being evident in human thought. Thus Greek ontology is based on the factualness of language, in that it conceives the essence of language in terms of statements.

On the other hand, however, it must be emphasized that language has its true being only in dialogue, in *coming to an understanding*. This is not to be understood as if that were the purpose of language. Coming to an understanding is not a mere action, a purposeful activity, a setting up of signs through which I transmit my will to others. Coming to an understanding as such, rather, does not need any tools, in the proper sense of the word. It is a life process in which a community of life is lived out. To that extent, coming to an understanding through human conversation is no different from the understanding that occurs between animals. But human language must be thought of as a special and unique life process since, in linguistic communication, "world" is disclosed. Reaching an understanding in language places a subject matter before those communicating like a disputed object set between them. Thus the world is the common ground, trodden by none and recognized by all, uniting all who talk to one another. All kinds of human community are kinds of linguistic community: even more, they form language. For language is by nature the language of conversation; it fully realizes itself only in the process of coming to an understanding. That is why it is not a mere means in that process.

For this reason invented systems of artificial communication are never languages. For artificial languages, such as secret languages or systems of mathematical symbols, have no basis in a community of language or life; they are introduced and applied only as means and tools of communication. For this reason they always presuppose a prior agreement, which is that of language. It is well known that the consensus by which an artificial language is introduced necessarily belongs to another language. In a real community of language, on the other hand, we do not first decide to agree but are always already in agreement, as Aristotle showed.[82] The object of understanding is not the verbal means of understanding as such but rather the world that presents itself to us in common life and that embraces everything about which understanding can be reached. Agreeing about a language is not the paradigmatic case but rather a special case—agreeing about an instrument, a system of signs, that does not have its being in dialogue but serves rather to convey information. The fact that human experience of the world is verbal in nature broadens the horizon of our analysis of hermeneutical experience. What we saw in the case of translation and the possibility of communication across the frontiers of our own languages is confirmed: the verbal world in which we live is not a barrier that prevents knowledge of being-in-itself but fundamentally embraces everything in which our insight can be enlarged and deepened. It is true that those who are brought up in a particular linguistic and cultural tradition see the world in a different way from those who belong to other traditions. It is true that the historical "worlds" that succeed one another in the course of history are different from one another and from the world of today; but in whatever tradition we consider it, it is always a human—i.e., verbally constituted—world that presents itself to us. As verbally constituted, every such world is of itself always open to every possible insight and hence to every expansion of its own world picture, and is accordingly available to others.

This is of fundamental importance, for it makes the expression "*world in itself*" problematical. The criterion for the continuing expansion of our own world picture is not given by a "world in itself" that lies beyond all language. Rather, the infinite perfectibility of the human experience of the world means that, whatever language we use, we never succeed in seeing anything but an ever more extended aspect, a "view" of the world. Those views of the world are not relative in the sense that one could oppose them to the "world in itself," as if the right view from some possible position outside the human, linguistic world could discover it in its being-in-itself. No one doubts that the world can exist without man and perhaps will do so. This is part of the meaning in which every human, linguistically constituted view of the world lives. In every worldview the existence of the world-in-itself is intended. It is the whole to which linguistically schematized experience refers. The multiplicity of these worldviews does not involve any relativization of the "world." Rather, the world is not different from the views in which it presents itself. The relationship is the same in the perception of things. Seen phenomenologically, the "thing-in-itself" is, as Husserl has shown,[83] nothing but the continuity with which the various perceptual perspectives on objects shade into one another. A person who opposes "being-in-itself" to these "aspects" must think either theologically—in which case the "being-in-itself" is not for him but only for God—or he will think like Lucifer, like one who wants to prove his own divinity by the fact that the whole world has to obey him. In this case the world's being-in-itself is a limitation of the omnipotence of his imagination.[84] In the same way as with perception we can speak of the "linguistic shadings" that the world undergoes in different language-worlds. But there remains a characteristic difference: every "shading" of the object of perception is exclusively distinct from every other, and each helps co-constitute the "thing-in-itself" as the continuum of these nuances—whereas, in the case of the shadings of verbal worldviews, each one potentially contains every other one within it—i.e., each worldview can be extended into every other. It can understand and comprehend, from within itself, the "view" of the world presented in another language.

Thus, we hold, the fact that our experience of the world is bound to language does not imply an exclusiveness of perspectives. If, by entering foreign language-worlds, we overcome the prejudices and limitations of our previous experience of the world, this does not mean that we leave and negate our own world. Like travelers we return home with new experiences. Even if we emigrate and never return, we still can never wholly forget. Even if, as people who know about history, we are fundamentally aware that all human thought about the world is historically conditioned, and thus are aware that our own thought is conditioned too, we still have not assumed an unconditional standpoint. In particular it is no objection to affirming that we are thus fundamentally conditioned to say that this affirmation is intended to be absolutely and unconditionally true, and therefore cannot be applied to itself without contradiction. The consciousness of being conditioned does not supersede our conditionedness. It is one of the prejudices of reflective philosophy that it understands matters that are not at all on the same logical level as standing in propositional relationships. Thus the reflective argument is out of place here. For we are not dealing with relationships between judgments which have to be kept free from contradictions but with life relationships. Our verbal experience of the world has the capacity to embrace the most varied relationships of life.[85]

Thus the sun has not ceased to set for us, even though the Copernican explanation of the universe has become part of our knowledge. Obviously we can keep seeing things in a certain way while at the same time knowing that doing so is absurd in the world of understanding. And is it not language that operates in a creative way, reconciling these stratified living relationships? When we speak of the sun setting, this is not an arbitrary phrase; it expresses what really appears to be the case. It is the appearance presented to a man who is not himself in motion. It is the sun that comes and goes as its rays reach or leave us. Thus, to our vision, the setting of the sun is a reality (it is "relative to Dasein"). Now, by constructing another model, we can mentally liberate ourselves from the evidence of our senses, and because we can do this we can see things from the rational viewpoint of the Copernican theory. But we cannot try to supersede or refute natural appearances by viewing things through the "eyes" of scientific under-standing. This is pointless not only because what we see with our eyes has genuine reality for us, but also because the truth that science states is itself relative to a particular world orientation and cannot at all claim to be the whole. But what really opens up the whole of our world orientation is language, and in this whole of language, appearances retain their legiti-macy just as much as does science.

Of course this does not mean that language is the cause of this intellectual power of persistence, but only that the immediacy of our worldview and view of ourselves, in which we persist, is preserved and altered within language because we finite beings always come from afar and stretch into the distance. In language the reality beyond every individual consciousness becomes visible.

Thus the verbal event reflects not only what persists but what changes in things. From the way that words change, we can discover the way that customs and values change. In the German language-world, for example, the word Tugend ("virtue") now nearly always has an ironic significance.[86] If we use other words instead to discreetly express the continuance of moral norms in a world that has turned away from established conven-tions, then such a process is a mirror of what is real. Poetry, too, often becomes a test of what is true, in that the poem awakens a secret life in words that had seemed to be used up and worn out, and tells us of ourselves. Obviously language can do all this because it is not a creation of reflective thought, but itself helps to fashion the world orientation in which we live.

We have, then, a confirmation of what we stated above, namely that in language the world itself presents itself. Verbal experience of the world is "absolute." It transcends all the relative ways being is posited because it embraces all being-in-itself, in whatever relationships (relativities) it appears. Our verbal experience of the world is prior to everything that is recognized and addressed as existing. *That language and world are related in a fundamental way does not mean, then, that world becomes the object of language.* Rather, the object of knowledge and statements is always already enclosed within the world horizon of language. That human experience of the world is verbal does not imply that a world-in-itself is being objectified.[87]

The world of objects that science knows, and from which it derives its own objectivity, is one of the relativities embraced by language's relation to the world. In it the concept of "being-in-itself" acquires the character of a *determination of the will.* What exists in itself is independent of one's own willing and imagining. But in being known in its being-in-itself, it is put at one's disposal in the sense that one can reckon with it—i.e., use it for one's own purposes.

As we can see, this idea of being-in-itself is only the apparent equivalent of the Greek concept of kath' hauto. The latter means primarily the ontological difference between what an entity is in its substance and its essence and what can exist in it and is subject to change. What belongs to the permanent nature of an entity can certainly always, in a preeminent sense, be known—i.e., it always has a prior association with the human mind. But what exists "in itself" in the sense of modern science has nothing to do with this ontological difference between the essential and the inessential; rather, it is determined as certain knowledge, which permits us to control things. The certified facts are like the object (Gegenstand) and its resistance (Widerstand) in that one has to reckon with them. What exists in itself, then, as Max Scheler has shown, is relative to a particular way of knowing and willing.[88]

This does not imply that some particular science is concerned in a special way with dominating what exists and, on the basis of this will to dominate, determining the real meaning of being-in-itself. Scheler rightly emphasized that the world model of mechanics is related in a special way to the capacity to make things.[89] But the knowledge of all the natural sciences is "knowledge for domination." This can be seen with particular clarity where modern science sets new goals of research that not only try to be methodologically different from the unitary method of modern physics, but also claim to embody a different attitude to research. Thus, for example, the environmental studies of the biologist von Üxküll contrasted the world of physics to a universe of life composed of the manifold living worlds of plants, animals, and men.

Such biological inquiry claims to overcome the naive anthropocentricity of the earlier study of animals by investigating the particular structures of the habitats in which living things have their being. Like animal environments the human world is built of elements that are available to human senses. If "worlds" are to be thought of as biological plans, however, this not only assumes the existence of the world of being-in-itself that is made available through physics, in that one is working out the selective principles according to which the various creatures construct their worlds out of material that "exists in itself"; it also derives the biological universe from the physical universe by a kind of re-styling, and it indirectly assumes the existence of the latter. Certainly this constitutes a new kind of inquiry. It is a line of research generally known today as behavioral biology. Logically it would embrace the human species as well. It has now developed a physics by means of which one can conceive human beings' perceptions of time and space as a special case—distinctive to a specifically human orientation—of much more complicated mathematical structures, much as today we perceive the world of bees, whose capacity to orient themselves we explain by recourse to their sensitivity to ultraviolet light. This creates the impression that the "world of physics" is the true world that exists in itself, the absolute reality, as it were, to which all living things are related, each in its own way.

But is it really the case that this world is a world of being-in-itself where all relativity to Dasein has been surpassed and where knowledge can be called an absolute science? Is not the very concept of an "absolute object" a contradiction in terms? Neither the biological nor the physical universe can, in fact, deny its concrete existential relativity. In this, physics and biology have the same ontological horizon, which it is impossible for them, as science, to transcend. They know what is, and this means, as Kant has shown, as it is given in space and time and is an object of experience. This even defines the progressive knowledge that science aims for. The world of physics cannot seek to be the whole of what exists. For even a world equation that contained everything, so that the observer of the system would also be included in the equations, would still assume the existence of a physicist who, as the calculator, would not be an object calculated. A physics that calculated itself and was its own calculation would be self-contradictory. The same thing is true of biology, which investigates the environments of all living things, including, therefore, the human environment. What is known in it certainly also embraces the being of the scientist, for he too is a living creature and a man. But from this it in no way follows that biological science is a mere product of life and only has meaning as such. Rather, biology studies what exists in exactly the same way as does physics; it is not itself what it studies. The being-in-itself toward which research, whether in physics or biology, is directed is relative to the way being is posited in its manner of inquiry. There is not the slightest reason, beyond this, to admit science's metaphysical claim to know being-in-itself. Each science, as a science, has in advance projected a field of objects such that to know them is to govern them.

We find quite another situation when we consider man's relationship to the world as a whole, as it is expressed in language. The world that appears in language and is constituted by it does not have, in the same sense, being-in-itself, and is not relative in the same sense as the object of the natural sciences. It is not being-in-itself, insofar as it is not characterized by objectivity and can never be given in experience as the comprehensive whole that it is. But as the world that it is, it is not relative to a particular language either. For to live in a linguistic world, as one does as a member of a linguistic community, does not mean that one is placed in an environment as animals are. We cannot see a linguistic world from above in this way, for there is no point of view outside the experience of the world in language from which it could become an object. Physics does not provide this point of view, because the world—i.e., the totality of what exists, is not the object of its research and calculation. Nor does comparative linguistics, which studies the structure of languages, have any non-linguistic point of view from which we could know the in-itself quality of what exists and for which the various forms of the linguistic experience of the world could be reconstructed, as a schematized selection, from what exists in itself—in a way analogous to animal habitats, the principles of whose structure we study. Rather, every language has a direct relationship to the infinity of beings. To have language involves a mode of being that is quite different from the way animals are confined to their habitat. By learning foreign languages men do not alter their relationship to the world, like an aquatic animal that becomes a land animal; rather, while preserving their own relationship to the world, they extend and enrich it by the world of the foreign language. Whoever has language "has" the world.

If we keep this in mind, we will no longer confuse the factualness (Sachlichkeit) of language with the *objectivity (Objektivität) of science*. The distance involved in a linguistic relationship to the world does not, as such, produce the objectivity that the natural sciences achieve by eliminating the subjective elements of the cognitive process. The distance and the factualness of language, of course, are also genuine achievements and do not just happen automatically. We know how putting an experience into words helps us cope with it. It is as if its threatening, even annihilating, immediacy is pushed into the background, brought into proportion, made communicable, and hence dealt with. Such coping with experience, however, is obviously something different from the way science works on it, objectivizing it and making it available for whatever purposes it likes. Once a scientist has discovered the law of a natural process, he has it in his power. No such thing is possible in the natural experience of the world expressed in language. Using language by no means involves making things available and calculable. It is not just that the statement or judgment is merely one particular form among the many other linguistic orientations—they themselves remain bound up with man's life orientation. Consequently, objectivizing science regards the linguisticality of the natural experience of the world as a source of prejudices. With its methods of precise mathematical measurement the new science, as we learn from the example of Bacon, had to make room for its own constructs by directly opposing the prejudice of language and its naive teleology.[90]

On the other hand, there is a positive connection between the factualness of language and man's capacity for science. This becomes especially clear in ancient science, whose specific merit and specific weakness was that it originated in the linguistic experience of the world. In order to overcome this weakness, its naive anthropocentrism, modern science has also renounced its merit, namely its place in man's natural world-orientation. The concept of "*theory*" can illustrate this very well. It would seem that what modern science calls "theory" has scarcely anything to do with the way the Greeks approached seeing and knowing the order of the world. Modern theory is a tool of construction by means of which we gather experiences together in a unified way and make it possible to dominate them. We are said to "construct" a theory. This already implies that one theory succeeds another, and from the outset each commands only conditional validity, namely insofar as further experience does not make us change our mind. Ancient theoria is not a means in the same sense, but the end itself, the highest manner of being human.[91]

Nevertheless there are close connections between the two. In both cases the practical or pragmatic interest that views whatever happens in the light of one's aims and purposes, is overcome. Aristotle tells us that the theoretical attitude could emerge only when all the necessities of life were already available.[92] Even the theoretical attitude of modern science does not direct its questions to nature for particular practical purposes. True, the manner of its questions and investigations is aimed at dominating what exists and so must in itself be called practical. But the application of his knowledge is secondary in the mind of the individual scientist, in the sense that the application follows from the knowledge yet only comes afterward, so that no one who discovers a piece of knowledge needs to know for what purpose it is to be used. Nevertheless, despite the similarities, the meaning of the words "theory" and "theoretical" is now obviously different. In modern usage the idea of the theoretical is almost a privative idea. Something is meant only theoretically when it does not have the definitively binding quality of a goal of action. On the other hand, the projected theories themselves are dominated by the idea of construction—i.e., theoretical knowledge is itself conceived in terms of the will to dominate what exists; it is a means and not an end. "Theory" in the ancient sense, however, is something quite different. There it is not just that existing orders as such are contemplated, but "theory" means sharing in the total order itself.[93]

This difference between Greek theoria and modern science is based, in my opinion, on different orientations to *verbal experience of the world*. Greek knowledge, as I pointed out above, was so much within language, so exposed to its seductions, that its fight against the dunamis ton onomaton never led it to develop the ideal of a pure symbolic language, whose purpose would be to overcome entirely the power of language, as is the case with modern science and its orientation toward dominating the existent. Both the letter symbols Aristotle uses in logic and his proportional and relative way of describing the course of movements in physics are obviously quite different from the way in which mathematics comes to be applied in the seventeenth century.

We cannot ignore this fact, however much we emphasize that the Greeks were the founders of science. The days should be finally past when modern scientific method was taken as a criterion, when Plato was interpreted in terms of Kant, the Idea in terms of natural law (neo-Kantianism), or when Democritus was praised as the founder of the true, "mechanical" knowledge of nature. We have only to consider Hegel's fundamental refutation of the rationalist position by means of the idea of life in order to see the limitations of this approach.[94] As I see it, in *Being and Time* Heidegger attains a position from which both the differences and the similarities between Greek science and modern science can be considered. When he showed that the concept of presence-at-hand is a deficient mode of being and viewed it as the background of classical metaphysics and its continuance in the modern concept of subjectivity, he was pursuing an ontologically correct connection between Greek theoria and modern science. Within the horizon of his temporal interpretation of being, classical metaphysics as a whole is an ontology of the present-at-hand, and modern science is, unbeknownst to itself, its heir. But in Greek theoria there was undoubtedly another element as well. Theoria grasps not so much the present-at-hand as the thing itself, which still has the dignity of a "thing." The later Heidegger himself emphasized that the experience of the thing has as little to do with merely establishing simple presence-at-hand as with the experience of the so-called experimental sciences.[95] Thus we must keep the dignity of the thing and the referentiality of language free from the prejudice originating in the ontology of the present-at-hand as well as in the concept of objectivity.

Our starting point is that verbally constituted experience of the world expresses not what is present-at-hand, that which is calculated or measured, but what exists, what man recognizes as existent and significant. The process of understanding practiced in the moral sciences can recognize itself in this—and not in the methodological ideal of rational construction that dominates modern mathematically based natural science. If we said that historically effected consciousness is realized in language, this was because language characterizes our human experience of the world in general. As little as "world" is *objectified* in language, so little is historical effect the *object* of hermeneutical consciousness.

Just as things, those units of our experience of the world that are constituted by their suitability and their significance, are brought into language, so the tradition that has come down to us is again brought to speak in our understanding and interpretation of it. The linguistic nature of this bringing into language is the same as that of the human experience of the world in general. This is what has finally led our analysis of the hermeneutical phenomenon to the discussion of the relationship between language and world.

That human experience of the world is linguistic in nature was the thread underlying Greek metaphysics in its thinking about being since Plato's "flight into the logoi." We must inquire how far the answer given there—an answer that lasted until Hegel—does justice to the question we are concerned with.

This answer is theological. In considering the being of beings, Greek metaphysics regarded it as a being that fulfilled itself in thought. This thought is the thought of nous, which is conceived as the highest and most perfect being, gathering within itself the being of all beings. The articulation of the logos brings the structure of being into language, and this coming into language is, for Greek thought, nothing other than the presencing of the being itself, its aletheia. Human thought regards the infinity of this presence as its fulfilled potential, its divinity.

We do not follow this way of thinking in its splendid self-forgetfulness, and so we will have to consider to what extent we can follow its revival based on the modern idea of subjectivity as found in Hegel's absolute idealism. For we are guided by the hermeneutical phenomenon; and its ground, which determines everything else, is the *finitude of our historical experience*. In order to do justice to it, we followed the trail of language, in which the structure of being is not simply reflected; rather, in language the order and structure of our experience itself is originally formed and constantly changed.

Language is the record of finitude not because the structure of human language is multifarious but because every language is constantly being formed and developed the more it expresses its experience of the world. It is finite not because it is not at once all other languages, but simply because it is language. We have considered important turning points in European thought concerning language, and from these we have learned that the event of language corresponds to the finitude of man in a far more radical sense than is brought out in Christian thinking about the Word. It is from *language as a medium* that our whole experience of the world, and especially hermeneutical experience, unfolds.

A word is not simply the perfection of the "species" (Lat.), as medieval thought held. When a being is represented in the thinking mind, this is not the reflection of a pregiven order of being, the true nature of which is apparent to an infinite mind (that of the Creator). But neither is a word an instrument, like the language of mathematics, that can construct an objectified universe of beings that can be put at our disposal by calculation. No more than an infinite mind can an infinite will surpass the experience of being that is proportionate to our finitude. It is the medium of language alone that, related to the totality of beings, mediates the finite, historical nature of man to himself and to the world.

Only now can the great dialectical puzzle of the one and the many, which fascinated Plato as the negation of the logos and which received a mysterious affirmation in medieval speculation on the Trinity, be given its true and fundamental ground. When Plato realized that the word of language is both one and many, he took only the first step. It is always *one* word that we say to one another and that is said to us (theologically, "the" Word of God)—but the unity of this word, as we saw, always unfolds step by step in articulated discourse. This structure of the logos and the verbum, as recognized by the Platonic and Augustinian dialectic, is simply the reflection of its logical contents.

But there is another dialectic of the word, which accords to every word an inner dimension of multiplication: every word breaks forth as if from a center and is related to a whole, through which alone it is a word. Every word causes the whole of the language to which it belongs to resonate and the whole world-view that underlies it to appear. Thus every word, as the event of a moment, carries with it the unsaid, to which it is related by responding and summoning. The occasionality of human speech is not a casual imperfection of its expressive power; it is, rather, the logical expression of the living virtuality of speech that brings a totality of meaning into play, without being able to express it totally.[96] All human speaking is finite in such a way that there is laid up within it an infinity of meaning to be explicated and laid out. That is why the hermeneutical phenomenon also can be illuminated only in light of the fundamental finitude of being, which is wholly verbal in character.

Above we spoke of the way the interpreter *belongs* to his text and described the close relationship between tradition and history that is expressed in the concept of historically effected consciousness; we can now define more exactly the idea of belonging on the basis of the linguistically constituted experience of world.

As was to be expected, this involves us in a number of questions with which philosophy has long been familiar. In metaphysics *belonging* refers to the transcendental relationship between being and truth, and it conceives knowledge as an element of being itself and not primarily as an activity of the subject. That knowledge is incorporated in being is the presupposition of all classical and medieval thought. What is, is of its nature "true"—i.e., present before an infinite mind—and only for this reason is it possible for finite human thought to know beings. Thus, here thought does not start from the concept of a subject that exists in its own right and makes everything else an object. On the contrary, Plato defines the being of the "soul" as participating in true being—i.e., as belonging to the same sphere of being as the idea—and Aristotle says that the soul is, in a certain sense, everything that exists.[97] In this thinking there is no question of a self-conscious spirit without world which would have to find its way to worldly being; both belong originally to each other. The relationship is primary.

Earlier thought took account of this by giving teleology a universal ontological function. In a practical context it is not by chance that the intermediate agencies through which something is achieved prove suited to achieve the end; rather, they are chosen from the outset as suitable means. Thus the ordering of means to ends is prior. We call this purposiveness, and we know that not only rational human action is purposive in this way; but also where there is no question of setting up goals and choosing means—as in all living relationships—such relationships can be conceived only within the concept of purposiveness, as the reciprocal harmony of all the parts with one another.[98] Here, too, the whole in its relations is more original than the parts. Even in the theory of evolution we may use the concept of adaptation only with caution, inasmuch as this theory assumes that the natural situation is one of lack of adaptation—as if creatures were placed within a world to which they had belatedly to adapt themselves.[99] Just as being already adapted actually constitutes the creature's relation to life, so the concept of knowledge, dominated by thought of ends and means, is defined as the natural co-ordination of the human mind to the nature of things.

In modern science this metaphysical conception of how the knowing subject belongs to the object of knowledge is without justification.[100] Its methodological ideal ensures that every one of its steps can be retraced to the elements from which its knowledge is built up, while the teleological units of significance such as "thing" or "organic whole" lose their legitimacy. In particular, the critique of the verbalism of Aristotelian and Scholastic science that we touched on above dissolved the old co-ordination between man and world that lay at the basis of logos philosophy.

But modern science has never entirely denied its Greek ancestry, however much, since the seventeenth century, it has become conscious of itself and of the boundless possibilities that open up before it. Descartes' real treatise on method, his "Rules," the veritable manifesto of modern science, did not appear, as we know, until a long time after his death. However, his thoughtful meditations on the compatibility of the mathematical knowledge of nature with metaphysics set a task for an entire age. German philosophy from Leibniz to Hegel constantly tried to supplement the new science of physics with a philosophical and speculative science in which the legacy of Aristotle would be revived and preserved. We need only recall Goethe's objection to Newton, which was shared by Schelling, Hegel, and Schopenhauer.

Hence it is not surprising if, after another century of critical experiences provided by modern science and especially by the self-awareness of the historical sciences, we again take up this legacy. If we are to do justice to the subject, the hermeneutics of the human sciences—which at first appears to be of secondary and derivative concern, a modest chapter from the heritage of German idealism—leads us back into the problems of classical metaphysics.

This can be seen in the role that the concept of *dialectic* plays in nineteenth-century philosophy. It testifies to the continuity of the problem from its Greek origin. When it is a question of understanding the suprasubjective powers that dominate history, the Greeks have something over us, for we are entangled in the aporias of subjectivism. They did not try to base the objectivity of knowledge on subjectivity. Rather, their thinking always regarded itself as an element of being itself. Parmenides considered this to be the most important signpost on the way to the truth of being. Dialectic, this expression of the logos, was not for the Greeks a movement performed by thought; what thought experiences is the movement of the thing itself. The fact that this sounds like Hegel does not mean that there has been any false modernization but shows, rather, the historical connection. In the situation of modern thought that we have described, Hegel has consciously taken up the model of Greek dialectic.[101] Hence whoever wants to learn from the Greeks always has to learn from Hegel first. Both his dialectic of the determinations of thought and his dialectic of the forms of knowledge explicitly repeat the total mediation between thought and being that was formerly the natural element of Greek thought. In that our hermeneutical theory seeks to show the interconnection of event and understanding, it sends us back to Parmenides as well as to Hegel.

When we thus take the concept of belonging which we have won from the aporias of historicism and relate it to the background of general metaphysics, we are not trying to revive the classical doctrine of the intelligibility of being or apply it to the historical world. This would be a mere repetition of Hegel which would not hold up, either in the face of Kant and the experiential standpoint of modern science, or primarily in the face of an experience of history that is no longer guided by the knowledge of salvation. We are simply following an internal necessity of the thing itself if we go beyond the idea of the object and the objectivity of understanding toward the idea that subject and object belong together. Our critique of aesthetic and historical consciousness drove us to critique the concept of the objective, to detach ourselves from the Cartesian basis of modern science, and to revive ideas from Greek thought. But we cannot simply follow the Greeks or the identity philosophy of German idealism: we are thinking out the consequences of language as medium.

From this viewpoint the concept of belonging is no longer regarded as the teleological relation of the mind to the ontological structure of what exists, as this relation is conceived in metaphysics. Quite a different state of affairs follows from the fact that the hermeneutical experience is linguistic in nature, that there is dialogue between tradition and its interpreter. The fundamental thing here is that something occurs (etwas geschieht).[102] Neither is the mind of the interpreter in control of what words of tradition reach him, nor can one suitably describe what occurs here as the progressive knowledge of what exists, so that an infinite intellect would contain everything that could ever speak out of the whole of tradition. Seen from the point of view of the interpreter, "occurrence" means that he is not a knower seeking an object, "discovering" by methodological means what was really meant and what the situation actually was, though slightly hindered and affected by his own prejudices. This is only an external aspect of the actual hermeneutical occurrence. It motivates the indispensible methodological discipline one has toward oneself. But the actual occurrence is made possible only because the word that has come down to us as tradition and to which we are to listen really encounters us and does so as if it addressed us and is concerned with us. I have elaborated this aspect of the situation above as the hermeneutical logic of the question and shown how the questioner becomes the one who is questioned and how the hermeneutical occurrence is realized in the dialectic of the question. I recall this here in order to define correctly the meaning of belonging as it pertains to our hermeneutical experience.

For on the other side, that of the "object," this occurrence means the coming into play, the playing out, of the content of tradition in its constantly widening possibilities of significance and resonance, extended by the different people receiving it. Inasmuch as the tradition is newly expressed in language, something comes into being that had not existed before and that exists from now on. We can illustrate this with any historical example. Whether a given traditionary text is a poem or tells us of a great event, in each case what is transmitted re-emerges into existence just as it presents itself. There is no being-in-itself that is increasingly revealed when Homer's *Iliad* or Alexander's Indian Campaign speaks to us in the new appropriation of tradition; but, as in genuine dialogue, something emerges that is contained in neither of the partners by himself.

If we are trying to define the idea of belonging (Zugehörigkeit) as accurately as possible, we must take account of the particular dialectic implied in *hearing* (hören). It is not just that he who hears is also addressed, but also that he who is addressed must hear whether he wants to or not. When you look at something, you can also look away from it by looking in another direction, but you cannot "hear away." This difference between seeing and hearing is important for us because the primacy of hearing is the basis of the hermeneutical phenomenon, as Aristotle saw.[103] There is nothing that is not available to hearing through the medium of language. Whereas all the other senses have no immediate share in the universality of the verbal experience of the world, but only offer the key to their own specific fields, hearing is an avenue to the whole because it is able to listen to the logos. In the light of our hermeneutical inquiry this ancient insight into the priority of hearing over sight acquires a new emphasis. The language in which hearing shares is not only universal in the sense that everything can be expressed in it. The significance of the hermeneutical experience is rather that, in contrast to all other experience of the world, language opens up a completely new dimension, the profound dimension from which tradition comes down to those now living. This has always been the true essence of hearing, even before the invention of writing: that the hearer can listen to the legends, the myths, and the truth of the ancients. In comparison, the written, literary transmission of tradition, as we know it, is nothing new; it only changes the form and makes the task of real hearing more difficult.

Here the concept of belonging takes on a new definition. Belonging is brought about by tradition's addressing us. Everyone who is situated in a tradition—and this is true, as we know, even of the man who is released into a new apparent freedom by historical consciousness—must listen to what reaches him from it. The truth of tradition is like the present that lies immediately open to the senses.

The mode of being of tradition is, of course, not sensible immediacy. It is language, and in interpreting its texts, the hearer who understands it relates its truth to his own linguistic orientation to the world. This linguistic communication between present and tradition is, as we have shown, the event that takes place in all understanding. Hermeneutical experience must take everything that becomes present to it as a genuine experience. It does not have prior freedom to select and reject. Nor can it maintain an absolute freedom by leaving undecided matters specific to what one is trying to understand. It cannot unmake the event that it is itself.

This structure of the hermeneutical experience, which so totally contradicts the idea of scientific methodology, itself depends on the character of language as event that we have described at length. It is not just that the use and development of language is a process which has no single knowing and choosing consciousness standing over against it. (Thus it is literally more correct to say that language speaks us, rather than that we speak it, so that, for example, the time at which a text was written can be determined more exactly from its linguistic usage than from its author.) A more important point is the one to which we have constantly referred, namely that what constitutes the hermeneutical event proper is not language as language, whether as grammar or as lexicon; it consists in the coming into language of what has been said in the tradition: an event that is at once appropriation and interpretation. Thus here it really is true to say that this event is not our action upon the thing, but the act of the thing itself.

This confirms the similarity of our approach to that of Hegel and the Greek world, which we have already noted. Our inquiry started from our dissatisfaction with the modern concept of methodology. But this dissatisfaction found its most significant philosophical justification in *Hegel's explicit appeal to the Greek concept of methodology*. He criticized the concept of a method that dealt with the thing but was alien to it, calling it "external reflection." The true method was an action of the thing itself.[104] This assertion does not, of course, mean that philosophical cognition is not also an activity, even an effort that calls for the "effort of the concept." But this activity and this effort consist in not interfering arbitrarily—latching onto this or that ready-made notion as it strikes one—with the immanent necessity of the thought. Certainly, the thing does not go its own course without our thinking being involved, but thinking means unfolding what consistently follows from the subject matter itself. It is part of this process to suppress ideas "that tend to insinuate themselves" and to insist on the logic of the thought. Since the Greeks we have called this *dialectic*.

In describing the true method, which is the activity of the thing itself, Hegel quotes Plato, who loved to show his Socrates in conversation with young men, because they were ready to follow where Socrates' questions led, without regard for current opinions. He illustrated his own method of dialectical development by these "malleable youths," who did not parade their own ideas but rather avoided obstructing the path on which the subject matter led them. Here dialectic is nothing but the art of conducting a conversation and especially of revealing the mistakes in one's opinions through the process of questioning and yet further questioning. Here, then, the dialectic is *negative*; it confuses one's opinions. But this kind of confusion means at the same time a clarification, for it opens one's eyes to the thing. Just as in the famous scene in the *Meno* where, after all the slave's untenable suppositions have collapsed, he is led out of his confusion to the right solution of the mathematical task he has been set, so also all dialectical negativity contains an adumbration of what is true.

Not only in all pedagogical dialogue but in all thought, only pursuing what consistently follows from the subject matter can bring out what lies in it. It is the thing itself that asserts its force, if we rely entirely on the power of thought and disregard obvious appearances and opinions. Thus Plato linked the Eleatic dialectic, which we know chiefly from Zeno, with the Socratic art of dialogue and raised it in his *Parmenides* to a new reflective level. That things change and become their opposite as one consistently thinks them through, that thought acquires the power of "testing what follows from contraries, without knowing the what,"[105] is the experience of thought Hegel appeals to when he conceives of method as the self-unfolding of pure thought to become the systematic whole of truth.

Now the hermeneutical experience that we are endeavoring to think from the viewpoint of language as medium is certainly not an experience of thinking in the same sense as this dialectic of the concept, which seeks to free itself entirely from the power of language. Nevertheless, there is something resembling dialectic in hermeneutical experience: an activity of the thing itself, an action that, unlike the methodology of modern science, is a passion, an understanding, an event that happens to one.

The hermeneutical experience also has its own rigor: that of uninterrupted listening. A thing does not present itself to the hermeneutical experience without an effort special to it, namely that of "being negative toward itself." A person who is trying to understand a text has to keep something at a distance—namely everything that suggests itself, on the basis of his own prejudices, as the meaning expected—as soon as it is rejected by the sense of the text itself. Even the experience of reversal (which happens unceasingly in talking, and which is the real experience of dialectic) has its equivalent here. Explicating the whole of meaning towards which understanding is directed forces us to make interpretive conjectures and to take them back again. The self-cancellation of the interpretation makes it possible for the thing itself—the meaning of the text—to assert itself. The movement of the interpretation is dialectical not primarily because the one-sidedness of every statement can be balanced by another side—this is, as we shall see, a secondary phenomenon in interpretation—but because the word that interpretatively fits the meaning of the text expresses the whole of this meaning—i.e., allows an infinity of meaning to be represented within it in a finite way.

That this is dialectic, conceived on the basis of the medium of language, needs more exact discussion, as does the way in which this dialectic differs from the metaphysical dialectic of Plato and Hegel. Following a usage that we can find in Hegel, we call what is common to the metaphysical and the hermeneutical dialectic the *"speculative element."* The word "speculative" here refers to the mirror relation.[106] Being reflected involves a constant substitution of one thing for another. When something is reflected in something else, say, the castle in the lake, it means that the lake throws back the image of the castle. The mirror image is essentially connected with the actual sight of the thing through the medium of the observer. It has no being of its own; it is like an "appearance" that is not itself and yet allows the thing to appear by means of a mirror image. It is like a duplication that is still only the one thing. The real mystery of a reflection is the intangibility of the image, the sheer reproduction hovering before the mind's eye.

If we now use the word "speculative" as it was coined by philosophers around 1800 and say, for example, that someone has a speculative mind or that a thought is rather speculative, behind this usage lies the notion of reflection in a mirror. Speculative means the opposite of the dogmatism of everyday experience. A speculative person is someone who does not abandon himself directly to the tangibility of appearances or to the fixed

461

determinateness of the meant, but who is able to reflect or—to put it in Hegelian terms—who sees that the "in-itself" is a "for-me." And a thought is speculative if the relationship it asserts is not conceived as a quality unambiguously assigned to a subject, a property to a given thing, but must be thought of as a mirroring, in which the reflection is nothing but the pure appearance of what is reflected, just as the one is the one of the other, and the other is the other of the one.

Hegel has described speculative thought in his masterly analysis of the logic of the philosophical proposition.[107] He shows that only in its external form is the philosophical proposition a judgment—i.e., a predicate ascribed to a subject-concept. In fact the philosophical proposition does not pass over from the subject-concept to another concept that is placed in relation to it; it states the truth of the subject in the form of the predicate. "God is one" does not mean that it is a property of God's to be one, but that it is God's nature to be unity. Here the movement of definition is not tied to the fixed base of the subject, "from which it runs back and forth." The subject is not defined both as this and as that, in one respect like this, and in another like that. This would be the mode of imagistic thinking, not of the concept. In conceptual thinking, by contrast, the natural movement of definition beyond the subject of the proposition is prevented and "suffers a setback, as it were. Starting from the subject, as if this remained the basis throughout, it finds that, since the predicate is rather the substance, the subject has passed into the predicate and has thus been superseded. And since what seems to be predicate has become the whole independent mass, thought cannot roam freely, but is stopped by this weight."[108] Thus the form of the proposition destroys itself since the speculative proposition does not state something about something; rather, it presents the unity of the concept. The philosophical proposition has, as it were, two peaks by reason of this counterthrust of the predicate; Hegel compares it to the rhythm that follows from the two elements of meter and accent, and produces the same floating harmony.

The unaccustomed blockage that thought undergoes when the contents of a proposition compel thought to give up its cognitive habits constitutes, in fact, the speculativeness of all philosophy. Hegel's great history of philosophy shows that from the beginning, philosophy is speculation in this sense. If it expresses itself in the form of predication—i.e., using fixed ideas of God, soul, and world—then it fails to understand its own nature and is pursuing a one-sided "view of the understanding of the objects of reason." According to Hegel this is the nature of pre-Kantian dogmatic metaphysics and is characteristic of the "modern ages of nonphilosophy. Plato is certainly not such a metaphysician; still less is Aristotle, although sometimes the contrary is thought to be true."[109]

For Hegel the important thing is to *represent expressly* this inner block that thought undergoes when its habit of running away with ideas is interrupted by the concept. Non-speculative thought can, as it were, demand this. It has "a valid right that is not, however, respected in the mode of the speculative proposition." What it can demand is that the dialectical self-destruction of the proposition be expressed. "With other knowledge the proof constitutes this side of expressed inwardness. But since dialectic has been separated from proof, the concept of philosophical proof has, in fact, been lost." Whatever Hegel means by this,[110] he is, at any rate, trying to re-establish the meaning of philosophical proof. This takes place in the account of the dialectical movement of the proposition. This is what is *really* speculative, and speculative presentation consists in expressing this alone. The speculative relation, then, must pass into dialectical presentation. This, for Hegel, is the demand of philosophy. What is here called expression and presentation is not actually someone's act of demonstration or proof; rather, the object itself demonstrates itself, by so expressing and presenting itself. Thus dialectic is truly experienced when thought undergoes the incomprehensible reversal into its opposite. The very act of holding onto what consistently follows in the thought leads to this surprising movement of the reversal—as when, for example, a person seeking justice discovers that adhering strictly to the idea of justice becomes "abstract" and proves to be the greatest injustice (summum ius summa iniuria).

Hegel here distinguishes between the speculative and the dialectical. The dialectical is the expression of the speculative, the presentation of what is actually contained in the speculative, and to this extent it is the "truly" speculative. But since, as we have seen, the presentation is no adventitious activity but the emergence of the thing itself, the philosophical proof itself belongs to the thing. It is true that it emerges, as we have seen, from a demand of ordinary thinking and imagining. Hence it is a presentation for the external reflection of the understanding. But despite this, such a presentation is in fact by no means external. It considers itself such only as long as thought does not know that it proves finally to be the reflection of the thing in itself. Accordingly, Hegel emphasizes the difference between speculative and dialectical only in the Preface to his *Phenomenology*.

Because this distinction is in fact superseded, Hegel no longer retains it subsequently, from the viewpoint of absolute knowledge.

This is the point at which the proximity of our own inquiry to the speculative dialectic of Plato and Hegel meets a fundamental barrier. The supersession of the distinction between speculative and dialectical that we find in Hegel's speculative science of the concept shows how much he considered himself as the heir to the Greek philosophy of the logos. What he calls dialectic and what Plato called dialectic depends, in fact, on subordinating language to the "statement." The concept of the statement, dialectically accentuated to the point of contradiction, however, is antithetical to the nature of hermeneutical experience and the verbal nature of human experience of the world. In fact, Hegel's dialectic also follows the speculative spirit of language, but according to Hegel's self-understanding he is trying to take a hint from the way language playfully determines thought and to raise it by the mediation of the dialectic in the totality of known knowledge, to the self-consciousness of the concept. In this respect his dialectic remains within the dimension of statements and does not attain the dimension of the linguistic experience of the world. These are just a few indications of the way in which the dialectical nature of language pertains to the problems of hermeneutics.

Language itself, however, has something speculative about it in a quite different sense—not only in the sense Hegel intends, as an instinctive prefiguring of logical reflection—but, rather, as the realization of meaning, as the event of speech, of mediation, of coming to an understanding. Such a realization is speculative in that the finite possibilities of the word are oriented toward the sense intended as toward the infinite. A person who has something to say seeks and finds the words to make himself intelligible to the other person. This does not mean that he makes "statements." Anyone who has experienced an interrogation—even if only as a witness—knows what it is to make a statement and how little it is a statement of what one means. In a statement the horizon of meaning of what is to be said is concealed by methodical exactness; what remains is the "pure" sense of the statements. That is what goes on record. But meaning thus reduced to what is stated is always distorted meaning.

To say what one means, on the other hand—to make oneself understood—means to hold what is said together with an infinity of what is not said in one unified meaning and to ensure that it is understood in this way. Someone who speaks in this way may well use only the most ordinary and common words and still be able to express what is unsaid and is to be said.

Someone who speaks is behaving speculatively when his words do not reflect beings, but express a relation to the whole of being. This is connected with the fact that someone who repeats what is said, just like someone who takes down statements, does not need to distort consciously, and yet he will change the meaning of what is said. Even in the most everyday speech there appears an element of speculative reflection, namely the intangibility of that which is still the purest reproduction of meaning.

All this is epitomized in the poetic word. Here, of course, it is legitimate to see the actual reality of poetic speech in the poetic "statement." For here it is really meaningful and necessary that the sense of the poetic word is expressed in what is said as such, without invoking the aid of occasional knowledge. If in the process of reaching understanding between people the notion of the statement is distorted, here the concept of the statement achieves its fulfillment. The detachment of what is said from any subjective opinion and experience of the author constitutes the reality of the poetic word. But what does this statement state?

It is clear, first of all, that everything that constitutes everyday speech can recur in the poetic word. If poetry shows people in conversation, then what is given in the poetic statement is not the statement that a written report would contain, but in a mysterious way the whole of the conversation is as if present. The words put into the mouth of a literary character are speculative in the same way that the speech of daily life is speculative: as we said above, in his speech the speaker expresses a relationship to being. Moreover, when we speak of a poetic statement, we do not mean the statement that is put into someone's mouth in a work of literature, but the statement that the work itself, as poetic word, is. But the poetic statement as such is speculative, in that the verbal event of the poetic word expresses its own relationship to being.

If we take "the poetic spirit's mode of proceeding," as, say, Hölderlin has described it, then it becomes immediately clear in what sense the verbal event of literature is speculative. Hölderlin has shown that finding the language of a poem involves totally dissolving all customary words and modes of expression. "In that the poet feels himself seized in his whole inner and outer life by the pure tone of his original sensation and he looks about him in his world, it is new and unknown to him, the sum of all his experiences, his knowledge, his intuitions and memories, art and nature, as it presents itself within and without him; everything is present to him as if for the first time, for this very reason ungrasped, undetermined, dissolved into sheer material and life. And it is supremely important that he does not at this moment accept anything as given, does not start from anything positive, that nature and art, as he has learned to know and see them, do not *speak* before a language is there for *him*. . . . " (Note how close this is to Hegel's critique of positivity.) As a successful work and creation, the poem is not the ideal but the spirit reawakened from infinite life. (This is also reminiscent of Hegel.) It does not describe or signify an entity, but opens up a world of the divine and the human for us. The poetic statement is speculative inasmuch as it does not reflect an existent reality, does not reproduce the appearance of the *species* (Lat.) in the order of essence, but represents the new appearance of a new world in the imaginary medium of poetic invention.

We have discerned the speculative structure of the event of language both in daily speech and poetic speech. The inner resemblance that thus appears, linking the poetic word with everyday speech as an intensification of the latter, has already been noted, from its subjective, psychological side, in idealistic philosophy and its revival in Croce and Vossler.[111] If we stress the other aspect, the fact of something's coming into language, as what really occurs in the event of language, we are preparing a place for the hermeneutical experience. As we have seen, the way tradition is understood and expressed ever anew in language is an event no less genuine than living conversation. What distinguishes them is only that the productivity of the verbal orientation to the world finds new application to an already verbally mediated content. The hermeneutical relation is a speculative relation, but it is fundamentally different from the dialectical self-unfolding of the mind, as described by Hegel's philosophical science.

Since hermeneutic experience implies an event of language that corresponds to dialectical presentation in Hegel, it too partakes of dialectic —namely the dialectic, elaborated above,[112] of question and answer. As we have seen, the understanding of a traditionary text has an essential inner relationship to its interpretation, and although this is always a relative and incomplete movement, understanding still finds its relative fulfillment there. Accordingly, as Hegel teaches, the speculative content of a philosophical statement needs the corresponding dialectical presentation of the contradictions it contains if it is to become genuine science. There is a real correspondence here, for interpretation shares in the discursiveness of the human mind, which is able to conceive the unity of the object only in successiveness. Thus interpretation has the dialectical structure of all finite, historical being, insofar as every interpretation must begin somewhere and seeks to supersede the one-sidedness which that inevitably produces. It seems to the interpreter that some particular must necessarily be said and made explicit. All interpretation is motivated in this way and derives its significance from the context of its motivation. Through its one-sidedness it puts too much emphasis on one side of the thing, so that something else has to be said to restore the balance. As philosophical dialectic presents the whole truth by superseding all partial propositions, bringing contradictions to a head and overcoming them, so also hermeneutics has the task of revealing a totality of meaning in all its relations. The individuality of the sense intended corresponds to the totality of all definitions. One thinks here of Schleiermacher, who based his dialectic on the metaphysics of individuality and in his hermeneutical theory constructed the process of interpretation from antithetical directions of thought.

However, the correspondence between hermeneutical and philosophical dialectic, as it seems to follow from Schleiermacher's dialectical construction of individuality and Hegel's dialectical construction of totality, is not a real correspondence. For this parallel fails to take account of the real nature of the hermeneutic experience and the radical finitude that is its basis. It is true that interpretation has to start somewhere, but it does not start just anywhere. It is not really a beginning. We saw that the hermeneutical experience always includes the fact that the text to be understood speaks into a situation that is determined by previous opinions. The hermeneutical situation is not a regrettable distortion that affects the purity of understanding, but the condition of its possibility. Only because between the text and its interpreter there is no automatic accord can a hermeneutical experience make us share in the text. Only because a text has to be brought out of its alienness and assimilated is there anything for the person trying to understand it to say. Only because the text calls for it does interpretation take place, and only in the way called for. The apparently thetic beginning of interpretation is, in fact, a response; and the sense of an interpretation is determined, like every response, by the question asked. *Thus the dialectic of question and answer always precedes the dialectic of interpretation. It is what determines understanding as an event.*

From this it follows that hermeneutics cannot have any *problem of a beginning,* as the problem of the beginning of science is found in Hegel's logic.[113] Wherever it arises, the problem of the beginning is, in fact, the problem of the end. For it is with respect to an end that a beginning is defined as a beginning of an end. Given infinite knowledge, given speculative dialectic, this may lead to the fundamentally unsolvable problem of what one is to start with. For every beginning is an end, and every end is a beginning. At any rate, given this kind of perfect circularity, the speculative question of the beginning of philosophical science is seen fundamentally in terms of its fulfillment.

It is quite different with historically effected consciousness, in which hermeneutical experience reaches its consummation. It knows about the absolute openness of the event of meaning in which it shares. Here too, certainly, there is a standard by which understanding is measured and which it can meet: the content of the tradition itself is the sole criterion and it expresses itself in language. But there is no possible consciousness—we have repeatedly emphasized this, and it is the basis of the historicity of understanding—there is no possible consciousness, however infinite, in which any traditionary "subject matter" would appear in the light of eternity. Every appropriation of tradition is historically different: which does not mean that each one represents only an imperfect understanding of it. Rather, each is the experience of an "aspect" of the thing itself.

The paradox that is true of all traditionary material, namely of being one and the same and yet of being different, proves that all interpretation is, in fact, speculative. Hence hermeneutics has to see through the dogmatism of a "meaning-in-itself" in exactly the same way critical philosophy has seen through the dogmatism of experience. This certainly does not mean that every interpreter considers himself speculative—i.e., he is conscious of the dogmatism contained in his own interpretative intention. What is meant, rather, is that all interpretation is speculative as it is actually practiced, quite apart from its methodological self-consciousness. This is what emerges from the linguistic nature of interpretation. For the interpreting word is the word of the interpreter; it is not the language and the dictionary of the interpreted text. This means that assimilation is no mere reproduction or repetition of the traditionary text; it is a new creation of understanding. If emphasis has been—rightly—placed on the fact that all meaning is related to the I,[114] this means, as far as the hermeneutical experience is concerned, that all the meaning of what is handed down to us finds its concretion (i.e., is understood) in its relation to the understanding I—and not in reconstructing the originally intending I.

The intimate unity of understanding and interpretation is confirmed by the fact that the interpretation that reveals the implications of a text's meaning and brings it into language seems, when compared with the given text, to be a new creation, but yet does not maintain any proper existence apart from the understanding process. I have already pointed out above[115] that the interpretive concepts are superseded in the fullness of understanding because they are meant to disappear. This means that they are not just tools that we take up and then throw aside when we are done using them, but that they belong to the inner articulation of the subject matter (which is meaning). What is true of every word in which thought is expressed, is true also of the interpreting word, namely that it is not, as such, objective. As the realization of the act of understanding it is the actuality of the historically effected consciousness, and as such it is truly speculative: having no tangible being of its own and yet reflecting the image that is presented to it.

Compared with the immediacy of understanding between people or the word of the poet, the language of the interpreter is undoubtedly a secondary phenomenon. It is language related again to language. And yet the language of the interpreter is at the same time the comprehensive manifestation of language, embracing all forms of language usage and structure. Our starting point was that understanding is inseparable from language and that language is related to reason of every kind, and we can now see how the whole of our investigation is subsumed under this rubric. The development of the problem of hermeneutics from Schleiermacher, through Dilthey, to Husserl and Heidegger, which we have outlined, confirms from the historical side what we have now found to be the case: namely that philology's conceiving itself as a method raises a fundamental philosophical problem.

(C) THE UNIVERSAL ASPECT OF HERMENEUTICS

Our inquiry has been guided by the basic idea that language is a medium where I and world meet or, rather, manifest their original belonging together. We have also shown that this speculative medium that language is represents a finite process in contrast to the infinite dialectical mediation of concepts. In all the cases we analyzed—in the language of conversation, of poetry, and also of interpretation—the speculative structure of language emerged, not as the reflection of something given but as the coming into language of a totality of meaning. This drew us toward the dialectic of the Greeks, because they did not conceive understanding as a methodic activity of the subject, but as something that the thing itself does and which thought "suffers." This activity of the thing itself is the real speculative movement that takes hold of the speaker. We have sought the subjective reflection of it in speech. We can now see that this activity of the thing itself, the coming into language of meaning, points to a universal ontological structure, namely to the basic nature of everything toward which understanding can be directed. *Being that can be understood is language.* The hermeneutical phenomenon here projects its own universality back onto the ontological constitution of what is understood, determining it in a universal sense as *language* and determining its own relation to beings as interpretation. Thus we speak not only of a language of art but also of a language of nature—in short, of any language that things have.

Above we have already brought out the curious link between literary interpretation and the study of nature that accompanied the beginnings of modern science.[116] Here we are getting to the foundations. It is not by accident that one could talk about the "book of nature," which contained just as much truth as the "book of books." That which can be understood is language. This means that it is of such a nature that of itself it offers itself to be understood. Here too is confirmed the speculative structure of language. To come into language does not mean that a second being is acquired. Rather, what something presents itself as belongs to its own being. Thus everything that is language has a speculative unity: it contains a distinction, that between its being and its presentations of itself, but this is a distinction that is really not a distinction at all.

The speculative mode of being of language has a universal ontological significance. To be sure, what comes into language is something different from the spoken word itself. But the word is a word only because of what comes into language in it. Its own physical being exists only in order to disappear into what is said. Likewise, that which comes into language is not something that is pregiven before language; rather, the word gives it its own determinateness.

We can now see that this speculative movement was what we were aiming at in the critique of both aesthetic and historical consciousness that introduced our analysis of hermeneutical experience. The being of the work of art is not a being-in-itself that is different from its reproduction or the contingency of its appearance. Only by a secondary thematization of the two things is it possible to make this kind of "aesthetic differentiation." Similarly, whatever offers itself for our historical study from tradition or as tradition—the significance of an event or the meaning of a text—is not a fixed object existing in itself, which we have simply to establish. In fact, historical consciousness too involves mediation between past and present. By seeing that language is the universal medium of this mediation, we were able to expand our inquiry from its starting point, the critiques of aesthetic and historical consciousness and the hermeneutics that would replace them, to universal dimensions. For man's relation to the world is absolutely and fundamentally verbal in nature, and hence intelligible. Thus hermeneutics is, as we have seen, a *universal aspect of philosophy*, and not just the methodological basis of the so-called human sciences.

The objectifying procedures of natural science and the concept of being-in-itself, which is intended in all knowledge, proved to be an abstraction when viewed from the medium that language is. Abstracted from the fundamental relation to the world that is given in the linguistic nature of our experience of it, science attempts to become certain about entities by methodically organizing its knowledge of the world. Consequently it condemns as heresy all knowledge that does not allow of this kind of certainty and that therefore cannot serve the growing domination of being. By contrast, we have endeavored to liberate the mode of being of art and history, and the experience corresponding to them, from the ontological prejudice implied in the ideal of scientific objectivity; and, in view of the experience of art and history, we were led to a universal hermeneutics that was concerned with the general relationship of man to the world. We formulated this universal hermeneutics on the basis of the concept of language not only in order to guard against a false methodologism that infects the concept of objectivity in the human sciences but also to avoid the idealistic spiritualism of a Hegelian metaphysics of infinity. The fundamental hermeneutical experience was articulated for us not merely by the tension between strangeness and familiarity, misunderstanding and correct understanding, such as dominated Schleiermacher's project. Rather, it was ultimately apparent that because of his doctrine that understanding is consummated in divination Schleiermacher came close to Hegel. If we start from the fact that understanding is verbal, we are emphasizing, on the contrary, the finitude of the verbal event in which understanding is always in the process of being concretized. The language that things have—whatever kind of things they may be—is not the logos ousias, and it is not fulfilled in the self-contemplation of an infinite intellect; it is the language that our finite, historical nature apprehends when we learn to speak. This is true of the language of the texts handed down to us in tradition, and that is why it was necessary to have a truly historical hermeneutics. It is as true of the experience of art as of the experience of history; in fact, the concepts of "art" and "history" are modes of understanding that emerge from the universal mode of hermeneutical being as forms of hermeneutic experience.

Obviously it is not peculiar to the work of art that it has its being in its presentation, nor is it a peculiarity of the being of history that it is to be understood in its significance. Self-presentation and being-understood belong together not only in that the one passes into the other, and the work of art is one with the history of its effects, and tradition is one with the present of its being understood; speculative language, distinguishing itself from itself, presenting itself, language that expresses meaning is not only art and history but everything insofar as it can be understood. The speculative character of being that is the ground of hermeneutics has the same universality as do reason and language.

With the ontological turn that our hermeneutical inquiry has taken, we are moving toward a metaphysical idea whose significance we can show by going back to its origins. *The concept of the beautiful*—which shared the central place in eighteenth-century aesthetics with the sublime, and which was to be entirely eliminated in the course of the nineteenth century by the aesthetic critique of classicism—was once a universal metaphysical concept and had a function in metaphysics, the universal doctrine of being, that was by no means limited to the aesthetic in the narrower sense. We will see that this ancient conception of the beautiful can also be of service to the comprehensive hermeneutics that has emerged from the critique of the methodologism of the human sciences.

Even an analysis of the word's meaning shows that the concept of the beautiful has a close connection with the inquiry we have been pursuing. The Greek word for beautiful is kalon. There is no exact equivalent for this in German, not even if we use pulchrum as an intermediary term. But Greek thought in part determines the history of the meaning of the German word schön, so that the meanings of the two words overlap to some extent. Thus we say, for example, die "schönen" Künste ("the fine arts"). By adding the adjective schön we distinguish these arts from what we call "technology"—i.e., from mechanical arts that make useful things. It is the same with phrases such as schöne Sittlichkeit ("superior moral-ity"), schöne Literatur (belles lettres), schöngeistig (aesthete). In all these usages the word is in the same antithesis as is the Greek kalon to the idea of chresimon. Everything that is not part of the necessities of life but is concerned with the "how," the eu zen—i.e., everything that the Greeks reckon part of paideia—is called kalon. Beautiful things are those whose value is of itself evident. You cannot ask what purpose they serve. They are desirable for their own sake (di' hauto haireton) and not, like the useful, for the sake of something else. Thus even linguistic usage shows the special status accorded to what is called kalon.

But even the ordinary antithesis that determines the idea of the beautiful, the antithesis to the ugly (aischron), points in the same direction. The aischron is what cannot be looked at. The beautiful is what can be looked at, what is good-looking in the widest sense of the word. In German ansehnlich (good-looking) is also used to express magnitude (cf. "fair-sized"). And in fact the use of the word schön—both in Greek and in German—always implies a certain majestic size. Because the element of the ansehnlich points to the whole sphere of the decorus, the moral, its meaning comes close to being defined by its antithesis to the useful (chresimon).

Hence the idea of the beautiful closely approximates that of the good (agathon), insofar as it is something to be chosen for its own sake, as an end that subordinates everything else to it as a means. For what is beautiful is not regarded as a means to something else.

Thus Platonic philosophy exhibits a close connection, and sometimes even a confusion, between the idea of the good and the idea of the beautiful. Both transcend everything that is conditional and multiform: the loving soul encounters the beautiful-in-itself at the end of a path that leads through the beautiful that is multiform. The beautiful-in-itself is the one, the uniform, the boundless (Symposium), just like the idea of the good that lies beyond everything that is conditional and multiform—i.e., good only in a certain respect (Republic). The beautiful-in-itself shows itself to be as much beyond all beings as is the good-in-itself (epekeina). Thus the order of being that consists in the orientation toward the one good agrees with the order of the beautiful. The path of love that Diotima teaches leads beyond beautiful bodies to beautiful souls, and from there to beautiful institutions, customs, and laws, and finally to the sciences (e.g., to the beautiful relations of numbers found in mathematics), to this "wide ocean of beautiful utterance"[117]—and leads beyond all that. We may ask whether the movement beyond the sphere of what is perceptually visible into that of the "intelligible" really involves a differentiation and increase of the beauty of the beautiful and not just of the being that is beautiful. But Plato obviously means that the teleological order of being is also an order of beauty, that beauty appears more purely and clearly in the sphere of the intelligible than in that of the visible, which is muddied by the inharmonious and the imperfect. Similarly, medieval philosophy linked the idea of the beautiful so closely with that of the good, the bonum, that it failed to understand a classical passage from Aristotle on the kalon: the translation here simply rendered the word kalon as bonum.[118]

The basis of the close connection between the idea of the beautiful and that of the teleological order of being is the Pythagorean and Platonic concept of measure. Plato defines the beautiful in terms of measure, appropriateness, and right proportions; and Aristotle states that the elements (eide) of the beautiful are order (taxis), right proportions (summetria), and definition (horismenon), and he finds these paradigmatically exemplified in mathematics. Further, the close connection between the mathematical orders of the beautiful and the order of the heavens means that the cosmos, the model of all visible harmony, is at the same time the supreme example of beauty in the visible sphere. Harmonious proportion, symmetry, is the decisive condition of all beauty.

As we can see, this kind of definition of the beautiful is a universal ontological one. Here nature and art are not in antithesis to each other. This means, of course, that in regard to beauty the priority of nature is unquestioned. Art may take advantage of gaps in the natural order of being to perfect its beauties. But that certainly does not mean that "beauty" is to be found primarily in art. As long as the order of being is itself seen as divine or as God's creation—and the latter is the case until the eighteenth century—the exceptional case of art can be seen only within the horizon of this order of being. We have described above how it was only in the nineteenth century that the problems of aesthetics were transferred to art. We can now see that there was a metaphysical process behind this. This switch to the point of view of art ontologically presupposes a mass of being thought of as formless or ruled by mechanical laws. The artistic mind of man, which mechanically constructs useful things, will ultimately understand all beauty in terms of the work of his own mind.

Accordingly, only at the frontiers of the mechanical constructibility of being has modern science been reminded of the independent ontological value of the Gestalt and now introduces the idea of the Gestalt as a supplementary principle of knowledge into the explanation of nature —chiefly into the explanation of living nature (biology and psychology). This does not mean science abandons its fundamental attitude but only that it tries to reach its goal—the domination of being—in a more subtle way. This must be emphasized against the self-conception of modern natural science.[119] At the same time, however, science accepts the beauty of nature, the beauty of art, and the disinterested pleasure they give—but only at its own frontiers, the frontiers of the achieved domination of nature. When describing the reversal of the relationship between the beauty of nature and the beauty of art, we discussed the shift whereby the beauty of nature finally lost its priority to such an extent that it is conceived as a reflection of the mind. We might have added that "nature" came to be conceived in the way it has been ever since Rousseau: as the mirror image of the concept of art. As the counterpart of the mind, as the non-I, nature became a polemical concept, and as such it has none of the universal ontological dignity possessed by the cosmos, the order of beautiful things.[120]

Certainly no one will want simply to reverse this development and try to re-establish the metaphysical dignity of the beautiful that we find in Greek philosophy by reviving the last embodiment of this tradition, the eighteenth-century aesthetics of perfection. However unsatisfactory is the development of aesthetics toward subjectivism that began with Kant, he has convincingly proved the untenability of aesthetic rationalism. Still, it is incorrect to base the metaphysics of the beautiful solely on the ontology of measure and the teleological order of being to which the rationalist aesthetic of rules, which seems so classical, ultimately appeals. The metaphysics of the beautiful is not, in fact, identical to this application of aesthetic rationalism. The return to Plato brings out quite a different aspect of the phenomenon of the beautiful, and this is what is of interest in our hermeneutical inquiry.

However closely Plato has linked the idea of the beautiful with that of the good, he is still aware of a difference between the two, and this difference involves the *special advantage of the beautiful*. We have seen that the intangibility of the good finds an analogue in the beautiful—i.e., in the harmony between the thing and its attendant disclosure (aletheia)—in that it too has an ultimate effulgence. But Plato can say, moreover, that in the attempt to grasp the good itself, the good takes flight into the beautiful.[121] Thus the beautiful is distinguished from the absolutely intangible good in that it can be grasped. It is part of its own nature to be something that is visibly manifest. The beautiful reveals itself in the search for the good. It is the mark distinguishing the good for the human soul. That which manifests itself in perfect form attracts the longing of love to it. The beautiful disposes people in its favor immediately, whereas models of human virtue can be only obscurely descried in the unclear medium of appearances, because they have, as it were, no light of their own. Thus we often succumb to impure imitations and appearances of virtue. The case of the beautiful is different. It has its own radiance, so that we are not seduced here by deceptive copies. For "beauty alone has this quality: that it is what is most radiant (ekphanestaton) and lovely."[122]

Through the anagogical function of the beautiful, which Plato has described in unforgettable terms, a structural characteristic of the being of the beautiful becomes visible, and with it an element of the structure of being in general. Obviously what distinguishes the beautiful from the good is that the beautiful of itself presents itself, that its being is such that it makes itself immediately evident (einleuchtend). This means that beauty has the most important ontological function: that of mediating between idea and appearance. This is the metaphysical crux of Platonism. It finds its concrete form in the concept of participation (methexis) and concerns both the relation of the appearance to the idea and the relation of the ideas to one another. As we learn from the *Phaedrus*, it is not accidental that Plato likes to illustrate this controversial relation of "participation" by the example of the beautiful. The idea of the beautiful is truly present, whole and undivided, in what is beautiful. Hence, through the example of the beautiful, the "parousia" of the eidos that Plato has in mind can be made evident and, by contrast to the logical difficulties of participation in the "being" of "becoming," the thing itself can be offered in evidence. "Being present" belongs in a convincing way to the being of the beautiful itself. However much beauty might be experienced as the reflection of something supraterrestrial, it is still there in the visible world. That it really is something different, a being of another order, is seen in its mode of appearance. It appears suddenly; and just as suddenly, without any transition, it disappears again. If we must speak with Plato of a hiatus (chorismos) between the world of the senses and the world of ideas, this is where it is and this is where it is also overcome.

The beautiful appears not only in what is visibly present to the senses, but it does so in such a way that it really exists only through it—i.e., emerges as one out of the whole. The beautiful is of itself truly "most radiant" (to ekphanestaton). The sharp division between the beautiful and what has no share in the beautiful is, moreover, a fact that is well established phenomenologically. Aristotle[123] says of "well-formed works" that nothing can be added to them and nothing taken away. The sensible mean, exactness of proportion, is part of the oldest definition of the beautiful. We need only think of the sensitivity to the tonal harmonies from which music is constructed.

"Radiance," then, is not only one of the qualities of the beautiful but constitutes its actual being. The distinguishing mark of the beautiful —namely that it immediately attracts the desire of the human soul to it—is founded in its mode of being. The proportionateness of the thing does not simply let it be what it is but also causes it to emerge as a harmonious whole that is proportioned within itself. This is the disclosure (aletheia) of which Plato speaks in the *Philebus* and which is part of the nature of the beautiful.[124] Beauty is not simply symmetry but appearance itself. It is related to the idea of "shining" (scheinen: also, to appear). "To shine" means to shine on something, and so to make that on which the light falls appear. Beauty has the mode of being of *light*.

This means not only that without light nothing beautiful can appear, nothing can be beautiful. It also means that the beauty of a beautiful thing appears in it as light, as a radiance. It makes itself manifest. In fact the universal mode of being of light is to be reflected in itself in this way. Light is not only the brightness of that on which it shines; by making something else visible, it is visible itself, and it is not visible in any other way than by making something else visible. The reflective nature of light was already brought out in classical thought,[125] and correlatively the idea of reflection that plays such an important role in modern philosophy originally belongs to the sphere of optics.

Obviously it is because of its reflective nature that light combines seeing and the visible, so that without light there can be neither seeing nor anything visible. We recognize the consequences of this trivial observation when we consider the relation of light to the beautiful and the extent of the meaning covered by the beautiful. It is actually light that makes visible things into shapes that are both "beautiful" and "good." But the beautiful is not limited to the sphere of the visible. It is, as we saw, the mode of appearance of the good in general, of being as it ought to be. The light in which not only the realm of the visible but also that of the intelligible is articulated, is not the light of the sun but the light of the mind, of nous. Plato's profound analogy[126] already alluded to this; from it Aristotle developed the doctrine of nous and, following him, medieval Christian thought developed that of the intellectus agens. The mind that unfolds from within itself the multiplicity of what is thought is present to itself in what is thought.

The Christian doctrine of the word, the verbum creans, which we have considered at some length above, follows the Platonic and Neoplatonic metaphysics of light. We have described the ontological structure of the beautiful as the mode of appearing that causes things to emerge in their proportions and their outline, and the same holds for the realm of the intelligible. The light that causes everything to emerge in such a way that it is evident and comprehensible in itself is the light of the word. Thus the close relationship that exists between the shining forth (Vorscheinen) of the beautiful and the evidentness (das Einleuchtende) of the understandable is based on the metaphysics of light.[127] This was precisely the relation that guided our hermeneutical inquiry. The reader will recall that the analysis of the nature of the work of art led to the question of hermeneutics and that this expanded into a universal inquiry. All this took place without any reference to the metaphysics of light. If we now consider the connection between the latter and our inquiry, we are helped by the fact that the structure of light can obviously be detached from the Neoplatonic and Christian metaphysical theory of the at once sensible and intellectual source of light. This is already clear from Augustine's dogmatic interpretation of the creation story. Augustine notes[128] that light is created before the differentiation of things and the creation of the light-giving heavenly bodies. But he puts special emphasis on the fact that the first creation of heaven and earth takes place without the divine word. Only when light is created does God *speak* for the first time. Augustine interprets this speech, by means of which light is commanded and created, as the coming into being of mental light, by means of which the difference among created things is made possible. It is only through light that the formlessness of the first created mass of heaven and earth is rendered capable of being shaped into a multiplicity of forms.

In Augustine's ingenious interpretation of Genesis we can discern the first hint of the speculative interpretation of language that we have elaborated in the structural analysis of the hermeneutical experience of the world, according to which the multiplicity of what is thought proceeds only from the unity of the word. We can also see that the metaphysics of light brings out a side of the classical concept of the beautiful that is justified apart from the context of substance metaphysics and the metaphysical relationship to the infinite divine mind. Thus our analysis of the place of the beautiful in classical Greek philosophy shows that this aspect of metaphysics has a productive significance for us also.[129] That being is self-presentation and that all understanding is an event, this first and last insight transcends the horizon of substance metaphysics as well as the metamorphosis of the concept of substance into the concepts of subjectivity and scientific objectivity. Thus the metaphysics of the beautiful has implications for our inquiry. Now it is no longer a question, as it seemed in the nineteenth century, of justifying the truth claim of art and the artistic, or even that of history and the methodology of the human sciences, in terms of theory of science. Now we are concerned, rather, with the much more general task of establishing the ontological background of the hermeneutical experience of the world.

The metaphysics of the beautiful can be used to illuminate two points that follow from the relation between the radiance of the beautiful and the evidentness of the intelligible. The first is that both the appearance of the beautiful and the mode of being of understanding have the character of an event; the second, that the hermeneutical experience, as the experience of traditionary meaning, has a share in the *immediacy* which has always distinguished the experience of the beautiful, as it has that of all evidence of *truth*.

1. First, against the background of traditional speculation on light and beauty, let us justify our assigning primacy to the activity of the thing in hermeneutical experience. It is now clear that we are not concerned here with either mythology or a mere dialectical reversal in the manner of Hegel, but with the continuing influence of an ancient truth that has been able to assert itself against modern scientific methodology. This is seen from the very etymology of the concepts we use. We have said that, like everything meaningful, the beautiful is einleuchtend ("clearly evident," "shining in"). This concept of evidentness belongs to the tradition of rhetoric. The eikos, the verisimilar, the "probable" (wahrscheinliche: "true shining"), the "evident," belong in a series of things that defend their rightness against the truth and certainty of what is proved and known. Let us recall that we assigned a special importance to the sensus communis.[130] Also there may be an echo of the mystical, pietistic-sounding illuminatio, illumination (Erleuchtung) in the idea of Einleuchten (an echo that can also be heard in the sensus communis, for instance in Oetinger[131]). At any rate it is not by chance that the metaphor of light is used in both spheres. The thing itself compels us to speak of an event and of an activity of the thing. What is evident (einleuchtend) is always something that is said—a proposal, a plan, a conjecture, an argument, or something of the sort. The idea is always that what is evident has not been proved and is not absolutely certain, but it asserts itself by reason of its own merit within the realm of the possible and probable. Thus we can even admit that an argument has something evidently true about it, even though we are presenting a counterargument. How it is to be reconciled with the whole

of what we ourselves consider correct is left open. It is only said that it is evident "in itself"—i.e., that there is something in its favor. The connection with the beautiful is manifest. The beautiful charms us, without its being immediately integrated with the whole of our orientations and evaluations. Indeed, just as the beautiful is a kind of experience that stands out like an enchantment and an adventure within the whole of our experience and presents a special task of hermeneutical integration, what is evident is always something surprising as well, like a new light being turned on, expanding the range of what we can take into consideration.

The hermeneutical experience belongs in this sphere because it too is the event of a genuine experience. This is in fact always the case when something speaks to us from tradition: there is something evident about what is said, though that does not imply it is, in every detail, secured, judged, and decided. The tradition asserts its own truth in being understood, and disturbs the horizon that had, until then, surrounded us. It is a real experience in the sense we have shown. The event of the beautiful and the hermeneutical process both presuppose the finiteness of human life. We might even ask whether the beautiful can be experienced by an infinite mind in the same way that it can be by us. Can this mind see anything other than the beauty of the whole that lies before it? The "radiance" of the beautiful seems to be something reserved to finite human experience. There was a similar problem in medieval thought, namely how beauty can be in God if he is one and not many. Only Nicholas of Cusa's theory of the complicatio of the many in God offers a satisfactory solution (cf. the "sermo de pulchritudine" of Nicholas of Cusa, cited above [p. 473]). From this it seems to follow that, as in Hegel's philosophy of infinite knowledge, art is a form of representation that is superseded in the concept and in philosophy. Similarly, the universality of the hermeneutical experience would not be available to an infinite mind, for it develops out of itself all meaning, all noeton, and thinks all that can be thought in the perfect contemplation of itself. The God of Aristotle (as well as the Spirit of Hegel) has left "philosophy," this movement of finite existence, behind. None of the gods philosophizes, says Plato.[132]

The fact that we have been able to refer several times to Plato, even though Greek logos philosophy revealed the ground of hermeneutical experience only in a very fragmentary way, is due to this feature of the Platonic view of beauty, which is like an undercurrent in the history of Aristotelian and Scholastic metaphysics, sometimes rising to the surface, as in Neoplatonic and Christian mysticism and in theological and philosophical spiritualism. It was in this tradition of Platonism that the conceptual vocabulary required for thought about the finiteness of human life was developed.[133] The continuity of this Platonic tradition is attested by the affinity between the Platonic theory of beauty and the idea of a universal hermeneutics.

2. If we start from the basic ontological view that being is *language—i.e., self-presentation*—as revealed to us by the hermeneutical experience of being, then there follows not only the event-character of the beautiful and the event-structure of all understanding. Just as the mode of being of the beautiful proved to be characteristic of being in general, so the same thing can be shown to be true of the *concept of truth*. We can start from the metaphysical tradition, but here too we must ask what aspects of it apply to hermeneutical experience. According to traditional metaphysics the truth of what exists is one of its transcendental qualities and is closely related to goodness (which again brings in beauty). Thus we may recall St. Thomas' statement that the beautiful is to be defined in terms of knowledge, the good in terms of desire.[134] The beautiful is that in the vision of which desire comes to rest: cuius ipsa apprehensio placet. The beautiful has an orientation not only toward goodness but towards the cognitive faculty: addit supra bonum quemdam ordinem ad vim cognoscitivam. The "radiance" of the beautiful appears here like a light that shines over what is formed: lux splendens supra formatum.

By again appealing to Plato, we can again attempt to free this statement from its connection to the metaphysical doctrine of forma. Plato was the first to show that the essential element in the beautiful was aletheia, and it is clear what he means by this. The beautiful, the way in which goodness appears, reveals itself in its being: it presents itself. What presents itself in this way is not different from itself in presenting itself. It is not one thing for itself and another for others, nor is it something that exists through something else. Beauty is not radiance shed on a form from without. Rather, the ontological constitution of the form itself is to be radiant, to present itself in this way. From this, then, it follows that in regard to beauty the beautiful must always be understood ontologically as an "image." It makes no difference whether it "itself" or its copy appears. As we have seen, the metaphysical distinction of the beautiful was that it closed the gap between the idea and the appearance. It is certainly an "idea"—i.e., it belongs to an order of being that rises above the flux of appearances as something constant in itself. But equally certain is that it is itself that appears. As we saw, this is by no means an objection to the doctrine of ideas but the concentrated exemplification of its problem. Where Plato appeals to the evidentness of the beautiful, he does not need to insist on the contrast between "the thing itself" and its copy. It is the beautiful itself that both creates and supersedes this contrast.

Plato is likewise important for the problem of truth. In analyzing the work of art we have endeavored to show that self-presentation is to be regarded as the true being of the work of art. To this end we invoked the concept of play, and this directed us into more general contexts. For we saw there that the truth of what presents itself in play is properly neither "believed" nor "not believed" outside the play situation.[135]

In the aesthetic sphere this is obvious. Even when the poet is honored as a seer, his poetry—e.g., Hölderlin's song of the return of the gods—is not actually regarded as a prophecy. Rather, the poet is a seer because he himself presents what is, was, and will be, and hence he himself attests to what he proclaims. It is true that poetic utterance has something ambiguous about it, like an oracle. But this is precisely where its hermeneutical truth lies. If we regard it as something that is simply aesthetic, nonbinding, and lacking in existential seriousness, we are obviously failing to see how fundamental is the finitude of man for the hermeneutical experience of the world. It is not the weakness but the strength of the oracle that it is ambiguous. Whoever would put Hölderlin or Rilke to the proof to see if they really believe in their gods or angels is missing the point.[136]

Kant's fundamental definition of aesthetic pleasure as disinterested pleasure has not only the negative implication that the pleasurable object cannot be employed as something useful or desired as something good but also the positive one that "really existing" can add nothing to the aesthetic content of pleasure, to the "sheer sight" of a thing, because aesthetic being is, precisely, self-presentation. Only from the moral standpoint is there an interest in the real, factual existence of the beautiful—e.g., in the song of the nightingale, the imitation of which was, for Kant, somehow morally offensive. Whether, from the fact that aesthetic being is so constituted, it really follows that truth must not be sought here because nothing is known here, is the question. In our analyses of the aesthetic we discussed the narrowness of the concept of knowledge that limited Kant's position in this matter, and from the question of the truth of art we found our way into hermeneutics, where art and history were combined for us.

Even with regard to the hermeneutical phenomenon it seemed an unjustified limitation to regard the process of understanding solely as the immanent effort of a philological consciousness that is indifferent to the "truth" of its texts. On the other hand, it was clear that the understanding of texts did not mean that the question of truth was decided in advance from the standpoint of a superior knowledge of the subject matter, or that in understanding one was enjoying one's own superior knowledge of the object. Rather, the whole value of hermeneutical experience—like the significance of history for human knowledge in general—seemed to consist in the fact that here we are not simply filing things in pigeonholes but that what we encounter in a tradition says something to us. Understanding, then, does not consist in a technical virtuosity of "understanding" everything written. Rather, it is a genuine experience (Erfahrung)—i.e., an encounter with something that asserts itself as truth.

The fact that such an encounter takes place in verbal interpretation, for reasons we have discussed, and that the phenomenon of language and understanding proves to be a universal model of being and knowledge in general, enables us to define more exactly the meaning of the truth at play in understanding. We have seen that the words that bring something into language are themselves a speculative event. Their truth lies in what is said in them, and not in an intention locked in the impotence of subjective particularity. Let us remember that understanding what someone says is not an achievement of empathy in which one divines the inner life of the speaker. Certainly it is true of all understanding that what is said acquires its determinacy in part through a supplementing of meaning from occasional sources. But this determination by situation and context, which fills out what is said to a totality of meaning and makes what is said really said, pertains not to the speaker but to what is spoken.

Accordingly, poetic utterance proved to be the special case of a meaning that has dissolved into and been embodied in the utterance. The coming into language that occurs in a poem is like entering into relationships of order that support and guarantee the "truth" of what is said. All coming into language, and not just the poetic, has about it something of this quality of self-attestation. "Where the word breaks off, no thing may be." As we emphasized, speaking is never just subsuming individual things under universal concepts. In using words what is given to the senses is not put at our disposal as an individual case of a universal; it is itself made present in what is said—just as the idea of the beautiful is present in what is beautiful.

What we mean by truth here can best be defined again in terms of our concept of *play*. The weight of the things we encounter in understanding plays itself out in a linguistic event, a play of words playing around and about what is meant. *Language games* exist where we, as learners—and when do we cease to be that?—rise to the understanding of the world. Here it is worth recalling what we said about the nature of play, namely that the player's actions should not be considered subjective actions, since it is, rather, the game itself that plays, for it draws the players into itself and thus itself becomes the actual subjectum of the playing.[137] The analogue in the present case is neither playing with language nor with the contents of the experience of the world or of tradition that speak to us, but the play of language itself, which addresses us, proposes and withdraws, asks and fulfills itself in the answer.

Thus, understanding is not playing, in the sense that the person understanding playfully holds himself back and refuses to take a stand with respect to the claim made on him. The freedom of self-possession necessary for one to withhold oneself in this way is not given here, and this, in fact, is what applying the concept of play to understanding implies. Someone who understands is always already drawn into an event through which meaning asserts itself. So it is well founded for us to use the same concept of play for the hermeneutical phenomenon as for the experience of the beautiful. When we understand a text, what is meaningful in it captivates us just as the beautiful captivates us. It has asserted itself and captivated us before we can come to ourselves and be in a position to test the claim to meaning that it makes. What we encounter in the experience of the beautiful and in understanding the meaning of tradition really has something of the truth of play about it. In understanding we are drawn into an event of truth and arrive, as it were, too late, if we want to know what we are supposed to believe.

Thus there is undoubtedly no understanding that is free of all prejudices, however much the will of our knowledge must be directed toward escaping their thrall. Throughout our investigation it has emerged that the certainty achieved by using scientific methods does not suffice to guarantee truth. This especially applies to the human sciences, but it does not mean that they are less scientific; on the contrary, it justifies the claim to special humane significance that they have always made. The fact that in such knowledge the knower's own being comes into play certainly shows the limits of method, but not of science. Rather, what the tool of method does not achieve must—and really can—be achieved by a discipline of questioning and inquiring, a discipline that guarantees truth.

Notes

1 If one transposes oneself into the position of another with the intent of understanding not the truth of what he is saying, but him, the questions asked in such a conversation are marked by the inauthenticity described above (pp. 355f.).

2 We have here the problem of "alienation," on which Schadewaldt has important things to say in the appendix to his translation of the *Odyssey* (RoRoRo-Klassiker, 1958), p.324.

3 Droysen, *Historik*, ed. Hübner (1937), p.63.

4 Hegel, *Die Vernunft in der Geschichte*, ed. Lasson, p.145.

5 Pp. 185ff. and 295ff. above.

6 Plato, *Seventh Letter*, 341c, 344c, and *Phaedrus*, 275.

7 This is the reason for the enormous difference that exists between what is spoken and what is written, between the style of spoken material and the far higher demands of style that something fixed as literature has to satisfy.

8 Kippenberg relates that Rilke once read one of his *Duino Elegies* aloud in such a way that the listeners were not at all aware of the difficulty of the poetry.

9 Cf. the correspondence that followed Fichte's essay "Über Geist und Buchstabe in der Philosophie" (Fichte, *Briefwechsel*, II, ch. 5).

10 Cf. pp. 273f.

11 Cf. p.354 above, in particular the quotation from Friedrich Schlegel.

12 Cf. my note on H. Rose's *Klassik als Denkform des Abendlandes*, in *Gnomon*, (1940), pp. 433f. [*GW*, V, 353–56]. I now see that the methodological introduction to "Platos dialektische Ethik" (1931) [*GW*, V, 6–14] implicitly makes the same criticism.

13 [On the distinction between "reading" and "performing," see "Zwischen Phänomenologie und Dialektik: Versuch einer Selbstkritik," *GW*, II, 3–23, and

"Text and Interpretation," in *The Gadamer-Derrida Encounter: Texts and Comments*, ed. Diane Michelfelder and Richard Palmer (Albany: SUNY Press, 1988).]

14 Cf. pp. 305ff. above [and the essays in *GW*, II, section 4].

15 Johannes Lohmann in *Lexis* III and elsewhere.

16 Cf. Ernst Cassirer, *Wesen und Wirkung des Symbolbegriffs* (1956), which chiefly contains the essays published in the Warburg Library Series. R. Hönigswald, *Philosophie und Sprache* (1937), starts his critique here.

17 Hönigswald puts it in this way: "Language is not only a fact, but a principle" (op. cit., p.448).

18 This is how Lohmann, op. cit., describes the development.

19 There is a still valuable account of it in Hermann Steinthal's *Die Geschichte der Sprachwissenschaft bei den Griechen und Römern mit besonderer Rücksicht auf die Logik* (1864). [One can now mention as representative of many works K. Gaiser, "Name und Sache in Platons 'Kratylos,'" *Abhandlungen der Heidelberger Akademie der Wissenschaften, philos.–histor. Klasse*, no. 3 (1974).]

20 *Cratylus*, 384d.

21 *Cratylus*, 388c.

22 *Cratylus*, 438d–439b.

23 *Seventh Letter*, 342ff.

24 *Sophist*, 263e, 264a.

25 [On "mimesis," see above pp. 113f., and note the significant change from "mimesis" to "methexis," which Aristotle records in *Metaphysics*, I, 6, 987 b 10–13.]

26 *Cratylus*, 385b, 387c.

27 *Cratylus*, 432a ff.

28 *Cratylus*, 434e.

29 *Cratylus*, 429bc, 430a.

30 *Cratylus*, 430 d 5.

31 Hegel, *Jenenser Realphilosophie*, I, 210. [Now in *Gesammelte Werke*, VI, *Jenaer Systementwürfe*, I (Düsseldorf, 1975), 287.]

32 The importance of the grammar of the stoics and the formation of a Latin conceptual language to mirror Greek is pointed out by Johannes Lohmann in his *Lexis*, II passim.

33 Wilhelm von Humboldt, *Linguistic Variability and Intellectual Development*, tr. George C. Buck and Frithjof A. Raven (Coral Gables: University of Miami Press, 1971),§9.

34 Let us recall Aristotle's use of the word *phronesis*: because he uses it in nontechnical senses, it is risky to draw conclusions about his thought based on a developmental historical approach, as I once tried to show against Werner Jaeger, "Der Aristotelische Protreptikos," *Hermes* (1928), pp. 146ff. [*GW*, V, 164–86].

35 Cf. Leibniz, "Dialogus de Connexione inter res et verba, et veritatis realitate," *Opera philosophica*, ed. Johann Eduard Erdmann (2 vols. in one; Berlin: 1839–40), p.77.

36 Leibniz, "De cognitione, veritate et ideis" (1684), *Opera philosophica*, ed. Erdmann, pp. 79ff.

37 We know that in his letter to Mersenne of November 20, 1629, which Leibniz knew, Descartes had already developed, on the model of the creation of numerical symbols, the idea of such a sign language of reason that would contain the whole of philosophy. There is even a rudimentary form of the same idea, though in a Platonized form, in Nicholas of Cusa's *Idiota de mente*, III, 6.

38 *On the Posterior Analytics*, II, 19.

39 [I am not unaware that the "linguistic turn," about which I knew nothing in the early '50's, recognized the same thing. See my reference to it in "The Phenomenological Movement," *Philosophical Hermeneutics*, tr. David E. Linge (Berkeley: University of California Press, 1976), pp. 130–81.]

40 St. Thomas, *Summa Theologica*, I, ques. 34, and elsewhere.

41 In what follows I use the instructive article "Verbe" in the *Dictionnaire de Théologie Catholique*, as well as Lebreton's *Histoire du dogme de la Trinité*.

42 The parrots: Sextus Empiricus, *Adversus mathematicos*, VIII, 275.

43 *Assumendo non consumendo*, Augustine, *De Trinitate*, XV, 11.

44 For the following, see Augustine, *De Trinitate*, XV, 10–15. [In an excellent study, G. Ripanti has shown that the *De doctrina christiana* contains the outlines of a biblical hermeneutics, not as theological methodology, but as a description of the mode of experience of Bible-reading. See his *Agostino teoretico dell'interpretazione* (Brescia, 1980).]

45 Cf. *Commentarium in Johannem*, ch. 1, titled *De differentia verbi divini et humani*, and the difficult and important opusculum, compiled from genuine texts by Thomas, called *De natura verbi intellectus*, on which we shall mainly draw in what follows.

46 Plato, *Sophist*, 263e.

47 Cf. Christoph Wagner, *Die vielen Metaphern und das eine Modell der plotinischen Metaphysik* (unpub. diss., Heidelberg, 1957), which investigated the ontologically important metaphors of Plotinus. On the concept of the "fountain," cf. Appendix V below.

48 One cannot fail to note that the patristic and Scholastic interpretation of Genesis to some extent repeats the discussion of the correct understanding of the *Timaeus* that took place among Plato's pupils. [See my "Idea and Reality in Plato's *Timaeus*," in *Dialogue and Dialectic: Eight Hermeneutical Studies on Plato*, tr. P. Christopher Smith (New Haven: Yale University Press, 1980), pp. 156–93.]

49 There is some excellent material on this subject in Hans Lipps' *Untersuchungen zu einer hermeneutischen Logik* (1938) and in J. L. Austin, *How to Do Things with Words* (Oxford, 1962).

50 G. Rabeau's interpretation of Thomas, *Species Verbum* (Paris, 1938), seems to me rightly to emphasize this.

51 Theodor Litt rightly emphasizes this in his article "Das Allgemeine im Aufbau der geisteswissenschaftlichen Erkenntnis," *Berichte der sächsischen Akademie der Wissenschaften*, 93, no. 1 (1941).

52 Ludwig Klages saw this very clearly. Cf. Karl Löwith, *Das Individuum in der Rolle des Mitmenschen* (1928), pp. 33ff. [and my review, *Logos*, 18 (1929), 436–40 (*GW*, IV)].

53 This image suggests itself involuntarily and thus confirms Heidegger's demonstration of the closeness of meaning between *legein* "to say," and *legein*, "to gather" (first mentioned in "Logos [Heraclitus, Fragment B 50]" (1951), in *Early Greek Thinking*, tr. David Farrell Krell and Frank A. Capuzzi (New York: Harper and Row, 1975), pp. 59–78).

54 Plato, *Phaedo*, 99e.

55 Cf. J. Stenzel's important article on Speusippus in Pauly-Wissowa, *Real-Encyclopädie der Altertumswissenschaft*.

56 *Poetics*, 22, 1459 a 8.

57 *Topics*, I, 18, 108 b 7–31 treats in detail the *tou homoiou theoria*.

58 See p.416 above.

59 Thus we must view the terminological statements of the *Peri Hermeneias* in the light of the *Politics*, e.g., 1, 2.

60 *Posterior Analytics*, II, 19; cf. pp. 350ff. above.

61 *Stoicorum Veterum Fragmenta*, ed. Arnim, II, 87.

62 Cf. the theory of *diastema*, rejected by Aristotle, *Physics*, IV, 4, 211 b 14ff.

63 Johannes Lohmann has recently made some interesting observations, according to which the discovery of the "ideal" world of notes, figures, and numbers produced a special kind of word formation and hence the beginnings of a consciousness of language. Cf. his essays in the *Archiv für Musikwissenschaft*, 14 (1957), 147–55, and 16 (1959), 148–73, 261–91, *Lexis*, IV, 2, and finally, "Über den paradigmatischen Charakter der griechischen Kultur," *Festschrift* for Gadamer (1960). [See now *Musike und Logos* (Stuttgart, 1970), which satisfies only in small part the need for a collection of Lohmann's very important work.]

64 Cf. K. Volkmann-Schluck, who seeks primarily to establish the place of Nicholas in the history of thought on the basis of the idea of the "image": *Nicolaus Cusanus* (1957), esp. pp. 146ff. [and likewise J. Koch, *Die ars coniecturalis des Nicolaus Cusanus* (Arbeitsgemeinschaft für Forschung des Landes Nordrhein-Westfalen, 16) and my "Nicolaus von Cues und die Philosophie der Gegenwart," *Kleine Schriften*, III, 80–88, and "Nicolaus von

Cues in der Geschichte des Erkenntnisproblems," *Cusanus-Gesellschaft*, 11 (1975), 275–80 (both repr. in *GW*, IV).]

65 *Philosophi quidem de Verbo divino et maximo absoluto sufficienter instructi non erant ... Non sunt igitur formae actu nisi in Verbo ipsum Verbum ... , De docta ignorantia*, II, 9.

66 Cf. p.425 above.

67 Cf. Cassirer, *Philosophy of Symbolic Forms*, tr. Ralph Manheim (3 vols.; New Haven: Yale University Press, 1953), I, 290.

68 The most important evidence followed here is Nicholas of Cusa's *Idiota de mente*, III, 2: *Quomodo est vocabulum naturale et aliud impositum secundum illud citra praecisionem. ...*

69 Cf. the instructive account by J. Koch, op. cit., n. 64 above.

70 [See my "Wahrheit des Wortes," *GW*, VIII.]

71 Cf. for what follows *Linguistic Variability and Intellectual Development* [first published 1836], tr. George C. Buck and Frithjof A. Raven (Coral Gables: University of Miami Press, 1971).

72 Op. cit., §6.

73 Op. cit., §22.

74 Op. cit., §13.

75 Op. cit., § 9.

76 Ibid.

77 Op. cit., §9 (*Über die Verschiedenheit des menschlichen Sprachbaus* [1836], p.60).

78 Op. cit., §9 (*Über die Verschiedenheit des menschlichen Sprachbaus* [1836], p.59).

79 [See *GW*, II, part 3, "Ergänzungen," 121–218.]

80 Max Scheler, Helmut Plessner, Arnold Gehlen.

81 Aristotle, *Politics* 1, 2, 1253 a 10ff. [See also "Man and Language," *Philosophical Hermeneutics*, tr. David E. Linge (Berkeley: University of California Press, 1976), p.59.]

82 Cf. pp. 429f. above [and *GW*, II, 16, 74].

83 *Ideen*, 1, §41.

84 Hence it is a sheer misunderstanding if one appeals against idealism—whether transcendental idealism or "idealistic" philosophy of language—to the being-in-itself of the world. This is to miss the methodological significance of idealism, the metaphysical form of which can be regarded, since Kant, as outmoded. Cf. Kant's "disproof of idealism" in the *Critique of Pure Reason*, B 274ff.

85 Karl-Otto Apel, "Der philosophische Wahrheitsbegriff einer inhaltlich orientierten Sprachwissenschaft," *Festschrift* for Weisgerber, pp. 25f. (repr. in Apel, *Transformationen der Philosophie* [2 vols.; Frankfurt, 1973], 1, 106–37), shows correctly that what men say about themselves is not to be understood as objective assertions concerning a particular being. Hence it is meaningless to

refute such statements by showing their logical circularity or contradictoriness.

86 Cf. Max Scheler's essay "Zur Rehabilitierung der Tugend," in *Vom Ursprung der Werte* (1919).

87 [The next three pages are slightly revised. See "Zwischen Phänomenologie und Dialektik: Versuch einer Selbstkritik," *GW*, II, 3ff.]

88 This remains true, even though Scheler wrongly takes transcendental idealism as productive idealism and regards the "thing-in-itself" as the antithesis of the subjective production of the object.

89 Cf. chiefly Scheler's essay "Erkenntnis und Arbeit," in *Die Wissensformen und die Gesellschaft* (1926) [repr. in his *Gesammelte Werke*, VIII].

90 Cf. pp. 342f. above.

91 [See my "Lob der Theorie," in *Lob der Theorie* (Frankfurt, 1983), pp. 26–50 (*GW*, X).]

92 *Metaphysics*, I, 1.

93 Cf. pp. 121f. above.

94 The fact is that Hegel's synchronistic account of the rationalist position, which sees Plato's ideas, as the calm realm of laws, on the same level as the knowledge of nature obtained by modern mechanics, corresponds exactly to the neo-Kantian view (cf. my speech in memory of Paul Natorp in Natorp, *Philosophische Systematik*, XVII, n., repr. in my *Philosophical Apprenticeships*, tr. Robert R. Sullivan [Cambridge, Mass.: MIT Press, 1985], pp. 21–26) with the difference that the neo-Kantians elevated into an absolute methodological ideal what, for Hegel, was only a truth that was to be superseded. [On the theory of atoms, see my "Antike Atomtheorie" (1934), *GW*, V, 263–79.]

95 On "the thing," see *Vorträge und Aufsätze*, pp. 164f. Here, in accordance with his later line of inquiry, Heidegger breaks with the summary comprehensive view of "theoria" in terms of the "science of the present-at-hand," which had been undertaken in *Being and Time* (see *Vorträge*, pp. 51f.). [See my "Einführung" to Heidegger, *Der Ursprung des Kunstwerks* (Stuttgart: Reclams Universal-Bibliothek, 1960), pp. 102–25, repr. in my *Heideggers Wege: Studien zum Spätwerk* (Tübingen, 1983), pp. 81–92 (now *GW*, III).]

96 In his "hermeneutical logic," Hans Lipps burst the narrow bounds of the traditional propositional logic and revealed the hermeneutical dimension of logical phenomena.

97 Plato, *Phaedo*, 72; Aristotle, *De anima*, III, 8, 431 b 21.

98 Even Kant's critique of the teleological faculty of judgment allows for this subjective necessity.

99 Cf. Hans Lipps on Goethe's theory of colors in *Die Wirklichkeit des Menschen*, pp. 108ff.

100 [In my view, it is a mere confusion to say that "indeterminacy" in quantum physics, which arises because the "energy" originating with the observer interferes with the observed object, and which itself appears as an element in the measured values, is a "constituent part of the subject."]

101 Cf. on this my "Hegel and the Dialectic of the Ancient Philosophers," in *Hegel's Dialectic: Five Hermeneutical Studies*, tr. P. Christopher Smith (New Haven: Yale University Press, 1976), pp. 5–34.

102 [On the priority of conversation over discursive statement, see the essays in *GW*, II, 121–217, gathered under the title "Ergänzungen."]

103 Aristotle, *De sensu*, 473 a 3, and also *Metaphysics*, 980 b 23–25. The primacy of hearing over seeing is due to the universality of the *logos*, which does not contradict the specific primacy of sight over all the other senses, which Aristotle often emphasizes (*Metaphysics*, I, 1 and elsewhere). [See my "Sehen, Hören, Lesen," *Festschrift* for Sühnel (Heidelberg, 1984).]

104 Hegel, *Logik*, ed. Meiner, II, 330.

105 Aristotle, *Metaphysics*, XII, 4, 1078 b 25. Cf. pp. 356–57 above.

106 Cf. for this derivation of the word *speculum* Thomas Aquinas, *Summa theologica*, II, 2, ques. 180, 3, reply to obj. 2, and the clever illustration of the "speculative counterpart" in Schelling, *Bruno* (*Werke*, part I, IV, 237): "Imagine the object and the image of the object that is thrown back by the mirror . . . "

107 [See my *Hegels Dialektik: Sechs hermeneutische Studien* (2nd ed., Tübingen, 1980) (*GW*, III).]

108 Hegel, "Vorrede," *Phänomenologie des Geistes*, ed. Hoffmeister, p.50.

109 Hegel, *Encyclopedia*, §36.

110 "Vorrede," *Phänomenologie*, ed. Hoffmeister, p.53. Does he mean Aristotle or Jacobi and the romantics? Cf. my essay cited above, n. 101. On the concept of "expression," cf. pp. 330–31f. above and Appendix VI below.

111 Cf. Karl Vossler, *Grundzüge einer idealistischen Sprachphilosophie* (1904).

112 Cf. pp. 361ff. above.

113 Hegel, *Logik*, I, 69f.

114 Cf. Stenzel's fine study *Über Sinn, Bedeutung, Begriff, Definition* (Darmstadt: Wissenschaftliche Buchgesellschaft, 1958).

115 Pp. 398f. above.

116 See pp. 181, 231f. above.

117 *Symposium*, 210d: "utterance" = "relations" [see my "Unterwegs zur Schrift," *GW*, IX].

118 Aristotle, *Metaphysics*, XII, 4, 1078 a 3–6. Cf. Grabmann's introduction to Ulrich von Strassburg's *De pulchro, Jahrbuch der bayerischen Akademie der Wissenschaften* (1926), p.31, as well as the valuable introduction by G. Santinello to Nicholas of Cusa's *Tota pulchra es, Atti e Mem. della Academia*

Patavina, LXXI. Nicholas goes back to pseudo-Dionysius and Albert, who were the decisive influences on medieval thought concerning the beautiful.

119 [This distinction needs to be applied more broadly. The issue of form or Gestalt is not confined to the human life sciences. Concepts of "symmetry," "forms of order," and "system" likewise cannot be grasped on the basis of the concept of mechanical construction. And even here the "beauty" which rewards the researcher is no mere self-encounter of a human being with himself.]

120 [See the forthcoming lectures by Wien, "Die Philosophie und die Wissenschaft vom Menschen" (1984), and Lund, "Naturwissenschaft und Hermeneutik" (1986).]

121 *Philebus*, 64 e 5. In *Platos dialektische Ethik*, §14 (*GW*, V, 150f.), I have considered this passage in more detail. Cf. also Gerhard Krüger, *Einsicht und Leidenschaft*, pp. 235f.

122 *Phaedrus*, 250 d 7.

123 *Nicomachean Ethics*, II, 6, 1106 b 10: "hence the common remark about a perfect work of art, that you could not take from it nor add to it" (tr. Rackham).

124 Plato, *Philebus*, 51d.

125 *Stoicorum Veterum Fragmenta*, ed. Arnim, II, 24, 36, 36, 9.

126 *Republic*, 508d.

127 The Neoplatonic tradition that influenced Scholasticism via pseudo-Dionysius and Albert the Great is thoroughly familiar with this relationship. For its previous history cf. Hans Blumenberg, "Licht als Metapher der Wahrheit," *Studium generale*, 10, no. 7 (1957), 432–47.

128 In his commentary on Genesis.

129 It is worthy of note in this context that patristic and Scholastic thought can be interpreted productively in Heideggerian terms, e.g., by Max Müller, *Sein und Geist* (1940), and *Existenzphilosophie in geistigen Leben der Gegenwart*, 2nd ed., pp. 119ff., 150ff.

130 Cf. pp. 17ff. above.

131 [See my "Oetinger als Philosoph," *Kleine Schriften*, III, 89–100 (*GW*, IV).]

132 *Symposium*, 204 a 1.

133 Cf. the importance of the school of Chartres for Nicholas of Cusa [which is stressed especially by R. Klibanksy. See also *De arte coniecturis*, ed. J. Koch (Cologne, 1956).]

134 St. Thomas, *Summa theologica*, 1, ques. 5, 4, and elsewhere.

135 Cf. pp. 104f. above.

136 Cf. my criticism of R. Guardini's book on Rilke, cited above, Part Two, n. 316. [See my "Rainer Maria Rilke nach fünfzig Jahren," in *Poetica: Ausgewählte*

Essays (Frankfurt: Insel, 1977), pp. 77–101 (*GW,* IX).]

137 Cf. above, pp. 102ff., and Eugen Fink, *Spiel als Weltsymbol* (1960) and my review, *Philosophische Rundschau,* 9 (1962), 1–8.

Appendices and Supplements

APPENDIX I

(To p.34)

The concept of style is one of the undiscussed assumptions on which historical consciousness lives. A brief glance at the fairly unexplored history of the word will tell us why this is so. The concept has arisen, as generally happens, by a word being lifted out of the original sphere of its application. Now this new sense is not primarily historical but normative. Thus in the modern tradition of classical rhetoric, the word "style" replaces what was called in the latter the genera dicendi and is therefore a normative concept. Different modes of speaking and writing are appropriate to particular purposes and contents, and their special demands. These are called different styles. It is clear that this view of different styles and their right application also implies the possibility of a wrong application.

A person who possesses the art of writing and expressing himself needs to observe a correct style. It appears that the concept of style first emerged in French jurisprudence and meant the manière de procéder—i.e., the way of conducting a trial that satisfied particular legal requirements. After the sixteenth century the word is used in a general way to describe the manner in which something is presented in language.[1] Obviously behind this usage is the view that certain apriori demands—especially, for example, unity —are made of artistic representation, and these are independent of the content of what is represented. The examples compiled by Panofsky[2] and

W. Hofmann[3] mention, apart from the word *stile*, the words *maniera* and *gusto* for this normative idea, which establishes a generic ideal of style.

But beyond this there is also, from the outset, the personal use of the word. A style is also the individual hand that is recognizable everywhere in the works of the same artist. This transferred meaning probably comes from the ancient practice of canonizing classical representatives of particular genera dicendi. Viewed in terms of the concept, the use of the word "style" for a so-called personal style is in fact a logical application of the same meaning; for "style" in this sense also designates a unity in the variety of the works—i.e., the way in which an artist's characteristic mode of representation distinguishes him from any other.

This emerges also in Goethe's use of the word, which became generally accepted. Goethe derives his concept of style from a distinction between it and the concept of "manner" and obviously combines both elements.[4] An artist creates a style when he is no longer just engaged in imitation but is also fashioning a language for himself. Although he ties himself to the given phenomenon, this is not a fetter for him. He can still express himself in the process. Rare though the correspondence is between "faithful imitation" and an individual manner (or way of understanding), this is precisely what constitutes style. Thus a normative element is also included in the idea of personal "style." The "nature," the "essence" of things remains the basic foundation of knowledge and art, from which the great artist cannot move away; and because of this connection with the nature of things, for Goethe the personal use of the word "style" still clearly retains a normative sense.

Here it is easy to recognize the classicist ideal. But Goethe's usage reveals the conceptual content that the word "style" always has. Style is by no means a mere peculiarity of expression; it always refers to something fixed and objective that is binding on individual forms of expression. This also explains how this idea comes to be applied as a historical category. For the retrospective historical gaze regards the taste of a particular time as something binding, and hence applying the concept of style to the history of art is a natural consequence of historical consciousness. It is true, however, that here the sense of the aesthetic norm that was originally implied in the concept of style (vero stile) has been lost in favor of a descriptive function.

This by no means settles the question whether the idea of style deserves the exclusive place it has won in the history of art—nor whether it can be applied, apart from the history of art, to other historical phenomena—e.g., political action.

As far as the first of these questions is concerned, the historical concept of style seems undoubtedly legitimate wherever the only aesthetic criterion is the connection with a dominant taste. Thus it is true primarily of all decoration, the fundamental purpose of which is not to exist for itself but for something else, and to bring it into conformity with the unity of a life context. It is obvious that the decorative is a subsidiary quality that belongs to something that has another purpose—i.e., a use.

We may ask ourselves, however, whether it is right to extend the point of view of the history of style to so-called free works of art. We have already seen that even a so-called free work of art has its original place in a life context. A person who wants to understand it cannot use it to give him particular experiences, but must find the right attitude, and that means primarily the right historical attitude, to it.

Therefore even here there are stylistic demands that cannot be infringed. But this does not mean that a work of art has significance only in terms of a history of style. Here Sedlmayr is quite right with his critique of the history of style.[5] The classificatory interest satisfied by the history of style really has nothing to do with the artistic element. Nevertheless the concept of style still retains its significance for the proper study of art. For even the aesthetic structural analysis that Sedlmayr calls for must obviously, through what it calls the right attitude (Einstellung), take account of the demands made by the history of style.

This is quite clear in the case of arts that require performance (music, theater, dance, etc.). The performance must be stylistically faithful. We must know what is called for both by the style of the time and by the personal style of a master. Of course this knowledge is not everything. A performance that was "historically faithful" would not be a genuine artistic performance—i.e., the work would not present itself to us in it as a work of art; rather, it would be—insofar as such a thing is at all possible—a didactic product or merely material for historical research, which the recordings conducted by the master himself will finally become. Nevertheless, even the most vital re-creation of a work is subject to certain limitations as a result of the question of the right historical style, and it must not fail to take account of these. Style belongs, in fact, to the fundamental bases of art; it is one of its inevitable conditions, and what emerges in the question of performance is obviously true also for our general receptive attitude to art of all kinds (performance, after all, is nothing but a particular kind of mediation facilitating our reception of art). Like that of taste, with which it is related (cf. the word Stilgefühl—"feeling for style"), the concept of style is inadequate to describe the experience of art and the scholarly understanding of it—it is adequate only in the sphere of decoration—but it is necessarily presupposed wherever art is to be understood.

This concept can now also be applied to political history. Actions can have style, and a style can be expressed even in a series of events. The word is meant here primarily in a normative sense. If we say of an action that it has great style or real style, then we are judging it from an aesthetic point of view.[6] Even if we are trying to describe a particular style of political action, this is fundamentally an aesthetic concept of style. In manifesting this style in action, we are making ourselves visible to others, so that they know with whom they have to deal. Here, too, style means a unity of expression.

However let us consider whether we can use this concept of style as a historical category. Transferring the concept of style from the history of art to history in general involves viewing historical events not in their own significance but in relation to a totality of forms of expression characteristic of their time. But the historical significance of an event does not have to be identical with its cognitive value as an expression of its time, and it is misleading to imagine that we have understood it if we have understood it solely in this way, as an expressive phenomenon. If, in fact, we extend the concept of style to history in general—as has been discussed by Erich Rothacker in particular—and expect this to yield us historical knowledge, then we are compelled to assume that history itself obeys an inner logos. This may be true for particular lines of development that we pursue, but this kind of history is not really history. It is the construction of ideal types which, as Max Weber's critique of the organologues has shown, is legitimate only as a description. Viewing events in terms of the history of style, like viewing art only in terms of the history of style, fails to take account of the essential fact that something is taking place in it and we are not just being presented with an intelligible series of events. Here we have reached the limits of intellectual history (Geistesgeschichte).

APPENDIX II

(To p.141)

Occasionality must appear as a meaningful element within a work's total claim to meaning and not as the trace of the particular circumstances that are, as it were, hidden behind the work and are to be revealed by interpretation. If the latter were the case, this would imply that it would be possible to understand the meaning of the whole only by re-establishing the original situation. If, however, occasionality is an element of meaning within the work itself, then the reverse is the case, namely that understanding the meaning of the work also makes it possible for the historian to experience something of the original situation into which the work speaks. Our fundamental analyses of the nature of aesthetic being have given the idea of occasionality a new justification that goes beyond all its particular forms. The play of art is not as transcendent of space and time as the aesthetic consciousness maintains. Even if we recognize this in principle, however, we cannot speak of time erupting into the game, as does Carl Schmitt in regard to *Hamlet* in his book *Der Einbruch der Zeit in das Spiel*.

No doubt the historian can take an interest in investigating those relations in the forming of the play of art that weave it into its time. But in my view Schmitt underestimates the difficulty of this task. He thinks that it is possible to recognize that fissure in the work through which contemporary reality shines and which reveals the contemporary function of the work. But this procedure is full of methodological difficulties, as the example of Platonic scholarship teaches us. Although it is right, in principle, to exclude the prejudices of a pure aesthetics of experience (Erlebnis) and to situate the play of art within its historical and political context, it seems to me wrong to expect one to read *Hamlet* like a roman à clef. An eruption of time into the play which would be recognizable as a fissure within it is, it seems to me, precisely what we do not have here. For the play itself there is no antithesis of time and art, as Schmitt assumes. Rather, the play draws time into its *play*. This is the great power of literature which makes it possible for it to belong (angehört) to its own time and through which its time listens (hört) to it. In this general sense, it is true, *Hamlet* is full of political relevance. But if we are reading out of it the poet's concealed support for Essex and James, then the work can hardly prove this. Even if the poet really belonged to this party, the play he has written would conceal his partisanship so that even the perspicacity of Schmitt would fail to see it. If he wanted to reach his public, the poet undoubtedly had to consider the counter-party within it. So what we are really seeing here is the eruption of play into time. Since the play is ambiguous, it can have its effect, which cannot be predicted, only in being played. Its nature is not to be an instrument of masked goals that need only have be unmasked in order to be unambiguously understood, but it remains, as an artistic play, in an indissoluble ambiguity. The occasionality it contains is not a pregiven relation through which alone everything acquires its true significance; on the contrary, it is the work itself whose expressive power fills out this, like every other, occasion.

Thus, in my opinion, Schmitt falls victim to a false historicism when, for example, he interprets politically the fact that Shakespeare leaves the question of the Queen's guilt open, and sees this as a taboo. In fact it is part of the reality of a play that it leaves an indefinite space around its real theme. A play in which everything is completely motivated creaks like a machine. It would be a false reality if the action could all be calculated out like an equation. Rather, it becomes a play of reality when it does not tell the spectator everything, but only a little more than he customarily understands in his daily round. The more that remains open, the more freely does the process of understanding succeed—i.e., the process of transposing what is shown in the play to one's own world and, of course, also to the world of one's own political experience.

To leave an enormous amount open seems to me the essence of a fruitful fable and myth. Thanks precisely to its open indeterminacy, myth is able to produce constant new invention from within itself, with the thematic horizon continuously shifting in different directions. (We need only think of the many attempts to treat the Faust theme, from Marlowe to Paul Valéry.)

If we see a political intention in leaving things open, as Carl Schmitt does when he speaks of the taboo of the Queen, then we are failing to recognize the nature of artistic play, namely the playing itself out by trying out possibilities. The self-playing-out of play does not take place in a closed world of aesthetic appearance, but as a constant integration in time. The productive ambiguity that constitutes the essence of a work of art is only another way of expressing the play's essential characteristic of continually becoming a new event. In this fundamental sense understanding in the human sciences moves very close to the immediate experience of the work of art. Scholarly understanding too allows the meaningful dimension of tradition to play itself out and consists in testing it. Precisely for this reason it is itself an event, as is shown in the course of our present investigation.

APPENDIX III

(To p.253)

Löwith's discussion of Heidegger's interpretation[7] of Nietzsche, though it raises some objections that are justified in detail, suffers from the general weakness that, without realizing it, he is playing off Nietzsche's ideal of naturalness against the principle of the formation of ideals. This is to make unintelligible what Heidegger means when, with conscious exaggeration, he places Nietzsche in the same line as Aristotle—and this does not mean that he places him at the same point. On the other hand, however, Löwith is led by this short circuit to the absurdity of himself treating Nietzsche's doctrine of the eternal return as a kind of Aristotle redivivus. Indeed, for Aristotle the eternal cycle of nature was a self-evident aspect of being. For him the moral and historical life of mankind remains related to the order represented pre-eminently by the cosmos. There is no question of this in Nietzsche. He, rather, conceives the cosmic cycle of being entirely in terms of its contrast to human life. The eternal return of the same is significant as a lesson for man—i.e., as something tremendous that has to be accepted by the human will, something which destroys all illusions of a future and of progress. Thus Nietzsche conceives the doctrine of the eternal return in order to encounter man in the tension of his will. Nature is here conceived in terms of man, as that which does not take any account of him.

But we cannot, as in a recent transposition, again play off nature against history if we are seeking to understand the unity of Nietzsche's thought. Löwith himself does not get past establishing the unresolved conflict in Nietzsche. But must we not, in view of this, ask the further question how it was possible to get caught thus in a blind alley—i.e., why was it not for Nietzsche himself an imprisonment and a failure but the great discovery and liberation? The reader finds no answer in Löwith to this further question. But this is precisely what one would like to understand, that is, to carry out, through one's own thinking. Heidegger has done this; he has constructed the system of relations, on the basis of which Nietzsche's statements are ordered among themselves. That this relational system is not directly expressed in Nietzsche himself is part of the methodological significance of this kind of reconstruction. And, paradoxically, we see Löwith himself doing what he can regard, in Nietzsche, only as a failing: he reflects about unreflectiveness; he philosophizes against philosophy in the name of naturalness and appeals to common sense. But if common sense were really a philosophical argument, then that would be the end of all philosophy and, with it, the end of any appeal to common sense. It is impossible for Löwith to get out of this difficulty except by acknowledging that an appeal to nature and naturalness is neither nature nor natural.

APPENDIX IV

(To p.268)

Löwith's persistent refusal to understand the transcendental significance of Heidegger's position on understanding[8] seems to me wrong on two counts. He does not see that Heidegger has discovered something that exists in all understanding and is a task that cannot be dismissed.[9] Further, he does not see that the violence done by many of Heidegger's interpretations by no means follows from this theory of understanding. It is, rather, a productive misuse of the texts, which betrays something more like a lack of hermeneutical awareness. Obviously it is the weight of his concern for his own subject matter that makes certain aspects of the texts considered over-resonate and distorts their proportions. Heidegger's impatient attitude to traditional texts is so little the consequence of his hermeneutical theory that it resembles more that of those great figures who have been responsible for the development of intellectual life and who, before the development of historical consciousness, assimilated tradition "uncritically." It is only the fact that Heidegger takes account of the criteria of science and from time to time tries by literary critical means to justify his productive assimilation of tradition which challenges such criticism. This does not affect the accuracy of his analysis of understanding, but is a fundamental confirmation of it. It is always part of understanding that the view that has to be understood must assert itself against the power of those tendencies of meaning that dominate the interpreter. Precisely because the thing itself makes a claim on us, it is necessary for us to exert ourselves hermeneutically. But on the other hand, it is impossible to understand tradition without accepting the claim of its subject matter, unless in the total indifference of psychological or historical interpretation to the subject matter which supervenes when we no longer in fact understand.

APPENDIX V

(To p.421)

It is strange that such a fine Plotinus scholar as Richard Harder criticizes, in his last lecture before his death, the idea of the *source* because of its "scientific origin" ("Quelle oder Tradition?" *Sources de Plotin, Entretiens Fondation Hardt* V, vii, [1960], 325–39). However justified the criticism of a superficial source study, the concept of the source has a better justification than that. As a *philosophical* metaphor it is of Platonic and Neoplatonic origin. The dominant image is that of the springing up of pure and fresh water from invisible depths. This is seen in, among other things, the frequent combination of pege kai arche (Phaedrus 245c, as well as often in Philo and Plotinus). As a *philological* term the concept of fons was first introduced in the age of humanism, but there it does not primarily refer to the concept that we know from the study of sources; rather, the maxim "ad fontes," the return to the sources, is to be understood as a reference to the original undistorted truth of the classical authors.[10] This, again, confirms our observation that, in its dealings with texts, philology understands what is found in them as truth.

The transition of the concept into the technical meaning familiar to us doubtless retains something of the original connotation, in that the source is distinguished from a faulty reproduction or assimilation. This explains, in particular, why we use the concept of "source" only in regard to the tradition of literature. Only what has come down to us in language gives us constant and full information about what it contains; it is not merely to be interpreted, like other documents and remnants, but allows us to draw directly from the source—i.e., to measure later derivations against and by the source. These are not scientific images, but come from the spirit of language. They offer fundamental confirmation of Harder's remark that sources need not become muddied by being used. There is always fresh water pouring out of a source, and it is the same with the true sources of the human spirit that we find in tradition. Studying them is so rewarding precisely because they always have something more to yield than has yet been taken from them.

APPENDIX VI—ON THE CONCEPT OF EXPRESSION

(To pp. 330 and 462)

The whole of our investigation shows why the concept of expression must be purified of its modern subjectivist flavor and referred back to its original grammatical and rhetorical sense. The word "expression" corresponds to the Latin expressio, exprimere which is used to describe the mental origin of speech and writing (verbis exprimere). But in German the word Ausdruck has an early history in the language of mysticism, pointing back to Neoplatonic coinage, that is still in need of investigation. Outside the writings of mysticism the word comes into general usage only in the eighteenth century. Then its meaning is expanded and it passes into aesthetic theory also, where it supplants the concept of imitation. But there is still no trace of the subjectivist element that an expression is the expression of something interior, namely of an experience (Erlebnis).[11] The dominant aspect is that of communication and communicability—i.e., it is a question of finding the expression.[12] But to find the expression means to find an expression that aims at making an impression—that is, it is not an expression in the sense of an expression of an experience. This is particularly true in the terminology of music.[13] Eighteenth-century musical theory of the emotions does not imply that one expresses oneself in music, but that music expresses something—namely emotions—which, in their turn, are to make an impression. We find the same thing in aesthetics with, say, Sulzer (1765): Expression is not to be understood primarily as an expression of one's own feelings, but as an expression that arouses feelings.

Nevertheless, the second half of the eighteenth century is already far along the path toward the subjectification of the concept of expression. When, for example, Sulzer attacks the younger Riccoboni, who regards the art of the actor as that of representation and not of feeling, he is already considering sincerity of feeling as essential in aesthetic representation. Similarly he supplements the espressivo of music with the psychological substructure of the composer's feeling. We are here confronted with a transition from the rhetorical tradition to the psychology of experience (Erlebnis). However, the concern with the essence of the expression, and of aesthetic expression in particular, still remains related to the metaphysical context, which is of Neoplatonic origin. For an expression is never merely a sign that points back to something else, something within; rather, what is expressed is itself present in the expression—e.g., anger is present in angry furrows in the face. The modern diagnostics of expression knows this as well as Aristotle did. Obviously it is part of the nature of living things that the one is present in the other in this way. This has been specifically recognized in philosophical usage, as when Spinoza sees exprimere and expressio as a fundamental ontological concept and when, following him, Hegel sees the true reality of the mind in the objective significance of expression as representation and utterance, and uses this to support his critique of the subjectivism of reflection. So also do Hölderlin and Sinclair, for whom the concept of the expression acquires a central place.[14] Language as the product of creative reflection, which produces a poem, is "the expression of a living, but particular whole." The meaning of this theory of expression has obviously been wholly distorted by the subjectivizing and psychologizing process of the nineteenth century. In fact, both with Hölderlin and Hegel, the rhetorical tradition is far more important. In the eighteenth century "expression" replaces "the act of expression" and refers to the lasting form that remains behind as, for example, the impression of a seal. The context of this image becomes quite clear from a passage in Gellert which refers to the fact "that our language is not capable of certain kinds of beauty and is a brittle wax that often shatters when we seek to impress on it the images of the spirit."[15]

This is ancient Neoplatonic tradition.[16] The point of the metaphor is that the impressed form is not partially but wholly present in all the impressions. This is also the basis of the application of the idea in the "emanationist thinking" which, according to Rothacker,[17] is everywhere the basis of our historical view of the world. It is clear that the critique of the psychologization of the concept of expression runs through the whole of our present investigation and is at the basis of our critique both of "the art of experience (Erlebnis)" and of romantic hermeneutics.[18]

Notes

1 Cf. also *Nuevo Estilo y Formulario de Escribir* as the title of a collection of formulas for letter writers. In this usage observance of style is almost the same as in the *genera dicendi*. But the transfer to all modes of expression, of course in a normative sense, is obvious.

2 Erwin Panofsky, *Idea: A Concept in Art Theory*, tr. Joseph J. S. Peake (Columbia, S.C.: University of South Carolina Press, 1968), p.238, n. 5 to ch. 6.

3 W. Hofmann, *Studium Generale*, 8, no. 1 (1955), 1.

4 Cf. Schelling, III, 494.

5 [See *Kunst und Wahrheit: Zur Theorie und Methode der Kunstgeschichte* (2nd ed., enl.; Mäander, 1978).]

6 [See Hegel, *Nürnberger Schriften*, p.310.]

7 In ch. 3 of *Heidegger: Denker in dürftiger Zeit* (Frankfurt, 1953). See also the new ed. of Löwith's *Nietzsches Lehre von der ewigen Wiederkehr* [and now the vol. on Nietzsche in his *Sämtliche Schriften* (Stuttgart, 1986)].

8 Cf. Löwith, *Heidegger: Denker in dürftiger Zeit* (Frankfurt, 1953), pp. 80f.

9 [Derrida would particularly deny this, since he regards Heidegger's interpretation of Nietzsche as a relapse back into metaphysics. See my "*Destruktion* and Deconstruction" in *The Gadamer-Derrida Encounter: Texts and Comments*, ed. Diane Michelfelder and Richard Palmer (Albany: SUNY Press, 1988).]

10 [I am indebted to E. Lledo for interesting evidence on the expression "ad fontes" in Spanish humanism: he shows its relation to the Psalms.]

11 The counterpart to the concept of *expressio* in Scholastic thinking is, rather, the *impressio speciei*. It is, of course, the nature of the *expressio* that takes place in the *verbum* that, as Nicholas of Cusa was probably the first to point out, *mens* is expressed in it. Thus it is possible for Nicholas to say that the word is *expressio exprimentis et expressi* (*Comp. theol.*, VII). But this does not mean an expression

of inner experiences, but the *reflective structure* of the *verbum*, namely of making everything visible, including itself in the act of expression—just as light makes all things visible, including itself. [See now the entry by Tonelli, "Ausdruck," *Historisches Wörterbuch der Philosophie*, ed. Joachim Ritter, I, 653–55.]

12 Kant, *KdU*, B 198.

13 See the instructive essay of H. H. Eggebrecht, "Das Ausdrucksprinzip im musikalischen Sturm und Drang," *Deutsche Vierteljahrschrift für Literaturwissenschaft und Geistesgeschichte*, 29 (1955), 323–49.

14 Ed. Hellingrath, III, 571ff.

15 *Schriften*, VII, 273.

16 See, for example, *Dionysiaka*, I, 87.

17 Erich Rothacker, *Logik und Systematik der Geisteswissenschaften* (*Handbuch der Philosophie*, III), p.166. Cf. above, p.78, the concept of life in Oetinger, and pp. 234ff. above, in Husserl and Count Yorck as well as pp. 227ff., 239ff.

18 Similar points are also made in some of my earlier writings, e.g., "Bach und Weimar" (1946), pp. 9ff. [*Kleine Schriften*, II, 75–81 (*GW*, IX)] and "Über die Ursprünglichkeit der Philosophie" (1947), p.25 [*Kleine Schriften*, I, 11–38 (*GW*, IV)].

SUPPLEMENT I
Hermeneutics and Historicism (1965)

In previous philosophical reflection on the basis of the human sciences there has been hardly any mention of hermeneutics. Hermeneutics was merely an ancillary discipline, a canon of rules regarding the way to handle texts. The only distinctions made were to account for the special nature of particular texts—e.g., biblical hermeneutics. And finally there was a rather different ancillary discipline called hermeneutics in the form of legal hermeneutics. It contained the rules for filling gaps in a codified law, and hence had a normative character. But the central philosophical problem presented by the human sciences was considered to be epistemological—by analogy to the natural sciences and their foundation in Kantian philosophy. Kant's *Critique of Pure Reason* had justified the apriori elements in the experiential knowledge of the natural sciences. Thus the task was to provide a corresponding theoretical justification for the mode of knowledge of the historical sciences. In his *Historik* J. G. Droysen outlined a very influential methodology of the historical sciences that was to be the equivalent of the Kantian task; and from the outset W. Dilthey, who was to work out the philosophy proper of the historical school, consciously pursued the task of a critique of historical reason. Thus even his own self-conception was epistemological. As we know, he viewed the epistemological foundation of the so-called human sciences in terms of a "descriptive and analytical" psychology purified of all alien domination by the natural sciences. In carrying out this task, however, Dilthey was led beyond his original epistemological starting point, and so it was he who introduced hermeneutics into philosophy. True, he never entirely gave up the epistemological foundation that he had sought in psychology. His view that experiences (Erlebnisse) are characterized by inner awareness—so that there is not the problem of knowledge of the other, of the non-I, that lay behind Kant's inquiry—remained the basis on which he sought to construct the historical world in the human sciences. But the historical world is not a coherent experience in the way that, in autobiography, history presents itself to the inner world of the subjective consciousness. Historical coherence must, in the end, be understood as a coherence of meaning that wholly transcends the horizon of the individual's experience. It is like an enormous alien text that one needs the help of hermeneutics to decipher. Thus Dilthey is compelled by the nature of the subject matter to search for the passage from psychology to hermeneutics.

In endeavoring to provide this hermeneutical foundation for the human sciences Dilthey found himself in marked contrast to that epistemological school that was attempting at the time to establish a foundation of the human sciences on a neo-Kantian basis: the philosophy of value developed by Windelband and Rickert. The epistemological subject seemed to him a bloodless abstraction, but however much he was himself inspired by the desire for objectivity in the human sciences, he could not get away from the fact that the knowing subject, the understanding historian, does not simply stand over against his object, historical life, but is himself part of the same movement of historical life. Especially in his later years Dilthey did more and more justice to the idealistic philosophy of identity, because the idealistic concept of the mind contained the same substantial communion between the subject and the object, between the I and the Thou, that was contained in his own concept of life. What Georg Misch shrewdly defended against both Husserl and Heidegger as the standpoint of life philosophy[1] obviously shared with phenomenology the critique of a naive historical objectivism and the latter's epistemological justification by the philosophy of value promulgated in southwest Germany. The constitution of historical fact by a value relation, convincing as it was, took no account of the way historical knowledge is interwoven with historical events.[2]

Let us recall here that the monumental body of work left by Max Weber and first published under the title *Wirtschaft und Gesellschaft* in 1921 had been planned by him as a *Grundriß der verstehenden Soziologie*.[3] Those parts of this sociological study—prepared for the outline of social economics —that were almost completed are concerned with the sociology of religion, law, and music, whereas political sociology, for example, is treated only in a very fragmentary way. Here we are concerned primarily with the introductory section, written between 1918 and 1920, which is now called

"A sociological theory of categories." It is an impressive catalogue of concepts on an extremely nominalistic basis, which incidentally—unlike his well-known essay on the logos of 1913—avoids the concept of value (and hence a total reliance on south-west German neo-Kantianism). Max Weber calls this "interpretive (verstehend) sociology" inasmuch as its object is the common meaning of social action. It is true that the meaning that is "subjectively intended" in the area of social and historical life cannot be only that which is actually meant by the individual actors. Thus instead of the hermeneutical and methodological concept we have the conceptually constructed pure type (the "ideal-typical construction"). The whole edifice rests on this basis, which Max Weber calls "rationalistic," an edifice which is, in its conception, "value free" and neutral, a monumental bastion of "objective" science, which defends its methodological clarity by a classificatory system and, in those parts that he completed, leads to a great systematic survey of the world of historical experience (Erfahrung). Genuine involvement in the problematic of historicism is avoided by the ascetic approach of his methodology.

But the further development of hermeneutical reflection is, in fact, dominated by the question of historicism and hence starts from Dilthey, whose collected works in the twenties soon over-shadowed even Ernst Troeltsch's influence.

The fact that Dilthey started with romantic hermeneutics, which in our century was combined with the revival of the speculative philosophy of Hegel, introduced a multipronged criticism of historical objectivism (Yorck, Heidegger, Rothacker, Betti, and others).

It also left visible traces in historical philological research, for the romantic ideas that had been hidden by the scientific positivism of the nineteenth century again emerged within science.[4] For example, the problem of classical mythology is taken up again in the spirit of Schelling by Walter F. Otto, Karl Kerenyi, and others. Even such an abstruse scholar as J. J. Bachofen, a victim of the monomania of his own intuitions and whose ideas fostered modern ersatz religions (for instance, via Alfred Schuler and Ludwig Klages they influenced Stefan George), won new scientific respect. In 1925 there appeared, under the title *Der Mythos von Orient und Occident, eine Metaphysik der alten Welt*, a systematically edited collection of Bachofen's main writings, for which Alfred Baeumler wrote an eloquent and significant introduction.[5]

Even if we open the historical collection of de Vries' *Forschungsgeschichte der Mythologie*,[6] we gain the same impression, namely of how the "crisis of

509

historicism" has brought about a revival of mythology. De Vries' survey is noted for its breadth of horizon and well-chosen texts, which give a good illustration of the modern period in particular, with the omission of the history of religion, though there is sometimes an overslavish and sometimes an overly free observance of chronology. It is interesting to see how Walter F. Otto and Karl Kerenyi are clearly recognized as forerunners of a new development in scholarship that takes myth seriously.

The example of mythology is only one among many. In the concrete work of the human sciences it would be possible to show many places where there is the same turning away from a naive methodologism, the equivalent of which in philosophical reflection is the explicit criticism of historical objectivism or positivism. This development became particularly important where originally normative aspects are combined with science. This is the case both in theology and jurisprudence. Theological discussion in recent decades has placed the problem of hermeneutics in the foreground precisely because it has had to combine the heritage of historical theology with new theological and dogmatic departures. Karl Barth's commentary on Paul's *Epistle to the Romans* was the first revolutionary eruption,[7] a "critique" of liberal theology, which was less concerned with critical history as such than with the inadequacy of a theology that regarded its findings as an understanding of Scripture. Thus despite all his disaffection for methodological reflection, Barth's *Romans* is a kind of hermeneutical manifesto.[8] Though he has not much time for Rudolf Bultmann and his thesis of the demythologization of the New Testament, it is not his interests that separate him from Bultmann. Rather, I think, Bultmann's combination of historical-critical research with theological exegesis and his reliance on philosophy (Heidegger) for methodological self-awareness prevents Barth from recognizing himself in Bultmann's method. What the situation requires, however, is not simply denying the heritage of liberal theology but mastering it. Contemporary discussion of the hermeneutical problem within theology—and not of the hermeneutical problem only—is, therefore, determined by the conflict between the inalienable intention of theology and critical history. Some consider it necessary to find a new defense of historical inquiry in the face of this situation, while others—for example, the work of Ott, Ebeling, and Fuchs—place less emphasis on the importance of theology as research than on its "hermeneutical" assistance to the proclamation.

If a layman wants to consider the development within the legal discussion of the hermeneutical problem, it will not be possible for him to study in detail the legal works in this field. All he can do is make the general observation that in every field jurisprudence is retreating from legal positivism, as it is called, and it regards as a central question the extent to which the concrete application of law presents a special juridical problem. Kurt Engisch (1953) gives a comprehensive survey of this problem.[9] That this problem is emerging into the foreground in reaction to extreme forms of legal positivism is also historically understandable, as we can see from Franz Wieacker's *Privatrechtsgeschichte der Neuzeit* or Karl Larenz's *Methodenlehre der Rechtswissenschaft*.[10] Thus we can see in the three fields in which hermeneutics has played a part from the beginning—in the historical and philological sciences, in theology, and in jurisprudence—that the critique of historical objectivism or "positivism" has given new importance to the hermeneutical aspect.

Fortunately for us, the extent of the hermeneutical problem has recently been surveyed and systematized in the important work of an Italian scholar. The legal historian Emilio Betti has produced an enormous work, *Teoria Generale della Interpretazione*,[11] the main ideas of which have been developed in German in a "hermeneutical manifesto" under the title of *Zur Grundlegung einer allgemeinen Auslegungslehre*.[12] It provides an account of the issue that is remarkable for the breadth of its horizon, its impressive knowledge of detail, and its clear systematic arrangement. As a legal historian who is also himself a teacher of law, and as a compatriot of Croce and Gentile who is equally at home in German philosophy, so that he speaks and writes perfect German, he was, in any case, safe from the dangers of a naive historical objectivism. He is in a position to reap the great harvest of hermeneutical reflection that has ripened over the years since Wilhelm von Humboldt and Schleiermacher.

Clearly reacting against Benedetto Croce's extreme position, Betti seeks the mean between the objective and the subjective element in all under-standing. He formulates a complete canon of hermeneutical principles, at the head of which stands the text's autonomy of meaning, according to which the meaning—i.e., what the author intended to say—can be gained from the text itself. But he also emphasizes with equal clarity the principle of the currency of understanding—i.e., its adequacy to the object. This implies that he views the interpreter's being inevitably tied to a particular perspective as an integrating element in hermeneutical truth.

As a lawyer he is safe from overestimating subjective intention—e.g., the historical accidents that have led to formulating a particular law—and from automatically equating this with the meaning of law. On the other hand, he follows the "psychological interpretation" founded by Schleier-macher, to the extent that his hermeneutical position is constantly in danger of becoming vague. However much he tries to overcome this psychological narrowness and recognizes the task of reconstructing the mental context of values and significant contents, he is able to justify this task—which is the real hermeneutical one—only by a kind of *analogy with psychological interpretation*.

Thus he writes, for example, that understanding is a re-cognition and reconstruction of the meaning, and he explains this by saying that it is an understanding "of a mind speaking through the forms of its objectification to another thinking mind, with the former considering itself related to the latter in their common humanity; it is a process of leading back and together, and reuniting those forms with the inner whole that has brought them forth and from which they have become separated, an interiorizing of these forms, in which process their content passes into a subjectivity that is different from the one that originally contained them. Accordingly in the process of interpretation we are concerned with a reversal or inversion of the creative process, a reversal in which the interpreter has to make his hermeneutical way back along the creative path, carrying on this process of *rethinking* within himself" (p. 93f.). Here Betti is following Schleier-macher, Boeckh, Croce, and others.[13] Curiously, he imagines that he is ensuring the "objectivity" of understanding by this strict psychologism with its romantic flavor, an objectivity that he regards as threatened by all those who, following Heidegger, regard binding meaning to subjectivity as mistaken.

In his debate with me, which has also been presented in Germany,[14] he sees nothing in my work but equivocations and conceptual confusions. This generally means that the critic is relating the author to a question that he does not intend. And this seems to be the case here. He was fearful for the scientific nature of interpretation, as I presented it in my book. I showed him in a private letter that this concern was unnecessary, and he was good enough to print the following passage from it in his treatise:

"Fundamentally I am *not proposing a method*; I am describing *what is the case*. That it is as I describe it cannot, I think, be seriously questioned. . . . For example, when you read a classic essay by Mommsen you immediately know its era, the only era when it could have been written. Even a master of the historical method is not able to keep himself entirely free from the prejudices of his time, his social environment, and his national situation, etc. Is this a failing? And even if it were, I regard it as a necessary philosophical task to consider why this failure always occurs wherever anything is achieved. In other words, I consider the only scientific thing is to *recognize what is,* instead of starting from what ought to be or could be. Hence I am trying to go beyond the concept of method held by modern science (which retains its limited justification) and to envisage in a fundamentally universal way what *always* happens."

But what does Betti say to this? That I am, then, limiting the hermeneutical problem to a quaestio facti ("phenomenologically," "descriptively") and do not at all pose the quaestio iuris. As if when Kant raised the quaestio iuris he intended to prescribe what the pure natural sciences ought to be, rather than to justify their transcendental possibility as they already were. In the sense of this Kantian distinction, to think beyond the concept of method in the human sciences, as my book attempts, is to ask the question of the "possibility" of the human sciences (which certainly does not mean what they really ought to be). This fine scholar is here confused by a strange resentment against phenomenology. That he can conceive the problem of hermeneutics only as a problem of method shows that he is profoundly involved in the subjectivism which we are endeavoring to overcome.

Obviously I have not succeeded in convincing Betti that a philosophical theory of hermeneutics is not a methodology—right or wrong ("dangerous"), as the case may be. It may be misleading when Bollnow calls understanding an "essentially creative act"—although Betti does not hesitate to so describe the elaborative interpretation of law. But it is quite certain that to follow the aesthetics of genius, as Betti himself does, is not sufficient. The theory of inversion cannot really overcome what Betti (following Droysen) rightly recognizes as a psychologizing constriction. And so he does not quite get beyond the ambiguity between psychology and hermeneutics that held Dilthey captive. If, in order to explain the possibility of understanding in the human sciences, he has to presuppose that only a mind on the same level can understand another mind, the inadequacy of this psychological-hermeneutical ambiguity becomes apparent.[15]

Even if we are basically clear about the difference between psychic particularity and historical significance, it obviously remains difficult to find the transition from the narrowness of psychology to a historical hermeneutics. Even Droysen was already clear about the task (*Historik* §41), but up to now that transition has been given a firm basis only in

Hegel's dialectical combination of subjective and objective mind in absolute mind.

Even where one remains very close to Hegel, as does R. G. Collingwood, who was strongly influenced by Croce, we find the same thing. We now have two works by Collingwood in German translation: his autobiography, which has been published in Germany under the title *Denken* after having had a great success in the original,[16] and also his posthumous work, *The Idea of History*, translated into German under the title *Philosophie der Geschichte*.[17]

I have made some observations on the autobiography in the introduction to the German edition, and therefore will not repeat them here. The posthumous work contains a history of historical writing from classical times to the present day, ending significantly with Croce. Part 5 comprises a separate theoretical discussion. I shall limit myself to this last part, since the historical sections are, as often happens, so influenced by national traditions of thinking that they are almost unintelligible to a reader of another nationality. For a German reader the chapter on Wilhelm Dilthey, for example, is most disappointing:

"Dilthey has come up against the question which Windelband and the rest had not the penetration to recognize: the question how there can be knowledge, as distinct from an immediate experience, of the individual. He has answered that question by admitting that there cannot be such a knowledge, and falling back on the positivistic view that the only way in which the universal (the proper object of knowledge) can be known is by means of natural science or a science constructed on naturalistic principles. Thus in the end he, like the rest of his generation, surrenders to positivism" (pp. 173–174). Whatever truth there is in this judgment is made almost unrecognizable by the reason that Collingwood gives for it.

The kernel of the systematic theory of historical knowledge is undoubtedly the theory of the re-enactment of the experience of the past. In this Collingwood stands in the ranks of those who protest against "what may be called a positivistic conception, or rather misconception of history" (p. 228). The proper task of the historian is that "of penetrating to the thought of the agents whose acts they are studying" (p. 228). It is particularly difficult in German translation to decide exactly what Collingwood means here by "thought" (Denken). Obviously the concept of Akt in German ("act" in English) has quite a different connotation from what the English author intends. The re-enactment of the thought of the protagonists of history (or of the thinkers also) does not mean, for Collingwood, actually the real psychic acts of these people but their thoughts—i.e., that which can be rethought. Now thought includes "the corporate mind of a community or an age" (p. 219). But this "thought" seems to have a strange life of its own, as when Collingwood describes biography as anti-historical because it is not based on "thought" but on a natural process. "Through this framework—the bodily life of the man, with his childhood, maturity and senescence, his diseases and all the accidents of animal existence—the tides of thought, his own and others', flow crosswise, regardless of its structure, like sea-water through a stranded wreck" (p. 304).

Who is actually behind this "thinking"? Who are the protagonists of history whose thinking we have to penetrate? Is it the particular intention that a man is pursuing in his action? This is what Collingwood[18] seems to mean: "This depends on the assumption that his acts were done on purpose. If they were not, there can be no history of them. . . . " (p. 310). But is the reconstruction of intention really an understanding of history? We can see how Collingwood gets involved, against his will, in psychological particularity. He cannot get out of it without a theory of someone who acts as "representative of the world spirit"—i.e., without Hegel.

He would not be pleased to hear that. For all metaphysics of history, even that of Hegel, seems to him nothing more than a system of pigeonholes (p. 264) without any genuine historical truth value. Moreover, I am not quite clear how his thesis on a radical historicism is compatible with his theory of re-enactment, when he rightly sees, on the other hand, that the historian himself "is a part of the process he is studying, has his own place in that process, and can see it only from the point of view which at this present moment he occupies within it" (p. 248). How does that fit with the defense of the re-enactment of a transmitted "thought," which Collingwood illustrates by the example of Plato's critique of sensualism in the *Theaetetus?* I am afraid that the example is wrong and proves the opposite.

If in the *Theaetetus* Plato proposes the thesis that knowledge is exclusively perception by the senses, then, according to Collingwood, I do not, as a reader today, know the context that led him to this view. In my mind this context is a different one: namely the discussion that emerges from modern sensualism. But since we are concerned with a "thought," this does not matter. Thought can be placed in different contexts without losing its identity (p. 301). One should like to remind Collingwood here of the critique of statements in his own "logic of question and answer" (*Denken,* pp. 30–43). Is not the re-enactment of Plato's idea, in fact, successful only if we grasp the true Platonic context (which I think is that of a mathematical theory of evidence that is not yet quite clear about the intelligible mode of being of mathematics)?[19] And who will be able to grasp this context if they do not explicitly hold in abeyance the preconceptions of modern sensualism?[20]

In other words, Collingwood's theory of re-enactment avoids the particularity of psychology, but the dimension of hermeneutical mediation which is passed through in every act of understanding still escapes him.

In the context of a critique of historical objectivism the works of Erich Rothacker are remarkable. In one of his last writings in particular, *Die dogmatische Denkform in den Geisteswissenschaften und das Problem des Historismus*,[21] he developed his earlier ideas, which maintain Dilthey's hermeneutical concern against all psychologism (like Hans Freyer in the *Theorie des objektiven Geistes*). The concept of the dogmatic thought form is intended entirely as a hermeneutical concept.[22] Dogmatics is defended as a productive method of knowledge in the human sciences, insofar as it elaborates the immanent context that determines an area of significance. Rothacker appeals to the fact that the concept of dogmatics has by no means a merely critical and pejorative sense in theology and jurisprudence. But unlike the case of these systematic disciplines the concept of dogmatics is not intended here to be merely a synonym for systematic knowledge—i.e., for philosophy—but signifies "another attitude," to be defended as something separate from the historical inquiry, which tries to understand processes of development. But then, for Rothacker, the concept of "dogmatics" has its fundamental place within the total historical attitude and receives its relative justification from it. It is ultimately what Dilthey's concept of the structural context had formulated in general, in its particular application to historical methodology.

Such dogmatics, then, exercises its corrective function where there is historical thinking and knowledge. There can be no dogmatics of Roman law until there is a history of law. Walter F. Otto's *Götter Griechenlands* was possible only after historical research had made of Greek mythology a multiplicity of different pieces of knowledge concerning the history of religion and myth, and if Wölfflin's "classical art"—unlike his "fundamental concepts of art history"—is described by Rothacker as dogmatics, this kind of description seems to me only relative. The difference between it and baroque aesthetics, especially mannerism, is the secret starting point of this "dogmatics," but this implies that, from the outset, it is less believed and known than meant historically.

In this sense dogmatics is, in fact, an element in our historical knowledge. Indeed, Rothacker has emphasized this element as the "only source of our intellectual knowledge" (p. 25). We must establish a comprehensive context of meaning, as presented in this dogmatic approach, and find it self-evident. We must, at least, not find it impossible that it might be "true" if we really want to understand it. Of course, as Rothacker shows, this poses the problem of the multiplicity of such dogmatic systems or styles, and this is the problem of historicism.

Rothacker proves to be an energetic defender of the latter. Dilthey tried to banish the danger of historicism by deriving different worldviews from the complexity of life. Rothacker follows him in this by calling dogmatic systems explanations of lived worldviews or of stylistic directions, and basing the latter on the fact that man acts within a perspective and is tied to a particular view. Thus they are all, from different perspectives, irrefutable (p. 35). Applied to science, this means that relativism has clear limitations rather than boundless sway. It does not endanger the immanent "objectivity" of research. Its starting point is the variability and freedom of scientific inquiries, which develop from the variable ways in which lived worldviews create significance. From this point of view, modern science itself is seen as the dogmatics of a quantifying worldview (p. 53) as soon as we allow that there can be another way of knowing nature.[23]

It is by no means self-evident that legal hermeneutics belongs within the context of the problem of general hermeneutics. It is not, properly speaking, concerned with any question of methodological reflection, as is the case with philology and scriptural hermeneutics, but of a subsidiary legal principle itself. It is not its task to understand valid legal propositions but to discover law—i.e., to so interpret the law that the legal order fully penetrates reality. Because interpretation has a normative function here, it is sometimes—for example by Betti—entirely separated from literary interpretation, and even from that historical understanding whose object is legal (constitutions, laws, and so on). That the interpretation of the law is, in a juridical sense, an act that creates law cannot be contested. The different principles that are to be applied in this act—e.g., the principle of analogy or the principle of filling in gaps in the law, or finally the productive principle that lies in the legal decision itself—i.e., that depends on the particular legal case—do not merely present methodological problems but reach deeply into the matter of law itself.[24]

Obviously a legal hermeneutics cannot seriously be satisfied with using the subjective principle of the meaning and original intention of the lawgiver as a canon of interpretation. Often it cannot avoid applying objective concepts—e.g., that of the notion of law expressed in a particular law. It is obviously an entirely lay idea to regard applying the law to a concrete case as the logical process of subsuming the individual under the universal.

Legal positivism, which would like to limit legal reality entirely to the established law and its correct application, probably has no supporters today. The distance between the universality of the law and the concrete legal situation in a particular case is obviously essentially indissoluble. Nor does it seem satisfactory to consider the power of the individual case to create law as something deductively predetermined—an ideal dogmatics in the sense of a dogmatics that would contain, at least potentially, all possible legal truths in a coherent system. Even the "idea" of this kind of perfect dogmatics seems senseless, quite apart from the consideration that the power of the individual case to create law is, in fact, responsible for constantly new codifications. What is remarkable about the situation is this: that the hermeneutical task of bridging the distance between the law and the particular case still pertains, even if no change in social conditions or other historical variations cause the current law to appear old-fashioned or inappropriate. The distance between the law and the individual case seems to be absolutely indissoluble. To this extent, it is possible to divorce the hermeneutical problem from the consideration of the historical dimension. It is no mere unavoidable imperfection in the process of legal codification when it leaves free play for its application to concrete instances, as if this free play could, in principle, be reduced at will. To be "elastic" enough to leave this kind of free play seems rather to be in the nature of legal regulation as such, indeed of legal order generally.

If I am not mistaken, Aristotle was quite clear about this when he ascribed an exclusively critical function to the idea of natural law rather than a positive, dogmatic one. It has always been felt to be shocking (when it was not denied outright, by misinterpreting Aristotle's text) that he distinguishes between conventional and natural law, yet goes on to claim that natural law can be changed.[25]

Natural law and law established by statute are not "equally changeable." Rather, by considering comparable phenomena it is explained that even what is just by nature is changeable, without on that account ceasing to be different from that which is established by mere statute. Obviously traffic regulations, for example, are not changeable to the same but to a much higher degree than something naturally just. Aristotle seeks not to detract from this view but to explain how to distinguish what is naturally just in the unstable human world (in contrast to that of the gods). Thus he says that the distinction between what is naturally right and what is legal or conventional is as evident—despite the changeability of both—as the distinction between the right hand and the left. There too by nature the right is the stronger, and yet this natural priority cannot be described as unchangeable, since, within limits, it can be removed by training the other hand.[26]

"Within limits," that is, within a certain area of free play. To leave this kind of area, far from destroying the meaning of right order, belongs rather to the essential nature of the situation: "The law is universal and cannot therefore answer to every single case."[27] The disposition of the case does not result from the codification of laws but, on the contrary, the codification of laws is possible only because laws are, in themselves and by nature, universal.

Perhaps we must ask at this point whether the inner connection between hermeneutics and writing is not to be regarded as a secondary one.[28] It is not the fact of its being written as such that makes an idea need interpretation, but the fact of its being in language; but that includes the universality of meaning from which, in turn, follows the possibility of its being written down. Thus both codified law and written tradition point to a deeper connection that is concerned with the relation between understanding and application, as I think I have shown. It should not surprise us that Aristotle is the supreme witness to this. His critique of the Platonic idea of the good is, in my opinion, the root of the whole of his own philosophy. Without being "nominalism," it contains a radical revision of the relation between the universal and the particular, as it is implied in the Platonic doctrine of the idea of the good—at least as it is presented in the Platonic dialogues.[29]

But this does not exclude the fact that in addition to this essential distance between the universal and the concrete, there is also the historical distance, which has its own hermeneutical productivity.

I am not so bold as to decide whether this is also true of legal hermeneutics, in the sense that a legal order which historical change has rendered in need of interpretation (e.g., with the aid of the principle of analogy) contributes to a more just application in general, namely to a refinement of the feeling for law that is guiding interpretation. In other fields, however, the matter is clear. It is beyond all doubt that the "significance" of historical events or the rank of works of art becomes more apparent with the passage of time.

At present, discussion of the hermeneutical problem is probably nowhere so lively as in the area of Protestant theology. Here also the concern, in a certain sense, as in legal hermeneutics, is with interests that go beyond science, in this case with faith and its right proclamation. Consequently the hermeneutical discussion is interwoven with exegetical and dogmatic questions on which the layman can make no comment. But as with legal hermeneutics the advantage of this situation is clear: that it is not possible to limit the "meaning" of the text to be understood to the supposed opinion of its author. In his great work *Church Dogmatics*, Karl Barth contributes to the hermeneutical problem explicitly nowhere and indirectly everywhere.[30] It is a somewhat different matter in the case of Rudolf Bultmann, who favors methodological discussions and who, in his collected essays, often refers explicitly to the problem of hermeneutics.[31] But in his case too the emphasis is immanently theological, not only in the sense that his exegetical work constitutes the experiential basis and sphere of application of his hermeneutical principles, but above all also in the sense that a major issue in contemporary theological debate—the question of a demythologization of the New Testament—is too much bound up with dogmatic tensions to be conducive to methodological reflection. I am convinced that the principle of demythologization has a purely hermeneutical aspect. According to Bultmann this program is not supposed to decide dogmatic questions in advance—e.g., how much of the contents of the scriptural writings are essential for the Christian proclamation and hence for faith and how much might be sacrificed; rather, it is a question of understanding the Christian proclamation itself, of the sense in which it must be understood if it is to be "understood" at all. Perhaps, indeed certainly, it is possible to understand "more" in the New Testament than Bultmann has understood. But this can only emerge by understanding this "more" equally *well*—i.e., *really understanding* it.

Historical biblical criticism and its scientific elaboration in the eighteenth and nineteenth centuries have created a situation that requires constant re-adjustment between the general principles of the scientific understanding of a text and the particular tasks of the self-understanding of the Christian faith. It is good to remind ourselves of the history of these harmonizing efforts.[32]

At the beginning of the nineteenth-century development stands Schleiermacher's *Hermeneutik*, which offers a systematic basis for the essential similarity among interpretive procedures in relation to Scripture and to all other texts, which Semler had already envisaged. Schleiermacher's special contribution was psychological interpretation, according to which every idea in a text has to be related to its context in the personal life of its author, as a moment in his life, if it is to be fully understood. In the meantime, we have acquired a more detailed insight into the history of the growth of Schleiermacher's hermeneutical ideas since the Berlin manuscripts, from which Lücke composed his edition, have been excellently reproduced by the Heidelberg Academy of Sciences.[33] The exploitation of the original manuscripts in this way is not revolutionary, but it is not without significance. In his introduction Kimmerle shows that the early manuscripts emphasize the identity of thought and speech, while the later elaboration views speech as individualizing utterance. In line with this, there is also the slow emergence and final domination of a psychological viewpoint over the genuinely linguistic viewpoints of "technical" interpretation ("style").

We know well enough that even in the dogmatic system of Schleiermacher, which has been made available to us in a fine edition produced by Martin Redeker (*Der christliche Glaube*),[34] Schleiermacher's psychological and subjective orientation challenges theological criticism. The "self-consciousness of faith" is a dangerous basis for dogma. Christoph Senft's book discusses the development from Schleiermacher to the liberal theology of Ritschl with great insight and gives us a good idea of this.[35] On page 42, Senft writes of Schleiermacher, "Despite his effort to obtain living concepts in order to grasp the historical, the dialectic between speculation and empiricism remains for him a static one. The reciprocal influence between history and the person studying it is unproblematic and critical; those who examine history are safe from any fundamental cross-examination."

Nor has F. C. Baur, as Senft shows, advanced the hermeneutical problem any more in this direction, even though he has made the historical process the subject of his investigation, for he maintains the autonomy of self-consciousness as an unrestricted basis. But Hofmann—and this comes out well in Senft's account—in his hermeneutics takes the historicality of revelation hermeneutically seriously. The doctrine that he develops is the "explanation of the Christian faith, the presupposition of which 'lies outside us' yet not outside us in a legal sense, but in such a way that what lies outside us is revealed 'experientially' as its own history" (Senft p.105). But this ensures at the same time that "as the monument of a history—i.e., of a particular nexus of events—and not as a text-book of general doctrines, the Bible is the book of revelation." Thus we may say that by making the dogmatic unity of the Bible highly problematical and by destroying the rationalistic-dogmatic assumption of a scriptural "doctrine," the criticism that historical-scriptural studies have exercised on the canon has set the theological task of recognizing biblical history *as history*.

In my view, modern hermeneutical debate gets its orientation from this. Faith in this history must itself be understood as a historical event, as an appeal of the word of God. This is true even for the relationship between the Old and the New Testaments. It can be understood (according to Hofmann) as the relationship between prophecy and fulfillment, so that the prophecy that fails in history is determined in its significance only by its fulfillment. But the historical understanding of the Old Testament's prophecies in no way impairs the New Testament's significance as procla-mation. On the contrary, the redemptive event that the New Testament proclaims can be understood as a real event only if prophecy is not a mere "image of future fact" (Hofmann in Senft, p.101). But especially with respect to the concept of the self-understanding of faith, basic to Bult-mann's theology, is it true that it has a historical (and not an idealistic) sense?[36]

Self-understanding refers to a historical decision and not to something one possesses and controls. Bultmann has constantly emphasized this. Hence it is quite wrong to understand Bultmann's concept of fore-understanding—being caught up in prejudices—as a kind of pre-knowl-edge.[37] This is a purely hermeneutical concept, developed by Bultmann on the basis of Heidegger's analysis of the hermeneutical circle and the general fore-structure of human Dasein. It refers to the openness of the horizon of inquiry within which alone understanding is possible, but it does not mean that one's own fore-understanding should not be corrected by the encoun-ter with the word of God (or, indeed, with any other word). On the contrary, the purpose of this concept is to display the movement of understanding as precisely this process of correction. It must be noted that this "corrective" process is, in the case of the call of faith, a specific one that is of hermeneutic universality only in its formal structure.[38]

This is where the theological concept of self-understanding comes in. This idea also has obviously been derived from Heidegger's transcendental analysis of existence. The being that is concerned with its being presents itself, through its understanding of being, as a means of access to the question of being. The movement of the understanding of being is itself seen to be historical, as the basic nature of historicity. This is of decisive importance for Bultmann's concept of self-understanding.

This concept is different from that of self-knowledge not only in the "psychologistic" sense that what is known in self-knowledge is already present, but in the deeper speculative sense that is behind the concept of "mind" or "spirit" in German idealism, according to which perfect self-consciousness knows itself in other being. Certainly the development of this self-consciousness in Hegel's phenomenology is decisively made possible by the recognition of the other. The growth of the self-conscious mind is a fight for recognition. What it is, is what it has become. However, the idea of self-understanding appropriate to theology is concerned with something else.[39]

What is extra nos, other than us and not at our disposal, is part of the inevitable essence of this self-understanding. The self-understanding that we acquire in constantly new experiences of the other and of others remains, from a Christian point of view, non-understanding in an essential sense. All human self-understanding has its absolute boundary in death. This really cannot be used as a serious argument against Bultmann (Ott, p.163) in an attempt to find a sense of "conclusion" in Bultmann's idea of self-understanding. As if the self-understanding of faith were not precisely the experience of the eventual failure of human self-understanding. This experience of failure need not necessarily be understood in Christian terms. Human self-understanding is deepened by every such experience. In every case it is an "event" and the concept of self-understanding a historical concept. But according to Christian doctrine, there is a "final" failure. The Christian meaning of proclamation, the promise of resurrection that sets us free from death, consists precisely in bringing the constantly repeated failure of self-understanding—its eventual collapse in death and finiteness—to an end in faith in Christ. Certainly this does not mean that one steps outside one's own historicity, but rather that faith is the eschatological event. In his *History and Eschatology* Bultmann writes, "The paradox that Christian existence is at once eschatological, unworldly, and historical has the same meaning as Luther's statement: Simul iustus simul peccator."[40] It is in this sense that self-understanding is a historical concept.

The contemporary hermeneutical discussion that starts from Bultmann seems in one particular direction to be moving beyond him. If, according to Bultmann, the appeal of the Christian proclamation to man is that he should give up his right to dispose of himself as he chooses, this appeal is like a privative experience of human self-determination. In this way Bultmann has interpreted Heidegger's concept of the inauthenticity of Dasein in a theological way. In Heidegger, of course, authenticity is connected with inauthenticity not only in the sense that fallenness is as much part of human life as "resoluteness," sin (unbelief) just as much as belief. The fact that for Heidegger authenticity and inauthenticity have the same origin points quite beyond the starting point in self-understanding. This is the first form in which, in Heidegger's thought, being itself has come into language as the antithesis of "disclosure" and "concealment."[41] Just as Bultmann relied on the existential analysis of Dasein in Heidegger in order to explain the eschatological existence of man between belief and unbelief, so it is possible to use as a theological starting point this dimension of the question of being that has been worked out more exactly by the later Heidegger, namely by going into the central significance that language has, in this event of being, for the "language of faith." Already in Ott's very skillful speculative hermeneutical discussion, there is, following Heidegger's "Letter on Humanism," a critique of Bultmann. It corresponds to his own positive thesis on page 107: "The language in which reality 'comes into language,' in and with which all reflection on existence takes place, accompanies existence in all epochs of its realization." The hermeneutical ideas of the theologians Fuchs and Ebeling seem, similarly, to start from the late Heidegger by putting more emphasis on the concept of language.

Ernst Fuchs has given us a *hermeneutics* that he calls a "Sprachlehre des Glaubens"—i.e., a grammar of faith.[42] His starting point is that language is the illumination of being. "Language contains the decision about what stands open to us as existence, as the possibility of what can become of us if we remain responsive as men." Thus he starts from Heidegger in order "to get over the modern entanglement in the subject-object schema." But while Heidegger is thinking of the "attraction of language itself that comes from its original source and returns to it," Fuchs thinks of the inner attraction of language in listening to the New Testament "as the attraction of the word of God."

With this listening is associated the awareness that we cannot say that we are the last for whom God's word is intended. But from this there follows that "we must let ourselves be shown our historical limitations, as they emerge in our historical understanding of the world. But this means that we have the self-same task that has always existed for the self-understanding of faith. We share this task with the authors of the New Testament." Thus Fuchs acquires a hermeneutical basis that can be justified by New Testament scholarship itself. The proclamation of the word of God in preaching is a translation of the statements of the New Testament, the justification of which is theology.

Theology here almost becomes hermeneutics, since—following the development of modern biblical criticism—it does not take as its object the truth of revelation itself, but the truth of the statements or communications that are related to God's revelation (p. 98). Hence the chief category is *communication*.

Fuchs follows Bultmann in seeing that the hermeneutical principle and the understanding of the New Testament must be neutral in regard to faith, for its only presupposition is the question about ourselves. But it reveals itself as God's question to us. A grammar of faith must deal with what actually happens when the call of God's word is heard. "To know what takes place in this encounter does not mean that one can automatically say what one knows" (p. 86). Thus the task is finally not only to hear the word, but also to find the word that is a response. We are concerned with the *language* of faith.

An essay, "Übersetzung und Verkündigung," makes it clearer how this hermeneutical theory seeks to get beyond the existential interpretation of Bultmann.[43] It is the hermeneutical principle of translation that shows the direction. It cannot be denied that "translation should create the same space as a text intended to create when the spirit was speaking in it" (p. 409). But the bold and yet unavoidable consequence is that the word has primacy over against the text, for it is a linguistic event. Here he obviously means to say that the relation between word and thought is not that the word expressing it belatedly catches up to the thought. The word, rather, is like a flash of lightning—it strikes. Accordingly, as Ebeling once put it, "The hermeneutical problem is epitomized in the act of preaching."[44]

We cannot here go into the way in which "the hermeneutical movements in the New Testament" are presented on this basis. We can see that the real point is that, for Fuchs, theology in the New Testament already "starts from the struggle between language itself and a thinking in terms of law or order that is a threat from the start."[45] The task of proclamation is that of transformation into the word.[46]

There is one thing common to all contemporary criticism of historical objectivism or positivism, namely the insight that the so-called subject of knowledge has the same mode of being as the object, so that object and subject belong to the same historical movement. The subject-object antithesis is legitimate where the object, the res extensa, is the absolute other of the res cogitans. But historical knowledge cannot be appropriately described by this concept of object and objectivity. The important thing, to use Count Yorck's words, is to grasp the "generic" difference between "ontic" and "historical"—i.e., to recognize the so-called subject in the mode of being of historicity that is appropriate to it. We saw that Dilthey did not break through to the full consequence of this insight, even if it is in his wake that the consequence is drawn. Moreover, the conceptual pre-suppositions for the problem of overcoming historicism, as expounded by, say, Ernst Troeltsch, were lacking.

Here the work of the phenomenological school has proved fruitful. Today, now that the various stages in the development of Husserl's phenomenology can be seen,[47] it seems clear to me that Husserl was the first to take the radical step in this direction, by showing the mode of being of subjectivity as absolute historicity—i.e., as temporality. Heidegger's epoch-making work *Being and Time*, to which one generally refers on this point, had a quite different and far more radical intention, namely of revealing the inadequate ontological preconception that dominates modern understanding of subjectivity or of "consciousness" even in its extreme form of the phenomenology of temporality and historicity. This critique served the positive task of asking in a new way the question of "being," to which the Greeks gave, as a first answer, metaphysics. *Being and Time*, however, was not understood in this, its real intention, but in what Heidegger had in common with Husserl. It was seen as a radical defense of the absolute historicity of Dasein, which is, in fact, a consequence of Husserl's analysis of the primal phenomenality of temporality ("flowing"). The argument runs, more or less, thus: the mode of being of Dasein is defined in an ontologically positive way. It is not presence-at-hand but futurity. There are no eternal truths. Truth is the disclosure of being that is given with the historicity of Dasein.[48] Here, then, were the foundations from which the critique of historical objectivism occurring in the sciences themselves could receive its ontological justification. It is, as it were, a second-degree historicism which not only opposes the historical relativity of all knowledge to the absolute claim of truth but works out its ground—namely the historicity of the knowing subject—and hence can no longer see historical relativity as a limitation of the truth.[49]

Even if this is correct, it still does not follow that all philosophical knowledge has only the significance and value of a historical expression in the sense of Dilthey's philosophy of world-views, or that it is therefore on the same plane as art, which is concerned with genuineness and not with truth. Heidegger's own question is far from seeking to sacrifice metaphysics to history, or the question of truth to that of the genuineness of expression. Rather, he seeks to inquire back behind the problematic of metaphysics. The fact that the history of philosophy thereby appears in a new way as the interior of world history, namely as the history of being, or better the history of the forgetfulness of being, still does not mean that this is a metaphysics of history of the kind that Löwith has shown to be a secular form of Christian history,[50] the most logical elaboration of which idea, on the basis of the modern Enlightenment, is Hegel's philosophy of history. Nor is Husserl's historical critique of the "objectivism" of modern philosophy in the Crisis a metaphysics of history. "Historicity" is a transcendental concept.

If one adopts the standpoint of a theological metaphysics, it is very easy to argue against this kind of "transcendental" historicism which, in the style of Husserl's transcendental reduction, takes its stand in the absolute historicalness of subjectivity, in order to understand, on this basis, everything accorded existential status as an objectification by this subjectivity. If being-in-itself exists, which alone could limit the universal historical movement of successive views of the world, it must obviously be something that surpasses all finite human perspectives, as it appears to an infinite spirit. But this is the order of creation, which thus remains an ordering prior to all human projections. It is thus that some years ago Gerhard Krüger interpreted the dual aspect of Kant's philosophy, namely the idealism of phenomena and the realism of the thing in itself,[51] and even in his latest works has sought to defend the rights of teleological metaphysics against modern subjectivism on the basis of mythical or religious experience.

The question becomes much more difficult, however, if we are not prepared to accept the consequences that culminate in the Christian account of creation, and yet would still like to oppose the old teleological cosmos, for which the so-called natural awareness of the world continues to argue, to the mutability of human history.[52] It is obviously the case that the nature of historicity became conscious to the human mind only with the Christian religion and its emphasis on the absolute moment of the saving action of God, and that, nevertheless, the same phenomena of historical life were known before that. But they were understood in an "unhistorical" way, whether by deriving the present from a mythical past or by seeing the present in relation to an ideal and eternal order.

It is true that the historical writing of, say, Herodotus, even of Plutarch, is able to describe very well the ebb and flow of human history, as a great variety of moral exempla, without reflecting on the historicity of their own present and on the historicity of human life in general. The model of the cosmic order, in which everything that is divergent and opposed to the norm passes quickly away, as it is ironed out in the great harmonizing process of a natural cycle, can also be used as a description of the course of human affairs. The best order of things, the ideal state, is in conception just as permanent an order as the cosmos, and even if an ideal realization of it does not endure, but is superseded by the new confusion and disorder that we call history, this is the result of an error in calculation by human reason, which knows what the right thing is. The right order has no history. History is always a history of disintegration and, sometimes, of the restoration of the right order.[53]

In regard to actual human history, then, historical skepticism—even in the Christian, reformed view—is the only attitude that can be taken. This was the intention and insight behind Löwith's revelation of the theological, and especially eschatological, assumptions on which the European philosophy of history is based, which he expounded in his *Weltgeschichte und Heilsgeschehen*. For Löwith, to conceive a unity of world history is the false need of the Christian and modernistic spirit. For him the eternal God and his plan of salvation for man need not be sought if we really take the finitude of man seriously. We should look at the eternal cycle of nature, in order to learn from it the equanimity that alone is appropriate to the minuteness of human life in the universe. The "natural concept of the world" that Löwith uses against both modern historicism and modern science, is clearly of Stoic origin.[54] No other Greek text seems to illustrate Löwith's intention as well as the pseudo-Aristotelian (Hellenistic-Stoic) work *On the Cosmos*. This is not surprising, for obviously the modern author is, like his Hellenistic predecessor, interested in the course of nature only insofar as it is the antithesis of the desperate disorder of human affairs. A person who defends the naturalness of this natural view of the world in this way no more starts from the eternal return of the same than did Nietzsche, but from the absolute finitude of human life. His rejection of history is a reflection of fatalism—i.e., despair of this life having any meaning. It is not a denial of the significance of history but of the possibility of its being interpreted at all.

Leo Strauss' criticism of modern faith in history, which appears in a number of outstanding books on political philosophy, seems to me more radical. He is Professor of Political Philosophy at Chicago, and it is one of the encouraging features of our world, increasingly restricted as it is in its area of freedom, that such a radical critic of the political thought of our contemporary world works there. We are familiar with the querelle des anciens et des modernes, which dominated the minds of the literary public in seventeenth-and eighteenth-century France. Although it is primarily a literary quarrel that displayed the defenders of the excellence of the Greek and Roman classical poets competing with the literary self-confidence of the writers who were at that time introducing a new classical period of literature at the court of the Sun King, the tension of this argument finally ended in a sense of historical awareness. For it was necessary to limit the absolute exemplariness of the classical world. That querelle was, as it were, the last form of an unhistorical debate between tradition and the modern age.

It is not by accident that one of Leo Strauss' first works, *Spinoza's Critique of Religion* (1930), was concerned with this quarrel. His whole impressive and learned life's work is devoted to the task of reviving this quarrel in a more radical sense—i.e., confronting modern historical self-consciousness with the clear rightness of classical philosophy. When Plato inquires into the best state—and even the extended political empiricism of Aristotle preserves the priority of this question—this may have little to do with the concept of politics that dominates modern thought since Machiavelli. And in his book *Natural Law and History* Strauss apparently goes back to the antithesis of the modern historical worldview, namely natural law; the purpose of his book is, in fact, to exhibit the Greek classics of philosophy, Plato and Aristotle, as the true founders of natural law, and to accept neither the Stoic nor the medieval form of natural law, to say nothing of that of the Enlightenment, as being philosophically correct.

Strauss is motivated here by his insight into the catastrophe of modern times. So elementary a human concern as the distinction between "right" and "wrong" assumes that man is able to raise himself above his historical conditionedness. When classical philosophy foregrounds the uncondi-tional nature of this distinction in its inquiry into justice, it is clearly right, and a radical historicism that historically relativizes all unconditional values cannot be right. Thus one's arguments have to be tested in the light of classical philosophy.

Now Strauss cannot, of course, mean that he could undertake this task in the same way that Plato undertakes his critique of sophism. He is himself too familiar with the modern historical awareness to defend classical philosophy in a naive way. Thus his argument against what he calls historicism is itself based primarily on historical grounds. He appeals to the fact (as does Löwith after him) that historical thought itself has historical conditions of growth. This is true both of naive historicism—i.e., of the development of a historical sense in the study of tradition—and of its refined form, which takes account of the existence of the knowing subject in his historicity.

Although this is unquestionably correct, so is the conclusion that the historical phenomenon of historicism, just as it has had its hour, could also one day come to an end. This is quite certain, not because historicism would otherwise "contradict itself," but because it takes itself seriously. Thus we cannot argue that a historicism that maintains the historical conditionedness of all knowledge "for all eternity" is basically self-contradictory. This kind of self-contradiction is a special problem.[55] Here also we must ask whether the two propositions—"all knowledge is historically conditioned" and "this piece of knowledge is true unconditionally"—are on the same level, so that they could contradict each other. For the thesis is not that this proposition will always be considered true, any more than that it has always been so considered. Rather, historicism that takes itself seriously will allow for the fact that one day its thesis will no longer be considered true—i.e., that people will think "unhistorically." And yet not because asserting that all knowledge is conditioned is meaningless and "logically" contradictory.

Strauss, however, does not take up the question thus. Simply to show that the classical philosophers thought differently—i.e., unhistorically —says nothing about the possibility of thinking unhistorically today. There are sufficient reasons for regarding the possibility of thinking unhistorically not simply as a mere possibility. The many correct "physiognomic" observations that Ernst Jünger has made on this subject suggest that humanity has reached "the time wall."[56] What Strauss is concerned with is still conceived within historical thought and has the significance of a corrective. What he criticizes is that the "historical" interpretation of traditional thought claims to be able to understand the thought of the past better than it understood itself.[57] Whoever thinks like this excludes from the outset the possibility that the thoughts that are handed down to us could simply be true. This is the practically universal dogmatism of this way of thought.

The image of the historicist that Strauss here outlines and opposes corresponds, it seems to me, to that ideal of complete enlightenment that I described in my own inquiry into philosophical hermeneutics as the guiding idea behind the historical irrationalism of Dilthey and the nineteenth century. Is it not the utopian ideal of a present in the light of which the whole of the past will, as it were, be entirely revealed? Historical thinking does not at all seem best characterized as applying the superior perspective of the present to the whole of the past; that is rather the obstinate positivity of a "naive" historicism. Historical thinking has its dignity and its value as truth in the acknowledgment that there is no such thing as "the present," but rather constantly changing horizons of future and past. It is by no means settled (and can never be settled) that any particular perspective in which traditionary thoughts present themselves is the right one. "Historical" understanding, whether today's or tomorrow's, has no special privilege. It is itself embraced by the changing horizons and moved with them.

By contrast, the view of literary hermeneutics that one must understand an author better than he understood himself comes, as I have shown, from the aesthetics of genius, but it is originally a simple formulation of the Enlightenment ideal of clarifying obscure ideas by conceptual analysis.[58] Its application by historical consciousness is secondary and creates the false appearance of an unsurpassable superiority in the particular interpreter of the moment, which Strauss rightly criticizes. But I think when Strauss argues that in order to understand better it is necessary first to understand an author as he understood himself, he underestimates the difficulties of understanding, because he ignores what might be called the dialectic of the statement.

We have seen this in another place, where he defends the ideal of "objective interpretation" by saying that the author, at any rate, understood what he said in only one way, "assuming that he was not confused in his mind" (p. 67). We must still ask whether the contrast implied here between "clear" and "confused" is as obvious as Strauss assumes. Does he not here, in fact, share the point of view of full historical enlightenment and miss the real hermeneutic problem? He seems to consider it possible to understand what one does not understand oneself but what someone else understands, and to understand only in the way that the other person himself understood. And he also seems to think that if a person says something, he has necessarily and fully understood "himself" in the process. In my view these cannot both be true. In order to grasp its valid meaning, it is necessary to detach the dubious hermeneutical principle of having to understand an author "better" than he understood himself, from the presupposition of perfect enlightenment.

Let us then consider Strauss' defense of classical philosophy from a hermeneutic point of view. We will consider one example. Strauss shows very well that the I-Thou-We relation, as it is called in modern thinking, is known in classical political philosophy by a quite different name: *friendship*. He sees correctly that the modern way of talking about the "problem of the Thou" is based on the fundamental primacy of the Cartesian ego cogito. Strauss now thinks he sees why the ancient concept of friendship is correct and the modern formulation false. It is quite legitimate for someone who is attempting to discover the nature of the state and society to consider the role of friendship. But he cannot talk with the same legitimacy about the "Thou." The Thou is not something about which one speaks but that to which one speaks. By taking the function of the Thou as a basis, instead of the role of friendship, one is missing the objective communicative nature of the state and society.

I find this a very happy example. In Aristotelian ethics, the indeterminate position of the concept of friendship between the doctrine of virtue and of the good has long been for me, and for very similar reasons, a basis for recognizing the limitations of modern as compared with classical ethics.[59] Thus I fully agree with Strauss' example, but I ask: Does this insight emerge because we "read" the classics with an eye that is trained by historical science, reconstructing their meaning, as it were, and then considering it possible, trusting that they are right? Or do we see truth in them because we ourselves are thinking as we try to understand them—i.e., because what they say seems true to us when we consider the corresponding modern theories that are invoked? Do we understand them at all without at the same time understanding them as more correct? If the answer is no, then I go on to ask: is it not then meaningful to say of Aristotle that he could not understand himself in the way that we understand him if we find what he says more correct than those modern theories (which he could not know)?

The same thing could be shown to hold for the distinction Strauss rightly insists on between the concept of the state and that of the polis. That the institution of the state is something very different from the natural living community of the polis is not merely correct; something is revealed here—again from this experience of difference—that would remain incomprehensible not only for modern theory, but also in our understanding of the classical texts, were these not understood in terms of the contrast with modern times. If this is called "revitalization" or "reliving," these terms seem to me just as inexact as Collingwood's "re-enactment." The life of the spirit is not like that of the body. It is no false historicism to admit this, but in the closest accord with Aristotle's epidosis eis auto. In this respect I do not seriously differ from Strauss, inasmuch as he also regards the "fusion of history and philosophical questions" as inevitable in our thought today. I agree with him that it would be a dogmatic assertion to regard this as an absolute prerogative of the modern age. Indeed, how many unacknowledged assumptions govern us when we think in our concepts, so full of traditional ideas, and how much can we learn by going back to the fathers of thought? This is shown clearly by the instances we have mentioned, instances that can be multiplied from Strauss' writings.

In any case, we must not be led into the error of thinking that the problem of hermeneutics is posed only from the viewpoint of modern historicism. It is true that the classic authors did not discuss the opinions of their predecessors as historically different but as contemporary. But the task of hermeneutics—i.e., the task of interpreting transmitted texts —would still present itself, and if such interpretation always includes the question of truth, then this is perhaps not as far from our own experience in dealing with texts as the methodology of historical and philological science would have it. The word "hermeneutics" points back, as we know, to the task of the interpreter, which is that of interpreting and communicating something that is unintelligible because it is spoken in a foreign language—even if it is the language of the signs and symbols of the gods. The capacity to perform this task has always been the object of possible reflection and conscious training. (This can, of course, take the form of an oral tradition as, for example, with the Delphic priesthood.) But when it is a question of writing, the task of interpretation is quite clearly imposed. Everything that is set down in writing is to some extent foreign and strange, and hence it poses the same task of understanding as what is spoken in a foreign language. The interpreter of what is written, like the interpreter of divine or human utterance, has the task of overcoming and removing strangeness and making its assimilation possible. It may be the case that this task is complicated when the historical distance between the text and the interpreter becomes conscious; for this means that the tradition that supports both the transmitted text and its interpreter has become fragile and fissured. But I think that under the weight of the false methodological analogies suggested by the natural sciences, "historical" hermeneutics is separated far too much from "prehistorical" hermeneutics. I tried to show that they have at least one important trait in common: the structure of application.[60]

It would be fascinating to investigate the Greek beginnings of the essential connection between hermeneutics and writing. It is not just that according to Plato both Socrates and his opponents, the Sophists, engaged in the interpretation of poets; it is more important that Plato himself explicitly relates the whole of Platonic dialectics to the problems of writing, and that even within the dialogue it often explicitly assumes a hermeneutical character, whether the dialectical dialogue is introduced by a mythical tradition through priests and priestesses, by Diotima's instruction, or simply by the observation that the ancients did not worry at all that we should understand them, and hence left us as helpless as if we were dealing with fairy tales. We need to consider the reverse as well, namely the extent to which Plato's own myths belong to the dialectic and hence themselves have the character of interpretation. Thus constructing a Platonic hermeneutics that would advance the beginnings made by Hermann Gundert could be extremely instructive.[61]

But Plato is still more important as the *object* of hermeneutical reflection. As an artistic creation the dialogue form of the Platonic writings curiously stands halfway between the variety of characters of dramatic writing and the authenticity of the pedagogical work. In this respect the last decades have given us a high degree of hermeneutical awareness, and Strauss astonishes us by often brilliantly deciphering hidden relationships in the Platonic dialogues. However much we have been helped by form-analysis and other linguistic methods, the proper hermeneutical basis here is our own relation to the actual problems that concern Plato. Even Plato's artistic irony can be understood only by someone who shares his knowledge of the subject matter (as is the case with all irony). The result of this situation is that such deciphering interpretation remains "uncertain." Its "truth" cannot be demonstrated "objectively," except in terms of that agreement about the subject matter that links us with the interpreted text.

Strauss indirectly made a further important contribution to hermeneutic theory by investigating a particular problem, namely the question of how far in trying to understand a text one should take into account the conscious camouflaging of the true meaning due to the threat of persecution by the authorities or by the church.[62] It was mainly studies on

Maimonides, Halevy, and Spinoza that gave rise to this question. I do not want to question Strauss' interpretations—I largely agree with them—but I should like to make a countersuggestion that is perhaps justified in these cases, but is quite certainly so in others—e.g., in the case of Plato. Is not conscious distortion, camouflage, and concealment of the proper meaning in fact the rare extreme case of a frequent, even normal situation?—just as persecution (whether by civil authority or the church, the inquisition, or any other agency) is only an extreme case compared to the intentional or unintentional pressure that society and public opinion exert on human thought. Only if we are conscious of the uninterrupted transition from one to the other are we able to estimate the hermeneutic difficulty of Strauss' problem. How are we able to establish clearly that a distortion has taken place? Thus, in my opinion it is by no means clear that when we find contradictory statements in a writer, it is correct to take the hidden meaning—as Strauss thinks—as his true opinion. There is an unconscious conformism of the human mind to considering what is universally evident as really true. And there is, by contrast, an unconscious tendency to try out extreme possibilities, even if they cannot always be combined into a coherent whole. The experimental extremism of Nietzsche bears irrefutable witness to this. Contradictions are an excellent criterion of truth but, unfortunately, they are not an unambiguous criterion when we are dealing with hermeneutics.

Hence, for example, it is quite clear to me that despite its apparent obviousness, Strauss' statement that if an author contains contradictions that a schoolboy of today could spot immediately, then these are intentional and even meant to be seen through, cannot be applied to the so-called mistakes in argument by Plato's Socrates. Not because we are concerned here with the beginnings of logic (to say this is to confuse logical thought with logical theory), but because it is the nature of a dialogue directed toward an object to risk illogicality.[63]

The question has general hermeneutical consequences. We are concerned with the concept of "the author's meaning." I am disregarding the help that jurisprudence might offer here with its doctrine of legal interpretation. All I want to say is that at any rate Platonic dialogue is a model of writing that embraces many meanings and inner relationships, among which Strauss is often able to make important discoveries. Are we to so underestimate the mimetic truth that the Socratic dialogue has for Plato that we do not see this multifariousness of meaning in itself, even in Socrates himself? Does an author really know so exactly and in every sentence what he means? The curious chapter of philosophical self-interpretation—I think, for example, of Kant, Fichte, and Heidegger—seems to speak for itself. If the alternative suggested by Strauss is true—namely that a philosophical author has either an unambiguous meaning or is confused—then there is, I fear, in many controversial points of interpretation only one hermeneutical consequence: we must concede that there is confusion.

In considering the structure of the hermeneutical process I have explicitly referred to the Aristotelian analysis of phronesis.[64] Basically, I have followed here a line that Heidegger began in his early years in Freiburg, when he was concerned with a hermeneutics of facticity, against neo-Kantianism and value philosophy (and, probably ultimately, against Husserl himself). It is true that Aristotle's ontological basis became suspect for Heidegger even in his early investigations, a basis on which the whole of modern philosophy, especially the idea of subjectivity and that of consciousness, as well as the aporias of historicism, is founded (what in *Being and Time* is called the "ontology of the present-at-hand"). But in one point Aristotelian philosophy was at that time much more than a mere countermodel for Heidegger; it was a real vindicator of his own philosophical purposes: in the Aristotelian critique of Plato's "universal eidos" and, positively, in the demonstration of the analogical structure of the good and the knowledge of the good that is required in the situation of action.

What surprises me most about Strauss' defense of classical philosophy is the degree to which he tries to understand it as a unity, so that the extreme contrast that exists between Plato and Aristotle with regard to the nature and the significance of the good does not seem to cause him any trouble.[65] The early stimulation that I received from Heidegger has been valuable to me; for, among other reasons, Aristotelian ethics quite unexpectedly made it easier to understand the hermeneutical problem more deeply. I think it is true to say that this is not a misuse of Aristotelian thought, but shows what can be learned from it, a critique of the abstract and universal that—without being driven to a dialectical extreme, as in the manner of Hegel, and hence without the untenable consequence presented by the concept of absolute knowledge—has become essential for the hermeneutical situation after the rise of historical consciousness.

In his book *Die Wiedererweckung des geschictlichen Bewußtseins*, which appeared in 1956, Theodor Litt has presented under the title "Der Historismus und seine Widersacher" (historicism and its opponents) an energetic critique of Krüger and Löwith (though unfortunately not of

Strauss) that seems to have a difficulty at this point.[66] I think that Litt is right when he sees the danger of a new dogmatism in the philosophical opposition to history. The desire for a fixed, constant criterion "that points the way for those called to action" always has particular force if failures in moral and political judgment have had grave consequences. The question of justice, the question of the perfect state, seem to spring from an elementary need of human existence. Nevertheless everything depends on the way this question is intended and asked, if it is to bring clarification. Litt shows that it cannot refer to any universal norm under which the particular case of practical political action could be subsumed.[67] It is, however, a pity that he does not avail himself of Aristotle's assistance, for Aristotle made the same objection to Plato.

I am convinced of the fact that, quite simply, we need to learn from the classics, and it is greatly to be appreciated that Strauss not only makes this demand but also in large measure fulfills it. However, among the things that we need to learn from them is that there is an absolute distinction between a politike techne and a politike phronesis. Strauss does not in my opinion give this sufficient weight.

Here too Aristotle can help us avoid falling into an apotheosis of nature, naturalness, and natural law that would be nothing but an impotently doctrinaire critique of history, and he can help us acquire instead a more appropriate relationship to the historical tradition and a better understanding of what is. Incidentally, I do not regard the problem raised by Aristotle as in any way disposed of. It might well be that Aristotle's critique, like so many critiques, is right in what it says, but not against whom it says it.[68] But that is a large—and different—question.

Notes

1 Georg Misch, "Lebensphilosophie und Phänomenologie: Eine Auseinanderset-zung der Diltheyschen Richtung mit Heidegger und Husserl," *Philosophische Anzeiger 1929/30* (2nd ed., Leipzig and Berlin, 1931).

2 [A renewed awareness of Dilthey arose in 1983 with the publication of materials for the 2nd vol. of his *Einleitung in die Geisteswissenschaft* (*Gesammelte Werke*, XVIII and XIX). See also my recent work on Dilthey, *GW*, IV.]

3 This posthumous work now exists, with a rearrangement of the enormous material, carried out by Johannes Winckelmann (4th ed., 1st and 2nd half vols.; Tübingen, 1956) [a massive critical edition of Max Weber's work is now appearing].

4 A useful survey of the self-reflection carried out in modern historical science —with express reference to historical research in England, America, and France—is to be found in Fritz Wagner, *Moderne Geschichtsschreibung: Ausblick auf eine Philosophie der Geschichtswissenschaft* (Berlin, 1960). It appears that in every field, naive objectivism is no longer sufficient and that hence a need for theory is recognized that goes beyond mere epistemological methodologism. [See K.–G. Faber, *Theorien der Geschichtswissenschaft* (Munich, 1971) and Reinhard Koselleck, *Futures Past: On the Semantics of Historical Time*, tr. Keith Tribe (1979; Cambridge, Mass.: MIT Press, 1985).]

The individual studies on Ranke, Friedrich Meinecke, and Litt by W. Hofer, collected under the title *Geschichte zwischen Philosophie und Politik: Studie zur Problematik des modernen Geschichtsdenkens* (Stuttgart, 1956), as well as the political use of history by the National Socialists and the Bolsheviks, belong in this context. Hofer seeks to illustrate both the dangers and the productive potentialities of this intensified self-awareness that historical thinking gains from being brought into relation with politics.

Here we should especially refer to Reinhard Wittram, *Das Interesse an der Geschichte* (Kleine Vandenhoekreihe, 59/60/61; Göttingen, 1958). These lectures decisively pose the question of the "truth in history" that goes beyond mere "correctness" and give wide references in the notes to modern writing on the subject, particularly the important periodical essays.

5 In 1956, i.e., thirty years later, a photostatic reprint of this work by Bachofen appeared (2nd ed., Munich, 1956).

If we look back at this work, we see that its reprinting had real success, since it was followed by a critical edition of Bachofen, which has, for the most part, appeared. On the other hand, we read the enormously long introduction by Baeumler with a strange mixture of admiration and bewilderment. In it Baeumler has undoubtedly increased interest in Bachofen by shifting the emphases in the history of German romanticism. He makes a sharp division between the aesthetic romanticism of Jena, which he sees as the harvest of the eighteenth century, and the religious romanticism of Heidelberg (cf. my "Hegel und die Heidelberger Romantik" in *Hegels Dialektik* [1971], pp. 71–81). He shows Görres to be its leader, whose interest in early German history became one of the factors that paved the way for the national rising of 1813. There is a lot of truth in what he says, and for this reason Baeumler's work still deserves respect today. But like Bachofen himself, his interpreter moves in a sphere of psychic experience that he relates to a false scientific framework (as Franz Wieacker says in his review of Bachofen in *Gnomon*, 28 (1956), 161–73).

6 Jan de Vries, *Forschungsgeschichte der Mythologie* (Freiburg-Munich, n.d.). [See the useful collection of sources in mythology edited by F. Schupp and also Hans-Georg Gadamer and Heinrich Fries, "Mythos and Wissenschaft," in *Christlicher Glaube in moderner Gesellschaft*, ed. Franz Böckle, et al., II (Freiburg, Basel, Vienna: Herder, 1981), 8–38. An impressive testimony to the hermeneutic dimension of myth is Hans Blumenberg's entire book, *Work on Myth*, tr. Robert M. Wallace (Cambridge, Mass.: MIT Press, 1985).]

7 1st ed., 1919.

8 Cf. Gerhard Ebeling, "Wort Gottes und Hermeneutik," *Zeitschrift für Theologie und Kirche*, 56 (1959), 228ff.

9 *Die Idee der Konkretisierung in Recht und Rechtswissenschaft unserer Zeit, Abhandlungen der Heidelberger Akademie der Wissenschaften, philosophisch-historische Klasse* (1953), no. 1, p.294. Cf. also his *Einführung in das juristische Denken* (Stuttgart, 1956), in particular, p.520.

10 [In addition to the influential views in K. Larenz, *Methodenlehre* (3rd ed.), J. Esser's work has become the starting point for controversies in jurisprudence. See his *Vorverständnis und Methodenwahl in der Rechtsfindung: Rationalitätsgarantien der richterlichen Entscheidungspraxis* (Frankfurt, 1970) and *Juristisches*

Argumentieren im Wandel des Rechtsfindungskonzepts unserers Jahrhunderts (*Sitzungsberichte der Heidelberger Akademie der Wissenschaften, philosophisch-historische Klasse* [1979], no. 1).]

11 2 vols., Milan, 1955.

12 *Festschrift* for E. Rabl, II (Tübingen, 1954).

13 Ibid., n. 19 and p.141.

14 Emilio Betti, "L'Ermeneutica storica e la storicità dell intendere," *Annali della Faculta di Giurisprudenza* (Bari), 16 (1961), and *Die Hermeneutik als allgemeine Methodik der Geisteswissenschaften* (Tübingen, 1962).

15 Cf. also Betti's essay in *Studium Generale*, 12 (1959), 87, with which Franz Wieacker has no difficulty agreeing (see his review cited in n. 5 above). [Betti's great merit and my objections to his view are restated in my "Emilio Betti und das idealistische Erbe," *Quaderni Fiorentini*, 7 (1978), 5–11.]

16 Introduced by H.–G. Gadamer (Stuttgart, 1955).

17 Ibid.

18 See pp. 370ff. above.

19 [See my "Mathematik und Dialektik bei Plato," shortened version in *Festschrift* for C. F. von Weizsäcker (Munich, 1982), pp. 229–40 (complete version, *GW*, VII).]

20 I recall the great advance in knowledge achieved by Hermann Langerbeck's study "Doxis Epirusmie," *Neue philologische Untersuchungen*, 11 (1934), which the sharp criticism by E. Kapp in *Gnomon* (1935) should not prevent us from seeing. [See my review, now in *GW*, V, 341ff.]

21 *Abhandlungen der geistes– und sozialwissenschaftlichen Klasse der Akademie der Wissenschaften und Literatur* (Mainz), 6 (1954).

22 That Rothacker sees the necessity of detaching the hermeneutical problem of meaning from all psychological investigation of "intention"—i.e., including the "subjective meaning" of a text—is apparent from his essay "Sinn und Geschehnis" in *Sinn und Sein: Ein philosophisches Symposion* (1960).

23 It is not clear to me why Rothacker bases the *a priori* character of these lines of significance on Heidegger's ontological difference, instead of on the transcendental apriorism that phenomenology shares with neo-Kantianism.

24 If we look at the textbook by Karl Larenz, *Methodenlehre der Rechtswissenschaft* (Berlin, 1961), the excellent historical and systematic survey it gives shows us that this methodology has something to say in every case about undecided legal questions, and is consequently a kind of ancillary discipline of legal dogmatics. This is its importance in our context. [The 3rd ed. of this work has now appeared and includes an expanded discussion of philosophical hermeneutics. See also the comprehensive monograph by G. Zaccaria, *Ermeneutica e giurisprudenza* (Milan, 1984), which presents in two vols. my theoretical views and J. Esser's application of them to jurisprudence.]

25 *Nicomachean Ethics*, V, 7, 1134 b 27ff.

26 This passage has been considered by Leo Strauss with reference to the theory of the extreme situation which he knows probably from the Jewish tradition (*Naturrecht und Geschichte*, with a foreword by G. Leibholz, [Stuttgart, 1956]). H. Kuhn, *Zeitschrift für Politik*, new ser. 3, no. 4 (1956), 289ff. (see *GW*, II, 302ff.), has taken up a position against Strauss and sought to revise the Aristotelian text, following H. H. Joachim, so that Aristotle would no longer assert without qualification the changeability of natural law. In fact, the sentence 1134 b 32–33 seems immediately acceptable if we do not relate the controversial "equally" to the changeability of natural law and conventional law, but to the following word "obviously" (*delon*).

Recently W. Bröcker, *Aristoteles* (3rd ed.), pp. 301ff., has contributed to this discussion, but he succumbs, in my opinion, to a sophism, when "in the case of a conflict between natural and positive law" he defends the validity of the positive law as Aristotle's view. Of course it is "valid," but not "just," when Creon "overrides" the natural law. And this is precisely the question: namely whether or not it is meaningful to recognize, beyond what is "positively" legal and in view of its sovereign claim to validity, an appeal to the authority of natural law, before which what is "valid" is unjust. I have tried to show that there is such an appeal, but that its function is solely critical.

27 Kuhn, op. cit., p.299.

28 [See my "Unterwegs zur Schrift," *Mündlichkeit und Schriftlichkeit*, ed. A. Assmann and J. Assmann (Munich, 1983), pp. 10–19 (*GW*, VIII).]

29 Cf. also the excellent study by Joachim Ritter, "Naturrecht bei Aristoteles," *Res publica*, 6 (1961), which demonstrates at length why there cannot be in Aristotle any such thing as a dogmatic natural law: because nature entirely determines the whole human world and consequently also the legal constitution. Whether Ritter accepts the emendation that I presented in Hamburg in October, 1960, is not quite clear (p. 28), especially as he quotes H. H. Joachim's treatment of the chapter without any critical qualification (n. 14). But in the matter itself he agrees with my view (see above pp. 315ff.), as, apparently, does W. Bröcker, who translates the passage, op. cit. (n. 26 above), p.302, without, however, accepting my emendation. Ritter goes on to develop very instructively the metaphysical background of the "political" and "practical" philosophy of Aristotle. [What is here only cautiously suggested I have now proposed in a detailed study, *The Idea of the Good in Platonic-Aristotelian Philosophy*, tr. P. Christopher Smith (New Haven: Yale University Press, 1986). In sum, I doubt Plato ever conceived the idea of the good in the form criticized by Aristotle.]

30 Cf. the evaluation of an important aspect of this work by H. Kuhn, *Philosophische Rundschau*, 2 (1955), 144–52, and 4 (1957), 182–91.

31 *Glauben und Verstehen*, II, 211ff., III, 107ff. and 142ff., and also *History and Eschatology*, ch. 8; cf. also the essay by Hans Blumenberg, *Philosophische*

Rundschau, 2 (1955), 121–40 [and G. Bornkamm's critical comment, *Philoso-phische Rundschau*, 29 (1963), 33–141.]

32 Heinz Liebing, *Zwischen Orthodoxie und Aufklärung: Über den Wolffianer G. B. Bilfinger* (Tübingen, 1961), shows us how different was the relationship between theology and philosophy before the rise of historical Bible criticism, insofar as the New Testament was understood directly as dogmatics, i.e., as an epitome of universal truths of faith, and hence could be related (sympathet-ically or otherwise) to the systematic mode of proof and to the form of presentation in rational philosophy. Bilfinger seeks the systematic foundation for the scientific quality of his theology in a modified Wolffian metaphysics. The fact that in this he is aware of the limits set by his temporal situation and by his insight is the only hermeneutical element of his theory of science that points to the future, namely to the problem of history.

Cf. also my introduction to F. C. Oetinger's *Inquisitio in sensum communem* (Frommann-Verlag, 1964), pp. v–xxviii, repr. in *Kleine Schriften*, III, 89–100 [*GW*, IV].

33 The reproduction of the Berlin manuscripts, the oldest of which are very difficult to read, has been supervised by Heinz Kimmerle. See the supplemen-tary "Nachbericht" to the Heidelberg edition of 1968. [Thanks to Manfred Frank, *Das individuelle Allgemeine: Textstrukturierung und –interpretation nach Schleiermacher* (Frankfurt, 1977), the debate about Schleiermacher remains ongoing. See my remarks in opposition to Frank in "Zwischen Phänomenolo-gie und Dialektik: Versuch einer Selbstkritik," *GW*, II, 3ff.]

34 Berlin, 1960. [M. Redeker has now made available the preliminary materials Dilthey left for the second volume of his biography of Schleiermacher. See Dilthey, *Gesammelte Werke*, XIV, parts 1 and 2.]

35 Senft, *Wahrhaftigkeit und Wahrheit: Die Theologie des 19. Jh. zwischen Orthodoxie und Aufklärung* (Tübingen, 1956).

36 Cf. my "On the Problem of Self-Understanding," pp. 44–58, and "Martin Heidegger and Marburg Theology," pp. 198–212, both in *Philosophical Herme-neutics*, tr. David E. Linge (Berkeley: University of California Press, 1976).

37 In his *Grundlegung*, op. cit. (n. 72, p.265 above), p.115, n. 47a, Betti seems to make the mistake of thinking that "fore-understanding" is called for by Heidegger and Bultmann because it helps understanding. The fact is, rather, that we need to become *conscious* of the fore-understanding that is *always* operative in any case about which we use the word "scientific" in a serious sense.

38 Lothar Steiger, *Die Hermeneutik als dogmatisches Problem* (Gütersloh, 1961), an excellent dissertation from the school of H. Diem, seeks to show the peculiar characteristics of theological hermeneutics by tracing the continuity of the transcendental approach in theological understanding from Schleiermacher

via Ritschl and Harnack to Bultmann and Gogarten, and confronting it with the existential dialectic of the Christian *kerygma.*

39 Ott's analysis in *Geschichte und Heilsgeschehen in der Theologie R. Bultmanns* (Tübingen, 1955) is in many ways fruitful, but n. 2 on p.164 shows how much he fails to see the methodological distinction between a metaphysical concept of self-consciousness and the historical meaning of self-understanding. I should prefer not to go into whether Hegel's thought speaks less to the point about self-consciousness than does Bultmann's about self-understanding, as Ott seems to think. But no "living dialogue with tradition" should lose sight of the fact that they are different—as different as are metaphysics and Christian faith.

40 These Gifford Lectures of Rudolf Bultmann are of special interest, since they relate Bultmann's own hermeneutical position to that of other authors, especially to Collingwood and H. J. Marrou, *De la connaissance historique* (1954) (cf. *Philosophische Rundschau,* 8, 123).

41 [See my "Heidegger and Marburg Theology," cited n. 36 above.]

42 Bad Cannstatt, 1954, with a supp. for the 2nd ed., 1958. Cf. also *Zum hermeneutischen Problem in der Theologie: Die existenziale Interpretation* (Tübingen, 1959) and *Marburger Hermeneutik* (1968).

43 "Zur Frage nach dem historischen Jesus," *Gesammelte Aufsätze,* II (Tübingen, 1960).

44 "Wort Gottes und Hermeneutik," *Zeitschrift für Theologie und Kirche* (1959), 228ff.

45 Cf. my "Heidegger and Marburg Theology," cited n. 36 above.

46 Perhaps what Fuchs and Ebeling call the "new hermeneutical position" will become most apparent if we exaggerate it. In an attractive and serious little book, Helmut Franz raised the question of *Kerygma und Kunst* (Saarbrücken, 1959). He moves largely within the linguistic framework of the later Heidegger and sees the task as one of bringing art back to genuine kerygmatic being. From its enclosure in the framework (*Ge-stell*) of the art industry, art must again become "e-vent." The writer is probably thinking particularly of music and its essential connection with the space in which it is played, or rather which it makes resound. But there is no doubt that he does not mean only music or only art: he means the church itself and also its theology, when he sees the *kerygma* as being threatened by "industry." The question is, though, whether theology and the church can be absolutely characterized by being transformed into "event." [See also *The New Hermeneutics,* ed. J. B. Cobb and J. M. Robinson (New York, 1964).]

47 *Husserliana,* I–VIII. Cf. the essays in *Philosophische Rundschau* by H. Wagner (1 [1954], 1–23, 93–123), D. Henrich (6 [1959], 1–25), L. Landgrebe (9 [1962], 133), and myself (10 [1963], 1–49). The criticism that I made there of some aspects of the approach of Herbert Spiegelberg unfortunately erred in certain

points. As regards the maxim "to the things themselves" (*zu den Sachen selbst*) and as regards Husserl's concept of reduction, Spiegelberg adopts the same position as I do in the face of current misunderstandings, as I would like to acknowledge explicitly here. [It should be explicitly noted that the interpretation of Husserl has also grown as a result of the progress of the edition of Husserl's work and that younger scholars are contributing.]

48 But this does not mean: "There is nothing eternal. Everything that exists, is historical." Rather, the mode of being of what is eternal or timeless—God or numbers, for instance—can only be determined correctly by "fundamental ontology," which brings out the meaning of the being of Dasein. See Oskar Becker's *Mathematische Existenz* (Jahrbuch für Philosophie und phänomenologische Forschung, 8; Halle: Niemeyer, 1927).

49 Cf. Friedrich Meinecke's concept of "dynamic historicism," *Entstehung des Historismus*, pp. 499ff.

50 *Weltgeschichte und Heilsgeschehen* (Stuttgart, 1953) [now in his *Sämtliche Schriften*, II (Stuttgart, 1983), 7–239].

51 *Philosophie und Moral in der kantischen Kritik* (Tübingen, 1931).

52 Cf. Löwith's critique of Krüger, *Philosophische Rundschau*, 7 (1960), 1–9.

53 In reference to Günther Rohr's *Platons Stellung zur Geschichte* (Berlin, 1932), I formulated this as follows: "If the correct *paideia* were effectual in a state, there would not be what we call 'history': the alternation of growth and death, growth and decline. Above the laws of decline in historical process which are confirmed by the facts, there would emerge a continuing, preserved situation. And only if we see that this kind of *permanence* can also be called 'history' can we understand Plato's 'view of history': the nature of history would be fulfilled as the immortality of the repeated preserving, in the permanent reflection of a permanent model, in a political cosmos within the natural one" (*Deutsche Literaturzeitung* [1932], col. 1982ff. [*GW*, V, 327–31]). (Recall the beginning of the *Timaeus*.) Since then, Konrad Gaiser has treated the problem again in *Platos ungeschriebene Lehre* (1963). [See my "Platos Denken in Utopien," *Gymnasium*, 90 (1983), 434–55 (*GW*, VII).]

54 "Der Weltbegriff der neuzeitlichen Philosophie," *Sitzungsberichte der Heidelberger Akademie der Wissenschaften, philosophisch-historische Klasse*, no. 4 (1960).

55 Cf. above Part Three, n. 85.

56 Cf. also Arnold Gehlen's analysis of modern art, which speaks of the *post-history* "into which we are passing" (see my review of his *Zeit-Bilder*, *Philosophische Rundschau*, 10, nos. 1/2 = *Kleine Schriften*, II, 218–226 (*GW*, IX).

57 *What Is Political Philosophy?* (Glencoe, 1959), p.68.

58 Cf. above, pp. 191ff.

59 Cf. my "Über die Möglichkeit einer philosophischen Ethik," *Kleine Schriften*, I, 179–91 (*GW*, IV). [See also my "Freundschaft und Selbsterkenntnis," in the

Festschrift for Uvo Hölscher (Würzburg, 1985) (*GW*, VII), and my review of recent books on ethics in *Philosophische Rundschau*, 32 (1985), 1–26.]

60 See above pp. 309ff.

61 In the *Festschrift* for O. Regenbogen (Heidelberg, 1952) and *Lexis* II.

62 *Persecution and the Art of Writing* (Glencoe, 1952).

63 The discussion of this problem still does not seem to me always to start from the right basis, as can be seen from the otherwise remarkable review of R. K. Sprague's *Plato's Use of Fallacy* by K. Oehler, *Gnomon*, 36 (1964), 335–40.

64 See above pp. 309ff.

65 [In my *The Idea of the Good in Platonic-Aristotelian Philosophy* (cited n. 29 above), I tried to resolve this alleged contradiction, with which Leo Strauss was presumably quite content.]

66 Heidelberg, 1956.

67 "It is a hopeless undertaking to start from the idea of the 'true' state, indicate the norm of justice, and then seek to establish *what* particular ordering of communal matters would help the universal demand to be realized here and now" (p. 88). Litt gives more detailed reasons for this in his essay "Über das Allgemeine im Aufbau der geisteswissenschaftlichen Erkenntnis" (1940).

68 [See n. 63 above.]

SUPPLEMENT II
To what extent does language preform thought?

We may begin by explaining why the question in the title is asked at all. What suspicion, what critique of our thought, is hidden behind it? It is, in fact, the fundamental doubt about the possibility of our escaping from the sphere of influence of our education which is linguistic, of our socialization which is linguistic, and of our thought which is transmitted through language, as well as the doubt about our capacity for openness to a reality which does not correspond to our opinions, our fabrications, our previous expectations. In our contemporary situation, faced as we are with an increasingly widespread anxiety about the future of mankind, the issue is the suspicion slowly seeping into the consciousness of all that, if we go on this way, if we pursue industrialization, think of work only in terms of profit, and turn our earth into one vast factory as we are doing at the moment, then we threaten the conditions of human life in both the biological sense and in the sense of our own ideals for being human, even to the extreme of self-destruction. So we are led to ask with increasing urgency whether a primordial falsity may not be hidden in our relation to the world; whether, in our linguistically mediated experience, we may not be prey to prejudices or, worse still, to necessities which have their source in the linguistic structuring of our first experience of the world and which would force us to run with open eyes, as it were, down a path whence there was no other issue than destruction. Slowly this becomes clear: if we continue thus, we can—without, of course, being able to calculate the precise day—predict with certainty the fact that life on this planet will become impossible; predict it with as much certainty as we can predict, from astronomical calculations, our collision with another planet. It is, then, a geniune question of contemporary importance to discover whether it is really because of the baleful influence of language that we find ourselves in our present predicament.

No one will deny that our language influences our thought. We think with words. To think is to think something with oneself; and to think something with oneself is to say something to oneself. Plato was, I believe, quite correct to call the essence of thought the interior dialogue of the soul with itself. This dialogue, in doubt and objection, is a constant going beyond oneself and a return to oneself, one's own opinions and one's own points of view. If anything does characterize human thought, it is this infinite dialogue with ourselves which never leads anywhere definitively and which differentiates us from that ideal of an infinite spirit for which all that exists and all truth lies open in a single moment's vision. It is in this experience of language—in our growing up in the midst of this interior conversation with ourselves, which is always simultaneously the anticipation of conversation with others and the introduction of others into the conversation with ourselves—that the world begins to open up and achieve order in all the domains of experience. But this implies that we know of no other way of ordering and orientation than that which, from the data of experience, leads eventually to those terms of orientation which we name the concept or the universal and for which the concrete is a particular case.

In a brilliant image, Aristotle illustrates this passage from experience to the knowledge of the universal.[1] I refer to the description in which he shows how a unified experience arises from many perceptions and how, from the multiplicity of experiences, there arises something like a consciousness of the universal which endures through the changing aspects of the life of experience. For this he finds an elegant comparison. How does one come to the knowledge of the universal? By the mere fact that experiences accumulate and one recognizes that they are the same? Doubtless; but what does it mean to recognize them "as the same," and when does that become the unity of the universal? It is like an army in flight. Finally one soldier looks back to see how close the enemy are, discovers that they are not as close as all that, stops a moment, and then another stops. The first, the second, the third—these are not yet the whole army and yet, in the end, the whole army regroups. Now the same is true of learning to speak. There is no first word and yet, while learning, we grow into language and into world. Doesn't it follow that everything depends on the way we grow into the pre-schematization of our future orientation to the world when we learn a language and grow into everything we learn by way of conversation? This is the process that is nowadays called "socialization": growth into the social. Of necessity it is likewise growth into conventions, into a social life regulated by conventions, and so language is open to the charge of being an ideology. Just as learning language means constantly practicing modes of expression and arguments, so our formation of convictions and opinions is also a way of introducing us into a set of preformed articulations of meanings. Where is truth in all this? How are we to succeed in making these preformed expressions and phrases into living, fluid speech? How can we attain to that rare feeling of having said fully what we wanted to say?

As for language, so for the rest of living: a world conventionally preformed becomes familiar, and the question is to know whether or not, in our understanding of ourselves, we can ever arrive at that point to which, in those rare cases of perfect speech to which I have just now referred, we think we have come: namely when we really say what we want to say. In other words, do we ever arrive at the point where we understand what really is? These two—total understanding and expression adequate to it—are limit cases of our orientation in the world and of our infinite interior dialogue with ourselves. And yet I want to say, precisely because this dialogue is infinite, because this orientation to things, given in the preformed schemas of discourse, enters into our spontaneous process of coming to an understanding both with one another and with ourselves, there is opened to us the infinity of what we understand in general and what we can make part of our own minds. There are no limits to the interior dialogue of the soul with itself. With this thesis I would oppose the suspicion that language is an ideology.

I want to argue that the act of understanding and speaking has a claim to universality. We can express everything in words and can try to come to agreement about everything. That we are limited by the finitude of our capacities and that only a truly infinite conversation could entirely redeem this claim is of course true. But it is self-evident. The real question is: does not a whole series of opposing arguments arise against the universality of our linguistically mediated experience of the world? There is, for instance, American relativism, derived from Humboldt and given a new lease on life in a new spirit of empirical research, according to which the different languages are so many different images of the world and perspectives on the world, and none can escape that particular image and that particular schematization within which he is imprisoned. Among Nietzsche's aphorisms in the *Will to Power*, there occurs the apt remark that God's truly creative act was the creation of grammar, implying that he initiated us into these schemas of mastery of the world in such a way that we can never get behind them. Is it not the case, therefore, that the dependence of thought on the possibilities of speech and linguistic habits is restrictive? And what fateful meaning lies in the fact that if we look about us, the world is tending to such a global cultural leveling that we no longer speak as a matter of course only about Western philosophy? Hence do we not ponder the insight that the whole of our conceptual philosophical language and its derivative, the conceptual language of modern science, are only one of these perspectives on the world, and indeed in the final analysis of Greek origin? It is the language of metaphysics with whose categories we are familiar from grammar—subject and predicate, nomen and verbum, noun and verb. Today, with our newly awakened global consciousness, we may incline to feel that in such a concept as "verb" there resounds a pre-schematization of our whole European culture. And so, behind all this, there lurks the uneasy question whether, in all our thought, even in the critical dissolution of all metaphysical concepts such as substance, accident, the subject and its properties, and so on, predicative logic included, we are doing anything more than thinking through to its conclusion that which built up the linguistic structure and relation to the world of the Indo-Germanic peoples millennia before any written tradition? We raise this question today just when we are, perhaps, at the end of our linguistic culture—an end slowly advanced by technological civilization and its mathematical symbolisms.

Thus we are not involved in idle suspicions directed against language. We have reached the point where we must ask to what extent everything from this historical moment is predetermined. Even before the game of world history began, did some cast of the dice fatally compel us by means of our language to our way of thinking, and if things continue so, will humankind destroy itself by technology? Against this, one might ask whether this suspicion about ourselves does not artificially put our reason under tutelage. Do we not stand on common ground here and feel certain that we are speaking of something real and that this is no mere gloomy picture painted by a philosopher living in Cloud-cuckooland, if I speak of a self-endangerment of humankind that originated long ago and if I see a fatal coherence in Western history, which Heidegger in particular has taught us to discern? That line of thought will one day be part of the common knowledge of humanity. We see with increasing clarity today—as Heidegger especially has taught us to see—that Greek metaphysics is the beginning of modern technology. Concept formation, born of Western philosophy, has led the will to dominance as the fundamental experience of reality along a lengthy historical path. Even so, do we really mean to say that what we begin to understand in these terms sets up an insurmountable barrier?

A second objection has been developed by Habermas against my own theories. The question is whether the extralinguistic modes of experience are not underestimated when one asserts, as I do, that it is in language that we articulate the experience of the world as something we hold in common. The multiplicity of languages does not affect the issue. This relativity is not one which holds us in unbreakable shackles, as those of us who can think to some extent in a different language know quite well. But are there not other experiences of reality that are non-linguistic? The experience of domination and the experience of work are obvious enough. These are the two arguments that Habermas[2] more or less opposes to hermeneutics' claim to universality, and in doing so he interprets linguistic understanding—why, I do not know—as a sort of immanent movement of meaning within a closed circle, and he calls that the cultural tradition of peoples. Now the cultural tradition of peoples is pre-eminently the heritage of forms and techniques of domination, of ideals of liberty, of objectives of order and the like. Who denies that our specific human possibilities do not subsist solely in language? One would want to admit, instead, that every linguistic experience of the world is experience of the world, not experience of language. And is what we articulate in verbalized disagreements not somehow an encounter with reality? The encounter with domination and unfreedom leads us to develop our political ideas, and it is the world of work—the world of "our capability"—that we experience in mastering techniques of working, which are, we find, ways of discovering our own nature. It would be a false abstraction to say that it was not through and in the concrete experiences of our human existence which we gain in domination and work, and only here, that our human understanding of ourselves, our evaluations, our conversations with ourselves, find their concrete fulfillment and critical function. The fact that we move in a linguistic world and grow up into the world through an experience pre-formed by language does not at all remove the possibilities of critique. On the contrary, the possibility of going beyond our conventions and beyond all those experiences that are schematized in advance opens up before us once we find ourselves, in our conversation with others, faced with opposed thinkers, with new critical tests, with new experiences. Fundamentally in our world the issue is always the same as it was in the beginning: in language we are trained in conventions and social norms behind which there are always economic and hegemonic interests. But this is precisely the world we as humans experience: in it we rely on our faculty of judgment, that is, on the possibility of our taking a critical stance with regard to every convention. In reality, we owe this to the linguistic virtuality of our reason. Now it is certainly the case that our experience of the world does not take place only in learning and using a language. There is a prelinguistic experience of the world, as Habermas, referring to Piaget's research, reminds us. The language of gesture, facial expression, and movement binds us to each other. There are laughter and tears (Helmut Plessner has worked out a hermeneutics of these). There is the world of science within which the exact, specialized languages of symbolism and mathematics provide sure foundations for the elaboration of theory, languages which have brought with them a capacity for construction and manipulation which seems a kind of self-representation of homo faber, of man's technical ingenuity. But even these forms of self-representation must constantly be taken up in the interior dialogue of the soul with itself.

I acknowledge that these phenomena demonstrate that behind all the relativities of language and convention there is something in common which is no longer language, but which looks to an ever-possible verbalization, and for which the well-tried word "reason" is, perhaps, not the worst. Nevertheless, there remains something that characterizes language as such, and that is precisely the fact that language as language can be contrasted with every other act of communication. We call this difference writing and graphic transcription. The persuasive speech which binds one man with another or even with himself in so intuitive and living a way that they seem inseparable from one another can nevertheless take on the rigid form of written relations. These latter can be deciphered and read and raised into a new enactment of meaning, indeed so much so that our whole world is more or less—although perhaps not for much longer—a literary one, that is, one administered by means of writing and transcription. Setting aside for the moment all the differences within transcription, I would say that everything in writing, to be understood, requires something like a kind of heightening for the inner ear. This is obviously true for poetry and the like, but for philosophy too I take care to tell my students: you must sharpen your ear, you must realize that when you take a word in your mouth, you have not taken up some arbitrary tool which can be thrown in a corner if it doesn't do the job, but you are committed to a line of thought that comes from afar and reaches on beyond you. What we do is always a kind of changing back, which I want to call in a very wide sense "translation." Think a moment what it means to "translate"—i.e., to transpose a dead thing in a new act of understanding that "reads" it, or even to transpose into our own or another language what was recorded only in a foreign language and given as a text.

The translation process fundamentally contains the whole secret of how human beings come to an understanding of the world and communicate with each other. Translation is an indissoluble unity of implicit acts of anticipating, of grasping meaning as a whole beforehand, and explicitly laying down what was thus grasped in advance. All speaking has something of this kind of laying hold in advance and laying down. Heinrich von Kleist's fine essay "On the Progressive Elaboration of Thoughts in Discourse" describes his experiences in Berlin at the time of his licentiate examination. (I think every examiner should be asked to swear that he has read this essay!) At that time these examinations were public but were attended—then as now—only by those whose turn was yet to come. Kleist describes how the examination runs, how the professor asks a question out of the blue, and how the candidate has to answer on the spot. Yet, as we all know, only fools can answer questions whose answers everybody knows. A question must be posed—i.e., it contains an opening for a possible answer. Computers and parrots can give the "right" answer much quicker. Kleist has a good phrase to describe this experience: the balance wheel of thoughts must be set in motion. In speaking, one word brings forth another, and hence our thinking gets promulgated. A word becomes real when it proffers itself in our speaking on its own out of however thoroughly pre-schematized a thesaurus and customary usage. We speak that word and it leads to consequences and ends we had not perhaps conceived of. The background of the universality of this linguistic access to the world is that our recognition of the world—to use an analogy—does not present itself to us as an infinite text which we painfully and piecemeal learn to recite. The word "recite" should make us realize that speaking is something quite different. Reciting is the opposite of speaking. When we recite, we already know what is coming, and the possible advantage of a sudden inspiration is precluded. All of us have had the experience of listening to a bad actor and getting the impression that he was already thinking of the next word. That is not speaking. Speaking is only speaking if we accept the risk of positing something and following out its implications. To sum up, I would say that the misunderstanding in the question of the linguisticality of our understanding is really one about language—i.e., seeing language as a stock of words and phrases, of concepts, viewpoints and opinions. In fact, language is the single word, whose virtuality opens for us the infinity of discourse, of speaking with one another, of the freedom of "expressing oneself" and "letting oneself be expressed." Language is not its elaborated conventionalism, nor the burden of pre-schematization with which it loads us, but the generative and creative power to unceasingly make this whole once again fluent.

Notes

1 [*Posterior Analytics*, II, 19, 100 a 3ff.]
2 [Jürgen Habermas, "The Hermeneutic Claim to Universality," tr. Josef Bleicher, in Josef Bleicher, *Contemporary Hermeneutics: Hermeneutics as Method, Philosophy and Critique* (London: Routledge and Kegan Paul, 1980), pp. 181–211, and my "The Universality of the Hermeneutical Problem," in *Philosophical Hermeneutics*, tr. David E. Linge (Berkeley: University of California Press, 1976), pp. 3–17.]

Afterword

When I finished the present book at the end of 1959, I wondered whether it had not come "too late"—that is, whether its attempt to reassess the value of traditional and historical thought was not by then almost superfluous. Signs of a new wave of technological animosity to history were increasing. Correlatively, increased receptiveness toward Anglo-American theory of science and analytic philosophy, and finally the fresh impetus which the social sciences, particularly social psychology and sociolinguistics, were receiving offered no hope for the humanistic tradition of the romantic Geisteswissenschaften. But that was precisely the tradition from which I set out. It represented the experiential ground of my theoretical work—though not at all its limit or even its goal. But even the classical historical Geisteswissenschaften were undergoing a reorientation toward the new statistical and formal methods, so that the pressure toward scientific planning and the technical organization of research was unmistakable. A new "positivistic" self-conception was emerging, fostered by the acceptance of Anglo-American methods and modes of inquiry.

It was, of course, a flat misunderstanding when people accused the expression "truth and method" of failing to recognize the methodical rigor of modern science. What hermeneutics legitimates is something completely different, and it stands in no tension whatever with the strictest ethos of science. No productive scientist can really doubt that methodical purity is indispensable in science; but what constitutes the essence of research is much less merely applying the usual methods than discovering new ones—and underlying that, the creative imagination of the scientist. This is not true only in the so-called Geisteswissenschaften.

Moreover, the hermeneutical reflection undertaken in *Truth and Method* is just the opposite of mere conceptual play. It has grown everywhere out of the concrete practice of the sciences for which methodological considerations such as controllable procedure and falsifiability are taken to be self-evident. Further, such hermeneutical reflection has manifested itself everywhere in the practice of science. To situate my work within the philosophy of this century, it must be kept in mind that I have endeavored to mediate between philosophy and the sciences; and I have especially tried to extend the radical questioning of Martin Heidegger (to whom I am indebted for the decisive matters) over the broad expanse of scientific experience, as far as I am able to survey it. That, of course, necessitated transcending the restricted horizon of scientific theory and its methodology. But can it be held against a philosophical approach that it does not consider scientific research as an end in itself but, rather, thematizes the conditions and limits of science within the whole of human life? In a time when science penetrates further and further into social practice, science can fulfill its social function only when it acknowledges its own limits and the conditions placed on its freedom to maneuver. Philosophy must make this clear to an age credulous about science to the point of superstition. On just this depends the fact that the tension between truth and method has an inescapable currency.

Thus philosophical hermeneutics participates in a philosophical movement of our century that overcame the one-sided orientation toward the scientific fact, taken for granted by neo-Kantianism as well as by the positivism of that time. Hermeneutics also has relevance to theory of science in that hermeneutic reflection discloses conditions of truth in the sciences that do not derive from the logic of scientific discovery but are prior to it. This is especially, though not exclusively, true in the so-called Geisteswissenschaften, whose English equivalent, "moral sciences," already indicates that these sciences make their object into something that necessarily belongs to the knower himself.

Perhaps this ultimately pertains to the "real" sciences as well. Still, to me some distinctions seem necessary here. If in modern microphysics the observer cannot be eliminated from the results of measurement and must appear in its reports, this has a precisely determinable sense that can be formulated mathematically. If in modern behavioral science the researcher discovers structures that determine his own behavior on the basis of phylogenetic heritage, then perhaps he learns something about himself, but precisely because he looks at himself with eyes other than those of his "practice" and his self-consciousness; and to that extent he succumbs to neither overglorifying nor depreciating mankind. If, by contrast, every historian's own standpoint is always discernible in his findings and valuations, then this discovery implies no criticism of his claim to be scientific. It says nothing about whether the historian has erred by being bound to a standpoint and has misunderstood or misprized tradition or whether, thanks to the advantage of his standpoint, he succeeded in putting something hitherto unobserved in its proper light because of its similarity to something observable in immediate contemporary experience. Here we are in the middle of a hermeneutic problematic—but this scarcely implies that there are no scientific methods whereby to distinguish the true from the false, to avoid error, or to reach truth. In the "moral" sciences this is not a whit different from the "real" sciences.

The same holds for the empirical social sciences. Here it is apparent that a "fore-understanding" guides their inquiry. They are concerned with a highly developed social system which accepts the validity of norms that cannot be scientifically demonstrated but that have developed historically. They present not only the object but also the sphere of empirical rationality within which methodical work takes place. For the most part research gets its topics of inquiry from disturbances in the existing social system or through ideological critique, which opposes existing structures of domination. Undoubtedly, here too scientific research leads to a corresponding scientific management of the local systems that are its subject matter; but just as undeniable is that the social sciences are tempted to extrapolate their results to more complex systems. Succumbing to such temptation is all too easy. However uncertain are the factual bases on which rational management of social life might be possible, a will to believe impels the social sciences onward and drives them far beyond their limits. Perhaps we can clarify this by considering the classic paradigm that J. S. Mill proposes for the application of inductive logic to the social sciences, namely that of meteorology. It is not just the fact that long-range forecasts valid for large areas have gained very little in certainty through the modern means of data collection and analysis; even if we had complete control of atmospheric events—or, better, since we basically have this dominion already, if data collection and analysis were enormously increased, and more reliable forecasts thereby made possible—at that point new complications would arise. It belongs to the very nature of the scientific management of processes that they can be made to serve any of several purposes. That is, there would arise the problem of influencing the weather, and with it would ensue a struggle among socio-economic interests (of which the current state of prognostics has given us only a little foretaste: the occasional attempt by interested parties to influence the weekend forecast). Transferred to the social sciences, the "manageability" of social processes necessarily leads to a "consciousness" of the social engineer that tries to be scientific and yet can never completely deny its share in the social partnership. Here lies a special complication that derives from the social function of the empirical social sciences: on the one hand is the tendency to extrapolate the results of empirical and rational research to complex situations too quickly merely in order to plan things scientifically; on the other hand are the pressures which the social partners exert on science in order to influence the social process as they see fit.

The absoluteness of the ideal of "science" in fact exercises a powerful fascination, and it repeatedly leads people to believe that hermeneutic reflection is completely without an object. The narrowing of perspective that results from concentrating on method is almost imperceptible to the scientist. He is always already oriented toward the methodological correctness of his procedure—but also, conversely, away from reflection. Even when, by defending his methodology, he acts in a genuinely reflective manner, he does not allow this reflection itself to be consciously thematized. A philosophy of the sciences that understands itself as a theory of scientific method and dismisses any inquiry that cannot be meaningfully characterized as a process of trial and error does not recognize that by this very criterion it is itself outside science.

It is in the nature of the case, then, that the dialogue between philosophy and philosophy of the sciences never really succeeds. The Adorno-Popper debate, like that between Habermas and Albert, shows this all too clearly.[1] By raising "critical rationality" to the status of an absolute measure of truth, empirical theory of science regards hermeneutic reflection as theological obscurantism.[2]

Fortunately, there can be agreement about the fact that there is only one "logic of scientific investigation"—but also that it is not sufficient, since at any given time the viewpoints that select the relevant topics of inquiry and foreground them as subjects of research cannot themselves be derived from the logic of investigation. What is remarkable is that, for the sake of rationality, theory of science here abandons itself to complete irrationality and considers philosophical reflection on certain aspects of practical cognition to be illegitimate; it even charges the philosophy that does so with immunizing its contentions against experience. It fails to recognize that it is itself complicit with a much more fatal immunization against experience—for example, against that of common sense and the experience one gains in living. It always does so when it promotes the uncritical expansion of scientific management beyond specific contexts—for example, when it assigns responsibility for political decisions to experts. The contention between Popper and Adorno still has something unsatisfying about it, even after Habermas analyzed it. I agree with Habermas that a hermeneutic fore-understanding is always in play and that it therefore requires reflexive enlightenment. But that is as far as I go with "critical rationality" because I consider perfect enlightenment illusory.

Given this situation, two points need to be re-emphasized: What is the significance of hermeneutic reflection for the methodology of the sciences? and, How does the duty to think critically bear on the fact that understanding is determined by tradition?

In my work, heightening the tension between truth and method had a polemical intent. Ultimately, as Descartes himself realized, it belongs to the special structure of straightening something crooked that it needs to be bent in the opposite direction. But what was crooked in this case was not so much the methodology of the sciences as their reflexive self-consciousness. The post-Hegelian historiology and hermeneutics which I have described show this, I think, clearly enough. It is a naive misunderstanding (furthered by Betti's adherents[3]) to fear that the hermeneutic reflection I practice will mean a weakening of scientific objectivity. Here Apel, Habermas,[4] and the representatives of "critical rationality" are in my opinion equally blind. They all mistake the reflective claim of my analyses and thereby also the meaning of application which, as I have tried to show, is essential to the structure of all understanding. They are so caught up in the methodologism of theory of science that all they can think about is rules and their application. They fail to recognize that reflection about practice is not methodology.

The subject of my reflection is the procedure of the sciences themselves and the restriction of objectivity that is to be discerned (and not at all commended) in them. It seems to me that nothing less than scientific integrity, to which the philosopher must be accountable, demands that we acknowledge the productive meaning of such restrictions—in the form of productive prejudices, for example. How can a philosophy that makes this conscious be accused of encouraging people to proceed uncritically and subjectively in science! To me that seems just as nonsensical as expecting mathematical logic, conversely, to advance logical thinking, or expecting the scientific theory of critical rationalism that calls itself "logic of scientific investigation" to advance scientific research. Rather, theoretical logic and philosophy of science satisfy a philosophical demand for legitimation; they remain secondary to scientific practice. Despite all the differences between the natural sciences and the Geisteswissenschaften, there is really no disagreement between them about the immanent validity of critical methodology in the sciences. Even the most extreme critical rationalist will not deny that, prior to the application of scientific methodology, there are determining factors pertaining to choice of topics and modes of inquiry.

The final confusion that dominates methodology of the sciences is, I think, the degeneration of the concept of practice. This concept lost its legitimacy in the age of science with its ideal of certainty. For since science views its purpose as isolating the causes of events—natural and historical—it is acquainted with practice only as the application of science. But that is a "practice" that requires no special account. Thus the concept of technology displaced that of practice; in other words, the competence of experts has marginalized political reason.

As we can see, it is not only the role of hermeneutics in the sciences that is in question here but also mankind's understanding of itself in the modern age of science. One of the most important lessons the history of philosophy offers for this current problem consists in the role played in Aristotelian ethics and politics by practice and the knowledge that enlightens and leads it, the practical acuteness or wisdom that Aristotle called phronesis. The sixth book of the *Nichomachean Ethics* remains the best introduction to this buried problematic. On this topic I can point to a more recent essay, "Hermeneutics and Practical Philosophy," my contribution to the collection *Zur Rehabilitierung der praktischen Philosophie*, edited by M. Riedel.[5] Philosophically regarded, what emerges from the background of the great tradition of practical (and political) philosophy reaching from Aristotle to the turn of the nineteenth century is that practice represents an independent contribution to knowledge. Here the concrete particular proves to be not only the starting point but also a continuing determination of the content of the universal.

We are acquainted with this problem in the form Kant gave it in the *Critique of Judgment*. There he differentiates between determinative judgment, which subsumes the particular under a given universal, and reflective judgment, which seeks a universal concept for a given particular. Now Hegel, I think, has rightly shown that to separate these two functions of judgment is a mere abstraction, and that judgment is really always both. The universal under which the particular is subsumed continues to determine itself through the particular. Thus the legal meaning of a law is determined through adjudication, and fundamentally the universality of the law is determined through the concreteness of the case. For this reason, as is well known, Aristotle has even gone so far as to claim that the Platonic idea of the good is vacuous, and rightly so, if we really have to think of the good as a being of the highest universality.[6]

Relying on the tradition of practical philosophy helps guard us against the technological self-understanding of the modern concept of science. But that does not exhaust the philosophical intention of my endeavors. In the hermeneutic dialogue in which we stand, I would like to see more attention given to this philosophical intention. The concept of play, which I wrested decades ago from the subjective sphere of the "play impulse" (Schiller) and which I employed to critique "aesthetic differentiation," involves an ontological problem. For this concept unites event and understanding in their interplay, and also the language games of our world experience in general, as Wittgenstein has thematized them in order to criticize metaphysics. My inquiry can appear as an "ontologization" of language only when the presupposition of the instrumentalization of language is left completely unexamined. Hermeneutic experience in fact poses a problem of philosophy for us: to disclose the ontological implications involved in the "technical" concept of science and to bring about theoretical recognition of hermeneutic experience. Philosophical dialogue must proceed in this direction in order to renew not Platonism but a dialogue with Plato that inquires behind the ossified concepts of metaphysics and their unacknowledged continuance. Whitehead's "footnotes to Plato" could become important in this respect, as Wiehl has rightly recognized (see his introduction to the German edition of Whitehead's *Adventures of Ideas*). In any case, my intent was to connect philosophical hermeneutics with the Platonic—not the Hegelian—dialectic. The title of the third volume of my *Kleine Schriften* indicates what that means: *Idea and Language*. Modern study of language deserves respect, but the technical self-understanding of modern science prevents it from perceiving the hermeneutic dimension and the philosophical task involved in it.

Through the breadth of its contributions, *Hermeneutics and Dialectics*, the collection dedicated to me, gives a good indication of the range of philosophical problems that hermeneutic inquiry comprehends. In the meantime, however, philosophical hermeneutics has also become a partner in a continuing dialogue with the several branches of hermeneutic methodology.

Discussion about hermeneutics has spread primarily to four branches of science: juridical hermeneutics, theological hermeneutics, literary theory, and logic of the social sciences. Within this body of literature, which is slowly becoming vast, I can mention only a few works that take up an explicit position with regard to my own contribution. In juridical hermeneutics:

Franz Wieacker in "Das Problem der Interpretation," (*Mainzer Universitätsgespräche*, pp. 5ff.)

Fritz Rittner in "Verstehen und Auslegen," *Freiburger Dies Universitatis*, 14 (1967).

Joseph Esser in *Vorverständnis und Methode in der Rechtsfindung* (1970).

Joachim Hruschka, "Das Verstehen von Rechtstexten," *Münchener Universitätsschriften, Reihe der juristischen Fakultät*, 22 (1972).

In the realm of theological hermeneutics I should name, in addition to those mentioned above, the recent contributions of:

Günter Stachel, *Die neue Hermeneutik* (1967).

Ernst Fuchs, *Marburger Hermeneutik* (1968).

Eugen Biser, *Theologische Sprachtheorie und Hermeneutik* (1970).

Gerhard Ebeling, *Einführung in die theologische Sprachlehre* (1971).

In theory of literature, among Betti's foremost successors is Hirsch's *Validity in Interpretation*, and a whole series of other attempts to emphasize the methodical element in theory of interpretation. See for example, S. W. Schmied-Kowarzik, "Geschichtswissenschaft und Geschichtlichkeit" in *Wiener Zeitscrift für Philosophie, Psychologie, Pädagogik* 8 (1966), pp. 133ff.; D. Benner, "Zur Fragestellung einer Wissenschaftstheorie der Historie," in *Wiener Jahrbuch für Philosophie*, 2 (1969), pp. 52 ff. A fine analysis of what method means in the process of interpretation I found recently in Thomas Seebohm, *Zur Kritik der hermeneutischen Vernunft* (1972); to be sure, he evades the claim of philosophical hermeneutics when he foists on it a speculative concept of a given totality.

Other contributions: H. Robert Jauss, "Literaturgeschichte als Provocation" (1970); Leo Pollmann, "Theorie der Literatur" (1971); and Harth, *Philologie und praktische Philosophie* (1970).

J. Habermas, above all, has offered a critical evaluation of the significance of hermeneutics in the social sciences. See his report *Logik der Sozialwissenschaften* in the supplement to the *Philosophische Rundschau*, and the collection *Hermeneutik und Ideologiekritik* in the Suhrkamp series on "Theory."

Also important is the number of *Continuum* in which Frankfurt critical theory is confronted with hermeneutics. A good overview of the problem in the historical sciences is contained in Karl-Friedrich Gründer's lecture before the 1970 congress of historians (Saeculum).

But back to theory of science. The problem of relevance certainly cannot be limited to the Geisteswissenschaften. In the natural sciences too what are called facts are not arbitrary measurements but measurements that represent an answer to a question, a confirmation or refutation of a hypothesis. So also an experiment to measure certain quantities is not legitimated by the fact that these measurements are made with utmost exactitude, according to all the rules. It achieves legitimacy only through the context of research. Thus all science involves a hermeneutic component. Just as in the realm of history a question or fact cannot be considered in isolation, so also the same is true in the realm of natural science. But this scarcely means that the rationality of its procedure, insofar as such is possible, would be thereby curtailed. The paradigm of "posing and testing hypotheses" pertains to all research, in the historical sciences too, and even in philology; and it always presents the danger that the rationality of procedure will be taken for a sufficient legitimation of the significance of what is "known" through it.

But when one comes to acknowledge the problematic of relevance, the notion of value-free inquiry developed by Max Weber must be surpassed. The blind decisionism concerning ultimate ends that Max Weber propagated is unsatisfactory. Here methodological rationalism ends in crude irrationalism. To connect it to so-called philosophy of existence mistakes the matter entirely. The opposite is true. What Jaspers had in mind with the concept of existential elucidation was, rather, precisely to subject ultimate decisions to rational elucidation—otherwise he could not have considered "reason and existence" inseparable—and Heidegger drew a still more radical conclusion when he clarified the ontological difficulty in differentiating value and fact, and dissolved the dogmatic concept of "fact." Still, the question of value plays no role in the natural sciences. The special context of their research, as I have mentioned, is subordinate to hermeneutically clarifiable contexts. But they do not thereby overstep the limits of their methodological competence. In at most a single point does something analogous come into question—namely whether scientific inquiry really is completely independent of the language world in which the scientist lives as a scientist, and in particular whether it is independent of the linguistic world schema of his own mother tongue.[7] But in another sense hermeneutics comes into play here too. Even if the language of science could be regularized so that all the overtones of the mother tongue were filtered out, there would always remain the problem of "translating" scientific knowledge into common language, which is the only way the natural sciences acquire their communicative universality and thereby their social relevance. Yet that consideration would not pertain to research as such; rather, it would only indicate that research is not "autonomous" but instead takes place in a social context. The same holds true for all sciences. One need not ascribe a special autonomy to the "interpretive" sciences, and yet we cannot overlook the fact that in them prescientific knowledge plays a much greater role. Of course one can gratify oneself by denigrating all such knowledge in these sciences as "unscientific" and untested.[8] But it is just this that must be recognized as constituting these sciences. One must face the objection, then, that what constitutes the special nature of these sciences is precisely the prescientific knowledge which is considered the sad vestige of unscientificity; and in any case it much more fully determines the practical and social life of mankind—including the fundamental conditions for the practice of science—than the increasing rationalization of human life can achieve or even want to achieve. For do we really want to entrust the decisive questions of social and political, as well as private and personal, life to an expert? For the application of his science, even the expert would employ not his science but rather his practical reason. And why should that be greater in an expert, even if he were the ideal social engineer, than in other people?

Thus it seems to me really revealing when people mock the hermeneutic sciences by harping on the accusation that they want to restore the qualitative worldview of Aristotle.[9] We can disregard the fact that modern science does not always apply quantitative procedures—for example, in the morphological disciplines. But I can appeal to the fact that the fore-knowledge stemming from the way language orients us in the world (which was in fact the basis of the so-called "science" of Aristotle) comes into play wherever the experience of life is assimilated, linguistic tradition is understood, and social life goes on. Such fore-knowledge is certainly no higher court where science is tried; it is itself exposed to every critical objection that science raises, but it is and remains the vehicle of all understanding. Thus it leaves its impress on the methodological unique-ness of the interpretive sciences. They manifestly present the task of delimiting the formation of technical terminologies and, instead of building special languages, they cultivate the ways common language is spoken.[10]

Here, perhaps, I can introduce the "Logical Propaedeutic" of Kamlah and Lorenzen,[11] which demands of philosophers the methodical definition of all concepts meant to be used in scientifically verifiable statements; but even the "Logical Propaedeutic" is not exempt from the hermeneutic circle of presupposed linguistic fore-knowledge and the need to purify linguistic usage critically. There can be no objecting to the ideal of such a scientific language, for it has undoubtedly clarified many disciplines, especially logic and theory of science; and insofar as it promotes responsible expression, no limits can be imposed on it in the field of philosophy either. What Hegel's *Logic* undertook, in the name of philosophy comprehending all science, is just what Lorenzen is seeking in reflecting on "research" and in renewing the attempt to justify it logically. This is certainly a legitimate task. But I would like to defend the idea that the knowledge and fore-knowledge that derive from the interpretation of the world sedimented in language would retain their legitimacy even if one imagined a perfected scientific language —and the same holds for "philosophy" as well. Against the historical elucidation of concepts that I advocate in my book and practice as well as I can, Kamlah and Lorenzen object that the court of tradition can pronounce no sure and unequivocal verdict. Indeed not. But to be responsible before that court—that is, not to invent a language commensurate with new insights but rather to retrieve it from living language —seems to me a legitimate demand. Philosophy can fulfill it only when the path from word to concept and from concept to word is kept open in both directions. It seems to me that, in defense of their own procedure, even Kamlah and Lorenzen appeal to the authority of linguistic usage. Of course it yields no methodical construction of a language through the gradual instauration of concepts. But making the implications of conceptual words conscious is a method too—and, I think, one commensurate with the subject matter of philosophy. For the subject of philosophy is not limited to the reflexive clarification of scientific procedure. It does not consist in "summing up" the multiple facets of modern knowledge and rounding them out into a whole "worldview." It does pertain to the whole of our experience of life and our world, but like no other science—rather like our very experience, articulated in language, of life and the world. I hardly want to assert that the knowledge of this totality is certain or that it does not need to be thoughtfully submitted to constant critique. But still, one cannot ignore such "knowledge," in whatever form it expresses itself: in religious or proverbial wisdom, in works of art or philosophical thought. Even Hegel's dialectic—I do not mean its schematization into a method of philosophical proof, but the experience basic to it of the "reversal" of concepts which claim to comprehend the whole in their opposite[12]—belongs to these forms of inner self-enlightenment and to the intersubjective representation of human experience. In my book I made vague use of Hegel's vague model, and can now refer to a recent publication, *Hegel's Dialectic: Five Hermeneutical Studies* (Tübingen, 1971), which contains a more precise exposition but also a certain justification for that vagueness.

It has often been objected that the language of my investigations is too inexact. In this I see not only the disclosure of a deficiency—which may exist often enough. I still think it appropriate to admit that the conceptual language of philosophy cannot be extricated from the whole of the language world and that, even at the expense of delimiting concepts precisely, its living relation to the whole must be preserved. That is the positive implication of the "indigence of language" inherent in philosophy from its beginnings. At very special moments and under very special circumstances that are not to be found in Plato or Aristotle, Meister Eckart or Nicholas of Cusa, Fichte or Hegel, but perhaps in Aquinas, Hume, and Kant, this linguistic indigence is concealed under the smooth surface of a conceptual system, and it emerges only—but then of necessity—when we thoughtfully follow the movement of thought. On this topic I refer to my Düsseldorf lecture, "History of Ideas and the Language of Philosophy."[13] The expressions used in philosophical language and sharpened to conceptual precision always convey meaning in certain respects like an "object language" and therefore remain somewhat inappropriate. But the context of significance that resounds in every word of living language likewise enters into the semantic potential of the conceptual word. That is unavoidable whenever the common expressions for concepts are used. But it is without consequence for the formation of concepts in the natural sciences, for in them experiment regulates conceptual usage, and thus commits them to the ideal of unambiguousness and pre-arranges the logical content of statements.

The situation is different in philosophy and wherever the pre-scientific knowledge that comes to us from language enters into cognition. There, language has a different function than the maximally univocal designation of the data (Gegebenem); it is "self-giving" (selbstgebend) and brings its own gift (Selbstgabe) into the communication. In the hermeneutic sciences, a verbal formulation does not merely refer to something that could be verified in other ways; instead it makes something visible in the how of its meaningfulness. The special demand placed on verbal expression and concept formation consists in the fact that they must also indicate the context of understanding in which the subject matter means something. Thus the connotations of an expression do not muddy its intelligibility (because they do not indicate what is meant unequivocally) but increase it insofar as the intended context as a whole gains in intelligibility. It is a *whole* that is constructed by words here, and it can be given in words alone.

This is traditionally regarded as a mere question of style, and such phenomena are consigned to the realm of rhetoric, which is concerned with persuading by means of exciting the feelings. Or one begins with modern aesthetic concepts. Then "self-giving" appears to be an aesthetic quality that derives from the metaphorical nature of language. One would rather not admit that a cognitive moment is involved in it. But to me the dichotomy between "logical" and "aesthetic" seems questionable when real speaking is at issue, instead of the logical construction of an ortholanguage such as Lorenzen proposes. It is, I think, a no less logical task to acknowledge the interaction between all elements of special languages, artificial expressions, and ordinary language. That is the hermeneutic task: as it were, the other pole that determines the appropriateness of words.

This leads me to the history of hermeneutics. I reviewed this history in my work essentially for the preparatory purpose of filling in the background. Consequently, my presentation displays a certain one-sidedness. That is already true of Schleiermacher. His lecture on hermeneutics, as we read it in Lücke's edition of the works, but also in the original materials that H. Kimmerle has edited in the Proceedings of the Heidelberg Academy of Sciences (and has since completed in a careful critical supplement[14]), and in his Academy lectures, which engage in an incidental polemic with Wolf and Ast—none of these are comparable in theoretical importance for philosophical hermeneutics to what is contained in Schleiermacher's lecture on dialectic, especially its discussion of the connection between thought and speaking.[15]

But we have since acquired new materials from the pen of Dilthey that present Schleiermacher's philosophy and sketch its contemporary background in Fichte, Novalis, and Schlegel in an especially masterly way. We are obliged to M. Redeker for gathering a second volume of Dilthey's *Life of Schleiermacher* from the posthumous manuscripts in a careful critical edition.[16] In it appears the first publication of Dilthey's famous and til now not widely known presentation of the prehistory of hermeneutics in the seventeenth and eighteenth centuries, which the well-known Academy Proceedings of 1900 only summarized. By its thorough source studies, broad historical horizon, and detailed presentation, it overshadows all others, not only my own modest labors[17] but also the well-known standard work of Joachim Wach.[18]

Recently it has become possible for us to learn about the earlier history of hermeneutics in still another way, through Lutz Geldsetzer's series of hermeneutical reprints.[19] Apart from Meier, there are important theoretical excerpts from Flacius and the elegant Thibaut, which have now been made conveniently accessible; others—for example, Chladenius, to whom I have given close attention—have since been included. Geldsetzer has supplemented these reprints with very careful, astonishingly erudite introductions. Of course, Dilthey and Geldsetzer's introductions accent somewhat different things than I did on the basis of important examples, especially Spinoza and Chladenius.

The same is true of new works about Schleiermacher, especially the contributions of H. Kimmerle, H. Patsch,[20] and the book by G. Vattimo.[21] Perhaps I overemphasized Schleiermacher's tendency toward psychological (technical) interpretation rather than grammatical-linguistic interpretation.[22] Nevertheless, that is his peculiar contribution, and so his school was based on psychological interpretation. This could be demonstrated beyond doubt by reference to the examples of Hermann Steinthal and Dilthey's emulation of Schleiermacher.

The theoretical intent of my inquiry determined the important place Dilthey occupies in it and my marked emphasis on his ambivalent attitude to the inductive logic of the century on the one hand and to the romantic-idealistic heritage on the other, which for the late Dilthey included not only Schleiermacher but the young Hegel. Newer emphases are noteworthy in this regard. With the opposite aim, Peter Krausser[23] has explored Dilthey's extensive scientific interests and has illustrated them in part from posthumous material. Of course, to emphasize these interests would occur only to a generation that came to know Dilthey exclusively through his late currency during the 1920s. For those who initially thematized Dilthey's interest in historicity and in placing the Geisteswissenschaften on a theoretical basis of their own—e.g., for Misch, Groethuysen, Spranger, and also Jaspers and Heidegger—it was always self-evident that Dilthey was deeply interested in the natural sciences of his time, especially anthropology and psychology. Now Krausser develops Dilthey's theory of structure by means of an almost cybernetic analysis, so that the Geisteswissenschaften are completely modeled on the natural sciences —though of course on the basis of such vague data that any cyberneticist would have to cross himself.

Rather than to the later Dilthey, M. Riedel stays closer to Dilthey's critique of historical reason, especially as it can be documented from the Breslau period, though he presents Dilthey's late work in his reprint of "The Construction of the Historical World in the Geisteswissenschaften."[24] He emphasizes the critical aspect of Dilthey's social interests and locates Dilthey's real relevance so exclusively in his inquiry into theory of science that to him the irrationalism imputed to Dilthey as the champion of life philosophy seems a mere misunderstanding. It was in precisely the opposite sense that I articulated the ambivalence in Dilthey's position, his indecision between theory of science and life philosophy: in this author's view emancipatory reflection remains not only the strongest and most profound but also, strangely, the most productive impulse in Dilthey.[25]

But the weightiest objection against my outline of a philosophical hermeneutics is that I have allegedly derived the fundamental significance of agreement from the language dependence of all understanding and all coming to an understanding, and thereby have legitimated a prejudice in favor of existing social relations. Now, that is in fact right, and in my view it remains a real insight: namely that coming to an understanding can only succeed on the basis of an original agreement, and that the task of understanding and interpretation cannot be described as if hermeneutics had to overcome the opaque unintelligibility of the transmitted text or even primarily the errors of misunderstanding. To me such a description seems inaccurate with regard both to the occasional hermeneutics of the early period, which did not reflect on its other presuppositions, and to Schleiermacher and the romantic break with tradition, for which mis-understanding is fundamental to all understanding. All coming to under-standing in language presupposes agreement not just about the meanings of words and the rules of spoken language; much remains undisputed with regard to the "subject matter" as well—i.e., to everything that can be meaningfully discussed. My insistence on this point is taken to demon-strate a conservative tendency and to deter hermeneutic reflection from its proper—critical and emancipatory—task.

Clearly an essential issue is at stake here. Discussion of it has been conducted primarily between Habermas as the developer of "critical theory" on the one side and me on the other.[26] On both sides it is agreed that ultimate, scarcely examined presuppositions come into play—though on the one side there is also the faith in "unconstrained dialogue," the ideal of Habermas and many others who follow the old Enlightenment slogan: to dissolve obsolete prejudices and overcome social privileges through thought and reflection. In this context Habermas makes the fundamental supposition of a "contrafactual agreement." On my side, by contrast, there is a deep skepticism about the fantastic overestimation of reason by comparison to the affections that motivate the human mind. When I considered the conflict between hermeneutics and ideology together with the powerful role played by rhetoric, this was no literary accident but instead a well-considered sketch of a thematic whole. Marx, Mao, and Marcuse—whose names are inscribed together on many walls these days—certainly do not have "unconstrained dialogue" to thank for their popularity.

What distinguishes the process of refining hermeneutic practice from acquiring a mere technique, whether it is called social technology or critical method, is that in hermeneutics history co-determines the consciousness of the person who understands. Therein lies an essential reversal: what is understood always develops a certain power of convincing that helps form new convictions. I do not at all deny that if one wants to understand, one must endeavor to distance oneself from one's own opinions on the matter. Whoever wants to understand does not need to affirm what he understands. Still, I think that hermeneutic experience teaches us that the effort to do so succeeds only to a limited extent. Rather, what one understands always speaks for itself as well. On this depends the whole richness of the hermeneutic universe, which includes everything intelligible. Since it brings this whole breadth into play, it forces the interpreter to play with his own prejudices at stake. These are the winnings of reflection that accrue from practice, and practice alone. The philologist's world of experience and his "Being-toward-the-text" that I have foregrounded are only an example and field of illustration for the hermeneutic experience that is woven into the whole of human practice. Within it, clearly, understanding what is written is especially important, but writing is only a late and therefore secondary phenomenon. In truth hermeneutic experience extends as far as does reasonable beings' openness to dialogue.

I would like to see more recognition of the fact that this is the realm hermeneutics shares with rhetoric: the realm of arguments that are convincing (which is not the same as logically compelling). It is the realm of practice and humanity in general, and its province is not where the power of "iron-clad conclusions" must be accepted without discussion, nor where emancipatory reflection is certain of its "contrafactual agreements," but rather where controversial issues are decided by reasonable considera- tion. The arts of rhetoric and argumentation (and their silent analogue, thoughtful deliberation with oneself) are at home here. If rhetoric appeals to the feelings, as has long been clear, that in no way means it falls outside the realm of the reasonable. Vico rightly assigns it a special value: copia, the abundance of viewpoints. I find it frighteningly unreal when people like Habermas ascribe to rhetoric a compulsory quality that one must reject in favor of unconstrained, rational dialogue. This is to underestimate not only the danger of the glib manipulation and incapacitation of reason but also the possibility of coming to an understanding through persuasion, on which social life depends. Even the scientific culture of our time can illustrate this. To the practice of human understanding it has assigned the increasingly mountainous task of integrating the particular realm that science dominates at any given time into the practice of social reason: the modern mass media enter in here.

Only a narrow view of rhetoric sees it as mere technique or even a mere instrument for social manipulation. It is in truth an essential aspect of all reasonable behavior. Aristotle had already called rhetoric not a *techne* but a *dunamis* because it belongs so essentially to the general definition of humans as reasonable beings. However extensive their effects and how- ever broad their manipulation, the institutionalized means of forming public opinion which our industrial society has developed in no way exhaust the realm of reasonable argumentation and critical reflection that social practice occupies.[27]

Recognizing this situation, of course, presupposes the insight that the concept of emancipatory reflection is much too vaguely defined. What is at issue is a simple problem: the appropriate interpretation of our experience. What role does reason play in the context of human practice? In every case it takes the general form of reflection. That means it does not merely apply reasonable, efficient means in order to achieve pregiven purposes and ends. It is not confined to the realm of purposive rationality. On this point hermeneutics is at one with ideology critique against "theory of science," insofar as the latter considers its immanent logic and the application of research results as sufficient to define the principle of social practice. Hermeneutic reflection makes ends conscious as well, and not in the sense of a knowledge of previously established ultimate ends, followed by reflection about the legitimacy of means. That is rather a temptation that derives from the realm of technological reason: to be concerned only with choosing the right means and to consider questions about ends as already decided.

In an ultimate sense, certainly, something is predecided for all human practice, namely that the individual as well as society is oriented toward "happiness." That appears a natural, manifestly reasonable statement. But we must concede to Kant that happiness, this ideal of the imagination, cannot be satisfactorily defined. Practical reason demands, however, that we think about our ends with just as much precision as about their corresponding means; that is, in our actions we can consciously prefer one way of acting over another and ultimately subordinate one purpose to another. Far from simply presupposing a given order of social life and making our practical choices within that given framework, in every decision we make we are responsive to a consistency of quite a different kind.

Consistency is an obligation for every kind of rationality, even the technical, which always tries to pursue circumscribed ends in a rational manner. But consistency plays its fullest role in practical experience—outside efficiency-oriented, technological rationality. Here consistency is no longer the self-evident rationality of choosing means—which, as Max Weber has powerfully demonstrated, obtains in the emotionally distorted field of sociopolitical action. What is at issue is rather the consistency of desire itself. Anyone who finds himself in a situation of genuine choice needs a standard of excellence to guide reflection in coming to a decision. The result is always something more than only correct subordination to the guiding standard. What one considers the right decision determines the standard itself, and not only in such a way that it becomes the precedent for future decisions but also that the commitment to particular goals of action is thereby developed. Here consistency ultimately means continuity, which alone gives content to one's identity with oneself. This is the truth that Kant's reflection on moral philosophy demonstrated to be the formal character of moral law in contrast to all utilitarian and technical calculation. But with Aristotle and a tradition reaching down to the present, one can derive an image of right living from this definition of "the right"; and one would have to agree with Aristotle that this guiding image, socially preformed though it is, continually determines itself further when we make "critical" decisions—even to the point of such determinacy that we can no longer consciously will any alternative; that is, our "ethos" has become a second "nature."[28] It is thus that the guiding image of the individual as of the society is formed, and in such a way that the ideals of a younger generation, precisely in differing from those of the older, determine them further—that is, establish them—through the concrete practice of their own behavior within their own field of play and context of ends.

Where is emancipatory reflection effectual here? I would say everywhere—of course in such a way that in dissolving the old ends, it concretizes itself again in new ones. It thereby accords with the law of gradualness that governs historical and social life itself. It would become vacuous and undialectical, I think, if it tried to think the idea of a completed reflection, in which society would lift itself out of the continuing process of emancipation—the process of loosening itself from traditional ties and binding itself to newly constructed validities—so as to achieve an ultimate, free and rational self-possession.

To describe emancipation as dissolving compulsions by making them conscious is a very relative way of speaking. Its content depends upon what compulsions are in question. The psychological process of socializing the individual, we know, is necessarily connected with the repression of drives and the renunciation of desires. The social and political life of mankind, on the other hand, is constituted by a social order that exercises a predominant influence on what is considered right. In the psychological realm there can certainly be neurotic distortions that incapacitate the individual for social communication. Here the compulsoriness of the communication disorders can be dissolved by clarifying them and making them conscious. Yet, in effect, this is nothing but reintegrating the disturbed person back into the world of social norms. Now there is something comparable in social and historical life. There, forms of domination can be experienced as compulsions, and making them conscious certainly means awakening desire for a new identification with the universal. Hegel's critique of positivity—of Christendom, of the German constitution, of vestigial feudalism—offers an excellent example of this. But such an example, in my opinion, cannot confirm what my critics postulate: that becoming conscious of existing structures of domination always has an emancipatory effect. Becoming conscious can also transform modes of behavior implanted by authority into guiding images that determine one's own free behavior. Hegel is an excellent example of this too, which appears reactionary only to those predisposed to think so. Tradition is not the vindication of what has come down from the past but the further creation of moral and social life; it depends on being made conscious and freely carried on.

What can be submitted to reflection is always limited in comparison to what is determined by previous formative influences. Blindness to the fact of human finitude is what leads one to accept the Enlightenment's abstract motto and to disparage all authority—and it is a momentous misunderstanding when the mere recognition of this fact is taken to express a political position, a defense of the status quo. In truth, the talk about progress or revolution—or even conservation—would be mere declamation if it laid claim to an abstract, apriori saving knowledge. It may be that under revolutionary conditions the emergence of the Robespierres, the abstract moralists who want to remake the world according to their reason, will win applause. But it is just as certain that their hour is appointed. I can only consider it a fatal confusion when the dialectical character of all reflection, its relation to the pregiven, is tied to an ideal of total enlightenment. To me that seems just as mistaken as the ideal of fully rational self-clarity, of an individual who would live in full consciousness and control of his impulses and motives.

Clearly the concept of meaning in idealist philosophy of identity is fatal in this context. This concept narrows the province of hermeneutic reflection to the so-called "cultural tradition"—in the line of Vico, as it were, who held that only what man makes can be understood by man. But the hermeneutic reflection that gives point to my whole investigation tries to show that such a conception of the understanding of meaning is erroneous, and in this respect I have had to qualify even Vico's famous definition.[29] Both Apel and Habermas seem to me to fixate on this idealist conception of understanding, which does not correspond to the whole movement of my analysis. It is not by accident that I oriented my investigation toward the experience of art, whose "meaning" cannot be exhausted by conceptual understanding. The fact that I began my inquiry into philosophical hermeneutics with a critique of aesthetic consciousness and a reflection on art—and not with the so-called Geisteswissenschaften—in no way indicated an evasion of the demand for scientific method but rather a genuine attempt to survey the full range which the hermeneutic question possesses and which does not so much distinguish certain sciences as hermeneutic as bring to light a pre-ordered dimension that precedes all application of scientific methods. To this end, the experience of art was important for several reasons. How does this pertain to the superiority to time that is claimed by art as the content of our aesthetic consciousness? Doesn't a doubt arise here whether this aesthetic consciousness that intends "art"—even the pseudo-religiously inflated concept of "art"—constricts our experience of the work of art, just as historical consciousness and historicism constrict our historical experience?

This problem is concretized in Kierkegaard's concept of "contemporaneity," which precisely does not mean omnipresence in the sense of something's being historically re-presented; rather, it sets a task that I later called application. Against von Bormann's objection,[30] I would like to defend the idea that the distinction between contemporaneity and aesthetic simultaneity which I employ is Kierkegaardian, though of course applied in a different way. When the note in his diary says, "The situation of contemporaneity is successfully brought about," I am saying the same thing when I say "total mediation," that is, immediate co-incidence. Naturally, to those who recall the vocabulary of Kierkegaard's polemic against "mediation," that sounds like backsliding into Hegelianism. Here one runs into the obstacles that the closure of Hegel's system throws in the way of all attempts to keep one's distance from its conceptual force. This pertains to Kierkegaard as well as to my own attempt to formulate, with the help of a Kierkegaardian concept, my distance from Hegel. Indeed I followed Hegel in order to stress the hermeneutic dimension of the mediation of past and present in opposition to the naive non-conceptuality of the historical view. In this sense I confronted Schleiermacher with Hegel.[31] Actually I followed Hegel's insight into the historicity of spirit a step further. Hegel's concept of a "religion of art" indicates exactly what motivates my hermeneutic doubt about aesthetic consciousness. For it, art exists not as art but as religion, as the presence of the divine, its own highest possibility. But if Hegel considers all art as something past, it is as it were absorbed by historical, rememorative consciousness; and as something past, it achieves aesthetic simultaneity. Insight into this context set me the hermeneutic task of employing the concept of aesthetic non-differentiation to distinguish the real experience of art—which does not experience art as art—from aesthetic consciousness. This seems to me a legitimate problem, one that does not result from idolizing history but is unmistakable in our experience of art. To regard "art" either as originally contemporary with all times and outside history or as a way of attaining culture through the experience of history is to impose a false dichotomy.[32]

Hegel is right. Thus today I can no more accept Oskar Becker's critique[33] than any other historical objectivism, though it certainly has a limited validity: the task of hermeneutic integration remains. It could be said that this corresponds more to Kierkegaard's ethical stage than to the religious. There, perhaps, von Bormann is right. But even in Kierkegaard, doesn't the ethical stage retain a certain conceptual predominance—and is it not transcended by the religious stage though only by "drawing attention"? (nicht anders als aufmerksam machend)

Today Hegel's aesthetics is once again receiving careful consideration. Rightly so, since it presents what until now has been the only real solution to the conflict between art's claim to be timeless and the historical uniqueness of the work and world, because it thinks both together and thereby makes art as a whole "memorial" (erinnerlich). Clearly two things belong together here: since the emergence of Christendom, art has not been the highest form of truth, the manifestation of the divine, and has therefore become reflective art; and second, the stage to which the mind has progressed—idea and concept, revealed religion and philosophy —leads to conceiving art henceforth as nothing but art. The transition from reflective art to the art of reflection, the way they flow into each other, seems to me not a confusion of different things (Wiehl[34]) but rather consitutes the objectively demonstrable content of Hegel's insight. Reflective art is not merely a late phase in the epoch of art but already the transition into knowledge, whereby art becomes art for the first time.

Here arises a special question that has been generally neglected until now: whether the special place of the verbal arts within the hierarchy of kinds of art is not indicated by the fact that they make this transition manifest.[35] R. Wiehl has convincingly demonstrated that the connecting link between art and the dramaturgy of dialectical thought is to be found in the concept of action, which is central to dramatic art. In fact, that is one of the profound insights that glimmer through the conceptual systematization of Hegel's aesthetics. I consider it no less significant that this transition is already indicated where linguisticality emerges as such for the first time, and that is in the lyric. In lyrics, action is not represented, to be sure; and in what is today called the "speech act," which describes the lyric as well, the quality of action is not obtrusive. In all verbal arts, what constitutes the enigmatic effortlessness of the work, in comparison to the recalcitrant materials in which the plastic arts realize themselves, is that no one thinks of speaking as an action. Wiehl rightly says, "The lyric is the presentation of a pure speech act, not the presentation of an action in the form of a speech act" (as is the case in drama).

But that means: language as language here comes into view.

In this way a relation between word and concept comes into play that precedes the relation between drama and dialectic which Wiehl has worked out.[36] It is in the lyric that language appears in its pure essence, so that all the possibilities of language, and even of the concept, are as it were germinally contained within it. Hegel had already had this fundamental insight when he recognized that, by contrast to the "material" of other arts, language signifies a totality. That insight had already led Aristotle, despite the precedence that seeing has among the natural senses, to ascribe special precedence to hearing because hearing takes in language and thus everything, not just the visible.

To be sure, Hegel did not specially distinguish the lyric in respect to this precedence of the linguistic. He was too much influenced by the ideal of naturalness that Goethe represented for his age, and he therefore viewed the lyrical poem only as a subjective expression of inwardness. But in truth the lyrical word is language in a paradigmatic sense. This is especially evident from the fact that the lyrical word can be raised to the ideal of poésie pure. That pertains not to the developed form of dialectic, as drama does, but to the speculative basis of all dialectic. The same self-presence of mind occurs in the verbal movement of speculative thought as in the verbal movement of the "pure" poem. Adorno too has rightly called attention to the affinity between the lyrical and the speculative-dialectical statement—and, above all, Mallarmé himself has done so.

There is something else that points in the same direction, and that is the degree to which various kinds of poetry are translatable. The standard of "action" that Wiehl derived from Hegel himself is almost the opposite of this standard. In any case, it is agreed that the more the lyric approximates the ideal of poésie pure, the less translatable it is: clearly, sound and meaning are here interwoven to the point of being indivisible.

I have since worked further in this direction, though certainly not alone. The distinction between "denotative and connotative" employed by Wellek and Warren plainly calls for more precise analysis. I have looked into the various modes of linguisticality, and especially the significance of writing for the ideality of language. Recently Paul Ricoeur has come to the same conclusion: writtenness confirms the identity of sense and dissolves the psychological side of speaking. It thus becomes clear, in passing, why hermeneutics in the line of Schleiermacher, and especially Dilthey—despite their preoccupation with psychology—did not take over the romantic project of grounding hermeneutics in living dialogue but rather returned to the "utterances of life fixed in writing" emphasized by the older hermeneutics. Correlatively, Dilthey regarded the interpretation of poetry as the triumph of hermeneutics. By contrast, I have pointed to "dialogue" as the structure of verbal understanding and characterized it as a dialectic of question and answer. That proves to hold completely true for our "Being-toward-the-text." In interpreting, the questions a text puts to us can be understood only when the text, conversely, is understood as an answer to a question.

It is not by accident that the verbal work of art (sprachliche Kunstwerk) comes into the foreground here. Quite independent of the historical question of oral poetry, it is in a fundamental sense oral art as literature (Sprachkunst as Literatur). I call texts of this kind "eminent" texts.

What has occupied me for years and what I have pursued in various still unpublished lectures ("Image and Word," "The Being of Poems," "On the Truth of the Word," "Philosophical, Religious, and Poetic Speaking"), are the special problems of eminent texts. Such a text fixes the pure speech act and therefore has an eminent relation to writing. In it language is present in such a way that its cognitive relation to the given disappears, just as does the communicative relation to the addressee. The universal hermeneutic process of horizon-formation and fusion, which I have made conceptually explicit, applies to such eminent texts as well. I am far from wanting to deny that the way a work of art speaks to its time and world (what H. R. Jauss calls its "negativity"[37]) co-determines its meaning, that is, the way it speaks to us. This was precisely the point of historically effected consciousness: to think the work and its effect as a unity of meaning. What I described as the fusion of horizons was the form in which this unity actualizes itself, which does not allow the interpreter to speak of an original meaning of the work without acknowledging that, in understanding it, the interpreter's own meaning enters in as well. One misunderstands this basic hermeneutic structure when one thinks that a historical or critical method could be used to "break" the circle of understanding (as Kimmerle has recently contended[38]). What Kimmerle has described is not at all different from what Heidegger called "coming into the circle in the *right way*"—that is, neither by anachronistically updating it nor distorting it to fit one's own preconceptions. Working out the historical horizon of a text is always already a fusion of horizons. The historical horizon cannot be determined by itself in advance. In more recent hermeneutics, that is known as the problematic of fore-understanding.

Now in the case of the eminent text something else requiring hermeneutic reflection is in play. The "suspension" of the immediate relation to reality—which the English, with their nominalistic orientation to thought and language, designate by the word "fiction"—really manifests no suspension, no weakening of the immediacy of the speech act, but, just the opposite, its "eminent" realization. In all literature, that holds for the implied "addressee"—which does not mean the receiver of a message but everyone who is receptive today and tomorrow. Even though classical tragedies were written for a certain festival and certainly spoke to a particular social present, they were not like stage props to be used only once or even kept in storage for later use. They could be performed in new productions and very soon read as texts not because of historical interest, certainly, but because they still had something to say.

It was not defining some canon of content specific to the classic that encouraged me to designate the classical as the basic category of effective history. Rather, I was trying to indicate what distinguishes the work of art, and particularly the eminent text, from other traditionary materials open to understanding and interpretation. The dialectic of question and answer that I elaborated is not invalidated here but modified: the original question to which a text must be understood as an answer has, as suggested above, an originary superiority to and freedom from its origins. This hardly means that the "classical work" is accessible only in a hopelessly conventional way or that it encourages a reassuringly harmonious conception of the "universally human." Rather, something "speaks" only when it speaks "originarily," that is, "as if it were saying something to me in particular." This hardly means that what speaks in this way is measured by an suprahistorical norm. Just the reverse is true: what speaks in this way sets the standard. And that is the problem. In such cases the original question that the text is understood as answering claims an identity of meaning which has always already mediated the distance between its origin and the present. In my Zürich lecture of 1969, "The Being of the Poetical," I indicated the hermeneutic distinctions necessary for such texts.[39]

But the hermeneutic dimension seems to me relevant to current discussions of aesthetics in other respects as well. Precisely when "anti-art"—such as pop art and the happening—became the rage, and when, even in traditional genres, forms of art were sought that thumb their noses at traditional conceptions of the work and its unity and that defy all univocal understanding, hermeneutic reflection must ask what is the point of such pretensions. The answer will be that the hermeneutic conception of the work remains viable so long as such productions can be described as identifiable, repeatable, and worth repeating. So long as such productions as these try to be are governed by the fundamental hermeneutic structure of understanding something as something, their constitutive form is nothing radically new. Such "art" is not really different from certain long-since recognized forms of performing art, such as dance, which are evaluated in such a way that even improvisation, which is never repeated, tries to be "good"—and that means ideally repeatable and confirming itself as art in the repetition. Here a sharp distinction needs to be drawn from mere trick and legerdemain. Even in them something is to be understood. It can be conceptualized; it can be imitated. It even tries to be adept and good. But its repetition, in Hegel's words, becomes "insipid, like a piece of legerdemain that has been seen through." The dividing line between a work of art and piece of artifice may be quite fluid, and often contemporaries may not know whether the charm of a production is a mere trick or artistic richness. Also, artistic media are often used as media in merely practical contexts, for example in poster art and other forms of commercial and political advertisement.

From such functions of artistic media, what we call a work of art remains quite distinct. Even if, for example, statues of gods, choral songs, and attic tragedy and comedy are found within cultural systems, and even if every "work" belongs originally to a context of life that has passed away, nevertheless the doctrine of aesthetic non-differentiation implies that this relation to the past is, as it were, retained in the work itself. Even in its origin it had gathered its "world" in itself and was therefore "intended" as itself, as this statue of Phidias, this tragedy of Aeschylus, this motet of Bach. The hermeneutic constitution of the unity of the work of art is invariant among all the social alterations of the art industry. That holds as well for the apotheosis of art into the religion of culture, symptomatic of the bourgeois period. Even Marxist literary analysis must take heed of this invariance, as Lucien Goldmann, for example, has rightly emphasized.[40] Art is not merely a tool of the sociopolitical will; art documents a social reality only when it is really art, and not when it is used as an instrument.

In my work, I brought "classical" concepts such as "mimesis" and "representation" into play not in order to defend classical ideas but to transcend the bourgeois conception of the aesthetic as cultural religion. This has been understood as a kind of back-sliding into a Platonism definitively superseded by the modern view of art. But it does not seem quite so simple to me. The doctrine of recognition on which mimetic representation is based only hints at what it would mean to grasp the claim to being of artistic representation. Aristotle, who derives the mimetic nature of art from the pleasure of learning, considers the poet different from the historian in that he portrays things not as they happened but as they could happen. Thus he ascribes to poetry a universality that has nothing to do with the substantialist metaphysics underlying the classical aesthetic of imitation. The Aristotelian idea of concept formation, the hermeneutic legitimacy of which seems to me indisputable, points rather to the dimension of the possible, and therefore also to the critique of reality (of which not only ancient comedy has given us a strong taste)—even though so much classical theory of imitation claims Aristotle as its model.

But I will stop here. The ongoing dialogue permits no final conclusion. It would be a poor hermeneuticist who thought he could have, or had to have, the last word.

Notes

1 *Der Positivismusstreit in der deutschen Soziologie*, ed. T. W. Adorno et al. (Neuwied, 1969).

2 Hans Albert, *Traktat über praktische Vernunft* (1968) [*Treatise on Critical Reason*, tr. Mary Varney Rorty (Princeton: Princeton University Press, 1985)].

3 I have already discussed his polemic—useful, though distorted by emotion—in "Hermeneutics and Historicism," Supplement I above.

4 See Apel, Habermas, and others in the collection *Hermeneutik und Ideologiekritik*, ed. Jürgen Habermas (Frankfurt: Suhrkamp, 1971), which includes my reply, pp. 283–317 [*GW*, II, 250–75].

5 *Zur Rehabilitierung der praktischen Philosophie* (1972) [*GW*, IV].

6 In this connection I can mention my essay, "Amicus Plato Magis Amica Veritas," pp. 194–218, and "Plato's Unwritten Dialectic," pp. 124–55, both in *Dialogue and Dialectic: Eight Hermeneutical Studies on Plato*, tr. P. Christopher Smith (New Haven: Yale University Press, 1980). [See also my *The Idea of the Good in Platonic-Aristotelian Philosophy*, tr. P. Christopher Smith (New Haven: Yale University Press, 1986).]

7 Werner Heisenberg in particular has repeatedly discussed this question.

8 See the important essay by Viktor Kraft, "Geschichtsforschung als strenge Wissenschaft," now in *Logik der Sozialwissenschaften*, ed. E. Topitsch, pp. 72–82.

9 Thus H. Albert, *Traktat über praktische Vernunft*, p.138.

10 D. Harth, *Deutsche Vierteljahrsschrift*, Sept., 1971, has rightly emphasized this in a solid study.

11 Wilhelm Kamlah, Paul Lorenzen, *Logische Propädeutik: Vorschule des vernünftigen Redens* (1967).

12 Popper does not consider this experience at all, and so criticizes a concept of

"method" that Hegel does not employ. See "Was ist Dialektik?" in *Logik der Sozialwissenschaften*, ed. E. Topitsch, pp. 262–90.

13 In *Arbeitsgemeinschaft für Forschung des Landes Nordrhein-Westfalen*, 170 (1971). [*Kleine Schriften*, IV, 1–16; *GW*, IV.]

14 Heinz Kimmerle, afterword to the edition of F.D.E. Schleiermacher's *Hermeneutik* (Heidelberg, 1968), with an appendix "Zur Datierung, Textberichtigungen, Nachweise."

15 Despite the work of Halpern and Odebrecht, unfortunately we still have no satisfactory edition of Schleiermacher's *Dialektik*. So the edition of Jonas in the *Werke* is still indispensable. It is to be hoped that these omissions will soon be rectified; in particular, the editorial side of the matter would be of fundamental interest because of its analogy to the still awaited edition of Hegel's lectures.

16 Dilthey, *Das Leben Schleiermachers*, II, parts 1 and 2 (Berlin, 1966).

17 [See now *Seminar: Philosophische Hermeneutik*, ed. H.–G. Gadamer and G. Boehm (Frankfurt: Suhrkamp, 1976).]

18 [J. Wach, *Das Verstehen: Grundzüge einer Geschichte der hermeneutischen Theorie im 19. Jahrhundert* (3 vols.; 1926; repr. Hildesheim, 1966).]

19 *Instrumenta philosophica. Series hermeneutica*, I–IV (Düsseldorf, 1965).

20 Herman Patsch in *Zeitschrift für Theologie und Kirche*, 63 (1966), 434–72.

21 Gianni Vattimo, *Schleiermacher filosofo dell-interpretazione* (Milan, 1968).

22 [See the work of Manfred Frank, *"Das individuelle Allgemeine": Text-strukturierung und –interpretatio nach Schleiermacher* (Frankfurt, 1977).]

23 *Diltheys Kritik der endlichen Vernunft* (1970).

24 Frankfurt: Suhrkamp, 1970.

25 [On recent Dilthey studies, see my essays in *GW*, III.]

26 [See *Hermeneutik und Ideologiekritik* and the essays collected in sec. IV, "Weiterentwicklungen" in *GW*, II.]

27 I consider the works of Chaim Perelman and his students a valuable contribution to philosophical hermeneutics (especially his *Traité de l'argumentation*, with L. Olbrecht-Tyteca), and recently, *Le Champ de l'argumentation* (both Brussels: Presses Universitaires) [and see Perelman, *The New Rhetoric and the Humanities: Essays on Rhetoric and its Applications* (Boston: Dordrecht, 1979)].

28 See my "Über die Möglichkeit einer philosophischen Ethik," *Kleine Schriften*, I, 179ff. [and now, "Gibt es auf Erden ein Mass?" parts I and II, *Philosophische Rundschau*, 31 (1984), 161–77, and 32 (1985), 1–26].

29 Pp. 17ff. above.

30 Now in *Hermeneutik und Ideologiekritisk*, ed. J. Habermas, pp. 88ff.

31 [Pp. 158ff. above.]

32 Helmut Kuhn's *Wesen und Wirken des Kunstwerks* (1960) seems to me to be handicapped by this abstract opposition between art and religion. Conversely, Walter Benjamin seems to me to recognize the fundamental pastness of art when he speaks of the "aura" of the work of art. But he proclaims a new

political function for the work of art in the age of mechanical reproduction, one which completely revolutionizes the meaning of art and against which Theodor Adorno raises pertinent objections in his *Aesthetic Theory*.

33 *Philosophische Rundschau*, 10 (1963), 225–37.

34 Reiner Wiehl, "Uber den Handlungsbegriff als Kategorie der Hegelschen Aesthetik," *Hegel-Studien*, 6 (1971), 135–70, esp. 138.

35 [See my "On the Contribution of Poetry to the Search for Truth," pp. 105–15, and "Philosophy and Poetry," pp. 131–39, in *The Relevance of the Beautiful*, tr. Nicholas Walker (Cambridge: Cambridge University Press, 1986); and more recently, "Die Poesie im Hegelschen System der Künste," *Hegel-Studien*, 21 (1986).]

36 [See "Text and Interpretation," tr. Dennis Schmidt, in *The Gadamer-Derrida Encounter: Texts and Comments*, ed. Diane Michelfelder and Richard Palmer (Albany: SUNY Press, 1988).]

37 Hans Robert Jauss, "Literaturgeschichte als Provokation" (1970) [and *Asthetische Erfahrung und literarische Hermeneutik* (Frankfurt, 1979)].

38 Heinz Kimmerle, *Die Bedeutung der Geisteswissenschaft für die Gesellschaft* (1971), pp. 71ff.

39 See also "Wahrheit und Dichtung," *Zeitwende*, 6 (1971) [*GW*, VIII].

40 Lucien Goldmann, *Dialektische Untersuchungen* (1968).

Subject Index

Absolute knowledge, 161, 207, 223, 224, 227, 275, 299, 348, 463, 535
Abstraction, 23, 77, 100, 243, 427
Academy, 566, 567
Addressee, 328–329
Adventure, 479
Advice, 319
Aesthetic consciousness, 328, 497, 573
Aesthetic differentiation, 74–77, 115–116, 124, 128, 130, 135, 141, 145–146, 153, 399, 469, 560
Aesthetic immediacy, 82
Aesthetic object,
  See Work of art
Alienation/Estrangement, 311, 318, 340, 361, 391, 394, 484
Allegory, 61–70, 97, 170
Ambiguity, 498–499
Analogy, 3, 65, 428, 476, 516
Analysis notionum, 415
Anamnesis, 14, 113
Answer,
  See Question
Anticipatio, 342
Appearance, aesthetic, 474
Application/Applicatio, 533
Arabesque, 40, 41, 80

Architecture, 75, 149–151
Arete, 309
Ars inveniendi, 25, 414
Art, 39–49, 70–85, 222–223, 464–465, 470, 481, 574
  history of, 494, 496
  of experience, 496, 503
  of questioning and of dialectic, 356–359
  of understanding, 157–158, 178–179, 364–370, 579
  of writing, 493, 577
  See also Techne/Technique
Artist/Artistic, 73–81, 113, 125, 186–187, 473, 478
Assimilation, 243
Authority, 7, 273–274, 277–281
Autobiography, 58, 218, 277, 507
Axiom, 354, 363

Baroque, 8, 62, 68–69, 286, 515
Beauty,
  free v. dependent, 39–41
  of nature and of art, 39, 43–44, 48–49
Being, 83, 86, 87, 102–105, 245–247, 446, 469

585

Author Index